ROUTLEDGE HANDBOOK OF BEHAVIORAL ECONOMICS

There is no doubt that behavioral economics is becoming a dominant lens through which we think about economics. Behavioral economics is not a single school of thought but representative of a range of approaches, and, uniquely, this volume presents an overview of them.

In the wide spectrum of international contributors, each provides an exploration of a central approach, aspect, or topic in behavioral economics. Taken together, the whole volume provides a comprehensive overview of the subject which considers both key developments and future possibilities.

Part One presents several different approaches to behavioral economics, including George Katona, Ken Boulding, Harvey Leibenstein, Vernon Smith, Herbert Simon, Gerd Gigerenzer, Daniel Kahneman, and Richard Thaler. This section looks at the origins and development of behavioral economics, and compares and contrasts the work of these scholars who have been so influential in making this area so prominent. Part Two presents applications of behavioral economics, including nudging; heuristics; emotions and morality; and behavioral political economy, education, and economic innovation.

The *Routledge Handbook of Behavioral Economics* is ideal for advanced economics students and faculty who are looking for a complete state-of-the-art overview of this dynamic field.

Roger Frantz is Professor of Economics at San Diego State University, USA.

Shu-Heng Chen is Professor at the Department of Economics at National Chengchi University, Taiwan.

Kurt Dopfer is Professor at the Department of Economics, University of St. Gallen, Switzerland.

Floris Heukelom is Assistant Professor at Nijmegen School of Management, Radboud University Nijmegen, the Netherlands.

Shabnam Mousavi is Assistant Professor at the Johns Hopkins Carey Business School, Johns Hopkins University, USA.

ROUTLEDGE HANDBOOK OF BEHAVIORAL ECONOMICS

Edited by Roger Frantz, Shu-Heng Chen, Kurt Dopfer, Floris Heukelom, and Shabnam Mousavi

Routledge
Taylor & Francis Group
LONDON AND NEW YORK

First published 2017 by Routledge

2 Park Square, Milton Park, Abingdon, Oxfordshire OX14 4RN
52 Vanderbilt Avenue, New York, NY 10017

Routledge is an imprint of the Taylor & Francis Group, an informa business

First issued in paperback 2019

British Library Cataloguing in Publication Data
A catalogue record for this book is available from the British Library

Library of Congress Cataloging in Publication Data
Names: Frantz, Roger S., editor.
Title: Routledge handbook of behavioral economics/edited by Roger Frantz, Shu-Heng Chen, Kurt Dopfer, Floris Heukelom and Shabnam Mousavi.
Description: Abingdon, Oxon ; New York, NY: Routledge, 2016.
Identifiers: LCCN 2016004972|ISBN 9781138821149 (hardback) | ISBN 9781315743479 (ebook)
Subjects: LCSH: Economics–Psychological aspects.
Classification: LCC HB74.P8 R68 2016 | DDC 330.01/9–dc23LC record available at http://lccn.loc.gov/2016004972

ISBN: 978-1-138-82114-9 (hbk)
ISBN: 978-0-367-32185-7 (pbk)

Typeset in Bembo
by Sunrise Setting Ltd., Brixham, UK

CONTENTS

FIGURES

TABLES

CONTRIBUTORS

Morris Altman, Newcastle Business School, Department of Behavioural and Institutional Economics, University of Newcastle

Michelle Baddeley, Department of Economics and Finance, University College London

Nina Bandelj, Department of Sociology, University of California

Anna Bayona, Department of Economics, Finance, and Accounting, ESADE Business School, Ramon Liull University

Georg Blind, Institute of Asian and Oriental Studies, University of Zurich

Shu-Heng Chen, AI-ECON Research Center, Department of Economics, National Chengchi University

Bin-Tzong Chie, Department of Industrial Economics, Tamkang University

Richard Curtin, Institute for Social Research, University of Michigan

Peter E. Earl, School of Economics, University of Queensland

Gigi Foster, Department of Economics, University of New South Wales

Roger Frantz, Department of Economics, San Diego State University

Daniel Friedman, Economics Department, University of California

Paul Frijters, Department of Economics, University of Queensland

Gerd Gigerenzer, Max Planck Institute for Human Development

Thomas Grebel, Department of Economics, Fredrich-Schiller University

Floris Heukelom, Department of Economics, Radboud University

Hamid Hosseini, School of Public Affairs, Penn State University

Ying-Fang Kao, AI-ECON Research Center, Department of Economics, National Chengchi University

Stefan Kesting, Department of Economics, Leeds University

Reza Kheirandish, Department of Economics, Clayton State University

Julie Kim, Department of Sociology, University of California

Sean Leaver, School of Economics, Finance and Marketing, RMIT University

Shabnam Mousavi, School of Business, Johns Hopkins University

Matthias Mueller, Department of Business, Economics, and Social Sciences, University of Hohenheim

Rosemarie Nagel, Department of Economics, University of Pompeu Fabra

Jason Potts, School of Economics, Finance and Marketing, RMIT University

Andreas Pyka, Department of Business, Economics, and Social Sciences, University of Hohenheim

Devjani Roy, Kennedy School of Government, Harvard University

Manuel Scholz-Wäckerle, Department of Socioeconomics, WU—Vienna University of Economics and Business

Esther-Mirjam Sent, Department of Economics, Radboud University

Michael Stützer, Department of Economics, Leeds University

Cass R. Sunstein, Harvard Law School

Chung-Ching Tai, Department of Economics, Tunghai University

Zaibu Tufail, Department of Sociology, University of California

Ragupathy Venkatachalam, AI-ECON Research Center, Department of Economics, National Chengchi University

Xianghong Wang, Department of Economics, Renmin University

Richard Zeckhauser, Kennedy School of Government, Harvard University

PART I

Scientists in the field of behavioral economics

Introduction

The first and last articles in Part one are of a broader nature about the history of behavioral economics: Peter Earl, "The evolution of behavioural economics," and Morris Altman, "A bounded rationality assessment of the new behavioral economics." Earl's chapter, which opens the book, goes into more detail about the history/evolution of behavioral economics. Alfred Marshal is older than "old" behavioral economics, but the others Earl discusses are old behavioral economics: Simon, Leibenstein, Baumol, Winter, Katona, and Shackle. The "new" behavioral economics that he discusses is Kahneman and Tversky, and Thaler and Sunstein. The *New York Times* in 2001 may have implicitly declared the "old behavioral economics to be irrelevant," but Earl obviously disagrees. Altman's chapter is much more focused on the relative strengths and weaknesses of two approaches to behavioral economics. The old behavioral economics of Simon or the new behavioral economics of Kahneman and Tversky. Altman also discusses Vernon Smith, Akerlof, and others. Altman appreciates both the old and the new behavioral economics but when push comes to shove he prefers Simon's approach.

There are two chapters on George Katona. Richard Curtin was a student and friend of Katona where both worked at the University of Michigan. Richard Curtin's chapter, Chapter 2, "George Katona: a founder of behavioral economics," reviews Katona's career in behavioral economics beginning in the 1940s, but does more than that. He shows how Katona's idea of frames of reference preceded Kahneman and Tversky's idea of framing by 25 years, and how his ideas of intervening variables preceded Akerlof's ideas on intervening variables by 50 years. These facts should not go unnoticed by anyone interested in the "real' history of behavioral economics. Hamid Hosseini's chapter, "George Katona's contributions to the start of behavioral economics," Chapter 10, shows that Katona was writing about psychology and business decisions as early as 1945, and that in 1977 the American Psychological Association acknowledged Katona with developing a new field of research bridging the gap between psychology and economics. Hosseini also shows the various ways in which Katona's research methodology and underlying assumptions were different in several respects from the then standard neoclassical theory. Finally, Hosseini discusses why economists affiliated with the Cowles Commission did not appreciate Katona's work, while others such as James Tobin acknowledged the debt owed to Katona by the economics profession.

Ken Boulding is the subject of Stefan Kesting's chapter, Chapter 3, titled "Ken Boulding: the image as a precursor to framing?" Similar to Curtin putting Katona's work in historical perspective with younger behavioral economists, Kesting shows how both Boulding's image, and Kahneman and Tversky's concept of framing rely on mental accounting, with Boulding preceding the latter by about 25 years. Chapter 4 focuses on Harvey Leibenstein, who similar to Boulding began writing about behavioral economic themes in the 1950s. Leibenstein's work in the area of behavioral economics began with his 1950 article on the social context of individual decision making, specifically how others' behavior served as intervening variables between prices and quantities demanded. Akerlof discussed this in 2007, while Vernon Smith discussed it in his book, *Rationality and Economics* in 2009, both writing almost 60 years after Leibenstein's 1950 *QJE* article. Of course, the focus of the chapter is Leibenstein's X-efficiency theory, a theory which attempted to ask what are the implications for economic theory when we drop the assumptions of perfect rationality, maximizing behavior, and efficiency as meaning only allocative efficiency. Leibenstein dropped all three and opened the "black box" which is the neoclassical/non-behavioral economics firm. These three are also the foundations of the then neoclassical theory, and which helped open the conversation for a later advancement, not a beginning, of behavioral economics.

There are four papers discussing the work of Herbert Simon. One is Altman's paper which we have already mentioned. The paper by Grebel and Stützer, "Schumpeter, Kirzner, Knight, Simon, and others: behavioral economics and entrepreneurship," Chapter 13, mentions Simon's theory of bounded rationality as the reason why entrepreneurs are not globally rational. The third paper is by Esther-Mirjam Sent, Chapter 5. Sent's paper discusses Simon's contributions, including his work on: complex hierarchical systems; aggregation, causality, and identifiablility in econometrics; cognitive psychology; artificial intelligence; bounded rationality; and his differences with Kahneman and Tversky. Chapter 12 is by Manuel Scholz-Wäckerle, a Senior Lecturer of Socioeconomics in Vienna University, and is about "meso behavior." Meso behavior is defined/described as

> a particular kind of economic behavior that is not integral part of the homo oeconomicus model. This behavior is called meso because it is neither part of micro- nor of macroeconomics alone and it is shaped systemically through interactive socio-economic associations. Thereafter meso is characterized through structure as well as process components of dynamic change.

In the fourth section it is shown that Veblenian and Schumpeterian agents are basically acting in terms of Simon's approach to satisficing behavior, a "precondition for . . . meso-structured behavior." Scholz-Wäckerle also discusses meso behavior in the writings of 2009 Nobel Prize winner Elinor Ostrom. Elinor Ostrom is also featured in Chapter 11, "Behavioral rules: Veblen, Nelson–Winter, Ostrom, and beyond" by Georg Blind.

Two chapters are on the founders of experimental economics: Reinhard Selten and Vernon Smith, Selten's work beginning in the late 1950s and Smith in the early 1960s. Selten received the Nobel Prize in 1994 and Smith in 2002. Selten's work was applied to both fully rational and not-so-fully rational players. His work with C. C. Berg in 1970 described framing, 11 years before the same concept was published by Kahneman and Tversky. In Chapter 6 Rosemarie Nagel et al. describe Selten as a "dualist" because he presented economics from both a normative (assuming rationality) and a descriptive (conducting experiments and developing behavioral models) approach. In Chapter 7 Shabnam Mousavi presents Vernon Smith and Gerd Gigerenzer on ecological rationality and heuristics. She compares Smith and Gigerenzer with respect to ecological rational, bounded rationality, heuristics and experiments.

Floris Heukelom provides chapters on two more recent names in the history of behavioral economics: Richard Thaler (Chapter 8), and Daniel Kahneman (Chapter 9), winner of the Nobel Prize in 2002. Heukelom takes us chronologically through Kahneman's very productive career, saying that "it is easy to observe that the central idea in Kahneman's work is that human decision making is best understood as the combined outcome of two cognitive systems," which Kahneman refers to as System 1 and System 2. Heukelom also takes us chronologically through Thaler's career, saying that

> one could argue that Thaler's economic world view has been remarkably constant over the course of his career of now almost forty years. Economic theory tells us how we should behave in the economy, and economists should be more concerned with finding out if and when people behave along those lines. If not, economists should devise ways to help individuals do so.

1
THE EVOLUTION OF BEHAVIOURAL ECONOMICS

Peter E. Earl

Introduction

There are many ways in which one might tell the story of behavioural economics. It has a much longer history than many of its current proponents realise, a history that behavioural economics itself can be used to understand (for an early attempt to offer a reflexive analysis of the state of behavioural economics, see Earl, 1983a). If judging purely from the advance reviews by Chip Heath and Daniel Kahneman of Richard Thaler's (2015) book *Misbehaving*, one would believe that it was Thaler who invented behavioural economics. This might indeed be true for what nowadays typically passes for behavioural economics. However, such claims contrast sharply with the perspective offered by Baddeley (2013), who begins her textbook with a survey of psychological perspectives on choice that goes back to eighteenth-century contributions by David Hume and Adam Smith. Yet, despite such a long historical sweep, Baddeley's account is very light on what Sent (2004) calls 'old behavioural economics'—that is, behavioural economics pre-Thaler or recent behavioural contributions in the spirit of the 'old' approach. The same can be said of Cartwright (2014), who similarly sees behavioural economics as beginning with Adam Smith's (1759) *Theory of Moral Sentiments*.

In the present survey, the focus is not on how 'new' behavioural economics has evolved but on the earlier contributions that have been left behind rather than being integrated with the new approach. The inclusion of 'evolution' in the title provides a clue to the approach that is taken and why the starting point is the publication of Alfred Marshall's (1890) *Principles of Economics*, ninety years before Thaler's (1980) seminal paper in the first issue of the *Journal of Economic Behaviour and Organisation*. Marshall not only built his analysis on his knowledge of actual behaviour, as a behavioural economist would, but he is increasingly being recognised as one of the founding fathers of evolutionary economics, a research programme that is both closely related to 'old behavioural economics' and is instructive for understanding how what is viewed as behavioural economics has changed since 1980.

Marshall and evolutionary analysis

Marshall's thinking was greatly influenced by evolutionary biology (see Hart, 2013). This arm of biology views the evolution of species populations as arising via the following process: (i) genetic mutations occur, (ii) mutations affect survival chances of the organisms in which they are embodied, and (iii) a mutation may be passed down to later generations if the organism in which it is embodied breeds and its progeny survive into adulthood. Inspired by evolutionary biology, Marshall ended up concerned with the struggle of firms to get established and remain competitive in a world where gradual change, not equilibrium, was the order of the day. He thus likened the competitive struggles of firms in an industry to those of trees within a forest where many plants fail to get enough sunlight and nutrition to enable them to grow to maturity. He did not go as far as later writers, most notably Nelson and Winter (1982), who assigned to routines in economic and social systems a role akin to that of genes in biological system as the key elements that get passed from one generation to the next. Innovative routines may give a firm a competitive edge over rivals, enabling it to earn greater profits; indeed, radically different routines may greatly disrupt an established order that had been evolving steadily. If new routines are retained and come to be employed more widely (for example, via internal growth of the firm or by being spread over a wider geographical area via a franchise system), then the new way of doing business may account for a growing share of economic activity. This will continue until routines that are even better suited to passing the test of the market are developed and applied. Where Marshall emphasised gradual change, modern evolutionary economists have emphasised, via Schumpeter's (1943) notion of 'creative destruction', the possibility that the history of economic systems may be punctuated by revolutionary shifts in which one way of doing business comprehensively renders another obsolete.

There are obvious parallels between the evolutionary gradualism of Marshall's analysis and the notions of 'normal science' and the use of 'scientific research programmes' in scientific inquiry, and between the idea of game-changing new business modes and Kuhn's (1962) analysis of 'scientific revolutions'/'paradigm shifts'. However, if we apply the perspective of evolutionary economics to the market for economic ideas, it becomes apparent that good ideas may fail to be transmitted down the generations if they fail to survive the selection process, including the process of selection into the educational equivalent of franchise manuals; namely, the textbooks that themselves have to survive the test of the market. What is retained and replicated via today's textbooks in behavioural economics thus could be—and, indeed, is—very different from what might have been in them if the evolutionary mutation and selection processes had worked differently. A key factor here is the role of purposive individuals as creative agents and marketers of new potential routines for doing economics: unlike in biology, the mutations do not happen randomly. Instead, routines and personality-related factors may affect which elements are used to create novel contributions and how they are presented to potential adopters.

Marshallian behavioural economics

Marshall's own legacy illustrates the haphazard processes at work in the market for economic ideas. Most economists think of him as a key player in the development of the marginalist, supply-and-demand framework of mainstream equilibrium economics, not as a pioneer of evolutionary economics. Such received wisdom is the result of not reading Marshall at first hand and of the efforts of Marshall's successor, Pigou, and those whom he influenced, to remove the evolutionary aspects of Marshall's thinking from what they passed on from his *Principles* (see Hart, 2013). However, Marshall also deserves to be recognised as one of the pioneers of behavioural economics. His approach was not to employ convenient axioms in the manner of an 'armchair economist' but to build his analysis on what he had been able to discover from business people about the way that business worked. This led him to place learning—by consumers, about what they needed and how to source it reliably for a reasonable price, and by producers, about production methods and how to win customers for their output—at the heart of his analysis

(Loasby, 1978; Hart, 2013). He also viewed firms as organisations, not as black boxes. He emphasised the managerial succession problems faced by firms, along with the forces of inertia in large, well-established businesses that could make it easier for new firms to start winning customers despite having limited resources, experience or reputation (Marshall, 1923: 317–18).

Although Marshall's way of thinking was not retained by his Cambridge successor, Pigou, it resurfaced from the late 1930s onwards in the work of members of the Oxford Economists' Research Group (OERG) (see Wilson and Andrews, 1951; Young and Lee, 1993), particularly in the work of P. W. S. Andrews (1949). Central to this approach was getting to know business managers and administering questionnaires to them. The data thereby obtained raised questions about the interest-elasticity of investment and the role of marginal revenue and marginal cost in pricing choices. Decades before the 'contestable markets' revolution in industrial economics led by Baumol et al. (1982), it was clear to the Oxford post-Marshallians that competition was much on the minds of managers, even if they did not have large numbers of existing rivals. The managers seemed ever-fearful of the possibility of cross-entry by firms diversifying from other sectors where the capability requirements were rather similar to those required in their own lines of business. This led them to focus on developing long-term goodwill relationships with customers and not to be greedy with profit margins, in order to deter potential entrants.

Marshall argued that prices in an industry track the average costs of the industry's 'representative firm' in the long run, falling with accumulated experience and growth in the scale of production. The Oxford economists reworked this in terms of prices being the result of simple decision rules being used for dealing with complex competitive situations. They saw price-setting as involving the use of a conventional mark-up on 'full' or 'normal' costs. Firms would use their own costs as proxies for the costs of prospective entrants, adjusted in light of any information they had about their relative standing among existing players. Hence more (less) efficient firms would tend to operate with bigger (smaller) profit margins. The tendency for costs and prices to fall in real terms through time would be enhanced not merely by the effects that external competitive pressure had on the rate at which firms discovered better ways of doing things but also by what Andrews called 'internal competition'; that is, workers trying to improve their promotion prospects by demonstrating their abilities to see ways of improving productivity.

Although Andrews's research led him to emphasise the power of competition and to criticise models of imperfect/monopolistic competition (Andrews, 1964), he emphasised the use of targets by profit-seeking firms as a means of dealing with uncertainty. Failure to meet target levels of sales would normally result in experimentation with different marketing strategies rather risking spoiling the market via destructive price competition. His highly discursive analysis was rich in content and saw simple decision rules as effective for dealing with the complexity of the manager's choice problem. However, it was typically seen as lacking in rigour and was misunderstood by mainstream economists (Irving, 1978).

In the US, the project closest in style to the OERG's behavioural research was Lester's (1946) investigation of firms' labour hiring practices and whether they were consistent with marginal productivity theory. This met with much the same fate as the Oxford work, even though the key critic, Fritz Machlup, was not actually opposed to behavioural research in principle. Machlup's (1946) critique was based on the view that Lester should have done a longer field study, more akin to an anthropological piece of research, before reaching his heretical conclusions (see Lavoie, 1990).

Bounded rationality and the behavioural theory of the firm

The work of the OERG and the Lester–Machlup debate were both noted in the early pages of Cyert and March's (1963) *A Behavioural Theory of the Firm*. Just as in Marshall's work, this took an organisational view of the firm, and it gave a key role to simple decision rules, showing how they could be used in modelling firm behaviour via computer simulations. This book was a logical economics descendant of Simon's (1945) management classic *Administrative Behaviour* and was born out of close interaction between Cyert, March and Simon at Carnegie Institute of Technology, later Carnegie-Mellon University, in Pittsburgh.

Simon had provided a more formal ground than the post-Marshallians for building a theory of the firm around decision rules. He argued that the human mind lacks the cognitive capacity to do the kinds of computations that would be required for optimal decision-making, especially in the face of organisational deadlines. Simplifying decision rules have to be used to avoid getting bogged down when engaging in problem-solving: one decision typically contains many sub-decisions—such as how, and how long, to search for possible solutions, and what to infer about the prospective performance of rival possible solutions—rather than just a choice between given means to given ends. In the face of inevitable 'bounded rationality', decision-makers have to engage in 'satisficing' behaviour, setting targets ('aspiration levels') and searching, initially locally, until a prospective means of meeting them is discovered. To survive in a competitive environment, where optimal choices may be impossible to discover or to identify as such even if they have been made, the decision-maker simply needs to find solutions that are good enough, given the strength of the competitive pressures, as Alchian (1950) had noticed.

Soon after *A Behavioural Theory of the Firm* was published, Harvey Leibenstein (1966) offered the first of his many papers (collected in Button 1989) on what he called '*X*-efficiency'. He was trying to get economists to shift from viewing inefficiency in terms of deadweight losses caused by relative prices being distorted by monopoly power, towards something more akin to the layperson's view of it as a situation in which a firm was operating with higher costs than were necessary. Though he did not portray it as such, his thinking can be viewed as bringing together elements of Marshall's view (of how firms differ in what they know about production methods, and the role of managers in shaping a firm's performance) and the Carnegie School's view of firms as composed of individuals each pursuing their own interests.

Like Cyert and March, Leibenstein recognised that employees in an organisation might make the most of any opportunities to enjoy a quiet life. Internal competition among workers could be attenuated if workers suspected that efforts to stand out by being unusually industrious would be matched by their peers or would result in them being penalised socially for acting as rate-busters. However, if competitive pressure increased, productivity increases might follow. With their idea of 'organisational slack', Cyert and March had also recognised that firms could be achieving lower profits than they might have earned, and operating with higher production costs than they might discover under pressure. They saw this slack as resulting from lags in the adjustment of aspirations into line with higher attainments, combined with the different interest groups in the firm being reluctant to incur the downside risks of trying to extract more for themselves when they were meeting their aspirations. Leibenstein's *X*-inefficiency notion complemented this view but he emphasised more the scope for reducing unit costs via better management and better knowledge of best-practice methods (or improving on them) rather than merely changing the distribution of returns to the different members of the coalition that made up the firm.

These views of the firm implied an approach to economic policy rather different from Thaler and Sunstein's (2008) liberal paternalism. The latter centres on using gentle nudges to steer consumers towards better choices. However, if limited search and experimentation result in needlessly low performance levels, then the way to stimulate productivity improvements is to put in place policies that make it harder to reach aspiration levels and/or to prevent firms from selecting their normal default options. Policies based on offering rewards could be of limited use if firms do not notice or respond to the incentives that are offered (Cyert and George, 1969). The 'old behavioural' approach is consistent with Hayekian policies of market liberalisation and the corporatisation, privatisation or outsourcing of public sector activities, which are all aimed at increasing competitive pressure. But it could also imply that regulatory policies could be used to jolt firms into discovering ways of operating in a leaner and fitter manner. For example, Loasby's (1967) field research on how the UK's regional policies affected managers' decisions showed that when firms were denied Industrial Development Certificates for their preferred locations this prompted their managers to have a major rethink, as a result of which they discovered better ways of running their firms. Nowadays, we might recognise that environmental regulations could have benefits, not merely in terms of the environment but also via the pressure that they posed on firms to find better ways of doing what they do.

As is evident from the thousands of studies of efficiency and productivity employing data envelope analysis and stochastic frontier analysis techniques, econometricians have proved open to the idea that firms differ in efficiency and frequently may not be operating at best-practice levels of productivity. (After a rather slow start in the twentieth century, research specifically aiming to measure *X*-efficiency has taken off strongly in the new millennium—about 175 studies are reported in a survey by Frantz, 2015.) But the same cannot be said for economists, despite the potential contradiction between advocating neo-liberal policies to improve economic performance and believing that firms should be modelled 'as if' they maximise profits. Adopting the satisficing view entails adopting a general framework that asserted that choices are based on decision rules (including rules for adjusting aspiration levels) that can take many forms. One can guess what these rules might be in a particular situation, and model their implications for behaviour, but to know whether one's analysis might be a good approximation it would be necessary to begin by studying the kinds of rules people actually use in the context in question—and it might be the case that people are using a diverse set of decision rules. This is very different from the standard approach of trying to derive results from preference orderings and production functions of a very generalised kind and assuming that consumers or firms are all alike.

It is important to note that the behavioural economics of the 1950s and 1960s was not offered with calls that mainstream economists needed to start again from scratch. Leibenstein considered himself to be a neoclassical economist who was simply asking his peers to acknowledge the presence of selective rationality and X-inefficiency, and to try to take account of these phenomena in their work. Simon viewed his bounded rationality/satisficing approach as a constructive contribution to mainstream economics (see the correspondence from Simon to Earl quoted in Earl and Peng, 2012). But it was impossible to incorporate it into the increasingly tightly defined core of microeconomic theory because it clashed with the view that all economising behaviour should be viewed as an act of constrained optimisation. To argue that in *some* situations satisficing was a rational way of choosing, whereas in simple, pre-defined choices optimisation would be feasible, would be problematic for a 'one size fits all' approach to economics. Hence, the only way for rule-based behaviour to be rendered acceptable to the mainstream economist was by modelling computational limitations as an additional constraint and then theorising in terms of optimal decision rules. This was done by Baumol and Quandt (1964) and is essentially what has happened with modern-day models of bounded rationality.

From an evolutionary standpoint, Simon's view of decision-making poses an even more fundamental challenge to the mainstream. Winter (1964) realised that if humans take time to gather and process information, then those who try to speed up and simplify their choices by using decision rules might be able to out-compete those who try to find optimal solutions, since the latter's choices may be out of date by the time they materialise. The firms that survive competitive selection processes might thus be the satisficers, not those that sought to optimise. It could thus be unwise to model markets 'as if' populated by firms that maximised profits.

This view contradicts the famous claims of Friedman (1953) (which had been based on a misinterpretation/misrepresentation of Alchian, 1950—see Kay, 1995) that competitive pressures would ensure firms ended up maximising profits even if they did not actually do the kinds of calculation presumed in the orthodox theory of the firm. However, the 'as if' approach was kept alive via Day's (1967) paper, where it was argued that, via a succession of iterative adjustments, satisficing firms could, sooner or later, stumble upon the best choices. Such a conclusion required the choice environment to be static, which, as Winter (1971) point out, it would not be in a world of Schumpeterian innovating entrepreneurs. But since the mainstream economists were focused on static equilibrium configurations and had not bought into Schumpeter's world-view, they felt they could ignore Winter's contributions (if they were aware of them) and appeal to Day's paper if the need arose to reject critiques based on satisficing ideas. Ironically, Day himself went on to spend much of the rest of his career making major contributions to the analysis of technical change and chaotic, dynamic systems, consistent with Winter's perspective.

Thus, although Simon was awarded the 1978 Alfred Nobel Memorial Prize in Economic Sciences for his analysis of decision-making in organisations, and although Cyert and March's behavioural theory of the firm has achieved well over 20,000 citations on Google Scholar, the Carnegie approach to behavioural economics, like that of the Oxford post-Marshallians, failed to become incorporated into mainstream economics. (Leibenstein fared no better at persuading mainstream economists to adopt his *X*-efficiency approach, despite his 1966 paper notching up over 4,500 Google Scholar hits.) However, the mainstream is going to find it hard to argue with the burgeoning empirical findings surveyed in Frantz (2015). The Carnegie School's citations mostly ended up coming via research in management and organisational behaviour. The main long-term carry forward of the ideas of Simon, Cyert and March within economics was to be via the evolutionary analysis that developed from Nelson and Winter's (1982) book *An Evolutionary Theory of Economic Change*.

Post-Marshallian inputs have also been significant to the evolutionary research programme, in the form of the analysis of corporate growth and industrial organisation offered by Penrose (1959) and Richardson (1972). Both base their analysis on detailed case knowledge (see Finch, 1999) and emphasise that firms differ in their capabilities, with Penrose also highlighting how limits to the rate at which managers can learn affect the rate at which firms can grow successfully. However, both of these contributions have had a bigger impact in research on business strategy, with many of their citations being as foundations for the 'resource-based view of the firm' and coming from business school scholars rather than from economists.

Change of focus: behavioural analysis of consumer choice

Focused as they were on opening up the black box of the firm, the Carnegie School did little to extend their behavioural analysis of decision-making to the realm of consumer behaviour. That it might be wise to do this ought to have become apparent after the publication of Lancaster's (1966) reformulation of standard consumer theory into a model of household choices framed in terms of the characteristics offered by products. Viewing choice in this way was an aspect of Marshall's thinking (Loasby, 1978) and was also proposed by Ironmonger (1972) in a book based on his Cambridge PhD dissertation that predated Lancaster's much better-known work. Framing choices in terms of selecting from rival bundles of characteristics provided a way of making sense of how consumers could deal with novel products (as more efficient new means of producing outputs on various existing characteristics axes). However, with a large range of products that promised significantly different combinations of characteristics outputs, consumers would face a major computational challenge if they were aware of all of their possible options and tried to weigh up all of the different combinations of characteristics in order to work out which product offered the best mix. In reality, their search processes might limit the scale of the information-processing task by causing them to stop well short of discovering all the available options and, if even a partial list left them with information overload, they might cope by applying simplifying rules and routines.

Potential for a Carnegie-style behavioural theory of the consumer was seized in marketing and approaches based on problem-solving decision cycles rapidly found its way into marketing textbooks (Nicosia, 1966; Engel, Kollat and Blackwell, 1968) and monographs (most notably Bettman, 1979) before being attempted in economics (Earl, 1983b). Although presenting consumers as if they went through problem-solving decision cycles with the aid of simplifying decision heuristics, the information-processing view of choice came to recognise that precisely which procedures were used would depend upon the context of choice (Earl, 1986; Payne, Bettman and Johnson, 1993). In some situations, a checklist or a process of filtering out products in terms of a priority based set of aspiration levels might lead to a decision despite there being many options, whereas in other cases such 'non-compensatory' procedures might be used to produce a short-list from which it would then be possible to make a selection by means more in keeping with Lancaster's (compensatory) view of performances on characteristics being traded off against each other. With only a few relevant characteristics and a few rival products, it might even be possible to choose not merely by working out overall evaluations in a manner akin to that envisaged by Lancaster but also with such evaluations being a function of some assessment of how social referents would view the selection of each option, weighted by the chooser's motivation to comply with the such social pressures, as presumed in the Fishbein and Ajzen (1975) model of behavioural intentions that has been frequently employed in the marketing literature.

These contributions failed to have any impact on how economists typically viewed consumer behaviour. This is not surprising: they emphasise the impact of the context of choice on decision-making processes, often rejected the principle of gross substitution (i.e., the idea that 'everyone has their price') and present choices as commonly being made in a filtering manner without all available information necessarily being used. Mainstream economists did not merely squander the potential for the characteristics-based approach to consumer choice to bring together economics and marketing (recognised by Ratchford, 1975); they even resisted replacing their traditional utility functions with the kind of characteristics-based approach that Lancaster and Ironmonger had offered, and it was not discussed in orthodox textbooks.

The most significant modern research on decision-making that tries to understand how ordinary people cope with the complex challenges of real life is arguably that of psychologist Gerd Gigerenzer and his colleagues on 'fast and frugal decision-making' (Gigerenzer et al., 1999; Gigerenzer and Brighton, 2009). This can be seen as a revival of the evolutionary perspective that emerged from Winter's (1964, 1971) challenge to the constrained optimisation paradigm. Like the 'new' behavioural economics, it assigns a key role to simple heuristics but its focus is on the vital role that heuristics play in facilitating effective decision-making. This contrasts sharply with the 'new' view that heuristics produce biased judgments that result in needlessly poor choices. Just as Kahneman (2011) has little to say about Simon's contributions, except insofar as Simon's work on expert chess players is consistent with his view of choices that are based on 'thinking fast', so he relegates any remarks about Gigerenzer's research to endnotes. In the 'new' behavioural economics of consumer behaviour, the focus has been on finding inherited heuristics that make all humans 'predictably irrational' (Ariely, 2009) in the same way, whereas the 'old' approach (such as Earl, 1986) was more like that of a clinical psychologist focusing on how individuals' personally constructed systems of rules for coping with life could in some cases prove dysfunctional. Where the 'old' approach was open to marketing's strategy of segmenting consumers into groups with similar modes of operating, the 'new' approach has, in effect, used empirical evidence of heuristics and biases as the basis for continuing with the mainstream 'representative agent' method.

Confidence and uncertainty

The behavioural theory of the firm portrayed corporate decision-makers as engaging in 'uncertainty avoidance' and attempts to eliminate uncertainty via measures (for example, lobbying policymakers) aimed at achieving a 'negotiated environment'. However, Keynes (1936, 1937) had earlier suggested that when faced with situations in which 'we simply do not know' about the future, people tend to use simplifying procedures, such as copying the behaviour of those believed to have better capacities for choosing, or simply extrapolating the past into the future, or making leaps into the unknown on the basis of 'animal spirits' if the surrounding mood was one of confidence. Keynes's emphasis on the psychological underpinnings of investment and business cycles has carried into modern-day behavioural economics far better than the 'old behavioural' analyses considered previously, as is evident via its influence on Akerlof and Shiller's (2009) book *Animal Spirits*.

Before Keynes's writings on confidence came significantly to influence behavioural economics, it was psychologist George Katona who was well known in that connection (for a survey of Katona's life and work, see Wärneryd, 1982). Katona pioneered surveys of consumer sentiment at his Survey Research Centre at the University of Michigan, having realised that, in an affluent economy in which consumers enjoy discretionary spending, consumption demand depends not merely on the ability of consumers to spend but also on their willingness to do so. The animal spirits idea thus also needed to be applied to consumer choice: with consumer durables often being discarded before they are worn out, the timing of purchases could be affected by consumers being uncertain about their job prospects and abilities to service credit commitments. Business cycles could thus be driven by shifts in consumer sentiment ahead of any shift in the animal spirits of the business sector.

In *The Powerful Consumer* (1960), and in many of his other publications, Katona argued that the evidence shows that corporate advertising cannot control consumer demand (contrary to Galbraith, 1958) and that macroeconomic policy measures could be rendered ineffectual by consumer sentiment. Katona's work had widespread impacts, provoking both academic and business researchers to construct indices of consumer confidence. His ideas were well-established in economic psychology and in the kind of behavioural economics that was being done in the 1980s (see the macroeconomics volume of the handbook edited by Gilad and Kaish, 1986). However, Katona's view of the importance of the psychology of saving has not carried into 'new' behavioural economics. Akerlof and Shiller do not refer to him. For 'new' behavioural economists, the focus for applying psychology to saving behaviour is not on modelling shifts in consumer sentiment but on using nudges to ensure that consumers achieve the self-control that is necessary in saving up for retirement.

Modern behavioural economics has also failed to employ contributions by G. L. S. Shackle, one of the earliest converts to Keynes's view of the significance of confidence as a determinant of aggregate spending. Shackle's approach was more like modern contributions in that it employed psychological concepts within formal models (his life and work are surveyed in Earl and Littleboy, 2014). Shackle (1939) swiftly set out to understand how entrepreneurs decide, in the face of uncertainty, whether or not to embark on what he came to label 'crucial experiments'—choices that could have irreversible major consequences and which do not lend themselves to analysis in terms of statistical probabilities. In the absence of probabilistic knowledge, decision-makers have to use their imaginations to derive conjectures about what might be possible and what could get in the way of imagined possibilities. Bounds to human imaginative capacities open up potential for surprise, and Shackle saw expectation-formation as involving reflection on how surprising imagined possibilities would be if they actually occurred. Assessments of potential surprise took the place of probabilities in Shackle's analysis but he did not view them as being used in an additive manner.

In his early work on potential surprise, Shackle presaged the Carnegie School's view that decision-makers use aspiration levels to discriminate between acceptable and unacceptable outcomes, for he saw the problem of choice being resolved with reference to thresholds of tolerance for poor outcomes and for potential surprise. However, after a decade of developing his ideas, he ended up with a different approach, more akin to Kahneman and Tversky's (1979) prospect theory (see Earl and Littleboy, 2014, chapter 8). In contrast to the subjective utility models that were offered as the mainstream way of dealing with absent data on objective probabilities, Shackle (1949) presented decision-makers as framing their conjectures in terms of gains and losses relative to a reference point. He also offered a theory of attention which predicted that, for each scheme under consideration, the decision-maker would end up focusing on one gain and one loss, thereby ignoring both less dramatic possibilities and outer possibilities that were harder to take seriously. Following such cognitive simplification, the decision-maker would rank the rival schemes on the basis of these pairs of 'focus outcomes', with Shackle's 'ascendancy function' view of the allocation of attention seeming to imply an S-shaped utility function akin to that in prospect theory.

Although Shackle's approach to choice under uncertainty initially attracted attention from leading economists such as Arrow and Klein, this interest was short-lived and economists adopted the subjective utility approach instead. Shackle's work did not go unnoticed by those who developed the behavioural theory of the firm, being cited favourably by Cyert and March (1963). However, Shackle made no attempt to try to align himself with the Carnegie School despite potential complementarities between the bounded rationality perspective and his view of the limitations to imagination and of focusing induced by finite attention. Rather, he objected to Simon's way of discussing rationality in terms of 'fully posed' problems (Shackle, 1969: 100). Later, Shackle (1985) attacked Simon for rejecting expected utility theory for its failure to address computational complexity rather than because the probability notion makes no sense in situations in which people do not repeatedly face the same kind of problem.

With the shift of the 'old' behavioural approach towards consumer behaviour, Shackle's framework was adapted into a satisficing, characteristics-based framework by Earl (1983b, 1986). Today, however, Shackle's analysis has become part of Austrian and post-Keynesian economics, whereas 'new' behavioural economists employ prospect theory, seemingly unaware of Shackle's contributions. As Kahneman (2011: 278–9) reports, the reference point idea around which prospect theory was built came to him and Tversky as a result of realising that, contrary to the assumptions of the subjective expected utility model, they had rather vague ideas about their total wealth but could more readily assess the implications of outcomes in terms of changes in their wealth.

The contrast between Shackle's failure to win converts for his potential surprise view and the success of prospect theory is striking. But so, too, is the extent to which the latter is based on a watered down view of the nature of choice—as were the experiments of Kahneman and Tversky that underpinned its assumptions (such as the impact of the endowment effect on the shape of the utility function). Genuine uncertainty, computational challenges and emotionally charged hopes and fears were all absent.

In not admitting any role for focusing or filtering process in choices involving complex payoff matrices, prospect theory fails to encompass bounded rationality. Moreover, it assigns no role for the imagination to consider what might be possible or for life-changing choices that entail 'crucial experiments'. Loss aversion and the endowment effect came from experiments that revealed contradictions between what people would pay to get something and what they would then require as compensation for parting with up after they had been given it. From Shackle's perspective, choice experiments would need to entail high stakes, but he would have had very mixed views about the pioneering attempt of Slonim and Roth (1998) to do this by spending their research dollars on studying an ultimatum game in a low-wage economy. Shackle did not just reject probability; his view of the role of the imagination in the choice process also led him to reject game theory on the basis that real-life games frequently involve potential for surprising the opposition via innovative ploys and for differing conjectures being constructed about the underlying payoff matrix.

Conclusion: behavioural economics as a tragedy of missed opportunities

On 9 February 2001 Herbert Simon died. Two days later, a pair of articles in the *New York Times* signalled that 'old' behavioural economics had been forgotten and the term 'behavioural economics' now applied only to the 'new' approach. Such coverage signified that the new approach had become mainstream. One of the articles (Lowenstein, 2001) was about Richard Thaler's long but ultimately successful attempt to get his ideas established. The other (Uchitelle, 2001) was about the work of David Laibson, of a younger generation and a rising star at Harvard. Neither article mentioned Simon at all. Simon had collected his Nobel Prize but had not focused his efforts on changing economics, whereas Thaler had been tireless at doing this despite initially succeeding in making an impact more in marketing and finance. Though heretical in his use of anecdotes, he succeeded by devising a version of behavioural economics that could be accepted by the mainstream by enabling it do deal with anomalies through a twisted version of the rational choice model. Others followed, and textbook franchises were established. 'Old' behavioural economics did not enjoy such evolutionary fitness.

All this seems tragic to 'old' behavioural economists. Instead of creating a general view of choice based on the application of rules and routines that may, depending on context, be fast and frugal or dysfunctional, most modern behaviourists have ended up with a focus on the systematic and predictable incompetence of consumers. Where once the behavioural theory of the firm offered potential for doing industrial economics mindful that firms are complex evolving organisations, we have modern behavioural industrial economics focusing on how firms behave strategically to exploit the failings of consumers—unless prevented from doing so by policies emerging from behavioural law and economics. And research has focused predominantly on closed decision problems, often with simple payoff matrices involving insignificant (or, if larger, merely hypothetical) betting choices, rather than on the kinds of situations in which decision-makers use their imaginations to envisage possibilities.

In terms of behavioural economics itself, the fact that this has happened should be no more surprising than the failure of 'old' behavioural economics to become part of every economist's core theoretical toolkit. Academia is not populated by humble maximisers of the growth of socially useful knowledge in their research fields. Rather, academics are boundedly rational individuals who have their own goals to pursue and incomplete, heuristics-driven knowledge of relevant literatures. In the face of time pressure, what matters is knowing enough to produce papers that referees, with similar limitations, will deem acceptable. Search rules and cognitive heuristics may ensure that economists fail to discover alternative approaches and that they form biased assessments of the merits of what they encounter or of their own research. The modern behavioural economist ends up doing behavioural economics in the modern way, which typically means doing it oblivious of earlier traditions or their extension into modern evolutionary economics. Textbook writers have a key role in determining whether a more radical grand synthesis will emerge and become widespread.

Bibliography

Akerlof, G., & Shiller, R. (2009). Animal Spirits: How Human Psychology Drives the Economy, and Why it Matters for Global Capitalism. Princeton, NJ: Princeton Univeristy Press.

Alchian, A. (1950). Uncertainty, evolution, and economic theory. Journal of Political Economy, 58(3), 211–21.

Andrews, P. W. S. (1949). Manufacturing Business. London: Macmillan.

Andrews, P. W. S. (1964). On Competition in Economic Theory. London: Macmillan.

Ariely, D. (2009). Predictably Irrational: The Hidden Forces that Shape Our Decisions. New York: HarperCollins.

Baddeley, M. (2013). Behavioural Economics and Finance. London and New York: Routledge.

Baumol, W. J., & Quandt, R. E. (1964). Rules of thumb and optimally imperfect decisions. American Economic Review, 54(2), 23–46.

Baumol, W. J., Panzar, J., & Willig, R. (1982). Contestable Markets and the Theory of Industrial Structure. New York: Harcourt Brace Jovanovich.

Bettman, J. R. (1979). An Information Processing Theory of Consumer Choice. Reading, MA: Addison–Wesley.

Button, K. (Ed.). (1989). The Collected Essays of Harvey Leibenstein, Volume 2: X-efficiency and Microeconomic Theory. Aldershot: Edward Elgar.

Cartwright, E. (2014). Behavioral Economics (2nd edn.). London and New York: Routledge.

Cyert, R. M., & George, K. D. (1969). Competition, growth and efficiency. Economic Journal, 79(March), 23–41.

Cyert, R. M., & March, J. G. (1963). A Behavioral Theory of the Firm. Englewood Cliffs, NJ: Prentice-Hall.

Day, R. H. (1967). Profits, learning and the convergence of satisficing to marginalism. Quarterly Journal of Economics, 81(2), 302–11.

Earl, P. E. (1983a). A behavioral theory of economists' behavior. In: A. S. Eichner (Ed.), Why Economics is Not Yet a Science (90–125). Armonk, NY: M. E, Sharpe (London, Macmillan).

Earl, P. E. (1983b). The Economic Imagination: Toward a Behavioural Analysis of Choice. Brighton: Wheatsheaf.

Earl, P. E. (1986). Lifestyle Economics: Consumer Behaviour in a Turbulent World. Brighton: Wheatsheaf.

Earl, P. E., & Littleboy, B. (2014). G. L. S. Shackle. Basingstoke: Palgrave Macmillan.

Earl, P. E., & Peng, T.-C. (2012). Brands of economics and the Trojan horse of pluralism. Review of Political Economy, 24(3), 451–67.

Engel, J. F., Kollat, D. T., & Blackwell, R. D. (1968). Consumer Behavior. Hinsdale, IL: Dryden Press.

Finch, J. H. (1999). The methodological implications of post Marshallian economics. In S. C. Dow & P. E. Earl (Eds.), Contingency, Complexity and the Theory of the Firm (156–77). Cheltenham: Edward Elgar.

Fishbein, M. A., & Ajzen, I. (1975). Belief, Attitude, Intention and Behavior: An Introduction to Theory and Research. Reading, MA: Addison–Wesley.

Frantz, R. (2015). 50 years of X-efficiency research. Department of Economics, San Diego State University, available online at www-rohan.sdsu.edu/~frantz/docs/Sibiu.%202015.%2050%20Years.pdf.

Friedman, M. (1953). The methodology of positive economics. In M. Friedman (Ed.), Essays in Positive Economics (3–43). Chicago, IL: University of Chicago Press.

Galbraith, J. K. (1958). The Affluent Society. London: Hamish Hamilton.

Gigerenzer, G., & Brighton, H. (2009). Homo heuristicus: Why biased minds make better inferences. Topics in Cognitive Sciences, 1(1), 107–43.

Gigerenzer, G., Todd, P. M., & the ABC Research Group (1999). Simple Heuristics that Make Us Smart. New York: Oxford University Press.

Gilad, B., & Kaish, S. (Eds.). (1986). Handbook of Behavioral Economics: Volume A Behavioral Microeconomics; Volume B Behavioral Macroeconomics. Greenwich, CT: JAI Press.

Hart, N. (2013). Alfred Marshall and Modern Economics. Basingstoke: Palgrave Macmillan.
Ironmonger, D. S. (1972). New Commodities and Consumer Behaviour. Cambridge: Cambridge University Press.
Irving, J. (1978). P. W. S. Andrews and the Unsuccessful Revolution. (PhD), University of Wollongong, New South Wales, Australia.
Kahneman, D. (2011). Thinking, Fast and Slow. New York: Farrar, Straus and Giroux.
Kahneman, D., & Tversky, A. (1979). Prospect theory: An analysis of decision under risk. Econometrica, 47(2), 263–91.
Katona, G. A. (1960). The Powerful Consumer: Psychological Studies of the American Economy. New York: McGraw-Hill.
Kay, N. M. (1995). Alchian and 'the Alchian thesis'. Journal of Economic Methodology, 2(2), 281–6.
Keynes, J. M. (1936). The General Theory of Employment, Interest and Money. London: Macmillan.
Keynes, J. M. (1937). The general theory of employment. Quarterly Journal of Economics, 51(2, February), 209–23.
Kuhn, T. S. (1962). The Structure of Scientific Revolutions. Chicago, IL: University of Chicago Press.
Lancaster, K. J. (1966). A new approach to consumer theory. Journal of Political Economy, 75(April), 132–57.
Lavoie, D. (1990). Hermeneutics, subjectivity and the Lester/Machlup debate: Towards a more anthropological approach to empirical economics. In W. J. Samuels (Ed.), Economics as Discourse: An Analysis of the Language of Economics (167–84). New York: Springer.
Leibenstein, H. (1966). Allocative efficiency vs. "X-efficiency". American Economic Review, 56(3, June), 392–414.
Lester, R. A. (1946). Shortcomings of marginal analysis for wage–employment problems. American Economic Review, 36, 63–82.
Loasby, B. J. (1967). Making location policy work. Lloyds Bank Review, 83(January), 34–47.
Loasby, B. J. (1978). Whatever happened to Marshall's theory of value? Scottish Journal of Political Economy, 25(1), 1–12.
Lowenstein, R. (2001). Exuberance is rational. New York Times Magazine, 11 February.
Machlup, F. (1946). Marginal analysis and empirical research. American Economic Review, 36, 519–34.
Marshall, A. (1890). Principles of Economics. London: Macmillan.
Marshall, A. (1923). Industry and Trade (4th edn.). London: Macmillan.
Nelson, R. R., & Winter, S. G. (1982). An Evolutionary Theory of Economic Change. Cambridge, MA: Belknap Press of Harvard University Press.
Nicosia, F. M. (1966). Consumer Decision Processes: Marketing and Advertising Implications. Englewood Cliffs, NJ: Prentice–Hall.
Payne, J. W., Bettman, J. R., & Johnson, E. J. (1993). The Adaptive Decision Maker. Cambridge: Cambridge University Press.
Penrose, E. (1959). The Theory of the Growth of the Firm. Oxford: Basil Blackwell.
Ratchford, B. T. (1975). The new economic theory of consumer behavior: An interpretive essay. Journal of Consumer Research, 2(September), 65–75.
Richardson, G. B. (1972). The organisation of industry. Economic Journal, 82(327), 883–96.
Schumpeter, J. A. (1943). Capitalism, Socialism and Democracy. London: George Allen & Unwin (new edn, 1992, London and New York: Routledge).
Sent, E.-M. (2004). Behavioral economics: How psychology made its (limited) way back into economics. History of Political Economy, 36(4), 735–60.
Shackle, G. L. S. (1939). Expectations and employment. Economic Journal, 49(195), 442–52.
Shackle, G. L. S. (1949). Expectation in Economics. Cambridge: Cambridge University Press.
Shackle, G. L. S. (1969). Decision, Order and Time in Human Affairs (2nd edn.). Cambridge: Cambridge University Press.
Shackle, G. L. S. (1985). Book review note on 'Reason in Human Affairs' by Herbert A. Simon. Economic Journal, 95, 246.
Simon, H. A. (1945). Administrative Behavior. New York: Macmillan (3rd edn. 1976, Free Press).
Slonim, R., & Roth, A. E. (1998). Learning in high stakes ultimatum games: An experiment in the Slovak Republic. Econometrica, 66(3), 569–96.
Smith, A. ([1759] 1976). The Theory of Moral Sentiments (edited by D. D. Raphael and A. L. MacFie), Oxford: Clarendon Press.

Thaler, R. H. (1980). Toward a positive theory of consumer choice. Journal of Economic Behavior & Organization, 1(1), 39–60.
Thaler, R. H. (2015). Misbehaving: The Making of Behavioral Economics. New York: W. W. Norton.
Thaler, R. H., & Sunstein, C. R. (2008). Nudge: Improving Decisions about Health, Wealth and Happiness. New Haven, CT: Yale University Press.
Uchitelle, L. (2001). Some economists call behavior a key. New York Times, Business section, 11 February.
Wärneryd, K.-E. (1982). The life and work of George Katona. Journal of Economic Psychology, 2, 1–31.
Wilson, T., & Andrews, P. W. S. (Eds.). (1951).Oxford Studies in the Price Mechanism. Oxford: Clarendon Press.
Winter, S. G. (1964). Economic 'natural selection' and the theory of the firm. Yale Economic Essays, 4, 225–72.
Winter, S. G. (1971). Satisficing, selection and the innovating remnant. Quarterly Journal of Economics, 85(2), 237–61.
Young, W. L., & Lee, F. S. (1993). Oxford Economics and Oxford Economists. London: Macmillan.

2

GEORGE KATONA

A founder of behavioral economics

Richard Curtin

George Katona was a founder of behavioral economics. Katona first published a broad outline and agenda for the development of behavioral economics in the 1940s (1942a, 1944a, 1945, 1946a, 1946b, 1947, 1951a, 1951b). Katona conceived behavioral economics as a discipline within economics that was primary concerned with the human element in economic affairs. While some believe that the adjective "behavioral" is implicit and unnecessary in the title of any social science discipline, Katona thought it was necessary to emphasize that the centerpiece of this research was human decision making whereas a significant portion of economic theory was concerned with the behavior of markets. Katona did not attempt to replace economic theory but tried to bolster its findings with new insights from a more complete and accurate account of economic behavior (Katona, 1951a, 1963, 1967a, 1972a, 1974, 1976a, 1980). Katona was an empirical scientist who believed that understanding economic behavior through careful observation was the best foundation on which to base advances in economic theory. That same approach has persisted for most other researchers in behavioral economics who have followed Katona (Rabin, 2002).

George Katona was my mentor, friend, and colleague. Following Katona's death in 1981, several articles appeared describing his life and scholarly contributions (Wärneryd, 1982; Hosseini, 2011), including an article written by me (Curtin, 1984). These articles were written as intellectual biographies. While it is hard to completely avoid such details, this article will primarily assess the impact of the theories advanced by Katona on the subsequent development of behavioral economics. Founders of a scientific discipline can have a profound influence on its growth and maturation. This article will demonstrate that George Katona has had an enduring and extensive impact on the development of behavioral economics. To be sure, at times his theoretical insights and scientific methodology were the subject of intense debates during his lifetime. Those debates have reverberated over the years as the core principles that he advanced were repeatedly rediscovered by succeeding generations of researchers.

Katona viewed the scope of behavioral economics to include all human economic behavior: all types of consumer spending and saving behavior, entrepreneurship, and all work related behavior including job choice and investments in human capital, all types of business behavior ranging from decisions on prices, output, investment, finance, and preferences and reactions to economic policies and programs by consumers as well as businesses. In addition, the analysis could be focused on the micro or the macro level. Behavioral economics in the last fifty years, as even a casual observer could appreciate, has grown to encompass all these fields and many more. One might assume that the coverage of most aspects of economic behavior would naturally be associated with an underlying theory that would be seen as a competitor to economics. Katona never had that intention. He felt that all disciplines required subdisciplines that specialized in specific areas. Insights from behavioral economics would naturally be incorporated into the disciplines of economics as well as psychology.

There was a critical difference between Katona's scientific approach and that of conventional economics. Katona focused on the rationality of the *process* of decision making, while economics was mainly concerned with the rationality of the *outcomes*. This same difference in focus was identified by Herbert Simon as procedural versus substantive rationality. Process or procedural rationality emphasizes the appropriate deliberation and decision processes, outcome or substantive rationality emphasizes the realization of the appropriate results. This difference in perspectives is deeply rooted in the disciplines of psychology and economics. To be sure, a decision could be seen as rational by psychologists as well as by economists, but that coincidence would be irrelevant since the ultimate objective of each discipline is to focus on the rationality of either decision processes or decision outcomes, but not both.

A corollary of this difference is whether attention is given to equilibrium or to the process of disequilibrium adjustments. Economics used equilibrium conditions to define the appropriate outcomes, but psychology's main focus is on how people learn and adapt to a constantly changing environment. Economic theory posits that people learn from their mistakes, so that their behavior will ultimately converge to the rational and optimum outcomes in equilibrium. Psychologists are more likely to believe that the divergences from rationality are a permanent feature of the human condition. Unfortunately, there are no behavioral observations that can convincingly reject either of these opposing views given the fundamental differences in their underlying theoretical perspectives. Katona did not believe it was useful to simply categorize deviations from orthodox economic theories as anomalies. He thought science was best served by specifying the conditions under which each behavioral response was likely to occur. In contrast, conventional economics has demonstrated a preference for more compact and tractable models, despite a long and growing list of documented anomalies.

There is another distinctive aspect of Katona's views compared with later scholars in behavioral economics: Katona's research agenda was problem-oriented rather than discipline-oriented. Katona's research was motivated by unresolved economic problems of his era, including hyperinflation as well as crippling deflation, massive job losses, and the evaporation of wealth and incomes, all of which he personally experienced before reaching his mid-30s. Katona believed that these complex and multifaceted societal problems required the addition of behavioral factors to conventional economic models. In contrast, the next generation of behavioral economists, which Sent (2004) called the "new" behavioral economists, were more likely to base their research on how decisions differed from theoretical predictions based on the standard rationality postulates. While their results could be used to address unresolved economic problems, the motivation for their research was theoretical rather than problem-oriented. Katona's pragmatic approach was reaffirmed by Raj Chetty in his Ely Lecture on behavioral economics more than a half century later (Chetty, 2015). He argued that the starting point of behavioral economics was how to best resolve pressing economic problems, such as those Katona had addressed. Behavioral factors should be introduced insofar as they improved prediction and policy decisions. Comparable to Katona's earlier views, Chetty argued that as economics becomes more problem-oriented and empirical, behavioral economics will play an increasing role in determining its future scientific development.

When Katona first formulated his theories on behavioral economics in the 1940s, the Great Depression had significantly challenged the orthodox macroeconomic theory. Like many of his contemporaries, Katona's ideas were significantly influenced by the new theoretical approach advanced by John Maynard Keynes (1936). Keynesian theory provided what Katona viewed as a compelling explanation of how uncertainty and ambiguity influenced the expectations and decisions of economic agents. Keynes placed special emphasis on the decisions of business firms as well as how government policy makers acted to determine the course of the national economy. Katona thought that Keynes had made a significant omission by not extending that same influence over the macro economy to the consumer sector. Indeed, Keynes proposed the "fundamental psychological law" which essentially assumed that consumers were passive responders to current income, and he completely dismissed the importance of consumer investment expenditures as a factor in shaping the course of the macro economy. Katona disagreed on both counts. He believed that the consumer was a powerful and independent actor whose actions could influence whether the macro economy would expand or contract. While Katona's views about the power of the consumer sector has found worldwide support when it came to economic policy decisions, conventional economic theory still views the consumer as a passive responder whose actions cannot spark a recession or create an economic recovery. Katona long held that consumers had discretion in when and how much to spend, and these decisions could produce expansions or recessions. Consumption was not a passive, endogenous variable completely determined by the rational calculus of other economic factors.

Katona's main theoretical contributions involved the acquisition of information and learning to form economic expectations, the importance of consumer optimism and uncertainty to the functioning of the macro economy, and the role of economic aspirations in determining longer-term economic trends. Katona's research led to a number of advances associated with behavioral microeconomics as well as behavioral macroeconomics. He documented through careful observation by the early 1950s that the frame of reference and the context in which economic information is perceived determines its meaning, that all economic agents use relative rather than absolute reference standards, that psychological variables intervene between economic signals and responses to determine the behavioral outcomes, and that social influences on behavior are an inescapable part of economics. Most of these theoretical insights were advanced by Katona in the 1940s and 1950s. A half-century later, his theories were still widely accepted by behavioral economists.

Another critical component of Katona's contributions was his leadership in the development of the scientific infrastructure required for the robust measurement of economic behavior. When Katona began his research, most of the required tools for the new scientific discipline had yet to be developed. Probability methods of sample selection and advances in statistics were needed to draw nationally representative samples that could provide estimates with known sampling variances; observation and questionnaire methods needed to be developed that could yield valid and reliable measures across all population groups; and machine tabulation and analysis methods needed to be devised (with Angus Campbell, 1946c and 1953c; 1949c; with Janet Fisher, 1950; 1951a; 1954c; 1957a; 1957d; 1957f). Katona and his colleagues at the Survey Research Center at the University of Michigan, including Rensis Likert, Angus Campbell, Leslie Kish, Charles Cannell, and James Morgan, acquired the skills and built the necessary infrastructure. After nearly three-quarters of a century, the Survey Research Center is still in the forefront of advancing the methodology and research on behavioral economics. Katona's advances in theory and methods are so commonly accepted that his achievements represent the unquestioned scientific foundation of behavioral economics (Tobin, 1972).

Strength from adversity

George Katona was born on November 6, 1901 in Budapest, Hungary, and he died on June 18, 1981 in Berlin, Germany. Katona had a remarkable intellect. He was just 20 years old when he completed his PhD in psychology and won the Gauss Medal from the University of Göttingen. His early life was shaped by economic and political upheavals (Katona, 1972b; Curtin, 1984). His original plan was to get a law degree and take over his grandfather's law practice. When Bela Kun led a communist putsch and closed the University of Budapest, he switched to the University of Göttingen in Germany. After completing his PhD, Katona obtained a faculty position at the University of Frankfurt, and published an award winning monograph (Katona, 1924). The hyperinflation in the early 1920s in Germany forced him to seek additional employment, which he obtained at a bank. While employed at this bank, he was paid daily at noon and given a few hours to spend his salary before it became worthless. This experience prompted Katona to publish a paper on inflation as a form of mass hysteria in the *Frankfurter Zeitung*. This article was widely cited and demonstrated to Katona the potential contribution of psychology to the study of economic problems. Katona decided to move to Berlin to study economics, a discipline he soon mastered without the benefit of formal training. Gustav Stolper, who founded *Der Deutsche Volkswirt* (The German Economist), hired Katona in 1926 as an assistant editor, where Katona regularly published commentaries on the German economy. Katona also continued his research in Berlin on the psychology of perception and evaluation (1921, 1925, 1926, 1927, 1929, 1935) under the influence of Max Wertheimer, a founder of Gestalt psychology. Stolper and Wertheimer had a significant influence on the development of Katona's intellectual views.

The same pattern of political displacement and economic crisis was repeated once again in the 1930s. The *Volkswirt* was one of the first publications banned by Hitler's government, and this caused Katona to immigrate to the United States in 1933. The Great Depression of the 1930s reaffirmed the importance Katona placed on the study of macroeconomics. Katona and Stolper formed a business in New York to provide investment advice to Europeans. Katona's involvement ended when he was sidelined by a three-year battle with tuberculosis. He used this as an opportunity to return to an academic life to continue his research on perception and learning. Katona obtained a Carnegie grant to conduct his research, which culminated with the publication of *Organizing and Memorizing* in 1940, a book that was widely recognized for its advances in theory and scientific methodology (1940, 1942b, 1942c). This research, combined with his prior studies on perception and evaluation of information, eventually became the foundation of his theories about how economic expectations were formed, how they changed, and how they influence the course of the macro economy.

The life course of Katona was again interrupted by WWII, and he was drawn back to his interests in the psychology of inflation. Katona gave lectures at the New School for Social Research on that topic and published an influential book in 1942 called *War without Inflation*. This book marked the start of his lifelong efforts to develop a new interdisciplinary approach to the study of economic behavior. He was appointed in 1942 by Jacob Marschak of the Cowles Commission for Research in Economics at the University of Chicago to conduct studies of the reactions of businesses to price controls. This research was co-sponsored by the National Bureau of Economic Research. He related compliance or circumvention to both economic and psychological factors (1944b, 1945). Katona sent a draft of his chapter on survey methods to Rensis Likert, a leading survey expert at the US Department of Agriculture. Likert offered a job to Katona to direct the first nationwide survey of ownership of liquid assets in 1946. At the end of the war, Katona, Likert, and Angus Campbell moved to the University of Michigan to establish the Survey Research Center. Katona's avowed goal when he came to the University of Michigan was to develop the theory and methods of behavioral economics. Katona became a Professor of Psychology and Economics and remained active until his death in 1981.

Psychological foundations of economic behavior

Economic behavior is learned behavior and it is dependent on how people perceive and utilize information. The development of Katona's theories about how people learn was influenced by the Gestalt theories of Max Wertheimer and Kurt Lewin. The theory of information favored by economists is that the content of the individual elements defined its overall meaning. Katona held that this view was inconsistent with scientific observations about how people perceive and utilize economic information. Katona believed that perceptions of information taken in its entirety helped to define the meaning of its component parts, rather than the aggregation of the components defining the meaning of the overall perception. Although this Gestalt principle may have been controversial when Katona proposed it more than a half century ago, the fact that the perceived meaning of information is context dependent has since achieved widespread scientific acceptance across all social sciences. Everyone now recognizes that how information is framed determines its meaning.

The rise and fall of Keynesian economics closely parallels the controversy over the Gestalt principles. Keynes did not insist that macroeconomic theory be derived solely from microeconomic foundations of profit and utility maximization. Keynes believed that macroeconomics included some concepts that had no microeconomic representation, a position on which Katona agreed. By the late 1970s, however, the Keynesian view was displaced by the neoclassical consensus that held that micro foundations were paramount in defining macroeconomic theory (Lucas, 1972). The consensus favored this presumed principle of consistency despite the fact that a strictly applied principle of methodological individualism would eliminate a good deal of macroeconomic results that could not be reduced to their microeconomic foundations (Blaug, 1992). This difference in theoretical perspectives has yet to be resolved.

Context sensitive information processing

The first assumption challenged by Katona was the notion that the same economic information, say on income or prices, would be interpreted in the same way regardless of the context in which it was perceived. Katona believed the frame of reference or context could give the same change in an economic variable a unique meaning. In an article published in 1944, Katona (1944a: 340) stated that "Viewing a situation or problem within different frames of reference may account for different reactions to the same economic situation and different answers to the same economic problem." Recent work has come to the same conclusion about reference dependent standards (Sugden, 2003; Köszegi and Rabin, 2006; Farber, 2008). While people usually react to price or income changes in the manner expected by traditional economic theory, under certain conditions, people could react in a manner unanticipated by conventional economic theory. For example, although people may ordinarily react to escalating inflation in a defensive manner by postponing expenditures, under certain conditions, rising prices may cause more spending and advance buying. Katona argued that it was important to specify which conditions lead to one response and which to another response (1946b, 1949a, 1949b, 1951a, 1960a, 1964a, 1968a, 1968b, 1968c, 1975). Economists treated the perverse impact of "inflationary psychology" as an aberration. It was not a sufficient cause to modify accepted theory; indeed, such aberrations are specifically excluded from the equilibrium nature of economic theories. Katona thought that context dependent information processing was the standard response, and economic theory needed to be flexible enough to account for an event that had been repeatedly observed over the past century in economies throughout the world. He argued that describing a behavioral reaction as an "aberration" or due to "animal spirits" needlessly limits understanding of its causes and consequences as well as corrective policy reactions.

More than a quarter-century later, Kahneman and Tversky (1979) advanced the same basic idea but were much more successful in showing how the framing of a problem had a significant influence on people's perception of the information and the resulting decisions. They themselves framed their research in a way that proved more convincing to economists: they investigated departures from rationality caused by how framing influenced the decisions people make in response to an equivalent set of choices. Their experiments yielded convincing evidence that how decision problems were framed had a significant influence on choice outcomes. Perhaps the most important deviation from rationality was associated with a very common frame in economic decisions: whether the decision problem was framed as a gain or a loss. Kahneman and Tversky formalize these insights in *Prospect Theory* (1979), which has been widely adopted in behavioral economics. Ultimately, the anomalies Katona demonstrated were no more or less successful than those shown by Kahneman and Tversky in prompting a fundamental revision in orthodox economic theory. Nonetheless, the use of these insights have become commonplace as empirical studies have expanded to nearly every aspect of economic behavior.

Katona also held that frames of reference had an impact on how people learned about cyclical developments in the economy (Katona, 1951a, 1960a, 1964a, 1975, with Strümpel 1978, 1979). He hypothesized that people naturally use the stage of the economic cycle to direct their conscious awareness to ongoing economic developments. After a recovery turned into a robust expansion, people increasingly become less attentive to favorable economic news, and increasingly attend to potential negative trends. The opposite shift in attention-resources occurred near the end of a recessionary downturn. Katona described these shifts in the selective attention of consumers as partly reflecting the age-old maxim that "only what's new is news." Katona understood, however, that it is impossible for people to attend to every bit of economic news. Some mechanism was needed to provide a convenient means to quickly select which information deserved attention and which information could be ignored. Throughout Katona's life, such rational inattention was dismissed as an unreliable and unrealistic task since rationality was thought to require full and complete information. More recently, rational inattention has received much more robust theoretical attention by Christopher Sims (1998, 2003).

Intervening variables

Katona did not believe there was a direct and unchanging link between a change in an economic factor and a behavioral response. Other variables intervened between the stimulus and response that could modify how economic agents actually behaved. The link between income and consumption is an example that Katona frequently used to demonstrate the importance of intervening variables. Initially he focused on exceptions to the Keynesian "fundamental psychology law" and later on evidence that was contrary to Friedman's permanent income hypothesis. Most famously, Katona's hypothesis that economic optimism or pessimism was a critical intervening variable which determined macro trends in consumption was his most famed conjecture and most replicated finding worldwide. Katona theorized that a host of intervening variables conditioned the relationship between income and consumption, which at times opened a significant divergence between observed spending and the amount that would be expected based on the annuity value of wealth.

Perhaps the most common intervening variable Katona proposed was expectations. At the time, for example, most models estimated consumption as a function of income, both defined as current or past realizations. Katona thought that how people reacted to their current income was modified by how they expected their income to change in the future. Income expectations intervened and influenced the relationship between current income and consumption.

In response, economic theory quickly included the direct influence of income expectations as a predictor rather than use the concept of an intervening variable. The same sort of incorporation into economic models can be said for other intervening variables, such as aspirations and social norms.

Katona believed intervening variables played an important role in shaping responses to changes in economic factors. Disregarding the role of these intervening variables was not a loss to pure theory, but it was a determent to a full understanding of economic behavior. That same conclusion was offered by George Akerlof some fifty years later. Akerlof (2007) argued that other intervening variables, namely social norms, were the missing element in macroeconomics. The inclusion of social norms was necessary to resolve neutralities, such as the independence of consumption from current income or the independence of inflation and unemployment. Social norms could explain why consumption was not governed by permanent income, and social norms about nominal prices and wages could explain the correspondence of inflation and unemployment, for example. These social norms are manifestations of the economic environment that have evolved over many decades. The nature and function of what Akerlof called social norms are identical to what Katona called intervening variables. Indeed, Akerlof and Shiller (2010) used a wide range of concepts—using the Keynesian term "animal spirits"—to signify the impact from the same type of psychological antecedents on economic behavior that Katona called intervening variables. As Katona and later Akerlof and Shiller would emphasize, these intervening variables are shaped by economic as well as social factors.

Social influences

The impact of social factors is perhaps the single most striking difference between directly observing how consumers make their economic decisions and how the theory of utility maximization describes that process. Conventional economic theory holds that people behave as if they were isolated on economic islands so that what other people prefer, consume, or earn had no impact on their own economic decisions. Indeed, orthodox economic theory is unique among all of the social sciences in the limited formal recognition it accords to the social nature of human behavior. Needless to say, it is not that economists actually believe social factors are unimportant, but that economic models can quickly become intractable if each individual's utility is partly dependent on the outcomes achieved by every other person. But as Akerlof has shown, orthodox neoclassical theory is not consistent with empirical observation without assuming that social norms play a significant role in shaping economic behavior.

Katona emphasized social influences on perceptions and learning. Most social influences on behavior were well known before Katona applied them to the study of economic behavior, such as how group membership and reference standards affect preferences. The rise of social media and networking are likely to influence the formation of reference groups as well as the social influences on learning. Moreover, there is no need to highlight the fact that people acting in their roles as consumers, workers, or voters are likely to display a range of preferences and behaviors that are not fully consistent across their roles. Multiple and sometimes inconsistent motives are the norm. This meant that human behavior could neither be described as entirely rational nor completely capricious (Katona, 1953b).

Katona did note that the principle of methodological individualism was also a subject of debate in psychology. He used an older terminology, the molar (group) and the molecular (individual) to discuss the differences (Katona, 1951a). It is clearly true that only an individual can think, make a decision, and act; no group is capable of these tasks. Nonetheless, it is widely believed that at times the collective actions of groups of people cannot be surmised from summing what individual would do acting alone. Again, Katona used the principles of Gestalt psychology to assert that it is possible for not only the total to be different than the sum of its constituent parts, but the total can help to define its constituent parts.

While Katona never believed that other people's opinions were the only or even the prime determinant of their optimism or pessimism, he did recognize that changes in economic expectations were significantly influenced by other people's assessments. The social influences on people's expectations helped to produce synchronized wave of optimism and pessimism that made the consequent changes in spending and saving behavior potent determinants of whether the economy moved toward expansion or contraction.

Formation of expectations

Katona believed that there was no other concept that played a larger or more important role in shaping economic behavior than expectations. The importance of expectations as a determinant of behavior was largely missing in psychology (Newcomb, 1972). Katona believed that expectations had both cognitive as well as affective components, meaning expectations contained information about future states of economic variables as well as how people evaluated those expected outcomes. No one, Katona believed, could be indifferent about expected changes in their own income, job prospect, or cost of living. This combination of what change they anticipated and how they evaluated that expected change meant that people would be motivated to mediate their responses to economic signals to avoid losses or to achieve gains.

How expectations are formed has been long debated. Everyone agrees with the premise that economic expectations must be learned. Katona identified two forms of learning in his classic book *Organizing and Memorizing* (1940). The conventional explanation was that learning was accomplished by repetition or memorization. This nineteenth-century principle is now commonly referred to as learning by association. This theory was widely used as a justification for the primacy of past experience, with expectations formed by a process of extrapolation from past realization. The basic process was modified by many variants, such as differential weighting of past realizations and adjusting future expectations to account for past errors. All of these theories, however, meant that expectations would never be fully accurate predictors of the actual future outcomes (Curtin, 2010). Although most of these theories were couched as learning theories, by its complete dependence on the past, such learning would always produce biased expectations. While Katona believed many expectations were formed as a simple function of past realizations, not all expectations could be formed in this manner since Katona believed it defied the basic principle of rationality. Even ordinary consumers could take into account the impact of some change in the environment or economic policies on subsequent developments before it was reflected in market outcomes or official economic statistics.

Katona theorized that there was a second form of learning that was more powerful and flexible and not solely dependent on past experience. His experimental investigation of human learning and perception began with his doctoral dissertation in 1921 and this continued as his primary research interest over the next two decades. In his book *Organizing and Memorizing* (1940), Katona provided empirical support for another distinct form of learning due to an understanding of the organization or structure of the material. Katona found that this type of learning had high transferability to other similar situations. The greater transferability was based on understanding whole processes rather than memorizing specific associations. These insights had a significant influence on how he believed economic expectations were formed and how they changed.

Learning by organization and understanding was consistent with the formation of expectations that were not solely dependent on past trends. In addition, they could be more accurate by being based on an understanding of the relevant underlying factors. Instead of simply basing expectations on past results, Katona proposed in the 1940s that it would be more appropriate to directly ask economic agents about their economic expectations (1942, 1945, 1946a, 1947, 1951a). To be sure, Katona never believed that consumers had sufficient knowledge to form expectations about the vast majority of economic series that are of concern to the profession. He did believe that for a select few economic series, consumers paid a good deal of attention. Among those of greatest concern to consumers were trends in income, employment, inflation, and interest rates. Moreover, Katona believed that for these economic variables, consumers were less likely to extrapolate past trends and associations.

The initial reactions by the economics profession to Katona's theories were to dismiss them as naive. Economists doubted that consumers had the ability to acquire, understand, and effectively utilize information to form coherent economic expectations. Nonetheless, expectations increasingly garnered attention by economists. Indeed, expectations soon became central components in Modigliani and Brumberg's life-cycle theory of consumption (1954) and in Friedman's permanent income hypothesis (1957). While in theory, expectations were hypothesized to be forward-looking, in practice Friedman, for example, used averages of past income realizations to estimate future permanent income. The two essential ideas that Katona advanced were often denied: forming expectations was still viewed as dependent on past trends, and consumers were still thought to be incapable of forming realistic economic expectations.

John Muth (1961) used the methodological techniques pioneered by Katona to collect and analyze survey data on economic expectations. Based on his analysis, Muth proposed that economic agents did not simply extrapolate past changes but based their expectations on an understanding of the underlying economic theory. Muth proposed the same sort of learning that Katona had identified in 1940. He termed that learning process the rational expectations hypothesis. Economics has never been the same. By the early 1970s, Lucas (1972) criticized Keynesian theory for assuming that people reacted naively to economic policies—the position Katona had advocated thirty years earlier when he analyzed wartime price controls in 1942. Needless to say, Katona never believed in the rational expectations hypothesis, but he never believed that people were irrational either. One might have anticipated that Katona's theories and use of surveys to measure economic expectations would have finally convinced economists of the merits of his approach. It did not.

It should be no surprise that economics embraced the rational expectations hypothesis as it was the natural accompaniment of rational maximization of utility by consumers and profits by business. While each of these assumptions proved difficult to sustain empirically, it was the model's predictions rather than its assumptions that demonstrated its scientific merit. Although orthodox economists now judge the incorporation of the rational expectations hypothesis the most important innovation in economic theory in nearly the last half-century (Mankiw, 1988), just as many would agree that as a practical matter the investigation of specific economic problems or issues is best conducted with more realistic assumptions (Katona, 1980).

Once economic agents were assumed to rationally form expectations that were equivalent to the results of economic models, most economists concluded that there was no reason to actually measure the expectations agents held. Katona's views fit between the initial reactions that observed expectations were uninformed noise and the later reactions that expectations were fully rational and identical to econometric predictions. The empirical data on the accuracy of consumer inflation expectations compared with the predictions of professional economic forecasters were unanticipated, to say the least. The year-ahead inflation forecasts of consumers were slightly more accurate than those of the economists (Gramlich, 1983; Baghestani, 1992; Thomas, 1999; Mehra, 2002; Curtin, 2010). Each time, the predictive ability of consumer expectations was viewed as an anomaly. No one, however, could offer a convincing explanation of why ordinary consumers could match the skills, experience, and motivation of professional forecasters.

Aspirations

Katona intended the concept of aspirations to fill a gap in existing economic theory concerning economic growth. The orthodox theory of economic growth is dominated by the supply side: capital goods, technology, and labor productivity. It assumes an automatic and commensurate growth in the demand for goods and services. People's aspirations to consume more are assumed to be insatiable. The assumption that utility functions were defined by "given tastes and preferences" was always meant to include the latest and most advanced array of goods and services. Economists have long considered the determinants of "tastes and preferences" to be an inquiry more suited to psychology than economics, and more importantly, only influenced the specific products or services consumed by consumers, not the overall rate of economic growth. Katona disagreed and advanced a theory in the 1940s in which changes in consumers' aspirations could have an independent and significant impact on the overall rate of economic growth (Katona 1946a, 1951a, 1960a, 1964a, 1975).

In particular, Katona believed changes in aspirations had significantly influenced Americans' willingness to incur debt to achieve their consumption aspirations as well as to make additional investments in human capital and increase their participation in the workforce. These actions created substantial expansions in markets for a wide variety of goods and services that independently added to the pace of domestic economic growth. Moreover, the strong rise in material aspirations also increased the willingness of Americans to step up their labor force participation rates, which also acted to increase the pace of economic growth. These factors also created differences in economic cultures across countries. For example, Americans became known for higher consumption and lower savings, while Germans were noted for higher savings and lower consumption (Katona et al., 1971a). Even to the present time, growth in the German economy is more dependent on exports given the insufficiency of domestic consumption compared with its productive capacity.

Katona conceptualizes aspirations as motives that instigate and direct economic behavior (1951a, 1953b, 1975). Aspirations were not distant dreams or unrealistic hopes; Katona viewed aspirations as reality based. The aspirations that provide the strongest behavioral motives are those that are only modestly different from recent accomplishments. Aspirations are not static, but continually change in response to accomplishment and failure. Changes in aspirations are also sensitive to contextual factors and the performance of other people and groups. A critical part of Katona's theory is that he hypothesized an asymmetric dynamic to changes in aspirations: fulfillment quickly gives rise to new aspirations, but failure does not immediately result in diminished aspirations. Failure initially sparks renewed efforts toward attainment. No one easily or quickly gives up their aspirations. Aspirations are finally reduced only after prolonged frustration and failure. Declines in aspirations not only indicate that people judge the probability of failure higher than the probability of success, but that an unchanged aspiration will result in net losses in utility since maintaining those aspirations would misdirect behavioral decisions. Rational processing of feedback requires change.

This theory was largely ignored in the economic literature as irrelevant since material aspirations were always expected to increase. To be sure, some people may reduce their aspirations, but they would be more than offset by others that increased their aspirations. No one could imagine a coordinated reduction in material aspirations that could have a significant impact on economic growth, until secular stagnation challenged that view. Secular stagnation is usually defined by economists in terms of supply, an insufficiency of potential capital investments at current interest rates. Others have termed it an insufficiency of demand that persisted despite a wide array of spending incentives. Katona would have suggested that the weakness in spending as well as labor force participation, aside from an aging population, was related to reductions in material aspirations. Aspirations that had been reduced due to reversals in income and wealth as well as lessened prospects for renewed personal financial advancement due to rising inequality. Whether the Katona hypothesis is correct or not is not the basic issue. Rather it is whether economics persists with a one-sided "supply" hypothesis or adds another "demand" hypothesis to the determinants of economic growth.

Behavioral macroeconomics

Katona is widely known for advancing theories of behavioral macroeconomics. Macroeconomics became an established field of study following the 1936 publication by John Maynard Keynes on the *General Theory of Employment, Interest, and Money*. This book resonated with Katona since it was about solutions to the economic problems Katona had personally experienced. Katona agreed with the Keynesian emphasis on demand as the main determinant of trends in the overall economy, but disagreed with the belief of Keynes that consumers were passive actors in the macro economy. Keynes thought the primary determination of macroeconomic trends were the investment decisions of businesses as well as the government's monetary and fiscal policies. The consumer was assumed to be a passive actor, mechanistically translating income into consumption. Keynes assumed firms made investment decisions based on their expectations about future economic prospects and rates of return. While firms were forward-looking and thus could influence future trends in the overall economy, consumers were backward-looking and thus had no influence on future economic conditions. Keynes thought this was due to what he called a "fundamental psychological law." Consumers were viewed as simply automatons that mindlessly spend a certain portion of their income in good and bad times.

Katona argued that part of the Keynesian theory was based on flawed premises. The first was the assumption that investment spending by consumers was an unimportant cause of cyclical developments in macroeconomic conditions, especially when compared to business investment spending. The second was the notion that consumers did not command enough financial resources to vary the timing of their investment expenditures based on their own future financial prospects and economic expectations.

Purchases of homes, vehicles, and large household durables were common among consumers in the 1920s. Conventional economic theory treats these expenditures as investments as they have the same characteristics as business investments. These investment expenditures are typically excluded from "consumption" in empirical analyses. One might think that the aggregate size of consumer investments was completely dominated by business investments. In fact, the dollar size of consumer investments is slightly larger than the total investment expenditures of business. Even during the Great Depression of the 1930s, consumer expenditures for housing and durables accounted for 9.6% of total GDP compared with just 7.1% for business fixed investment. The same dominance of consumer investments over business investment was true in the 1940s and in subsequent decades up to the present time. Moreover, consumer and business investment spending over nearly the past century have exhibited similar cyclical patterns, including the degree of change from peak to troughs. Katona found no empirical justification for excluding cyclical variation in consumer investment spending as a determinant of economy-wide expansions or contractions. Instead, Katona challenged orthodox economic theory which still holds that consumer spending is endogenous and therefore not capable of causing a recession (Katona, 1951a, 1960a, 1964a, 1975).

There is no consensus among economists on the causes of recessions (Christiano and Fitzgerald, 1999). None of the usual suspects—monetary, credit, price, or technology shocks—account for the bulk of the cyclical fluctuations. Nonetheless, consumption shocks account for a relatively large share of the cyclical fluctuations (Cochrane, 1994). Given this troublesome finding, several explanations have been proposed. The first is that the consumption shock reflects information known to the consumer but unobserved by macro models. Economists typically assume that consumers base their economic expectations on the public information releases of governmental agencies; that is, on the same sources of information used by economists. Consumers, however, may base their forecasts on the information that they possess about their own prospects, or what is usually termed private information. It is this information that can produce the aggregate shock (Cochrane, 1994). This line of reasoning is compelling, but it may not be germane. It is not the mere possession of private information that is at issue, but the synchronization of changes in private information across many consumers that produce recessions.

While Katona recognized the fundamental investment character of expenditures on homes, vehicles, and other durables, he also viewed these purchases as a means households used to adjust their precautionary savings. Postponing the purchase of a new vehicle or new appliance has little immediate impact on living standards (assuming the current vehicle or appliance is still in working condition) but has a large and immediate impact on household saving (as a result of the purchase or the incurrence of debt). It is commonplace for consumers to describe the purpose of the timing of their investment expenditures as a means to adjust their precautionary savings. This observation led Katona to challenge conventional theories that held that the pattern of consumption should be independent from the pattern of income. Indeed, Katona hypothesized that varying the timing of investment expenditures was the dominant method used by households to adjust the amount of their precautionary savings, usually done in anticipation of potential cyclical developments (Katona, 1951a, 1960a, 1964a, 1975). Some years later more plausible assumptions about the utility function were advanced that hypothesized that consumers could be expected to accumulate precautionary savings as a hedge against uncertainty (Kimball, 1990), and prospect theory can incorporate income uncertainty as a response asymmetry between positive and negative income changes (Kahneman and Tversky, 1979).

The second flawed premise has to do with the lack of consumer discretion. While it could be suggested that by writing in the 1930s, Keynes was unduly influenced by the Depression era hardships, purchases of homes, vehicles, and household durables were already widespread during the prior decade of the 1920s, with consumers often using credit to make these purchases. Katona emphasized the accumulation of financial assets by consumers in the 1940s gave them latitude in the timing of their spending decisions. Katona found the extent of financial assets held by consumers in to be quite large in 1946, reflecting a personal saving rate that exceeded 20% from 1941 to 1944. It was these holdings of liquid assets that sparked the interest of the Federal Reserve Board in sponsoring the first Survey of Consumer Finances in 1946 under the direction of Katona. The basic issue was what consumers would do with the large amount of liquid assets they had at their disposal. If consumers attempted to quickly replenish their stocks of household goods depleted during the Great Depression and WWII, inflation could rapidly escalate and pose a policy challenge for the Fed. While there was a spending spurt following the war, Katona found that consumers also placed a high value on financial security and maintaining their savings and reserve funds. Rather than dismissing the importance of consumer investments and ignoring the growing financial latitude of households, Katona was convinced that it was necessary to closely monitor their expectations for signs of potential change. Katona expressed this view by his 1960 book title *The Powerful Consumer.* A decade later, James Tobin (1972: 55) agreed that "once consumption is not liquidity-constrained it is a highly psychological variable."

Measurement of consumer sentiment

Katona added questions on the 1946 survey to measure the economic expectations and spending intentions of consumers. The Federal Reserve Board was uninterested in the economic expectations of consumers, but was convinced by Katona's argument that they were necessary to build rapport and encourage truthful responses. Interviewers could not show up on someone's doorstep and announce the Federal Reserve wanted to know how much savings they had accumulated. While the Fed accepted the rapport rationale, they made it clear to Katona that they were not interested in the results from the questions on expectations and intentions, but only on the hard numbers on the household's financial balance sheets. Needless to say, shortly thereafter upon the success of Katona's expectation questions, they became quite interested and requested early tabulations for which they were willing to pay extra (Morgan, 1972; Curtin, 2004).

In the 1950s a committee was established under the auspices of the Federal Reserve Board to investigate the forecasting ability of Katona's measures of expectations (Smithies et al., 1955). The committee reasoned that for consumer expectations to have a creditable impact on macro economic trends would require the same data to predict spending on the micro level. The straightforward notion was that accurate macro predictions were simply the aggregation of relationships measured at the individual level. This is now known as establishing the micro foundations of macroeconomics, a principle also known as methodological individualism. Unfortunately, at the time of the evaluation, it was only possible to test the predictive ability of expectations at the micro level since just eight observations were available for the time-series tests. What the committee found based on an analysis of the panel data was that economic optimism or pessimism was unrelated to consumers' subsequent purchase behavior, but there was a relationship between purchase intentions and subsequent purchases. Although Katona considered intentions a subclass of expectations (about a person's own behavior), the panel data on individual responses did not convince him that it necessarily implied that expectations data would not be useful predictors of macroeconomic spending trends. Katona based his view on both methodological and theoretical considerations, with the importance of each of these factors depending on whether the tests were based on micro or macro data (Katona, 1957c, 1958b, 1959a, 1959b, 1960b, 1976b; Dechaux, 2015).

The methodological factors mainly involved measurement issues. In addition to measurement errors due to sampling and non-sampling factors involved in population surveys, accurate predictions of individual behavior required information on a wide array of factors. If the predictions were limited to the behavior of large subgroups or even the entire consumer sector, then the idiosyncratic factors would often cancel out in the aggregate. The complexity of the estimation problem would be significantly reduced if the focus was restricted to only those factors that were expected to change among all or most consumers. The selected factors may only have a trivial impact on any one individual's decision, but if the factor changed in the same manner across very many people at the same time, it could still have a significant impact on the macro economy (Katona, 1960a, 1964a, 1975).

The theoretical issue was more contentious. Katona did not agree with methodological individualism. He believed that in some aspects the macro economy could not be considered the simple aggregation of its micro constituents. Katona thought that the macro economy can display characteristics that are uniquely different than the sum of its micro units. While some economists agreed with this position, most still hold fast to the principle that all macro theory must be justified by its micro foundations (Lucas, 1972). This is true despite the fact that economic theory is guided by a comparable system-wide organizing principle: equilibrium. Equilibrium conditions are not properties of any of its micro participants but are only a property of the macro system itself. No simple summing of the economy's constituent parts can establish equilibrium. Only with the simplifying assumption of representative agents are they equivalent.

Katona also faced an empirical problem. Conventional economic models at that time used two additional simplifying assumptions that excluded the behaviors his theories were designed to explain. The first was the so-called "certainty equivalence" derived from the assumption of quadratic utility functions. This assumption meant that only the mean of the expected future income stream had an impact on current consumption decisions. The theory left no room for considerations of the potential impact of uncertainty about future income. The second simplifying assumption was that utility functions were additive and time separable. Based on this assumption, expenditures on vehicles, household durables, and homes were simply eliminated from the analysis since these expenditures do not fully represent current consumption but are more accurately described as investments (Curtin, 2004).

Perhaps the most interesting postscript to the debates of the 1950s is what has proven to be an effective leading indicator over the next half century. The presumed predictive ability of purchase intentions data was tested using large samples and with probability measures by the US Census Bureau in the 1960s. These surveys were discontinued due to their poor predictive performance, although the debates they spawned were also contentious (McNeil, 1974; Curtin, 2004; Dechaux, 2015). In contrast, the approach advocated by Katona has not only survived to this day in the US but has also been replicated by six dozen other countries in every inhabited continent in the world (Curtin, 2005). In the US, as in most other countries, consumer sentiment measures are recognized as leading economic indicators based on their predictive performance (for a summary, see Curtin, 2005). Notably, the predictive performances of Katona's measures were at their very best at the most critical times: when the economy was about to turn from expansion to contraction, or vice versa.

Prediction versus understanding

Scientific advancement requires not just models that can accurately predict behavior but also theories that represent a comprehensive understanding of the underlying causal pathways. Science is poorly served, for example, by only knowing that a certain medication has a high probability of curing a disease. Scientific advancement requires an understanding of the exact mechanisms and causal structures involved. Economics has long been satisfied with only prediction. Katona believed that research should be aimed at advancing our understanding of economic behavior. While Katona insisted that accurate predictions were an indispensable means to test new theories, there was no substitute for understanding the factors that shaped economic decision making. This placed a critical emphasis on observing how people made actual decisions. Katona also thought that the realism of the model's assumptions acted as the best guide for the subsequent revisions that are necessary for scientific advancement.

Katona justly deserves recognition as a founding father of behavioral economics. The comprehensive agenda he envisioned for the field in the 1940s has proven to be as prescient as his creation of new methodologies to observe and measure economic behavior. His theoretical advances in understanding the human element in economic affairs have prompted even more sophisticated advances in the quarter-century since his death. His cherished goal of creating an empirical discipline to improve the science of economics by focusing research attention on unresolved economic problems has surely been achieved.

Scientific publications of George Katona

Experimentelle Beiträge zur Lehre von den Beziehungen zwischen den achromatischen und chromatischen Sehprozessen. Zeitschrift für Sinnesphysiologie 53 (1921), 145–73.
Psychologie der Relationserfassung und des Vergleichens. Leipzig, Germany: Barth, 1924.
Experimente über die Grössenkonstanz. Zeitschrift für Psychologie 97 (1925), 215–51.
Experimentelle Untersuchungen über simultane und sukzessive Gesichtswahrnehmungen. Psychologische Forschung 7 (1926), 226–56.
Eine kleine Anschauungsaufgabe. Psychologische Forschung 9 (1927), 159–63.
Zur Analyse der Helligkeitskonstanz. Psychologische Forschung 12 (1929), 94–126.
Color-Contrast and Color-Constancy. Journal of Experimental Psychology 18 (1935), 49–63.
Organizing and Memorizing: Studies in the Psychology of Learning and Teaching. New York: Columbia University Press, 1940; 2nd edn, 1949. (Republished in 1967 by Hafner Publishing Company, New York. Also in Italian.)
War Without Inflation: The Psychological Approach to Problems of War Economy. New York: Columbia University Press, 1942a.
The Role of the Order of Presentation in Learning. American Journal of Psychology 55 (1942b), 328–53.
On Different Forms of Learning by Reading. Journal of Educational Psychology 33 (1942c), 335–55.
The Role of the Frame of Reference in War and Post-War Economy. American Journal of Sociology 49 (1944a), 340–7.
With Dickson H. Leavens. Price Increases and Upgrading. Journal of Business 17 (1944b), 231–43.
Price Control and Business. Bloomington, IN: Cowles Commission and Principia Press, 1945.
Psychology Analysis of Business Decisions and Expectations. American Economic Review 36 (1946a), 44–62.
With R. Likert. Relationship between Consumer Expenditures and Savings. Review of Economic Statistics 28 (1946b), 197–200.
With A. Campbell. A National Survey of Wartime Savings. Public Opinion Quarterly (Fall, 1946c), 373–81.
Contribution of Psychological Data to Economic Analysis. Journal of the American Statistical Association 42 (1947), 449–59.
Effect of Income Changes on the Rate of Saving. Review of Economics and Statistics 31 (1949a), 95–103.
Analysis of Dissaving. American Economic Review 39 (1949b), 673–88.
Financial Surveys among Consumers. Human Relations 2 (1949c), 3–11.
With J. A. Fisher. Post-war Changes in the Income of Identical Consumer Units. Studies in Income and Wealth, Vol. 13. New York: National Bureau of Economic Research, 1950.
Psychological Analysis of Economic Behavior. New York: McGraw-Hill, 1951a; paperback, 1963. (Also in German, French, Spanish, Italian, Japanese, and Yugoslav.)
Expectations and Decisions in Economic Behavior. In D. Lerner and H. D. Lasswell (eds.), The Policy Sciences: Recent Developments in Scope and Method. Stanford, CA: Stanford University Press, 1951b.
With J. N. Morgan. The Quantitative Study of Factors Determining Business Decisions. Quarterly Journal of Economics 66 (1952b), 67–90.
With E. Mueller. Consumer Attitudes and Demand: 1950–52. Ann Arbor: Survey Research Center, University of Michigan, 1953a.
Rational Behavior and Economic Behavior. Psychological Review 60 (1953b), 307–18.
With A. Campbell. The Sample Survey: A Technique for Social Science Research. In L. Festinger and D. Katz (eds.), Research Methods in the Behavioral Sciences. New York: Dryden Press, 1953c.
Economic Psychology. Scientific American 191(4) (1954a), 31–6.
With F. Mueller. A Study of Purchase Decisions. In L. H. Clark (ed.) Consumer Behavior, 1. New York: New York University Press, 1954b.
Variability of Consumer Behavior. In L. R. Klein (ed.), Contributions of Survey Methods to Economics. New York: New York University Press, 1954c.
The Predictive Value of Data on Consumer Attitudes. In L. H. Clark (ed.), Consumer Behavior, II. New York: New York University Press, 1955.
With E. Mueller. Consumer Expectations, 1953–1956. Ann Arbor: Survey Research Center, University of Michigan, 1956.
Attitudes toward Saving and Borrowing. Consumer Installment credit, Part II (Vol. 1). Washington, DC: National Bureau of Economic Research and Federal Reserve Board, 1957a.

With S. Steinkamp and A. Lauterbach. Business Looks at Banks: A Study of Business Behavior. Ann Arbor: University of Michigan Press, 1957b.
Federal Reserve Board Committee Reports on Consumer Expectations and Savings Statistics. Review of Economics and Statistics 39 (1957c), 40–6.
Public Opinion and Economic Research. Public Opinion Quarterly 21 (1957d), 117–28.
Consumer Buying Habits: Analysis of A Ten-Year Study. The Integrated Approach to Product Planning. American Management Association Marketing Series No. 101 (1957e), 56–8.
The Function of Survey Research in Economics. In Mirra Komarovsky (ed.), Common Frontiers of the Social Sciences. Glencoe, IL: Free Press/Falcon's Wing Press, 1957f.
Business Expectations in the Framework of Psychological Economics. In M. J. Bowman (ed.), Expectations, Uncertainty, and Business Behavior. New York: Social Science Research Council, 1958a.
Attitude Change: Instability of Response and Acquisition of Experience. Psychological Monographs 72(10), Whole No. 463, 1958b, 1–38.
The Psychology of Recession. American Psychologist 14 (1959a), 135–43.
Repetitiousness and Variability of Consumer Behavior. Human Relations 12 (1959b), 35–49
The Powerful Consumer: Psychological Studies of the American Economy. New York: McGraw-Hill, 1960a. (Also in German, Dutch, Italian, and Japanese.)
Changes in Consumer Expectations and their Origin. In The Quality and Economic Significance of Anticipations Data (National Bureau of Economic Research). Princeton, NJ: Princeton University Press, 1960b.
Principal editor of annual volumes entitled Survey of Consumer Finances. Ann Arbor: Survey Research Center, University of Michigan, 1960 through 1970.
The Relationship between Psychology and Economics. In S. Koch (ed.), Psychology: Study of a Science (Vol. 6). New York: McGraw-Hill, 1963
The Mass Consumption Society. New York: McGraw-Hill, 1964a. (Also in German, French, Dutch, Spanish, Swedish, and Japanese.)
With J. B. Lansing. The Wealth of the Wealthy. Review of Economics and Statistics 66(1) (1964b), 1–13.
Private Pensions and Individual Saving. Ann Arbor: Survey Research Center, University of Michigan, 1965.
What is Consumer Psychology? American Psychologist 22 (1967a), 219–26.
Anticipations Statistics and Consumer Behavior. American Statistician 21 (1967b), 12–13.
On the Function of Behavioral Theory and Behavioral Research in Economics. American Economic Review 58(1) (1968a), 146–50.
Consumer Behavior: Theory and Findings on Expectations and Aspirations. American Economic Review 58(2) (1968b), 19–30.
With E. Mueller. Consumer Response to Income Increases. Washington, DC: The Brookings Institution, 1968c.
Attitudes toward Fiscal and Monetary Policy. Public Policy 18(2) (1970), 281–8.
With B. Strümpel and E. Zahn. Aspirations and Affluence: Comparative Studies in the United States and Western Europe. New York: McGraw-Hill, 1971a. (Also in German, Dutch, and Japanese.)
Consumer Durable Spending: Explanation and Prediction. Washington: Brookings Papers on Economic Activity, 1 (1971b), 234–9.
The Human Factor in Economic Affairs. In A. Campbell and P. E. Converse (eds.), The Human Meaning of Social Change. New York: Russell Sage Foundation, 1972a.
Reminiscences. In B. Strümpel, J. N. Morgan, and E. Zahn (eds.), Human Behavior in Economic Affairs: Essays in Honor of George Katona. Amsterdam/New York: Elsevier, 1972b.
Theory of Expectations. In B. Strümpel, J. N. Morgan, and E. Zahn (eds.), Human Behavior in Economic Affairs: Essays in Honor of George Katona. Amsterdam/New York: Elsevier, 1972c.
Cognitive Processes in Learning: Reactions to Inflation and Change in Taxes. In L. Mandell et al. (eds.), Surveys of Consumers 1971–72. Ann Arbor: Survey Research Center, University of Michigan, 1973.
Psychology and Consumer Economics. Journal of Consumer Research 1 (1974) 1–8.
Psychological Economics. New York: Elsevier, 1975.
Economics as A Behavioral Science. In M. Pfaff (ed.), Frontiers in Social Thought: Essays in Honor of Kenneth E. Boulding. Amsterdam-New York: North Holland, 1976a.
Persistence of Belief in Personal Financial Progress. In B. Strümpel (ed.), Economic Means for Human Needs. Ann Arbor: Survey Research Center, University of Michigan, 1976b.
With B. Strümpel. A New Economic Era. New York: Elsevier, 1978.

Toward a Macropsychology. American Psychologist 34(2), (1979), 118–26.
Essays on Behavioral Economics. Ann Arbor: Survey Research Center, University of Michigan, 1980.

Bibliography

Akerlof, G. A. (2007). The Missing Motivation in Macroeconomics. American Economic Review 97(1), 5–31.

Akerlof, G. A., & Shiller, R. J. (2010). Animal Spirits: How Human Psychology Drives the Economy, and why it Matters for Global Capitalism. Princeton, NJ: Princeton University Press.

Baghestani, H. (1992). Survey Evidence on the Muthian Rationality of the Inflation Forecasts of US Consumers. Oxford Bulletin of Economic and Statistics 54, 173–86.

Blaug, M. (1992). The Methodology of Economics: Or, How Economists Explain (2nd edn). Cambridge: Cambridge University Press.

Chetty, R. (2015). Behavioral Economics and Public Policy: A Pragmatic Perspective. American Economic Review 105(5), 1–33.

Christiano, L. J., & Fitzgerald, T. J. (1999). The Business Cycle: It's Still a Puzzle. Economic Perspectives, Federal Reserve Bank of Chicago, 56–83.

Cochrane, J. H. (1994). Shocks. Carnegie-Rochester Conference Series on Public Policy 41, 295–364.

Curtin, R. T. (1984). Curtin on Katona. In H. W. Spiegel, & W. J. Samuels (eds.), Contemporary Economists in Perspective 1. New York: Jai Press, 495–522.

Curtin, R. T. (2004). Psychology and Macroeconomics. In J. S. House et al. (eds.), A Telescope on Society: Survey Research and Social Science at the University of Michigan and Beyond. Ann Arbor: University of Michigan Press.

Curtin, R. T. (2005). Consumer Sentiment Surveys: Worldwide Review and Assessment. Ann Arbor: University of Michigan.

Curtin, R. T. (2010). Inflation Expectations and Empirical Tests. In P. Sinclair (ed.), Inflation Expectations. New York: Routledge.

Dechaux, Pierrick (2015). Proving the Existence of Macropsychological Phenomena? The Katona-Tobin Controversy over the Predictive Value of Attitudinal Data. CES working papers, Université Panthéon-Sorbonne (Paris 1), Centre d'Economie de la Sorbonne. Available online at http://EconPapers.repec.org/RePEc:mse:cesdoc:15011.

Farber, H. S. (2008). Reference-Dependent Preferences and Labor Supply: The Case of New York City Taxi Drivers. American Economic Review 98(3), 1069–82.

Friedman, M. (1957). A Theory of the Consumption Function. Princeton, NJ: Princeton University Press.

Gramlich, E. M. (1983). Models of Inflation Expectations Formation. Journal of Money, Credit, and Banking 15, 155–73.

Hosseini, H. (2011). George Katona: A Founding Father of Old Behavioral Economics. Journal of Socio-Economics 40, 977–84.

Kahneman, D., & Tversky, A. (1979). Prospect Theory: An Analysis of Decision under Risk. Econometrica 47(2), 263–92.

Keynes, J. M. (1936). The General Theory of Employment, Interest, and Money. New York: Macmillan.

Kimball, M.S. (1990). Precautionary Saving in the Small and in the Large. Econometrica 58(1), 53–73.

Köszegi, B., & Rabin, M. (2006). A Model of Reference-Dependence Preferences. Quarterly Journal of Economics 121(4), 1133–65.

Lucas, R. (1972). Expectations and the Neutrality of Money. Journal of Economic Theory 4(2), 103–24.

Mankiw, N. G. (1988). Recent Developments in Macroeconomics: A Very Quick Refresher Course. Journal of Money, Credit and Banking, 20(3, Part 2), 436–49.

McNeil, J. M. (1974). Census Bureau Programs to Measure Consumer Purchase Expectations: 1959-1973. Bureau of the Census, US Department of Commerce, Technical Paper 36.

Mehra, Y. P. (2002). Survey Measures of Expected Inflation: Revisiting the Issue of Predictive Content and Rationality. Federal Reserve Bank of Richmond Economic Quarterly 88(3), 17–36.

Modigliani, F., & Brumberg, R. (1954). Utility Analysis and the Consumption Function: An Interpretation of Cross-Section Data. In K. Kurihara (ed.), Post-Keynesian Economics. Rutgers University Press.

Morgan, J. (1972). A Quarter Century of Research in Economics. In B. Strümpel, J. N. Morgan, E. Zahn (eds.), Human Behavior in Economic Affairs. San Francisco: Jossey-Bass.

Muth, J. F. (1961). Rational Expectations and the Theory of Price Movements. Econometrica 29(3), 315–35.

Newcomb, T. M. (1972). Expectations as a Social Psychological Concept. In B. Strümpel et al. (eds.), Human Behavior in Economic Affairs. San Francisco: Jossey-Bass.

Rabin, M. (2002). A Perspective on Psychology and Economics. European Economic Review 46, 657–85.

Sent, E. (2004). Behavioral Economics: How Psychology Made its (Limited) Way Back into Economics. History of Political Economy 36(4), 735–60.

Simon, H. A. (1957). Models of Man: Social and Rational. Models of a Man: Social and Rational. New York: Free Press.

Sims, C. A. (1998). Stickiness. Carnegie-Rochester Conference Series on Public Policy 49(1), 317–56.

Sims, C. A. (2003). Implications of Rational Inattention. Journal of Monetary Economics 50, 665–90.

Smithies, A, et al. (1955). Consumer Survey Statistics: Report to the Subcommittee on Economic Statistics of the Joint Committee on the Economic Report. Washington.

Sugden, R. (2003). Reference-Dependent Subjective Expected Utility. Journal of Economic Theory 111, 172–91.

Thomas Jr, L. B. (1999). Survey Measures of Expected US Inflation. Journal of Economic Perspectives 13 (4), pp. 125–44.

Tobin, J. (1972). Wealth, Liquidity, and the Propensity to Consume. In B. Strümpel et al. (eds.), Human Behavior in Economic Affairs: Essays in Honor of George Katona. Amsterdam: Elsevier, 37–56.

Tversky, A. & Kahneman, D. (1974). Judgement under Uncertainty: Heuristics and Biases. Science 185 (4157), 1124–31.

Wärneryd, K. (1982). The Life and Work of George Katona. Journal of Economic Psychology 2(1), 1–31.

3

KEN BOULDING

The image as a precursor to framing?

Stefan Kesting

Introduction

Boulding's scholarly work is manifold and has been highly innovative and interdisciplinary (Dolfsma and Kesting, 2013). He was also quite critical of mainstream economics and tried to contribute to the reform of the discipline (Boulding, 1950, 1958, 1962, 1969, 1975, 1986, 1988 and 1992; McCloskey, 2013). It is, therefore, not too surprising that parallels to behavioural economics should be found in his writings. Boulding and behavioural economics share the motivation of questioning and improving the basic concept of rationality in economics. Both share a common intellectual root and legacy in Keynes's exploration of real uncertainty and suggestion of how to deal with it in chapter 12 of his *General Theory* (1936). Because of its focus on our worldview and preconceptions (the image) directing our behaviour, Boulding's book *The Image* (1956) can be seen in some of its aspects as a precursor to Kahneman and Tversky's concept of framing and mental accounts (Kahneman, 2011). Both the image as well as framing are based on the idea that mental accounting, mapping, and modelling (Denzau and North, 1994) are guiding economic behaviour and not just the rational maximisation of given preferences. In this chapter, I will try to answer the following questions: In what way does Boulding's concept of the image pre-empt the framing, heuristic and bias effects as well as mental accounting emphasised in behavioural economics? And, in what way do both theories of economic behaviour differ? I have structured my argument in five parts: the first provides an introduction to the main features of the image, the second will explore the common intellectual roots in Keynes's microeconomics and the link to Herbert Simon, the third intends to focus on the communalities of the image with Kahneman's framing and mental accounting concepts. The fourth part concentrates on the differences and attempts to use Boulding's image as a platform to raise some critical points concerning behavioural economics. This chapter will close with a concluding summary.

Boulding's *The Image*

A short and at the same time inclusive definition of the image can be found in an article by Warren Samuels:

> The fundamental role of the image is to define the world. The image is the basic, final, fundamental, controlling element in all perception and thought. It largely governs our

definition of reality, substantively and normatively, in part as to what is actual and what is possible.

(Samuels, 1997: 311)

The image is the absolute starting point of human action. In Boulding's own words, set in italics in the introduction to the book: "*The first proposition of this work, therefore, is that behaviour depends on the image*" (Boulding, 1956: 6). The concept of the image incorporates value judgements:

> The image of value is concerned with the *rating* of the various parts of our image of the world, according to some scale of betterness or worseness. We, all of us, possess one or more of these scales. It is what the economists call a welfare function.
>
> *(ibid.: 11)*

So far, mainstream economists could nod and say: right, what then is the difference to our concept of individuals rationally maximising on the basis of stable preferences and welfare functions? The image is crucially different to standard neoclassical microeconomics because it is a social, interactive concept used by "semirational beings" (ibid.: 16) to cope with an uncertain world. Although Boulding names Hayek and Katona (see chapter 2) as his two main intellectual predecessors from economics (ibid.: 149–150), the influence of Keynes on his views is clearly apparent in his reference to liquidity preference (ibid.: 91) and his description of the general conditions for economic behaviour: "Our image of the consequences of our acts is suffused with uncertainty to the point where we are not even sure what we are uncertain about" (ibid.: 84). It is open to question whether the image remains stable or changes depending on the experiences of the individual and the influence of outside messages on it: "The image is part of—and changes within—an ongoing process in which experience and image and selective perception coevolve" (Samuels, 1997: 312). How does our image, containing our value judgements, visions of the future, preferences and welfare perception, change and how do others influence this evolutionary process? Boulding insists that human beings communicate with each other via symbols (i.e., communication that can become independent of the communicator) *and* face to face (Boulding, 1956: 65, 75 and 88) and that communication constitutes and changes our images: "It is this symbolic image and the communications which establish it and which change it which constitutes the peculiar quality of human society, a quality which no animal society shares" (ibid.: 44). Samuels highlights the linguistic character of the image in his interpretation: "Images are linguistic phenomena for mankind. Language is the material of images. Having an image, reducing it to words, talking about it—all this involves the use of language" (Samuels, 1997: 317). Image and language alike are at the same time intra- and inter-individual and their change takes place via correspondence of these levels:

> The basic bond of any society, culture, subculture or organisation is a "public image" that is, an image the essential characteristics of which are shared by the individuals participating in the group. ... Indeed, every public image begins in the mind of some single individual and only becomes public as it is transmitted and shared.
>
> *(Boulding, 1956: 64)*

It is no coincidence that Boulding stresses that organisations defined "as a structure of roles tied together by lines of communication" (ibid.: 57) are the primary providers of lasting public images. However, no single organisation in a society has a monopoly on creating and maintaining a certain worldview or public image, because "there is not a single public image, but there are many public images, as many indeed as there are cultures and subcultures within the great frame of the human race" (ibid.: 132). In fact, a subculture is nothing else than a group of people sharing a certain public image. On a societal level, a healthy competition of such subcultural public images in an open public discourse promotes economic and social progress.[1] Boulding writes that "Fortunately for the progress of mankind, monopolies of knowledge are notoriously unstable" (1956: 141) and highlights that: "The extraordinary rapidity with which images have changed in the last two hundred years is perhaps mainly a result of increased communication among previously isolated subcultures" (1956: 146). This change of public images is mediated by certain individuals whom Boulding praises: "Society owes an enormous debt to those marginal men who live uneasily in two different universes of discourse" (1956: 146).

This summary of the image as a discursive mechanism of social and economic evolution is important to keep in mind when we will move to the comparison with Kahneman's behavioural economics. However, in the same paragraph where Boulding emphasises that the image of a person is more or less the public image of the organisation where he or she plays a role, he also stresses that: "The image is always the property of the individual persons, not of the organisation" (1956: 28). The individual image is an instrument to avoid vagueness and uncertainty and as such prone to a habitual conservative bias and selective perception (ibid.: 86 and 12). It is characterised by an unself-conscious process of formation (ibid.: 123). On the other hand, the image is also self-reflective and self-conscious: "We not only know, but we know that we know" (ibid.: 25). So, the image has both latent and manifest elements and can fail as an instrument to understand and guide human behaviour (ibid.: 71).

All this leads to the conclusion that the image is an instrument to deal with uncertainty and problems of human cognition to arrive at decisions as well as direction for action and is put forward as an alternative concept to neoclassical self-interested calculation of utility.

From Keynes via Simon to Kahneman

As I have shown in the former section, the origin of Boulding's image lies at least in part in Keynes's ideas on real uncertainty as the typical human condition (Dow, 1995 and 2003; Lawson, 1994) and the behavioural implications that he describes in chapter 12 of his *General Theory* (1936). This is also true for Herbert Simon's concepts of bounded and procedural rationality. After describing Keynes's radical departure from classical economics through his emphasis on expectations and animal spirits in chapter 12 of the *General Theory* (Simon, 1997: 15), Simon exclaims: "Only the fear of pronouncing an egregious anachronism prevents me from claiming Keynes ... as the true originator of the economics of bounded rationality" (ibid.: 16). These parallel Keynesian roots and conceptual overlaps between Boulding and Simon are important for my comparison because Kahneman makes an implicit reference to Simon in the title of his speech on the occasion of receiving the Nobel Prize for economics in 2002: *Maps of Bounded Rationality: A Perspective on Intuitive Judgement and Choice*. I want to suggest here that the tribute paid to Simon could have equally been paid to Boulding.

Simon defines his core concept as resting on individuals trying to deal with real uncertain circumstances in the world and their awareness of the limits of their information about it and their limited cognitive abilities (ibid.: 26): "Procedural rationality is concerned with *how* the decision maker generates alternatives of action and compares them. It necessarily rests on a theory of human condition" (ibid.: 18). This human condition of bounded rationality forces individuals to engage in an evolutionary process of developing an appropriate image: "Bounded rationality says that each one of us, faced with living and making decisions, looks out in the world and tries to get a picture of it; and each one of us of course gains a different picture" (ibid.: 25). Note, that the word image could have been used in this quote by Simon instead of picture.

Like Boulding, Simon highlights the role of organisations in forming commonly held images (compare his second lecture, in Simon, 1997). What follows for Simon from bounded rationality is the need to develop a theory of the mind. Boulding's theory of the image is an attempt at such a theory. However, as I will try to show in the next section, Kahneman took this task to a higher level of sophistication in providing an empirical foundation for his theory of mind.

Kahneman and Tversky's behavioural economics and Boulding's *The Image*: common conceptual elements and theoretical distinctions

While Boulding developed *The Image* mainly based on introspection and participant observation, Kahneman followed Simon's methodological suggestion for developing procedural rationality (1997: 23) and used laboratory experiments to critically assess standard economic rationality and to develop his theory of the mind. The resulting concepts of framing and mental accounting resemble the image quite closely. Like Boulding, Kahneman sees them as an alternative to neoclassical rationality and an instrument to deal with uncertainty and limited cognitive abilities:

> The Econs of the rational agent model do not resort to mental accounting: they have a comprehensive view of outcomes and are driven by external incentives. For Humans, mental accounts are a form of narrow framing; they keep things under control and manageable by a finite mind.
>
> *(2011: 343)*

Kahneman's book *Thinking Fast and Slow* assembles a lifetime of experimental work to tease out and define the various psychological elements that shape mental frames and accounts. I can only highlight a few of these elements here which bear particular resemblance or contrast with *The Image*. The first is the influence of rare events on framing. In his description, Kahneman even uses Boulding's terminology: "You constructed the event in your mind, and the vivid *image* of the outcome exists there even if you know that its probability is low" (ibid.: 328, italics mine). The image in this instance leads to the neglect of calculating chances and imprints a dominant vivid imagery on the mind of the decision maker. A second related element is the influence of memories on the image or mental frame. Memories may or may not be an accurate representation of the actual experience in the past. So, Kahneman concludes: "Tastes and decisions are shaped by memories, and the memories can be wrong" (ibid.: 385).

The third element is the endowment effect. Following a critical account of neoclassical indifference curve analysis, Kahneman states that: "First, tastes are not fixed; they vary with the reference point. Second, the disadvantages of a change loom larger than its advantages, inducing a bias that favours the status quo" (ibid.: 292). Boulding's image was also meant to show that preferences are malleable and context specific. However, Kahneman's work specifies how, for instance in stressing loss aversion: "The fundamental ideas of prospect theory are that reference points exist, and that losses loom larger than corresponding gains" (ibid.: 297).

Kahneman shares with Boulding and Simon the focus on the potential advantages of organisations—if carefully designed—for the quality of decision making compared with individuals: "Organisations are better than individuals when it comes to avoiding errors, because they naturally think more slowly and have the power to impose orderly procedures" (ibid.: 417–18). He adds: "An organisation that seeks to improve its decision product should routinely look for efficiency improvements ... The operative concept is routine" (ibid.: 418). A conclusion and advice reminiscent of the evolutionary economics of Nelson and Winter (1982 and 2002).

One point of distinction and difference between Kahneman and Tversky's prospect theory and Boulding's approach is their vision of, and emphasis on, wrong or manipulated images or frames and mental accounts. While Boulding concedes that images can be manipulated and lead to misinterpretation and misunderstanding (1956: 71), his impetus is on demonstrating the decision enhancing potential of his concept of the image. In contrast, Kahneman's main interest is in showing how our ability to make rational decisions is tainted by: overconfidence (2011: 87), anchors which can be manipulated (ibid.: 126), confusing mere correlation with causation (ibid.: 182), illusions (ibid.: chapter 20), the media (ibid.: 138) and delusions (ibid.: 256), apart from the already aforementioned endowment, rare event and memory effects.

Another point of contention is their different views on how communication works in forming mental frames or images. Whereas from Boulding's perspective public debate and deliberation are the main instrument in forming, revising and improving public images (1956: chapter 9), Kahneman remains highly sceptical of communicative action: "The standard practice of open discussion gives too much weight to the opinions of those who speak early and assertively, causing others to line up behind them" (2011: 85).

Conclusion

Despite some conceptual areas of contention and disagreement, overall, not just Simon's but also Boulding's theoretical work can be viewed as paving the road to modern behavioural economics. Their frameworks contribute to the construction of an alternative microeconomic theory that is based on a cognitive theory biased by preconceptions and allowing for changing, context specific preferences.

Note

1 Boulding describes this as a "process of the mutual modification of images both relational and evaluational in the course of mutual communication, discussion, and discourse. The course of the discussion is punctuated by decisions which are essentially temporary in nature in the sense that they do not close the discussion, although they do, of course, have the effect of modifying it. In one sense, in a successful political process all decisions are interim. We live in a perpetual state of unresolved conflict. A decision is partial resolution of conflict. It should never be a complete resolution" (Boulding, 1956: 103).

Bibliography

Boulding, K. E. (1950). A Reconstruction of Economics. New York: Wiley & Sons.

Boulding, K. E. (1956). The Image: Knowledge in Life and Society. Ann Arbor: University of Michigan Press (reprinted 1997).

Boulding, K. E. (1958). The Skills of the Economist. London: Hamish Hamilton.

Boulding, K. E. (1962). The Relations of Economic, Political, and Social Systems. Social and Economic Studies (Jamaica), 11(4): 351–62. Reprinted as chapter 11 in: Boulding, K. E. (ed.): Beyond Economics: Essays in Society, Religion, and Ethics, Ann Arbor: University of Michigan Press, 98–111.

Boulding, K. E. (1969). Economics as a Moral Science, Presidential Address. American Economic Association, December 29, 1968, American Economic Review, 59(1): 1–12.

Boulding, K. E. (1975). Some Observations on the Learning of Economics, American Economic Review, 65(2): 428–30.

Boulding, K. E. (1986). What Went Wrong with Economics? American Economist, 30 (Spring): 5–12.

Boulding, K. E. (1988). What Do We Want in an Economics Textbook? Journal of Economic Education, 19(2): 113–32.

Boulding, K. E. (1992). Appropriate Methodologies for the Study of the Economy. In: Boulding, K. E. (ed.): Toward a New Economics: Critical Essays on Ecology, Distribution, and Other Themes, Aldershot: Edward Elgar, 98–112.

Denzau, A. T., & North, D. C. (1994). Shared Mental Models: Ideologies and Institutions. Kyklos, 47: 3–31.

Dolfsma, W., & Kesting, S. (2013, eds.). Interdisciplinary Economics: Kenneth E. Boulding's Engagement in the Sciences. London and New York: Routledge.

Dow, S. (1995). Uncertainty about Uncertainty. In Dow, S. and Hillard, J. (eds.): Keynes, Knowledge and Uncertainty, Aldershot: Edward Elgar, 117–27.

Dow, S. (2003). Babylonian Mode of Thought, in King, J. E. (ed.): The Elgar Companion to Post Keynesian Economics. Cheltenham and Northampton: Edward Elgar, 11–15.

Kahneman, D. (2002). Maps of Bounded Rationality: A Perspective on Intuitive Judgment and Choice, Nobel Prize Lecture, December 8, 2002. Available at: www.nobelprize.org/nobel_prizes/economic-sciences/laureates/2002/kahneman-lecture.pdf [accessed 18 November 2015].

Kahneman, D. (2011). Thinking Fast and Slow, New York: Farrar, Straus and Giroux.

Keynes, J. M. (1964[1936]). The General Theory of Employment, Interest, and Money, San Diego: Harcourt Brace Jovanovich.

Lawson, T., (1994). Uncertainty. In Hodgson, G. M., Samuels, W. J. and Tool, M. R. (eds.): The Elgar Companion to Institutional and Evolutionary Economics, Vol. II, Aldershot: Edward Elgar, 350–7.

McCloskey, D., (2013). Comment: What Went Wrong with Economics? A Quarter Century On. In: Dolfsma, W. and Kesting, S. (eds.): Interdisciplinary Economics: Kenneth E. Boulding's Engagement in the Sciences, London and New York: Routledge, 574–86.

Medema, S. G., & Samuels, W. J. (1997). Kenneth E. Boulding's The Image and Contemporary Discourse Analysis, in: Samuels, W. J., Medema, S. G. and Schmid, A. A. (eds.): The Economy as a Process of Valuation. Cheltenham, UK and Northampton, MA: Edward Elgar, 299–327.

Nelson, R. R., & Winter, S. G. (1982). An Evolutionary Theory of Economic Change. Cambridge, MA: Belknap Press.

Nelson, R. R., & Winter, S. G. (2002). Evolutionary Theorizing in Economics. Journal of Economic Perspectives, 16(2): 23–46.

Samuels, W. J. (1997). Kenneth E. Boulding's The Image and Contemporary Discourse Analysis, in Samuels, W. J., Medema, S. G. and Schmid, A. A. (eds.): The Economy as a Process of Valuation, Cheltenham and Lyme, US: Edward Elgar, 299–327.

Simon, H. (1997). An Empirically Based Microeconomics: Raffaele Mattioli Lectures, Delivered in Milan from 18 to 19 March 1993, Cambridge: Cambridge University Press.

4

HARVEY LEIBENSTEIN

A first generation behavioral economist

Roger Frantz

Behavioral economics. The integration of relevant insights from other disciplines, including but not limited to psychology, neuroscience, management, and sociology into economic models. Economics is best studied from an interdisciplinary perspective.

Introduction

It is not uncommon to read that behavioral economics began with scholars such as George Akerlof, Richard Thaler, Daniel Kahneman and Amos Tversky. It is not uncommon, but it is not correct. Behavioral economics began in the 1940s and 1950s with people such as George Katona, Herbert Simon, Harvey Leibenstein, and others. These scholars' behavioral economics, in general, does not "look" like the writings of Akerlof, Thaler, Kahneman or Tversky. But it represents the first building blocks of what became the "behavioral revolution."

In this chapter I will focus on, but not exclusively on, the behavioral economics of Harvey Leibenstein, whose name is synonymous with X-efficiency. Leibenstein integrated several theories from the fields of psychology and management into economic models and theories of organizational efficiency and human rationality. Efficiency and rationality are two of the foundations of economics. By challenging these foundations from the point of view of human behavior, Leibenstein ranks as one of the first generation of behavioral economists.

On the first page of his *General Theory of Employment, Interest, and Money*, Keynes (Keynes, 1936) explained the use of the word "general" in the title. His explanation was that it is about breaking down long held beliefs which Keynes found intellectually limiting. The same sentiment could have been expressed by Leibenstein about his behavioral economics in X-efficiency theory, or by Katona as he was developing psychological economics, or Simon while he was replacing the concept of perfect rationality with that of selective rationality. These three scholars, and others during their time, were breaking down long held barriers with their writing. Keynes says on page one that

> I have called this book the *General Theory of Employment, Interest and Money*, placing the emphasis on the prefix *general*. The object of such a title is to contrast the character of my arguments and conclusions with those of the *classical* theory of the subject . . . I shall argue that the postulates of the classical theory are applicable to a special case only and not to the general case, the situation which it assumes being a limiting point of the

> possible positions of equilibrium. Moreover, the characteristics of the special case assumed by the classical theory happen not to be those of the economic society in which we actually live, with the result that its teaching is misleading and disastrous if we attempt to apply it to the facts of experience.

As the postulates of classical theory are a limiting point, so are allocative efficiency and perfect rationality limiting points. The "charge" of the first generation of behavioral economists was to make the initial case for the "general theory of human behavior."

In the *Forward* to *X-Efficiency: Theory, Evidence and Applications* (Frantz, 1997), Leibenstein discusses Lionel Robbins's 1932 book, *An Essay on the Nature and Significance of Economic Science*. In this book, Robbins defines economics as the efficient allocation of scarce resources in their alternative uses. Leibenstein comments that in this definition,

> What got lost . . . was the businessman's idea and the engineer's idea of efficiency, which signify how well or poorly people and machines are working Once allocative efficiency is combined with the maximization-of-utility or profits postulate there is no longer any room for the businessman's and the engineer's concept of efficiency. Thus, the idea disappeared that suboptimal operations by the firm and inside the firm are possible . . . Businessmen, engineers, and psychologists are aware of suboptimal behavior, but standard economic theory somehow does not easily or readily lend itself to the possibility of suboptimal operations.
>
> *(Frantz, 1997: xvi)*

Leibenstein's preference is for an interdisciplinary approach to economics. His major work, X-efficiency theory, called for an interdisciplinary approach to the study of efficiency (and rationality), combining economics with psychology, management and engineering studies. His work to incorporate non-allocative, X, (in)efficiency and selective rationality into economics was largely ignored by a majority of the profession.

Robinson Crusoe replaced by socio-economic man

Robinson Crusoe had been a celebrated figure of pure economic reason for decades. In Leibenstein's 1950 article, "Bandwagon, Snob, and Veblen Effects in the Theory of Consumers' Demand," he presented a model whereby a consumer is interdependent, not independent, with others, taking cues from others before deciding how much to purchase in response to a price change.[1] In this article Leibenstein shows the influence of his Princeton mentor, Oscar Morgenstern. Morgenstern in his article, "Demand Theory Reconsidered," says that

> Collective demand is generally understood as a summation of individual demand schedules (for the same commodity). We shall in the following, unless otherwise stated, accept this additivity, but only as a first approximation. It is only valid if the demand functions of the various individuals are independent of each other. This is clearly not true universally. Current theory possesses no methods that allow the construction of aggregate demand curves when the various constituent individual demand curves are not independent of each other.
>
> *(Morgenstern, 1948: 175)*

This lacuna in the literature ended in 1950, although in his typical reserve, Leibenstein says that "My purpose, in this paper, is to take a step or two in that direction" (Leibenstein, 1950: 183). Interdependence took three forms: the desire to be "in style," the bandwagon effect; the desire for "exclusiveness," the snob effect; and, as an expression of conspicuous consumption, the Veblen effect. One result of his model is that a price change affects both quantity demanded *and* demand. In the case of Veblen effects, the demand curve is upward sloping to the right.

Being in style, being exclusive, or engaging in conspicuous consumption implies that the individual has knowledge of what others are doing and what is important to them. Leibenstein says about knowledge that,

> One of the difficulties in analyzing this type of demand involves the choice of assumptions about the knowledge that each individual possesses. This implies that everyone knows the quantity that will be demanded by every individual separately, or the quantity demanded by all individuals collectively at any given price—after all the reactions and adjustments that individuals make to each other's demand has *(sic)* taken place . . .
>
> *(Leibenstein, 1950: 190)*

Leibenstein's bandwagon, snob, and Veblen effects are about the foresight which one has about how others will react to a given price change. The existence of a bandwagon effect means that the more of *X* that others are expected to purchase, the more the individual will purchase at any price. That is, the bandwagon demand curve is more elastic than a demand curve without interdependent preferences. The existence of a snob effect means that the more of *X* that others are expected to purchase, the less will the individual purchase at any price. The snob demand curve is less elastic than a demand curve without interdependent preferences. The Veblen effect shows that an individual's knowledge and expectation about how others feel about highly priced goods can produce an upward sloping demand curve. An individual's behavior results in unintended consequences—the elasticity of the demand curve.

Leibenstein performs a *Gedankenexperiment*, gathering data from questionnaires. (Doing so, he violated the orthodox economic maxim of "watch what people do, not what they say.") The consumer is asked how much he or she would purchase if he or she expects total demand to be x1. The consumer then indicates how much he would purchase at a range of prices. The results from all of the consumers then yields a market demand curve based on the assumption that all consumers are purchasing a total of x1 units. Leibenstein calls this Survey 1. Survey 2 asks consumers how much they would purchase given that total demand is that yielded by Survey 1. The results from Survey 2 become the parameter for Survey 3 and so forth. The result of each survey beginning with Survey 2 is a separate market curve, each one based on a different expectation of total market demand. It does not seem an exaggeration to say that Leibenstein's analysis was a starting point for experimental economics (Dean and Perlman, 1998: 133).

Vernon Smith in his 2009 book *Rationality in Economics* discusses how experiments show that an individual's demand is dependent on others' demand, and how an individual's behavior results in unintended consequences. Smith says that,

> From the experiments, it is easier to see how people might hold a belief revealed in a survey, but that belief need not persist or be strong enough to change their myopically self-interested response in impersonal exchange. It also tells you, by implication, perhaps why someone might vote for a policy intentionally designed to change outcomes, but his or her market behavior creates outcomes contrary to those intentions.
>
> *(Smith, 2009: 165)*

In "The Economic Theory of Fertility Decline" (1975), Leibenstein "introduces a sketch of a new theory of consumption based on social status considerations" (Leibenstein, 1975: 2).

Leibenstein turned Robinson Crusoe into socio-economic man

Firm behavior. In Leibenstein's theory effort or productivity, and costs of production may be seen as the outcome of a "game." In his 1976 book, *Beyond Economic Man*, Leibenstein used the prisoner's dilemma game to illustrate the importance of interdependence, and the determinants of the level of X-efficiency (Leibenstein, 1976). Employees must decide on their effort levels. The firm must decide how well they treat the employees. The employees can work with great effort, average effort, or little effort. The firm can treat the employees with great concern, average concern, or little concern. Regardless of what the employees *expect* the firm to do: the less effort the employees display, the more utility they receive. Regardless of what the firm *expects* the employees to do: the less concern for the employees, the lower are their costs and the higher their profits. The interdependence of expectations and "rational" behavior results in low effort and low profits. Pareto optimal solutions are replaced by sub-optimal solutions as the norm. The invisible hand has a "sore thumb."

Work effort. Supervisors, peers, and the individual worker affect effort. Supervisors, sending "vertical" pressure down to the individual would typically like more effort. Peers create "horizontal" pressure for the individual to supply effort which falls within the group's norm. Individuals are often asked by peers to "follow the herd." Individuals exert pressure on themselves to work with a certain level of effort, a level which depends upon a myriad of things including expectations about themselves, their psychological make-up, and health status. What is the lowest level of effort given by the employee? It is an effort level that is acceptable to *both* the supervisor (s1), peers (p1), and self (i1). Individuals will produce with a minimum effort level which overlaps s1, p1, and i1. What is the highest level of effort acceptable to both supervisors (s2) and peers (p2), and self (i2)? Individuals will produce with a maximum effort which overlaps s2, p2, and i2. Individuals are subject to forces pushing them for more or less effort, and they compromise with themselves to satisfy the social forces with which they interact. In XE theory, Leibenstein called these ranges inert areas. Again, the social nature of production is evident in Leibenstein's writings. Leibenstein considered humans as social beings, with a psychological make-up that leads to watching what others do and what are their preferences, and then reacting. He applied these ideas to consumers, employees and supervisors, and fertility behavior.

X-efficiency theory: non-maximization/selective rationality

Non-profit maximizing models of the firm were not Leibenstein's creation. John R. Hicks (1935), Tibor Scitovsky (1943), William Baumol (1959), Robin Marris (1963, 1964), Oliver Williamson (1964), and Joseph Monsen and Anthony Downs (1965) were some of those scholars who wrote about "complex objective functions. Scitovsky and Marris wrote about utility maximization, Baumol about sales maximization, Williamson about "expense preference" functions, and Monsen and Downs about monetary and non-monetary lifetime income. Hicks is the author of the oft quoted comment that "The best of all monopoly profits is a quiet life" (Hicks, 1935). The orthodox view of the firm as a profit maximizer was being broken. But firms were maximizing something, some "complex objective function."

Leibenstein went one step further. Not only were firms not profit maximizers, but individuals were not maximizers *of anything*. Individuals were not (unboundedly) rational. We are not (necessarily) irrational: *we are selectively rational*. Our level of rationality ranges from 0 percent to

100 percent. The foundation upon which economics rests was thus challenged. Leibenstein's X-efficiency theory was, therefore, an attempt to spell out the implications of non-maximization/selective rationality for economic theory. It was one small step for an economist, one giant leap for the economics profession.

Leibenstein applied the concept of selective rationality to several fields, including fertility behavior. In "The Economic Theory of Fertility Decline" (1975). Leibenstein assumes that rationality is selective:

> For an economic theory to be valid, one need not assume that *typical* behavior is "rational." It is sufficient that behavior at critical junctures be of a "rational" type. Assume that the age of marriage and the birth of the final child depend on calculated considerations, although all intervening fertility behavior is "spontaneous," Note that under these conditions *average* typical behavior appears to be non-rational, but marginal behavior is rational . . . In addition, it is not required that all households behave this way. If a reasonable proportion do, then an economic theory that depends on rationality is significant.
>
> *(Leibenstein, 1975: 3)*

Otherwise, standard neoclassical theory which "rests" on the assumption of rational behavior may not be the most appropriate theory. In "An Interpretation of the Economic Theory of Fertility: Promising Path or Blind Alley?" Leibenstein (1974) explains selective rationality as the outcome of two conflicting forces. He says that his theory of selective rationality "assumes that there is a higher degree of substitution between the extent to which people indulge themselves in 'casual' decision-making and the point at which economic constraints force, or create strong pressure for calculated decision making" (Leibenstein, 1974: 475). Pressure pushes people to be *more* calculating, or *more* rational. Leibenstein calls it being selectively rational. About the beginnings of X-efficiency theory, Leibenstein says that it was

> Basically the outcome of an accident—having underutilized research assistants, who were willing to search out the details of technical reports on visits to enterprises in less developed countries . . . mostly from the ILO and the United Nations . . . Their work revealed a number of clear-cut, empirical examples of firms that appeared to be operating non-optimally and in other ways that contradict standard micro theory. It was forced by the data to reconsider my previously held positions.
>
> *(Frantz, 1997: xv)*

Non-optimality is also discussed in the first few sentences of Leibenstein's 1966 article, "Allocative Efficiency vs. 'X-Efficiency'" where he says that:

> At the core of economics is the concept of efficiency. Microeconomic theory is concerned with allocative efficiency. Empirical evidence has been accumulating that suggests that the problem of allocative efficiency is trivial. Yet it is hard to escape the notion that efficiency in some broad sense is significant.
>
> *(Leibenstein, 1966: 392)*

Leibenstein undertook a new definition to one of the most basic concepts in economics: efficiency. Allocative efficiency is an efficiency produced in the market, and exists when the price of a product equals the marginal cost of production. If a firm is X-efficient, then it is producing on their production and cost frontiers.

X-efficiency theory is based on several postulates. First, maximizing behavior/fully rational behavior is one point on a continuum. It is the point where standard economic theory "lives." The other end is completely irrational behavior. The degree of rationality is a variable, what Leibenstein called "selective" rationality. The degree of rationality depends on external and internal pressure for rational behavior. Pressure in X-efficiency theory is pressure from competitors, peers, supervisiors, and from one's personality. Rationality which is selective means that rationality varies among people and is subject to change over time. Hence, selective rationality, and the theory behind it, X-efficiency theory, is an evolutionary concept.

The human personality in X-efficiency theory has two parts, a superego and an id. The superego is the part of us which wants to do the best possible job. It is willing to be calculating, analytical, and logical, regardless of the dis-ease it creates. The id is the "California surfer dude," dude. Leibenstein also referred to the id as our "animal spirits" (Leibenstein, 1976: 79). The id wants to make the easiest possible decisions, does not want to be "hassled" with details, dude, wants to avoid headaches from calculating, being analytical, and logical. The superego is close to, if not fully rational. The id is, dude! The level of rationality is a compromise between the needs of the superego and the id, the behavior of peers, the demands of supervisors, and the level of competition in the product market. In other words, internal and external pressures.[2]

Second, behavior is subject to an "inert area." People get into a "comfort zone," a range of effort which they, their peers and supervisors, are comfortable with. Moving outside this range will be resisted. Given selective rationality, the maximum effort level will be achieved if and only if it is within the inert area. The inert area can shift over time, towards more effort if market pressures increase, or towards less effort if, for example, labor–management relations worsen. The inert area concept implies that at least some decisions are made passively.

Third, labor contracts are incomplete. Employers simply cannot control or stipulate all aspects of the labor contract. What activities the employee engages in must be at the discretion of the employee.

Fourth, production functions are not completely specified, meaning that a given amount of inputs outputs will fall within some range. The implications of X-efficiency theory are that output and cost are not determined by technology in a mechanical fashion. Firms operate below their output frontier and above their cost frontier. Economics becomes a bit messy. Messy is not good, and, ergo, X-efficiency must be rejected.

Fifth, within "reason" employees have effort discretion. In his 1945 article Hayek said that "the task of keeping costs from rising requires constant struggle, absorbing a great part of the energy of the manager" (Leibenstein, 1976: 200–1). The term "absorbing a great part" implies effort discretion. Leibenstein calls it the "struggle of the firm against effort entropy" (Leibenstein, 1976: 201).

Sixth, the proper level of analysis is the individual, neither the household or the firm. Leibenstein replaced the mechanical nature of economic theory with a version in which individuals were assumed to be social, not homo economicus, but human, and selectively rational.

The first empirical test of X-efficiency theory came in 1967 by John Shelton (Shelton, 1967). Since then there have been about 200 empirical studies in which the authors say that they are testing X-efficiency theory.[3] (There are hundreds of studies which are virtually identical to the 200 studies just mentioned but they do not mention X-efficiency. There are a few of the 200 studies that cite some XE literature but do not mention it within the text.) The studies support the XE hypothesis. Below is a sample of empirical studies on financial and non-financial institutions. Noting that these studies at times are comparing apples, movie tickets, and Honda Civics, the average level of X-efficiency is about 0.75. On average, firms produce about 25 percent below their production frontier and/or 25 percent above their cost frontier. Among financial institutions the average level of X-efficiency is in Australia (0.91), Taiwan (0.81), Western Europe

(0.80), US (0.75), China (0.73), Latin America (0.69), and the Middle East (0.69). These studies cover data from every continent in the world, from many industries. The results of these studies seems clear: XE X-ists, and is important (Frantz, 1997, 2007, 2015a, 2015b; Frantz et al. 2015).

The concept of allocative efficiency given to the profession by Robbins left out the internal efficiency or inefficiency of the firm, X-(in)efficiency. In addition, *allocative market inefficiency is small, maybe 0.001 percent of GDP to 0.0001 percent of GDP. And it is small as compared to X-inefficiency which has been estimated to be perhaps two or three percent of GDP.* Oscar Morgenstern's concept of rationality, VNM rationality, is that of an expected utility maximizing individual, whose behavior is consistent with several axioms, including completeness, transitivity, and independence. Kahneman and Tversky's "prospect theory" (Kahneman and Tversky, 1979) and empirical studies showing preference reversal behavior (Holt, 1986) have challenged expected utility theory as an explanation of real human behavior. Mellers (2001) discusses three other theories which contradict expected utility theory and offer empirical evidence: rank-dependent expected utility, cumulative prospect theory, and security potential and aspiration theory (Mellers, 2001). XE is larger than Robbins' allocative efficiency, and selective rationality seems more consistent with real human behavior than Morgenstern's VNM rationality.

Leibenstein and the Austrians

Leibenstein expressed several similarities with the Austrian economists. My point here is not that Harvey was an Austrian, but that the Austrians shared beliefs with Leibenstein (and other first generation behavioral economists). Expressing the Austrian philosophy of methodological individualism, Leibenstein points out that "only individuals make decisions, and not the socially or legally constituted entities we call firms and households, although individuals make some decisions in the name of such entities" (Leibenstein, 1976: 3). The "molecular" units of the economy are firms and households, but the more basic or "atomistic" units are individuals. He adds that "we can only understand the behavior of such molecular units through the study of the organization and structure of their atomistic constituents" (Leibenstein, 1976: 3). The basic unit of economic analysis is the individual, and the theory based on the individual is what Leibenstein called "micro-micro" theory.

In addition, the atomistic elements are neither objective nor physical quantities. Leibenstein is here expressing the Austrians' belief in subjectivity. For example, the supply of labor is the quantity of workers, hours worked, but also mental and physical effort. Only the individual knows best how much s/he is giving. Only the individual knows how much of their knowledge they are using. Knowledge is subjective. Hayek called subjective knowledge tacit knowledge. In his 1957 book, *Economic Backwardness and Economic Growth* (Leibenstein, 1957), Leibenstein speaks of knowledge as being so vague that:

> A man may have nothing more than a sense of its existence, and yet this may be the critical element. Given a sufficient inducement, he can search out its nature in detail and get it to a stage where he can use it. People normally operate within the bounds of a great deal of intellectual slack. Unlike underutilized capital, this is an element that is very difficult to observe.
>
> *(Leibenstein, 1976: 41)*

Hayek called vague knowledge unorganized or tacit knowledge, the knowledge of particular circumstances of time and place (Hayek, 1945). He believed that this was the most important form of knowledge and distributed throughout the population. It is neither objective nor easily communicated knowledge.

Hayek relates unorganized knowledge to phenomena which seem X-efficient-like. He says that unorganized knowledge includes knowing how "to put to use a machine not fully employed, or somebody's skill which could be better utilized ... the shipper ... using empty or half-filled journeys of tramp-steamers ..." (Hayek, 1945: 522). He also cites the ability of "an inefficient manager to dissipate the differentials on which profitability rests, and that it is possible, with the same technical facilities, to produce with a great variety of costs" (Hayek, 1945: 523). Leibenstein replaced the mechanical nature of economic theory where all variables are clearly defined and measurable with a more subjective theory in which important variables are not and perhaps cannot be known.

A third similarity with the Austrians is Leibenstein's lack of faith in the belief that prediction is the most important or the only way of evaluating a theory. He refers to this as the "romantic" view, calling it a "matter of faith or of taste" (Leibenstein, 1976: 13). Leibenstein preferred to evaluate a theory on whether it is able to

> obtain coherent explanations of phenomena and events ... Predictive capacity without explanatory capacity is worthless. ... Only predictive capacity that arises out of having coherent and communicable explanations has scientific standing. The power to predict is subsidiary to the power to explain. Explanation without prediction is sufficient, but prediction without explanation is of no consequence from a scientific standpoint.
>
> *(Leibenstein, 1976: 13)*

Leibenstein seems to mimic Hayek when he speaks about the fact that economics deals with a large number of variables and a large number of relationships among the variables. These variables include "economic" and "noneconomic" variables. The latter are particularly troubling because they "cannot be accounted for on the basis of existing knowledge" (Leibenstein, 1976: 14–15). And prediction, which requires accurate knowledge about the future, is very difficult. He says that

> a system that will predict what will actually happen – is, in principle, impossible. Even if we knew all the necessary initial data, as the system unfolds the environmental parameters would change; they would influence some of the variables within the system and the results would not be in accordance with what we would have predicted at the outset.
>
> *(Leibenstein, 1976: 15)*

Economists, says Leibenstein, cannot predict individual events; we can explain "general trends" (Leibenstein, 1976: 21). Hayek called this the "explanation of the principle."

According to Hayek, equilibrium is attained when people have perfect foresight about the behavior of others, and when the behavior of each follows a pattern which is comprehensible to others.

> Every person's plan is based on the expectation of just those actions of other people which those other people intend to perform and that all those plans are based on the expectation of the same set of external facts ... Correct foresight is then ... the defining characteristic of a state of equilibrium.
>
> *(Hayek, 1945: 42)*

According to Leibenstein, an individual's effort level in a multi-person organization depends on the effort level of others, and the pattern of effort must be understandable by others. Given these two prerequisites for effort equilibrium, an individual will conform to the group norm and put out a level of effort which falls within the norm. Leibenstein refers to this norm as the "inert area." Why do individuals stay within the inert area? According to Leibenstein, and Carl Menger before him, people remain within the inert area if the utility of leaving the inert area—producing more or less than the established norm—exceeds the utility of remaining within the inert area. Here Leibenstein shows his neoclassical side, and a fourth similarity with the Austrians.

The entrepreneur. Similarity number five involves Israel Kirzner's belief that neoclassical theory has no place for an entrepreneur, that Leibenstein's XE concept and his theory of the entrepreneur are important, and that some of Stigler's criticisms of XE are also important. According to Kirzner, entrepreneurs exist only when there are opportunities for earning economic profits. On the other hand, general equilibrium theory does not allow for such opportunities. Each person's plans are successfully completed, and no trades can leave two participants better off. In other words, there are no opportunities for economic profits, and hence there is no place for an entrepreneur. Leibenstein agrees with Kirzner about general equilibrium theory. Leibenstein says in chapter 6 of *Time, Uncertainty, and Disequilibrium: Exploration of Austrian Themes* that "If we want to get anywhere to solve the entrepreneurial puzzle, we have to stay away from the neoclassical general equilibrium syndrome" (Leibenstein, 1979: 129).

Kirzner says that,

> Scope for entrepreneurship, we have discovered, is present whenever error occurs. Pure profit opportunities exist whenever error occurs . . . X-inefficiency *is* possible, it reflects error, and is necessarily reflected in the availability of entrepreneurial profit opportunities and scope for entrepreneurial discovery and improvement.
>
> *(Kirzner, 1978: 70–1)*

Under conditions of equilibrium, X-inefficiency, "genuine disparities in efficiency among firms" (Kirzner, 1978: 72), cannot exist. "But under conditions of disequilibrium, when scope exists for entrepreneurial activity, there is no reason why genuine disparities may not exist among different producers, traceable . . . to differences to which producers have succumbed to error" (Kirzner, 1978: 73). So X-inefficiency x-ists under conditions of disequilibrium when there is a role for entrepreneurs. In Leibenstein's theory, entrepreneurs work when markets are in disequilibrium and are imperfect.

In Leibenstein's theory the entrepreneur interprets the "gaps" in (imperfect) markets. Entrepreneurs do not know where the gaps are. They discover them as a result of activity. Leibenstein thus concludes that in many ways entrepreneurs operate between markets. As in the Austrian theory of the entrepreneur, the entrepreneurial function in Leibenstein's theory is a process of discovery. Leibenstein replaced the emphasis of equilibrium with one of disequilibrium. Perfect markets were replaced with imperfect markets, and combined with disequilibrium lead to a role for the entrepreneur, a role which was all but lost in standard economic theory.

Was Leibenstein an Austrian economist? No, but he shared certain beliefs with them. Was he a neoclassical economist? I have given some examples showing Leibenstein to follow neoclassical thinking (e.g., people change their behavior patterns only if the marginal benefits exceed the marginal costs). But X-efficiency theory pulled him away from neoclassical theory, and the response of X-efficiency theory by some in the profession—X-efficiency is not consistent with neoclassical theory and, therefore, we reject it—pushed him even further away.

First generation behavioral economist

In his 1957 book *Economic Backwardness and Economic Growth*, Leibenstein, with a tip of the hat to Keynes, says that "In view of the framework of ignorance within which we are forced to work . . . " (Leibenstein, 1957: 3). In his 1960 book *Economic Theory and Organizational Analysis*, Leibenstein said that "we do not define firms as profit maximizing entities. Indeed, we want to leave the matter of objectives . . . free" (Leibenstein, 1957: 154). Before he published his 1966 article on X-efficiency Leibenstein was already convinced that ignorance and selective rationality are the proper framework for studying human behavior. In addition, firms are not profit maximizers, although he did leave it open that they may be maximizing something.

In the language of the id: rationality is, whatever dude! Michael Jensen, well known for several seminal ideas, including the agency theory of the firm and the capital asset pricing model, argued in 2008 that perhaps 50 percent of our lives are ruled by something other than rational behavior. In "Non-Rational Behavior, Value Conflicts, Stakeholder Theory, and Firm Behavior," he says that

> human beings are not rational in something on the order of 50 percent of their lives. I spent seven years with the Mind, Brain Behavior Initiative at Harvard (including membership on its steering committee) in my search for the source of the systematic non-rational behavior of human beings. And by that I mean not only people out there in the world, but every single person . . . , including me. The source of this non-rational behavior lies in the basic structure of the human brain. Neuroscientists have now uncovered the structure that leads all humans to engage in this non-rational behavior.
>
> *(Jensen, 2008: 169)*

Kenneth Arrow shared the 1972 Nobel Prize with John R. Hicks, for his work on general equilibrium and welfare theories. Which is why his 1987 article, "Rationality of the Self and Others in an Economic System," seems rather odd. Arrow argues against the monopoly of the rationality assumption in economics. In essence, he accepts the idea of selective rationality. He says that "Not only is it possible to devise complete models of the economy on hypotheses other than rationality, but in fact virtually every practical theory of macroeconomics is partly so based" (Arrow, 1987: 202). Even more, he says that the rationality assumption is not essential to economics, and when used must be supplemented by non-rationality assumptions. Thus, "the rationality hypothesis is by itself weak" (Arrow, 1987: 206). It is most useful when markets are competitive, in equilibrium, and when they are "complete." Under other conditions "the very concept of rationality becomes threatened, because perception of others and, in particular, of their rationality becomes part of one's own rationality" (Arrow, 1987: 203). In saying this, Arrow sounds very much like, Hayek (1945).

George Akerlof, 2001 winner of the Nobel Prize, and Janet Yellen, in their 1985 paper refer to this as "near" rationality. Near to rationality means that rationality is selective. In their paper they show that selective rationality has an effect on equilibrium solutions (Akerlof and Yellen, 1985). Richard Thaler refers to selective rationality as "quasi" rationality (Russell and Thaler, 2001). They say that

> Since rationality is *assumed,* there is little in the literature to suggest what would happen if some agents were not rational. This is surprising in light of the accumulating evidence

> that supports Herbert Simon's view that man should be considered at most boundedly rational.
>
> *(Russell and Thaler, 2001: 1071)*

Akerlof (1985), Arrow (1987), Thaler (1999), and Jensen (2008)—two Nobel Prize winners—add Herbert Simon (1957, 1976) and his theory of bounded rationality, and we have three Nobel Prize winners arguing against the notion of perfect rationality. Leibenstein argued against the same thing, writing before all of the above except Simon. Thaler and Akerlof put their "toe" into the conversation, talking about quasi and near rationality. They stayed close to the shore of neoclassical-beach. Simon waded up to his waist, talking about bounded rationality, which can mean anything from 1 percent to 99 percent rationality, but continuing to talk about maximizing given bounded rationality. But Leibenstein did not only put his "toe" into the conversation. Leibenstein jumped in, not close to, near or quasi to the shore of neoclassical-beach, not maximizing around bounded rationality. Not close to the shore, not bounded but maximizing. Not maximizing. Not perfectly rational, selectively rational, somewhere between 0 percent and 100 percent rational. What are the implications for economic theory? That was Leibenstein's agenda. Over lunch in Harvard Square, he once said to me that "My biggest mistake was not learning more math."

Conclusions

We can see behavioral elements in the writings of Leibenstein beginning in 1950. George Katona's contributions began in 1940. In Simon we see it beginning in 1947, certainly no later than 1955. Richard Nelson, 1961; Vernon Smith, 1962; Sidney Winter, 1964, Richard Day, 1967. And you can trace some of the major topics of these behavioral economists to Frederick Hayek's 1945 paper on knowledge. Here is the real beginning of behavioral economics.

In his *Principles of Economics*, Marshall discusses external economies of scale as an advantage of many people working in a relatively small geographical area. What occurs is that the "mysteries of the trade become no mysteries; but are as it were in the air, and . . . individuals (sic) learn many of them unconsciously" (Marshall, 1920: 271). Leibenstein, who was 80 percent wide and 20 percent clever, said in his 1957 book *Economic Backwardness and Economic Growth* that,

> some ideas, and these are difficult to acknowledge specifically, we may borrow almost imperceptibly from the intellectual climate in which we live and work. We do so almost without knowing it . . . it is impossible to acknowledge one's total intellectual indebtedness or even to acknowledge the most important instances, for these may well be the instances of imperceptible borrowing.
>
> *(Leibenstein, 1957: viii)*

A lot of people have borrowed from Leibenstein, Simon, Katona, and the other first generation behavioral economists, whether they are conscious of it or not.

Notes

1 In *A Theory of Economic-Demographic Development* (1954) Leibenstein says that the interdependence also includes that among economics and other social sciences: "One of the most significant facts of economics and the other social sciences is mutual interdependence" (Leibenstein, 1954: 2–3).

2 I once asked Leibenstein whether he was attempting to incorporate Freudian concepts, superego and id, into economics. His response was a definitive, "No."

3 There are hundreds of studies which are virtually identical to the 200 studies just mentioned but they do not mention X-efficiency. There are a few of the 200 studies that cite some XE literature but do not mention it within the text.

Bibliography

Akerlof, G., & Yellen, J. (1985). A Near-Rational Model of the Business Cycle, with Wage and Price Inertia. Quarterly Journal of Economics 100(Supplement), 823–38

Arrow, K. (1987). Rationality of Self and Others in an Economic System. In Hogarth, R., & Reder, M., Rational Choice: The Contrast between Economics and Psychology, Chicago: University of Chicago Press, 201–16.

Baumol, W. (1959). The Revenue Maximization Hypothesis. In Business Behavior, Value, and Growth, New York: Macmillan, 45–53.

Day, R. (1967). Profits, Learning and the Convergence of Satisficing to Marginalism. Quarterly Journal of Economics, 81(May): 302–11.

Dean, J., and Perlman, M. (1998). Harvey Leibenstein as a Pioneer of Our Time. The Economic Journal, 108(446), 132–52.

Frantz, R. (1997). X-Efficiency Theory: Theory, Evidence, and Applications. Norwell, MA: Kluwer Academic.

Frantz, R. (2007). Renaissance in Behavioral Economics: Essays in Honor of Harvey Leibenstein. London: Routledge.

Frantz, R. (2015a). Antitrust and X-Efficiency. Antitrust Bulletin, 60(3), 221–30.

Frantz, R. (2015b). 50 Years of X-Efficiency Research. Working Paper.

Frantz, R., Churchill, B., & Mackay, T. (2015). X-Efficiency among Chinese Banks. Open Journal of Social Sciences, 3(3): 69–75.

Hayek, F. A. (1945). Economics and Knowledge. Economica, New Series, 4(13), 33–54.

Hicks, J. R. (1935). Annual Survey of Economic Theory: The Theory of Monopoly. Econometrica, 3(January), 1–20.

Hogarth, R., & Reder, M. (1987). Rational Choice: The Contrast between Economics and Psychology. Chicago: University of Chicago Press.

Holt, C. (1986). Preference Reversals and the Independence Axiom. American Economic Review, 76(3), 508–15.

Jensen, M. (2008). Non-Rational Behavior, Value Conflicts, Stakeholder Theory, and Firm Behavior. Business Ethics Quarterly, 18(2), 167–71.

Kahneman, D., & Tversky, A. (1979). Prospect Theory: An Analysis of Decision under Risk. Econometrica, 47(2), 263–91.

Katona, G. (1940). Organizing and Memorizing. New York: Columbia University Press.

Katona, G. (1951). Psychological Analysis of Economic Behavior. New York: McGraw-Hill.

Katona, G. (1975). Psychological Economics. New York: Elsevier.

Katona, G. (1980). Essays on Behavioral Economics. Ann Arbor: Institute for Social Research.

Keynes, J. M. (1936). The General Theory of Employment, Interest, and Money. Cambridge: Macmillan Cambridge University Press.

Kirzner, I. (1978). Economics and Error. In L. A. Spadaro (ed.), New Directions in Austrian Economics, Menlo Park, CA: Institute for Humane Studies, 57–76.

Leibenstein, H. (1950). Bandwagon, Snob, and Veblen Effects in the Theory of Consumer Demand. Quarterly Journal of Economics, 64(2), 183–207

Leibenstein, H. (1954). A Theory of Economic-Demographic Development. New York: Greenwood Press.

Leibenstein, H. (1957). Economic Backwardness and Economic Growth. New York: John Wiley & Sons.

Leibenstein, H. (1960). Economic Theory and Organizational Analysis. New York: Harper & Row.

Leibenstein, H. (1966). Allocative Efficiency and "X-Efficiency". American Economic Review, 56-(June), 392–415.

Leibenstein, H. (1974). An Interpretation of the Economic Theory of Fertility: Promising Path or Blind Alley? Journal of Economic Literature, 12(2), 457–79.

Leibenstein, H. (1975). The Economic Theory of Fertility Decline. Quarterly Journal of Economics, 89(1), 1–31.

Leibenstein, H. (1976). Beyond Economic Man. Cambridge: Harvard University Press.

Leibenstein, H. (1979). The General X-Efficiency Paradigm and the Role of the Entrepreneur. In M. Rizzo (ed.), Time, Uncertainty, and Disequilibrium. Exploration of Austrian Themes, Lexington, MA: Lexington Books, 127–39.
Marris, R. (1963). A Model of the Managerial Enterprise. Quarterly Journal of Economics, 77(May), 185–209.
Marris, R. (1964). The Economic Theory of Managerial Capitalism, New York: Free Press.
Marshall, A. (1920). Principles of Economics. 8th edn. C.W. Guillebaud, ed. New York: Macmillan.
Mellers, B., & McGraw, A. P. (2001). Anticipated Emotions as Guides to Choice. Current Directions in Psychological Science, 10(6), 210–14.
Monsen, R., & Downs, A. (1965). The Theory of a Large Managerial Firm. Journal of Political Economics, 73(June), 221–36.
Morgenstern, O. (1948). Demand Theory Reconsidered. Quarterly Journal of Economics, 62(2), 165–201.
Nelson, R. (1961). Uncertainty, Learning, and the Economics of Parallel Research and Development Efforts. Review of Economics and Statistics, 43(4), 351–64.
Nelson, R., & Winter, S. (1982). An Evolutionary Theory of Economic Change. Cambridge: Harvard University Press.
Robbins, L. (1932). An Essay on the Nature and Significance of Economic Science. New York: Macmillan.
Russell, T., & Thaler, R. (2001). The Relevance of Quasi Rationality in Competitive Markets. American Economic Review, 75(5), 1071–82.
Scitovsky, T. (1943). A Note of Profit Maximization and its Implications. Review of Economic Studies, 11(1), 57–60.
Shelton, J. (1967). Allocative Efficiency versus "X-Efficiency": Comment. American Economic Review, 57(December), 1252–8.
Simon, H. (1957). Models of Man. New York: John Wiley & Sons.
Simon, H. (1976). From Substantive to Procedural Rationality. In S. J. Latsis (ed.), Method and Appraisal in Economics. Cambridge: Cambridge University Press, 129–48.
Smith, V. (1962). An Experimental Study of Competitive Market Behavior. Journal of Political Economy, 70(2), 111–37.
Smith, V. (2009). Rationality in Economics. Cambridge: Cambridge University Press.
Thaler, R. (1999). Mental Accounting Matters. Journal of Behavioral Decision Making, 12(3), 183–206.
von Neumann, J., & Morgenstern, O. (1944). Theory of Games and Economic Behavior. Princeton: Princeton University Press.
Williamson, O. (1964). The Economics of Discretionary Behavior: Management Objectives in a Theory of the Firm, Englewood Cliffs, NJ: Prentice-Hall.
Winter, S. (1964). Economic "Natural Selection" and the Theory of the Firm. LEM Chapters Series. In: Yale Economic Essays, 225–72.

5

HERBERT SIMON'S BEHAVIORAL ECONOMICS

Esther-Mirjam Sent

Introduction

Behavioral economics and its focus on the interrelations between economics and psychology are attracting increasing attention and recognition (Heukelom, 2014; Sent, 2004b). Bounded rationality has made its way into the work of, for example, rational expectations economists such as Thomas Sargent and game theorists such as Robert Aumann (Sent, 1997; 2004b). Yet, in 1992 Herbert Simon noted that "[r]eaders would not be deceived by the claim that economists flocked to the banner of satisficing man with his bounded rationality. The 'flocking' was for a long time a trickle that is now swelling into a respectable stream" (Simon, 1992b: 266).

Bounded rationality, in all likelihood, first appeared in print in *Models of Man* (Simon, 1957: 198; see Klaes and Sent, 2005). In his mature work, Simon used the concept to "designate rational choice that takes into account the cognitive limitations of the decision-maker—limitations of both knowledge and computational capacity" (Simon, 1987b: 266). Through the use of bounded rationality, Simon sought to criticize neoclassical economists for their lack of interest in the formal foundations of rationality. As Simon (1999: 23) reflected on this act of conceptual innovation, he began to use this concept after a while:

> You have to realize about the bounded rationality terminology that I began to use this as a label for the things that economists needed to pay attention to— and were not. It was never intended as a theory in any sense.

This is reminiscent of Harvey Leibenstein's introduction of X-efficiency theory (Frantz, 2007; Perelman, 2011).

Described by his colleague and friend Richard Cyert as a "true Renaissance man" Simon is the master of scientific border crossing. This chapter argues that "complexity" is the central theme of Simon's contributions to the various disciplinary domains (also see Frantz, 2003). Before turning to Simon's research in the third section, a brief second section will offer a biographical prolog. The section on the central theme of Simon's contributions is subsequently followed by one that highlights certain discontinuities. The fifth section next situates Simon's contributions within economics, while the last section concludes.

Biographical prolog

Born on June 15, 1916 in Milwaukee, Wisconsin, Simon was the second son of Arthur Simon, an immigrant German who was an electrical engineer and inventor, and Edna Merkel Simon, a third-generation American who was an accomplished pianist. Determined to become a mathematical social scientist, he bid farewell to Milwaukee at age seventeen to enter the halls of academe in Chicago, where he obtained his BA in 1936 and his graduate degree in 1943, both in political science. During his professional career, he was affiliated with the University of California at Berkeley, the Illinois Institute of Technology, the Cowles Commission, the RAND Corporation, and Carnegie Mellon University, which was still known as the Carnegie Institute of Technology when Simon moved there in 1949. At the time of his death in 2001, he was the Richard King Mellon Professor of Computer Science and Psychology at Carnegie.

In 1978, Simon received the Nobel Prize in economics for what the Nobel committee called "his pioneering research into the decision making process within economic organizations." Bounded rationality has received renewed attention in recent years from, among others, behavioral economists, game theorists, and rational expectations economists (Heukelom, 2014; Sent, 2004b). Yet, whereas Simon saw bounded rationality as an alternative to mainstream economics, many contemporary theorists attempt to use his ideas to solve some of the problems in their neoclassical program.

Starting off in political science and then moving through several disciplinary domains, such as management theory, economics, cognitive psychology, and artificial intelligence, Simon's entire academic career was focused on understanding human decision making and problem solving processes, and their implications for social institutions.

Continuities in Simon's contributions

There is a persistent reappearance of the theme of "complexity" in Simon's work. Indeed, Simon (1996a: ix) has counted himself among the partisans of complexity. Although several defining moments in complexity research may be distinguished, current enthusiasts tend to deal in concepts such as computational complexity, adaptive systems, genetic algorithms, classifier systems, and cellular automata (pp. ix, 169). In some instances, Simon has been cautious in his evaluation of these developments, arguing that "[i]t will be some time before we can assess its potential" (p. 181). Yet, in others, he has been much more forthcoming about the fundamental differences between these versions of complexity and his own.[1] Instead, Simon's (1996a: ix) own, idiosyncratic interpretation stressed "the particular hierarchical form of complexity,"[2] because "nature loves hierarchies" (Simon, 1973b: 5).[3] The reason for this, according to Simon (1996a: 196–7) is that "complex systems will evolve from simple systems much more rapidly if there are stable intermediate forms than if there are not. The resulting complex forms in the former case will be hierarchic."[4] For Simon, then, complexity was intimately connected with hierarchy, which, in turn, was closely related to ideas such as near decomposability, linkages, and frequency.[5]

Simon's complex, hierarchical system has linkages of different strengths or intensities among its components. Since he has maintained that effective hierarchies are nearly decomposable,[6] a complex, hierarchical system can be analytically divided into subsystems containing components with linkages of similar connectivity. The higher the subsystems are in the hierarchy, the lower is the frequency of interaction among their components. In other words, the weaker are the linkages among their elements. According to Simon (1973b: 10), "[m]otions of the system determined by low-frequency modes will be so slow that we will not observe them—they will be replaced by constants." Similarly, the lower the subsystems are in the hierarchy, the higher is the frequency of interaction among their components. In other words, the stronger are the linkages among their elements. For Simon (1973b: 10), "[m]otions of the system determined by the high frequency modes . . . will be so rapid that the corresponding subsystems will appear always to be in equilibrium . . . . In their relations with each other, the several subsystems will behave like rigid bodies . . . ". That is, Simon recommended treating slow behaviors at the higher levels as constants and fast behaviors at the lower levels as averages or equilibrium values. Hence, the analyzable subsystems with which Simon ended up are those in the middle, leading him to advocate theories of the middle level. In Simon's (1973b: 10–11) words:

> The middle band of frequencies, which remains after we have eliminated the very high and very low frequencies, will determine the observable dynamics of the system under study . . . . [W]e can build a theory of the system at the level of dynamics that is observable, in ignorance of the detailed structure or dynamics at the next level down, and ignore the very slow interactions at the next level up.

According to Simon, subsystems in the middle can be analyzed without reference to the subsystems below, since these are virtually in equilibrium, and the subsystems above, since these are essentially constant.[7] This description of Simon's interpretation of a complex, hierarchical system helps to understand the continuities in Simon's contributions to the various disciplinary domains.

First, Simon conceived of the organizations that he encountered in his political science and management theory research as complex, hierarchical systems.[8] The characteristics of these systems, as outlined in the previous paragraphs, allowed him to focus mostly on the middle levels of management. According to Simon (1960: 47), "the new developments in decision making will tend to induce more centralized decision making activities at middle management levels."[9] Therefore, Simon was mainly interested in how managers who find themselves situated in the middle make decisions, or, in how these managers manage to manage in complex, hierarchical systems. Simon (1960: 43) further noted that "[h]ierarchy is the adaptive form for finite intelligence to assume in the face of complexity." Consequently, just like systems can be divided into subsystems, goals can be divided into subgoals. Once these (moveable) subgoals have been set, the managers look for alternatives with which these can be met in a satisfactory manner. Therefore, satisficing allows the managers to determine when they are ready to move to the next subgoal, and heuristics inform the managers which branches to pursue from one subgoal to the next. Hence, managers are boundedly rational entities confronting the decisions they make in the complex, hierarchical systems in which they find themselves. Moreover, as suggested by Simon's later research in cognitive psychology and artificial intelligence, the problem solving skills of middle managers could be simulated and automated.[10] However, let us first follow Simon into economics.

Not unexpectedly, Simon also viewed economic systems as complex, hierarchical systems, thereby resonating with the contributions of Hayek to early complexity theory (Fiori, 2010).[11] Like the managers in political and administrative organizations, agents in economic systems are boundedly rational in dividing goals into subgoals, employing heuristics, and satisficing. Their choices do not stem from an examination of all possible alternatives. Instead, they climb on only certain branches of the tree; they can only explore subsystems of the complex, hierarchical system. In contrast, neoclassical economics[12] assumed that economic agents made choices: (a) among a given, fixed set of alternatives; (b) with (subjectively) known probability distributions of outcomes for each; and (c) in such a way as to maximize the expected value of a utility function. Instead, Simon wanted to model economic agents as making choices: (a') through a process for generating alternatives; (b') with strategies such as heuristics for dealing with uncertainty; and (c') in such a way as to satisfice relative to their aspiration levels. Hence, the nascent ideas inherent in Simon's early vision of science later blossomed into concepts that were to form the core of his criticism of neoclassical economics.[13]

Though perhaps unintended, Simon's ardent defense of theories of the middle level actually tended to immunize the neoclassical orthodoxy from damage from part of his attack. In addition to the above differentiation among levels of hierarchy, Simon further introduced a distinction between inner and outer environments. Just like subsystems higher up in the hierarchy can be analyzed without detailed descriptions of subsystems that are located lower down, one can evaluate the "outer environment with only minimal assumptions about the inner environment" (Simon, 1996a: 8). According to Simon, "[e]conomics illustrates well how outer and inner environment interact" (p. 25). Nevertheless, Simon's criticism of neoclassical economics seems to encounter some difficulties when he subsequently equated the outer environment with substantive, or neoclassical, rationality and the inner environment with procedural, or psychological, rationality, which tends to be the version modeled by himself (Simon, 1976).[14] If neoclassical economists propounded the idea that the outer environment could be evaluated without regard for the inner environment, they would have been given an argument for focusing on their preferred substantive as opposed to Simon's procedural rationality. Surely, Simon had not intended to bequeath this rationale to neoclassical economists![15] Furthermore, neoclassical economists have also employed some of Simon's mathematical results to their advantage in their own version of rationality. Again, these contributions were intimately related to Simon's focus on complex, hierarchical systems.

Consider Simon's valuable insights on causality and econometric identifiability.[16] What connects them to his research on managerial decision making and economic bounded rationality is, again, his interpretation of nearly decomposable systems.[17] Specifically, systems of simultaneous equations and sets of variables appearing in these equations can themselves be approached as complex, hierarchical systems. As a result, such systems can be divided into subsets of equations and subsets of variables. In particular, near decomposability is what allows the partitioning of both the equations and the variables of the system into relatively disjunct subsets for certain statistical purposes. The resulting hierarchies express the asymmetrical relationship among individual equations and their constituent variables. As Simon showed, they facilitate making a distinction between cause and effect and between endogeneity and exogeneity. In other words, hierarchy is intimately connected with causal ordering, which was closely related to econometric identifiability.

Next, consider Simon's useful contributions to the analysis of aggregation.[18] His conclusion that the possibility of consistent aggregation gives an insight into the difference between short run and long run dynamics again relied on the concept of complex, hierarchical systems.[19] As with his research on causality and identifiability, Simon started out with a system of variables that is nearly decomposable into subsystems. For reasons outlined previously, the interactions among the variables within a subsystem can be analyzed to a first approximation as though the links among the subsystems did not exist. Furthermore, interactions can be confined to different hierarchical levels, with the links among the variables within a subsystem represented by an index and the interactions among the indices representing subsystems may be evaluated without regard to the links within each subsystem. Simon further established that in the short run each subsystem can be studied (approximately) independently of the other systems and that in the long run the system can be studied by aggregating the variables of each subsystem into indices.

Finally, the conceptual framework of complex, hierarchical systems was extended in Simon's serial symbol processing hypothesis to cognitive psychology and artificial intelligence. In cognitive psychology, Simon's earlier argument that analyses of intermediate subsystems could be carried out without reference to the lower subsystems is reflected in his focus on the architecture of the mind at the symbolic level.[20] Specifically, Simon constructed a theory of the architecture of the mind and the characteristics of that architecture at the symbolic level in the absence of any but a very incomplete and primitive theory of how these symbolic processes were implemented by neuronal structures. Recall that Simon had earlier postulated that boundedly rational agents who find themselves in a complex, hierarchical system divide goals into subgoals, employ heuristics, and satisfice. In artificial intelligence, these same ideas enabled the development of simple problem solving procedures for computers.[21] In particular, they suggested that machines could be programmed to solve problems without specifying the solution for every class of problem in detail and that tasks could be divided into independent, hierarchically ordered subtasks. The result was a step-by-step, serial search through a vast problem space of possibilities, with each step guided by a heuristic rule of thumb. Moreover, his embrace of theories of the middle level led Simon to promote the resulting computer programs as tools for simulation.[22]

Branching from political science to management theory to economics to cognitive psychology to artificial intelligence, Simon saw complex, hierarchical systems everywhere. For Simon, these can be partitioned into suborganizations, subgoals, subsets of equations and variables, and subtasks. The subsystems in the middle consist of middle management, short run dynamics, the architecture of the mind at the symbolic level, and computer simulations of problem solving.[23] Heuristic rules of thumb guide managers, organizations, economic agents, human problem solvers, and computers. Moreover, each of these members of Simon's loosely coupled systems employ a satisficing strategy.

Whereas Simon saw complex, hierarchical systems everywhere, he also simultaneously conceptualized his own science as such a system (Simon, 1989b; 1991a: 368–87). The supposed near decomposability of this system allowed him to branch out in many diverse directions. However, this also left him the victim of unintended consequences and subverted intentions, perhaps because the bounded rationality of his audience prevented it from comprehending his science as a complex, hierarchical system. Although Simon himself could see the continuity in his scientific career, those less prone to cross scientific borders were more likely to observe discontinuities, as will be elaborated in the next section.

Discontinuities in Simon's contributions

Simon started out his career criticizing the theoretical outlook in political science and management theory (Simon, 1997a). He initially sought to supply much-needed in-depth empirical studies to a field infatuated with theory. Yet, his resulting contribution eventually still lay within the classical tradition in organization theory of observation, experience, and reflection, as he himself acknowledged (Simon, 1991a: 59n). Despite his expressed conviction that systematic observation and experimentation were badly needed in order for organizational theory to become scientific, Simon admitted that he often relied on facts derived mostly from common-sense observation and experience (p. 73). To be sure, Simon did apologize for this, arguing that a satisfactory theoretical framework was needed before the direction of empirical studies could be determined. Instead of supplying such studies in political science, though, Simon moved on to another subsystem.

In economics, Simon eloquently chided the failures of neoclassical economics and game theory, as elaborated in the next section.[24] Instead, he would seek to develop a much-needed alternative in the form of bounded rationality (Simon, 1982a, b; 1997b). Yet, Simon gradually withdrew from boundedly rational decision making in economics and left the alternative at the mercy of mainstream economists, who have instead used it in an attempt to strengthen neoclassical economics (Sent, 1998d; 2004a). For instance, rational expectations economists sought to reinforce the rational expectations hypothesis by focusing on convergence to this equilibrium through boundedly rational "learning". They have also used bounded rationality to deal with some of the problems associated with rational expectations, such as multiple equilibria and the computation of equilibria (Sargent, 1993; Sent, 1997; 1998a, b). Similarly, game theorists have sought to save the rationality of the Nash equilibrium by incorporating limited versions of bounded rationality. In particular, they have used bounded rationality to select among multiple equilibria, rule out unintuitive equilibria in the prisoner's dilemma game, and circumvent no-trade theorems (Sent, 2004a).

Moreover, many of the specific mathematical results of the self-avowed critic of neoclassical economics have repeatedly been used in an effort to strengthen neoclassical economics. For instance, some have argued that the papers by Emile Grunberg and Franco Modigliani (1954) and Simon (1954a) on the harmlessness of self-fulfilling public prediction were precursors to the general concept of rational expectations (Hands, 1990). In fact, Simon (1982d: 608) himself has acknowledged the connection between his own work on public prediction and the subsequent rise of rational expectations economics. Similarly, Simon's (1956b) introduction of certainty equivalence[25] facilitated attempts by new classical economists to link linear prediction and linear optimal control techniques (Sent, 1998b). Also, Simon (1979c: 505) himself has noted a close connection between his work on certainty equivalence and new classical economics.

Finally, Simon was one of the pioneers of the serial symbol processing hypothesis in cognitive psychology and artificial intelligence (Newell and Simon, 1972). Specifically, Simon's general-purpose computer model of human cognition sought to capture much of what went on in human problem solving (McCorduck, 1979). Yet, gradually, this interpretation of artificial intelligence has come under increasing attack because of its controversial use of symbols with propositional content.[26] For example, where do the symbolic concepts themselves come from? And, how do they evolve and grow? Or, how are they molded by feedback from the environment? Instead of trying to answer such philosophical questions, a newer generation of artificial intelligence researchers has moved away from symbol processing towards adaptive computing systems that simulate intelligence through neural networks, genetic algorithms, or classifier systems.[27] In their focus on connectionism and parallelism, this research is generally set in opposition to the contribution by Simon.

Conceptualizing his own science as a complex, hierarchical system, Simon constantly moved from one disciplinary subsystem to the next. For example, he came to the University of Chicago with the intent to major in economics, but left with a political science degree. The hurdle here was Simon's unwillingness to satisfy the accounting requirement accompanying the economics major. Simon came to the Cowles Commission as a critic of the rationality postulate in neoclassical economics, but gradually withdrew from his interest in boundedly rational decision making as a result of frequent visits to the RAND Corporation. Simon had been invited to work on decision making in organizational theory at RAND, but slowly shifted to focus on problem solving mediated through cognitive science.

Situating Simon's contributions within economics

What connected Simon's ventures into the different disciplinary domains was a search for complex, hierarchical systems. From this perspective, Simon (1998) criticized the four basic assumptions of neoclassical economics: (1) the presupposition that each economic agent had a well-defined utility or profit function; (2) the idea that all alternative strategies were presumed to be known; (3) the assumption that all the consequences that follow upon each of these strategies could be determined with certainty; and (4) the presumption that the comparative evaluation of these sets of consequences was driven by a universal desire to maximize expected utility or expected profit. For Simon, these four assumptions clashed with insights from psychology that there were external, social constraints and internal, cognitive limitations to decision making, upon which he based the opposing assumptions of his bounded rationality program.

Simon argued that, first, the bounded rationality program assumed that decision-makers were confronted by the need to optimize several, sometimes competing, goals. Second, Simon's bounded rationality program postulated a process for generating alternatives. Third, Simon argued that individuals mostly applied approximate solutions to problems. Finally, Simon's bounded rationality theory proposed a satisficing strategy, which sought to identify, in theory and in actual behavior, procedures for choosing that were computationally simpler and argued that individuals picked the first choice that met a preset acceptance criterion.

Partly due to his explicit efforts to distance himself from the mainstream, Simon's insights never caught on in economics "proper." Disillusioned, he left the Graduate School of Industrial Administration at Carnegie Mellon University in the 1970s for the psychology department at the same institution, noting: "My economist friends have long since given up on me, consigning me to psychology or some other distant wasteland" (Simon, 1991a: 385). However, psychology is no longer considered a distant wasteland, partly because later contributions to behavioral economics situated themselves squarely within the mainstream (Sent, 2004b). Whereas Simon started from a conviction that neoclassical economists were not all that serious about describing the formal foundations of rationality while he was, the more recent contributions to behavioral economics rely on the insights from Kahneman and Tversky that use the rationality assumption of mainstream economics as a benchmark from which to consider deviations (Heukelom, 2014). In addition, the mathematical difficulties encountered by mainstream economics facilitated not only the incorporation of psychological insights, in general, but also encouraged efforts to integrate some bounded rationality, in particular, into mainstream models to deal with problems such as multiple equilibria, no-trade theorems, and so on (Sent, 2004b).

Concluding comments

This paper has explored the continuities and discontinuities in Simon's science. Yet, there is certainly room for improvement. For instance, it is noteworthy that Simon has collaborated very extensively throughout his scientific career. Furthermore, he has been affiliated with many powerful scientific institutions and societies. Although this paper has touched on some of this, following Simon in his focus on individuals has kept it from a thorough appreciation of the rich detail of Simon's social interactions. Moreover, in stressing the centrality of scientists for complex, hierarchical systems, this paper has, in effect, placed them in the middle of the hierarchy. For, if it had not done so, there would have been little reason within Simon's theory of complexity for the focus on them as objects of explanation. Hence, ironically, it has tended to put them on an equal footing with middle management, and not with the CEO or entrepreneur, or the assembly-line worker or the laboratory technician.

Simon himself has explicitly applied his views concerning science to his own science. Not too surprisingly, he found a fixed point in which his own predictions were self-fulfilling. In his autobiography, Simon (1991a: 386) described the application of his insights concerning simulations of science to his own science, as follows: "Not only does it predict (explain) my behavior successfully, but . . . it has provided me for fifty-three years with a reliable set for conducting research." At the same time, it does not seem to have helped much in gaining a lasting influence in the various disciplinary domains through which Simon traveled, including economics.

Notes

1 See Simon (1992e: 574, 576; 1993: 644-6).
2 Also see Boumans (1998: 77, 79), Mirowski (1998: 21–2), and Simon (1960: 40–3; 1973b: 5, 27; 1996a: 184).
3 Also see Simon (1996a: 184): "[C]omplexity frequently takes the form of hierarchy . . . "
4 Also see Cohen (1995: 185–6) and Simon (1973b: 27; 1996a: 7–8).
5 Also see Mirowski (1998: 18–22) and Simon (1973b; 1989b: 385–6; 1996a: 183–216).
6 See Simon (1996b: 83): "[W]hat is important about nearly decomposable systems is that we can analyze them at a particular level of aggregation without detailed knowledge of the structures at the level below." Also see Simon (1973b: 11–15; 1996a: 198, 216).
7 In addition, near decomposability applies to the horizontal relations among subsystems as well: "The loose horizontal coupling permits each subassembly to operate dynamically in independence of the detail of the others" (Simon, 1973b: 16).
8 See Simon (1960: 40): "An organization can be pictured as a three-layered cake. In the bottom layer, we have the basic work processes. . . . In the middle layer, we have the programmed decision-making processes. . . . In the top layer, we have nonprogrammed decision-making processes . . . "
9 As a result, Simon's (1996a: 28) insights "have been applied mainly to business decisions at the middle levels of management." Also see Simon (1973b: 3).
10 See Simon (1960: xi, 47; 1997: 21, 28, 167, 173–4).
11 See Simon (1998: 266): "Bounded rationality . . . is deeply concerned with the ways in which the actual decision-making process influences the decisions that are reached."
12 In contemporary economics, the mainstream approach is known as neoclassical economics.
13 See Sent (1998d, e) and Simon (1982a, b; 1997b).
14 See Simon (1996a: 25): "[A]n intelligent system's adjustment to its outer environment (its substantive rationality) is limited by its ability . . . to discover appropriate adaptive behavior (its procedural rationality)."
15 Please note that this argument is not related to the distinction between microeconomics and macroeconomics. As noted by Simon, the distinction here is between outer environment (or substantive rationality) and inner environment (or procedural rationality). Also see note 17.
16 See Simon (1953). Also see Boumans (1998: 82), Mirowski (1998: 20n), and Simon (1989b: 386).
17 According to Simon (1953: 66), one can "decompose the system into complete subsets of equations of various orders . . . "
18 See Simon and Ando (1961). Also see Boumans (1998: 83) and Simon (1996a: 198).
19 See Simon and Ando (1961: 111): "Such a system can be represented as a superposition . . . [that] separates short-run from long-run dynamics . . . "
20 Simon (1993: 644) wanted "to characterize most of the higher-level and complex cognitive phenomena at the symbol level, rather than attempting to describe it all solely in neuronal terms." Also see Simon (1991a: 328; 1996a: 80–3).
21 See Mirowski (1998: 17–19) and Simon (1960: 19; 1973b: 6; 1991a: 328; 1991b: 146; 1996a: 13–15). In fact, when Simon's first computer program did not employ heuristics, he designed a new program that did operate as a search system within heuristic search spaces.
22 See, for example., Simon (1996a): "Because of its abstract character and its symbol manipulating generality, the digital computer has greatly extended the range of systems whose behavior can be imitated. Generally we now call the imitation 'simulation' . . . " (p. 13). Simon continued: "Simulation can be of . . . help to us when we do not know very much initially about . . . the inner system" (p. 15).
23 Simon (1991a) further sometimes saw himself as a subsystem in the middle in his personal life: "It even occurred to me that the mediating role I had sometimes played as a boy, when misunderstandings arose between my mother and grandmother, was not wholly unlike the role of the foreman as 'man in the middle' between blue-collar workers and management" (p. 73).
24 Though initially developed as an alternative to neoclassical economics, game theory has become part of the mainstream. Interestingly, Simon and contemporary game theorists share much criticism of earlier incarnations of game theory (see Sent, 2004a).
25 Certainty equivalence, sometimes called the separation principle, permitted the separation of the maximum problem facing an agent into two parts, an optimization or control part and a forecasting part. It is applicable when the objective function is quadratic, the constraints are linear, and the noise is Gaussian.
26 See, for example, Churchland and Churchland (1990), Dreyfus (1972; 1992), Dreyfus and Dreyfus (1986), Flores and Winograd (1986), and Searle (1980, 1990).

27 See, for example, Anderson and Rosenfeld (1998), Crevier (1993), Nadel et al. (1989), Rumelhart et al. (1986), and Sent (1998c).

Bibliography

Anderson, J. E. and Rosenfeld, E. (eds) (1998). Talking Nets: An Oral History of Neural Networks. Cambridge, MA: MIT Press.

Baars, B. J. (1986). Interview with Herbert A. Simon. In B. J. Baars, The Cognitive Revolution in Psychology. New York: Guilford Press, 361–81.

Boumans, M. (1998). Lucas and Artificial Worlds. History of Political Economy, 29, 63–88.

Churchland, P. M. & Churchland, P. S. (1990). Could a Machine Think? Scientific American, 262, 32–9.

Cohen, D. (1995). Interview with Herbert A. Simon. Psychologists on Psychology, 2nd edn. New York: Routledge, 181–94.

Crevier, D. (1993). AI: The Tumultuous History of the Search for Artificial Intelligence. New York: Basic Books.

Dreyfus, H. L. (1972) What Computers Can't Do: A Critique of Artificial Reason. New York: Harper & Row.

Dreyfus, H. L. (1992) What Computers Still Can't Do: A Critique of Artificial Reason. Cambridge, MA: MIT Press.

Dreyfus, H. L. and Dreyfus, S. E. (1986). Mind over Machine: The Power of Human Intuition and Expertise in the Era of the Computer. New York: Free Press.

Edwards, P. N. (1996). The Closed World: Computers and the Politics of Discourse in Cold War America. Cambridge, MA: MIT Press.

Fiori, S. (2010). Is H. A. Simon a Theoretician of Decentralized Planning? A Comparison with F. A. Hayek on Planning, Market, and Organizations. Constitutional Political Economy, 21, 145–70.

Flores, C. F. & Winograd, T. (1986). Understanding Computers and Cognition: A New Foundation by Design. Norwood, NJ: Ablex.

Frantz, R. (2003). Herbert Simon: Artificial Intelligence as a Framework for Understanding Intuition. Journal of Economic Psychology, 24, 265–77.

Frantz, R. (ed.) (2007) Renaissance in Behavioral Economics: Essays in Honour of Harvey Leibenstein. London: Routledge.

Fuller, S. (1991) Simon Says Put Your Foot in Your Mouth. Social Studies of Science, 21, 149–50.

Grunberg, E. (1986). Predictability and Reflexivity. American Journal of Economics and Sociology, 45, 475–488.

Grunberg, E. & Modigliani, F. (1954). The Predictability of Social Events. Journal of Political Economy, 62, 465–78.

Hands, D. W. (1990). Grunberg and Modigliani, Public Predictions and the New Classical Macroeconomics. Research in the History of Economic Thought and Methodology, 7, 207–23.

Heukelom, F. (2014) Behavioral Economics: A History. Cambridge: Cambridge University Press.

Klaes, M., & Sent, E.-M. (2005) A Conceptual History of the Emergence of Bounded Rationality. History of Political Economy, 37, 27–59.

Kulkarni, D. & Simon, H. A. (1988). The Processes of Scientific Discovery: The Strategy of Experimentation. Cognitive Science, 12, 139–75.

Langley, P., Simon, H. A., Bradshaw, G. L., & Zytkow J. M. (1987). Scientific Discovery: Computational Explorations of the Creative Processes. Cambridge, MA: MIT Press.

March, J. G. & Simon, H. A. (1993). Organizations. 2nd edn. New York, NY: Wiley.

McCorduck, P. (1979). Machines who Think: A Personal Inquiry into the History and Prospects of Artificial Intelligence. San Francisco: W.H. Freeman & Company.

Mirowski, P. E. (1998). What Should be Bounded when it Comes to Bounded Rationality? or, Automata vs. Simulacra. Unpublished working paper, Department of Economics, University of Notre Dame.

Mirowski, P. E. (2002) Machine Dreams: Economics Becomes a Cyborg Science. Cambridge: Cambridge University Press.

Nadel, L., Cooper, L., Culicover, P. & Harnish, M. (eds) (1989) Neural Connections, Mental Computations. Cambridge, MA: MIT Press.

Newell, A. & Simon, H. A. (1972). Human Problem Solving. Englewood Cliffs, NJ: Prentice-Hall.

Newell, A., Shaw, J. C. & Simon, H. A. (1958). Elements of a Theory of Human Problem Solving. Psychological Review, 23, 342–343. Reprinted in Simon (1989a), 6–19.

Newell, A., Shaw, J. C. & Simon, H. A. (1962). The Processes of Creative Thinking. In H. E. Gruber, G. Terrell, and M. Wertheimer (eds), Contemporary Approaches to Creative Thinking. New York: Atherton Press, 63–119. Reprinted in Simon (1979a), 144–74.

Okada, T. & Simon, H. A. (1995). Collaborative Discovery in a Scientific Domain. In J. D. Moore and J. F. Lehman (eds), Proceedings of the 17th Annual Conference of the Cognitive Science Society. Hillsdale, NJ: Erlbaum, 340–5.

Okada, T. & Simon, H. A. (1997). Collaborative Discovery in a Scientific Domain. Cognitive Science, 21, 109–46.

Perelman, M. (2011). Retrospectives: X-Efficiency. Journal of Economic Perspectives, 25, 211–22.

Qin, Y. and Simon, H. A. (1990). Laboratory Replication of Scientific Discovery Processes. Cognitive Science, 14, 281–312.

Rumelhart, D. E., McClelland, J. L., & The PDP Research Group (1986). Parallel Distributed Processing: Explorations in the Microstructure of Cognition. 2 vols, Cambridge, MA: MIT Press.

Sargent, T. J. (1993). Bounded Rationality in Macroeconomics. Oxford: Oxford University Press.

Searle, J. R. (1980). Minds, Brains, and Programs. Behavioral and Brain Sciences, 3, 417–58.

Searle, J. R. (1990). Is the Brain's Mind a Computer Program? Scientific American, 262, 26–31.

Sent, E.-M. (1997). Sargent versus Simon: Bounded Rationality Unbound. Cambridge Journal of Economics, 21, 323–38.

Sent, E.-M. (1998a). The Evolving Rationality of Rational Expectations: An Assessment of Thomas Sargent's Contributions. Cambridge: Cambridge University Press.

Sent, E.-M. (1998b). Engineering Dynamic Economics. History of Political Economy, 29, 41–62.

Sent, E.-M. (1998c). Artificial Intelligence. In J. B. Davis, D. W. Hands, and U. Mäki (eds), The Handbook of Economic Methodology. Cheltenham: Edward Elgar, 22–5.

Sent, E.-M. (1998d) Bounded Rationality. In J. B. Davis, D. W. Hands, and U. Mäki (eds), The Handbook of Economic Methodology. Cheltenham: Edward Elgar, 36–40.

Sent, E.-M. (1998e) Herbert A. Simon. In J. B. Davis, D. W. Hands, and U. Mäki (eds), The Handbook of Economic Methodology. Cheltenham: Edward Elgar, 457–58.

Sent, E. M. (2000). Herbert A. Simon as a Cyborg Scientist. Perspectives on Science, 8, 380–406.

Sent, E.-M. (2004a). The Legacy of Herbert Simon in Game Theory. Journal of Economic Behavior and Organization, 53, 303–17.

Sent, E.-M. (2004b). Behavioral Economics: How Psychology Made its (Limited) Way Back into Economics. History of Political Economy, 36, 735–60.

Shen, W.-M. & Simon, H. A. (1993). Fitness Requirements for Scientific Theories Containing Recursive Theoretical Terms. British Journal for the Philosophy of Science, 44, 641–52.

Simon, H. A. (1953). Causal Ordering and Identifiability. In W. C. Hood and J. C. Koopmans (eds), Studies in Econometric Method. New York, NY: John Wiley & Sons, chapter 3.

Simon, H. A. (1954a). Bandwagon and Underdog Effects and the Possibility of Election Predictions. Public Opinion Quarterly, 18, 245–53.

Simon, H. A. (1954b). Some Strategic Considerations in the Construction of Social Science Models. In P. F. Lazarsfeld (ed.), Mathematical Thinking in the Social Sciences. Glencoe, IL: Free Press, 388–415.

Simon, H. A. (1955). A Behavioral Model of Rational Choice. Quarterly Journal of Economics, 69, 99–118. Reprinted in Simon (1982b), 239–58.

Simon, H. A. (1956a). Rational Choice and the Structure of the Environment. Psychological Review, 63, 129–38. Reprinted in Simon (1957), 261–73.

Simon, H. A. (1956b). Dynamic Programming under Uncertainty with a Quadratic Objective Function. Econometrica, 24, 74–81.

Simon, H. A. (1957). Models of Man. New York: John Wiley.

Simon, H. A. (1959). Theories of Decision-Making in Economics and Behavioral Science. American Economic Review, 49, 253–83. Reprinted in Simon (1982b), 287–317.

Simon, H. A. (1960). The New Science of Management Decision. New York: Harper & Row.

Simon, H. A. (1966). Scientific Discovery and the Psychology of Problem Solving. In R. G. Colodny (ed.), Mind and Cosmos: Essays in Contemporary Science and Philosophy. Pittsburgh: University of Pittsburgh Press, 22–40. Reprinted in Simon (1977), 286–303.

Simon, H. A. (1973a). Does Scientific Discovery Have a Logic? Philosophy of Science, 40, 471–80.

Simon, H. A. (1973b). The Organization of Complex Systems. In H. H. Pattee (ed.), Hierarchy Theory. New York, NY: George Brazilier, 3–27.

Simon, H. A. (1976). From Substantive to Procedural Rationality. In S. J. Latsis (ed.), Method and Appraisal in Economics. Cambridge: Cambridge University Press, 129–48. Reprinted in Simon (1982b), 424–43.

Simon, H. A. (1977). Models of Discovery. Boston: D. Reidel.
Simon, H. A. (1979a). Models of Thought. Volume I. New Haven: Yale University Press.
Simon, H. A. (1979b). Rationality as Process and as Product of Thought. American Economic Review, 68, 1–18.
Simon, H. A. (1979c). Rational Decision Making in Business Organizations.American Economic Review, 69, 493–513.
Simon, H. A. (1982a). Models of Bounded Rationality. Volume 1. Cambridge, MA: MIT Press.
Simon, H. A. (1982b). Models of Bounded Rationality. Volume 2. Cambridge, MA: MIT Press.
Simon, H. A. (1982c). Election Predictions: Reply. Inquiry, 25, 361–4.
Simon, H. A. (1982d). Accurate Predictions and Fixed Point Theorems: Comments. Social Science Information, 21, 605–26.
Simon, H. A. (1987a). Is Scientific Discovery a Topic in the Philosophy of Science? In N. Rescher (ed.), Scientific Inquiry in Philosophical Perspective. New York, NY: University Press of America, 1–16.
Simon, H. A. (1987b). Bounded Rationality. In J. Eatwell, M. Milgate, & P. Newman (eds.). The New Palgrave Dictionary of Economics. Volume 1. London: Macmillan, 266–8.
Simon, H. A. (1989a). Models of Thought. Volume II. New Haven: Yale University Press.
Simon, H. A. (1989b). The Scientist as Problem Solver. In D. Klahr and K. Kotovsky (eds), Complex Information Processing: Essays in Honor of Herbert A. Simon. Hillsdale, NJ: Erlbaum, 375–98.
Simon, H. A. (1991a). Models of My Life. New York: Basic Books.
Simon, H. A. (1991b). Comments on the Symposium Computer Discovery and the Sociology of Scientific Knowledge. Social Studies of Science, 21, 143–8.
Simon, H. A. (1991c). Organizations and Markets. Journal of Economic Perspectives, 5, 25–44.
Simon, H. A. (1992a). Autobiographical Note. In A. Lindbeck (ed.), Economic Sciences, 1969–1980. Singapore: World Scientific, 339–42.
Simon, H. A. (1992b). Living in Interdisciplinary Space. In M. Szenberg (ed.), Eminent Economists: Their Life Philosophies. Cambridge: Cambridge University Press, 261–9.
Simon, H. A. (1992c). Scientific Discovery as Problem Solving. International Studies in the Philosophy of Science, 6, 3–14.
Simon, H. A. (1992d). Scientific Discovery as Problem Solving: Reply to Critics. International Studies in the Philosophy of Science, 6, 69–88.
Simon, H. A. (1992e). Review of "John von Neumann and the Origins of Modern Computing" by William Aspray. Minerva: A Review of Science, Learning, and Policy, 30, 570–77.
Simon, H. A. (1993). The Human Mind: The Symbolic Level. Proceedings of the American Philosophical Society, 137, 638–47.
Simon, H. A. (1995). Comment on Kagel. In G. Wolters and J. G. Lennox (eds), Concept, Theories, and Rationality in the Biological Sciences. Pittsburgh, PA: University of Pittsburgh Press, 359–66.
Simon, H. A. (1995/96a). Machine Discovery. Foundations of Science, 1, 171–200.
Simon, H. A. (1995/96b). Machine Discovery: Reply to Comments. Foundations of Science, 1, 225–32.
Simon, H. A. (1996a). The Sciences of the Artificial. 3rd edn. Cambridge, MA: MIT Press.
Simon. H. A. (1996b). Machine as Mind. In P. J. R. Millican and A. Clark (eds), Machines and Thought. New York: Oxford University Press, 81–102.
Simon, H. A. (1997a). Administrative Behavior: A Study of Decision-Making Processes in Administrative Organizations. 4th edn. New York: Free Press.
Simon, H. A. (1997b). Models of Bounded Rationality. Vol. 3. Cambridge, MA: MIT Press.
Simon, H. A. (1998). Bounded Rationality. In J. Eatwell, M. Milgate, and P. Newman (eds), The New Palgrave Dictionary in Economics. London: Macmillan, 266–7.
Simon, H. A. (1999). Interview with Herbert A. Simon. Working paper, CISTEMA, Copenhagen Business School.
Simon, H. A. & Andro, A. (1961). Aggregation of Variables in Dynamic Systems. Econometrica. 29, 111–38.
Simon, H. A. and Kotovsky, K. (1963). Human Acquisition of Concepts for Sequential Patterns. Psychological Review, 70, 534–46.
Simon, H. A., Valdés-Pérez, R. E., & Sleeman, D. H. (1997). Scientific Discovery and Simplicity of Method: Editorial. Artificial Intelligence, 91, 177–81.
Walton, D. (1995a). From the Invisible Hand to the Artificial Mind: Herbert Simon and the Economic Construction of Intelligence. Unpublished working paper.
Walton, D. (1995b). When an Economist is Not Just an Economist: From Management to Cybernetics and Back Again. Unpublished working paper.

6

REINHARD SELTEN, THE DUALIST

Rosemarie Nagel,[1] *Anna Bayona, Reza Kheirandish and Shabnam Mousavi*

> I am convinced of the necessity of reconstructing microeconomics on the basis of a more realistic picture of economic decision making. Moreover, I think that there are strong reasons for modeling boundedly rational economic behavior as non-optimizing.
>
> *(Selten, 2001: 14)*

Introduction

In this chapter, we weave a portrait of Selten, whose scientific work has emerged from a harmonious and ongoing bidirectional flow between theoretical game theory and the formalization of insights on (economic) behavior by using experimental methods. Delivering formal structures to now central elements of behavioral and experimental economics, such as descriptive learning models or the strategy method, alongside producing game theoretic concepts like subgame perfect equilibrium, Selten, the dualist,[2] stands out among the first generation of both behavioral economists and game theorists.

Reinhard Selten is a revolutionary, who has not only worked on the concept of economic rationality but also created an altogether new angle to formally describing human economic behavior through an innovative approach to game theoretical concepts. This chapter highlights a seeming contrast between the two perspectives of Selten's work and demonstrates how bounded rationality serves as a bridge between the two. In addition, it shows that many concepts currently used in game theory, its applied fields, and experimental economics can be traced back to his ingenious thinking. Selten's views on the structure of economic behavior are complex and multidisciplinary, and can be analyzed from the lenses of economic theory, experimental methods, biology, psychology, sociology, anthropology, and neuroscience, among others. He has played a major role in developing formalizations that expand the explanatory power of economic theory to include psychological understanding of human behavior. Working closely with psychologists, he has maintained a deep interest in studying individual human behavior and cognition, which was unusual in a profession so focused on outcome and aggregate phenomena.[3] At the same time he has also worked closely with prominent economic theorists. For his game theoretic contributions, he received the Nobel Prize in Economic Sciences in 1994, alongside John Nash and John Harsanyi. (He worked with Harsanyi for over 20 years.) Many scientists from different schools of thought have not recognized his parallel endeavor to enhance both game theory and experimentally driven work. In a remedial spirit, this chapter aims to introduce Selten's scientific achievements to a wider audience by illustrating this dual aspect of his contributions.

We present Reinhard Selten the dualist, who from the very beginning entertained economic problems both from an approach based on the rationality assumption and by using mathematics as a method of inquiry, and from a complementary approach, by conducting experiments and developing behavioral models. While an undergraduate student in mathematics, Selten developed interests in economics and psychology, and was later deeply influenced by the work of Herbert Simon on bounded rationality. Many consider Selten (in Europe) and Vernon Smith (in the US) to be the founders of experimental economics, originating from Selten working with Sauermann on oligopoly experiments (1959), and Smith on double oral auctions (1962). Describing himself as a slow researcher, Selten has been driven by a need to work in uncharted areas. For example, he started working on non-cooperative game theory when most of his peers were working on cooperative game theory (e.g., Selten, 1965). Similarly, in the 1980s, he began to work on cooperative bargaining problems of coalition formation (e.g., Selten & Uhlich 1998) when most experimental work was on non-cooperative bargaining, inspired by Kalisch et al. (1954). This work later inspired Nash, Nagel, Ockenfels, and Selten (2012), wherein the authors applied a non-cooperative approach to coalition formation based on Nash's (2008) paper on the agency method.

Since the start of his career, Selten's work has had a multifaceted character. For example, his theoretical dynamic oligopoly game that leads to the concept of the subgame perfect equilibrium (Selten, 1965) is practically concurrent with his analysis of actual behavior in this kind of game (Selten, 1967). Experimenters often quote the 1967 paper for the so-called *strategy method* it describes, which is now a standard tool for understanding the cognitive processes underlying a decision. His drive to understand human behavior led him to model complex games, analyze behavior mathematically, and take the games to the laboratory. In doing so, Selten developed new cognitive theories that provided a descriptive view of the behavior observed in the laboratory that reveals limitations of rationality. It is the union of these two approaches that makes Selten a unique researcher of human economic behavior.

In the foreword to Selten's (1999) *Game Theory and Economic Behavior: Selected Essays*, Al Roth elaborates:

> The reason Selten's contributions constitute one scientific career, and not two separate ones, is that he has been a leader in developing the theoretical implications of how games might be played by ideally rational players, and also, when these theories fail to be descriptive of observed behavior, in undertaking the related endeavor of proposing more descriptive theories.

In this chapter, we weave a portrait of Selten, whose scientific work has emerged from a harmonious and ongoing bidirectional flow between theoretical game theory and the formalization of experimental insights. Rather than integrating the knowledge acquired from these different disciplines into one, Selten chooses to work with them separately. This ongoing and active exchange is well illustrated in Selten (1991a), where he establishes an imaginary dialogue between discussants such as "the Bayesian," "the Experimentalist," "the Economist," "the Adaptationalist (biologist)," "the Naturalist", "the Population Geneticist" and "the Chairman" who moderates the dialogue. The dialogue encompasses each discussant's views on (Bayesian) optimization, cultural and biological evolution, experimentation, mathematical modeling, equilibration, adaptation, aspiration levels, learning, gene mutation, and many more concepts. The issue is not to determine which approach single-handedly best describes all possible aspects of a phenomenon but rather to acknowledge that there is a space (where), a reason (why), and a situation (when) for each view.

In his autobiographical note for the 1994 Nobel Prize, Selten wrote: "The structure of boundedly rational economic behavior cannot be invented in the armchair, it must be explored experimentally."[4,5] Selten's prominent and enduring contribution to future generations of scholars is that of establishing connections between multidisciplinary views in order to explain the structure of economic behavior in a more integrated manner. In particular, his earlier bounded rationality models have inspired the subsequent literature that has brought models of bounded rationality into mainstream economics. Furthermore, Selten introduced several game theoretic concepts to biology, such as a class of models for asymmetric conflicts. (Further examples and details can be found in Selten, 1980, 1983b, and Hammerstein & Selten, 1994.)

In contrast in 2001, Selten together with Gigerenzer edited *Bounded Rationality: The Adaptive Toolbox*, a collection of multidisciplinary chapters that explore how humans and animals make choices under limited time, information, and resources. The "adaptive toolbox" refers to the collection of learned or evolved mental capacities that can be exploited by heuristic decision rules to make judgments under conditions of uncertainty. The criterion to find decision rules was not that these are the outcome of an optimization problem but that subjects in the laboratory are observed to apply these rules. Fast, in that they lead to action under time constraints, and frugal, in that they require little information or calculation, heuristics nonetheless perform effectively in real world situations when used by boundedly rational agents.

The present chapter does not provide a comprehensive description of Reinhard Selten's ideas on the structure of economic thought, nor does it review all the work that his ideas have influenced and continue to influence. We draw on the original papers of Selten and co-authors, on excellent discussions of Selten's theoretical contributions to game theory by Gul (1997) and Güth (1995), and on a large collection of essays in *Selten's School of Behavioral Economics* edited by Sadrieh and Ockenfels (2010), in which leading scholars in the fields of experimental economic and biology together with Selten's former PhD students discuss their academic and personal interactions with Reinhard Selten.

The organization of this chapter is as follows. First, we depict Selten's interplay of economic theory and experimentation. From there, we illustrate his approach to developing descriptive boundedly rational models. We use the word *descriptive* in a general sense to mean a departure from the neoclassical model with its standard assumptions. We continue by elaborating on Selten's view of bounded rationality, which behavioral economics draws from in many ways, by specifying what he did *not* view as bounded rationality. Concluding remarks and open questions close our discussion and point to paths for future research.

The interplay of economic theory and experimentation

Selten clearly separates *game theoretic models* from *mathematical solution concepts*. Game theoretic models serve to describe situations by formalizing them. Their elements are the timing, the players, the information, the alternatives and their properties available to each player at each decision point and the payoff function. This follows the method originally developed by the fathers of game theory, von Neumann and Morgenstern, in their 1944 seminal book *Theory of Games and Economic Behavior*. Game theoretic models have been successful in structuring a large spectrum of situations that describe economic behavior. Prominent examples of game theoretic models are oligopoly, signaling and coordination, and derived concepts such as games of strategic complementarity it or substitutability.[6] For an experimenter, on the one hand, a theoretical (micro-founded) model can be easily transformed into an experiment by translating its assumptions and the key features of the game into instructions. *Mathematical solution concepts*, on the other hand, serve as benchmarks for predicting how a game will be played and are typically based on equilibrium concepts, assuming understanding of the rules of the game (or *game form recognition* à la Chou et al., 2009), rationality, often common knowledge of rationality, and optimization. The analysis of the game from a mathematical point of view provides a potential structure for the set of possible strategies and presents a starting point for organizing actual behavior. Two examples can be seen in Selten and Uhlich (1988) and Nash et al. (2012) on characteristic function games where they discuss different cooperative solutions and develop a bounded rationally guided solutions based on fairness criteria and reciprocity concepts.

The starting point of his major contribution to game theory was initialed by Sauermann and Selten (1959, 1960) who studied behavior from an experimental stance in a complicated oligopoly game with several variables and demand inertia without a theoretical solution. The aftermath of this joint work directed Selten to find a simplified theoretical framework for analyzing dynamic oligopoly contexts, which—according to the interview with Güth, Strobel, and Wickström (1997)—subsequently led to his consequential 1965 paper, which proposed the first refinement concept of this kind. In that paper, while searching for a backward induction solution Selten realized that the equilibrium he found had a special property. He named it the *subgame perfect equilibrium* (SPE)[7]. When a game has several Nash equilibria, rational players cannot coordinate. A Nash equilibrium is an SPE if it is a Nash equilibrium in every subgame. This concept eliminates the Nash equilibria of the dynamic game that contain non-credible threats and has been extensively analyzed in all areas of economics, including industrial organization (e.g., applications such as entry deterrence described in Vives, 1999) and macroeconomics (e.g., applications such as monetary policy reviewed in a collection edited by Grossman & Rogoff, 1995). Over time, the SPE concept has become the most widely used equilibrium refinement for non-cooperative, extensive form, and complete information games of strategic interaction.

In 1975, Selten noticed that in some games the notion of SPE was not sufficient to rule out non-credible threats. He then developed the concept of trembling-hand perfection (Selten, 1975), which is a further refinement of the SPE concept. To understand the trembling-hand concept, assume that each player can make a mistake (his hand trembles) with a small probability. An equilibrium satisfies the trembling-hand perfection if it is robust to such mistakes. Thus, the small perturbations from the equilibrium concept can eliminate some equilibria. In his review of the contributions of the game theory Nobel Prize winners of 1994, Gul (1997) claims that Selten's main contributions were

> That a small probability of mistakes could capture forward-looking rationality (that is, credibility and subgame perfection) in a dynamic interaction; that such strategy perturbations could be used to eliminate equilibria; and finally that a sensible definition of rationality must pay some attention to possible deviations from rationality by other players.
>
> *(p. 171)*

In addition, Harsanyi and Selten (1972, 1988) developed equilibrium selection concepts for bargaining games based on risk and payoff dominance. After receiving the Nobel Prize, Selten was asked by one of his students whether he had previously believed that his SPE concept was an important contribution. Selten replied that at the time he had in fact considered the game theoretic model of the duopoly game with demand inertia to be the most interesting contribution of the paper, but then went on to note the very special feature of his SPE concept developed in Selten (1965).

In Selten's work, scientific attention to game theoretical reasoning parallels the realistic approach to describing human economic behavior. This is well demonstrated in his 1978 paper on the "chain store paradox,"[8] wherein he describes the tension and contradictions between the "correct" game theoretic solution, which he calls *induction theory*, and the more realistic and intuitive behavioral story, which he calls *deterrence theory*. This important paper marks the juncture where Selten becomes aware of the limitations of the SPE as a descriptive model of behavior. In reaction, he proposes a heuristic behavioral model to explain the paradoxical tension between the two theories, induction and deterrence, drawing on Simon's idea of procedural rationality. In this heuristic model, three levels of decisions are made: routine, imagination, and reasoning. Routine decisions draw on past experience and do not demand conscious effort, whereas imagination uses routine knowledge and extends it to generate new outcome possibilities. Reasoning involves conscious considerations of information and the use of logic. A decision process starts at a routine level, where the decision maker "decides on how to decide." However, that does not necessitate following the solution generated from the highest (rational) level of decision. That is, a decision maker can know the rational solution but nevertheless choose a different lower-level solution. Sadrieh (2010) provides an elaborate discussion on how this decision making framework could be viewed in relation to the approaches of both classical and behavioral economics.

When establishing a dialogue between economic theory and experimentation, Selten maintains that the experimenter should not be blindly guided by game theoretic solutions but should instead explore what actual behavior is about. In his view, human economic behavior in the initial phases of a game cannot be realistically or accurately described by game theoretical reasoning. However, behavior might or might not converge to the mathematical solution through a boundedly rational adaptation process or by evolutionary forces. Of course, there are those who choose this theoretical solution consciously, typically the subpopulation of "economic theorists." Many times, those who act according to fully rational behavior fail to get high payoffs, especially in the beginning of the game, as shown, for example, in Bosch-Domènech et al. (2002) and Camerer and Fehr (2006).

Economic experiments have proven successful in determining the scope and limits of economic theory because they can both control the assumptions that are required for the economic model to hold and isolate the effects of various institutional features. While comparing theories of behavior (including game theoretic reasoning), Selten (1978b: 144) argues: "Probably one cannot form a sound intuitive judgment about the practical usefulness of different strategic recommendations without thinking about a concrete situation like the laboratory experiment where the payoffs are monetary payoffs." Harstad and Selten (2013) present two examples where economic theory has systematically failed to capture observed economic behavior. The first is in common value auctions, where there is robust experimental evidence for systematic violations of the equilibrium predictions, a phenomenon known as the *winner's curse* (Kagel & Levin, 1986; Kagel, 1995; Kagel, Levin, & Harstad, 1995). The second can be found in models that predict zero speculative trade with rational agents. An example of these theoretical predictions can be found in Milgrom and Stokey (1982) and experimental evidence of violations to these predictions in Smith, Suchanek, and Williams (1988).

Experiments are also useful for understanding strategic decision making in complex environments. From early on, Selten has been interested in complex models that reflect the richness of the environment being modeled, such as the behavior of the firm or macroeconomic models.[9] Sauermann and Selten (1959, 1960) were the first ever to run an oligopoly experiment with a high degree of complexity, reflecting features of the business environment.[10]

Another example of a complex experiment is presented in Selten, Pittnauer, and Hohnisch (2012), where subjects in a dynamic decision making problem are asked to maximize the long-term profit of a monopolist who can adjust 20 different parameters in a qualitative way. Following from the idea that the theorist has to provide a benchmark for rational behavior, the theorist can also simulate the optimal path of behavior, where all the features of the game are known. Figure 6.1 shows the optimal set of solutions for each parameter. For a human subject, to act in accordance with the optimal solution path is very difficult or nearly impossible. In the real world the decision maker typically does not know the mathematical relationship between the parameters. In the experimental design therefore, subjects do not know the parameters of the game (they only know the qualitative features of the game) whereas the theorist knows the values of the parameters, which is a prerequisite for a benchmark solution. Nonetheless, most subjects successfully completed the task by selecting reasonable goal systems in accordance with the aspiration adaptation theory. Figure 6.2 shows the features of the game, which are presented only qualitatively and were illustrated by a flowchart in the experimental instructions. However, a theorist would not know how to solve the game mathematically on the basis of the flowchart presented in Figure 6.2 alone. Complexity often requires the need for flowcharts that show causality between variables. Such experiments are unfortunately still very rare in experimental economics, which, however, can lead to interesting patterns of rich behavior. In another instance, Selten and Apesteguia (2005) provide a flowchart for the reader to understand the stability requirements of an imitation equilibrium in an experiment about price competition on the circle.

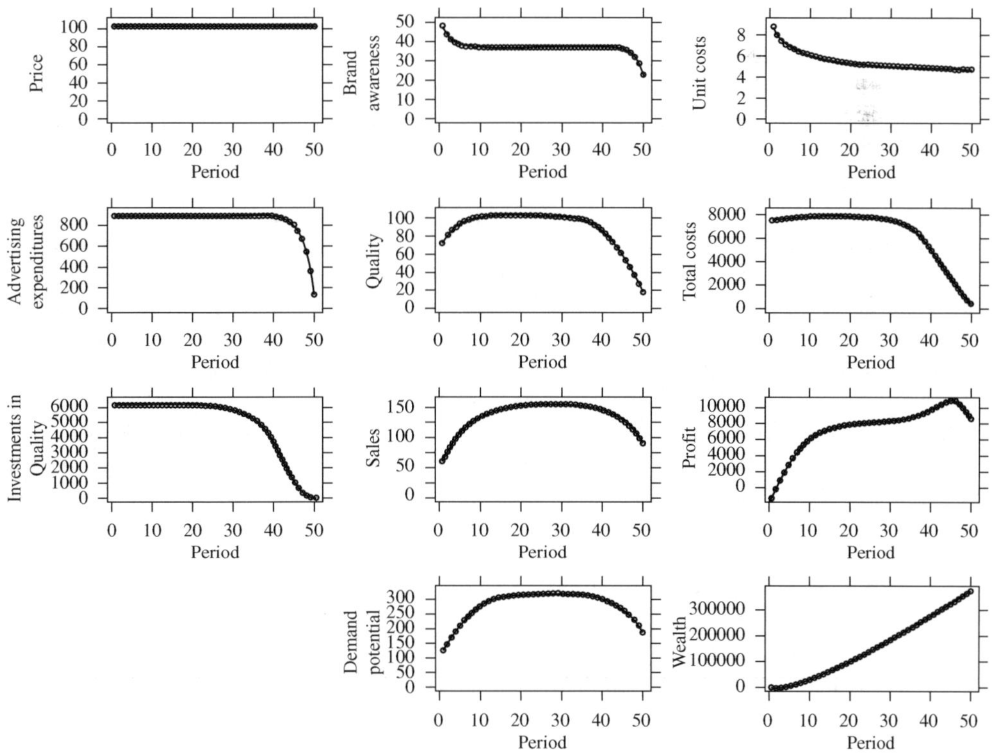

Figure 6.1 Optimal paths of the variables in the monopoly market model in Selten, Pittnauer, and Hohnisch (2012)

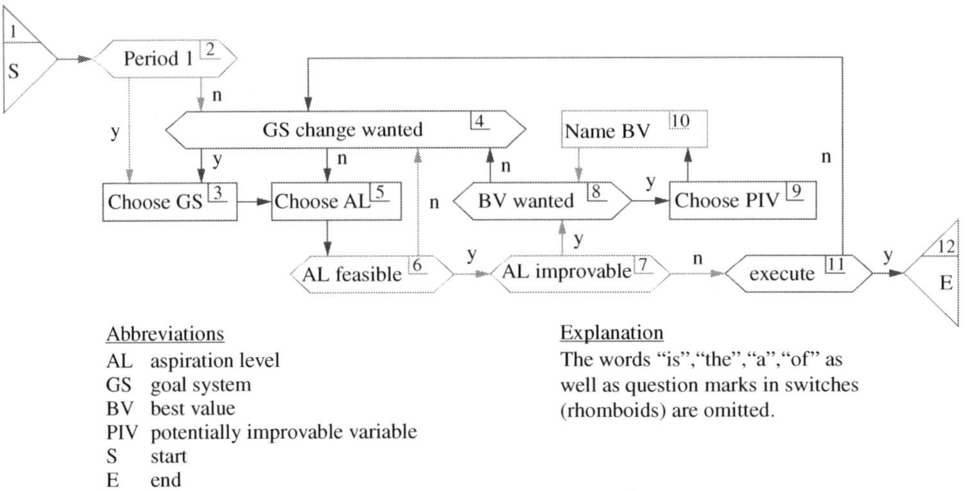

Figure 6.2 Flowchart representing the decision procedure of a participant in the experiment (y is yes and n is no) in Selten, Pittnauer, and Hohnisch (2012)

Selten's creativity comes across both on an organizational level and intellectual level. In 1984 Selten set up an experimental computer lab, the first in Europe. He was also a pioneer in developing and using many new concepts, useful tools, and interesting games. In the following, we focus on five examples.

First, Selten (1967) developed the concept of the strategy method, which is especially suitable for eliciting subjects' procedural thinking. In complex games the method consists of two main parts: a subject first has to become acquainted with the game by responding at the nodes of the games reached during an interaction with another player before being able to compose a complete strategy for playing the game (see, e.g., Selten et al., 1997, as discussed below). This means that the subject has to choose an action in each information set reachable in the game. The advantage of this method is that decisions have to be made at points that are typically not reached when the game is played in a sequential way, such as reactions to very small offers in ultimatum games, which are seldom observed. Selten et al. (2003) also applied this method to analyze how subjects play in a large set of different 3×3 games. The experiment was conducted within the curriculum of third- and fourth-year undergraduate students at the University of Bonn, who had to submit a programmed strategy that formed their grade after having played many of rounds of the game against other students. The results show that in games with a single pure strategy equilibrium, subjects learned to adjust their strategies over time so that at the end that equilibrium was played. When there were multiple pure equilibria, subjects tended to coordinate on the equilibrium with maximum joint payoffs. In simple games, a strategy can be constructed immediately, without the necessity of learning about the game. In this case, subjects provide a decision for each possible information set reached during the course of the game. Mitzkewitz and Nagel (1993) introduced this simplified form of the strategy method in an ultimatum game where receivers had incomplete information about the pie size.[11] In Selten and Buchta (1998), subjects had to draw bid functions (which can take any form) in private value auctions, which they could then adjust period by period. The strategy method was also applied by Fischbacher and Gächter (2010) to analyze voluntary contributions to public goods, where conditional cooperators who cooperate when others cooperate were found to be the major type of behavioral strategy.

These and similar games that use the simplified strategy method are reviewed in Brandts and Charness (2011).

The second example of Selten's innovative tools measures the predictive success in distinguishing between different area theories (Selten, 1991c).[12] Selten's measure of predictive success, derived axiomatically, also called *hit rate*, subtracts the relative size of the predicted range from the relative frequency of correct predictions. If the outcomes are randomly allocated within the predicted range then the hit rate is expected to be equal to the relative size of the predicted range. Hence, the measure of predictive success is the excess hit rate over the random hit rate (Selten, 1987). This kind of measure is especially interesting if the researcher explores and develops different descriptive theories (comprised of areas of different sizes) to characterize different kinds of behavior, a dominant theme in most of Selten's experimental papers (e.g., Selten et al. (2012) in the context of a dynamic decision making experiment or by Forsythe et al. (1999) in the context of financial markets with adverse selection).

Third, Selten emphasizes the importance of collecting subjects' comments during or at the end of the experiment in order to assess their thinking procedures, as applied for example to the beauty contest game with newspaper readers (Selten & Nagel, 1998; Bosch-Domènech et al., 2002). This method of analyzing subjects' comments remains relatively rare in experimental economics, where most experiments focus on merely observing and recording subjects' behavior. However, Selten himself did not stop at the point where he had a statistical mapping between game situations and behavior but always went beyond it to explore the reasoning processes that induce a certain behavior. Videotaping is an alternative way to obtain an introspection into subjects' reasoning processes. For example, Hennig-Schmidt et al. (2010) studied the effect of pro-social behavior in negotiations using a videotaping approach, which allows the researchers to analyze socio-emotional factors and interpersonal relations on group processes. Observing groups of players during discussions can bring to light the stages involved in the formation of complex cognitive processes, which cannot be achieved by eliciting written statements. Today, the technology of chatting between subjects in a free or more controlled way via computer chat rooms has made it possible to directly obtain comments for analysis in a much easier way than with audio or video tapes.

Fourth, Selten formally put forward some prominent behavioral effects that are now known and used frequently by behavioral economists before their appearance in behavioral literature. For instance, Selten attached importance to *presentation effects*, that is, the fact that the response to a decision task depends on how it is presented. In a first step, Selten and Berg (1970) ran continuous-time oligopoly experiments and found that the way the task was presented had a significant influence on behavior. Presentation effects were later analyzed in further detail and called *framing* by Tversky and Kahneman (1981). Consequently, Selten (1998) attributed this to boundedly rational reasoning and subjects' "superficial analysis". Similarly, the market entry game, introduced in Selten and Güth (1982), was independently developed by Kahneman (1988) and gained prominence afterwards.

Finally, Selten's scientific rigor was evident from his use of statistics and the way in which he insisted statistics should be used. He contended that experimenters should obtain a sufficient number of independent observations and analyze the individual raw data from all possible angles rather than applying statistical techniques, such as regression, in a mechanical way. In addition, Selten prefers non-parametric statistics to regressions, and has a clear notion of the appropriate summary statistics that can be used for analyzing experimental data. A firsthand example is the case of Rosemarie Nagel, who analyzed the guessing game data when Selten was her advisor. When she proposed using arithmetic averages to determine the cut-off values between levels of reasoning, Selten suggested that, given the structure of the thinking process, the geometric average was a much more appropriate measure.

Models of bounded rationality

Selten strives to operationalize cognitive processes that describe behavior and has made progress in developing and inspiring several formal models of boundedly rational behavior in games. These models have well-established foundations rooted in psychology, neurology, and other related disciplines. At the same time, Selten has explicitly expressed his reservations regarding the use of utility functions as a tool to explain behavior. For example, Sauermann and Selten (1962) propose that the behavior of the firm can be described by satisfaction of aspiration levels rather than by maximization of utility or profit; this has been subsequently applied, for example, by Tietz and Weber (1972) in the context of two-person bargaining. Aspiration adaptation theory is not based on outcomes alone but also encompasses elements of cognitive procedures, extending on Simon's (1976) distinction between substantive and procedural rationality, according to which decision makers reach a decision based on a goal system to which they attach aspiration levels. The following quote of Sadrieh (2010) best summarizes Selten's thoughts on the emergence of a decision process: "only partially non-routine choices [. . .] result from conscious deliberations. And even the deliberate choices, he believes, are not based on the optimization of an objective function, but on adaptation of aspirations to the perceived environment" (p. 284).

Selten's behavioral models are not based on the ideal optimization of classical economics. This can be seen in the experiment of a finite-period supergame of an asymmetric Cournot duopoly game in Selten et al. (1997). In this experiment, the authors developed a model based on the programmed strategies of experimental subjects who participated in an undergraduate seminar lasting 13 weeks; their strategies were seen to be not based on the optimization of expected profits given the expected strategies of the opponents. Let us cite a longer passage from the paper to emphasize the contribution of this work and Selten's critique of optimization:

> Typically, the participants tried to approach the strategic problem in a way which is very different from that suggested by most oligopoly theories. These theories almost always involve the maximization of profits on the basis of expectations of the opponent's behavior. It is typical that the final tournament strategies make no attempt to predict the opponent's reactions and nothing is optimized. Instead of this, a cooperative goal is chosen by fairness considerations and then pursued by an appropriate design of the strategy. Cooperative goals take the form of "ideal points". An ideal point is a pair of outputs at which a player wants to achieve cooperation with his opponent. Such ideal points guide the behavior in the main phase. A move of the opponent towards the player's ideal point usually leads to responses which move the player's output in the direction of his ideal point.
>
> *(Selten et al., 1997)*

Selten's editor wanted to eliminate the statement "nothing is optimized" but Selten refused. Notably, this kind of cognitive approach is in stark contrast to the game theoretic approach, which uses backward induction for finitely played games. Here, typical human subjects instead divide a repeated finite game into three phases: how to start and react to the opponent's starting behavior, thereby establishing the ideal point; a middle game of consolidation (called *measure for measure* policy); and an end game phase with a possible defection from cooperation. Selten et al. (1997: 538) note that: "A response guided by the principle 'measure for measure' protects against attempts to exploit one's own cooperativeness and rewards cooperative moves of the other player".

Selten's thoughts on cooperation, fairness, and reciprocity can be summarized in the following quote: "Fairness and reciprocity are very important for strategic reasoning" (Selten, 1998: 433). For example, fairness considerations may be important focal points in bargaining situations; at other times, the fairness principle may provide subjects with a benchmark. This idea is addressed in Selten (1983a), where he develops the theory of "equal division of payoff bounds" in order to describe the behavioral and cognitive reasons that influence players' aspiration levels in zero-normalized three-person games in the context of an experimental characteristic function game. The theory specifies three lower payoff bounds for the final payoffs of the three players. The lowest reasonable aspiration level for each of these three players corresponds to the equal division of payoff bounds. Thus, the theory of lower payoff bounds specifies the minimum aspiration that a player reasonably holds. In addition, Selten (1972, 1978a) operationalized the equity principle, which in the words of Hennig-Schmidt et al. (2010: 140) can be expressed as: "The amount in question is distributed to the parties involved in such a way that each party is treated equally according to a certain standard". Selten's ideas subsequently inspired a literature on the institutions and principles that foster the provision of public goods, reviewed in Fehr et al. (2010).

Models of bounded rationality in games aim to sketch out players' reasoning processes and are not necessarily equilibrium concepts because they do not require consistency of beliefs (although adaptive behavior may lead to such consistency). Additionally, game theoretical concepts are often circular, whereas boundedly rational reasoning typically avoids circular reasoning. An example of a model of boundedly rational behavior is the level-k model, which is a non-equilibrium model of strategic thinking originally proposed by Nagel (1995) to explain initial choices and behavior over time in the guessing game. It was inspired by Selten (1991b), a theoretical paper on anticipatory learning in 2×2 games, described below, and by Nagel's participation as a subject in the guessing game. Coricelli and Nagel (2010) recount Selten's influence on the development of the level-k model. The level-k model assumes that subjects instantiate their beliefs in a level-0 type, which is non-strategic, and adjust their behavior by performing *k* iterations of best responses. Most importantly, unlike equilibrium concepts, there is no requirement for consistent beliefs to be formed here. An earlier account can be found in Selten (1991a: 18):

> Experimentalist: Let me now say something about common knowledge or the lack of it. Consider a chain of the following kind:
>
> *I know, that he knows, that I know, that he knows, ...*
>
> Roughly speaking, common knowledge means, that such chains can be continued indefinitely. Does it really matter in practical decision situations whether I have common knowledge or whether I have to break off such chains after stage 4? I do not think so. As far as human decision behavior is concerned I dare say: A lack of common knowledge is not important; what often is important is a very common lack of knowledge.

We interpret this "very common lack of knowledge" in two dimensions. First, subjects may lack knowledge about the environment. Second, subjects may lack knowledge about the reasoning processes of other players. There exists an extensive body of literature that analyzes games in which subjects lack knowledge about the reasoning processes of other players by using the level-k model. The level-k model has been successfully applied to explain initial non-equilibrium behavior in many games with or without complete information such as the winner's curse in common value auctions (e.g., Crawford & Iriberri, 2007), as well as in market entry games. Also the model has been used in games wherein subjects receive signals, which often become reference points and distract subjects' attention from focusing on the reasoning processes of other players, and consequently result in very low levels of reasoning (e.g., Baeriswyl & Cornand, 2014; Bayona et al., 2016; and Benhabib et al., in press). In the same vein, Camerer, Ho, and Chong (2004) have developed a refinement of the level-k model, namely, the cognitive hierarchy model.[13] Finally, many experiments show that an average initial low level k is not increased through an adaptive learning process (see e.g. Nagel, 1995, Brocas et al., 2014), because "low level reasoners" do not die out. These or similar cognitive models have been subsequently formalized and re-introduced to economic theory among others in the work by Kets (2012) in epistemic game theory, by Strzalecki (2014) who discusses the robustness of models of bounded depth to the changes in specific assumptions about the distribution of higher order beliefs, and by Alaoui and Penta (2015), who introduce awareness costs, and García-Schmidt and Woodford (2015) in macroeconomic settings.

Selten was also the first to develop a systematic theory in yet another area: he made an important contribution in the field of boundedly rational learning in economics. Selten and Stoecker (1986) developed the so-called learning direction theory, a *qualitative* theory, based on their experiment of a 10 period prisoners' dilemma game (PD) where subjects played ten times against altering opponents. Subjects must first learn to cooperate and then learn the end effect of when to start defect in the ten period PD game. Their learning theory focuses on the concept of ex post rationality, and therefore follows a different approach to backward induction. According to this theory, a player calculates the ex post best response strategy to the previous strategy combination of other players and then adjusts the decision in this direction, knowing the payoff structure of the game.[14] Selten (1998: 422) describes it in the following way:

> Consider the example of an archer who wants to hit the trunk of a tree by bow and arrow. If the arrow misses the tree on the left-hand side, the archer will be inclined to aim more to the right. Similarly, a miss on the right-hand side will result in a tendency to aim more to the left. Of course, the archer may also not change his aim at all, because he may think of the miss as caused by temporary exogenous influences like a gust of wind. However, if the aim is changed, then it will have a tendency to be changed in the indicated direction.

For the PD game, this means the decision of which period to start defect will be based on the experience of defection of the opponent in the previous ten periods game.

Learning direction theory is based not on expectations about the future but rather on a cognitive procedure that is in turn based on past observations. One application of learning direction theory can be found in Selten and Buchta (1998), where players update their bidding functions according to whether they have won or lost in a private value auction. If they have won, then they would bid less aggressively, and vice versa. Around the same time, Selten developed a theoretical model of anticipatory learning, taking into account that the other player would also adjust his behavior in a similar manner (Selten, 1991b). Because it was not based on an experimental paper, Selten called it a "speculative attempt," which was later tested by Tang (2001).

The most prominent basic learning model in experimental economics is a reinforcement learning model that rests on minimal or no information about the environment and minimal rationality or cognition but strongly on the own payoffs received in the past. Ido Erev recounts that his interactions with Selten helped him see that mainstream behavioral economic research tends to overemphasize a few violations of the assumptions of rational economic theory and to ignore the fact that the rational model suffers from a more important shortcoming: in most natural settings the rational model is "not even wrong," seeing as almost any behavior can be justified as rational given certain prior beliefs or as including decision costs. This insight led Erev and Roth to focus on descriptive models of learning, which generated a line of work (e.g., Roth & Erev, 1995; Erev & Roth, 1998; Erev & Roth, 2014; Erev & Haruvy, 2016). Related research focuses on replicator dynamics of evolutionary game theory (Börgers & Sarin, 1997), its convergence (Beggs, 2005), and its properties with regard to the attainability of boundary points (Hopkins & Posch, 2005). Furthermore, learning direction theory has been incorporated together with elements of reinforcement learning, Cournot best response dynamics, and fictitious play in a more quantitative way, in the experience-weighted attraction (EWA) learning model of Camerer and Ho (1999).

Selten and co-authors have contributed to the formulation of the impulse balance theory, which incorporates the principles of learning direction theory and makes *quantitative* predictions, without outlining a complete learning model. Impulse balance theory is suitable in environments that are well described by repetitive decision tasks involving the same parameter, whereby a player receives sufficient feedback to calculate the ex post optimal choice to the last period's choice. If a higher (lower) value of the parameter increases the profit there is an upward (downward) impulse. The player is then expected to move in the direction of the impulse by an amount that is proportional to the strength of the impulse, which is measured by foregone profits. The theory then models the stationary distribution where expected upward and expected downward impulses balance out. It has been applied to the winner's curse for example, in Selten, Abbink, and Cox (2005), to price competition on a circle in Selten and Apesteguia (2005), to first price auctions in Ockenfels and Selten (2005) and in Neugebauer and Selten (2006), to experimental 2×2 games in Selten and Chmura (2008), and to the newsvendor game in Ockenfels and Selten (2014).

Nevertheless, Harstad and Selten (2013: 509) declare: "It is logically possible that descriptively accurate bounded rationality models of economic decision making are necessarily fragmented and incapable of representation in a single, coherent model". As a result, they argue that theoretical models of bounded rationality do not yet constitute an alternative to neoclassical models. More work is needed in this line of research to create an internally consistent body of work that is general enough to suit a wide variety of applications and thereby constitute a coherent alternative to neoclassical models. The reader is referred to Samuelson (2005) and Schotter (2006) for a foundation of how to integrate economic theory and experimental economics.

What bounded rationality is not

In the spirit of Simon (1957), or Leibenstein (1966), Selten maintains that models portraying the individual as boundedly rational or selectively rational and non-optimizing describe economic behavior more accurately. Selten (1998) discusses the roots of economic behavior and draws connections to motivation (the driving force of behavior), learning (routine adjustment without reasoning), and cognition (reasoning processes of the human mind, whether conscious or not). Approaching bounded rationality from a theoretical stance, Selten finds Simon's conception of bounded rationality to be comprised of three elements: search for alternatives, satisficing, and aspiration adaptation. Moreover, he notes that bounds of rationality are not limited to cognitive bounds, but extend to emotional and motivational ones. The formalization of the latter constitutes an even greater theoretical challenge, given that emotions and alternative motivations are capable of overturning a rational deliberation even if not subject to cognitive limits. As Selten elaborates: "A decision maker may think that a choice is the only rational one (e.g., to stop smoking) but nevertheless not take it" (Selten 2001: 15).

Selten calls attention to the lack of a theory that specifies what constitutes bounded rationality. In the absence of such a theory, he resorts to a discussion of what it is not. Bounded rationality is not irrationality, nor is it optimization under cognitive bounds or merely automatized behavior. Fehr et al. (2010: 170) elaborate on this insight:

> Reinhard Selten was very strict in correcting people when they named the observed non-rational behavior irrational behavior. He preferred to speak about boundedly

> rational behavior. He was also very definite in rejecting the view that deviations from rationality are caused by errors that can be wiped out by teaching or training people.

Selten finds less value in models of bounded rationality that add to the complexity of behavioral models. Such models are very popular because they require only minimal adjustments to the assumptions of the neoclassical theory. Although this is an attractive feature for modelers, Selten points out that these types of models in fact necessitate knowing even more than what is required by rational choice models. For example, reacting to Aumann and Sorin's (1989) analyses of supergames in which players face a much higher level of complexity solving a task under constraints (compared to without constraints), he calls it "a remarkable piece of work, but it is not a contribution to the theory of bounded rationality" (Selten, 2001: 15).

In the same vein, Selten views Sargent's (1993) book *Bounded Rationality in Macroeconomics* as another theoretically astute exercise that does not theorize bounded rationality.

> There, the assumption of rational expectations is replaced by least square learning but otherwise an optimization approach is taken without any regard to cognitive bounds of rationality. Here, too, we see a highly interesting theoretical exercise which, however, is far from adequate as a theory of boundedly rational behavior.
>
> *(Selten, 2001: 15)*

Nontheless, the research by Sargent and his co-authors has initiated a series of learning-to-forecast experiments by Sargent's PhD student Jasmina Arifovic, and others. The setting of the theoretical literature "[puts] the agents and the econometrician on the same footing" (Sargent, 1993) in the sense that neither knows the true data-generating model, and that subjects need to form beliefs based on past observed data. Although subjects in the laboratory do not literally apply econometric techniques, their forecasting behavior can in a large number of cases be better described by least square learning than rational expectations. In the meantime, however, experimenters have constructed other forms of adaptive learning models, which provide a more accurate description of experimental data (e.g., see Arifovic, 1996, for a genetic algorithm model; Hommes et al., 2005, for reinforcement of rules; Pfajfar & Zakelj, 2014, and Mauersberger, 2016, for a mean-variance learning model; and the extensive survey by Duffy, 2016). Notably, there is a parallel between these adaptive learning models and directional learning developed by Selten and Stoecker (1986).

In addition, there are many models of bounded rationality proposed in which individuals optimize an objective function with non-standard preferences that diverge from neoclassical models (the literature on these models and on level-k models is surveyed by Crawford, 2013). Models in this class that have strong psychological foundations include but are not limited to reference-dependent preferences (e.g., Kahneman & Tversky, 1979) and time-inconsistent preferences (e.g., O'Donoghue & Rabin, 1999). According to Selten, there is another stream of behavioral models that do not explicitly take into account the actual reasoning process but that expand the utility function or the equilibrium concept, such as McKelvey and Palfrey's (1995) quantal response equilibria introducing commonly known error terms, social preferences and reciprocity (e.g., Bolton & Ockenfels, 2000; Fehr & Schmidt, 1999), and Eyster and Rabin's (2005) cursed equilibrium concept. In Selten's view, these are not behavioral models but are instead neoclassical optimization models with non-standard preferences or allowing for errors. Selten strongly maintains that individuals do not optimize and also insists that one cannot speak of maximization if important information is ignored for example due to decision costs.

In face of the ideal of optimization, one may ask whether we humans are to despair because our rationality is bounded. The answer is a resounding "No!" On the contrary, it is the purely "rational man" who is doomed to despair when facing the complexities of real life with which boundedly rational humans have been grappling for ages. The first author of this chapter (Rosemarie Nagel), has translated her image of us as boundedly rational agents into poetic terms.

The Rational Man as a Tuning Fork[15]
The rational man we choose as our economic tuning fork
For it is bound to the fundamental tone
with high overtones, dying out quickly.
He is sent behind the veil of ignorance,
from where he reveals her body of knowledge,
common and pure, with perfect memory.
A blessing or hidden curse?
Now listen!
Here comes the sun (spot)
And sings out, in ancient mode,
extrinsically or, with intrinsic sentiments
The overtones for each instrument,
So different, each one.
A surprise at each occasion
Endless random shocks.
So unpredictable,
few with perfect pitch.
Yet there is a pattern,
with low to higher degrees.
No instrument would like to be a tuning fork
So poorly purely without overtones.
Thus see!
We proudly admit we are boundedly rational.
But the rational man is poorer, more bounded.
Pity him, not ourselves.
Yet value him. And still avail him wisely.
Aware!
In the end we're dependent on
the creatures we've created.
So, that's why we rise from our armchair,
And, experiment!

The poem turns around the traditional picture of the "rational man" who is omnipotent and infinitely capable of calculating all perfectly, far superior to human decision makers. This is what Reinhard Selten has taught economists: not to be ashamed of not being the "rational man." Instead, economists should explore the boundless possibilities of human behavior reflected, for example, in their subjects' behavior in experiments. Although Selten did not create a new term for the boundedness of human rationality, he endeavored to initiate a revolution by inverting the old one. For him, the definition of revolution is to turn something around quietly rather than violently (*revolvere* [Lat.] = to turn around). This illustrates Selten's legacy. He very critically discusses new concepts that have been developed and frequently does so with vehemence, but his ideas help to improve on what other economists find in their experimental and theoretical inquiry. While Selten has ultimately not left the strict bounds of science but has instead worked to expand its boundaries, he encourages his students to use their creativity in a non-scientific manner to explore new boundaries and features outside the paradigm of the *Zeitgeist* and to hopefully later turn these into more scientific findings.

Concluding remarks

Selten has been driven by a conviction:

> The picture of rational decision making underlying most of contemporary economic theory is far away from observed behavior. It is therefore necessary to develop theories of bounded rationality. Experimental results support some theories of limited range. However, an empirical-based general theory remains a task of the future.
>
> *(Selten, 1998: 414)*

This quote summarizes the central argument of our chapter wherein we focused on Selten's contribution to the interplay between economic theory and experimentation. Many of Selten's wishes became fulfilled. There exists today a good body of experimental work, psychological findings are important to understand human behavior, several descriptive cognitive theories have been developed, and some policy makers are interested in running laboratory or field experiments before implementing policies in the field. Many of the concepts developed by Selten have been extended upon by other scholars and found to be considerably fruitful.

By way of description of the scientific steps, we observed that theorists provide a model that qualifies certain strategies and that with a solution concept finds the equilibrium points, and in turn provides benchmarks for structuring behavior. Subsequently in the experimental design phase, experimenters adjust the theoretical model either by simplification or by specifying rules that are left unspecified in the model. Once the experiment is conducted, the experimenter needs to analyze the actual individual behavior and describe it by using behavioral procedures, which can be very different from the reasoning procedure or the theoretical outcomes originally specified by the theorist. Notwithstanding, adaptation might guide behavior towards (some of) the theoretical solution(s). Experimentally based processes and theoretical models have the potential to generate new insights that can further catalyze experiments and economic theories. An analogy helps to bring this point home. The Wright brothers recognized that flying with airplanes cannot be achieved with flapping wings but instead may be achieved through employing technologies that resembled their knowledge of bicycle riding. In the same way, Selten maintains that human subjects often use procedures to obtain their (multiple!) goals, which differ from what game theory suggests. One might add that for some (simple) situations these strategies might look like the "flapping wings," and the equivalent of bicycle techniques for boundedly rational procedures can (only) be found by conducting experiments.

How good are the experimental methods? Selten has pointed out deep shortcomings in the state of the art in experimental economics. For instance, many small games can encompass a large set of problems faced in the real world. Game theory seems to suggest that complex situations can be analyzed by splitting the problem into small games and studying them separately, often with more information than what is realistically possible, which is necessary to find mathematical solutions. This approach neglects the fact that complex decision making requires simultaneous updates of many parameters or variables that are not always commensurable, in addition to the interactions between them. What is needed is a theory that uses qualitative strategies rather than modeling the situation as a simple strategic game or decision problem (van Damme et al., 2014). More complex games are required for many situations of interest, such as how top managers decide how to allocate their company's resources. Unfortunately, such experiments are still very rare in experimental economics, while they hold great potential to shed light on interesting patterns of complex behavior.

The interaction between theory and experiments is of utmost importance, and the work of Reinhard Selten, the dualist, is a prime example. Many current experimenters appear to have moved away from studying theoretical problems based on microeconomic or macroeconomic models in the laboratory and have instead turned to problems inspired by psychology. One big commitment should be an ongoing exchange between theorists and experimenters while taking account of psychological findings when it comes to policy making. Efforts in this direction have been made, for example, in auctions (e.g., the work on FCC auctions by Cramton, 1997, and Klemperer, 2002), in institutional design (e.g., the matching applications developed in Roth, 1985, and 1986), in central banks with macroeconomic experiments (e.g., the Bank of Canada), and in public decision making (e.g. the behavioral insight team of the UK government). In this respect, the contribution of Selten is the design of "real" markets, such as the properties of the types of possible auctions for third-generation mobile telecommunication services in Britain; the results are published in Abbink et al. (2005).

Selten also introduced new ways of teaching economics. He clearly separated his theoretical lectures, where experiments played no role, from his experimental seminars lasting more than 10 weeks, where the students were asked to develop their own strategies, such as the work published in Selten, Mitzkewitz, and Uhlich (1997) and in Selten et al. (2003). Selten strongly believes that an experimental researcher has to also be trained by being a subject. In Bonn, Selten and his collaborators have invited undergraduate students to participate in research experiments in the computer laboratory "Spielend Geld verdienen" ("making money by playing"). His teaching methods have been further developed by his students and co-authors and many others, such as the approach described in Selten and Nagel (2014), how Güth and van Damme apply it in their game theory courses. A famous inspirational quote by Confucius enlightens us and seems like a summary of Selten's endeavors "By three methods we may learn wisdom: First, by reflection, which is noblest; second, by imitation, which is easiest; and third by experience, which is the bitterest."[16]

Selten's approach to understanding human economic behavior is based on this constant dialogue, with feedback loops between different schools of thought and different fields that deepen our knowledge of human economic behavior. As a result, his work is wide-ranging, covering many disciplines in which he has been a pioneer, such as introducing the SPE, then leaving this territory to others and moving on to other unexplored territories. When focusing his attention on a new problem, Selten devotes all of his creativity to it, including the invention of new names for new concepts, such as *trembling-hand* (Selten, 1975) or *measure for measure* (Selten et al., 1997). His age has never determined the speed and richness of his innovativeness and willingness to go against the flow. When asked by one of his students what the most noteworthy questions are, his avant-garde mind produced yet another question unexplored by economists: "What is consciousness?"

Acknowledgments

We thank José Apesteguia, Antonio Cabrales, Ron Harstad, Robin Hogarth, Felix Mauersberger, Axel Ockenfels, Avner Offer, Abdolkarim Sadrieh, Julia Swanson, Thomas Woiczyk, and Michael Woodford for their valuable comments and suggestions. We wish to emphasize that all the contents reflect the authors' views, and that maybe Selten himself does not agree with all our assessments about his contributions.

Notes

1 Rosemarie Nagel attended many of Selten's lectures during her undergraduate studies, and wrote her Master's thesis (Diplomarbeit) and her PhD thesis with him as an advisor.

2 In his blurb on the Bonn University website, Selten proclaims himself a "methodic dualist." That is a scientist with interest both in the normative theory of rational behavior, as well as (and increasingly so) in descriptive theories of boundedly rational agents (www.bonneconlab.uni-bonn.de/team/selten.reinhard/selten.reinhard.seite.forschungsinteresse). We wish to add a cautionary note for our philosophically inclined readers, to whom the term *dualist* brings to mind dualism as used by Descartes to dichotomize mind and body, or Searle's revisited dualism, which offers a scientific solution to the problem of consciousness. We emphasize that our use of the term is at the surface level of economics (not philosophy), wherein a dualistic view refers to having an eye on normative theory and the other eye on descriptive theory.

3 This has changed since the 1990s when psychologists and economists started working together.

4 The term *armchair economics* has been famously used earlier by Simon and Bartel (1986) in "The failure of armchair economics."

5 "Reinhard Selten – Biographical". Nobelprize.org. Nobel Media AB 2014. Web. 18 Sep 2015. www.nobelprize.org/nobel_prizes/economic-sciences/laureates/1994/selten-bio.html.

6 Actions are strategic complements if agents have an incentive to respond to higher actions of rivals with higher actions of their own, and they are substitutes if agents have an incentive to respond to higher actions of rivals with lower actions of their own. For the original definition, see Bulow, Geanakoplos, and Klemperer (1985).

7 Harsanyi (1967–8) developed the Bayesian Nash equilibrium concept for games of incomplete information.

8 The game played is as follows: Player A, the chain store incumbent, has a store in twenty different locations. Potential entrants, one in each market, sequentially decide whether to enter the market or not. After an entrant announces his decision, player A decides whether to cooperate or act aggressively. For the payoffs and rules of the game, refer to Selten (1978b).

9 See Abbink and Brandts (2010) for a discussion on the issue of simplicity versus complexity in oligopoly experiments.

10 Three asymmetric firms competed in quantities for 30 periods. The asymmetries were in capacities (known to firms) and cost conditions (private information of each firm). Firms can take on debt, which is private information. In addition, firms can acquire information about the private information of other firms. Demand is simulated and constant over time but not known for firms.

11 An ultimatum game is a game with two players, a proposer (player A) and a responder (player B). Player A proposes a division of a sum of money (size of the pie), which player B can either accept or reject. If the proposal is rejected, then both players get nothing; otherwise the proposed division is implemented. Suppose a subject has to decide what to do in each information set in the course of the game. In an ultimatum game in which only the proposer knows the pie size, he has to make a proposal for every possible pie. At the same time, the responder, knowing that these pies are drawn with equal probability, has to have a strategy for accepting or rejecting every possible proposal.

12 An area theory is a theory that predicts a subset of all possible outcomes (Selten, 1991a).

13 Also refer to Crawford and Iriberri (2007). For an excellent review of the recent developments in behavioral game theory, see Camerer (2003), Crawford (2013), and Crawford, Costa-Gomes, and Iriberri (2013).

14 This stands in contrast to reinforcement learning, where players do not need to know the payoff structure of the game.

15 A tuning fork is an acoustic resonator that emits a pure musical tone after a moment in which some high overtones first need to die out. The main reason for using the fork shape is that, unlike many other types of resonators, it produces a very pure tone, with most of the vibrational energy at the fundamental frequency, and little at the overtones (harmonics) Retrieved December 9, 2015, from Wikipedia website https://en.wikipedia.org/wiki/Tuning_fork. An overtone is "A musical tone which is a part of the harmonic series above a fundamental note, and may be heard with it." Retrieved December 9, 2015, Oxford Dictionary. www.oxforddictionaries.com/es/definicion/ingles/overtone.

16 Confucius. (n.d.). BrainyQuote.com. Retrieved December 9, 2015, from BrainyQuote.com website: www.brainyquote.com/quotes/quotes/c/confucius140548.html.

Bibliography

Abbink, K., & Brandts, J. (2010). Drei Oligopolexperimente. In A. Sadrieh & A. Ockenfels (Eds.), The Selten school of behavioral economics: A collection of essays in honor of Reinhard Selten. Heidelberg, Germany: Springer, 53–72.

Abbink, K., Irlenbusch, B., Pezanis-Christou, P., Rockenbach, B., Sadrieh, A., & Selten, R. (2005). An experimental test of design alternatives for the British 3G/UMTS auction. European Economic Review, 49(2), 505–30.

Alaoui, L., & Penta, A. (2015). Endogenous depth of reasoning. Review of Economic Studies, published online October 29, doi:10.1093/restud/rdv052.

Arifovic, J. (1996). The behavior of the exchange rate in the genetic algorithm and experimental economies. Journal of Political Economy, 104(3), 510–41.

Aumann R.J., & S. Sorin (1989). Cooperation and bounded recall. Games and Economic Behavior, 1(1), 5–39.

Baeriswyl, R., & Cornand, C. (2014). Reducing overreaction to central banks disclosure: Theory and experiment. Journal of the European Economic Association, 12(4), 1087–126.

Bayona, A., Brandts, J., & Vives, X., (2016), Supply function competition, market power and the winner's curse. Mimeo.

Beggs, A. W. (2005). On the convergence of reinforcement learning. Journal of Economic Theory, 122(1), 1–36.

Benhabib, J., Duffy, J., & Nagel, R. (in press). De-framing rules to (de)-anchor beliefs in beauty contest experiments. Mimeo.

Bolton, G. E., & Ockenfels, A. (2000). ERC: A theory of equity, reciprocity, and competition. American Economic Review, 90(1), 166–93.

Börgers, T., & Sarin, R. (1997). Learning through reinforcement and replicator dynamics. Journal of Economic Theory, 77(1), 1–14.

Bosch-Domènech, A., Montalvo, J. G., Nagel, R., & Satorra, A. (2002). One, two, (three), infinity, . . . : Newspaper and lab beauty-contest experiments. American Economic Review, 92(5), 1687–701.

Brandts, J., & Charness, G. (2011). The strategy versus the direct-response method: A first survey of experimental comparisons. Experimental Economics, 14(3), 375–98.

Brocas, I., Carrillo, J., Wang, S., & Camerer, C. (2014). Imperfect choice or imperfect attention? Understanding strategic thinking in private information games. Review of Economic Studies, 81(3), 944–70.

Bulow, J., Geanakoplos, J., & Klemperer, P. (1985). Multimarket oligopoly: Strategic substitutes and strategic complements. Journal of Political Economy, 93(3), 488–511.

Camerer, C. (2003). Behavioral game theory: Experiments in strategic interaction. Princeton, NJ: Princeton University Press.

Camerer, C. F., & Fehr, E. (2006). When does "economic man" dominate social behavior? Science, 311(5757), 47–52.

Camerer, C. & Ho, T., (1999). Experience-weighted attraction learning in normal-form games. Econometrica, 67(4), 827–74.

Camerer, C. F., Ho, T. H., & Chong, J. K. (2004). A cognitive hierarchy model of games. Quarterly Journal of Economics, 119(3), 861–98.

Chou, E., McConnell, M., Nagel, R., & Plott, C. R. (2009). The control of game form recognition in experiments: Understanding dominant strategy failures in a simple two person "guessing" game. Experimental Economics, 12(2), 159–79.

Coricelli, G., & Nagel, R. (2010). Walking with Reinhard Selten and the guessing game: From the origin to the brain. In A. Sadrieh & A. Ockenfels (Eds.), The Selten school of behavioral economics: A collection of essays in honor of Reinhard Selten. Heidelberg, Germany: Springer, 111–23.

Cramton, P. (1997). The FCC spectrum auctions: An early assessment. Journal of Economics & Management Strategy, 6(3), 431–95.

Crawford, V. P. (2013). Boundedly rational versus optimization-based models of strategic thinking and learning in games. Journal of Economic Literature, 51(2), 512–27.

Crawford, V. P., & Iriberri, N. (2007). Level-k auctions: Can a nonequilibrium model of strategic thinking explain the winner's curse and overbidding in private-value auctions? Econometrica, 75(6), 1721–70.

Crawford, V. P., Costa-Gomes, M. A., & Iriberri, N. (2013). Structural models of nonequilibrium strategic thinking: Theory, evidence, and applications. Journal of Economic Literature, 51(1), 5–62.

Duffy, J. (2016). Macroeconomics: A survey of laboratory research. Final draft for The handbook of experimental economics, volume 2.
Erev, I., & Haruvy, E. (2016). Learning and the economics of small decisions. Invited chapter submitted to Kagel, J. H. & Roth, A. E. (Eds.), The handbook of experimental economics. Princeton University Press.
Erev, I., & Roth, A. E. (1998). Predicting how people play games: Reinforcement learning in experimental games with unique, mixed strategy equilibria. American Economic Review, 88(4), 848–81.
Erev, I., & Roth, A. E. (2014). Maximization, learning, and economic behavior. Proceedings of the National Academy of Sciences, 111(Supplement 3), 10818–25.
Eyster, E., & Rabin, M. (2005). Cursed equilibrium. Econometrica, 73(5), 1623–72.
Fehr, E., & Schmidt, K. M. (1999). A theory of fairness, competition, and cooperation. Quarterly Journal of Economics, 114(3), 817–68.
Fehr, E., Gächter, S., Milinski, M., & Rockenbach, B. (2010). Institutions fostering public good provision. In A. Ockenfels & A. Sadrieh (Eds.), The Selten school of behavioral economics: A collection of essays in honor of Reinhard Selten. Heidelberg, Germany: Springer, 167–84.
Fischbacher, U., & Gächter S. (2010). Social preferences, beliefs, and the dynamics of free riding in public good experiments. American Economic Review, 100(1), 541–56.
Forsythe, R., Lundholm, R., & Rietz, T. (1999). Cheap talk, fraud, and adverse selection in financial markets: Some experimental evidence. Review of Financial Studies, 12(3), 481–518.
García-Schmidt, M. & Woodford, M. (2015): Are low interest rates deflationary? A paradox of perfect-foresight analysis. NBER Working Paper No. 21614.
Gigerenzer, G., & Selten, R. (Eds.). (2001). Bounded rationality: The adaptive toolbox. Cambridge, MA: MIT Press.
Grossman, G. & Rogoff, K., (1995), Handbook of international economics, volume 3, Amsterdam: Elsevier.
Gul, F., (1997). A Nobel Prize for game theorists: The contributions of Harsanyi, Nash and Selten. Journal of Economic Perspectives, 11(3), 159–74.
Güth, W. (1995). On ultimatum bargaining experiments: A personal review. Journal of Economic Behavior & Organization, 27(3), 329–44.
Güth, W., Strobel, M., & Wickström, B. A. (1997). Equilibrium selection in linguistic games: Kial ni (ne) parolas esperanton? In Understanding strategic interaction. Berlin, Heidelberg, Germany: Springer, 257–69.
Hammerstein, P., & Selten, R. (1994). Game theory and evolutionary biology. In R. Aumann & S. Hart (Eds.), Handbook of game theory with economic applications, volume 2. Amsterdam: Elsevier, North-Holland, 929–93.
Harsanyi, J. C., (1967–68). Games with incomplete information played by "Bayesian" players. Parts I-III, Management Science, 14 (3, 5, 7), 159–82, 320–34, 486–502.
Harsanyi, J. C., & Selten, R. (1972). A generalized Nash solution for two-person bargaining games with incomplete information. Management Science, 18(5), 80–106.
Harsanyi, J. C., & Selten, R. (1988). A general theory of equilibrium selection in games, volume 1. Cambridge, MA: MIT Press Books.
Harstad, R. M., & Selten, R. (2013). Bounded-rationality models: Tasks to become intellectually competitive. Journal of Economic Literature, 51(2), 496–511.
Hennig-Schmidt, H., Leopold-Wildburger, U., Ostmann, A., & van Winden, F. (2010). Understanding negotiations: A video approach in experimental gaming. In A. Ockenfels & A. Sadrieh (Eds.), The Selten school of behavioral economics: A collection of essays in honor of Reinhard Selten. Heidelberg, Germany: Springer, 127–66.
Hommes, C., Sonnemans, J., Tuinstra, J., & van de Velden, H. (2005). Coordination of expectations in asset pricing experiments. Review of Financial Studies, 18(3), 955–80.
Hopkins, E., & Posch, M. (2005). Attainability of boundary points under reinforcement learning. Games and Economic Behavior, 53(1), 110–25.
Kagel, J. H. (1995). Auctions: A survey of experimental research. In J. H. Kagel & A. E. Roth (Eds.), The Handbook of experimental economics. Princeton, NJ: Princeton University Press, 501–85.
Kagel, J. H., & Levin, D. (1986). The winner's curse and public information in common value auctions. American Economic Review, 76(5), 894–920.
Kagel, J., Levin, D. & Harstad, R, (1995). Comparative static effects of number of bidders and public information on behavior in second-price common value auctions. International Journal of Game Theory, 24(3), 293–319.

Kahneman, D. (1988). Experimental economics: A psychological perspective. In R. Tietz, W. Albers & R. Selten (Eds.), Bounded rational behavior in experimental games and markets: Proceedings of the Fourth Conference on Experimental Economics, Bielefeld, West Germany, September 21–25, 1986. Berlin, Germany: Springer-Verlag, 11–18.

Kahneman, D., & Tversky, A. (1979). Prospect theory: An analysis of decision under risk. Econometrica, 47(2), 263–91.

Kalisch, G. K., Milnor, J. W., Nash, J. F., & Nering, E. D. (1954). Some experimental n-person games. In R. M. Thrall, C. H. Coombs, & R. L. Davis (Eds.), Decision processes. New York: Wiley, 301–27.

Kets, W. (2012). Bounded reasoning and higher-order uncertainty. Mimeo. Available at SSRN: http://ssrn.com/abstract=2116626 or http://dx.doi.org/10.2139/ssrn.2116626.

Klemperer, P. (2002). What really matters in auction design. Journal of Economic Perspectives, 16(1), 169–89.

Leibenstein, H. (1966). Allocation efficiency vs. "X-efficiency". American Economic Review, 56(3), 392–415.

Mauersberger, F. (2016). Monetary policy rules in a non-rational world: A macroeconomic experiment. Mimeo.

McKelvey, R. D., & Palfrey, T. R. (1995). Quantal response equilibria for normal form games. Games and Economic Behavior, 10(1), 6–38.

Milgrom, P., & Stokey, N. (1982). Information, trade and common knowledge. Journal of Economic Theory, 26(1), 17–27.

Mitzkewitz, M., & Nagel, R. (1993). Experimental results on ultimatum games with incomplete information. International Journal of Game Theory, 22(2), 171–98.

Nagel, R. (1995). Unraveling in guessing games: An experimental study. American Economic Review, 85(5), 1313–26.

Nash, J. F. (2008). The agencies method for modeling coalitions and cooperation in games. International Game Theory Review, 10(4), 539.

Nash, J. F., Nagel, R., Ockenfels, A., & Selten, R. (2012). The agencies method for coalition formation in experimental games. Proceedings of the National Academy of Sciences, 109(50), 20358–63.

Neugebauer, T., & Selten, R. (2006). Individual behavior of first-price auctions: The importance of information feedback in computerized experimental markets. Games and Economic Behavior, 54(1), 183–204.

Ockenfels, A., & Selten, R. (2005). Impulse balance equilibrium and feedback in first price auctions. Games and Economic Behavior, 51(1), 155–70.

Ockenfels, A., & Selten, R. (2014). Impulse balance in the newsvendor game. Games and Economic Behavior, 86, 237–47.

O'Donoghue, T., & Rabin, M. (1999). Doing it now or later. American Economic Review, 89(1), 103–24.

Pfajfar, D. & Žakelj, B. (2014). Experimental evidence on inflation expectation formation. Journal of Economic Dynamics and Control, 44, 147–68.

Roth, A. E. (1985). The college admissions problem is not equivalent to the marriage problem. Journal of Economic Theory, 36(2), 277–88.

Roth, A. E. (1986). On the allocation of residents to rural hospitals: A general property of two-sided matching market. Econometrica, 54(2), 425–7.

Roth, A. E. (1999). Foreword. In R. Selten (Ed.), Game theory and economic behavior: Selected essays. Northampton, MA: Edward Elgar, ix–x.

Roth, A. E., & Erev, I. (1995). Learning in extensive-form games: Experimental data and simple dynamic models in the intermediate term. Games and Economic Behavior, 8(1), 164–212.

Sadrieh, A. (2010). Risky choice and the construction of preferences. In A. Ockenfels & A. Sadrieh (Eds.), The Selten school of behavioral economics: A collection of essays in honor of Reinhard Selten (pp. 283–95). Heidelberg, Germany: Springer.

Sadrieh, A. & Ockenfels, A. (Eds.) (2010). The Selten school of behavioral economics: A collection of essays in honor of Reinhard Selten. Heidelberg, Germany: Springer.

Samuelson, L. (2005). Economic theory and experimental economics. Journal of Economic Literature, 43(1), 65–107.

Sargent, T. J. (1993). Bounded rationality in macroeconomics. Oxford, UK: Oxford University Press.

Sauermann, H., & Selten, R. (1959). Ein Oligopolexperiment. Zeitschrift für die gesamte Staatswissenschaft/Journal of Institutional and Theoretical Economics, 115(3), 427–71.

Sauermann, H., & Selten, R. (1960). An experiment in oligopoly (translation of Sauermann & Selten (1959)). General Systems, 5, 85–114.

Sauermann, H., & Selten, R. (1962). Anspruchsanpassungstheorie der Unternehmung. Zeitschrift für die gesamte Staatswissenschaft/Journal of Institutional and Theoretical Economics, 118(4), 557–97.

Schotter, A. (2006). Strong and wrong: The use of rational choice theory in experimental economics. Journal of Theoretical Politics, 18(4), 498–511.

Selten, R. (1965). Spieltheoretische Behandlung eines Oligopolmodells mit Nachfrageträgheit: Teil i: Bestimmung des dynamischen Preisgleichgewichts. Zeitschrift für die gesamte Staatswissenschaft/ Journal of Institutional and Theoretical Economics, 121(2), 301–24.

Selten, R. (1967). Die Strategiemethode zur Erforschung des eingeschränkt rationalen Verhaltens im Rahmen eines Oligopolexperiments. In H. Sauermann (Ed.), Beiträge zur experimentellen Wirtschaftsforschung, volume I. Tübingen, Germany: J.C.B. Mohr (Paul Siebeck), 136–68.

Selten, R. (1972). Equal share analysis of characteristic function experiments. In H. Sauermann (Ed.), Beiträge zur experimentellen Wirtschaftsforschung, volume III. Tübingen, Germany: J.C.B. Mohr (Paul Siebeck), 130–65.

Selten, R. (1975). Reexamination of the perfectness concept for equilibrium points in extensive games. International Journal of Game Theory, 4(1), 25–55.

Selten, R. (1978a). The equity principle in economic behavior. In H. W. Gottinger & W. Leinfellner (Eds.), Decision theory and social ethics: Issues in social choice. Dordrecht, Holland: D. Reidel, 289–301.

Selten, R. (1978b). The chain store paradox. Theory and Decision, 9(2), 127–59.

Selten, R. (1980). A note on evolutionarily stable strategies in asymmetric animal conflicts. Journal of Theoretical Biology, 84(1), 93–101.

Selten, R. (1983a), Equal division of payoff bounds for 3-person characteristic function experiments. In R. Tietz (Ed.), Aspiration levels in bargaining and economic decision making. Springer Lecture Notes in Economics and Mathematical Systems, No. 213, Berlin, Germany: Springer-Verlag, 265–75.

Selten, R. (1983b). Evolutionary stability in extensive two-person games. Mathematical Social Sciences, 5(3), 269–363.

Selten, R. (1987). Equity and coalition bargaining in three-person games. In A. Roth (Ed.), Laboratory experimentation in economics: Six points of view. Cambridge, UK: Cambridge University Press, 42–98.

Selten, R. (1991a). Evolution, learning, and economic behavior. Games and Economic Behavior, 3(1), 3–24.

Selten, R. (1991b). Anticipatory learning in two-person games. In R. Selten (Ed.), Game equilibrium models I. Berlin, Heidelberg, Germany: Springer-Verlag, 98–153.

Selten, R. (1991c). Properties of a measure of predictive success. Mathematical Social Sciences, 21(2), 153–67.

Selten, R. (1998). Features of experimentally observed bounded rationality. European Economic Review, 42(3–5), 413–36.

Selten, R. (1999). Game theory and economic behavior: Selected essays. Northampton, MA: Edward Elgar.

Selten, R. (2001). What is bounded rationality? In G. Gigerenzer & R. Selten (Eds.), Bounded rationality: The adaptive toolbox. Cambridge, MA: MIT Press, 13–36.

Selten, R., & Apesteguia, J. (2005) Experimentally observed imitation and cooperation in price competition on the circle. Games and Economic Behavior, 51(1), 171–92.

Selten, R. & Berg, C. C., (1970). Drei experimentelle Oligopolspielserien mit kontinuierlichem Zeitablauf. In H. Sauermann (Ed.), Beiträge zur experimentellen Wirtschaftsforschung, volume II. Tübingen, Germany: J.C.B. Mohr (Paul Siebeck), 162–221.

Selten, R., & Buchta, J. (1998). Experimental sealed bid first price auction with directly observed bid functions. In D. Budescu, I. Erev, & R. Zwick (Eds.), Games and human behavior: Essays in honor of Amnon Rapoport. Mahwah, NJ: Lawrence Erlbaum, 79–104.

Selten, R., & Chmura, T. (2008). Stationary concepts for experimental 2×2-games. American Economic Review, 98(3), 938–66.

Selten, R., & Güth, W. (1982). Equilibrium point selection in a class of market entry games. In M. Deistler, E. Fürst, & G. Schwödiauer (Eds.), Games, economic dynamics, and time series analysis. Berlin, Heidelberg, Gemany: Springer-Verlag, 101–16.

Selten, R., & Nagel, R. (1998). Das Zahlenwahlspiel: Hintergründe und Ergebnisse. Spektrum der Wissenschaft, February, 16–22.

Selten, R., & Nagel, R. (2014). Werner Güth, an early, original behavioral theorist and experimental economist. In special issue for Werner Güth: How Werner Güth's ultimatum game shaped our understanding of social behavior. Journal of Economic Behavior & Organization, 108, 292–318.

Selten, R., & Stoecker, R. (1986). End behavior in sequences of finite Prisoner's Dilemma supergames: A learning theory approach. Journal of Economic Behavior & Organization, 7(1), 47–70.

Selten, R., & Uhlich, G. R. (1988). Order of strength and exhaustivity as additional hypotheses in theories for 3-person characteristic function games. Berlin, Heidelberg, Germany: Springer, 235–50.
Selten, R., Abbink, K., & Cox, R. (2005). Learning direction theory and the winner's curse. Experimental Economics, 8(1), 5–20.
Selten, R., Mitzkewitz, M., & Uhlich, G. R. (1997). Duopoly strategies programmed by experienced players. Econometrica, 65(3), 517–55.
Selten, R., Pittnauer, S., & Hohnisch, M. (2012). Dealing with dynamic decision problems when knowledge of the environment is limited: An approach based on goal systems. Journal of Behavioral Decision Making, 25(5), 443–57.
Selten, R., Abbink, K., Buchta, J., & Sadrieh, A. (2003). How to play (3×3)-games: A strategy method experiment. Games and Economic Behavior, 45(1), 19–37.
Simon, H. A. (1957). Models of man: Social and rational. New York: John Wiley & Sons.
Simon, H. A. (1976). From substantive to procedural rationality. In T. J. Kastelein, S. K. Kuipers, W. A. Nijenhuis, & G. R. Wagenaar (Eds.), 25 years of economic theory: Retrospect and prospect. New York: Springer-Verlag US, 65–86.
Simon, H. A., & Bartel, R. D. (1986). The failure of armchair economics. Challenge, 29(5), 18–25.
Smith, V. L. (1962). An experimental study of competitive market behavior. Journal of Political Economy, 70(2), 111–37.
Smith, V. L., Suchanek, G. L., & Williams, A. W. (1988). Bubbles, crashes, and endogenous expectations in experimental spot asset markets. Econometrica, 56(5), 1119–51.
Strzalecki, T. (2014). Depth of reasoning and higher order beliefs. Journal of Economic Behavior & Organization, 108, 108–22.
Tang, F. F. (2001). Anticipatory learning in two-person games: Some experimental results. Journal of Economic Behavior & Organization, 44(2), 221–32.
Tietz, R., & Weber, H. J. (1972). On the nature of the bargaining process in the Kresko-game. In H. Sauermann (Ed.), Contributions to experimental economics, volume III. Tübingen, Germany: J.C.B. Mohr (Paul Siebeck), 305–34.
Tversky, A., & Kahneman, D. (1981). The framing of decisions and the psychology of choice. Science, New Series, 211(4481), 453–8.
van Damme, E., Binmore, K, Roth, A., Samuelson, L., Winter, E., Bolton, G., Ockenfels, A., Dufwenberg, M., Kirchsteiger, G., Gneezy, U., Kocher, M., Sutter, M., Sanfey, A., Kliemt, H., Selten, R., Nagel, R., & Azar, O. (2014). How Werner Güth's ultimatum game shaped our understanding of social behavior. Journal of Economic Behavior & Organization, 108, 292–318.
Vives, X. (1999). Oligopoly pricing: old ideas and new tools. Cambridge, MA: MIT press.
von Neumann, J. & Morgenstern, O. (1944). Theory of games and economic behavior. Princeton, NJ: Princeton University Press.

7

GERD GIGERENZER AND VERNON SMITH

Ecological rationality of heuristics in psychology and economics

Shabnam Mousavi

An economist who is only an economist cannot be a good economist.

Hayek, 1956

Introduction

Behavioral economists use psychological findings to evaluate and revise economic decision theory, to build models that correspond directly to observations of behavior, and to develop descriptive accounts for deviations from principles of neoclassical rationality. One of the main sources of psychological insight is the heuristics and biases research program. This chapter introduces another source of psychological insights, the ecological rationality of fast-and-frugal heuristics, and is organized as follows. First, this chapter juxtaposes psychological (á la Gigerenzer) with economic (á la Smith) views of ecological rationality, thereby connecting fast-and-frugal heuristics to a major source of inspiration and motivation for behavioral economists, namely experimental economics. Then, it briefly reviews a collection of articles illustrating how the successful use of heuristics in business decision making can be understood by using ecological rationality as an investigative framework. Finally, it locates the field of inquiry for behavioral economics on a continuum of scientific problem solving in the interval that Weaver (1948) called *organized complexity*. Simple heuristics deserve special attention from behavioral economists because they work best in this very interval, where exact methods of optimization are structurally unfitting. Put together, these connections, examples, and arguments suggest that mainstream behavioral economics can gain from integrating this less explored psychological framework. Such integration starts by attempting to formulate effective decision rules as fast-and-frugal heuristics and exploring their ecological rationality.

Although our navigations through daily life involve numerous decisions under vague or changing criteria, most humans are not paralyzed by indecision. To account for this fact, social scientists have developed theories and constructed models that describe and predict behavior and strive to improve judgment. Both field and experimental studies have revealed that the human mind tends to ignore available information systematically and apply simple rules to make decisions in complex situations. Two psychology research programs have set out to accommodate these observations in scientific frameworks: the heuristics and biases program and the study of the ecological rationality of fast-and-frugal heuristics. For the main body of behavioral economists, the views of the heuristics and biases program inform their empirical and experimental studies. Their formalization techniques have been shaped under the influence of analytical advances in operational research, wherein optimization is the dominant method and where probability theory and logical relationships are the primary tools of investigation and validation. These studies concentrate on revealing deviations from the axioms and principles of the economic theory of rational decision making, and provide descriptions based on the heuristics and biases at work for phenomena considered puzzling from the viewpoint of the subjective expected utility framework. The heuristics and biases program views heuristics as suboptimal strategies arising from less-than-rational judgment. Furthermore, in this approach judgments are considered biased, that is, distorted because the mind is predisposed to making logical or statistical errors in a systematic manner. Accordingly, choice behavior is believed to improve when biases are diagnosed and removed (or diminished)—a process referred to as *debiasing*. However, there is little solid evidence that deviations from rational norms lead to real world loss or inefficiency.

In this chapter, an alternative psychological view of heuristic decision making is introduced that has yet to be adopted by mainstream behavioral economists, the fast-and-frugal heuristics approach. This approach overlaps in its central notion of ecological rationality with the experimental economics research pioneered by Vernon Smith. The next section presents parallels made between the psychological and economic views of ecological rationality. In the third section, an overview is given of a recent collection of articles on fast-and-frugal decision making across domains of business that provides examples of using the framework of ecological rationality. These illustrate the process and conditions of observed successful heuristic strategies made by different agents such as managers and consumers in financial, commercial, and labor markets.[1] The fourth section draws on a categorization of scientific problems with respect to their complexity that was put forward by Warren Weaver in 1948. Political problems and business and governmental economic decisions are areas of complexity where data are limited and certainty is absent. In these situations, scientific problem solving necessarily involves methods beyond optimization, statistical inference, and mathematical or logical truth benchmarks. By combining this view of complexity together with the effectiveness of heuristics' simplicity, the heuristics approach emerges as an efficient scientific method for solving problems of mid-range complexity. Finally, a summary and forward-looking remarks close the chapter.

Ecological rationality in economics and psychology

The very lecture that Vernon Smith delivered for his Nobel Prize (2002) was titled *Constructivist and Ecological Rationality in Economics*, as was the book that he published in 2008, which expanded the themes of that lecture. Therein, he elaborates:

> Ecological rationality refers to emergent order in the form of practices, norms, and evolving institutional rules governing action by individuals that are part of our cultural and biological heritage and are created by human interactions, but not by conscious human design . . . . in hundreds of market experiments, economically unsophisticated and naïve but proficient individuals produce rational outcomes without in fact having any knowledge of rationality and efficiency of the outcomes they produce. Their effectiveness is perhaps less surprising once we recognize that their human forbearers and contemporaries used their cultural and biological inheritance to create the institutional forms that we study in the experiments, but our neoclassical models (since the 1870s) failed to anticipate or even to appreciate this important development as we proceeded to

> construct the concept of an "institution free core" of economic analysis.[2]
>
> *(p. 2)*

The notion of ecological rationality is the junction at which Gigerenzer's and Smith's research programs meet. As Smith puts it,

> Paraphrasing Gigerenzer et al. . . . ecological rationality as it applies across the spectrum that I examine here can be defined as follows: The behavior of an individual, a market, an institution, or other social system involving collectives of individuals is ecologically rational to the degree that it is adapted to the structure of its environment.
>
> *(Ibid: 36)*

Whereas Gigerenzer's research has focused largely on individual aspects of the subject matter, Smith has applied this concept to elaborate on institutions and the market. Table 7.1 juxtaposes Gigerenzer's and Smith's views where they overlap and correspond on the notions of ecological rationality and heuristic decision making. These overlaps open potential venues of exploration for behavioral economics, especially given the fact that ecological rationality has been formalized in models of fast-and-frugal heuristics. Fast-and-frugal heuristics are partially unconscious decision rules that exploit learned or evolved capacities of our mind. One example is the gaze heuristic, which requires following a moving object against a noisy background—a difficult task for a machine but easy for humans, even infants, who can draw on their evolutionarily developed capacity of gaze. A heuristic is ecologically rational when it functionally matches the environment in which it is used.

Economics, as a science, has heavily relied on constructivist rationality, defined by Smith as "the deliberate use of reason to analyze and prescribe actions judged to be chosen" (Ibid.: 2). This form of rationality produces the normative ground for the realm of behavior explored thus far in mainstream behavioral economics. Again, in Smith's words,

> When applied to institutions, constructivism involves the deliberate design of rule systems to achieve desirable performance. The latter include the "optimal design" of institutions, where the intention is to provide incentives for agents to choose better actions than would result from alternative arrangements.
>
> *(Ibid.)*

Notice that constructivist rationality establishes its norms on the basis of statistical validity or logical veracity. In contrast, ecological rationality as a benchmark not only extends applicable notions of rationality to the evaluation of behavior but also suggests acquiring norms that go beyond statistics and logic. Unlike the positive economics norms used in as-if models, whose validity is cross-situational, such norms are sensitive to the context of the decision situation and to the content or wording that describes the particular situation (Mousavi & Gigerenzer, 2011; Gigerenzer, 1996).

Accordingly, the ecological rationality view seeks to enhance judgment not by nudging human beings, who are perceived as subject to cognitive limitations, but by boosting their abilities—for instance, by providing more accessible representations of information pertinent to the choice problem at hand (Grüne-Yanoff & Hertwig, 2015).

Constructing a formal theory of heuristic decision making that complements the existing statistics and logical framework is admittedly a long-term endeavor (Gigerenzer, 2008), and an ongoing one in the study of the ecological rationality of fast-and-frugal heuristics. An appeal

Table 7.1 Ecological rationality in economics (à la Smith) and psychology (à la Gigerenzer)

Subject	*Economic view à la Smith*	*Psychological view à la Gigerenzer*	*Overlap*
Ecological rationality	Ecological rationality is concerned with adaptations that occur within institutions, markets, management, and social and other associations governed by informal or formal rule systems.	A heuristic is ecologically rational to the degree that it is adapted to the structure of an environment. Humans have to adapt to a social and physical world, not to systems with artificial syntax, such as logic.	Smith uses the same definition of ecological rationality as Gigerenzer, wherein heuristics can be replaced by markets, management, or other rule systems
The normative aspect of constructivism and unbounded rationality	Constructivism or reason provides a variety of ideas to try out but often no relevant selection criteria, whereas the ecological process selects the norms and institutions that serve the stability of societies.	Unbounded rationality can generate optimal solutions for simple situations, such as tic-tac-toe; omniscience and omnipotence can also be used for theoretical examination of human behavior, but applying them as a universal standard of rationality is a scientific error.	Norms produced by unbounded or constructivist rationality are not useful as selection criteria in complex situations; the ultimate evaluation comes from the real world, not from theoretical sophistication.
Observation and experiments	Observing how people actually behave reveals unanticipated system rules, for example, the unexpected emergence of hubs (like an equilibrium) when airlines were deregulated.	Experimental games are bound to study social behavior as rule-obeying and not as rule-negotiating or rule-changing.	Rules are to be discovered as they emerge from social behavior. Formal models can be used to provide a possible description of what was observed.
Heuristic rules	Heuristics are a kind of cognitive capacity that we can access without being entirely aware of doing so.	Fast-and-frugal heuristics are strategies triggered by environmental situations and enabled by evolved or learned capacities.	The choice of heuristic strategy is often not fully deliberate. This does not exclude the possibility of training or altering the trigger conditions.

[Adopted with modification from Mousavi et al. (forthcoming). Based on interviews reported in Mousavi & Kheirandish (2014)].

of this pursuit for economists is the fact that heuristic strategies—not at a meta-level but as tools—have organically materialized as successful ways of making decisions in finance and business. Each of these instances can be regarded as a special case for a lower-level analysis of this claim. The next section provides a set of examples, where ecological rationality is used as a framework to study the success of heuristics in business decision making.

Ecological rationality as a framework for teasing out the elements of success

In a collection of studies (special section, *JBR* August 2014), fast-and-frugal heuristics are shown to be successfully used in a number of situations in which their ecological rationality clearly explains their success. Such instances are documented for consumer behavior in credit or goods markets, managerial judgment in pricing products and hiring employees, crisis management, entrepreneurial decisions, and organizational behavior. In each of the papers reviewed in this section, the authors apply ecological rationality as a framework, formulate the observed evolvement of successful strategies as heuristic processes, and argue how ecological rationality can help us understand the whens and whys of successful decision making.

Banks and financial sector

As major financial intermediaries in the monetary system, banks regularly engage in issuing lines of credit. Credit cards, which allow consumers to spend their future income, have been a concern for regulators because it has been shown time and again that repayment of credit card debt is a much more difficult task than perceived by credit card holders or the rational view of human decision making. Many cardholders quickly collect a considerable amount of debt on their credit cards and then pay high amounts of interest on their debt for extensive periods of time. Federal reserve board reports for American households indicate an average of above 15 percent of income being spent on financial obligation payments (www.federalreserve.gov/releases/housedebt/). For low- and middle-class Americans, this ratio can reach half of their disposable income. To protect consumers against this peril, in 2009, American lawmakers passed the credit card accountability, responsibility, and disclosure act (CARD). As a result, many banks hired consultants to implement their obligations. Shefrin and Nicols (2014) report their consulting process for the Chase Bank, where they developed the concept of financial styles for cardholder households. This is part of the Chase Blueprint Program designed to help cardholders better manage their spending and borrowing behavior. They note that "by nature, household decision making is a heuristic enterprise, as most household decision tasks are far too complex to be fully specified, let alone solved through optimization." Moreover, they observe that neoclassical preference ordering and the measurement tools based on it are concerned primarily with the consistency criterion of rational choice rather than "the quality of the decisions." At the same time, they note that their financial literacy questionnaires revealed that only half of those who self-assessed their mathematical skills as "high-level" were able to calculate interest rate and inflation correctly. Given the complexity of household decisions and these limitations of both technical measurement tools and customers' mathematical abilities, Shefrin and Nicols decided to use a fast-and-frugal decision rule to help Chase credit card holders find their personal financial styles, which would then match them with proper financial advice from a menu. After responding to a short series of binary questions, consumers are classified into one of the four categories: low control, minimum payer; high control, minimum payer; full balance paying, multiple cardholder; and full balance paying, single cardholder. This categorization task has four options and three cues, lending itself to an elimination heuristic process. Shefrin and Nicols (2014) report that this financial style categorization heuristic is more accessible to bank customers (especially the 25 percent with self-ranked low confidence in their online skills) and also technically advantageous over cluster analysis.

Let us turn now to another aspect of banking. Banks keep longitudinal and detailed data on their customers' financial choices. Thus, customer relationship management (CRM) in banking appears to be a perfect area for implementation of optimization methods based on customer lifetime valuation (CLV), which require such data. If this were true, banks should be using CLV routinely, and this should be contributing to improving relationships with their customers. Persson and Ryals (2014) examined the process of CRM at nine of the largest retail Nordic banks, and discovered that although these banks perform CLV calculations their decisions are made based on a handful of simple heuristics that deliberately ignore a large set of technically relevant results available from data analysis. Moreover, they report that customers prefer the banks that practice simple heuristic decision making to those that apply CLV. Providing a list of heuristics that can be applied to CRM, the authors determine their ecological rationality by specifying the conditions under which a certain heuristic succeeds or fails. For example, banks use simple rules to determine the active/inactive status of a customer, somewhat akin to the hiatus heuristic introduced by Wübben and von Wangenheim (2008), that use only one threshold value, such as a fixed number of inactivity months to drop a consumer from the list of active consumers, and ignore all other information.

Seeking financial consulting is prevalent among retail investors. To better understand the investor–advisor interaction and their respective perceptions, Monti et al. (2014) conducted interviews with 20 professional financial advisors and 99 active bank customers at an Italian corporate bank. Because these retailers admittedly lack the expertise for making investment decisions, they delegate financial decisions to the advisors. Interestingly, what they value in their advisors more than past performance record are trustworthiness, clarity, and attention. This is despite the fact that the retailers hold little confidence or trust in the financial system as a whole. Monti et al. (2014) propose a model of trust formation as the main vehicle for delegating financial decisions, which has little or no regard for standard economic metrics for evaluating financial choice. The analysis of their interview data resonates with the *honest signals* phenomenon of Pelligra (2010), where "honest signals are behaviors that are so expressive or so directly connected to our underlying biology that they become generally reliable indicators used by people to guide their own internal psychological production of trust." Thus, it is shown that advice taking is an adaptive behavior and that trust, as a simple heuristic, works well within cooperative environments. Monti et al.'s approach perceives trust as a public good that can in turn be understood as ecologically rational behavior in the complex financial environment. Non-expert retail investors in this study make decisions based on the trust engendered by their advisor's communication style. Moreover, these investors' perceptions of the investor–advisor relationship reflect portfolio decisions better than the risk–return trade-off.

Strategic corporate decision making

Innovation adoption in organizations is a complex strategic process. Nikolaeva (2014) uses a cognitive lens to observe this phenomenon that reveals the dominant use of two popular imitation heuristics, namely, *imitate the successful* and *imitate the majority*. Managers regularly copy predecessors for improving the status quo. The speed of innovation adoption depends on the interaction between the framing dictated by the status quo and the timing of the different imitation heuristics in use. Similarly, Berg (2014) shows that entrepreneurs choose their locations based on a combination of two simple heuristics, satisficing and imitation. When choosing where to locate, successful entrepreneurs form small consideration sets. Satisficing thresholds are set on the basis of imitation and are not updated along the search path.

Focusing on corporate strategic decision making, Azar (2014) specifies conditions under which firms follow the default heuristic, which kicks in when the cost of obtaining information is relatively high or the variation in possible outcomes is low. All in all, whether these decisions involve exploring new frontiers, such as in innovation adoption and entrepreneurial decisions, or routine choices such as setting corporate strategic policies, heuristic rules appear to guide the thrust of many important decisions.

Human resource and hiring decisions

Human resource (HR) managers routinely make hiring and delegation decisions based on incomplete information. Hu and Wang (2014), who view trust in HR decisions as a risky choice, propose that these decisions are frequently made by using simple heuristics. They investigate the use of four strategies by 120 HR managers, take-the-best (TTB), the minimum requirement heuristic (MR), likelihood expectancy (LE), and the Franklin rule (FR), and specify conditions for the best performance of each strategy. TTB was found to be most effective when the alternative options can be differentiated by the most valid cue. MR is a form of tallying that chooses the option that meets the higher number of minimum requirements and performs best when a limited number of cues are used as a minimum requirement for differentiating between options. By contrast, an LE user chooses the option with the higher LE score, that is, the one with the higher sum total of cues, and examines the space of cues exhaustively. The FR calculates a weighted sum of cue values and selects the one with the higher score. Hu and Wang's joint comparison of these four strategies in the context of HR management shows that the simple heuristics MR and TTB outperform the complex ones, LE and FR, in terms of predictive accuracy. Moreover, MR outperforms TTB overall because differentiation based on the most valid cue becomes more difficult in this environment, where cues often have a similar validity.

When hiring, would more interviewers increase the quality of hired employees? By observing corporate recruiting procedures and analyzing data from the recruitment procedures of several corporations, Fifić and Gigerenzer (2014) pursued a formal answer to this question. They show that in terms of hit rate, two interviewers are on average not superior to the best interviewer. That is, the chance of choosing higher quality interviewees from a pool of applicants by a single interviewer is higher than when more than one interviewer is involved. This finding manifests an instance of less-is-more phenomena and goes against a general consensus in the traditional approach, such as in the Condorcet jury theorem, which associates higher quality with more expert involvement. Furthermore, Fifić and Gigerenzer show that adding more interviewers will not increase the expected collective hit. This result provides additional insight to the free-rider explanation for inferior outcomes from collective choice processes (see, for example, Kerr & Tindale, 2004).

Pricing, marketing, and crisis management

Do managers' pricing choices show patterns and identifiable algorithms? Rusetski (2014) reports that a majority of managers (69%) rely on an identifiable heuristic when making their pricing decisions under limited information. His cluster analysis reveals that brand strength is a dominant input into intuitive decision-making algorithms, whereas product quality seems to play a relatively minor role in pricing. In fact, managers consistently price their products above, equal, or below those of their competitors instead of adjusting prices according to attributes such as quality. Observed pricing heuristics are ecologically rational because they rely on past experience and best practices for a given environment. When pricing decisions, which are typically made in complex environments, have to satisfy multiple criteria and are made under time pressure, frugal intuitive decisions are in fact more effective than those based on a full-fledged analysis.

Facing many products with many features in the markets, consumers use consider-then-choose decision processes with the help of heuristic decision rules. Hauser (2014) names these

Table 7.2 Observed crisis management heuristics formulated as simple decision rules

Heuristic	*Rule form*
Credibility heuristic	If the *conveyor* of the warning message passes a threshold of perceived credibility, then treat the message as being a signal from the target; if not, treat the message as being noise from a distracter.
Precedent heuristic	Search for precedent(s) for the unfolding event (i.e., historical analogue(s)), and if identified, then treat the current event in the same fashion as its precedent was treated.
Facts-trump-speculation heuristic	When faced with conflicting lines of evidence relating to a phenomenon, order them according to a predefined (but possibly implicit) hierarchy of evidence (cue validities), and treat the highest ranked line of evidence as true.

Based on MacGillivray (2014).

processes *consideration-set heuristics*. Marketing management, product development, and marketing communication decisions depend on the ability to identify such heuristics and to react properly to them. This requires understanding, quantifying, and simulating what-if scenarios for a variety of heuristics. Describing consumer choice processes by heuristic rules provides an effective tool for dealing with a broad set of managerial problems, including complex product categories with large numbers of product features and feature levels.

Heuristic rules are not always intuitive; managers can consciously develop and use them for dealing with crisis. MacGillivray (2014) gathers field evidence on crisis management rules in the water supply sector and explores these in the framework of fast-and-frugal heuristics. He highlights "the relations between rule-based reasoning and social, political and organizational structures." As such, he presents heuristic analysis as a powerful tool for understanding and justifying inferences and choices in given contexts, and for developing methods to persuade social actors in certain directions. Three heuristics for fast-and-frugal crisis management are specified: credibility, precedent, and facts-trump-speculation heuristics. As described in Table 7.2, credibility is used as a rule for discriminating between signal and noise, the precedent heuristic uses analogy as a rule for reasoning, and the facts-trump-speculation heuristic implements a noncompensatory approach to weighing evidence.

Observing heuristic rules used across domains of business and economics and teasing out their conditions of success comprises the agenda of studying the ecological rationality of fast-and-frugal heuristics. This method of study shifts the focus from the underlying biases associated with heuristics to exploring heuristic decision making as a legitimate approach to the study of choice under uncertainty alongside the more familiar approaches to this domain of scientific inquiry based on probability theory and logic (Gigerenzer, 2008).

The domain of behavioral economics

As a discipline, economics has been on a quest to become more scientific by mathematizing its methods and practices. The goal has been to make economics to the social sciences what physics is to the natural sciences. McCloskey (1991) argues that economics has moved away from its practical use of solving social, political, and market institution problems by its obsession for "becoming more mathematical":

> The problem is that the general theorem does not relate to anything an economist would actually want to know. We already know for example that if the world is not

> perfect the outcomes of the world cannot be expected to be perfect. This much we know by being adults. But economists arguing over the federal budget next year or the stability of capitalism forever want to know *how big* a particular badness or offsetting goodness will be. Will the distribution of income be radically changed by the abandonment of interest? It is useless to be told that if there is not a complete market in every commodity down to and including chewing gum then there is no presumption that capitalism will work efficiently. Yet that is a typical piece of information from the mathematical frontlines. It does not provide the economic scientist with a scale against which to judge the significance of the necessary deviations from completeness. Chewing gum or all investment goods: it does not matter for the proof.
>
> *(p. 9)*

Behavioral economics as a scientific movement has set out to bring realism back into economic theory and thus to enhance the relevance and applicability of economics to solving societal problems. Gaining sight of where social science stands in the spectrum of scientific inquiry is, therefore, of key importance to the development of behavioral economics. In what follows, a categorization of scientific problems is evoked and placed together with the study of heuristics in a space specified by different types of complexity and the range of variables. This exercise provides a perspective on how behavioral economics problems can be perceived and explored. One reason why heuristics work lies in the fact that their effective simplicity generates robustness, which in turn functions under certain forms of complexity. By demonstrating the power and range of the applicability of heuristics, we refute the misconception that heuristics are inferior to sophisticated optimization methods when it comes to a wide range of interesting practical problems.

The complexity continuum

Warren Weaver (1894–1978) is arguably one of the most influential scientists of the past century and unassumingly so. He also had a knack for spotting talent. In his thirty years of heading the natural science unit of Rockefeller Foundation he funded 15 out of 18 future Nobel Laureates in molecular biology (Sull & Eisenhardt, 2015). In his 1948 paper titled "Science and Complexity," he depicted his view of scientific inquiry and went on to foresee the function of science "in the developing future of man." Weaver views scientific problems in terms of the number of variables involved in solving them and locates them on a spectrum from simple to complex, where complexity can be either organized or disorganized. As he notes, physical science became significantly quantitative in the seventeenth century and since then has discovered the constant relationships between two, three, or four variables and thus almost exhausted *problems of simplicity* characterized by them. Picture this category of problems by one such instance: the motion of two balls hitting each other. Science in the twentieth century aimed at finding relationships that can describe the equivalent of the movement of billions of balls in many directions, where no specific information on an individual variable can be determined except in the form of distributions. To analyze average properties of the orderly systems that characterize these *problems of disorganized complexity*, scientists developed "powerful techniques of probability theory and of statistical mechanics." Such analysis can be easily applied to the financial stability of a life insurance company, but cannot be easily applied to many other economic and financial problems.[3] Weaver argues that the analytical achievements of statistical methods developed for dealing with the problems of disorganized complexity were so impressive that it became tempting to apply them to all sorts of problems with large numbers of variables. However, he cautions scientists about *an ignored vast middle ground,* where problems are complex but not disorganized. He keenly observes that these problems require a different approach:

> How can one explain the behavior pattern of an organized group of persons such as a labor union, or a group of manufacturers, or a racial minority? There are clearly many factors involved here, but it is equally obvious that here also something more is needed than the mathematics of averages. With a given total of national resources that can be brought to bear, what tactics and strategy will most promptly win a war, or better: what sacrifice of present selfish interest will most effectively contribute to a stable, decent, and peaceful world?
>
> These problems and a wide range of similar problems in the biological, medical, psychological, economic, and political sciences are just too complicated to yield to the old nineteenth century techniques which were so dramatically successful on two-, three-, or four-variable problems of simplicity. These new problems, moreover, cannot be handled with the statistical techniques so effective in describing average behavior in problems of disorganized complexity.
>
> These new problems, and the future of the world depends on many of them, requires science to make a third great advance, an advance that must be even greater than the nineteenth century conquest of problems of simplicity or the twentieth century victory over problems of disorganized complexity. Science must, over the next 50 years, learn to deal with these problems of organized complexity.
>
> *(pp. 5–6)*

An area characterized by solving these mid-range problems is the study of administrative and organizational behavior, a field pioneered by Herbert Simon (1947). Simon held that "satisficing," which entails setting and achieving an aspiration level, is a major decision tool used in organizations for solving complex problems. It can be applied to a wide variety of complex problems, from well-defined but intractable ones such as a game of chess to ill-defined daily problems that are full of surprises, such as choosing a career or planning a picnic.

Satisficing is one of the heuristics in the "toolbox" of the human mind. The descriptive study of fast-and-frugal heuristics comprises the study of the mind as an adaptive toolbox that contains heuristics, their building blocks, and evolved capacities. With heuristics, both experts and non-experts have tools to solve a vast set of problems with a mid-range of complexity. Figure 7.1 demonstrates an attempt to bring mid-range complexity and heuristic problem solving into one space, wherein the complexity of problems as categorized by Weaver is superimposed on the space of heuristic decision making. Notably, the overlaps and distinctions are not clear-cut. However, the critical role of simplicity captures a central feature of how to successfully deal with complexity in scientific and everyday problem solving.

The conjecture, here, is that discovering the structure of organization for given mid-range problems of *organized complexity*—which characterize most problems addressed in the social sciences, including economics—can reasonably be achieved by pursuing a scientific approach to heuristics. This endeavor entails developing testable models of heuristics and formulating existing observed phenomena as heuristic processes (as was shown in the third section). Using Figure 7.1, one can apply the concept of ecological rationality to Weaver's categorization of scientific inquiry: Mechanistic methods dealing with up to four variables are suitable for the *problems of simplicity*, whereas probability and statistical methods are suited to the investigation of problems with disorganized complexity and can at best generate knowledge of averages, not of specifics or

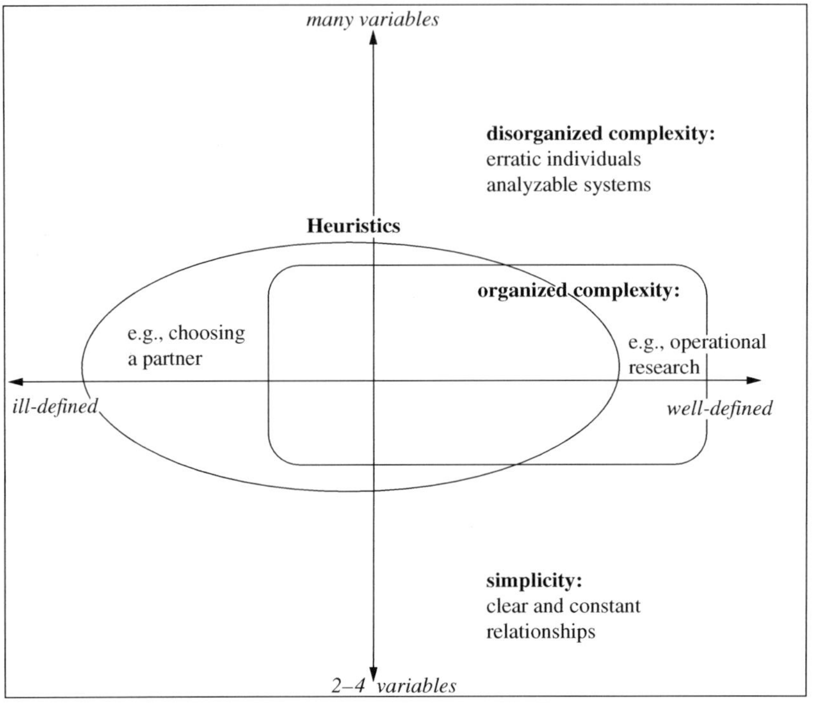

Figure 7.1 Placing heuristics in a space with degrees of complexity on the vertical axis versus the degree of definability of a problem on the horizontal axis

Graphics credit: Anoush Kheirandish.

single events of interest. Bearing in mind the superimposition of complexity over the range of definability as in Figure 7.1, one can view the study of the ecological rationality of heuristics as systematically exploring and revealing the "organization" of generalizable elements and features of many problems of *organized complexity*, from ill-defined to well-defined structures. Rigidly holding on to ideals of optimization and probability theory leaves one at one or the other end of the continuum of complexity and prevents one from *muddling through* a vast middle range of relevant economic and social problems with structured complexity that lend themselves to being modeled with the effective simplicity of heuristics.

Closing remarks

In its search for psychological insight to inform economic modeling of human behavior, behavioral economics has found it primarily in the heuristics and biases program, with which it shares the neoclassical benchmarks of rationality for evaluation of the choice behavior. Another school of thought in psychology, much less explored by behavioral economists, studies the functionality of fast-and-frugal heuristics. This approach evaluates behavior on the basis of its ecological rationality, where success is achieved through a functional match between heuristic strategies and the task environment. In this chapter, the economic and psychological conceptions of ecological rationality were juxtaposed, and some ways in which ecological rationality can be used as a framework for analyzing economic and business heuristic decision making were presented. The main message is that behavioral economists can benefit from adding the ecological rationality framework to their toolbox of methods and methodologies for the study of human behavior. In closing, a specific limitation of psychology merits attention: "When discussing psychological research, what surprises every economist or physicist is that psychology has no theory. It has many local ones but no overarching theory, not even a provisional one" (Gigerenzer, 2015: 252). By adopting psychological insights from a variety of psychology research programs, behavioral economics has the promising potential of contributing to theory building and theory integration in psychology, which in turn lends itself to the expansion of theory in behavioral economics.[4]

Notes

1 See chapter in this handbook for on overview of the fast-and-frugal heuristics study program.
2 See chapter 14 by Altman in this handbook on institutional economics and how it can inform behavioral economics.
3 Weaver's position agrees, independently, with Frank Knight's (1921) view that what is important to the student of business is not the problem of statistical probability, but those problems that do not lend themselves to the structural configuration of insurance in the market. Connections between Knight's typology of risk versus uncertainty and the study of fast-and-frugal heuristics have been worked out in Mousavi and Gigerenzer (2014).
4 An extensive exchange between economics and psychological views on this approach is presented in Mousavi, Neth, Meder, & Kheirandish, forthcoming, in *Behavioral Economics for Smart People*, Morris Altman (ed.).

Bibliography

Azar, O. H. (2014). The default heuristic in strategic decision making: When is it optimal to choose the default without investing in information search? Journal of Business Research, 67(8), 1744–8.
Berg, N. (2014). Success from satisficing and imitation: Entrepreneurs' location choice and implications of heuristics for local economic development. Journal of Business Research, 67(8), 1700–9.
Fifić, M. & Gigerenzer, G. (2014). Are two interviewers better than one? Journal of Business Research, 67(8), 1771–9.
Gigerenzer, G. (1996). On narrow norms and vague heuristics: A reply to Kahneman and Tversky. Psychological Review, 103, 592–6.
Gigerenzer, G. (2008). Why heuristics work. Perspectives on Psychological Science, 3, 20–9.
Gigerenzer, G. (2015). Simply rational: Decision making in the real world. New York: Oxford University Press.
Grüne-Yanoff, T. & Hertwig, R. (2015). Nudge versus boost: How coherent are policy and theory? Minds and Machines.
Hauser, J. R. (2014). Consideration-set heuristics. Journal of Business Research, 67(8), 1688–99.
Hayek, F. A. (1956). The dilemma of specialization. In L. White (ed.) State of the social sciences. Chicago: University of Chicago Press.
Hu, Z. & Wang, X. T. (2014). Trust or not: Heuristics for making trust-based choices in HR management. Journal of Business Research, 67(8), 1710–16.
Kerr, N. L. & Tindale, R. S. (2004). Group performance and decision making. Annual Review of Psychology, 55, 623–55.
Knight, F. H. (1921). Risk, uncertainty and profit. Dover 2006 unabridged republication of the edition published by Boston and New York: Houghton Mifflin.
MacGillivray, B. H. (2014). Fast and frugal crisis management: An analysis of rule-based judgment and choice during water contamination events. Journal of Business Research, 67(8), 1717–24.
McCloskey, D. (1991). Has formalization in economics gone too far? Methodus 3, 6–16.
Monti, M., Pelligra, V., Martignon, L. & Berg, N. (2014). Retail investors and financial advisors: New evidence on trust and advice taking heuristics. Journal of Business Research, 67(8), 1749–57.

Mousavi, S. & Gigerenzer, G. (2011). Revisiting the "error" in studies of cognitive errors. In Hofmann, D. A. and M. Frese (eds.), Errors in organizations, New York: Routledge, 97–112.
Mousavi, S. & Gigerenzer, G. (2014). Risk, uncertainty, and heuristics. Journal of Business Research, 67(8), 1671–8.
Mousavi, S. & Kheirandish, K. (2014). Behind and beyond a shared definition of ecological rationality: A functional view of heuristics. Journal of Business Research, 67(8), 1780–5.
Mousavi, S., Neth, H., Meder, B. & Kheirandish, S. (forthcoming). Heuristics: fast, frugal, and smart. In Altman, M., (ed.) Handbook of Behavioral Economics and Smart Decision-Making: Rational Decision-Making within the Bounds of Reason, Cheltenham: Edward Elgar Publishing.
Nikolaeva, R. (2014). Interorganizational imitation heuristics arising from cognitive frames. Journal of Business Research, 67(8), 1758–65.
Pelligra, V. (2010). Trust responsiveness: On the dynamics of fiduciary interactions. Journal of Socio-Economics, 39(6), 653–60.
Persson, A. & Ryals, L. (2014). Making customer relationship decisions: Analytics v rules of thumb. Journal of Business Research, 67(8), 1725–32.
Rusetski, A. (2014). Pricing by intuition: Managerial choices with limited information. Journal of Business Research, 67(8), 1733–43.
Shefrin, H. & Nicols, C. M. (2014). Credit card behavior, financial styles, and heuristics. Journal of Business Research, 67(8), 1679–87.
Simon, H. A. (1947). Administrative behavior: A study of decision making processes in administrative organization. Macmillan.
Smith, V. L. (2008). Rationality in economics: Constructivist and ecological forms. Cambridge: Cambridge University Press.
Sull, D. & Eisenhardt, K. M. (2015). Simple rules: How to thrive in a complex world. London: John Murray.
Weaver, W. (1948). Science and complexity. American Scientist, 36(4), 536–44.
Wübben, M. & von Wangenheim, F. (2008). Instant customer base analysis: Managerial heuristics often "get it right." Journal of Marketing, 72, 82–93.

8

RICHARD THALER'S BEHAVIORAL ECONOMICS

Floris Heukelom

Introduction

It is safe to say Richard Thaler (b. 1945) has been a key actor, if not the principal protagonist of the Kahneman and Tversky-inspired behavioral economics that emerged in the 1980s, and which arose as the most important alternative to mainstream economics in the 2000s. Building on Heukelom (2014), and complementing Thaler (2015), this chapter seeks to describe and explain Thaler's behavioral economics. I do so by discussing his work chronologically, and by showing which themes appeared when. The upcoming second section illustrates Thaler's economic thinking before he became acquainted with the work of Kahneman and Tversky, and what this reveals regarding the better known papers and theories that followed later. Section three will then discuss Thaler's documenting of descriptive fallacies of mainstream economics, which was the principal focus of the 1980s. The fourth section shows how this gathering of descriptive fallacies gradually developed into a program of designing actions and programs to make people behave more in accordance with the normative theory of mainstream economics in the 1990s, and how this eventually led to the formulation of a new overall program of libertarian paternalism, or nudging.

The normative power of mainstream economics

Richrad Thaler (b. 1945) conducted an MA and PhD in business administration at the University of Rochester. His dissertation, entitled *The Value of Saving a Life: A Market Estimate* (1974) was supervised by Sherwin Rosen (1938–2001), a labor economist. Although both equally turned to the question of how economics may explain the actual empirical phenomena observed in the economy, there does not seem to be an overly clear influence of Rosen on Thaler, or a lasting collaboration between the supervisor and the supervisee.

In contrast to the iconic, inward looking, mathematical economics of general equilibrium theory that dominated the 1970s, Thaler's work focused on everyday questions on the fringes of the economic discipline. Based on data of insurance purchases, Thaler's thesis provided an estimate of how much individuals apparently value their own lives (see also Rosen & Thaler, 1975). Following a part time affiliation with the Rochester-Monroe County Crimnal Justice Pilot City Porgram, Thaler's "An Econometric Analysis of Property Crime: Interaction between

Police and Criminals" (1977) explored the correlation between number of police cars in an area, and number of crimes reported and solved. Mayers and Thaler (1979) showed how sticky wages, an anomaly of economic rationality, could in fact be explained as resulting from rational employers and employees facing transaction costs.

The underlying stance in these early articles was that mainstream economic theory obviously presents a picture of how the economy and economic actors should work. In addition, however, the assumption was that in general the economy and economic actors actually do behave in this way. This first part of this understanding of economics was further sharpened in "Discounting with Fiscal Constraints: Why Discounting is Always Right" (1979). Contrary to what some US defense managers apparently believed, Thaler forcefully argued that also in the military future incomes and costs should always be discounted against appropriate rates. The fact that some managers sometimes refused to do so was not an invalidation of economic theory, but a signal of professional incapability. In other words, this key paper of Thaler also brought out more clearly another element of Thaler's thinking: if against all intuition and evidence individuals apparently fail to behave according to economic theory, then, well, they should be told so and if possible should be corrected in their behavior.

Descriptive fallacies

This line of thinking was taken a step further in the next year, when Thaler published "Towards a Positive Theory of Consumer Choice" (1980). This article is often taken to be the first in Thaler's behavioral economics program, including by Thaler himself. But however true this may be, it is at the same time part of a development of thinking that started a few years earlier, and that would continue to develop over subsequent years. As in his earlier articles, Thaler (1980) emphasized that individuals should behave according to the norms of economic theory. Why they should do so was, as before, never explicitly indicated, but nevertheless the obvious message was that they should do so because it is in their own best interest. However, taking this argument one step further, Thaler now for the first time argued that individuals systematically and predicatably deviate from the norms of economic behavior. The principal source for this claim was Daniel Kahneman and Amos Tversky's "Prospect Theory, An Analysis of Decision under Risk"(1979). Thaler took two messages from Kahneman and Tversky's work: that the economic theory according to which individuals should behave effectively constitutes a set of norms and hence constitutes a normative theory, and the observation that deviations from these norms are not accidental, but systematic and predictable.

Thus, although Thaler (1980) to some extent is one step in an ongoing development of thinking, it is equally true that here for the first time the core argument of the behavioral economics program is presented: individuals deviate systematically and predictably from the norms of rational economic theory. As a matter of fact, one could even claim very well that all of Thaler's articles in the next thirty years are restatements of this basic position, applied to different contexts and different empirical examples. For instance, in "Some Empirical Evidence on Dynamic Inconsistency" (1981) the traditional model of temporal discounting is introduced as the "normatively based" theory economists normally hold. Deviations from this model are understood as a problem of self-control. In addition, losses are hypothesized to be different from gains, in analogy with Kahneman and Tversky's prospect theory.

However, defying the tempting model of lineair scientific progress, in "An Economic Theory of Self-Control" (Shefrin and Thaler, 1981) Thaler returned to his stance of a few years earlier by offering a traditional "orthodox" explanation for observed behavior that is seemingly at odds with economic theory, such as Christmas funds bearing no interest and smoking clinics in which people pay several hundred (1980) dollars just to stop smoking. Within the individual, who in this regard could be likened to an organization, the interests of the far-sighted planner sometimes collide with the interests of the myopic doer, Thaler and Shefrin argued. Although both rationally strive to maximize their own utility, the eventual behavior of the individual will be in disaccord with one of these two actors. From the perspective of the actor who lost, the behavior will seem irrational, while in fact it was simply another part of the individual that won the battle to maximize utility.

In 1985 Thaler, together with Werner De Bondt published the much quoted "Does the Stock Market Overreact" which documented the since then well known "January effect". The (alleged) January effect shows stocks to systematically outperform in January compared to other months. Given that the stock market would seem to be a rational market if ever there was one, the effect is a clear demonstration of the descriptive shortcoming of mainstream, normative economics, according to De Bondt and Thaler.

The January effect article may in addition be understood as the start of behavioral finance. Delineating (sub)disciplines is never straightforward, but may be useful as one way of providing a quick grasp of ongoing developments. The subfield of behavioral finance is sometimes understood as a subdisicipline that is different from behavioral economics, as an empirically driven subliterature within finance (Samson, 2014). In relation to Thaler's work and (the chronology of) his academic development, however, it makes much more sense to understand behavioral finance as one branch within behavioral economics focusing on the descriptive fallacies of mainstream economics as applied to the world of finance. Throughout his career Thaler, for instance, easily packed together examples from the stock market, office restaurants, and studies of the availability of donor organs, to illustrate the descriptive shortcomings of mainstream economics. In other words, to Thaler descriptive fallacies within finance have always been but one important example of the problem with mainstream economics.

Another example is "Mental Accounting and Consumer Choice" (1985), in which Thaler presented the reader with four anecdotes which "illustrate a type of behavior" in which the "individual violate[s] a simple economic principle." The "standard economic theory" Thaler noted, "of course, is based on normative principles," and he offered prospect theory "as a substitute to the standard economic theory of the consumer" (Thaler, 1985: 200). All this made Thaler a great promoter of Kahneman and Tversky's work in economics and quickly turned him into a major recipient of, and influential voice in, the Alfred P. Sloan–Russell Sage behavioral economics program, which played a crucial role in establishing behavioral economics as a highly visible new sub-discipline in the 1980s and early 1990s.

As I have set out in much more detail elsewhere, the first, tentative summary of mainstream economic fallacies, and the explanation of these fallacies in terms of Kahneman and Tversky's behavioral psychology, received a strong boost through this Alfred P. Sloan and later Russell Sage Foundation's behavioral economics program, which ran from 1984 through 1992 (Heukelom, 2012, 2014). It is not possible to understand the rise of behavioral economics without assessing the role of the Sloan–Sage program. The primary contribution of the Sloan–Sage behavioral economics program was not the resources it provided, which were relatively modest. Instead, the program's contribution was to catalyze in the researchers it supported a sense of contributing to a new direction of the economic discipline.

Mid June 1984, the board of trustees of the Sloan Foundation officially installed the advisory committee and endowed it with $250,000 to fund a number of "seed projects" in subsequent years, to see if the program could work (Wanner's notes on the advisory committee meeting, 7 December 1984, RAC). As early as July 1984, Robert Abelson expressed a view that seems to have been shared by the other advisory committee members as well as by the program's director

Eric Wanner, namely that Kahneman and Thaler should be at the center of the new program: "Getting Thaler and Kahneman together is bound to produce progress. Their teamwork could be as seminal as the Tversky and Kahneman pairing, but more market oriented" (Abelson's letter to Wanner, 26 July 1984, RAC). The first behavioral economics meeting was planned for 7 December 1984 at the Waldorf-Astoria Hotel, New York. In addition to the advisory committee and Kahneman and Thaler the following economists and psychologists were invited: Hillel Einhorn, Baruch Fischoff, Donald Hood, Thomas Juster, Charles Plott, Howard Kunreuther, Howard Raiffa, Oliver Williamson, Richard Zeckhauser, and Herbert Simon.[1]

Another important element in this collaborative effort were Thaler's anomalies columns for the *Journal of Economic Perspectives* (*JEP*). In 1986, the journal's founding editors, Joseph Stiglitz (b. 1943), Carl Shapiro (b. 1955), and Timothy Taylor (b. 1960) decided that one element of their new journal would be "features," a series of short papers around one theme of which one would appear in every issue of the journal. As Taylor recalls

> We started with three features: a "Recommendations for Further Reading" feature written by Bernard Saffran, an "Economic Puzzles" feature written by Barry Nalebuff, and the "Anomalies" feature written by Richard Thaler. My memory is that Joe and Carl had Thaler in mind pretty much from Day 1. They had talked with Dick, and he had a list of potential topics pretty much ready to go . . .
>
> Our original plan with the "Anomalies" column was that it would include a range of anomalies: micro, macro, even theory or econometrics. However, getting authors to write these kinds of columns in JEP style proved tricky, and Dick and his co-authors generated a lovely stream of behavioral topics for us.
>
> *(Taylor, email to author, 6 April 2010)*

Thaler published two series of "anomalies" papers for the *JEP* that had the sole purpose of proclaiming that economics had serious problems regarding its theory of economic behavior. Each paper had a length of about 4000 words. The first series contained fourteen anomalies articles and appeared from the first issue of the journal in 1987 through to 1991.[2] The second series contained four publications and appeared between 1995 and 2001. Thaler's anomalies columns provided the core of the new Kahneman and Tversky-inspired behavioral economics with a highly visible platform, and arguably served as a strong catalyst for its development.

The first anomaly article in 1987 further documented the already mentioned January effect. When the market for stocks is in efficient equilibrium, in the neoclassical world the average monthly return should be equal for each month. There is no reason to expect that stocks would perform better just because it happens to be a certain month. However, this was exactly what was observed in the case of January. Especially for smaller firms stock returns were substantially higher in January compared with other months. How could this January effect be possible given the theory of efficient markets? The answer was that it was not possible, with the question left open how to solve this anomaly.

Loewenstein and Thaler (1989) showed that many similar anomalies existed in and outside the economy that have to do with intertemporal choice. For example, people prefer to pay too much tax in advance and to receive some back when the year is over instead of the reverse, even when the first option is subject to costs in terms of lost interest. Schoolteachers who can choose between being paid in nine months (September–June) or in twelve (September–August), choose the second option although from an economic perspective the first is more rational. But Loewenstein and Thaler also cited the dermatologist who lamented that her patients were unwilling to avoid the sun when she told them about the risks of skin cancer, but who were quick to stay out of the sun when she told them about the risk of getting "large pores and blackheads." This example, Loewenstein and Thaler argued, was also a violation of economic theory because it showed myopia in patients they should not have if they acted rationally. The implicit reasoning was that economic theory could be applied to every aspect of our lives and that therefore also violations of economic theory could be drawn from every corner of life: "where there are testable predictions, there are anomalies" (Loewenstein & Thaler, 1989: 183). The recurring message of the anomalies articles was that there are serious problems with economic theory which cannot be easily dismissed, and which need to be taken seriously.

In his anomalies columns, Thaler cited examples from finance that were clearly economic. The structure of the anomalies, however, was often similar to the biases produced by Kahneman and Tversky (e.g. Kahneman & Tversky, 1972, 1979, and Tversky & Kahneman, 1974, see also Heukelom, 2014). One anomaly that Thaler frequently investigated and that became one of the principal anomalies of behavioral finance was the "endowment effect" (e.g. Thaler, 1980, Kahneman, Knetsch, & Thaler, 1990, 1991). The endowment effect was an application of the framing effect of Kahneman and Tversky that showed that individuals' preferences are subject to an initial framing process. In other words, individuals' preferences depend on the quantity of the means they are endowed with. The experiment is as follows. Divide a group of subjects randomly into two sub-groups and give one of the two sub-groups a standard coffee mug. Subsequently, ask the sub-group with the mug what price they would minimally want to sell the mug for. Also ask subjects of the sub-group without mugs what price they would maximally want to pay for the mug. Typically, the willingness to accept (WTA) is about twice the willingness to pay (WTP). Apparently, people reframe their preferences after receiving the mug. In economics, this endowment effect could serve as an explanation for the often observed fallacy of taking into account sunk costs (see e.g. Thaler, 1980, 1987, Tversky & Kahneman, 1981). The endowment effect further falsified the Coase theorem, which says that in order to attain the efficient market allocation, the initial endowment of the goods should be irrelevant. The Coase theorem depends on the assumption that for every individual WTA equals WTP, so that trading will continue until the goods are in the hands of those with the highest WTP. But given the demonstrated systematic difference between WTA and WTP, the Coase theorem no longer held true: "Contrary to the assumptions of standard economic theory that preferences are independent of entitlements, the evidence presented here indicates that people's preferences depend on their reference positions" (Kahneman, Knetsch, & Thaler, 1990: 1344).

Meanwhile, 1991 saw the beginning of the Russell Sage Foundation Behavioral Economics books series. The first book to be published in this series was Thaler's *Quasi-Rational Economics* (1991). Eventually, eleven books were published, among which Loewenstein and Elster's *Choice over Time* (1992), and Thaler's *Advances in Behavioral Finance* (1993).

Libertarian paternalism, aka nudging

Thaler has never been primarily interested in finding better descriptive alternatives for mainstream economics. After exhaustively documenting descriptive failures, Thaler's next move was rather to devise ways to make people behave more in accordance with the normative economic theory. On the one hand, Thaler has always believed that individuals usually behave according to the normative economic theory. When they do not, it is however the individual who is to blame, and not economic theory. In contrast to, say, Herbert Simon, to Thaler the normative, universal validity of economic theory for rational behavior has never been in question. Quite the contrary; because economists know how best to behave in the economy, and because they observe individuals to make mistakes in that regard, economists are obliged in their capacity as fellow, moral human beings to help these failing individuals to behave more in accordance with the normative theory of rational economics.

Thaler's first article principally devoted to this policy implication of behavioral economics was "How to Get Real People to Save" (1992) in which he argued that to increase saving rates in the (American) economy, it is best to follow the common sense of mothers and empirical evidence of behavioral economists, and not the advice of mainstream economists. Mom and behavioral economists would, for instance, advise firms to make (larger) lump-sum bonuses, which people are more likely to save substantial parts of as compared to salaries smoothed out over time. In addition, Mom and behavioral economists would advise to increase withholding rates for the federal income tax. The resulting larger tax return would likely increase overall spending. Also, firms could offer payroll saving plans, as saving is easier when you do it automatically and do not see it happen in your account every month. Through these and other straightforward actions of mothers and behavioral economists, that, according to Thaler, seemed so foreign to mainstream economists in their everyday obviousness, individuals could be made to behave more in accordance to the mainstream economic theory.

In "Psychology and Savings Policies" (1994) Thaler provided an overview of why the standard life-cycle theory does not account for actual saving behavior, and which measures a government or employer could take to increase saving—such as providing more information as to how much you need to save to sustain consumption after retirement, and schemes to pre-commit oneself to send lump-sum payments to a savings scheme. That being said, the solutions remain theoretical solutions without practical evidence. Actual implemented behavioral economic saving policies emerged only in the early 2000s, first and foremost with Saving More Tomorrow (SMarT), in which people pre-commit to send an increasing amount of future pay-raises to a pension savings scheme (e.g. Benartzi & Thaler, 2001).

Rationality and nudging

Thaler's reinterpretation of Kahneman and Tversky's distinction between the normative and the descriptive in terms of a conflict within the economic decision maker had important consequences for welfare economics. Following Friedman (1953), and many others, most mainstream economists in the 1990s and 2000s associated welfare economics in one way or another with the term normative. That was one reason why Kahneman and Tversky's labels of normative and descriptive invoked confusion when inserted into the economics discourse. The reinterpretation of normative versus descriptive in terms of full rationality versus bounded rationality solved this confusion and in turn allowed behavioral economists to develop their own position on welfare economics (Heukelom, 2014).

Well known in this regard is Thaler and Sunstein's (2003) "Libertarian Paternalism." Libertarian paternalism can be understood as a paternalism that does not restrict individual freedom of choice. Thaler and Sunstein distinguished themselves explicitly from Paul Samuelson's revealed preference stance towards welfare issues.

> We clearly do not always equate revealed preference with welfare. That is, we emphasize the possibility that in some cases individuals make inferior choices, choices that they would change if they had complete information, unlimited cognitive abilities, and no lack of willpower.
>
> *(Thaler & Sunstein, 2003: 175)*

In other words, the justification for paternalistic policies was the fact that the decisions people actually make, their "revealed preferences," do not always match with their "true" preferences. Behavioral economists thus constructed a distinction between "revealed" and "true" preferences. This did not mean that preferences were considered context-dependent. Rather, it meant that it depended on the context whether the true preferences can and will be revealed appropriately. A source that was sometimes relied on in this regard was John C. Harsanyi who had argued that "in deciding what is good and what is bad for an individual, the ultimate criterion can only be his own wants and his own preferences," where the individual's "own preferences" were his "true" preferences: "the preferences he would have if he had all the relevant factual information, always reasoned with the greatest possible care, and was in a state of mind most conducive to rational choice" (quoted in Angner & Loewenstein, 2012: 679).

A more detailed and elaborate explication and defense of this new branch of behavioral economics can be found in Camerer et al. (2003) "Regulation for Conservatives: Behavioral Economics and the Case for 'Asymmetric Paternalism'." In this article, the five authors (Camerer, Issacharoff, Loewenstein, O'Donoghue, and Rabin) made a case for what they labeled "asymmetric paternalism," where "[a] regulation is asymmetrically paternalistic if it creates large benefits for those who make errors, while imposing little or no harm on those who are fully rational" (Camerer et al., 2003: 1212). Behavioral economics, then, "describes ways people sometimes fail to behave in their own best interests" (Camerer et al., 2003: 1217). These "apparent violations of rationality [. . .] can justify the need for paternalistic policies to help people make better decisions and come closer to behaving in their own best interests" (Camerer et al., 2003: 1218).

Thaler and Sunstein (2003) countered possible aversions to paternalism by economists and others by linking paternalism to libertarianism. Camerer et al. (2003), on the other hand, founded their defense of paternalistic policies on the need for asymmetry in the paternalistic policy. The definition of asymmetric paternalism resembled the Paretean improvement argument: "a policy is *asymmetrically paternalistic* if it creates large benefits for those people who are boundedly rational [. . .] while imposing little or no harm on those who are fully rational" (Camerer et al., 2003: 1219, emphasis in the original). Or, in other words, "asymmetric paternalism helps those whose rationality is bounded from making a costly mistake and harms more rational folks very little" (Camerer et al., 2003: 1254). Another way of putting it, Camerer et al. (2003) argued, is to see the limitedly rational individual as imposing negative externalities on his or her own demand curve. "When consumers make errors, it is as if they are imposing externalities on themselves because the decisions they make as reflected by their demand do not accurately reflect the benefits they derive" (Camerer et al., 2003: 1221). Hence, there was a need for a policy maker who could remove the externalities and redirect behavior in such a way that the externalities disappeared. Camerer et al. (2003) furthermore noted that firms could either consciously or unconsciously use the irrationality of individuals to gain more profit.

On the basis of these results, behavioral economists argued that economists are morally obliged to act against the violations of full rationality:

> As economists, how should we respond to the seemingly self-destructive side of human behavior? We can deny it, and assume as an axiom of faith that people can be relied upon to do what's best for themselves. We can assume that families paying an average of $1,000 per year financing credit card debt are making a rational tradeoff of present and future utility, that liquidity constraints prevent investing in employer-matched 401k plans, that employees prefer investing in their own company's stock instead of a diversified portfolio . . . that people are obese because they have calculated that the

> pleasures from the extra food, or the pain of the foregone exercise, is sufficient to compensate for the negative consequences of obesity.
>
> *(Loewenstein & Haisley, 2008: 213)*

According to Thaler and other behavioral economists, economics was particularly suited for solving the violations of full rationality because it possessed the knowledge of how to "steer human behavior in more beneficial directions while minimizing coercion, maximizing individual autonomy, and maximizing autonomy to the greatest extent possible" (Loewenstein & Haisley, 2008: 215). The role of the economist in this regard could be seen as analogous to the psychoanalytical therapist. "Just as the therapist endeavors to correct for cognitive and emotional disturbances that detract from the well-being of the patient, such as anxiety, depression, or psychosis, the economist/therapist endeavors to counteract cognitive and emotional barriers to the pursuit of genuine self-interest" (Loewenstein & Haisley, 2008: 216).

Thaler attempted to solve mankind's limited rationality problem by using phenomena similar to those that formed the basis for behavioral economics to begin with. The most important phenomenon in this regard was what was most commonly known in behavioral economics as framing. One of the central findings of Kahneman and Tversky's behavioral decision research and behavioral economics was that people are susceptible to the way in which a choice is presented to them. Depending on the "reference point," in Kahneman and Tversky's terms, or "frame," the term Thaler favored for behavioral economics, people change their preferences. The example taken from Thaler and Sunstein (2003) is of the cafeteria manager who can either place the desserts before the fruits or vice versa. If she frames this decision as fruits-before-desserts, then the fruit will be chosen more often. Thus, framing is used to influence people's behavior without affecting their freedom to choose in any significant way. Changing the default option from not-participating to participating in pension saving schemes is another often-quoted example.

Thus, when behavioral economics expanded, behavioral economists were both faithful to the Kahneman and Tversky legacy, while at the same time they sought to broaden its scope. Problematic in this regard were the labels of normative and descriptive, which were considered confusing in an economic context that already had created its own understanding of these concepts (e.g. Friedman, 1953). As a consequence, behavioral economists in the 1990s and 2000s reinterpreted the normative–descriptive distinction in terms of rationality. Thaler was well aware of the fact that the reinterpretation of economics in terms of normative versus descriptive raised the question concerning the definition of the descriptive theory when the normative theory is about rational behavior. However, Thaler was not very specific, or at least he did not offer a conclusive answer. Thaler referred to behavior that deviates from the normative solution on a number of occasions as "irrational" or "non-rational." Furthermore, he noted that he "would not want to call such choices rational" (Thaler, 2000: 138). On other occasions Thaler referred to the normative–descriptive distinction as rational versus emotional (see e.g. Shefrin & Thaler, 1988: 611).

But the main interpretation Thaler used in the 1980s and 1990s was the term "quasi-rationality," most prominently as the title of a collection of articles, *Quasi-Rational Economics* (1991). Quasi-rationality suggests a category of behavior somewhere in between the full rationality of the normative decision and irrational behavior. Regularly used in the 1980s and 1990s, quasi-rationality is perhaps best understood as the failed attempt of people to be rational, which is exemplified by the one suggested definition of the term that Thaler provided: "quasi-rational, meaning trying hard but subject to systematic error" (Thaler, 2000: 136). On another occasion it was characterized as "less than fully rational" (Thaler, 1991: xviii).

From the early 2000s onwards, the term increasingly favored by behavioral economists was "bounded rationality." The distinction that was made was that between the fully rational decision and the decision actually made that was deemed boundedly rational when deviating from the rational decision. Full rationality in behavioral economics was defined as follows:

> The standard approach in economics assumes "full rationality." While disagreement exists as to what exactly full rationality encompasses, most economists would agree on the following basic components. First people have well-defined preferences (or goals) and make decisions to maximize those preferences. Second, those preferences accurately reflect (to the best of the person's knowledge) the true costs and benefits of the available options. Third, in situations that involve uncertainty, people have well-formed beliefs about how uncertainty will resolve itself, and when new information becomes available, they update their beliefs using Bayes's law—the presumed ability to update probabilistic assessments in light of new information.
>
> *(Camerer et al., 2003: 1214–15)*

The most influential publication within this program of libertarian paternalism, has been Thaler and Sunstein's *Nudge* (2008). Nudge introduced the libertarian paternalism of behavioral economics to the wider public, and inspired policy makers from Democrat Barack Obama in the United States, to Conservative David Cameron in the United Kingdom, to a range of other social-democrats and social liberals elsewhere. In all this, the core idea remained: individuals may systematically and predictably deviate from the norms of economics—and scientific theories more generally—and that it is economists' and policy makers' job to ensure individuals act more rationally on their preferences.

Conclusion

The most important influence on Richard Thaler's thinking as an economist have been psychologists Kahneman and Tversky, who suggested that individuals may actually deviate predictably and systematically from economic theory, and who suggested economists might be more concerned with finding ways to help behave more in accordance with this normative economic theory. However, the firm belief that economics sets out how people should make their decisions predates Thaler acquaintance with the psychologists, and is visible from his earliest PhD papers onwards.

In fact, one could argue that Thaler's economic world view has been remarkably constant over the course of his career of now almost forty years. Economic theory tells us how we should behave in the economy, and economists should be more concerned with finding out if and when people behave along those lines. If not, then economists should devise ways to help individuals do so. From that perspective, the developments and nuances described above are refinements of an established point of view first of all.

Notes

1 As I have set out elsewhere, the term "behavioral economics" was first coined in 1943 by Clark Hull and has since then been employed by various (groups of) scientists in partly related, but also diverging ways (Heukelom, 2014,; Senn, 1966; Pooley, forthcoming, see also Hosseini, this volume). For instance, also the Society for the Advancement of Behavioral Economics (SABE) was founded in 1984.

2 The anomalies of the first series have been collected in *The Winner's Curse* (1992).

Bibliography

Angner, E. & Loewenstein, G. (2012). Behavioral Economics. Handbook of the Philosophy of Science, Volume 13, Philosophy of Economics. U. Maki. Amsterdam, Elsevier, 641–90.
Benartzi, S. & Thaler, R. H. (2001). Naive Diversification in Defined Contribution Savings Plans. American Economic Review, 91(1), 79–98.
Camerer, C., et al. (2003). Regulation for Conservatives: Behavioral Economics and the Case for "Asymmetric Paternalism." University of Pennsylvania Law Review, 151, 1211–54.
De Bondt, W. F. M. & Thaler, R. (1985). Does the Stock Market Overreact? Journal of Finance, 40(3), 793–805.
Friedman, M. (1953). The Methodology of Positive Economics. Essays in Positive Economics. Chicago, Chicago University Press, 3–43.
Heukelom, F. (2012). A Sense of Mission: The Alfred P. Sloan and Russell Sage Foundations' Behavioral Economics Program, 1984–1992. Science in Context, 25(2), 263–86.
Heukelom, F. (2014). Behavioral Economics: A History. Cambridge, Cambridge University Press.
Kahneman, D., et al. (1990). Experimental Tests of the Endowment Effect and the Coase Theorem. Journal of Political Economy, 98(6), 1325–48.
Kahneman, D., et al. (1991). Anomalies: The Endowment Effect, Loss Aversion, and Status Quo Bias. Journal of Economic Perspectives, 5(1), 193–206.
Kahneman, D. & Tversky, A. (1972). Subjective Probability: A Judgment of Representativeness. Cognitive Psychology, 3, 430–54.
Kahneman, D. &. Tversky, A. (1979). Prospect Theory: An Analysis of Decision under Risk. Econometrica, 47, 263–92.
Loewenstein, G. & Elster, J. Eds. (1992). Choice over Time. New York, Russell Sage Foundation.
Loewenstein, G. & Haisley, E. (2008). The Economist as Therapist: Methodological Ramifications of "Light" Paternalism. Perspectives on the Future of Economics: Positive and Normative Foundations. A. Caplin and A. Schotter. Oxford, Oxford University Press, 210–45.
Loewenstein, G. & Thaler, R. (1989). Anomalies: Intertemporal Choice. Journal of Economic Perspectives, 3, 181–93.
Mayers, D. & Thaler, R. H. (1979). Sticky Wages and Implicit Contracts: A Transactional Approach. Economic Inquiry, 17(4), 559–74.
Pooley, J. (forthcoming). A "Not Particularly Felicitous" Phrase: A History of the "Behavioral Sciences" Label.
Rosen, S. & Thaler, R. H. (1975). The Value of Saving a Life: Evidence from the Labor Market. Household Production and Consumption. N. Terleckyj, National Bureau of Economic Research, 265–98.
Samson, A. (2014). The Behavioral Economics Guide 2014 (with a foreword by G. Loewenstein and R. Sutherland). Retrieved from www.behavioraleconomics.com.
Senn, P. R. (1966). What is "Behavioral Science?" Notes Toward a History. Journal of the History of the Behavioral Sciences, 2(2), 107–22.
Shefrin, H. M. & Thaler, R. H. (1981). An Economic Theory of Self-Control. Journal of Political Economy, 89(2), 392–406.
Shefrin, H. M. & Thaler, R. H. (1988). The Behavioral Life-Cycle Hypothesis. Economic Inquiry, 26(4), 609–43.
Thaler, R. (1974). The Value of Saving a Life: A Market Estimate. Business Administration. Rochester, University of Rochester. PhD.
Thaler, R. (1985). Mental Accounting and Consumer Choice. Marketing Science, 4(3), 199–214.
Thaler, R. (1987). The Psychology of Choice and the Assumptions of Economics. Laboratory Experiments in Economics: Six Points of View. A. Roth. Cambridge, Cambridge University Press: 99–130.
Thaler, R., Ed. (1992). The Winner's Curse: Paradoxes and Anomalies of Economic Life. New York, Free Press.
Thaler, R., Ed. (1993). Advances in Behavioral Finance. New York, Russell Sage Foundation.
Thaler, R. H. (1977). An Econometric Analysis of Property Crime: Interaction between Police and Criminals. Journal of Public Economics, 8(1), 37–51.
Thaler, R. H. (1979). Discounting with Fiscal Constraints: Why Discounting is Always Right. Defense Management Journal, 2.
Thaler, R. H. (1980). Toward a Positive Theory of Consumer Choice. Journal of Economic Behavior and Organization, 1, 39–60.

Thaler, R. H. (1991). Quasi Rational Economics. New York, Russell Sage Foundation.
Thaler, R. H. (1992). How to Get Real People to Save. Personal Savings, Consumption, and Tax Policy. M. Kosters. Washington, DC, American Enterprise Institute.
Thaler, R. H. (1994). Psychology and Savings Policies. American Economic Review, 84(2), 186–92.
Thaler, R. H. (2000). From Homo Economicus to Homo Sapiens. Journal of Economic Perspectives, 14(1), 133–41.
Thaler, R. H. (2015). Misbehaving: The Making of Behavioural Economics. London, Penguin.
Thaler, R. H. & Sunstein, C. R. (2003). Libertarian Paternalism. American Economic Review, 93(2), 175–9.
Thaler, R. H. & Sunstein, C. R. (2008). Nudge, Improving Decisions about Health, Wealth, and Happiness. New Haven, Yale University Press.
Tversky, A. & Kahneman, D. (1974). Judgment under Uncertainty: Heuristics and Biases. Science, 185, 1124–31.
Tversky, T. & Kahneman, D. (1981). The Framing of Decisions and the Psychology of Choice. Science, 211, 453–8.

9

DANIEL KAHNEMAN AND THE BEHAVIORAL ECONOMICS OF COGNITIVE MISTAKES

Floris Heukelom

Introduction

Daniel Kahneman (b.1934) is one half of the Kahneman–Tversky dyad that rose to prominence in the 1970s through their work on heuristics, biases, and prospect theory. Subsequently, Kahneman, together with Richard Thaler (Chapter 8 this volume) and Eric Wanner in particular, initiated a new program on the border of economics and psychology, for which they quickly appropriated the label of behavioral economics. Based on these contributions, Kahneman received the Nobel Prize in economics in 2002. In this chapter I will first provide an overview of Kahneman's work, based on Heukelom (2014). Thereafter, I will briefly situate Kahneman's work in the history of the mind–body distinction, show how Kahneman's work is one example of the methodological problem that everything is evolution, and set out why Kahneman's work is best seen as an illustration of postwar American pragmatic liberalism.

The chronology of Kahneman's contributions

Kahneman obtained a BA from Hebrew University in 1956 while working as a psychologist in the Israeli army. In 1958 he moved to San Francisco and obtained a PhD from the University of California at Berkeley in 1961 under the supervision of Susan Ervin (b. 1927). After completing his PhD, Kahneman returned to the Psychology Department at Hebrew University where he would remain until 1978. In the meantime, however, he was among others a lecturer in the graduate program of the University of Michigan in 1968/9. While teaching at Michigan Kahneman invited his younger colleague Amos Tversky (1937–96) to lecture a class on recent developments in judgment and decision making (Kahneman, 2002).

Based on Kahneman's recollections in his autobiography and the one publication that emerged from it, his early work for the Israeli army in the early 1950s and at the Hebrew University is best characterized as correlational psychology (Kahneman and Ghiselli, 1962; Kahneman, 2002; Danziger, 1990, 1997; Gigerenzer, 1987a, 1987b). Correlational psychology builds theories on the basis of correlations in statistical data; for example, between IQ and the degree of education. Using methods developed by the British army in World War Two, the aim of Kahneman's early research was to develop reliable predictions about the future performance of people on the basis of character traits, be it in the army or in different kinds of jobs. For instance, to find out at an early stage which new recruits in the army would eventually be successful leaders on the future battlefield, tests were designed to evaluate the differences between recruits with respect to a few behavioral and personal characteristics that were thought to relate to leadership capacities.

It is not difficult to see that in this kind of research the ability of the researcher to predict the future performance of the subjects investigated is an important, and perhaps the only way to measure success. A classification of new recruits in the army along different dimensions might be an interesting exercise, but if it does not predict better than chance, then it is of no use. In his autobiography (Kahneman, 2002) Kahneman recalls how frustrating it was when time and again he was confronted with the fact that his predictions were anything but reliable. Extensive questionnaires and tests were set up, but in the end it turned out that the intuitive guesses of the staff members who conducted the tests and collected the questionnaires proved better than the scientific predictions.

Dissatisfied with the results of this research and eager to develop his research skills, Kahneman switched to the experimental psychology of vision, resulting in some twenty-five articles over a period of ten years, including two publications in *Science*, and a whole range more in prominent experimental psychology journals such as the *Journal of Experimental Psychology*. There is no one particular theme or article that stands out during the decade from 1961–71. Kahneman's overarching view of the human mind emerges when the different themes and articles are considered next to each other.

In 1962–3, Kahneman set up a vision lab at the Department of Psychology of Hebrew University (Kahneman, 2002: 6). Many of the articles he published in the following years were derived from the experimental results of this lab. In this research, Kahneman investigated the relationship between the "energy" of different stimuli and visual perception capacities. "Energy" was employed as a general concept to define the strength of a stimulus; the brighter, the more illuminated, the more contrasted, the longer and so forth the stimulus was, the more energy it had. Visual perception was measured in terms of the reaction times of the subjects. In the typical experiment, the subject had to decide as quickly as possible whether the opening of a so-called Landolt C was directed up-, down-, left-, or right-wards.[1] The conditions in terms of brightness, contrast, and so on in this setting could be varied in numerous ways. The visual task could also be combined with other cognitive tasks. Kahneman's textbook on the psychology of vision and attention, *Attention and Effort* (1973), was still used in the early twenty-first century as standard reference on the subject (Dawes—interview, 2008).

Examples of this research include Kahneman (1965a), "Control of Spurious Association and the Reliability of the Controlled Variable" and Kahneman's (1966), "Time-Intensity Reciprocity in Acuity as a Function of Luminance and Figure–Ground Contrast." In Kahneman and Norman (1964), the relation between the minimal amount of time subjects need to identify a visual stimulus (labeled the "critical duration" t_c) and the energy in terms of brightness and duration of the stimulus was investigated. It was shown that stimuli of equal energy do not necessarily produce the same critical duration and that a given visual stimulus does not trigger one but multiple sensory processes. The second conclusion particularly opposed the general view held in the psychophysical community that one stimulus triggers only one sensory process.

In the psychophysical paradigm Kahneman was working in, visual perception was seen as one of many cognitive tasks. Other cognitive tasks included conversation, or more generally, speech, learning, and calculation. How different cognitive tasks influence one another was investigated in Kahneman and Beatty (1966, 1967), Kahneman et al. (1967, 1968), and Kahneman, Peavler and Onuska (1968). The explicit emphasis in these articles was on how the combination of different cognitive tasks could lead to "errors of judgment." In Kahneman et al. (1967), for instance, it was shown that the capacity to visually perceive substantially decreases when subjects were engaged in other mental tasks such as speech or calculation. The "error of judgment" in these cases is very real, as it explains for instance why car drivers may miss a stop sign when engaged in conversation. It again illustrates Kahneman's focus on the psychology of mistakes.

Thus, in Kahneman's vision research an emphasis was placed on the question under which circumstances the human mind makes cognitive errors. Kahneman showed that there is a trade-off between different cognitive tasks in perception capacities, and that as a result people may sometimes "fail" to perceive the stimulus and make an error in judgment. Furthermore, the research conducted by Kahneman in the period between 1961 and 1971 was in line with the behaviorist drive to eliminate all introspection from psychology started in the interwar period (Danziger, 1997). In Kahneman's experiments self-reports were not necessary to establish how the cognitive system operates. The behavior of the cognitive system could be inferred from observed behavior and physical responses which cannot be controlled, such as pupil dilation and restriction. The human mind was considered to not permit introspective access, while its functioning could be inferred from the uncontrollable and unconscious responses made by the individual subjects.

Both elements are important in gaining an understanding of Kahneman's psychology and his subsequent influence on Thaler and other economists. The recurring theme of the cognitive errors shows that in Kahneman's view psychology was about discovering how people deviate from a norm behavior. This aspect of experimental psychology dates back to the beginning of experimental psychology in nineteenth century Germany. But in nineteenth century German and interwar American experimental psychology, this framework was adopted for the purpose of discovering what the true value was. The experimental psychologists wanted to know the true value of, for instance, the smallest amount of difference in weight people could perceive, and for this purpose devised a framework, which in spite of all the individual errors, could establish the true value (Fechner, 1860; Heidelberger, 2004; Boring, 1929). Thurstone, for instance, wanted to measure the attitude towards religion of a group of people, and for this purpose he constructed a method that would elicit the attitude from a series of observations in which each individually deviated from the true value (Thurstone and Chave, 1929). Thus, experimental psychology was explicitly modeled after experimental practice in physics, where the physicist tries to establish the true value of the temperature of boiling water by conducting a series of measurements in which each measurement individually deviates from the true value and from each other.

Kahneman employed the experimental psychological framework, but applied it differently. In Kahneman's work the true value was known. The true value was an accurate prediction of a recruit's future leadership capacities, or the true value was not running through a traffic light when driving a car. The question Kahneman then raised was how, when, and why the cognitive machinery fails to act according to the true value. Kahneman used an experimental psychological framework, but applied it with the opposite purpose. He did not want to find out what the true value was, but how people deviate from the true value. In Kahneman's research, the true value was always clear and determined by the experimenter. Kahneman knew how the cognitive machinery ideally responds, and investigated whether it actually does do so. In Kahneman's understanding, the scientist thus completely determined in each experimental situation what the good, optimal, or rational behavior should be. This was in line with the scientific desire to eliminate all introspection because it assumed that the experimental subject cannot judge whether it is giving the correct response or not. In Kahneman's experiments the experimenter determined how the subject should behave and determined how it did behave. All authority for judging behavior was placed in the hands of the scientist.

Because Kahneman has never provided an extensive theoretical exposition of the assumption that human beings often make cognitive errors, one could easily dismiss it as merely a nice way of illustrating theories which are perhaps not too exciting. But that would be a mistake. The key to understanding Kahneman's psychology lies in his conviction that human beings often make cognitive errors. Kahneman and his colleagues really believed that through their extensive studies they could accurately predict, or at least predict better than by mere chance, the future performance of different candidates for a job. The fact that they could not was for the young Kahneman a true cognitive illusion that he needed to correct for himself (Kahneman, 2002).

Another illustrative example recalled by Kahneman in his autobiography was the moment a flight instructor disagreed with the psychologists' theory that praise is more effective in developing skills than punishment. The flight instructor reasoned that although he praised the good performance of his recruits, the next time the performance would almost always be worse. Similarly, he would always punish recruits who had done a poor job, and this would almost always improve performance the next time. To Kahneman this was a clear cognitive illusion. A good performance is statistically more likely to be followed by a worse performance than by an equally good or even better performance, and vice versa. Also the truck or car driver described above who was engaged in a conversation and thus did not see a traffic light that he or she would otherwise not miss, really did make an error. His or her cognitive apparatus was tuned to noticing traffic lights, but it failed to do so.

To Kahneman it was and is a given fact of life that human beings often make cognitive errors. However, science could help in two ways. First, scientists could set out what the correct way of behaving is for each situation. For the truck driver, it is obvious what the correct behavior is, but for the flight instructor it may not be intuitively clear what the correct way of reasoning is. Scientists can, therefore, help to establish the correct way of reasoning. Second, scientists, and in particular psychologists, could help by investigating when, how and in what way human beings make cognitive errors and thus provide a basis for designing tools or education to help human beings correct these cognitive errors.

In 1969 Kahneman and Tversky started a collaboration that would result in 21 papers and two co-edited books, including one published together with Slovic. They continued to co-operate on different projects until Tversky's death in 1996, but the most productive and creative period was from 1969 to 1979, including the widely cited 1974 *Science* and 1979 *Econometrica* articles.[2] The cooperation was initiated by Kahneman, who was looking for new ways to experimentally test his intuition that an individual's cognitive apparatus systematically fails, and who tried to find a theory that might account for these cognitive errors.

Kahneman and Tversky's joint work became a mix of their earlier individual research. Tversky's work on decision theory, with its distinction between the normative and descriptive realm, became coupled with Kahneman's psychology of mistakes. For their first article, Tversky posed a set of questions to 84 participants who attended the 1969 meetings of the American Psychological Association and the Mathematical Psychology Group that meant to capture Kahneman's personal experience of incorrect research planning and unsuccessful replications. "Suppose," Kahneman and Tversky asked, "you have run an experiment on 20 Ss [subjects], and have obtained a significant result which confirms your theory ($z = 2.23$, $p < .05$, two-tailed). You now have cause to run an additional group of 10 Ss. What do you think the probability is that the results will be significant, by a one-tailed test, separately for this group?" (Kahneman and Tversky, 1972: 433). According to Kahneman and Tversky, the answer depends on the exact interpretation of the information provided. However, it should be below but close to 0.5, they argued. Nine out of the 84 participants gave answers between 0.4 and 0.6, which Kahneman and Tversky interpreted as "reasonable." The other 75, however, gave answers that exceeded 0.6. The median response of all participants was as high as 0.85. Thus, even those professionals who were trained and who were explicitly asked to give the normatively correct answer failed to calculate it correctly. Kahneman and Tversky felt justified in inferring the strong and bold thesis "that people have strong intuitions about random sampling; that these intuitions are wrong in fundamental respects; that these intuitions are shared by naïve subjects and by trained scientists; and that they are applied with unfortunate consequences in the course of scientific inquiry" (Tversky and Kahneman, 1971: 105).

To the retrospective outsider, the question seems much too detailed for conference participants asked to fill out a questionnaire in between conference sessions, even if they are professors of psychology. But while it is undoubtedly true that Kahneman and Tversky formulated the question such that the desired result would be likely to appear, the formulation of the question is also a testimony to the perceived superiority of scientific language, and science in general. To Kahneman and Tversky, as to many of their contemporaries, human behavior had to be measured and judged against the yardstick of science. Therefore, the scientific wording could not be bent too far in the direction of imperfect human understanding. However, where many of their contemporaries took similar experimental falsifications of individuals' capacity to reason along scientific lines as proof that something had to be wrong with the science (e.g. Ellsberg, 1961; Allais and Hagen, 1979; Baumol, 1951, 1958; Simon, 1955, 1959; Slovic and Lichtenstein, 1971), Kahneman and Tversky took it as evidence of a cognitive failure of the individuals tested. They found it appalling and fundamentally disturbing to see that even trained professionals failed to behave according to the dictates of normative theory.

Taking an idea from the learning theory of Estes (1964), Kahneman and Tversky hypothesized that individuals have the tendency to suppose that a sample from a population must represent the population in its general characteristics. In other words, they implicitly accounted for their results by supposing that the biological make-up of human beings makes individuals ignore the possibility that a sample of a population may not be an accurate representation of that population. Kahneman and Tversky hypothesized that this provides individuals with the wrong intuition and that as a result they fail to give the right answer. However, Kahneman and Tversky took the research of Estes (1964) a step further by concluding that if individuals systematically consider a sample to be representative of its population, then it could be thought of as a "heuristic." They advanced the idea the human mind uses this heuristic to base decisions on.

The reason why the majority of scientists and lay persons systematically deviated from the norm-answer that was given in Tversky and Kahneman, "Belief in the Law of Small Numbers" (1971), and further developed in Kahneman and Tversky, "Subjective Probability: A Judgment of Representativeness" (1972), was that human beings, in general, do not base their decisions on the normative laws of, in this case, probability theory and statistics, but instead use a "representative heuristic." Kahneman and Tversky described the representative heuristic as the phenomenon that "[t]he subjective probability of an event, or a sample, is determined by the degree to which it: (i) is similar in essential characteristics to its parent population; and (ii) reflects the salient features of the process by which it is generated" (Kahneman and Tversky, 1972: 430). In the example the individuals interrogated supposed the draw to be a good representation of the population the experiment was meant to say something about, and focused on the salient feature of the test, namely that it confirmed the theory significantly. As a result of this representative heuristic, most of the professional psychologists estimated the probability requested to be much higher than it actually was (as said, the median estimate was 0.85).

Because human beings have much more faith in small samples than they should, Kahneman and Tversky half jokingly labeled this phenomenon the "belief in the law of small numbers," in reference to the law of large numbers. The analogy with faith and belief cast the issue in terms of subjective religion, prejudice and limited knowledge versus objective, value-free science; it characterized the observation in terms of the incapable individual versus the rational, enlightened scientist. In other words, it expressed Kahneman and Tversky's view that an individual's erroneous behavior is the result of false beliefs for which the individual—including even the professor of psychology—cannot really be blamed. The "deviations of subjective from objective probability seem reliable, systematic, and difficult to eliminate" (Kahneman and Tversky, 1972: 431), and "[t]he true believer in the law of small numbers commits his multitude of sins against the logic of statistical inference in good faith. The representation hypothesis describes a cognitive or perceptual bias, which operates regardless of motivational factors" (Tversky and Kahneman, 1971: 109). In Kahneman and Tversky's framework, science, and in particular mathematics, decision theory and economics, determined what were the normatively correct decisions in each decision situation. In this framework, normative was equated with rational and objective. The actual decision made by the individual was part of a "descriptive" or "subjective" realm, and could be either in accord or in disaccord with the normative or rational benchmark. If in disaccord, this implied the individual had made an "error," "mistake," or, in the language of behavioral economics from the early 1980s onwards, an "ir-," "non-," "not fully," or "boundedly rational" decision.

The alternative theory Kahneman and Tversky proposed was their heuristics and biases theory, first labeled as such in Tversky and Kahneman (1974), "Judgment under Uncertainty: Heuristics and Biases." In this theory, people do not use the normative theories of probability and logic to make decisions under uncertainty, but instead rely on a number of heuristics, heuristics that sometimes lead to systematic deviations. In the often quoted definition of the theory, heuristics and biases "shows that people rely on a limited number of heuristic principles which reduce the complex tasks of assessing probabilities and predicting values to simpler judgmental operations. In general, these heuristics are quite useful, but sometimes they lead to severe and systematic errors" (Tversky and Kahneman, 1974: 1124). Kahneman and Tversky emphasized the importance and functioning of a few heuristics, such as representativeness, availability, and anchoring. But by no means was the heuristics and biases theory meant to remain confined to these few heuristics. There was no limit to the number of heuristics that possibly could be discovered in humans' minds. The heuristics and biases program summed up the many violations of the normative models Kahneman and Tversky had found, and provided a small, non-exhaustive list of explanations that might account for these violations.

The term "heuristic" appeared for the first time in 1971 without any precursors in either Kahneman's or Tversky's earlier work, and from the beginning was used without introduction as a natural term for an intuitive response. In the 1950s to the 1970s Herbert Simon had used "heuristic" and similar terms in his uncompromising attack on the—what he understood to be—behavioral foundations of neoclassical economics, and the alternative he proposed in the form of human decision making based on heuristics (e.g. Simon, 1955, 1959, 1963, 1986). It is, therefore, tempting to conclude that Kahneman and Tversky's use of the term somehow derived from Simon. But that would be a mistake. As illustrated by Kahneman and Tversky's use of the term, "heuristic" "was just a word from the language" (Kahneman—interview, 2009). Simon used the term in a different way and is moreover not mentioned in Kahneman and Tversky's research of the early 1970s.

It is useful to briefly set out the difference between the two. In Simon's view, individuals use rules of thumb or heuristics to make decisions. An example of a heuristic could be to set an aspiration price for the house one wishes to sell, and to go with the first offer that exceeds the aspiration price. Or, alternatively, the heuristic could be to accept the best among the first n offers (e.g. Simon, 1955). To Simon, such a heuristic was meant to optimize the decision made given all the constraints the individual faced in terms of information, cognitive capacity, and time. If the heuristic yielded a satisfactory outcome it would be maintained, if not it would be adjusted. Importantly, to Simon the heuristic's function was not to approximate the global optimum given all the possibly relevant information and computing capacity, but to achieve a satisfactory outcome given the information and capacity that one had.

In Kahneman and Tversky's approach, by contrast, the function of heuristics was to simplify and reorganize the decision problem in such a way that it was manageable for a not very sophisticated decision maker. The heuristics' objective was to approximate the optimum given all relevant information and full knowledge of statistics, logic, and expected utility theory. The heuristics did not yield the decision, but reorganized the informational input in such a way that a decision making process was possible. In the birth order problem, for instance, individuals, as said, commonly believe a family of G B G B B G instead of B G B B B B to be more likely because it better represents the individual's image of a family of six children (representativeness) or because it has such a family more readily available (availability). In other words, the availability heuristic links the incoming information to already present information about six-children families so as to simplify the decision. In this case, however, that organization of the information leads to the wrong conclusion. And because the heuristic is part of the biological make-up of the individual, it will not change. If the question is given more thought, the individual may opt for both options to be equally likely, particularly if the individual has just taken a course in logic and statistics. That is to say, the individual may override its own intuition using its capacity to reason. But the individual's initial intuitive response will always be the first option to be more likely.

In 1979 Kahneman and Tversky published their now famous article on "Prospect Theory: An Analysis of Decision under Risk" in *Econometrica*. The article marked a shift in emphasis away from probabilistic decision problems to an investigation of people's capacity to behave according to the normative theory of expected utility theory. It was the first attempt to produce a more complete descriptive theory of human decision making under uncertainty. Prospect theory has often been presented as being different from heuristics and biases (e.g. Kahneman, 2002), and it is certainly true that prospect theory brought the different heuristics into one overarching framework. But the foundation still was the idea that human beings rely on a set of heuristics for their decision making and that the use of these heuristics sometimes leads to systematic deviations from the normatively correct decision. In this regard it is to be noted that it took Kahneman and Tversky some five years to get the article published in *Econometrica*, and that the last four of these five years were used to tweak what was for the most part a finished argument to fit an economic audience (Kahneman, 2002, interview, 2009).[3]

Kahneman and Tversky made the connection with their earlier work in the first few lines of the 1979 article, which set out the conception of expected utility theory as a normative theory that also makes descriptive claims:

> Expected utility theory has dominated the analysis of decision making under risk. It has been generally accepted as a normative model of rational choice, and widely applied as a descriptive model of economic behavior. Thus it is assumed that all reasonable people would wish to obey the axioms of the theory and that most people actually do, most of the time.
>
> *(Kahneman and Tversky, 1979: 263)*

In a clever way, these opening sentences alluded to both the psychological and the economic framework. To psychologists these sentences restated a well-known normative–descriptive framework and signaled a contribution to an established field of research. Positivist economists in the line of Friedman (1953), on the other hand, might have raised their eyebrows at the injunction of the "normative," but they would certainly have agreed that reasonable people wish to obey the axioms of expected utility theory and that they actually do so, or at least most of the time. Note, furthermore, that Kahneman and Tversky carefully avoided the term "rational," and used "reasonable" instead. Invoking the term "rational" might have suggested that this was an article in the line of critique of economics. The use of "rational" would certainly have induced some economists to think that these two psychologists had the same research program as Simon, who had won the Nobel Memorial Prize in economics the year before. From the start, prospect theory was carefully constructed so as to be able to broaden the scope to economists especially.

The content of prospect theory is well-known. As in heuristics and biases, Kahneman and Tversky based their argument on a series of hypothetical questions they had presented to experimental subjects, in this case psychology students at Hebrew University. The problems the subjects were presented with were decision problems, involving different material outcomes and different probabilities. Most of the questions were reformulations or variants of Allais' decision problems (Allais, 1953; Allais and Hagen, 1979). One example of Kahneman and Tversky's use of an Allais-type approach is in the question where subjects were asked to state which of the following lottery options they preferred.

A: (4,000, .80) or B: (3,000)

That is, they were asked whether they preferred 4,000 shekel with a probability of 0.8, or 3,000 shekel for certain.[4] Most of the subjects in this case chose B. This implied that they did not maximize the expected monetary outcome. However, opting for the choice B could be explained by assuming that the decision maker was risk averse. Subsequently, subjects were asked which of the following two lottery options they preferred.

C: (4,000, .20) or D: (3,000, .25)

In this case, most of the subjects chose C and, hence, maximized the expected monetary outcome. This was problematic in combination with the first choice as it implied that subjects were sometimes risk averse, but on other occasions maximized the expected monetary outcome and hence were not risk averse. Note that the second choice is equal to the first with probabilities divided by four. With these and similar examples, Kahneman and Tversky illustrated that despite its normative status, expected utility theory as a descriptive theory was invalidated. In specific circumstances, people systematically deviated from the norms of expected utility theory. A new descriptive, "alternative account of individual decision making under risk," was therefore required. The alternative account was christened "prospect theory" (Kahneman and Tversky, 1979: 274).[5]

According to prospect theory, a human decision maker first employs a number of heuristics to make a decision problem manageable. This process was called the editing phase. Complicated decisions are broken down into different simpler decisions, different decisions are lumped together into one big decision, a benchmark is set with which the decision is compared, and so on. The purpose of this editing phase was to make the decision manageable. After this, the decision was evaluated in what was referred to as the evaluation phase. The evaluation phase had the same structure as the maximization of expected utility, but instead of the objective values of the material pay-off and probability, it used the individual's subjective perception of the material pay-off and probability. The subjective perception of the material pay-off was referred to as value (denoted v) and the subjective perception of probability was referred to as decision weight (denoted π). In expected utility theory, a subject who is faced with a choice between outcome x that occurs with probability p and outcome y that occurs with probability q derives utility according to the following function.

$$U(x,p;y,q) = p \cdot u(x) + q \cdot u(y) \quad (1)$$

in which utility u is a subjective valuation of the outcome according to the axioms of von Neumann and Morgenstern (1944) and Savage (1954). In other words, it defines how an individual values an outcome given its preferences if it behaves according to the normative rules of rational decision making. Furthermore, in the expected utility theory of equation (1) the individual perceives the probabilities of the outcomes as what they objectively are. In prospect theory, by contrast, a subject that following the editing phase faces the exact same choice will value this choice according to this function:

$$V(x,p;y,q) = \pi(p)v(x) + \pi(q)v(y) \quad (2)$$

in which v is similar to u, but based on empirical observations in experiments rather than axiomatically defined utilities; constructed with respect to an individual reference point, rather than to an objectively defined benchmark; and with a risk-seeking character in the loss-domain. In addition, the probabilities of the outcomes are not perceived as what they actually (i.e. objectively) are, but are also subject to a perception bias of the individual.[6]

The use of heuristics and the framework of psychophysics allowed Kahneman and Tversky to construct a theory in which individuals try to make the best decision, and yet could often be observed as making decisions that systematically deviate from the normatively correct decision. Individuals do their best, but because human beings apply heuristics to reconstruct decision problems to manageable proportions, and because they have a specific perceptual system which distorts the stimulus, their reasoned decisions may deviate from the normatively correct solution. Kahneman and Tversky had to cut the link between the normative and the descriptive theory in order to maintain the normative theory, while at the same time allowing for the conclusion that people systematically and persistently deviate from the norm. Human beings, who in Savage and Edwards' accounts were capable of normatively correct reasoning (i.e. normal healthy adults) could no longer be expected to behave according to the normative rules.

Ultimately, prospect theory was based on the authority of science, even if also scientists' first intuitive response could be mistaken. Prospect theory took the axioms of decision theory as the norm for behavior, and developed the measurement framework so that the experimental observations would fit. Deviations from the axiomatic norms were understood as errors or mistakes, and they bore no implications for the norms. Because of the clear separation between the normative and the descriptive, it was now possible to construct a separate account of decision making in the descriptive domain, without implications for the normative theory. In prospect theory, human beings were understood as having a biased perception of the relevant input of probabilities and pay-offs, just as they had a biased perception of sensory inputs such as temperature and weight.

Evaluation

Approaching Kahneman's work less from a historical, and more from a philosophical perspective, it is easy to observe that the central idea in Kahneman's work is that human decision making is best understood as the combined outcome of two cognitive systems. Different names and slightly different categorizations have been advanced by Kahneman over the years, with the labels System 1 and System 2 emerging as the definitive terms in the early 2000s. System 1 is the fast, energy efficient and intuitive system human beings rely on for frequently returning decisions that can be made without serious deliberations. Examples would be what to take for breakfast, and whether or not to bring an umbrella when going out. As System 1 is fast and energy efficient, it has its obvious advantages. However, because it is intuitive and relies on heuristics, or rules of thumb, System 1 leads to sub-optimal outcomes when these intuitions do not fit the decision at hand particularly well. System 2, by contrast, is slow, requires substantially more effort and energy, but also is less likely to produce sub-optimal outcomes. System 2 is not required for frequently returning decisions, such as what to take for breakfast, but is useful for infrequent, important, or especially difficult questions. Examples include buying a house, taking an exam, or inventing a driverless car.

So which part of the brain is System 1 and which is System 2? The behavioral economic subfield of neuroeconomics has attempted to answer this question, locating System 1 principally in the pre-frontal cortex, and System 2 everywhere else (e.g. Camerer et al., 2005; Kable, 2011). That sounds a lot like phrenology, discarded as scientifically meaningless by neuroscientists in the early twentieth century. But while not denouncing neuroeconomics directly, Kahneman has emphasized that the System 1 versus System 2 dichotomy is as much a description of the human decision making machinery, as it is a metaphor that should be judged by how successful it is when helping people to discuss their decision making around the proverbial water cooler in their offices. It is as much a theory as it is a tool (Kahneman, 2011). In addition, System 1 versus System 2 stands in a scientific tradition that goes back to the origins of Western thinking, the mind–body dichotomy.

The mind–body distinction that permeates (the history of) Western thinking, is usually first of all connected to René Descartes, but in various versions goes back to the ancient Greeks (e.g. Bennet and Hacker, 2003). Descartes posited that what distinguishes the mind from the body is its ability to think, to reason. The body is the province of emotions and intuitions, and is not capable of reason. As we humans are the only beings that possess a mind, reasoning is also what distinguishes us from the animal kingdom. Moreover, sometimes the body and its emotions and intuitions produce responses the mind judges inappropriate, not useful, or in some other sense not optimal given the situation at hand. In such cases, the mind overrides the impulsive response of the body. And as it is only human beings who possess a mind, it is also only human beings who are capable of overriding the body's intuitive, emotional response.

Western culture is full of parables and examples illustrating the eternal struggle between mind and body. Odysseus knew his body would succumb to the songs of the sirens, and that his mind would not be strong enough to prevent his body from steering the ship towards them, thus inevitably killing him. Yet he wanted to hear the sirens sing. He thus let himself be tied to the ship's mast before entering the sirens' waters. In other words, Odysseus' mind recognized in advance something very desirable to his body would come up, and foresaw the impossibility of using his mind to control his passionate body at the moment it most needed to. Yet, Odysseus neither wanted to forgo the bodily pleasure of the singing sirens, and so devised a solution to have both: hear the sirens without getting killed. The solutions Kahneman offers for the failures of System 1 stand in the line of this Odyssean element in Western culture. System 2 recognizes that something desirable to System 1 is coming up, for instance a loan check that could all be spent on clothing instead of also on paying down the mortgage and saving for retirement. In addition, System 2 realizes that when the moment is there it will be unable to control System 1, and hence devises a scheme or solution. For instance, asking the employer to deposit part of the check in a pension saving scheme prior to transferring the money (e.g. Thaler and Benartzi, 2004). This scheme partly gives System 1 what it wants, but controls the excess that imperils the individual.

Over the past twenty years, a range of authors have amended and criticized Descartes' dichotomy and the mind–body tradition in which it stands. Perhaps the most fundamental critique has arisen through the work of Antonio Damasio, Ap Dijksterhuis and others (e.g. Bennet and Hacker, 2003; Damasio, 2003; Dijksterhuis, 2006). These neurologists, psychologists, and philosophers offer two main criticisms of the Cartesian mind–body dichotomy. First of all, they argue that the distinction between mind and body is an illusion. Rather, the human brain, eyes, ears, stomach and feet are all part of one integral system which needs to be understood as such to effectively explain its output: human behavior. Second, these scientists reject the notion of a faculty of reason that is superior to emotions and intuitions. Instead, they argue that emotions and intuitions may be a different way of arriving at a decision, but that it often constitutes an effective, efficient, and perhaps even a superior way of arriving at a decision.

Although of course very well aware of these developments in neuroscience and psychology, Kahneman's work nevertheless clearly stands in a tradition of the Cartesian mind–body dichotomy. To Kahneman, emotions and intuitions may often be efficient ways of responding to everyday and well known tasks, when it becomes more difficult or the situation more unusual, support of the mind's reason, or System 2 is needed. In such cases, the mind's reason has to overrule the body's emotions and intuitions, as in the case of Odysseus.

Kahneman has connected this centuries-old dichotomy approach with insights from evolution theory. The basic principle of (Darwinian) evolution is simple enough. Given an environment with scarce resources, and a population of species in this environment the individuals of which slightly differ from each other due to random genetic variation, those individuals best adapted to random changes in the environment will produce the most offspring, and their genes will survive. Many amendments and extensions of this basic argument have been advanced, of course, but that is the basic principle (Hall and Hallgrimson, 2008).

As a thought experiment, this mechanism could be reversed. All plants and animals are the offspring of plants and animals which had an advantage over their peers at some point in the past. And so, if you have a plausible idea of the environment in the past for which the plant's shiny orange flowers, the animal's long neck, or the bird's particularly shaped beak produced a competitive advantage, you have explained why the plant or animal is thus shaped.

The same exercise could be conducted with the limits to the human cognitive machinery. Why does merely knowing a product brand increase the likelihood of selling its products? Because, throughout evolutionary history if you had encountered something several times and were still alive, the object encountered was probably good and safe (Dworschak and Grolle, 2012). Why do people often display herding behavior, and start selling shares only when all others are also selling shares? Because during the long time our ancestors spent in the dangerous surroundings of forests and savannas, it was generally very wise to first join your group in running away before carefully examining why they were running away.

The challenge arises when scientists' creative minds are combined with the little knowledge we have of past environments. For every (alleged) characteristic of every plant and animal a plausible past environment and evolutionary explanation is quickly conceived. The same holds for human beings. If you find that people are bad at statistics, because their intuitive, System 1 response is to answer based on which information is presented first (known as anchoring), our creative minds have little difficulty suggesting a plausible environment in which members of a hunter-gatherer society using the anchoring heuristics had an evolutionary advantage.

That would not be so bad, good even perhaps, if it were possible to test these evolutionary explanations. However, as it is neither possible to travel back in time to test these hypotheses, nor feasible to put some human beings in a pre-determined environment and see how they evolve over a few hundred thousand years, Kahneman's research and the research community to which it has given rise can only offer many partial explanations that it cannot decidedly validate or falsify.

Finally, Kahneman's research, and the behavioral economics to which it gave rise in particular, are best understood within the context of pragmatic liberalism in the United States—despite the fact that Kahneman was born in France, raised in Israel and only came to the United States in his early twenties. As will be well known, American society and science are strongly rooted in the seventeenth and eighteenth centuries' liberal ideals of the Enlightenment (Brands, 2010; Johnson, 1997). The Enlightenment sought to free individuals of the shackles of involuntary labor, autocratic leaders, religion, and morals.[7] A second dominant conviction in American society has been a naturalistic notion of the market. When freed to pursue their own interests, individuals will start to offer and buy products, and create the accompanying institutions they deem necessary to facilitate this economy. The market is a phenomenon that naturally emerges from a free, and liberated society. The institutions that will emerge include formal institutions such as courts and controls of quality, but also more informal institutions that facilitate the economic process (Acemoglu and Robinson, 2012; Friedman, 2005; McCloskey, 2006). And while for instance Continental European liberals changed to a more constructionist understanding of the market around the middle of the twentieth century (e.g. Nicholls, 1994; Hesse, 2010; Burgin, 2012), the dominant conception of the market in the United States has remained a naturalistic one up to the present.

That being said, something started to change in the late nineteenth century nevertheless (e.g. Pettit, 2013; Yarrow, 2010). Following a rapid economic development, including more fully developed industries and markets, the economically and politically freed Americans among others ran into the question what to do when a clever individual or company takes advantage of less well-informed consumers. Who takes precedence in the economy of liberated individuals, the free market or the free consumer?

From this perspective, the rise of American psychology in the late-nineteenth and early-twentieth century's, is best understood as an attempt to strengthen the individual in its dealings with the market (e.g. Capshew, 1999). On the one hand, this took the form of showing individuals how they might be deceived by malevolent market parties—and thus how to strengthen themselves against this element of the modern economy (e.g. Pettit, 2013). On the other hand, it took the form of testing and classifying individuals so as to improve their distribution across the different positions to be fulfilled in society (e.g. Mills, 1998). Both elements were captured under the label of mental, and later social or human engineering (Jordan, 1994; Lemov, 2005). In the words of James McKeen Cattel (1860–1944), the first professor of psychology in the United States at the University of Pennsylvania, the aim of psychology was "to describe, to understand, and to control human conduct" (Cattel, 1930: 31). The Second World War provided a strong catalyst to this engineering aspect of American society, with science and engineering stepping forth as primary components in winning the war and in organizing society. These developments also drew in psychology, boosting the discipline with a wealth of new funds, career opportunities, and areas of psychological research and application, while drawing the different branches of psychology together in one discipline of human engineering (Capshew, 1999; Cordeschi, 2002; Mindell, 2002).

Particularly explicit was Robert Yerkes (1876–1956), who stepped into the limelight during the war as the initiator and organizer of the Intersociety Constitutional Convention, which sought to reorganize the psychology profession on behalf of the American Psychological Association (APA) and a few other major associations. A gap existed, Yerkes argued, "between the human needs which are partially met by the physician and those which the clergyman or priest is expected to satisfy" (Yerkes, 1941: 535). Psychology, as the science concerned with the needs and requirements of the normal individual (as compared to the abnormal or severely maladjusted individual who required therapy or medial attention) "must stand as a basic science for such universally desirable expert services as the guidance and safeguarding of an individual's growth and development, education and occupational choice, social adjustments, achievement and maintenance of balance, poise, and effectiveness, contentment, happiness, and usefulness" (Yerkes, 1941: 536).

In *How Reason Almost Lost its Mind* (2013), Erickson et al. show how this American program of human engineering was reformulated in terms of rationality during the early postwar period. The objective of improving humans' capacity to deal with the complexities of the economy and modern life in general, was reformulated as the idea that while normal, healthy adults in general can be understood to be rational beings, they sometimes fail to make the rational decision due to an overload of information, or misconstrued organizational structures. Otherwise, however, the program by and large remained the same: it was the psychologist's job to figure out when the individual is prone to making mistakes, and how to correct these mistakes.

During the 1970s, the emphasis of this program shifted somewhat (Heukelom, 2014; Erickson et al., 2013). Instead of assuming that normal, healthy adults in general are pretty rational and only occasionally run into difficulties when the job becomes too demanding, a new generation of behavioral psychologists, including first and foremost Kahneman and Tversky, began to emphasize that perhaps it is rather the reverse: even normal, healthy adults often behave in ways that deviate systematically and predictably from the rational norm, they argued (e.g. Tversky and Kahneman, 1974). Moreover, individuals are much more difficult to correct into making the more rational decision than thought thus far. It is to be emphasized, however, that from the perspective of engineering psychology, this was a shift in emphasis only, albeit an important shift. The objective was and remained to support individuals in taking better care of their own interests and preferences amid the complexities of modern society.

In the 1980s, a new generation of economists, including first and foremost Richard Thaler introduced this engineering approach of the psychologists, and of Kahneman and Tversky in particular, to economics, thus creating what would become the new field of behavioral economics. The central objective of these behavioral economists became to enhance the rationality of individual consumers in the economy, and thereby to increase their welfare and their position versus other market participants, such as companies (e.g. Thaler and Sunstein, 2008; Heukelom, 2014). As such, Kahneman's behavioral economics became the last example of a century-old program of human engineering, that is, of pragmatic social science, even if now applied more explicitly to economic questions.

Conclusion

Throughout his career, Daniel Kahneman has been intrigued by the question of why individuals sometimes behave counter to the, sometimes very obvious, dictates of modern science. How does the decision making machinery of the human mind work? And, why does it sometimes fail systematically and predictably? Initially, Kahneman's research focused on traditional psychological topic, such as the assessments of military recruits and the visual system. Kahneman and Tversky's "Prospect Theory" article was the first, and very successful attempt to also include economic decisions in this research program. The hint was picked up quickly by Richard, who, together with Kahneman, built a new subfield of (micro) economics for which they successfully appropriated the label of behavioral economics.

Just as any other scientific work, Kahneman's research may be put into historical context. A first observation in that regard is that Kahneman's work stands in a line of a dichotomy between mind and body that goes back to the Greeks. Just like Odysseus used his mind to devise a scheme that would control his body amid stimuli that would risk it to self destruct, so Kahneman urges his readers to devise ways to solve the problems that the intuitive, bodily System 1 runs into when the situation at hand requires extra cognitive capacity, additional information, or more willpower. In that regard, Kahneman's work is in addition best understood as not sharing, and even implicitly opposing recent work by Damasio, Dijksterhuis, Bennet and Hacker, and others that denies the Greek–Cartesian mind–body dichotomy.

Second, Kahneman illustrates the difficulties in providing evolutionary explanations for human behavior. Given that it is relatively easy to come up with an adaptive strategy for "hunter-gatherers" that explains why human beings today tend to behave in a certain way, but at the same time difficult to validate or refute such hypotheses, explanations for the observed behavior proceed little beyond the speculative realm.

But perhaps that is not as problematic or destructive as it sounds. Kahneman's research also stands in a tradition of pragmatism and engineering that has been particularly influential in the United States, and which emphasizes the use of science in solving everyday problems of individuals and society, rather than providing fundamental explanations for why things are the way they are. Despite being a French-born Israeli, Kahneman's decades-long career in American academia has made him a principal product, as well as key contributing actor, to this particular American approach to the social sciences.

Notes

1 The Landolt C is one of the standard symbols used in psychophysics of vision and optometry. It consists of a C in which the opening can be varied, and which is either surrounded by bars the width of which equals the C's opening or not surrounded.

2 Tversky and Kahneman (1974), "Judgment under Uncertainty: Heuristics and Biases" and Kahneman and Tversky (1979), "Prospect Theory: An Analysis of Decision under Risk."

3 Initially, the article submitted to *Econometrica* was known as "Value Theory" (Kahneman, 2002).

4 At the time of the experiment, 4,000 shekel was about one third of the modal monthly Israeli income.

5 Kahneman (2002) recalls that they deliberately looked for a name that did not refer to any other theory or phenomenon in economics and psychology. Indeed, Jstor yields only one, idiosyncratic counter example. In 1977, Edmund W. Kitch of the University of Chicago developed a new economic theory for the patent system in the *Journal of Law and Economics*. "For expositional convenience, this view of the patent system will be called the prospect theory" (p. 266).

6 The experimentally induced subjective probability curve of Kahneman and Tversky (1979) suggested that the probabilities of one event space as perceived by the individual may not add up to 1, and hence violate Kolmogoroff's axioms (Kolmogoroff, 1933). Tversky and Kahneman (1992) offered solutions to this problem.

7 However, drawing on Jonathan Israel's three-tome history of the Enlightenment, among many others, we could ask just how radical the American version of the Enlightenment was (Israel, 2001, 2011). As Israel shows, some authors went further than others, with Baruch de Spinoza (1632–77) standing center stage as the first and most radical Enlightenment thinker, according to Israel. Adam Smith (1723–90), for instance, for various reasons did not want to liberate the individual as radically as did Spinoza (Israel, 2011). By and large, it seems fair to summarize that whereas freeing the individual from the economic and political shackles of Old World Europe was at the heart of the new American nation, cultural, religious and moral shackles were far less questioned.

Bibliography

Non published sources

Dawes, Robyn, interview with the author, Carnegie Mellon University, Pittsburgh, June 23, 2008.
Kahneman, Daniel, interview with the author, Princeton University, Princeton, April 16, 2009.

Published sources

Acemoglu, D. & Robinson, J. (2012). Why Nations Fail: The Origins of Power, Prosperity, and Poverty. New York, Crown.

Allais, M. (1953). Le Comportement de l'homme Rationnel Devant de le Risque: Critique des Postulats et Axioms de l'école Americaine. Econometrica, 21, 503–46.

Allais, M. & O. Hagen, O. Eds. (1979). Expected Uility Hypotheses and the Allais Paradox. London, D. Reidel.

Baumol, W. J. (1951). The Neumann–Morgenstern Utility Index: An Ordinalist View. Journal of Political Economy, 59(1), 61–6.

Baumol, W. J. (1958). The Cardinal Utility which is Ordinal. Economic Journal, 68, 665–72.

Bennet, M. R. & Hacker, P. M. S. (2003). Philosophical Foundations of Neuroscience. London, Blackwell.

Boring, E. C. (1929). A History of Experimental Psychology. New York, Century.

Brands, H. W. (2010). American Colossus: The Triumph of Capitalism. New York, Anchor Books.

Burgin, A. (2012). The Great Persuasion: Reinventing Free Markets since the Depression. Cambridge, Harvard University Press.

Camerer, C., et al. (2005). Neuroeconomics: How Neuroscience can Inform Economics. Journal of Economic Literature, 43, 9–64.

Capshew, J. H. (1999). Psychologists on the March: Science, Practice, and Professional Identity in America, 1929–1969. Cambridge, Cambridge University Press.

Cattel, M. (1930). Psychology in America. Psychological Review Ninth International Congress of Psychology, Proceedings and Papers: 12–32.

Cordeschi, R. (2002). The Discovery of the Artificial: Behavior, Mind, and Machines before and beyond Cybernetics. Dordrecht, Kluwer Academic.

Damasio, A. (2003). Looking for Spinoza: Joy, Sorrow, and the Feeling Brain. New York, Harcourt Books.

Danziger, K. (1990). Constructing the Subject: Historical Origins of Psychological Research. New York, Cambridge University Press.

Danziger, K. (1997). Naming the Mind: How Psychology Found its Language. London, SAGE.

Dijksterhuis, A. & Nordgren, L. F. (2006). A Theory of Unconscious Thought. Perspectives on Psychological Science, 1, 95–109.

Dworschak, M. & Grolle, J. (2012). Interview with Daniel Kahneman: Debunking the Myth of Intuition. Spiegel Online.

Ellsberg, D. (1961). Ambiguity, and the Savage Axioms. Quarterly Journal of Economics, 75(4), 643–69.

Erickson, P., et al. (2013). How Reason Almost Lost its Mind: The Strange Career of Cold War Rationality. Chicago, University of Chicago Press.

Estes, W. K. (1964). Probability Learning: Categories of Human Learning. A. W. Melton. New York, Academic Press.

Fechner, G. T. (1964/1860). Elemente der Psychophysik. Amsterdam, Bonset.

Friedman, B. (2005). The Moral Consequences of Economic Growth. New York, Alfred A. Knopf.

Friedman, M. (1953). The Methodology of Positive Economics. Essays in Positive Economics. Chicago, Chicago University Press, 3–43.

Gigerenzer, G. (1987a). The Probabilistic Revolution in Psychology: An Overview. The Probabilistic Revolution 2. L. Krüger, G. Gigerenzer and M. S. Morgan. Cambridge, MIT Press, 7–10.

Gigerenzer, G. (1987b). Survival of the Fittest Probabilist: Brunswik, Thurstone, and the Two Disciplines of Psychology. The Probabilistic Revolution 2. L. Krüger, G. Gigerenzer and M. S. Morgan. Cambridge, MIT Press, 49–72.

Hall, B. K. & Hallgrimsson, B. (2008). Strickberger's Evolution. Boston, Jones and Bartlett.

Heidelberger, M. (2004). Nature from Within: Gustav Theodor Fechner and his Psychophysical Worldview. Pittsburgh, University of Pittsburgh Press.

Hesse, J.-O. (2010). Wirtschaft als Wissenschaft: Die Volkswirtschaftslehre in der frühen Bundesrepublik Frankfurt am Main, Campus Verlag.

Heukelom, F. (2014). Behavioral Economics: A History. Cambridge, Cambridge University Press.

Israel, J. (2001). Radical Enlightenment: Philosophy and the Making of Modernity, 1650–1750. Oxford, Oxford University Press.

Israel, J. (2011). Democratic Enlightenment Philosophy Revolution and Human Rights 1750–1790. Oxford, Oxford University Press.

Johnson, P. (1997). A History of the American People. New York, HarperCollins.
Jordan, J. M. (1994). Machine-Age Ideology: Social Engineering and American Liberalism, 1911–1939. Chapel Hill, University of North Carolina.
Kable, J. W. (2011). The Cognitive Neuroscience Toolkit for the Neuroeconomist: A Functional Overview. Journal of Neuroscience, Psychology, and Economics, 4(2), 63–84.
Kahneman, D. (1965a). Control of Spurious Association and the Reliability of the Controlled Variable. Psychological Bulletin, 64(5), 326–9.
Kahneman, D. (1965b). Exposure Duration and Effective Figure–Ground contrast. Quarterly Journal of Experimental Psychology, 17, 308–14.
Kahneman, D. (1966). Time-Intensity Reciprocity in Acuity as a Function of Luminance and Figure–Ground contrast. Vision Research, 6, 207–15.
Kahneman, D. (1973). Attention and Effort. Englewoods Cliffs, Prentice Hall.
Kahneman, D. (2002). Autobiography. Available from http://nobelprize.org/economics/laureates/2002/kahneman-autobio.html.
Kahneman, D. (2011). Thinking, Fast and Slow. New York, Farrar, Straus and Giroux.
Kahneman, D. & Beatty, D. (1966). Pupil Diameter and Load on Memory. Science, 154, 1583–5.
Kahneman, D. & Beatty, D. (1967). Pupillary Responses in a Pitch-Discrimination Task. Perception and Psychophysics, 2, 101–5.
Kahneman, D. & Ghiselli, E. E. (1962). Validity and Nonlinear Heteroscedastic Models. Personnel Psychology, 15, 1–12.
Kahneman, D. & Norman, J. (1964). The Time-Intensity Relation in Visual Perception as a Function of Observer's Task. Journal of Experimental Psychology, 68, 215–20.
Kahneman, D. & Tversky, A. (1972). Subjective Probability: A Judgment of Representativeness. Cognitive Psychology, 3, 430–54.
Kahneman, D. & Tversky, A. (1979). Prospect Theory: An Analysis of Decision under Risk. Econometrica, 47, 263–92.
Kahneman, D., et al. (1967). Perceptual Deficit during a Mental Task. Science, 157, 218–9.
Kahneman, D., et al. (1968). Effect of Verbalization and Incentive on the Pupil Response to Mental Activity. Canadian Journal of Psychology, 22(3), 186–96.
Kahneman, D., Peavler, W. S. & Onuska, L. (1968). Effect of Verbalization and Incentive on the Pupil Response to Mental Activity. Canadian Journal of Psychology, 22(3), 186–96.
Kolmogoroff, A. (1933). Grundbegriffe der Wahrscheinlichkeitsrechnung. Berlin, Julius Springer.
Lemov, R. (2005). World as Laboratory: Experiments with Mice, Mazes, and Men. New York, Hill and Wang.
McCloskey, D. (2006). The Bourgeois Virtues: Ethics for an Age of Commerce. Chicago, University of Chicago Press.
Mills, J. A. (1998). Control: A History of Behavioral Psychology. New York, New York University Press.
Mindell, D. A. (2002). Between Human and Machine: Feedback, Control and Computing before Cybernetics. Baltimore, Johns Hopkins University Press.
Nicholls, A. J. (1994). Freedom with Responsibility: The Social Market Economy in Germany 1918–1963. Oxford, Clarendon Press.
Pettit, M. (2013). The Science of Deception: Psychology and Commerce in America. Chicago, University of Chicago Press.
Savage, L. J. (1954). The Foundations of Statistics. New York, John Wiley & Sons.
Simon, H. A. (1955). A Behavioral Model of Rational Choice. Quarterly Journal of Economics, 69(1), 99–118.
Simon, H. A. (1959). Theories of Decision-Making in Economics and Behavioral Sciences. American Economic Review, 49(1), 253–83.
Slovic, P. & Lichtenstein, S. (1971). Reversal of Preferences between Bids and Choices in Gambling Decisions. Journal of Experimental Psychology, 89, 46–55.
Thaler, R. H. & Benartzi, S. (2004). Save More Tomorrow: Using Behavioral Economics to Increase Employee Saving. Journal of Political Economy, 112, S164–87.
Thurstone, L. L. & Chave, E. J. (1929). The Measurement of Attitude: A Psychophysical Method and Some Experiments with a Scale for Measuring Attitude toward the Church. Chicago, University of Chicago Press.
Tversky, A. & Kahneman, D. (1971). Belief in the Law of Small Numbers. Psychological Bulletin, 76, 105–10.

Tversky, A. & Kahneman, D. (1974). Judgment under Uncertainty: Heuristics and Biases. Science, 185, 1124–31.

Tversky, A. & Kahneman, D. (1992). Advances in Prospect Theory: Cumulative Representation of Uncertainty. Journal of Risk and Uncertainty, 5, 297–323.

von Neumann, J. & Morgenstern, O. (2004 [1944]). Theory of Games and Economic Behavior. Princeton, Princeton University Press.

Yarrow, Y. L. (2010). Measuring America: How Economic Growth Came to Define American Greatness in the Late Twentieth Century. Massachusetts, University of Massachusetts Press.

Yerkes, R. M. (1941). Psychology and Defense. Proceedings of the American Philosophical Society, 84, 527–42.

10

GEORGE KATONA'S CONTRIBUTIONS TO THE START OF BEHAVIORAL ECONOMICS

Hamid Hosseini

Katona and the start of behavioral economics

Since the author of these pages considers George Katona as one of two founding fathers of behavioral economics, the other being Herbert Simon, this chapter begins with some introductory remarks about behavioral economics (see Hosseini, 2003 and 2011).

Behavioral economics is a type of economics, or an approach to doing economic research, that gradually emerged after WWII. According to Gilad, Kaish, and Loeb (1984), its name—that is, behavioral economics—was forged by George Katona. However, Angner and Loewenstein (2012) suggest that the name had first been used by Kenneth Boulding and Harold Johnson in their paper in 1958, and according to Esther-Mirjam Sent (2004), the term had been used by several (un-named) writers in the 1960s.

But what is behavioral economics and how do we define it? According to Herbert Simon (1986), it is a type of economics that augments and amends the existing body of classical and neoclassical economic theory to achieve a more realistic picture of economic process. In their 1986 *Handbook of Behavioral Economics*, Gilad, Kaish, and Loeb proposed three postulates in assessing the nature of behavioral economics. First, economic theory must be consistent with the accumulated body of knowledge in the behavioral sciences, including/especially psychology, which is at the root of the attempt to improve the assumptive realism of economic theory. Second, economic theory should concentrate on, and be able to explain, real world observed behaviors, thus requiring a shift of emphasis to what actually happens rather than the logical condition necessary for things to happen. A manifestation of this postulate is the survey-based research that Katona conducted at the University of Michigan. Third, economic theory must be empirically verifiable with field, laboratory, survey, and other microdata generating technicalities. Furthermore, Hosseini's 2003 paper cites a summary of the general attributes of behavioral economies according to a survey of SABE (Society for the Advancement of Behavioral Economics) members conducted by Gilad, Kuiska, and Loeb. The summary includes the following attributes associated with behavioral economics: first, behavioral economics rejects positivism as a methodological foundation for economic research; second, it refuses to use deductive reasoning as a sufficient basis of economic research; third, it dislikes a static analysis of equilibrium analysis, preferring a disequilibrium process; and finally, it especially objects to the use of the simplistic economic model of rational agents exhibiting optimizing behavior. This explains why Herbert Simon, as an alternate, introduced the notion of bounded rationality.

According to the author of this chapter, behavioral economics for the most part began in two American institutions—Carnegie Tech's Graduate School of Industrial Administration and the University of Michigan (Hosseini, 2003). However, Earl (1988), Sent (2004), and Angner and Loewenstein (2012) also add the UK universities of Oxford and Stirling. Whether behavioral economics emerged in two or four academic institutions, Hungarian born (former) University of Michigan professor George Katona should be viewed as one of the two founding fathers of this type of economics, the other being Carnegie's Herbert Simon.

Thanks to the popularity of Simon's bounded rationality and satisficing, not to mention that he was the recipient of Nobel Prize in economics in 1978, Herbert Simon is well known and needs no introduction. However, while in at least two papers this author (Hosseini, 2003 and 2011) has demonstrated the contributions of George Katona to the start of (old) behavioral economics, and Curtin had a chapter about him in 1984, contributions of this Hungarian born, psychology trained author to behavioral economics have for the most part been overlooked by historians of economics. And, as suggested by Jose Edwards (2010: 208), Katona was also misunderstood by some economists. This neglect was in spite of the fact that Katona was mentioned in Joseph Schumpeter's seminal book *History of Economic Analysis* as early as 1954 (p.24). In my view, George Katona and his contributions should not be overlooked. After all, according to Burkhard Strümpel (1972: 3), Katona was the father of behavioral economics or, according to Robert Pratt, Jr., virtually all research done in the field of behavioral economics is an outgrowth of the research done by Katona (p.193).

This chapter intends to demonstrate that George Katona was a founding father of behavioral economics, thus he made substantial contributions to the start of this type of economics. And, although historians of economics such as Esther-Mirjam Sent (2004) believe that Katona's contributions to behavioral economics were those related to macroeconomics, I would also argue that Katona's contributions to behavioral economics were also in microeconomics, more specifically regarding the theory of the firm. An example is his 1945 *AER* paper "Psychological Analysis of Business Decisions." Of course, Katona's contributions to macroeconomics, in particular to Keynesian consumption function, are more significant. This explains why James Tobin, a towering figure in macroeconomic theory, stated in 1972 that "The careers of consumption function and George Katona have been intertwined since 1945. The consumption–saving decision has been a major subject of theoretical and empirical inquiry to which no one has contributed more than Katona" (1972: 37).

George Katona: from experimental psychology to behavioral economics

Born in Budapest, Hungary in 1901, George Katona entered the University of Budapest in 1918. However, as a result of political turmoil in Hungary after WWI, Katona soon transferred to Germany's Göttingen University to study experimental psychology under prominent psychologist Müller. Concentrating on the role of experiments in the psychology of perception, Katona received his PhD in 1921. After graduation, he moved to Frankfurt to teach at the University of Frankfurt. To support his income, he also worked in the research department of a bank. In Frankfurt, he continued his research in experimental psychology which resulted in the publication of an award winning monograph in 1923. Working for a bank and witnessing the now famous German hyperflation when he lived in Germany, he also published a paper on the psychology of inflation in the same year, a paper that received a great deal of attention. According to Wärneryd (1982: 1), because of the success of that 1923 paper, his working for a bank and his observation of German hyperinflation, Katona became interested in the study of economics. It was because of his decision to learn more about economics that he decided to move to Berlin, and to also work for the Berlin Center of Gestalt Psychology. In Berlin, while learning gestalt psychology from Max Wertheimer, he also learned economics from economist Gustav Stolper (of the famous Stolper–Samuelson theorem). In fact, Stolper, who was at the time editing the weekly *German Economist* (*Der Deutsche Volkswirt*), asked Katona to be an assistant editor of that publication. As a result, and gradually, Katona become more interested in economic issues. In fact, between 1926 and 1933 (the year he immigrated to the United States), Katona published numerous articles and commentaries about economic issues, in addition to his paper on the psychology of perception. According to his 1972 published *Reminiscences*, he also wrote a lead editorial for that publication on the causes of stock market crash in the United States a day after the October 28, 1929 stock market crash.

Since that German weekly was one of the first German publications to be banned by Hitler's government in 1933, both Stolper and Katona immigrated to the United States in that year (Katona became a US citizen in 1939). Arriving in New York City, those two established an investment firm with the purpose of advising European investors in the United States. However, that collaboration ended in 1936 when Katona became very ill (with a severe case of tuberculosis), which lasted until 1939.

Psychologist Wertheimer, friend/mentor of Katona, had also immigrated to the United States to teach at the University in Exile (now New School University) in New York City. In 1939, Katona also joined the faculty at the University in Exile, to teach and do research in psychology. Supported by a grant from Carnegie Corporation while at that university, Katona published his important book in psychology in 1940. Because of his scholarship, Katona was invited by Jacob Marschak in 1942 to conduct and direct studies of business reaction to price controls during WWII at the University of Chicago's Cowles Commission for Research in Economics. This engagement enhanced his understanding of business sector behavior. In fact, as suggested by Richard Curtin, "The opportunity for direct observation and measurement of both the attitudes and the actions of business decision makers appealed to Katona" (1984: 501).

In 1944, at the invitation of Rensis Likert, who directed the US Department of Agriculture Division of Program Survey, Katona moved to Washington to utilize his knowledge of the survey method working for that division. It was in Washington, DC that Katona co-directed the first nation-wide survey of ownership of liquid assets in the United States (see Hosseini, 2011: 979). However, in 1947, Katona, Likert and other colleagues at the above-mentioned center moved to Ann Arbor, Michigan in order that they would create the University's Survey Research Center (SRC). Additionally, Katona was also appointed as Professor of Economics and Psychology at the University of Michigan. At SRC, Katona directed nationwide surveys of consumers for some twenty five years. Although officially retired in 1972, Katona remained active at SRC until his death in 1981, when visiting Berlin (at that time West Germany).

Katona: how did he contribute to behavioral economics?

As I argued in 2003 and 2011, Katona should be viewed as a founding father of behavioral economics. As an advocate of behavioral economics, Katona emphasized the psychological foundations of economic behavior, believing that this fact had been ignored in traditional economics. In his 1951 *Psychological Analysis of Economic Behavior*, Katona stated that: "economic process stems directly from human behavior and that this simple but important fact has not received its due in modern economic analysis" (quoted by Hosseini, 2011: 979). In fact, in the same paragraph, Katona stated his aim of helping to create what we now call behavioral economics. In his own words: "This author has set for himself the task of describing a psychological approach to economic analysis and the current research in the field of economic behavior" (Ibid).

The American Psychological Association (APA) acknowledged George Katona as a founding father of behavioral economics in 1977. In a citation by APA we read:

> Katona pioneered the development of a new body of knowledge bridging the gap between economics and psychology... His great methological innovation in behavioral economics was to explain changes in the economic system by analyzing actions and predispositions to action or the individual level of applying micro-data to macroeconomic analysis and prediction.
>
> *(quoted by Curtin, 2004: 496)*

Interestingly enough, Katona, in addition to being critical of "economics without psychology", was also critical of "psychology without economics."

Katona's contributions to behavioral economics appeared in many of his books and essays, especially in three of his books—his 1951 book *Psychological Analysis of Economic Behavior*, his 1975 *Psychological Economics*, and his 1980 book *Essays on Behavioral Economics* (in which he includes an essay by James Morgan). In his 1980 book, Katona identifies three attributes of behavioral economics. First, that behavioral economics is concerned with the actions of economic decision makers that function as consumers, workers, and entrepreneurs. These actions, to him, require the integration of psychological antecedents of economic behavior such as motives, attributes, and expectations (see Hosseini, 2011). Second, that behavioral economics emphasizes the study of the process of decision making rather than the economic consequences of human behavior. For example, how do individuals decide to make major purchases or new investments rather than the exact amounts consumed or invested. Third, behavioral economics is empirical and utilizes an inductive methodology (Ibid).

As an advocate of behavioral economics, Katona questioned some of the basic assumptions of conventional economics. For example, while neoclassical economics assumes a given/fixed utility function, Katona was interested in finding the empirical laws that could be able to describe individual behavior as accurately as possible. Or, while neoclassical economics assumes a close connection between rationality and the maximization of both utility and profit, like Simon, Katona "scrutinized the implications of departures of actual behavior from neoclassical assumptions" (Sent, 2004: 742). Katona, in fact, was critical of the neoclassical assumption of rationality as early as 1951. In his 1951 book, Katona stated that: "unlike pure (neoclassical) theorists, we shall not assume at the outset that rational behavior exists or that rational behavior constitutes the topic of economic analysis. We shall study economic behavior as we find it" (p. 16). He made a similar argument in his 1975 book (p. 218). However, contributions of Katona went through various stages, reflecting his life and economic experiences, as well as the various political and economic situations and events that he faced. While his 1923 essay on the psychology of hyperinflation reflected his reaction as a young psychologist living in Germany to that inflation, his 1924 award winning monograph reflected his exposure to the gestalt psychology of Max Wertheimer when living in Berlin. Katona's 1940 book in psychology was on the basis of his pre-WWII research in psychology while a professor at New School. However, the outbreak of WWII in Europe renewed his interest in economics. Describing that change of interest, he later wrote: "But I was not fully satisfied with research in psychology. In 1939 WWII broke out in Europe. It provided the opportunity to integrate my interest in economics and psychology" (quoted by Hosseini, 2011: 982). In fact, in 1942 he published a book entitled *War without Inflation* in which he applied his psychological arguments of his 1940 book to economic behavior, demonstrating that the psychological cause of inflation cannot be ignored.

As a result of his association with the Cowles Commission earlier, which coincided with the US involvement in WWII and its price controls, Katona became interested in the study of business behavior, thus the study of business reaction to price controls in the United States. This explains why, in his 1984 chapter, Curtin argued: "the opportunity for observation and measurement of both attitudes and actions of business decision makers greatly appealed to Katona" (1984: 501).

As a result of that interest, Katona collected and analyzed survey data on reactions to price controls on the part of business, whether produces, distributors, or retailers that provided/sold household durables, relating compliance or circumvention to both economic and psychological factors. In fact, Katona's 1945 book *Price Control and Business* reflected his association with the Cowles Commission, and his studies of business reaction to WWII price controls in the United States. As he stated, the book, which was based on his 1942 to 1944 study, was devoted to the analysis of the "actions of American businessmen as affected by price regulations and other wartime conditions" (1945: 2).

The study, as the basis of the 1945 book, had the following characteristics. In terms of method, this qualitative study included detailed interviews with a small sample of businessmen which he found to be better suited for discovering the types and motives of business adjustments than compiling quantitative data on prices, sales, costs, and profits. The sample included various manufacturers and distributors of a few important consumer goods in Chicago area, not all being affected by price controls (1945: 2). In his 2010 University of Paris dissertation, J. Edwards makes the mention that Katona had viewed his study as an alternative to NBER (National Bureau of Economic Research)-type of analysis whose purpose was twofold. Explaining those two purposes, Edwards wrote: "It was intended at the same time as a recollection of data to support war planning, and as a test of the potentiality of the method of interviews as a legitimate tool of economic research" (Edwards, 2010: 198–9).

At the time, the method used by Katona was rather innovative; it consisted of gathering data/information questionnaires designed (for the first time) to make businessmen discuss with qualified interviewers who were granted relatively wide freedom (Katona, 1945: 8). These data acquired contained information about different pricing procedures utilized for different types of activities. Katona found this method very fruitful. To him, the analysis of the motives and attitudes of businessmen was a worthwhile approach for the study of economic phenomena. And, the method of detailed interviews he found to be an appropriate tool of analysis for that purpose.

Moving to Michigan and establishing the Survey Research Center

As stated before, in 1947, Katona moved to Ann Arbor where, with the support of Likert and Angus Campbell, he founded the University of Michigan Survey Research Center (SRC). At SRC, at least during those immediate post WWII years, Katona's aim was to provide an empirical analysis of the attitudes and motives of consumers. More specifically, Katona's focus at SRC was to understand the role of the consumer in the transition from a wartime economy to "what all hoped would be a new era of peace and prosperity" (Curtin, 2004: 131). To understand Katona's purpose and appreciate that transition, one has to realize that at the end of WWII many, among both economists and the general public, were fearful that the mass unemployment and the deflationary spiral of the 1930s would return. Hosseini's 2011 paper includes a very long quotation from Katona's 1975 book which describes that false prediction (2011: 981). To many, during the war economic activity had been sustained by government purchases of war materials. Thus, when the war ends, government orders will cease, which would lead to another depression.

False prediction also existed on the inflation side, since others predicted that rapid inflation would emerge after the end of WWII. In fact, Katona also explained that false prediction in the same 1975 book. In his words:

> Some economists predicted rapid inflation. During the war an unprecedented large proportion of income had been saved. For several years in succession people had saved approximately a fourth of what they earned and most of the money had been put into war bonds and bank deposits which would be cashed or withdrawn without delay. When people would be spending both their incomes and their accumulated liquid assets, demand would exceed the supply of goods and runaway inflation develop.
>
> *(quoted by Hosseini, 2011: 981)*

Interestingly enough, Katona had argued that neither of those two catastrophes would occur. In his 1975 book, Katona explained why those catastrophes did not occur:

> Surveys conducted in 1945 and 1946 revealed that the American people did not think along those lines. In contrast to the experts, people on the whole were optimistic about economic development as well as about their own financial situation. They believed that the end of the war—a most welcome event—could not have any but good economic consequences . . . nor was rapid inflation expected.
>
> *(Ibid)*

In fact, many found those two inaccurate predictions problematic. As suggested by Curtin, many economists, as critics, were wondering "whether the underlying economic theory or statistical methodology or both were wrong" (2004: 31). Among those economist critics we can include Nobel Laureate Lawrence Klein who, in 1946, stated that "the order of magnitude of the error involved is great and, what is more serious, it is great enough to lead to disastrous policy recommendations" (1946: 291). To correct such grave mistakes by economists, Klein suggested better (macroeconomic) models with more detailed equations, fewer exogenous variables, and more dynamic specifications (Ibid).

Of course, Katona and his SRC colleagues, as proponents of behavioral economics, could not agree with what was suggested by Lawrence Klein. As demonstrated in both his 1946 *AER* essay and his 1951 book, Katona argued that, in addition to information about consumers' financial situations, forecasting (macroeconomic) models also require information on the psychological factors that shape changes in consumers' spending and saving decisions. In other words, according to Katona such economic models also require a correct and realistic psychological foundation.

As stated by Katona in 1975, by incorporating the Index of Consumer Sentiment in his Wharton econometrics model during the 1960s, Lawrence Klein took care of that problem (see Hosseini, 2011: 981). The Index of Consumer Sentiment (ICS), a tool that determines the general feelings of consumers towards the economy, was developed under the direction of George Katona at the University of Michigan's SRC during the late 1940s.

As a behavioral economist interested in macroeconomics, Katona challenged what he called the Keynesian "fundamental psychological law", one that deals with consumption behavior. Specifically, Katona's intent was to update Keynesian consumption function. In his 1946 *AER* essay, Katona wrote "J. M. Keynes, in describing psychological characteristics of human nature, did not borrow from psychologists but proposed, without their aid, what he called a psychological law referring to prosperity to assume under the influence of changes in income" (quoted by Hosseini, 2011: 981).

To appreciate Katona's contribution in the area of consumption behavior, the following statements by Rensis Likert are helpful:

> When Katona started his work, the prevailing view among economists was that the general level of the total economy and major changes in this level were controlled by the actions of business and government. Consumers were felt to have no influence, since their rate of expenditures was determined by their income, which in turn was controlled by the decisions of business and government.
>
> *(quoted by Hosseini, 2011)*

And:

> When Katona began his nationwide consumer surveys, the prevailing view was that the rate of consumer expenditures was not an independent factor affecting the level of economic activity. Increased or decreased rates of expenditures by business or government were viewed as the factor which determine whether we had good times and bad times. Consumers were felt to have little independent influence.
>
> *(Ibid)*

To emphasize Katona's contribution, Likert continues: "Amid considerable skepticism, Katona persevered in his view that consumers are important as an independent factor . . . " (Ibid).

Influenced by his 1940 book on psychology, Katona emphasized the role of expectations in macroeconomic analysis, especially as it relates to consumption behavior. Influenced by that 1940 book about psychology of learning, Katona related any type of expectations to psychology. This is obvious in his 1946 *AER* essay. In his own words: "The study of expectations forms part of the psychology of learning, since expectations are not innate or instinctive form of behavior but rather the result of experience" (Ibid: 982).

However, to Katona, the Keynesian consumption function was based on economics without psychology, since, to Keynes, variations in consumption and saving are only explainable by changes in income. Emphasizing psychology and expectations in the 1946 essay, Katona introduces psychology and expectations into the Keynesian notion of consumption and saving and remedies those notions in the following way: first, the volume of consumption and saving does not follow income in a mechanistic way, since it also depends on prevailing expectations; second, one's past experience is not the only factor shaping expectations, since expectations can also be influenced by present factors; and third, thus the average propensities to consume and save too can be influenced (Katona, 1946). To him, that influence could result from "certain types of public and private policies" (see Hosseini, 2011: 98). Katona's critique of the Keynesian consumption function was summarized by Robert Pratt. According to Pratt, for Katona, at any given time, willingness to spend varies according to the degree of optimism or pessimism felt by consumers; optimism and pessimism of consumers being psychological components (1972).

For Katona, consumers, as psychological beings, respond to various stimuli that include television and radio advertisement, packaging, extended warranties, point of purchase displays and others. To him, these stimuli are likely to differ among different individuals at a given time, and for the same person in different points of time. According to Katona, the reason is that individuals perceive and interpret stimuli differently. Here Katona is emphasizing what gestalt psychologsts have called intervening variables which include motives, beliefs, assumptions, prejudices, attitudes, aspirations, feelings, emotions, expectations, values, etc. According to Pratt, for Katona, intervening variables that play a dynamic part in a person's buying or not buying decisions provide the psychological framework within which perceived environmental stimuli are organized and interpreted (Pratt, 1972). On the basis of the arguments Katona had made in his 1940 book on psychology, he assumed that intervening variables are constantly changing; as a result of new learning and experiences acquired by individuals overtime. This analysis by Katona went beyond the Keynesian assumption that individual disposable income is the sole cause of consumption. Katona's conclusion was based on the sample interviews which he conducted with Likert, and using the first national survey on liquid assets. The purpose of that survey (sponsored by the Fed) was to explore the American household's use of the considerable amount saved during WWII (see Edwards, 2010: 204). The steps of the survey method used in those SRC surveys of consumption and savings of the United States' households were explained in the 1946 *Review of Economics and Statistics* paper by Katona and Likert. On the basis of those surveys, Katona (and Likert) concluded that while income may explain consumption behavior in the short run, however, it cannot explain it in the long run since people's behavior changes in the long run. In fact, Katona was surprised as to why Keynes could not see that difference. This surprise can be seen by what Katona wrote in 1951: "Keynes, who assigns great importance to the expectations of businessmen in shaping their policies, does not take expectations into account when he analyzes the factors influencing consumer behavior" (quoted by Hosseini, 2011: 982). Thus, it was Katona who insisted that consumers constitute an important and independent factor affecting the economy. For, as suggested by Likert, "the data he collected, and the analysis that he and colleagues made, gradually demonstrated even to the most skeptical that consumer perception, expectations and motivations can exercise a significant, independent impact on the economy" (1972: 8).

Obviously, what Katona did at the SRC, or his attempt in the creation of his version of behavioral economics, would not have been done without several crucial advances at the time—advances such as probability method of sample selection and other advances in statistics, valid and reliable survey instruments, and methods for machine tabulation and others, since he could not rely on established methods.

Conclusions: Katona's contributions and the economics profession

Katona's contribution to economics in general and to consumption behavior in particular was not appreciated by the economics profession at the beginning. This lack of initial appreciation of Katona's contributions by the economic profession was expressed by James Tobin, a Nobel laureate, and a macroeconomic theorist with many contributions in consumption theory, in his 1972 essay "Wealth, Liquidity, and the Propensity to Consume." In Tobin's words:

> A behavioral scientist by training and temperament, he [Katona] brought to economic research quite a different bag of tools and insights from those of technical economists. As a social psychologist, he was probably not surprised to find that he annoyed many of the brethren of his adopted scientific community. What put them off was his disdain for utility maximizing or profit maximizing models of individual behavior, and his failure to base his statistical inferences and macroeconomic conclusions on explicit formal system-wide models.

However, in the next sentence Tobin (obviously not a behavioral economist) appreciated Katona's contributions to economic theory by stating that: "But today we can appreciate, even from the perspective of economic theory and econometrics themselves, Katona's perception, prescience and persistence" (Tobin, 1972). According to Philip Miroswki, one should not be surprised that neoclassical economist associated with the Cowles Commission would not appreciate the contributions of Katona. The reason Mirowski gives is that: "the Cowles men had little respect for survey techniques or participation observation of social actors. This was illustrated in the cool reception given to the survey on war time price controls conducted by Katona . . . " (quoted by Edwards, 2010: 190). No doubt, Katona's contributions to economics were tremendous. In addition to helping to start (old) behavioral economics, he made substantial contributions at SRC (and its survey methods) and other aspects of economics and influenced various economic theories, as demonstrated in Hosseini's 2011 paper. For example, as argued by José Edwards (2010: 187), Katona's influence on economic analysis can be seen in the "Measurement without Theory" debate that began with Wesley Mitchell, and which later involved Tjalling Koopmans and Viring, as well as the full-cost controversies of the late 1940s and later. James Tobin, in the concluding remarks of his 1959 *Review of Economics and Statistics* paper, made the following comments about Katona's contributions at SRC and to consumption theory:

> I would not conclude without stressing the very considerable debt the profession owes George Katona and his colleagues at the Survey Research Center for the imaginative and pioneering work in the collection and interpretation of buying intentions and attitudinal data. Without their leadership, we must still be talking about the importance of consumer psychology for short-term business fluctuations and bemoaning our inability to measure it. Thanks to the experience they are accumulating, we can investigate the questions which attitudes are the most important ones to investigate in periodic surveys and what is the best way to use these data in combination with other economic information.
>
> *(1959: 144)*

Bibliography

Angner, E. & Loewenstein, G. (2012). Behavioral economics. Vol. 13. Handbook of the Philosophy of Science. Elsevier, Amsterdam, 641–90.

Curtin, R. (1984). Curtin on Katona. In: Spiegel, H., Samuels, W. (Eds) Contemporary Economics in Perspective. JAI Press, Greenwich, CT/London, England, 495–522.

Curtin, R. (2004). Psychology and macroeconomics. In: House, J., Juster, F., Kahn, R., Schuman, H., Singer, E. (Eds.) A Telescope on Society: Survey Research and Social Science at the University of Michigan and Beyond. University of Michigan Press, Ann Arbor.

Earl, P. (Ed.) (1988). Behavioral Economics. Vol. 1. Edward Elgar, Aldershot.

Edwards, J. (2010). Joyful Economics: Remarks on the History of Economics and Psychology from a Happiness Studies Perspective. PhD Dissertation (University of Paris), in English.

Gilad, B. & Kaish, S. (Eds.) (1986). Handbook of Behavioral Economics. Vols. A and B. JAI Press, London.

Gilad, B., Kaish, S. & Loeb, P. (1984). From economic behavior to behavioral economics. Journal of Behavioral Economics, 13, 1–24.

Hosseini, H. (2003). The arrival of behavioral economics: From Michigan, or the Carnegie School in the 1950s and the early 1960s. Journal of Socio-Economics, 23, 391–409.

Hosseini, H. (2011). George Katona: A founding father of old behavioral economics. Journal of Socio-Economics, 40(4), 977–84.

Katona, G. (1980). Essays on Behavioral Economics. University of Michigan Press, Ann Arbor, MI.

Katona, G. (1975). Psychological Economics. Elsevier, London.

Katona, G. (1964). Mass Consumption Society. McGraw-Hill, New York.

Katona, G. (1955). Business expectations in the framework of psychological economics: Toward a theory of expectations, 1958. In: Bowman, M. J. (Ed.), Expectations, Uncertainty and Business. Social Science Research Council, New York.

Katona, G. (1947). Contributions of psychological data to economic analysis. Journal of the American Statistical Association, 42(239), 449–59.

Katona, G. (1946). Psychological analysis of business decisions and expectation. American Economic Review, 36(1), 44–62.

Katona, G. (1945). Price Control and Business. Principia Press, Bloomington, IN.

Katona, G. (1942). War without Inflation. Columbia University Press, New York.

Katona, G. (1940). Organizing and Memorizing: Studies in the Psychology of Learning. Columbia University Press, New York.

Katona, G. & Likert, R. (1946). Relationships between consumer expectations and savings: The contribution of survey research. Review of Economics and Statistics, 28(4), 197–9.

Katona, G., with the collaboration of Albert Lauterbach and Stanley Steinkamp (1957). Business Looks at Banks: A Study of Business Behavior. University of Michigan Press, Ann Arbor, MI.

Katona, G., with the collaboration of Albert Lauterbach and Stanley Steinkamp (1951). Psychological Analysis of Economic Behavior. McGraw-Hill, New York.

Likert, R. (1972). Courageous pioneers: Creating a new field of knowledge. In Strümpel, B., Morgan, J. M., Zahn, E. (Eds.), Human Behavior in Economic Affairs. Jossey-Bass, San Francisco, 4–6.

Morgan, J. (1972). A quarter century of research in economics. In Strümpel, B., Morgan, J., Zahn, E. (Eds.), Human Behavior in Economic Affairs. Jossey-Bass, San Francisco, 15–34.

Pratt Jr., R. (1972). Marketing application of behavioral economics. In Strümpel, B., Morgan, J., Zahn, E. (Eds.). Human Behavior in Economic Affairs. Jossey-Bass, San Francisco, 15–34.

Sent, E.-M. (2004). Behavioral economics: How psychology made its (limited) way back into economics. History of Political Economy, 36(4), 735–60.

Strümpel, B., Morgan, J., & Zahn, E. (Eds.) (1972). Human Behavior in Economic Affairs. Jossey-Bass, San Francisco.

Tobin. J. (1972). Wealth, liquidity, the propensity to consume. In Strümpel, B. & Morgan, J. Zahn, E. (Eds.). Human Behavior in Economic Affairs. Jossey-Bass, San Francisco.

Tobin, J. (1959). On the predictive value of consumer intentions and attitudes. Review of Economics and Statistics, 41(1), 1–11.

Wärneryd, K.-E. (1982). The life and work of George Katona. Journal of Economic Psychology, 2, 1–30.

Wärneryd, K.-E. & Olander, F. (1972). The place for laboratory experiments and small-sample surveys in economic psychology. In: Strümpel, B., Morgan, J., Zahn, E. (Eds.). Human Behavior in Economic Affairs. Jossey-Bass, San Francisco.

Yang, B. & Lester, P. (1995). New directions for economics. Journal of Socio-Economics, 24, 443–56.

11

BEHAVIOURAL RULES

Veblen, Nelson–Winter, Ostrom and beyond

Georg Blind

Introduction

Any economist will agree with the definition of the discipline as the study of the behaviour of agents under conditions of scarcity. Anything beyond this common denominator, however, is subject to debate. Opinions start to diverge when economic behaviour is to be explained. For long and for many, the behaviour of economic agents has been understood as being driven by the pursuit of self-interest and as being guided by the rule of law.

While rules were seen as simply being decreed by the "benevolent dictator" in neoclassical economics, more recent scholarship inquires how legislation comes about (Brennan and Buchanan 1985). A common understanding of the term rule is equivalent to "law and regulation". The analytical reach of such reasoning thus remains limited to rules that control the *social* behaviour of agents. In its most general reading, however, a rule represents a condition–action statement linking a condition to a specific outcome. Accepting this definition, rules may equally well govern *individual* behaviour of agents.

Orthodox economists typically have little interest in rules governing individual agent behaviour, for the simple reason that the pursuit of self-interest continues to serve the purpose of such rule. Individual agent behaviour would be thus be controlled by a single rule that reads: "for deciding upon one's economic behaviour, that is, one's operations, consider your self-interest".

In the course of the last decades, concerns have been rising whether one single rule may actually suffice to explain individual behaviour of economic man in a meaningful way. Criticism to the single-rule approach has two predominant sources: theoretical objections and empirical counter-evidence. Concentrating on the latter, the remainder of this chapter discusses a selection of milestones in the development of a multi-rule approach for explaining individual agent behaviour. Sections 2 to 4 document the "reasoning about rules" that can be found in the works of Veblen, Ostrom and Nelson–Winter. Section 5 then shows how their understanding of rules can serve as building blocks for a general multi-rule approach that promises three important analytical merits: heterogeneous agents (between-heterogeneity), heterogeneous behaviour in individual agents (within-heterogeneity), and change in the behaviour of agents.

Thorstein Veblen: determinism of economic behaviour

"The whole canon of his work and thought was beyond economics and fell primarily in the realm of cultural anthropology" (Ault and Ekelund 1988: 431). This assessment of Veblen's work points to the "nature of man" as being centre-stage in Veblenian analysis. While being known best for his analysis of institutions, his works actually build on a distinct concept of individual behaviour. Veblen sees the economic agent as "a coherent structure of propensities and habits" (1919b: 74). By the term "habit", he denotes what contemporary scholarship considers a behavioural rule. Importantly, his analysis of institutions equally builds on behavioural rules. As Veblen puts it, "institutions are an outgrowth of habit" (1909: 628).

Heterogeneous habits as evolving patterns of behaviour

Veblen figures as one of the earliest opponents of a single-rule system in economics. For orthodox economics, he identifies "a preconception of normality", that is, an "archaic habit of thought" to reduce "facts and events to terms of fundamental truth" and to make them "square with the requirements of definitive normality" (1898b: 378–9). In essence, "definitive normality" precludes the very existence of heterogeneity: "the human material with which the inquiry is concerned is conceived [. . .] in terms of a passive and substantially inert and immutably given human nature" (1898b: 389).

Criticising this "state of economic science", Veblen observes "the apparatus being invested with a tendency to equilibrium at the normal, and the theory being a formulation of the conditions under which this putative equilibrium supervenes" (1898b: 383). Significantly, for Veblen, "the scheme arrived at is spiritually binding on the behaviour of the phenomena contemplated" (ibid: 383–4). Accordingly, "Features of the process that do not lend themselves to interpretation of the formula are abnormal cases [. . .] and are neatly avoided" (ibid: 384).

In contrast, Veblen himself understands of such "abnormal" features as representing entirely natural elements of a developmental course in the economic system. In his view, "each society and each stage of society had its own set of habits" (Ault and Ekelund 1988: 435). This qualifies behaviour as being heterogeneous not only in a historical, but also in a spatial dimension. What is more, the term "set" hints at Veblen's understanding of economic man as a "multi-rule agent". This worldview of Veblen's, obviously, originates from his fortunate reasoning as a "cultural anthropologist".

Veblen's recognition of a multitude of behavioural rules becomes even more apparent in one of his early qualitative empirical studies on "the instinct of workmanship" (1898a). Veblen starts his argument by pointing out a central axiom of orthodox economics: "men desire above all things to get the goods produced by labour and to avoid the labour by which the goods are produced" (1898a: 187). From the observation that many individuals work beyond the degree required to secure their livelihood, Veblen derives the existence of the said "instinct of workmanship". As a behavioural rule, it rivals the rule of "status" followed by members of what Veblen later identifies as a "leisure class" in his *opus magnum* (1899b).

Institutions as groups with shared rules

In Veblen's understanding, the very same "leisure class" represents an institution (Veblen 1899b: 22) and he equally counts "ownership" and "money" as institutions (1899b: ibid, 1899a: 405). From this, it becomes obvious that institutions in a Veblenian reading are not restricted to formal organisations. For Veblen, an institution refers to the sharing of a specific rule by a group of stable size where the rule may be considered "the dominant economic and legal feature of the community's life" (1899b: 117). In the case of the leisure class, "consumption for status" is the shared behavioural rule, for ownership the social rule of "respecting property", and for (fiat) money the cognitive rule of "trade goods against paper". In essence, Veblen's understanding of institutions follows a population approach.

Evolution of rules as innovation and adaptation

A witness of the industrial revolution, Veblen was sceptical about the contemporary neglect of technological progress in economic theory: to assume that "the state of the arts remains unchanged, [. . .] is [. . .] an exclusion of the main fact" (Veblen 1899a: 421–2). Veblen also specifies the "locus of change" in the process of evolution: "The physical properties of the materials accessible to man are constants: it is the human agent that changes—his insight and his appreciation of what these things can be used for is what develops" (1898b: 387–8).

In Veblen's understanding, behavioural rules in large part are "handed down from the past" (1899b: 191). During this process, however, rules may become subject to change through adaptation, and such change potentially causes further change:

> The growth of culture is a cumulative sequence of habituation, and the ways and means of it are the habitual response of human nature to exigencies that vary incontinently, cumulatively, but with something of a consistent sequence in the cumulative variations that so go forward—incontinently, because each new move creates a new situation which induces a further new variation in the habitual manner of response.
>
> *(1909: 628)*

Veblen only hints at some of the mechanisms through which rules are changing:

> Not only is the individual's conduct [. . .] directed by his habitual relations to his fellows in the group, but these relations [. . .] vary [. . .]. The wants and desires, the end and aim, the ways and means, the amplitude and drift of the individual's conduct are [. . .] of a highly complex and wholly unstable character.
>
> *(1909: 629)*

The behaviour of agents, thus, is seen to depend on the social context, which—in turn—is subject to change. This interdependency lies at the heart of what Veblen sees as a path-dependent process:

> The economic life history of the individual is a cumulative process of adaptation of means to ends that cumulatively change as the process goes on, both the agent and his environment being at any point the outcome of the past process.
>
> *(1898b: 391)*

Limitations

Veblen's work has been criticised for being "an economics [. . .] without theory" (Langlois 1986: 5). While he employs the concept of rules (habits) and rule populations (institutions) in a consistent way, it is true that he did not spend much effort on generalising his findings. Consequently,

Veblen's works may be disappointing to the reader looking for explicit theoretical and analytical guidance.

In spite of these limitations, contemporary rule economics is much indebted to Veblen in two respects. First, Veblen's voice was among the early scholarship questioning the appropriateness of single-rule theorising. Through his qualitative empirical work on the development of societies, he impressively documented the emergence of a behavioural rule which has largely replaced "profit maximisation" in growing layers of society: status. Secondly, his analyses of change in individual agents and of the historical development of societies represent important groundwork for the endogenisation of the processes of rule adoption and diffusion.

Nelson–Winter routines building on behavioural rules

In their own words, Nelson–Winter's "real concern is with organisations" (1982: 72). And indeed these scholars are known for their groundbreaking research on the behaviour of organisations. Importantly, however, their understanding of organisational routines builds on an analogy to individual behaviour:

> We propose that individual skills are the analogue of organisational routines, and that an understanding of the role that routinisation plays in organisational functioning is therefore obtainable by considering the role of skills in individual functioning.
>
> *(1982: 73; similar 2002: 30)*

Nelson–Winter's use of the term "skill" is particular and slightly differs from its common use: "skills [are] considered as units of purposive behaviour" and are "programmatic", in the sense that they involve specific procedures. This exactly corresponds to the definition of "behavioural rules" in current discourse.

To understand why Nelson–Winter only sparsely and rather accidentally[1] use the term "rule" for designating recurring patterns of individual behaviour, reflecting on their situation in the early 1980s is helpful. As is the case with every new theorising, Nelson–Winter were carefully developing their language. In fact, "rule" was not even a candidate in their list of alternative denominations: "plan", "script", "habit",[2] "routine" and "program" (1982: 74). At that time, the term "rule" had two predominant uses: as a near equivalent to "law and regulation" in the studies of constitutional political economy (see, for instance, Brennan and Buchanan 1985), and for designating the process quality of decisions through the compound noun of "decision rule". In fact, Nelson–Winter conform to the latter use in their discussion of evolutionary modelling and growth theory, and to the former when discussing policy.

Multi-dimensional heterogeneity in behavioural rules

Drawing on Alchian (1950), Nelson–Winter see *imitation* as one important route for the adoption of behavioural rules. They hold that in the presence of tacit knowledge, the effectiveness of *instruction* will be significantly limited (1982: 77). Recurring operations based on behavioural rules then enable their retention, or, in Nelson–Winter's more succinct words, prevents the skill from becoming "rusty" (1982: 124). The set of skills, that is, of behavioural rules, which an agent has adopted and retains for operations, is defined in Nelson–Winter as the "repertoire" of an individual (1982: 98). Naturally, every agent acquires an individual repertoire which leads to acknowledging "between-agent" heterogeneity.

With Michael Polanyi, Nelson–Winter share the view that behavioural rules might be followed subconsciously (1982: 78). Nelson–Winter even argue that "the choice among behaviour options that takes place in the exercise of a skill typically involves no deliberation and it is a constituent of the capability that the skill represents" (1982: 82). These arguments are in line with the empirical findings from research on consumers who frequently have difficulty in explaining their choices. Nelson–Winter see behavioural rules as being "context-dependent in various ways" and hold that their effectiveness "is particularly dependent upon detailed features of the *social* context" (1982: 87). They also observe that the use of rules for operations depends on a spatial dimension: "It is the differences between the environment in which a skill (and associated terminology) is developed and a relatively novel environment in which it is exercised that highlight its operational (and semantic) ambiguities" (1982: 91). In essence, this implies two more dimensions of heterogeneity: rules chosen for operations differ between agents in different environments, and even *within* individual agents depending on the respective situational social context.

Nelson–Winter then propose that the aggregate of the skills of individuals makes for organisational capabilities. This, they argue, poses important coordination problems (1982: 124–6). Organisations are countering these by using control tools such as "selection, modification, monitoring and adaptation" (1982: 114). As will be discussed later, a contemporary approach to understanding these control tools relies on conceptualising them as *social rules*.

Dynamics

In contrast to their initial conceptualisation of organisational routines that strongly builds on individual skills, Nelson–Winter do not draw on behavioural rules for theorising about evolution. In their works, the modelling of innovation refers entirely to organisational routines aimed at achieving technological progress (see 1982: 14; 2002). In Nelson–Winter's view, innovation is one possible reaction to "changed market conditions", with changes in prices serving as their predominant example (1975: 163; 1982), the other possible reaction being "routinised response". For describing "the variety of processes, mostly intentional but some not, by which rule changes take place", Nelson–Winter use the term "search" (1982: 171). In their view, search is equally conducted according to rules. As I will discuss later, such "innovation rules" are conceived as second order rules in contemporary rule-based economics. With Schumpeter, Nelson–Winter hold that "reliable routines of well-understood scope provide the best components for new combinations" (1982: 131).

Limitations

Nelson–Winter's reasoning about rule innovation is strongly guided by two concerns: the intent to position their theorising against orthodoxy; and their focus on analysing the evolution of rules in organisations. Consequently, their work contains no substantial cues about the processes of change in rules retained by individuals such as the behavioural rules discussed here. In essence, behavioural rules in Nelson–Winter merely serve as a building block for their reasoning about organisational routines in terms of decision rules.

Regardless of these limitations and of some definitional issues, Nelson–Winter's concept of "skills" contains important clues for our understanding of behavioural rules. Firstly, behavioural rules are seen as units of programmatic behaviour that consciously and subconsciously guide economic operations. Secondly, in rule-based economic theory, there is multi-dimensional heterogeneity: the *repertoire* of rules retained differs between agents, and the choice of rules for operations by an individual agent differs depending on the social context and a spatial dimension. And most importantly, the *repertoire* of individual agents is subject to change, that is, it evolves.

Elinor Ostrom's conceptual legacy

Elinor Ostrom is best known for her analyses of common-pool resources. In her *opus magnum Governing the Commons* Ostrom uses case studies as "an empirical basis for learning more about the effects of institutions on behaviours" (1990: xv) and aims to provide "more relevant theories of institutional change for policy analysis" (1990: 191). When it comes to criticising economic orthodoxy, Ostrom is less outspoken than Nelson–Winter—let alone Veblen—typically giving implicit reference only: "Where behaviour and outcomes are substantially different from the predicted, are there behavioural regularities that can be drawn upon in the development of improved theories?" (Ostrom, Gardner et al. 1994: jacket).

Definitions

In her 1986 presidential address to the Public Choice Society, Ostrom noted: "Rules, as I wish to use the term, are potentially linguistic terms that refer to prescriptions" (1986: 5). With policy design as one of her main research subjects, it is not surprising that her understanding of rules at that time closely corresponds to that of scholars in constitutional political economy. In her later writings, however, Ostrom pledges for a broad application of the concept of rules:

> Contemporary scholarship tends to focus on rules that are formally prescribed by a national government, but we must understand the process of rule change at a community level as well, even when the rules-in-use are not formally written by those using them to structure their daily interactions.
>
> *(2011: 322)*

Such broad understanding of the rules has important consequences for empirical research: "the rules affecting much of our behaviour are relatively invisible, which challenges our ability to identify and measure them" (2011: 318). From this follows the need for extensive qualitative fieldwork in inquiries of complex rule systems: "One needs to examine a full rule configuration, rather than a single rule" (Ostrom et al. 1994: 77).

With Veblen Ostrom shares the understanding of institutions as resulting from rules "commonly known and used by a set of participants to order repetitive, interdependent relationships" (Ostrom 1986: 5). Thus, by referring to "sets of participants", Ostrom implicitly endorses Veblen's population approach to the definition of institutions.

Ostrom's rules are for organising individuals

Arguably owing to her research focus on local communities, Ostrom holds that rules always exist for a social purpose: "All rules are the result of [. . .] efforts to achieve order and predictability among humans" (1994: 38). In Ostrom's view, behavioural rules are thus always pertaining to the social behaviour of agents. Rules exist for the plain purpose of defining a system design. In these designs, social behaviour features as the *object* of rules. Accordingly, rules pertaining to individual agent behaviour as a *subject* are not considered in Ostrom's approach.

Her empirically developed framework for the analysis of rule systems consists of seven "classes" (1994: chapter 2), or "types" (2011: 323–4) of rules:

- position rules describing conditions and rights for a position in a social system,
- boundary rules regulating entry to and exit from the system,
- choice rules prescribing choice conditions for specific positions,
- aggregation rules specifying voting processes,
- information rules indicating transparency levels for specific positions,
- pay-off rules controlling the distribution of rents, and
- scope rules specifying quantitative limitations of operations where monitoring of actions is difficult.

With all these types of rules referring to the agent as an object, Ostrom's understanding of rules closely resembles Nelson–Winter's organisational routines. As is shown through her empirical studies of common-pool resource systems, this framework is powerful for mapping the functioning of complex social organisations.

Ostrom's agent: implicitly heterogeneous and individually rational

Ostrom does not explicitly argue that agents in a community may be heterogeneous. However, she implicitly acknowledges analytically significant differences between agents. This becomes obvious where she states the necessity to distinguish "subsets of appropriators", that is, of agents in her empirical analyses of common-pool resource systems (1990: 210).

In a similarly implicit manner, Ostrom hints at differences in the set of rules adopted by individual agents where she comments on some of the difficulties in her empirical work: "Rule following or conforming actions are not as predictable as biological or physical behaviour explained by physical laws" (1994: 40).

The only type of heterogeneity that Ostrom explicitly acknowledges refers to a spatial dimension. Thus subscribing to a localist approach (see also Blind 2012a), Ostrom calls for "specialized rules that apply to localities" (1990: 214). Note that this type of heterogeneity again does not refer to individual agents but to agent communities.

In contrast to Nelson–Winter, Ostrom sees agents as being entirely conscious of their rules and rule-following. In her view, this results from a need to "formulate" rules (1994: 40). If agents eventually act unconsciously, then they follow what Ostrom refers to as "internalised norms" (1990: 193). In Ostrom's view, however, both cases are still in line with "a general conception of rational action" (1990: ibid).

Ostrom's "defence of rationality" continues in her interpretation of yet another empirical observation. Studying the development of rule systems she observes that the choice criterion in many agents is sufficiency, rather than optimality: "if individuals find rules that work relatively well, they may have little motivation to continue the costly process of searching for rules that will work even better" (1990: 211).

Evolution of rule system as a semi-conscious search process

In Ostrom's view, the need for theorising about change in rule systems arises from the simple observation that "rules can be changed while physical [. . .] laws cannot" (1986: 6). With Nelson–Winter, Ostrom shares a critical stance where it comes to explaining change in rule systems by means of orthodox theory:

> Profit maximisation is a useful theoretical tool for predicting behaviour in static market situations; it does not enable a theorist to predict which firms are most likely to survive or to predict innovative technological or institutional changes [...] It is thus not a judicious theoretical strategy to presume that choices about rules are made to maximise some single observable variable.
>
> *(Ostrom 1990: 207)*

Ostrom's opinionated statement builds on her general understanding of rule configurations as complex systems with feedback mechanisms: "Change in one rule affects the working of others" (1994: 77). As another feature of such complexity, Ostrom points to different layers of rules active in a configuration: "A theory of self-organisation and self-governance of smaller units within larger political systems must overtly take the activities of surrounding political systems into account in explaining behaviour and outcomes" (1990: 190).

In conceptualising the potential origins of change in rule systems, Ostrom relaxes the "consciousness condition" that she upholds for rule action: "Rule changes may result from self-conscious choice or may evolve over time" (1994: 77). In her late writings one finds explicit notion of change in rule configurations "as a result of many self-conscious or unconscious mechanisms" (2011: 325). Notably, the latter are seen to "include forgetting" (ibid: 326).

In the course of change in rule configurations, Ostrom identifies "variables that are most likely to affect decisions about continuing or changing rules", citing "expected benefits, expected costs, internalised norms, and discount rates" (1990: 192–3). The first two of these obviously reduce to the net benefit of a discrete change in rules and are entirely operational. Equally, discount rates reflect a single cognitive rule, namely the rule of preferring current over future pay-offs. From the perspective of contemporary behavioural rule economics, her notion of "internalised norms" is key. These norms represent cognitive rules of normative content that govern the individual behaviour of agents. For the adoption and retention of this class of rules Ostrom identifies "internal psychic and external social cost" (1990: 206) as the main influencing factors. Unfortunately, Ostrom only devotes but a single page on this in the exposition of her inductively derived theoretical framework (1990: chapter 6).

Limitations

Ostrom's inductively derived theoretical framework is only general to the analysis of common-pool resource systems. While it may be extended to cover other systems of social rules as well, it remains highly specific in its contribution to a rule-based economics. In essence, Ostrom's work is essential to the scholar concerned with the design and enforcement of rules for governing the *social* behaviour of agents. It is, however, much less instructive in explaining the evolution of rules.[3] Also, Ostrom's work hardly contributes to understanding the rules guiding agents" *individual* behaviour.

Adding to her empirical focus on common-pool resource systems, one can identify Ostrom's preoccupation with game-theoretic argument as explaining the origin of these limitations. Game theory—for all its merits—hardly allows for quality and heterogeneity to be accommodated. It is only in her reasoning about rule choice and rule innovation that Ostrom briefly departs from the track of game theory. In essence, this means that most of her work remains loyal to the single (behavioural) rule dogma of orthodox economics: self-interest.[4]

In spite of these limitations, her work represents a groundbreaking step towards a theory of rule-based economics. First, because she has demonstrated how "reasoning with rules" allows for obtaining superior empirical results. Second, and likely even more importantly, because her work delivers strong argument supporting the cause of heterogeneity in economic theorising. This becomes evident where she argues that a rule-based economics should strive for "a framework rather than a model [. . .] because one cannot encompass (at least with current methods) this degree of complexity within a single model" (1990: 214).

Reflections and synthesis

One finds hardly any explicit reference to Veblenian thought in the works of Nelson–Winter and Ostrom. While the former derive much inspiration from Schumpeter's writings, their *opus magnum* does not mention Veblen a single time (see Fagerberg 2003: 128).[5] Equally, Ostrom's *Governing the Commons* does not relate to Veblen at all. This finding also extends to both Nelson and Winter's and Ostrom's other works.

For understanding such absence of explicit references, it may help to reflect on the intentions of Nelson–Winter and Ostrom. Through their corresponding works, they aimed at diffusing radically new ideas into a wider audience in economics. In pursuing this objective, they have avoided overtly making reference to scholarship discredited in the view of many economists, such as Veblen's.[6] Put simply, these authors may have consciously avoided referencing Veblen (see also endnote 2) for the sake of propagating their own ideas more effectively.

However, the absence of such manifest linkages has little—if any—significance for the existence of implicit commonalities. At closer inspection, one finds important linkages between the works of Veblen and those of Nelson–Winter and Ostrom. Nelson–Winter share with Veblen two fundamental convictions. First, they acknowledge Veblen's view that economic agents act according to a multitude of rules in contrast to the singular rule world purported in much of received economic thinking. Second, they share Veblen's understanding that rules do not represent a *fixum*, but that they evolve. Ostrom, in turn, endorses Veblen's understanding of institutions as a community of rule followers. Thus, commonalities refer to the heterogeneity of agents and agency, of the historicity of economic development and of institutions as rule populations.

As another observation from the study of the works of Nelson–Winter and Ostrom, cross-references between these contemporaries are scarce and of a rather general nature. This absence may be seen as a "side-effect" of the strong focus on their respective research areas: large organisations (Nelson–Winter), and resource governance systems (Ostrom). As a consequence of such focus on very complex phenomena and the analytical depth of their models, producing an integrated theoretical approach to the study of rules governing economic behaviour in general was but a secondary objective to them.

Late in her career, Elinor Ostrom addressed the need for such generalisation: "If we are to make headway in understanding how rule systems change, and develop a general theory of institutional change, we must widen our view and study a much more diverse set of rule systems" (2011: 335). For furthering that purpose, she designates Dopfer and colleagues" deductively derived theoretical framework (Dopfer 2001; Dopfer 2004; Dopfer 2005; Dopfer and Potts 2008; Dopfer 2012) as a "very interesting approach" (2011: 333).

A unified rule taxonomy

Continuing the quest for a common terminology in rule-based economics (see Ostrom 1986: 4) Dopfer has developed a unified concept of rules. His rule-based approach (RBA), Dopfer argues, may be referred to as a "Schumpeter–Veblen program" (Dopfer 2012: 157) and unites the essentials of the works introduced here.

The RBA proposes a taxonomy of four classes of rules (Dopfer and Potts 2008: 6–10): cognitive, behavioural, social and technical. As a mutually exclusive and collectively exhaustive concept, this taxonomy allows for fully capturing the diversity of economic phenomena and helps to resolve definitional issues such as Veblen's "mental habits" (see 1898b; 1919a: 40), Nelson–Winter's "decision rules" and Ostrom's distinction of strategies from rules (2011: 321–2), which may all be more aptly understood of as cognitive rules. In a similar vein, Nelson–Winter's "organisational routines" and "control mechanisms" as well as Ostrom's "information rules" (2011: table 2), pertain to the category of social rules. And prominently, Nelson–Winter's skills and Ostrom's "internalised norms" correspond to the behavioural rules discussed here. Appendix 11.1 specifies these commonalities.

The RBA captures evolution as a diffusion process of a novel rule during which an increasing number of agents adopts that novel rule; potentially at the expense of a pre-existing rule. In that context, Veblen's understanding of a "leisure class" and of "ownership" as institutions (Veblen 1899b: 22), mirrors the RBA reading of institutions as rule populations with stable adoption rates. To provide another example, consider the problem of the reach of rules coded in law from the introduction to this article. By the theoretical concept of populations of agents retaining a rule, the RBA conceives of "abiding to law" as a rule in itself.[7]

Adding to the distinction of rule classes, the RBA introduces *three orders of rules,* similar but fully general to Nelson–Winter's hierarchy of rules (1982: 18). They help to understand the different ways in which rules are active in the economic system. At the centre of orders, "1st order operational rules" provide the direct base for operations and represent a direct equivalent to Ostrom's earlier "operational rules" (Ostrom 1990: 50) including her "choice", "position" and "pay-off rules" (Ostrom and Basurto 2011: table 2). In turn, rules controlling the overall functioning of an economy are designated as "0th order constitutive rules". They represent the constituent basis on which all economic activity takes place and define the "opportunity space of permissible 1st order operations" (Dopfer and Potts 2008: 9). In Ostrom's writings, this order of rules is referred to as "constitutional choice rules" (1990: 50) and as "boundary rules" (2011: table 2). Finally, there are rules pertaining to change and innovation in a social system. Nelson and Winter refer to these as "search rules" (1982: 20). In Ostrom, we find examples of this order of rules where she refers to "collective choice rules" (1990: 50). The RBA restates these mechanisms in a more general terminology by denoting as "2nd order mechanism rules" any rule that impacts on the propensity to create, adopt and retain new rules. Appendix 11.2 summarises these correspondences.

Beyond this helpful unification of terminology, the RBA generalises an important number of further phenomena. For instance, it makes explicit the distinction between rules and corresponding operations that is still partly implicit in both Nelson–Winter's and in Ostrom's writings. It also fully generalises processes of change and employs heterogeneous agents open to learning. It thus represents a fully general framework to "the study of the evolution of human societies" as envisioned by Ostrom (2011: 333).

Back to the field: the RBA in empirical research

As the RBA itself does not include practical guidance on how it can be used for developing hypotheses in empirical research, and on how the analysis can be operationalised, I have elsewhere developed a corresponding methodological template (Blind and Pyka 2014). We propose a four-stage methodology that starts with setting a response rule population, an investigation period (owing to historic time), as well as a spatial delimitation (owing to the susceptibility of agents to the social context).

In the second stage, we establish the ensemble of rules potentially influencing the size of the response rule population that Ostrom refers to as "rule configuration". To identify these rules, we suggest that the extant theoretical work in economics should be connected to that of other disciplines, and to include insights derived from interviews of experts, as well as of rule adopters and rejecters.

The third stage commits to the extraction of those rules from the configuration that have effectively caused change in the response rule populations. In essence, this represents an *ex ante* significance test. To effect this test, we propose to assess all rules in the configuration against two criteria for identifying instances of change during the investigation period: (a) change in the size of the respective rule populations, and (b) change in the strength of influence on the response rule population. Rules, for which either or both criteria are different from zero, qualify as part of a changing sub-system, that is, as part of the causal core of the model of change.

Finally, in the fourth stage we develop and test corresponding hypotheses pertaining to causal relationships between factor rules and the responses. To do so, we suggest that the subgroups of agents should be distinguished in the response rule population, an approach that has already been successfully employed by Ostrom.

A number of recent empirical investigations have built their inquiries on Dopfer and Potts" RBA (Blind 2012b; Grebel 2013; Wäckerle 2013). For example, in a study of entrepreneurial attitudes in contemporary Japan (Blind 2012b), the RBA was instrumental for conceiving of such attitudes as a 2nd order cognitive rule. Relying on the methodology sketched above, it was also possible to quantitatively evidence the sustained influence of a rule pertaining to the status of self-employment, or in Veblen's words "employment proper to the several classes" (1899b: 1).

Conclusion and outlook

For a long time, orthodox preconceptions have prevailed as the dominant cognitive rule that has effectively hindered the furthering of economic theory. Veblen was one of the early observers of this phenomenon: "having once been accepted and assimilated as real, though perhaps not as actual, it becomes an effective constituent in the inquirer's habits of thought, and goes to shape his knowledge of facts" (1899a: 422). The reasoning about behavioural rules in Veblen, Nelson–Winter and Ostrom presented here has documented their respective contributions to the project of liberating economic theory from these preconceptions.

"Diversity and change" may serve as common label for the empirical work of Veblen, Nelson–Winter and Ostrom. Veblen's stance is representative of this: For him, each society and each stage of society has its own set of habits. Here, the "set of habits" encompasses "diversity", and the "stages of society" result from "change". In turn, Nelson–Winter have used firms for an integrated analysis of both phenomena. Arguing that firms have different "search processes", they posit that change will occur, and that it will occur in diverse ways. Among the three contributions discussed here, it is Ostrom's work that relies most strongly on empirical observation for (inductive) theoretical reasoning. Employing a less general concept of discrete heterogeneity—through agent subgroups—she arrives at a fully operational framework for dynamic studies of common-pool resource systems. Recently, Dopfer and Potts have achieved systematic synthesis of the main theoretical postulates of Veblen, Nelson–Winter and Ostrom in their *General Theory of Economic Evolution* (Dopfer and Potts 2008).

While Ostrom once argued that "no one can legislate a language for a scientific community" (1986: 5), Dopfer and Potts have offered the heterodox community a common terminology for accommodating the theoretical body of Veblen, Ostrom, Nelson–Winter and Schumpeter. At the same time, the RBA represents what Ostrom had asked for: an analytical framework, rather than a theory. Combined with an appropriate empirical methodology (e.g., Blind and Pyka 2014), this promises to become an influential device in the adjustment process of some prevailing "preconceptions", which—as Veblen holds—happens "only tardily and concessively" (1925: 49).

Notes

1 Compare, for instance, phrases like "the distinction (and relationship) between a behavioral routine or rule and a particular action" (1982: 42).
2 Note the missing citation of Veblen's corresponding concept.
3 The theoretical contribution describing factors likely to enhance rule innovation in terms of "institutional innovativeness" spans less than one page in her *opus magnum* (1990: 211).
4 Note how even the adoption of norms (rules guiding individual behaviour) enter her model in terms of "internal psychic and external social cost" (Ostrom 1990: 206).
5 In spite of both Veblen and Winter holding a Yale PhD!
6 For instance, Lionel Robbins' 1932 *Essay on the Nature and Significance of Economic Science* contains a representative judgment on Veblen's work: "In the history of applied Economics, the work of a Jevons, a Menger, a Bowley, has much more claim on our attention than the work of, say, a Schmoller, a Veblen, or a Hamilton. And this is no accident. The fruitful conduct of realistic investigations can only be undertaken by those who have a firm grasp of analytical principle and some notion of what can and what cannot legitimately be expected from activities of this sort" (compare p. 116 of Robbins' 1945 extended and revised 2nd edition).
7 The extent to which this latter rule has been adopted and retained in a society also aptly explains the existence of "institutional voids".

Bibliography

Alchian, A. (1950). Uncertainty, evolution, and economic theory. Journal of Political Economy, 58, 211–21.

Ault, R. W. & Ekelund, R. B. (1988). Habits in economic analysis: Veblen and the neoclassicals. History of Political Economy, 20(3), 431–45.

Blind, G. D. (2012a). Culture and Economic Explanation: Economics in the US and Japan. By Donald Katzner. Journal of East Asian Studies, 12(1), 150–3.

Blind, G. D. (2012b). Investigating entrepreneurial spirit with the rule approach: Why self-employment is on the decline in Japan. Evolutionary and Institutional Economics Review, 9(1), 183–98.

Blind, G. & Pyka, A. (2014). The rule approach in evolutionary economics: A methodological template for empirical research. Journal of Evolutionary Economics, 24(5), 1085–105.

Brennan, G. & Buchanan, J. M. (1985). The Reason of Rules. Cambridge: Cambridge University Press.

Dopfer, K. (2001). Evolutionary economics: Framework for Analysis. K. Dopfer. The Evolutionary Foundations of Economics. Boston, Dordrecht, London: Kluwer Academic, 1–44.

Dopfer, K. (2004). The economic agent as rule maker and rule user: Homo Sapiens Oeconomicus. Journal of Evolutionary Economics, 14, 177–95.

Dopfer, K. (2005). Evolutionary economics: A theoretical framework. The Evolutionary Foundations of Economics. K. Dopfer. Cambridge: Cambridge University Press, 3–55.

Dopfer, K. (2012). The origins of meso economics. Journal of Evolutionary Economics, 22(1), 133–60.

Dopfer, K. and Potts, J. (2008). The General Theory of Economic Evolution. London: Routledge.

Fagerberg, J. (2003). Schumpeter and the revival of evolutionary economics: An appraisal of the literature. Journal of Evolutionary Economics, 13(2), 125–59.

Grebel, T. (2013). On the tradeoff between similarity and diversity in the creation of novelty in basic science. Structural Change and Economic Dynamics, 27, 66–78.

Langlois, R. (1986). The new institutional economics: An introductory essay. Economics as a Process: Essays in the New Institutional Economics. R. Langlois. Cambridge: Cambridge University Press, 1–25.

Nelson, R. R. & Winter, S. G. (1975). Factor price changes and factor substitution in an evolutionary model. Bell Journal of Economics, 6, 466–86.

Nelson, R. R. and Winter, S. G. (1982). An Evolutionary Theory of Economic Change. Cambridge MA: Harvard University Press.

Nelson, R. R. & Winter, S. G. (2002). Evolutionary theorizing in economics. Journal of Economic Perspectives, 16(2), 23–46.

Ostrom, E. (1986). An agenda for the study of institutions. Public Choice, 48(1), 3–25.
Ostrom, E. (1990). Governing the Commons. Cambridge: Cambridge University Press.
Ostrom, E. and Basurto, X. (2011). Crafting analytical tools to study institutional change. Journal of Institutional Economics, 7(3), 317–43.
Ostrom, E., Gardner, R. & Walker, J. (1994). Rules, games, and common-pool resources. Ann Arbor: University of Michigan Press.
Veblen, T. (1898a). The instinct of workmanship and the irksomeness of labor. American Journal of Sociology, 4(2), 187–201.
Veblen, T. (1898b). Why is economics not an evolutionary science? Quarterly Journal of Economics, 12(4), 373–97.
Veblen, T. (1899a). The preconceptions of economic science. Quarterly Journal of Economics, 13(4), 396–426.
Veblen, T. (1899b). The Theory of the Leisure Class: An Economic Study of Institutions. New York: Macmillan.
Veblen, T. (1909). The limitations of marginal utility. Journal of Political Economy, 17(9), 620–36.
Veblen, T. (1919a). The intellectual pre-eminence of Jews in modern Europe. Political Science Quarterly, 34(1), 33–42.
Veblen, T. (1919b). Why is economics not an evolutionary science? The Place of Science in Modern Civilization and Other Essays. T. Veblen. New York: Russell & Russell: 56–81.
Veblen, T. (1925). Economic theory in the calculable future. American Economic Review, 15(1 Suppl.): 48–55.
Wäckerle, M. (2013). On the bottom-up foundations of the banking-macro nexus. Economics: The Open-Access, Open-Assessment E-Journal, 7(2013-40), 1–45.

Appendix 11.1: Rule classes in Veblen, Nelson–Winter, Ostrom and Dopfer–Potts

	Classes of rules			
	Subject rules		*Object rules*	
Dopfer–Potts	Cognitive	Behavioural	Social	Technical
Veblen	Mental habits	Instincts (e.g. of workmanship); ideal of conduct	–	–
Nelson–Winter	Decision rules (e.g., investment rule)	Skills	Organisational routines; capabilities; control mechanisms	Technology
Ostrom	Strategies	Internalised norms	Information rules	–

Appendix 11.2: Orders of rules in Veblen, Nelson–Winter, Ostrom and Dopfer–Potts

	Orders of rules		
Dopfer–Potts	0th order Constitutional rules	1st order Operational rules	2nd order Mechanism rules
Veblen		Habits	
Nelson–Winter	"Institutional matters" (e.g., property rights, contracts)	Procedure rules	Search rules
Ostrom	Constitutional choice rules	Operational rules; position rules; pay-off rules	Collective choice rules; information rules

12
GENERATING MESO BEHAVIOUR

Manuel Scholz-Wäckerle

Introduction

In this chapter I will discuss a particular kind of economic behaviour that is not an integral part of the homo oeconomicus model. This behaviour is called meso because it is neither part of micro- nor of macroeconomics alone and it is shaped systemically through interactive socioeconomic associations. Thereafter, meso is characterized through structure as well as process components of dynamic change. In the second section I will identify some prototypic descriptions of such behaviour in the work of T.B. Veblen and J.A. Schumpeter in order to motivate an analytical discussion for generating meso behaviour. These prototypes include the instinct of workmanship and innovative entrepreneurship, as well as financing the means of the latter. It is argued that meso behaviour transforms the economy from within (i.e., leading to structural change including the possibility of economic crisis). However, the aforementioned scholars did not have analytical tools that were effective to translate these narratives into didactic analytical models. For this very reason, appropriate concepts and tools are discussed in order to ease the involved complexities for generating meso behaviour in models and simulations.

In the third section the chances and pitfalls of equilibrium, as well as rule-based approaches are highlighted in respective modelling attempts. It turns out that both of these analytical approaches lack systemic conceptions to meet the demands raised in the previous motivation. Therefore, I go beyond a rules-in-equilibrium approach and will discuss the meso framework originally developed by Dopfer et al. (2004). Structure as well as process rules are involved in the dynamic generation of meso behaviour, as proposed by Ostrom (2005) as well as Dopfer and Potts (2008). These rules work simultaneously on a horizontal (structure) and a vertical (process) axis, allow multiple associations between heterogeneous economic agents and relate agent systems to each other. An emerging meso unit corresponds to one of such potential networked systems that cannot be specified per se as an institution or as a social structure but involves agency and creative/adaptive response to changes in its environment. In this section I will compare the analytical concept of a meso unit (Dopfer et al., 2004; Dopfer and Potts, 2008) and that of a meso-sized interaction arena (Elsner, 2010; Elsner et al., 2015). The former takes an evolutionary economic approach and emphasises the innovation of generic rules. Once a novel rule originates in a micro agent, is carried and adopted by a share of the whole population, I speak of a meso unit as the generic rule and its carrier population. The latter draws otherwise on the concept of complexity where meso behaviour emerges from coordination in social-dilemma type situations.

In section four I will follow Simon (1987) and show that the Veblenian and Schumpeterian agents are not be understood as optimizing but as satisficing agents, a precondition for micro behaviour enhancing meso-structured behaviour thereafter. This notion makes a theory of meso behaviour intelligible to us, since it is not the behaviour of the representative agent transforming the economy but the (de)coordination of heterogeneous satisficing agents that are assigning agency to a meso unit through shared characteristics eventually. To model and generate meso behaviour on behalf of satisficing behaviour, it is suggested to combine evolutionary and complexity foundations as highlighted by Simon (1962). In this modular framework I will emphasise the role of intermediate stable complex forms such as meso units. The bounded rationality of involved agents drives them to collaborate in modular meso units to change the economy in response to emerging novel needs. As a consequence, imitation, adaptation, innovation as well as resistance gain a central role in this behavioural economics.

Agents are computationally designed in this respect and feature characteristics as emphasised by Gilbert (2008). In this final section I will emphasise that meso behaviour can be generated and modelled via the agent-based methodology. Agent-based modelling is considered as a generativist approach by Epstein (2006), a methodology featuring the growing of artificial worlds in algorithmic form from bottom up. Meso behaviour can be modelled as an irreversible and path-dependent process by linking micro with macro. Finally, I will emphasise the potential of this approach in inventing a new kind of agent-based meso-founded macroeconomics, compare Dosi et al. (2010), Ciarli et al. (2010), Cincotti et al. (2010), Delli Gatti et al. (2011), Chen et al. (2014) as well as Rengs and Wäckerle (2014). The final fifth section concludes.

Prototyping meso behaviour: Veblen and Schumpeter

This section will introduce the central prototypes of meso behaviour in relation to the Veblenian and Schumpeterian conceptualization of economic behaviour. Veblen and Schumpeter have highlighted economic behaviour in a systemic and to some degree evolutionary perspective that is alien to the homo oeconomicus model, foremost because preferences are formed endogenously via social interaction. This aspect alone involves complexities for modelling and simulation that we confront in this book chapter. Social learning, imitation, innovation and local adaptation are central tenets of meso behaviour and make it time and space dependent. It is important to address that we understand a meso unit as sufficiently autonomous to behave in its own right and that it is capable of agency. Meso behaviour triggers systemic feedbacks on the micro behaviour of the agents involved, on other associated meso units and their structural relations that are composing macro (the whole economy) thereafter. Veblen and Schumpeter had the most significant influence in this regard and it seems appropriate to take a closer look into their picture of human behaviour.

In general, Veblen's theory (especially Veblen, 1899) takes an approach to economics where social values are central for the creation of behavioural patterns and their interconnections (Bush, 1987: 1078). In this anthropological system of thought, Veblen identifies two types of habitual culture in the American society of his times. There is the pecuniary interest of status-seeking imitation, on the one hand, and the industrial interest in the common production of commodities, on the other hand. He associates the former with ceremonial proclivities to be found in the business class and the latter with instrumental or technological proclivities to be found in the industry class. In this regard there are two institutional systems considered, "they are institutions of acquisition or of production . . . they are pecuniary or industrial institutions" (Tool, 1977: 827).

These proclivities are conceived as instincts by Veblen, which can be either supportive in terms of progress as in the case of the "instinct of workmanship", "parental bent" or "idle curiosity" or obstruct constructive properties along "practices of exploit, prowess or mastery (warfare), ownership (material acquisition), and in pecuniary control of industry" (Tool, 1977: 825–6). The instrumental values of the industrial arts are driving technological progress and let society prosper for the common good. The ceremonial values of the business enterprise drive economic behaviour into status-seeking lock-ins and, thereby, lead to inertia of technological and consequential institutional change. This type of dialectics lead to conflicting behaviours that are subject to evolving power relations (Samuels, 1995: 571), such as the habits of conspicuous leisure, consumption and waste (Veblen, 1899: 63–4).

In terms of meso behaviour, it is the habits of thought in the industry class that lead to an emergent meso unit and its further stabilization. "These include 'idle curiosity,' which in industrial society signifies critical inquiry, 'the parental bent,' which means altruism, and 'the instinct of workmanship,' which denotes taking pride in and obtaining gratification from the craftsman like performance of work" (Sheehan and Tilman, 1992: 200–1). These habits of thought are enhancing micro behaviour that enables the emergence of meso. However, they are not conceptualized as constant ends, they are rather part of an "ends–means continuum" (ibid.). For instance, altruism cannot represent a behavioural end in constant terms, once established it becomes a new means for a different end, such as individual well-being, social welfare or sustainable development. Nevertheless, for Veblen it is the instinct of workmanship that has the most significant impact on meso behaviour.

> This alien factor is the instinct of workmanship. Other circumstances permitting, that instinct disposes men to look with favour upon productive efficiency and on whatever is of human use. It disposes them to deprecate waste of substance or effort.
>
> *(Veblen, 1899: 64)*

The instinct of workmanship brings us a step closer to Schumpeter with a similar vision about human behaviour in an industrial society. Innovative entrepreneurship generates meso behaviour that is creative but also destructive (Schumpeter, 1942: 82–3). Schumpeter studied the evolution of capitalism as civilization and his analysis breaks with the rather static description of economic behaviour within the circular flow. There are roughly two institutions that are significant for generating meso behaviour, the first refers to economic behaviour as entrepreneurial action and the second to financing the means to this action. Entrepreneurship is understood as the "carrying out of new combinations" (Schumpeter, 1934: 66) that is a "lasting condition" till the business is settled and not subject to social class.

> Because being an entrepreneur is not a profession and as a rule not a lasting condition, entrepreneurs do not form a social class in the technical sense, as, for example, landowners or capitalists or workmen do. ... It can also put its stamp on an epoch of social history, can form a style of life, or systems of moral and aesthetic values; but in itself it signifies a class position no more than it presupposes one.
>
> *(Schumpeter, 1934: 78)*

Therefore, the entrepreneur is substantially different from the homo oeconomicus in terms of behaviour. Quite similar to Veblen, Schumpeter insists on creativity, curiosity but also on a motive "to succeed for the sake, not of the fruits of success, but of success itself" (Schumpeter, 1934: 93) as central drivers of innovative behaviour striving for novelty. The entrepreneurial agent represents the focal source for generating meso behaviour, because it is dynamically breaking with existing standard behaviour and traditions. This kind of innovative behaviour is by far not of stochastic nature, on the contrary it is about choice. Hanappi (2008) argues that strategic interaction plays a dominant role for innovative behaviour because it depends on the communication of different mental models that indicate inputs for choices eventually. Innovative behaviour is subject to the social mediation of meso thereafter, a notion emphasising the Marxian roots of Schumpeterian thought. Meso behaviour is generated within power relations, where individual contradictory choices enforce the emergence of novelty. This idea of meso behaviour relates to the significance of a heterogeneous conception of economic agents that I will emphasise in section three. Consequently, modellers have to make explicit assumptions about information and communication within and between heterogeneous agents.

The commonality between Veblenian and Schumpeterian economic behaviour relates to the creative enhancement of meso-structured behaviour by the "socially shared imagination" (Dopfer, 2004: 190) or more generally by the development of a "common consciousness" (Hanappi, 2008: 2079). Complementarities in Veblenian and Schumpeterian meso behaviour have led to significant innovations in the history of capitalism. The most important were established by combining the usage of a new source of energy with a new a medium of communication. Examples are given by the use of coal for the steam engine and the development of steam-powered printing presses that have considerably enhanced literacy among all social classes. Another example is given by the use of fossil fuels in the combustion engine and the development of broadcast communication such as radio and TV. This combination has led to the Fordist accumulation regime of mass production and consumption, responsible for the after war boom in economic welfare. Foster (2011) shows how such complementarities have driven the development of capitalism by the collective usage and co-evolutionary relationship between new knowledge stemming from novel media and free energy. The behavioural response to this "autocatalytic interaction" is given by evolving "units of identification" (ibid: 94–6) forming on behalf of newly developed aesthetics and thereby generating novel meso behaviour. Foster (2011: 98) argues that aesthetics connects "energy throughput and the application of knowledge" and this process of economic structuration leads to "the reduction of accessible free energy gradients" (ibid.: 88). This hypothesis is considered as foundational for economic behaviour and relates to the problem of economic growth and sustainable development.

The "dilemma of growth" (Jackson, 2011: 49–66) has evidently shown that not every kind of innovation is beneficial and that innovative behaviour needs to be appraised in terms of energy usage, biodiversity loss, carbon emissions and environmental pollution. Jackson (2011: 87–102) emphasises that the complementarities of Veblenian and Schumpeterian economic behaviour may lead us into an "iron cage of consumerism", a state that is similar to a technological and institutional lock-in. To avoid such lock-ins, many authors argue in favour of installing and deploying a third industrial revolution built on novel meso behaviour. Perez (2013) argues that this time of multiple crises needs the "installation and deployment of a new golden age" (ibid.: 10–12), that is combining the usage of renewable forms of energy—such as solar and wind energy—with the use of novel information technology (i.e. the Internet). The most crucial role in this evolutionary economic project is probably given by global finance as indicated by Perez (2013: 13–15), who considers Minsky (1986) as a third complementarity in this regard.

Minsky argued that "Our economy is unstable because of capitalist finance" (Minsky, 1986: 244). Instability emerges endogenously in prosperous times of tranquil stability where margins of safety decline or even erode. Central to Minsky's theory of financial behaviour is the speculative motive that was originally introduced by Keynes (1936: 126) in his theory of endogenous money. In this view "money is created in the process of financing investment and positions in capital assets" (Minsky, 1986: 131). Schumpeter (1934) developed a very similar view on money where banks create purchasing power in order to finance innovative behaviour.

> This method of obtaining money is the creation of purchasing power by banks. ... It is always a question, not of transforming purchasing power which already exists in someone's possession, but of the creation of new purchasing power out of nothing ...
>
> *(Schumpeter, 1934: 72–3)*

Minsky owes his analytical precision both to Keynes and Schumpeter (Knell, 2015), he could truly master a synthesis of these two great economists and could explain why Schumpeter could not develop a full-fledged endogenous theory of money. In many respects Hyman Minsky has anticipated the role of herding behaviour in destabilizing the economy. Basically, a Schumpeter–Minsky meso unit consists of complementary micro behaviours of entrepreneurs and bankers that are providing the financial means for innovative behaviour, but this meso unit may quickly destabilize the economy if speculative or Ponzi schemes are adopted by a larger group of agents. The necessary choices for generating a meso unit are made under true uncertainty and this "is largely a matter of dealing today with a future that by its very nature is highly conjectural" (Minsky, 1986: 207).

Analysing meso behaviour: equilibria, rules and meso

The previous section has discussed prototypes of meso behaviour in the work of Veblen and Schumpeter. Their models have remained in the realm of prose, certainly within the more thought-provoking chapters of economic prose filled with grand pieces of ironic satire. Still, they build up scholarly entry barriers for students of economics as well as applicants of economic theory. To this extent, the aim of this section is to emphasise concepts that make meso behaviour intelligible to us and can bridge between semantic content, analysis, modelling and simulation.

The previously discussed problem structures can neither be associated solely with micro nor macro approaches, thereby they demand an intermediate level of analysis such as meso. A traditional way of addressing problem structures of this type is followed in institutional economics (Hodgson, 2004). Institutions are diverse, ubiquitous and manifold (Ostrom, 2005), who involve processes of social valuation and thereby evolve, since values are not constant ends. Hodgson (2015: 501) defines institutions as "integrated systems of rules that structure social interactions" and provides thereby a necessary working definition and "demarcation criterion to distinguish institutions from other social phenomena" (ibid.). The notion of "shared systems of rules" (ibid.) is essential in this regard and an interesting approach was developed by Masahiko Aoki (2001: 10), who articulates a game-theoretical approach and characterizes an institution as a "self-sustaining system of shared beliefs". In this conceptualization the author incorporates a "rules-in-equilibrium" approach (Hindriks and Guala, 2014) with special attention to the "rules of the game" as the

> way by which the game is repeatedly played ... We regard these rules as being endogenously created through the strategic interactions of agents, held in the minds of agents, and thus self-sustaining – as the equilibrium-of-the-game theorists do.
>
> *(Aoki, 2001: 10)*

The unique criterion in this approach is given by "repeated games" where pairwise interaction gains dynamic momentum, albeit Aoki (2001: 185–206) does not use a generative bottom-up but a closed-form evolutionary game theory approach (see also Bowles, 2004). Hodgson (2015: 500) considers this attempt fruitful since "the resulting game equilibria themselves establish possible rules" and thereby link to processes in contrast to deterministic outcomes. The advantage of

Aoki's (2001) approach to institutional change and more generically to meso behaviour is given by its analytical tractability:

> One of the great advantages of this equilibrium-based approach to institutions is that it becomes analytically tractable to deal endogenously with types of institutions that may emerge across different domains as well as possible interlinkages among institutions.
>
> *(Aoki, 2001: 207)*

Aoki (2001) has shown how we can apply this methodology in static terms to a diversity of real-world problems, ranging from governance, finance, to innovation. The issue of finance is, for instance, analysed as a topic of "relational-contingent governance" (Aoki, 2001: 307) in the context of the Asian banking crises in the 1990s, especially the case of Japan. Concerning Japan, I speak of the emergence of a rather stable and subsidized (see also Pagano, 2011: 387) firm–bank network on behalf of cross-shareholding and a main bank system in the second half of the twentieth century. This system emerged out of organisational disequilibrium and has reduced uncertainty to provide the means for innovative activity, job security as well as purchasing power. Aoki (2001: 329) highlights that institutional stability depends on "institutional complementarities and co-emergence", institutions that are already existing or co-emerging in order to sustain the performance of an institution, understood "in the economist's language as unintended subsidies coming from different selection domains" (Pagano, 2011: 377).

The concept of "interlocking complementarities" is not just useful in explaining stability but moreover in explaining the emergence of a novel set of institutions. Pagano (2011: 379–83) emphasises this complex interrelation with complementary dialectics between technology and property rights. This complementarity leads to an "organisational Nash equilibrium" where "the interactions between technology and property rights have a built-in inertia" that can prohibit development and keep the system "in a long period of stasis". Therefore, as argued by Pagano (2011: 383), "because of interlocking complementarities, we should expect the formation of new organisational species to require allopatric conditions of major external subsidies."

Consequently, it is historical specificity and path-dependency that matters for stabilizing rule-following behaviour, as was highlighted by Elinor Ostrom at several occasions: "As Ostrom (1990, 2000) insisted, they must be rules in actual or potential use in a community, and not merely rules in form" because "There is also the question of the guiding role of habit in rule-following" (Hodgson, 2015: 503). This intervention is significant for a theory of meso behaviour because it demonstrates the necessity of populating the economic space with agents carrying and sharing particular rules in heterogeneous actions. Ostrom's (2005: 135–216) attempt in assessing rules in collective action problems highlights the relevance of their underlying evolutionary processes. Her strategy to cope with the evolving diversity of different rules is to establish a generic rule-based approach (Ostrom, 2005: 181–4) working on two axes, a horizontal and a vertical one. The former focuses on the structural components, as given by position, boundary or aggregation rules (among others), and the latter on process components, such as operational, collective choice and constitutional-choice levels (Ostrom, 2005: 186–215). In a similar vein, Dopfer and Potts (2008: 6–10) discuss generic rules as cognitive, behavioural, social and technical rules on the structural axis and the order of rules on the process axis; constitutive, operational and mechanism rules.

Ostrom's (2005: 222) analysis focuses on the rules-at-use in common-pool resource regimes, Dopfer and Potts (2008) use their terminology to develop an evolutionary economic theory where knowledge is not constant, not exogenous and evolves. A further difference to Ostrom's rule-based approach deals with the structural component of object rules. In Dopfer and Potts (2008), objects such as institutions and organisations have agency but also technical artefacts, machines or even techniques. The latter typology signifies the material turn in the social sciences as discussed recently by D'Adderio (2011) who is working with the Latourian ontology of actor-network theory (Latour, 2005). To this extent, meso behaviour organises not just on behalf of typical individual micro carriers such as households but also, strictly speaking, in coordination with social carriers such as institutions and organisations as well as object carriers such as artefacts or machines within a flat ontology.

At the core of this model we find a meso unit that consists of a generic rule and its carrier population. A generic rule represents the analytical form of an idea: "A rule is defined as the idea that organises actions and resources into operations" (Dopfer and Potts, 2008: 6). However, it is not the rule that stands in the center of attention but the carrying agent. The micro theory within this approach is elaborated by Dopfer (2004) where carriers are both rule-makers and rule followers. With this conception agents face different micro trajectories, or life-cycles with distinct behavioural patterns rendering them as active entrepreneurs and/or passive adopters. It is crucial that in such a picture of economic behaviour agents are not aggregated into representative agents anymore and behaviour is of heterogeneous nature. Dopfer and Potts (2008: 5) argue that the micro entity is neither influenced solely by internal (e.g. preferences) nor external (e.g. institutions) signals as primary sources for behavioural response.

It is rather this bimodality between internal and external signals establishing the agents as different decision makers, an argument that is very close to the already discussed notion of choice in Hanappi (2008). Therefore, the agent is not just a carrier "of rules for operations" but "the locus for originating, adopting and retaining new rules" (Dopfer and Potts, 2008: 5). A significant puzzle stone for discussing the relation between micro and meso is given by similar research on routines as developed originally by Nelson and Winter (1982: 14-19). Relevant implications for routines are considered as "pertaining to organised groups, rather than individuals", "involving the notion of procedural memory", "recurrent interaction patterns" and "involving change driven by individuals" (Lazaric, 2011: 147). The concept of routines seems to be important for meso behaviour, because they act as "generative structures and behavioural patterns at one at the same time" (Vromen, 2011: 186). And, most importantly, "Only multi-agent collectives such as groups and organisations can have routines. ... 'Routines' are reserved exclusively to denote possible properties of collectives" (ibid.). Routines retain novel rules in organisational context and stabilize a meso unit to establish behaviour on its own.

Meso behaviour depends on several micro trajectories, but originates its own trajectory that is adopted or shared by many carriers of different kind. Direct aggregation from micro to macro is rejected thereby, the relation works rather "via the emergence and self-organisation of meso populations and structures" (Dopfer and Potts, 2008: 22). Meso behaviour governs the translation between micro and macro, if and only if we speak of diversity among meso units. Ostrom and Basurto (2011: 333–7) argue that a theory of meso seems to be promising for further investigation, in context of empirical research as well as agent-based modelling. The same argument has been made by Delli Gatti et al. (2010: 119) from a macroeconomic perspective. Recent explicit attempts in this direction were implemented by Blind (2012), Wäckerle (2013) or Blind and Pyka (2014). A more generic example of generating meso behaviour is illustrated by Dopfer (2012) in terms of Schumpeter's legacy. It is conceptualized as a "meso trajectory" consisting of a structure and a process component. The former is conceived as a rule-structure (the way that we think about our economy, deal with it and categorize it). The structure is real once it is actualized via operations and this constitutes the latter, the process component of economic change.

> In combination, we get an integrated elementary unit that can serve as an instrument for the description of both structure and process of an economy. ... The idea can serve as

> structure component, the set of physical actualizations as process component. The bimodal nature of the elementary unit breaks up with the traditional micro-macro dichotomy.
>
> *(Dopfer, 2012: 145–6)*

In summary Schumpeterian meso behaviour can be sketched as a process consisting of six phases:

I Origination

Sub-phase 1: creation of novel idea, that is, invention
Sub-phase 2: search, discovery and recognition process, microscopic selection

II Adoption

Sub-phase 3: first adoption, that is, innovation, chaotic environment, bifurcation, uncertain outcome
Sub-phase 4: macroscopic adoption of "seed", selective environment, path-dependence

III Retention

Sub-phase 5: retention of adopted "seed", meta-stability of actualization process
Sub-phase 6: existing regime as breeding ground for novel potential(s), link to phase I (Dopfer, 2012: 148).

As outlined by Dopfer (2012), this kind of meso dynamics depends on social interaction in a heterogeneous population of agents and it cannot be reduced to a diffusion process of a "single valued variable, but as a process in which individuals interact with an emergent population in a self-reinforcing way" (ibid.: 149). This aspect indicates the complementarities with Veblen's concept of cumulative causation of habits of thought and signifies the potential for a common theory of meso behaviour. The ways that meso behaviour is generated are different in terms of its actualizations but in its generic nature they share common conceptions of structure and process components.

Elsner and Heinrich (2009), and Elsner (2010) take a similar point of departure as Aoki (2001) but elaborating more on the potential mechanisms leading to an emergent meso-sized population. Elsner (2010: 447) considers co-evolutionary components as essential for the emergence of a meso-sized population, that is: "(1) a complex incentive structure, (2) experienced expectations, indicative (in varying degrees) of (3) the group size, and (4) the institution as such (as both quest and outcome of the individual's effort)." In this context, the author analysed the strategic behaviour of micro agents playing a pairwise prisoner dilemma. It is suggested to employ dynamics of critical mass processes as Schelling (1978: 102–10) emphasises in terms of "tipping" phenomena. In this analytical realm, Elsner (2010) is not obliged to introduce heterogeneous agents basically, because meso appears here as a problem of size primarily, a "minimum critical mass" within a given population. However, even quite simple extensions to the game-theoretical model show how the emergence of a meso-sized interaction arena can be supported endogenously, such as "contingent trust", "memory and monitoring", "reputation chain" and "partner selection" Elsner (2010: 466–72). Elsner's (2010) conceptualization of meso follows institutionalists' arguments with regards to instrumental and life-enhancing habits of thought. These allow a pragmatist mode of collective reasoning and decision-making necessary for institutionalization. The cumulative process of meso reproduces stylized facts investigated by other evolutionary economists researching the complexity of technological change (e.g. Arthur, 1989). Recently, Arthur (2015: 16) has acknowledged the potential of a common meso theory as developed by Dopfer and Potts (2008), and Elsner and Heinrich (2009). In these terms, I propose combining the evolutionary with the complexity foundations of meso behaviour. A candidate for such an analytical endeavour is given by the agent-based methodology as also indicated by Gräbner (2015).

Modelling meso behaviour: growing artificial economies as complex adaptive systems

Following these derived concepts, it is proposed to model the generation of meso behaviour on behalf of interactions between different economic agents in a given environment. The complexity is, therefore, not intrinsic to the agent itself. For this very reason, it is important to investigate the relations between the involved agents and how they build up systems creating agency on their own. Complex systems are hierarchical because they consist of subsystems which consist of subsystems themselves.

> By a *hierarchic system,* or hierarchy, I mean a system that is composed of interrelated subsystems, each of the latter being, in turn, hierarchic in structure until we reach some lowest level of elementary subsystem. In most systems in nature, it is somewhat arbitrary as to where we leave off the partitioning, and what subsystems we take as elementary. ... We shall want to include systems in which there is no relation of subordination among subsystems. ... For lack of a better term, I shall use hierarchy in the broader sense introduced in the previous paragraphs, to refer to all complex systems analyzable into successive sets of subsystems, and speak of "formal hierarchy" when I want to refer to the more specialized concept.
>
> *(Simon, 1962: 468)*

Simon's (1962) understanding of formal hierarchy—as "partitioning in conjunction with the relations that hold among its parts"—is essential for any concept of meso behaviour because it assumes a flat ontology of components, subsystems and systems where all the objects and subjects stand "next to each other" without any assumed authoritative subordination. From this point of departure, Simon (1962: 473) underpins the topic of complexity with evolutionary arguments and shows that complex systems evolve on behalf of simple systems and "much more rapidly if there are stable intermediate forms than if there are not." In economics, such stable intermediate forms are meso units. Hierarchy leads us to the notion of decomposability, in particular that of "nearly decomposable systems" (ibid.). The latter terminology refers to the interactions among and between subsystems. Hierarchy in near-decomposable systems informs us on the frequency of interactions, thus frequency increases by magnitude of one or two when we go one step downward in the formal hierarchy of a system and vice versa. This conclusion seems intuitive when we consider economic systems and their hierarchies. The frequency of interactions between households (micro) is much higher than that of interactions between regions, organisations, industries or political economic networks (meso) or of states or monetary unions (macro). Nearly decomposable systems share the characteristics of weak but not negligible interactions among subsystems, as also argued by Csermely (2009) in the context of "nestedness" and "weak links". The most noteworthy implications for meso behaviour and its analytical generation deal with the time horizon.

> (a) in a near-decomposable system, the short-run behaviour of each of the component subsystems is approximately independent of the short-run behaviour of other

> components; (b) in the long-run, behaviour of any one of the components depends in only an aggregate way on the behaviour of the other components.
>
> *(Simon, 1962: 474)*

Meso behaviour involves autonomous action and the interaction of meso units informs on the long-run macro behaviour. Veblen and Schumpeter considered different time horizons in their work and have always emphasised the sociohistorical context of development. Concerning the Schumpeterian case, the emergence and stabilization of a meso unit is effected by its short-run behaviour, which strongly depends on the interactions of the entrepreneur, its financier and its adopters. This type of meso behaviour is connected to Schumpeter Mark I (Schumpeter, 1934). Otherwise, in the long-run the meso behaviour depends in an aggregate way on the behaviour of other meso units within the whole economy, as considered in Schumpeter Mark II (Schumpeter, 1942: 79–82).

The processes of widening (Mark I) and deepening (Mark II) meso behaviour relate to Simon's (1962: 476–477) remarks on the "width of hierarchic span"; a hierarchic span is thereby understood as an indicator for the modularity of such nearly decomposable systems (Callebaut, 2005). According to Simon (2005) these systems are more likely to adapt in local niches. Formal hierarchical modularization makes systems more flexible to adapt and more robust to changes in a given environment. Generating meso behaviour depends strongly on the modularity of the modelled system. To begin with, it is proposed to assume rather simple satisficing heuristics (Simon, 1987; March, 1991; Winter, 2000) for the behaviour of micro agents rather than optimizing decision rules. This conception of micro agents is also highlighted by Beinhocker (2007: 118), who follows a quite similar route in combining evolutionary and complexity foundations for analysing economic behaviour on different scales.

Beinhocker (2007: 293) addresses the notion of economic evolution as algorithmic and synthetic where "instructions bind Physical Technologies and Social Technologies together into modules under a strategy." Satisficing micro behaviour enforces agents to collaborate and create but also contradict nested modules or meso units. Modelling such agent properties and the corresponding initialization of their systemic environment is necessary to develop a complex adaptive system. It is suggested to follow a computational approach that, moreover, allows the generation of meso behaviour in formal hierarchical terms. In particular, I want to emphasise prospects of the bottom-up or agent-based approach in computational economics (see Velupillai et al. (2011) for an overview of different approaches in computable economics).

As shown in Table 12.1, the bottom-up approach in computational economics differs substantially from traditional modelling tools. Characteristics such as the process-oriented design, as well as the possibility to model adaptive agents, feature in synergistic terms the systemic development of structure and process components of meso behaviour. Of course, algorithms represent artificial rules and stand only as proxies for more complex behavioural patterns, as discussed previously. Nevertheless, the modelling architecture focuses on space and time contextualization of agents and allows, for example, routinisation. What is the role of the computer in this respect? Holland (1992) summarizes quite illustratively:

> For example, the equation-based methods that work well for airplanes have a much more limited scope for economies. ... Despite the disparities and the difficulties, we are entering a new era in our ability to understand and foster such systems. The grounds for optimism come from two recent advances. First, scientists have begun to extract a common kernel from these systems: each of the systems involves a similar "evolving structure". ... The second relevant advance is the new era in computation ... This advance will allow experts who are not computer savvy to "flight-test" models of

Table 12.1 Modelling potential of the bottom-up approach

Traditional tools	*Agent-based objects*
Precise	Flexible
Little process	Process oriented
Timeless	Timely
Optimizing	Adaptive
Static	Dynamic
1,2, or ∞ agents	1,2, . . . , N agents
Vacuous	Spacey/networked
Homogeneous	Heterogeneous

Source: Miller and Page (2007: 79).

particular complex adaptive systems. For example, a policy maker can directly examine a model for its "reality", without knowing the underlying code.

(*Holland, 1992: 17*)

The first point raised by John Holland refers to the potential of the computational approach to generate meso behaviour that is dependent on evolving/modular structure. The second point is not of lower importance—quite the opposite—it highlights the didactic power of simulations in exploring complex adaptive systems and their potential path-dependent developments. Simulation (Gilbert and Troitzsch 2005: 5) particularly allows the investigation of emergence, "path-dependence, nonergodicity and cumulativity in processes of change" (Elsner et al., 2015: 10–11). Nevertheless not every simulation technique is appropriate in this regard. Figure 12.1 illustrates the development of simulation techniques and arranges them in two broad categories, where the grey-shaded area contains equation-based models and the white area contains either object, event or agent-based models. Among these techniques, we find cellular automata and agent-based models that are suitable to simulate the aforementioned dynamics. Agent-based models fall under the category of multi-agent models with communication between multiple agents as well as a sufficient degree of complexity concerning the individual heterogeneous agent. A typical example for such a multi-agent model is given by the "Sugarscape" model developed by Epstein and Axtell (1996: 21–53). The model consists of resources as well as social rules and heterogeneous individual metabolisms. In its most basic form "Sugarscape" already implies meso behaviour, since the distribution of wealth develops endogenously by influencing the "cultural" behaviour of individual agents thereafter. This case becomes even more evident with particular extensions allowing the emergence of trade and credit networks (Epstein and Axtell, 1996: 94–137).

Computational simulation suits the social sciences better than mathematics. A big part of this advantage is given by the usage of programming languages that are more expressive and less abstract than mathematical techniques. Programs are modular and deal more easily with "processes without a well-defined order of actions" (Gilbert and Troitzsch, 2005: 7). Elsewhere, Gilbert (2008) highlights the power of programming languages in designing artificial agents for proper use in agent-based models. The most important characteristics for agents and their micro trajectories in such models are given below:

- Autonomy – There is no global controller dictating what an agent does; it does whatever it is programmed to do in its current situation.

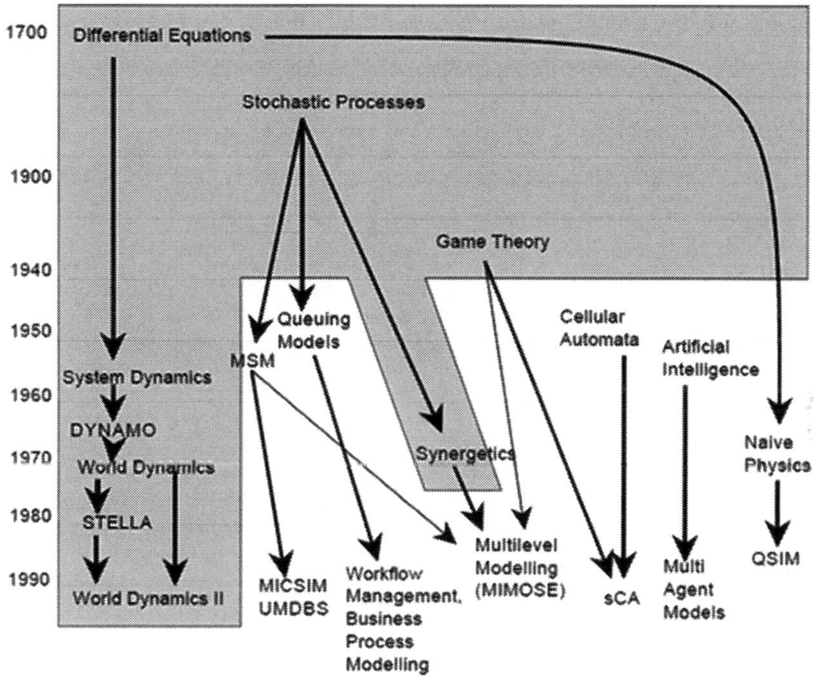

Figure 12.1 Development of different simulation techniques in the social sciences

Source: Gilbert and Troitzsch (2005: 7).

- Social ability – It is able to interact with other agents.
- Reactivity – It is able to react appropriately to stimuli coming from its environment.
- Proactivity – It has a goal or goals that it pursues on its own initiative.
- Perception – They can perceive their environment, possibly including the presence of other agents in their vicinity. In programming terms, this means that agents have some means of determining what objects and agents are located in their neighbourhood.
- Performance – They have a set of behaviours that they are capable of performing. Often, these include the following:
    - Motion – They can move within a space (environment).
    - Communication – They can send messages to and receive messages from other agents.
    - Action – They can interact with the environment, e.g. "picking up food".
- Memory – They have a memory, which records their perceptions of their previous states and actions.
- Policy – They have a set of rules, heuristics, or strategies that determines, given their present situation and their history, what behaviours they will now carry out (Gilbert, 2008: 21).

These distinctive properties stand in the foreground when it comes to generating meso behaviour, because they enhance the ontological correspondence between computational agents and real-world actors. The benefit of this approach relates to the development of modularity by growing the system from the bottom up, a principle that is considered as generative.

> Situate an initial population of autonomous heterogeneous agents in a relevant spatial environment; allow them to interact according to local rules, and thereby generate – or "grow" – the macroscopic regularity from the bottom-up.
>
> *(Epstein, 2006: 7)*

To grow and generate a system, it is necessary to change the language structure from mathematical equations to computational algorithms and programs. Social interaction is too complex to represent it in comprehensive and recognizable recursive equation systems, here the agent-based methodology is more intelligible and accessible to us. Meso behaviour is then generated via growing artificial societies from the bottom up, modelled via heterogeneous agents that imitate, innovate, adapt, adopt or even resist. An emerging meso unit differs substantially from other meso units due to its distinct rule-structure. To this extent it is worthwhile to differentiate between heterogeneity and diversity (D'Ippoliti, 2011), where the former is associated with micro agents and the latter with meso units. Meso behaviour differs from group- or system-based behaviour because it underlies explicitly an evolutionary process of origination, adoption and retention, with regards to distinctive shared rules transforming its structure and process components.

In the literature, we find several examples of agent-based generated meso behaviour, which mostly deal with aspects of imitation, adaptation and innovation. I highlight Elsner and Heinrich (2011) or Wäckerle et al. (2014) in relation to institutional economics, Janssen and Ostrom (2006) or Safarzynska (2013) in relation to ecological economics, Gilbert et al. (2001) in relation to innovation economics and Fagiolo et al. (2007) in relation to social policy. Dosi et al. (2010) present an agent-based macroeconomic model with a distinctive capital goods market and model the development of Schumpeterian innovative behaviour in complexes that we can consider as meso units. Ciarli et al. (2010) deliver an agent-based macroeconomic model that features both consumption and production on the micro level, as well as income distribution, and investigate structural change and growth thereby. Cincotti et al. (2010) provide a similar framework with regards to scope and scale but highlight more the Minskian financial aspects of credit-driven investment and systemic risk. Rengs and Wäckerle (2014) have particularly addressed the notion of Veblenian institutional consumption dynamics and its effects on firm organisation in a political economy with social classes. Delli Gatti et al. (2011) provide otherwise a very detailed instruction into macroeconomics from the bottom up. Together, this type of research develops a new kind of agent-based meso-founded macroeconomics by focusing on the progressive behavioural elements of development.

Concluding remarks

In this chapter I have highlighted why a theory of meso behaviour is important and why it is distinct from the homo oeconomicus model. I have motivated this endeavour on behalf of a brief tour through the history of economic thought, in particular through the work of Veblen and Schumpeter. Both of these seminal scholars have highlighted non-aggregate aspects of a dynamic, systemic and to some degree evolutionary economics. At the core of their economic models, I locate meso behaviour as the agency and adaptive/creative response of a meso unit that emerges on behalf of coordination and organisation of individual heterogeneous economic agents in social systems. I have emphasised the instrumental, creative and life-affirming proclivities of agents in the industrial society that enforce generative micro behaviour for meso, as found in the prototypes of the Veblenian engineer or the Schumpeterian entrepreneur. Analytical categories have been introduced to model social interaction, such as origination, imitation, innovation, adaptation, adoption and resistance. The framework of mesoeconomics is discussed in detail, highlighting formal preliminaries for generating meso behaviour. Thereby, a meso unit is on the one hand understood as a generic rule and its carrier population that goes through different stages of behaviour during its trajectory and interacts with other micro, meso or macro entities. Meso behaviour is thereby understood in a Schumpeterian understanding of innovation. On the other hand, meso refers to a platform size and interaction arena where individual agents coordinate to overcome social-dilemma type problems. This conception of meso relates to institutional economics and the pragmatist approach to collective action problems. To generate meso behaviour, it is necessary to think about agents in a Simonian understanding of satisficing behaviour. Such heterogeneous agents are furthermore part of a modular structure of systems, where complex systems adapt more rapidly if there are stable and intermediate forms in between. This architecture of complexity demands computational and algorithmic techniques for appropriate models and simulations. I have summarized some central properties of agents and systemic environments in such models, and have indicated how meso behaviour can be generated from the bottom up in such artificial economies.

Bibliography

Aoki, M. (2001). Toward a comparative institutional analysis. Cambridge, MA: MIT Press.

Arthur, W.B. (1989). Competing technologies, increasing returns, and lock-in by historical events. The Economic Journal, 99(394), 116–31.

Arthur, W.B. (2015). Complexity economics: A different framework. In Arthur, W.B. (ed.), Complexity and the economy. Oxford: Oxford University Press, 1–29.

Beinhocker, E.D. (2007). The origin of wealth: Evolution, complexity and the radical remaking of economics. London: Random House.

Blind, G.D. (2012). Investigating entrepreneurial spirit with the rule approach: Why self-employment is on the decline in Japan. Evolutionary Institutional Economic Review, 9(1), 183–98.

Blind, G.D. and Pyka, A. (2014). The rule approach in evolutionary economics: A methodological template for empirical research. Journal of Evolutionary Economics, 24(5), 1085–105.

Bowles, S. (2004), Microeconomics: Behavior, institutions, and evolution. New York: Princeton University Press.

Bush, P.D. (1987). The theory of institutional change. Journal of Economic Issues, 21(3), 1075–116.

Callebaut, W. (2005). The ubiquity of modularity. In Callebaut, W. and Rasskin-Gutman, D. (eds.), Modularity: Understanding the development and evolution of natural complex systems. Cambridge, MA: MIT Press, 1–28.

Chen, S.H., Chang, C.L. & Wen, M.C. (2014). Social networks and macroeconomic stability. Economics: The Open-Access, Open-Assessment E-Journal, 8(2014–16), 1–40.

Ciarli, T., Lorentz, A., Savona, M. & Valente, M. (2010). The effect of consumption and production structure on growth and distribution: A micro to macro model. Metroeconomica, 61(1), 180–218.

Cincotti, S., Raberto, M. & Teglio, A. (2010). Credit money and macroeconomic instability in the agent-based model and simulator Eurace. Economics: The Open-Access, Open-Assessment E-Journal, 4, 2010–26.

Csermely, P. (2009). Weak links: The universal key to the stability of networks and complex systems. Berlin: Springer-Verlag.

D'Adderio, L. (2011). Artifacts at the centre of routines: Performing the material turn in routines theory. Journal of Institutional Economics, 7(2), 197–230.

D'Ippoliti, C. (2011). Economics and diversity. London: Routledge.

Delli Gatti, D., Gaffeo, E. & Gallegati, M. (2010). Complex agent-based macroeconomics: A manifesto for a new paradigm. Journal of Economic Interaction and Coordination, 5(2), 111–35.

Delli Gatti, D., Desiderio, S., Gaffeo, E., Cirillo, P. & Gallegati, M (2011). Macroeconomics from the bottom-up. Berlin: Springer-Verlag.
Dopfer, K. (2004). The economic agent as rule maker and rule user: Homo sapiens oeconomicus. Journal of Evolutionary Economics, 14(2), 177–95.
Dopfer, K. (2012). The origins of meso economics: Schumpeter's legacy and beyond. Journal of Evolutionary Economics, 22(1), 133–60.
Dopfer, K. & Potts, J. (2008). The general theory of economic evolution. London: Routledge.
Dopfer, K., Foster, J. & Potts, J. (2004). Micro-meso-macro. Journal of Evolutionary Economics, 14, 263–79.
Dosi, G., Fagiolo, G. & Roventini, A. (2010). Schumpeter meeting Keynes: A policy-friendly model of endogenous growth and business cycles. Journal of Economic Dynamics and Control, 34(9), 1748–1967.
Elsner, W. (2010). The process and a simple logic of "meso": Emergence and the co-evolution of institutions and group size. Journal of Evolutionary Economics, 20, 445–77.
Elsner, W. & Heinrich, T. (2009). A simple theory of meso: Co-evolution of institutions and platform size. Journal of Socio-Economics, 38(5), 8433–58.
Elsner, W. & Heinrch, T. (2011). Coordination on "meso"-levels: On the co-evolution of institutions, networks and platform size. In Mann, S. (ed.), Sectors matter! Exploring mesoeconomics. Berlin: Springer-Verlag, 115–63.
Elsner, W., Heinrich, T. & Schwardt, H. (2015). The microeconomics of complex economies: Evolutionary, institutional, neoclassical, and complexity perspectives. Oxford: Academic Press.
Epstein, J. (ed.) (2006), Generative social science: Studies in agent-based computational modeling. Princeton, NJ: Princeton University Press.
Epstein, J.M. & Axtell, R. (1996). Growing artificial societies: Social science from the bottom up. Washington, DC: Brookings Institution Press.
Fagiolo, G., Valente, M. & Vriend, N.J. (2007). Segregation in networks. Journal of Economic Behavior and Organization, 64(3–4), 316–36.
Foster, J. (2011) Energy, aesthetics and knowledge in complex economic systems. Journal of Economic Behavior and Organization, 80, 88–100.
Gilbert, N. (2008). Agent-based models. Quantitative Applications in the Social Sciences 153. London: Sage Publications.
Gilbert, N. & Troitzsch, K.G. (2005). Simulation for the social scientist. Maidenhead: Open University Press.
Gilbert, N., Pyka, A. & Ahrweiler, P. (2001). Innovation networks: A simulation approach. Journal of Artificial Societies and Social Simulation, 4(3), 1–13.
Gräbner, C. (2015). Agent-based computational models – a formal heuristic for institutionalist pattern modelling? Journal of Institutional Economics, 12(1), 241–61.
Hanappi, H. (2008). The concept of choice: Why and how innovative behavior is not just stochastic. Journal of Evolutionary Economics, 18, 275–89.
Hindriks, F. & Guala, F. (2014). Institutions, rules and equilibria: A unified theory. Journal of Institutional Economics, 11(3), 459–80.
Hodgson, G.M. (2004). The evolution of institutional economics: Agency, structure and Darwinism in American institutionalism. London: Routledge.
Hodgson, G.M. (2015). On defining institutions: Rules versus equilibria. Journal of Institutional Economics, 11(3), 497–505.
Holland, J.H. (1992). Complex adaptive systems. Daedalus, 121(1), 17–30.
Jackson, T. (2011). Prosperity without growth. Abingdon: Routledge.
Janssen, M. & Ostrom, E. (2006). Governing social-ecological systems. In K.L. Judd and L. Tesfatsion (eds.), Handbook of computational economics II: Agent-based computational economics, Amsterdam: Elsevier, 1465–509.
Keynes, J.M. (2008) [1936]. The general theory of employment, interest and money. Milton Keynes: BN Publishing.
Knell, M. (2015). Schumpeter, Minsky and the financial instability hypothesis. Journal of Evolutionary Economics, 25(1), 293–310.
Latour, B. (2005). Reassembling the social: An introduction to actor-network theory. Oxford: Oxford University Press.
Lazaric, N. (2011). Organizational routines and cognition: An introduction to empirical and analytical contributions. Journal of Institutional Economics, 7(2), 147–56.
March, J.G. (1991). Exploration and exploitation in organizational learning. Organization Science, 2, 71–87.

Miller, J.H. & Page, S.E. (2007). Complex adaptive systems: An introduction to computational models of social life. Princeton, NJ: Princeton University Press.
Minsky, H.P. (2008) [1986], Stabilizing an unstable economy. New York: McGraw Hill Books.
Nelson, R. & Winter, S. (1982). An evolutionary theory of economic change. Harvard: Belknap Press.
Pagano, U. (2011). Interlocking complementarities and institutional change. Journal of Institutional Economics, 7(3), 373–92.
Perez, C. (2013). Unleashing a golden age after the financial collapse: Drawing lessons from history. Environmental Innovation and Societal Transitions, 6, 9–23.
Ostrom, E. (2005). Understanding institutional diversity. Princeton, NJ: Princeton University Press.
Ostrom, E. & Basurto, X. (2011). Crafting analytical tools to study institutional change. Journal of Institutional Economics, 7(3), 317–43.
Rengs, B. & Wäckerle, M. (2014). A computational agent-based simulation of an artificial monetary union for dynamic comparative institutional analysis. Proceedings of the 2014 IEEE Conference on Computational Intelligence for Financial Engineering & Economics (CIFEr), 427–34.
Safarzynska, K. (2013). The coevolution of culture and environment. Journal of Theoretical Biology, 322, 46–57.
Samuels, W.J. (1995). The present state of institutional economics. Cambridge Journal of Economics, 195(4), 569–90.
Schumpeter, J.A. (2012) [1934]. The theory of economic development. New Brunswick, NJ: Transaction Publishers.
Schumpeter, J.A. (2008) [1942]. Capitalism, socialism and democracy. 3rd edn. New York: Harper Perennial.
Sheehan, M.F. & Tilman, R. (1992). A clarification of the concept of "instrumental valuation" in institutional economics. Journal of Economic Issues, 26(1), 197–208.
Simon, H.A. (1962). The architecture of complexity. Proceedings of the American Philosophical Society, 106(6), 467–82.
Simon, H.A. (1987). Satisficing. In Eatwell, J., Millgate, M. and Newman, P. (eds) The new palgrave dictionary of economics 4. New York: Stockton Press, 243–45.
Simon, H.A. (2005). Foreword by Herbert A. Simon. In Callebaut, W. and Rasskin-Gutman, D. (eds.), Modularity: Understanding the development and evolution of natural complex systems. Cambridge, MA: MIT Press, iv–xiii.
Tool, M.R. (1977). A social value theory in neoinstitutional economics. Journal of Economic Issues, 11(4), 823–46.
Veblen, T. (2009) [1899]. The theory of the leisure class. Oxford: Oxford University Press.
Velupillai, K.V., Zambelli, S. & Kinsella, S. (eds.) (2011). The Elgar companion to computable economics. The International Library of Critical Writings in Economics. Cheltenham: Edward Elgar.
Vromen, J. (2011). Routines as multilevel mechanisms. Journal of Institutional Economics, 7(2), 175–96.
Wäckerle, M. (2013). On the bottom-up foundations of the banking-macro nexus. Economics: The Open-Access, Open-Assessment E-Journal, 7(40), 1–45.
Wäckerle, M., Rengs, B. & Radax, W. (2014) An agent-based model of institutional life-cycles. Games, 5(3), 160–87.
Winter, S.G. (2000). The satisficing principle in capability learning. Strategic Management Journal, 21, 981–96.

13

SCHUMPETER, KIRZNER, KNIGHT, SIMON, AND OTHERS

Behavioral economics and entrepreneurship

Thomas Grebel and Michael Stützer

Introduction

The common ground of behavioral economics and entrepreneurship research lies in answering two related questions: What drives economic behavior? And what makes entrepreneurial behavior different from other people's behavior? Although both behavioral economics and entrepreneurship research start out with different foci, they encounter the same challenges. Both put the homo oeconomicus as an optimizing representative agent into perspective. Whereas the homo oeconomicus manages to maximize subjective utility, human mankind evidently has a hard time in doing so. In general, a lack of information, uncertainty, and bounded capabilities thwart such kinds of behavior. In this chapter we will lay out the behavioral and psychological foundations of entrepreneurship theory, and refer to a selection of behavioral approaches in the entrepreneurship literature.

Behavioral foundations in entrepreneurship theory

What makes an entrepreneur and what drives entrepreneurial behavior, if it is not the dispassionate maximizing behavior of the economic man? In literature, there are many different views of the role of the entrepreneur in economy: the entrepreneur as industrial leader, manager, organizer, decision maker, supplier of financial capital, and so on (Hébert and Link, 1982; Barreto, 1989; Grebel, 2004). Most concepts highlight the functional role of the entrepreneur.[1] Some of them explicitly abandon the maximization hypothesis and envision a behavioral framework of the entrepreneur.

Schumpeter's conduct model

One of the most prominent concepts of the entrepreneur, which delivers behavioral foundations to entrepreneurship, arose from the seminal work by Joseph A. Schumpeter. His discontent with the static picture of neoclassical economics on economy made him develop a theory of economic change (Schumpeter, 1911), which put the entrepreneur in the center of an ever-changing economy. The entrepreneur, according to Schumpeter, destroys an equilibrium by innovating and thus induces economic change. This not only put the entrepreneur in the center of an endogenous theory of economic change, it also led to a quite heroic picture of the entrepreneur, very different to that of a pure maximizer. "It is more by will than by intellect that the leaders fulfill their function, more by 'authority,' 'personal weight,' and so forth than by original ideas" (Schumpeter, 1939: 88). Schumpeter incorporated passion, confidence and psychological aspects into the entrepreneur's profile, which Fritz Machlup named the "conduct model of the dynamic entrepreneur".[2] With his conduct model, Schumpeter paved the way to many behavioral approaches, some of them to be addressed later on.

Kirzner's arbitrageur

The concept by Kirzner describes the entrepreneur as someone who is alert to new opportunities, discovers arbitrage options, and functions as an equilibrator. In contrast to Schumpeter's concept where the entrepreneur is a disruptive element in economy, Kirzner's (1999) entrepreneur is not; in contrast, "the entrepreneurial discovery process is one whose tendency is systematically equilibrative" (Kirzner, 1999: 6). Before equilibrium is reached, a lack of knowledge and deficient capabilities have to be overcome. Both sides, suppliers and demanders, are prone to such deficiencies and thus furnish the market process. In this process the entrepreneur plays a special role as he is the one buying "in one market in order to resell, possibly at a considerably later date, in a second market" (Kirzner, 1999: 172). In so doing, the entrepreneur equilibrates the market while compensating for imperfect knowledge and creating new knowledge.

Knightian uncertainty

In Schumpeter's concept of the entrepreneur, uncertainty was irrelevant (Endres and Woods, 2010). Although Kirzner also neglected the role of uncertainty in his theory (Kirzner, 1999), his entrepreneur was a learning agent prone to error. Knight (1921) filled this gap and saw the main characteristic of an entrepreneur as a bearer of uncertainty. If there were perfect knowledge, optimization would be the dominant behavioral rule leading to a unique outcome (i.e., equilibrium). However, the higher the degree of uncertainty, the less likely it will be for unique behavioral rules to occur. Then, economic behavior inevitably becomes heterogeneous.[3] Economic actors have different kinds of knowledge, make different judgments, and differ in their capacity and/or willingness to make forecasts about the future.[4] Only a small group of people with superior managerial ability in terms of foresight and the capacity of ruling others, only those with confidence in their judgment and disposition to "back it up" in action perform entrepreneurial behavior (Knight, 1921: 269). The majority of the population simply furnishes the entrepreneurs with their productive services, whereas the entrepreneurs promise a fixed compensation while they bear the consequences of uncertainty (Knight, 1921: 271).

Knight (1921) classified three types of uncertainty: when (1) the probability distribution and future outcomes are known so that expected values can be calculated, when (2) probability distribution exists but is unknown ex ante so that actors can perform repeated trials to find out, and (3) when the future is unknown, which Knight calls "true uncertainty."

Simon: bounded rationality

On the grounds of uncertainty, one pervasive question remains to be answered: How do entrepreneurs make decisions? Normative decision theory supplies many techniques for optimization. If the probability distribution and all future outcomes are known, or at least can be inquired by repeated trials, then the expected outcome of entrepreneurial decisions can be calculated.

Under true uncertainty this is impossible. Without having information about probabilities and future outcomes to conceive of economic behavior as optimal behavior is futile.

In contrast to Friedman's (1979) rational expectation hypothesis, which suggests that decisions are right on average, so that optimization would be feasible, Simon (1955) claims that "businessmen" do not behave rationally on a global basis. He rejects this methodological approach (Simon, 1963) and coined an alternative concept called "bounded rationality". Decision makers either do not have or are incapable of retrieving all relevant information. Their cognitive capacity to process all information is limited, and therefore they cannot help "satisficing", that is, making suboptimal but simpler decisions (Schwartz, 2002).

With the bounded rationality approach Simon set the foundation for behavioral economics (Schwartz, 2002). His work has been conducive for many related theories such as the behavioral theory of the firm elaborated by Cyert et al. (1963). The fact that psychology has become more intertwined with economics is to a large extent due to Simon, who was inspired by psychology and incorporated many psychological aspects into economic theory. The extent to which psychology has influenced entrepreneurship theory will be presented in the next section.

Psychological foundations in entrepreneurial theory

As mentioned above, a further main approach to entrepreneurship comes from the discipline of psychology. Contrary to economics, the psychology of entrepreneurship is not so much concerned about who the entrepreneur is but rather how and why entrepreneurs act the way they do (Frese et al., 2000; Hisrich et al., 2007). The question of how entrepreneurs act is often related to specific entrepreneurial tasks such as risk-taking. We discuss aspects of the avoidance and taking of risks in the next section. The question of why entrepreneurs act concerns the motivation of entrepreneurial behavior. The personality approach in psychology offers some insights into what drives human behavior with respect to entrepreneurship.

Prospect theory

Entrepreneurial behavior is often accompanied by risk-taking. There is simply a high chance that a new venture fails—estimates vary between 30 percent and 50 percent failure rate in the first years after starting up. This calls for theories explaining the nature and extent of risk-taking of entrepreneurs. One of these theories is expected utility theory which predicts that if certain rationality axioms are satisfied (Morgenstern and von Neumann, 1953) people decide between risky alternatives based on the expected utility (Friedman and Savage, 1948). An interesting feature that makes expected utility theory useful for entrepreneurship is that people can be risk-averse, which means that they either shy away from a lottery with an expected value of zero or risk-loving which means accepting even a lottery with a negative expected value.

Although, expected utility theory is impressively elegant and mathematically rigorous, over time, scholars have discovered paradox situations where people's decisions deviate from the predictions of expected utility theory. An alternative model which describes human decision making more accurately was developed by Kahneman and Tversky (1979), which is called *prospect theory*. Key to prospect theory is that it depends on the reference point against which alternative outcomes are evaluated. Quite often the reference point is the status quo—for example the absolute level of wealth or income before starting a firm.[5] The reference point might also be the worst case scenario of losing all investments in the start-up. Based on the reference point, potential outcomes of the lottery are assigned to a value via a subjective value function. Typically, negative deviations from the reference point (=losses) hurt more than positive deviations (=gains).

They instead bring joy. Another feature of prospect theory is the subjective weighting of the probabilities attached to the lottery outcomes. Individuals differ in their subjective evaluation of small objective probabilities. For example, firm founders often overrate the small probability of founding a multi-million dollar company compared to the objective probability that the start-up firm goes bankrupt (Forlani and Mullins, 2000).

Big Five

The personality approach is one of the most established approaches to entrepreneurship. Even prominent economists such as Schumpeter (1934) and Sombart (1909) have speculated that the entrepreneur differs in personality from other people. Psychology research differentiates between several levels of personality: personality traits and characteristic adaptations. We start with the Big Five dispositional traits which refer to individual differences in behavior, thought, and feeling that account for general consistencies across situations and over time (McAdams and Pals, 2006: 212). The Big Five personality traits have a strong genetic base, remain relatively stable over lifetime and they are cross-culturally validated (Costa Jr and McCrae, 2006). According to this personality model, individual personality can be described by five broad dimensions: openness, extraversion, conscientiousness, neuroticism, and agreeableness. Each of these broad dimensions consists again of a cluster of more specific factors which are usually assessed by self-reports or observations. It should be kept in mind that the Big Five personality traits do not dictate individual behavior. In contrast, they are best understood as dispositional—making certain actions of people more likely or less likely. With respect to entrepreneurship, all Big Five traits seem to be related to entrepreneurial behavior (Zhao and Seibert, 2006, for a comprehensive description). In a nutshell, openness—the individual tendency to seek new experiences and explore novel ideas—is important for entrepreneurial behavior because it fosters idea generation and creativity. Extraversion—the individual tendency to engage with the outside world—fosters entrepreneurship, as a substantial part of the entrepreneurial task is to engage with customers, suppliers, financiers, and employees in order to run the business. Conscientiousness—the individual degree of self-control, persistence and motivation—is critical for entrepreneurial behavior because entrepreneurs work in a self-directed environment. Neuroticism (=the opposite of emotional stability) —the individual inability to cope with stress and the tendency to experience negative emotions—is detrimental for entrepreneurship as starting a business is a risky endeavor spiked with substantial challenges. Agreeableness—the individual tendency to trust, to compromise with others and to strive for social harmony—might be negative for entrepreneurship as entrepreneurial behavior is often associated with doing things differently than before and to challenge incumbent firms.

Entrepreneurial personality profile

The concept of the entrepreneurial personality profile builds on the Big Five personality traits. The intra-individual configuration of such personality traits (Block, 1971; Magnusson and Torestad, 1993) influences human action in general and entrepreneurial behavior in particular. Consequently, instead of looking at a single trait, it is the specific constellation of the Big Five traits which are in the center of psychology-based entrepreneurship research.

Following the above described relationships of the traits to entrepreneurship, an entrepreneurial personality profile consists of a high level of openness, extraversion, conscientiousness, and a rather low level of neuroticism and agreeableness (Schmitt-Rodermund 2004). Individuals scoring high on this profile should be more inclined to entrepreneurial behavior.

Empirical evidence for this relationship has been growing over the last decade (Obschonka et al., 2010, 2011).

The vast majority of research on traits and entrepreneurship is at the individual level—relating individual differences in entrepreneurial behavior to individual differences in traits. An interesting twist to trait research is the very recent development to look at regional personality differences where regional personality is simply measured by the mean of the individual traits/profile across a regional populace (Talhelm et al., 2014). Specific traits such as openness and the entrepreneurial personality profile are not randomly distributed across regions and countries but clustered in space (Obschonka et al., 2013; Rentfrow et al., 2008). The spatial clustering of certain entrepreneurial traits can become persistent as they get expressed by, for example, the creation of formal and informal institutions such as entrepreneurship friendly bankruptcy laws, the willingness to provide venture capital, and the general social approval of entrepreneurship as a career option which in turn again fuels entrepreneurial activity (Audretsch, 2007; Rentfrow et al., 2008). Given these characteristics, the regional personality structure features elements of several cultures.

Characteristic adaptations: self-efficacy and passion

Beside the dispositional Big Five traits, psychology research has identified numerous other personality characteristics related to entrepreneurship that fall into the category of characteristic adaptations (Frese and Gielnik, 2014). Because of space limitations, we focus on the following adaptations: self-efficacy, locus of control and entrepreneurial passion. These show very high correlations with entrepreneurial behavior and success. In general, characteristic adaptations differ from the above described personality traits in three important ways. First, the characteristic adaptations are more closely related to the entrepreneurial task than the more general personality traits. This close relation manifests itself in high correlations with entrepreneurship indicators. Second, characteristic adaptations do not remain as constant over time as the personality traits but are more likely to change over the lifetime. Characteristic adaptations are thus best understood as "specific motivational, social-cognitive, and developmental variables that are contextualized in time, situations, and social roles" (McAdams and Pals, 2006: 212). Third, the characteristic adaptations arise from the dispositional traits (McAdams and Pals, 2006).[6] Thus, characteristic adaptations can be regarded as "lower-order" dimensions of human personality.

Self-efficacy is defined as a person's beliefs in their own capabilities to master a task (Bandura, 1977). While this general self-efficacy affects the complete range of human behavior, the more domain-specific construct of entrepreneurial self-efficacy—the person's belief in their own capabilities to master the task of starting a business—is expected to be related to entrepreneurial behavior and success. This characteristic adaptation comprises sub-components such as identifying a business opportunity and marshalling the necessary financial and human resources to start-up (McGee et al., 2009). Self-efficacy is crucial for entrepreneurial behavior as self-efficacy affects whether a person engages in a task, how much effort is invested to succeed, and whether the individual shows perseverance in face of obstacles.

Passion is defined "as consciously accessible, intense positive feelings experienced by engagement in entrepreneurial activities" (Cardon et al., 2009: 517). In contrast to the dispositional traits, entrepreneurial passion is directly linked to the self-identity of the entrepreneur (Cardon et al., 2009). Passion is thought to influence entrepreneurial behavior in a number of ways. Most importantly, passion will make people work long hours during the start-up process in times of high uncertainty (Baum and Locke, 2004). Passion is also important to make other stakeholders (potential customers, financiers and employees) believe in the emerging venture, arguably leading to higher contributions of these stakeholders and keep them committed.

Behavioral approaches in entrepreneurship research

Entrepreneurship research is still a young research discipline. This comes at the cost that there is no full-fledged theoretical body such as consumption theory or production theory in microeconomics. We can only discuss some of the most prominent behavioral approaches embedded in entrepreneurship research. First, we introduce each behavioral approach; and second, we show links to the above discussed behavioral and psychological foundations.

Sarasvathy: causation and effectuation

The degree of uncertainty is crucial in any decision making process. Particularly for entrepreneurs, whose daily business is to deal with true uncertainty (Knight, 1921). Sarasvathy (2001) focuses on the question how entrepreneurs deal with an unpredictable future. She coined the concept of *causation* and *effectuation*. Both terms describe alternative processes of decision making. Causation denotes the process where an entrepreneur tries to accomplish a predefined effect or goal by choosing among different means to accomplish this effect or goal. On the contrary, causation describes a process in which the entrepreneur has to deal with a set of given means and chooses which goals can be achieved with these means. More precisely:

> Entrepreneurs following an effectuation approach might begin the new venture process with general aspirations to create a new venture, but as they make decisions and observe the results of those decisions, they utilize this new information to change course. Because the future is unpredictable, entrepreneurs using an effectuation approach may try different approaches in the marketplace before settling on a business model.
>
> *(Chandler et al., 2011: 377)*

Both causation and effectuation processes are relevant for all human decision making processes, whereas entrepreneurs tend to be more inclined to apply effectuation processes. Effectuation processes can be described by four core principles: 1) affordable loss, 2) strategic alliances, 3) exploitation of contingencies, and 4) controlling an unpredictable future. Regarding the first principle, effectuation predicts that entrepreneurs consider how much of the available resources they want to put at risk in the entrepreneurial activity rather than trying to maximize expected returns from the activity (this would resemble causation). The affordable loss dimension can be linked to prospect theory. The reference point is the actual wealth from which the entrepreneur starts. The value function is quite flat in the gain region but rather steep in the loss region, as the entrepreneur does not try to maximize expected returns but will not risk more money than he or she can afford to lose. In addition, the second principle—strategic alliances—can be linked to psychological approaches in entrepreneurship research. Forming strategic alliances is a way to gain commitment and secure resources from partners for the venture. Passionate entrepreneurs might have an advantage forming such strategic alliances, as their passion can be contagious and make others believe in the venture.

The same reasoning can be applied to one of the Big Five traits: extraversion. Unfortunately, there are no empirical studies available linking Big Five traits or passion to effectuation principles which is because of still remaining issues in measuring effectuation (Chandler et al., 2011, Read et al., 2009). The fourth principle—controlling an unpredictable future—builds directly on the Knightian uncertainty. In situations of true uncertainty where outcomes and probabilities are unknown, optimization strategies cannot be applied. Effectuation now predicts that the entrepreneur should focus on his or her own knowledge as well as capabilities and conduct short-term experiments (e.g., testing the market with different versions of a product). The knowledge gained through these experiments can then guide future action. In this way, the entrepreneurs keep control in uncertain environments while still making progress through learning from successful and unsuccessful experiments. Support for this kind of reasoning comes from Chandler et al. (2011) who show that experimentation is more likely in uncertain situations. From a theoretical stance, for example, Bhave (1994) gives insights into the venture creation process.

Bricolage

Bricolage is a behavioral approach explaining how entrepreneurs deal with resource scarcity and constraints. While a disproportionate share of research has focused on the small share of growth-oriented entrepreneurship in high-tech or ICT sectors—start-ups such as Google or Facebook that can "tap" (capital) markets, the vast majority of entrepreneurial endeavors are started with very limited resources. Nevertheless, these resource-constrained firms often flourish against the odds, raising the question of "how they can create something from nothing" (Baker et al., 2005: 1). According to Baker et al. (2005: 333), the entrepreneurs engage in bricolage behavior which is defined as "making do by applying resources at hand to new problems and opportunities". This definition emphasizes three elements: 1) making do, which refers to active engagement and action instead of analyzing and long search processes for optimal solutions; 2) using resources at hand, which means that entrepreneurs reuse resources that they have immediate access to or can acquire at low costs through markets or from the personal network; and 3) applying the resources to new purposes, which means entrepreneurs reuse those resources for problems they were never intended to be applied to. The solutions created by bricolage behavior can be brilliant and unforeseen, as depicted by many studies (Baker et al., 2003; Garud and Karnøe, 2003). However, there are limits to bricolage. Although it creates workable solutions which might be "good enough" in the short run, it might prove rather inferior to solutions gained through systematic problem solving. Relying too much on bricolage can end in a sea of patchwork solutions, which might not be appealing to customers, impedes long-term growth and innovativeness (Baker et al., 2005; Senyard et al., 2014). Bricolage behavior can be linked to two of the above described theories. Most importantly, there is a Schumpeterian (1934) element in bricolage behavior. Bricoleurs—individuals engaged in bricolage behavior—recombine available resources in innovative ways to create new solutions to existing problems. By doing so, they become agents of change because they create new products, new methods of production, new sources of supply, or new ways to organize business. In this way, bricolage can be regarded as a mechanism of how entrepreneurs bring Schumpeterian change within an environment of scarce resources. From a theoretical point of view (there are no empirical papers on sources of bricolage behavior) we can envision linkages between the psychological theories and bricolage. For example, the Big Five trait of openness should foster bricolage behavior because openness is about exploring novel ideas. Extraversion can also lead to more bricolage behavior because extraverted entrepreneurs might find easy access to resources via their social networks. Conversely, entrepreneurs scoring high in agreeableness might engage in less bricolage behavior because they are easily satisfied with the status quo.

Entrepreneurial opportunities

In contrast to the *Oxford English Dictionary*, which defines an opportunity as "a time, juncture, or condition of things favorable to an end or purpose, or admitting of something being done or effected," entrepreneurship theory usually conceives the term opportunity as a reference to situations conducive to profit making. While there are several definitions of "entrepreneurial opportunity", the definition favored by Shane (2000: 220) has gained popularity in the last years. According to this "entrepreneurial opportunities are those situations in which new goods, services, raw materials, and organizing methods can be introduced and sold at a greater price than their cost of production". This definition is accompanied by a framework which does not solely focus on opportunities but also includes the individuals pursuing these opportunities. The so-called nexus of opportunity and the enterprising individual are at the heart of entrepreneurship research. Shane and Venkataraman's approach has triggered much discussion—most importantly about the nature of entrepreneurial opportunities and their role in the entrepreneurial process (Alvarez and Barney, 2007; Alvarez et al., 2010; Davidsson, 2005; McMullen et al., 2007; Sarasvathy et al., 2010; Singh, 2001). The central issue focuses on the question of whether entrepreneurial opportunities can be discovered by individuals or are created by individuals. Shane (2000) as well as Eckhardt and Shane (2003) are proponents of the discovery view, which maintains that opportunities can be detected by alert individuals. The discovery view builds on the notion that profitable opportunities are "out there" waiting to be picked by an enterprising individual who recognizes the existing deficiency in allocation. The decision making context is, therefore, risky because some information about the already existing opportunity is available (Alvarez and Barney, 2007). Here, the Kirznerian (1973) entrepreneur assumes the role of arbitrageur. Of course, this does not mean that the entrepreneur is blessed with perfect knowledge and foresight. Knowledge remains dispersed among individuals (Hayek, 1945) and there are individual differences in the cognitive processes related to discovery. Consequently, research has looked at sources of knowledge necessary for discovery. A robust finding is that both prior knowledge from past experience (Shane, 2000) and an advantageous position in networks (Burt, 1992) are important determinants for connecting the dots to identify entrepreneurial opportunities (Baron, 2006). Beyond the differences in objective individual characteristics, believing in these differences also seems to be important for opportunity discovery. For example, Krueger and Dickson (1994) found that self-efficacy is positively associated with the discovery of opportunities. In addition, passion has been related to opportunity perception and exploitation (Klaukien et al., 2013). The discovery view is opposed by the creation view whose proponents argue that the entrepreneurial process is more complex than simply picking up opportunities like a $10 bill. Conversely, opportunities are not ready-made available artifacts but have to be created by action (Alvarez and Barney, 2007). As individuals work on, reframe, and evaluate ideas, they create an opportunity (O'Connor and Rice, 2001). Central to creation theory is the notion that the opportunity does not exist independently from the entrepreneur since they come into existence because the entrepreneur devotes his vision, knowledge, and effort into it. Opportunities are thus inseparably linked to the entrepreneur (Dimov, 2007; Klein, 2008). As Knightian uncertainty suggests, "opportunities do not exist until they are created" (Alvarez and Barney, 2007: 16).

When optimal decisions cannot be made, entrepreneurs must resort to some kind of heuristic. Whether entrepreneurs manage to choose the best heuristic seems to depend on the entrepreneurial personality profile. As, for example, empirical evidence from Stuetzer et al. (2013) shows, entrepreneurs that score high on the entrepreneurial personality profile are better equipped to make more progress in the process of creating an opportunity through starting up than entrepreneurs with a lower score in their entrepreneurial personality profile.

Conclusion

The history of entrepreneurship research shows that uncertainty and personality traits play an important role in entrepreneurial behavior. All traditional concepts, such as by Schumpeter,

Kirzner, or Knight, make reference to these aspects to a greater or a lesser extent. Behavioral economics, however, has made the focus on these aspects more explicit. As the examples in this chapter suggest, we may expect a lot of further insights in entrepreneurship theory from behavioral economics.

Notes

1 Compare Endres and Woods (2010).
2 See Endres and Woods (2010: 585).
3 Compare Grebel (2004: 32).
4 Other authors also emphasize the role of personal effort, such as Leibenstein (1978). See Frantz (2007) to get an overview.
5 Grebel et al. (2003), for example, substantiate this idea in their model on the decision-making process of start-up firms.
6 With respect to entrepreneurial intentions, Goethner et al. (2012) provide a good example for the interplay between psychological factors such as attitudes, perceived behavioural control and norms on the one hand and economic factors such as experience gained elsewhere on the other.

Bibliography

Alvarez, S. A. & Barney, J. B. (2007). Discovery and creation: Alternative theories of entrepreneurial action, Strategic Entrepreneurship Journal 1(1–2), 11–26.

Alvarez, S. A., Barney, J. B. & Young, S. L. (2010). Debates in entrepreneurship: Opportunity formation and implications for the field of entrepreneurship, Handbook of entrepreneurship research, Springer, pp. 23–45.

Audretsch, D. B. (2007). The entrepreneurial society, OUP Catalogue.

Baker, T., Gedajlovic, E. & Lubatkin, M. (2005). A framework for comparing entrepreneurship processes across nations, Journal of International Business Studies 36(5), 492–504.

Baker, T., Miner, A. S. & Eesley, D. T. (2003). Improvising firms: bricolage, account giving and improvisational competencies in the founding process. Research Policy, 32(2), 255–76.

Bandura, A. (1977). Self-efficacy: Toward a unifying theory of behavioral change. Psychological Review, American Psychological Association, 84, 191.

Baron, R. A. (2006). Opportunity recognition as pattern recognition: How entrepreneurs "connect the dots" to identify new business opportunities. The Academy of Management Perspectives, 20(1), 104–19.

Barreto, H. (1989) The entrepreneur in microeconomic theory. London and New York: Routledge.

Baum, J. R. & Locke, E. A. (2004). The relationship of entrepreneurial traits, skill, and motivation to subsequent venture growth. Journal of Applied Psychology, 89, 587–98.

Bhave, M. P. (1994). A process model of entrepreneurial venture creation. Journal of Business Venturing, 9(3), 223–42.

Block, J. (1971). Lives through times. Berkeley, CA: Bancroft Books.

Burt, R. (1992). Structural holes: The social structure of competition. Cambridge, MA: Harvard University Press.

Cardon, M. S., Wincent, J., Singh, J. & Drnovsek, M. (2009). The nature and experience of entrepreneurial passion. Academy of Management Review, 34(3), 511–32.

Chandler, G. N., DeTienne, D. R., McKelvie, A. & Mumford, T. V. (2011). Causation and effectuation processes: A validation study. Journal of Business Venturing, 26(3), 375–90.

Costa Jr, P. T. & McCrae, R. R. (2006). Age changes in personality and their origins: Comment on Roberts, Walton, and Viechtbauer.

Cyert, R. M., et al. (1963). A behavioral theory of the firm. Englewood Cliffs, NJ: Prentice-Hall.

Davidsson, P. (2005). Researching entrepreneurship. Volume 5. New York: Springer Science & Business Media.

Dimov, D. (2007). From opportunity insight to opportunity intention: The importance of person–situation learning match. Entrepreneurship Theory and Practice, 31(4), 561–83.

Eckhardt, J. T. & Shane, S. A. (2003). Opportunities and entrepreneurship. Journal of Management, 29(3), 333–49.

Endres, A. M. & Woods, C. R. (2010). Schumpeter's conduct model of the dynamic entrepreneur: Scope and distinctiveness. Journal of Evolutionary Economics, 20(4), 583–607.
Forlani, D. & Mullins, J. W. (2000). Perceived risks and choices in entrepreneurs' new venture decisions. Journal of Business Venturing, 15(4), 305–22.
Frantz, R. (2007). Renaissance in behavioral economics: Essays in honour of Harvey Leibenstein, Abingdon: Routledge.
Frese, M. & Gielnik, M. M. (2014). The psychology of entrepreneurship. Annual Revue of Organizational Psychology and Organizational Behaviour, 1(1), 413–38.
Frese, M., van Geldern, M. & Ombach, M. (2000). How to plan as a small scale entrepreneur: Psychological process characteristics of action strategies and success.
Friedman, B. M. (1979). Optimal expectations and the extreme information assumptions of "rational expectations" macromodels. Journal of Monetary Economics, 5(1), 23–41.
Friedman, M. & Savage, L. J. (1948). The utility analysis of choices involving risk. Journal of Political Economy, 56(4), 279–304.
Garud, R. & Karnøe, P. (2003). Bricolage versus breakthrough: Distributed and embedded agency in technology entrepreneurship. Research Policy, 32(2), 277–300.
Goethner, M., Obschonka, M., Silbereisen, R. K. & Cantner, U. (2012). Scientists' transition to academic entrepreneurship: Economic and psychological determinants. Journal of Economic Psychology, 33(3), 628–41.
Grebel, T. (2004). Entrepreneurship: A new perspective. London and New York: Routledge.
Grebel, T., Pyka, A. & Hanusch, H. (2003). An evolutionary approach to the theory of entrepreneurship. Industry & Innovation, 10(4), 493–514.
Hayek, F. A. (1945). The use of knowledge in society. American Economic Review, 35(4), 519–30.
Hébert, R. F. & Link, A. N. (1982). The entrepreneur: Mainstream views and radical critiques. 2nd edn. New York: Praeger.
Hisrich, R., Langan-Fox, J. & Grant, S. (2007). Entrepreneurship research and practice: A call to action for psychology. American Psychologist, 62(6), 575.
Kahneman, D. & Tversky, A. (1979). Prospect theory. Econometrica, 47, 263–91.
Kirzner, I. (1973). Competition and entrepreneurship. Chicago: University of Chicago Press.
Kirzner, I. (1999). Creativity and/or alertness: A reconsideration of the Schumpeterian entrepreneur. Review of Austrian Economics, 11, 5–17.
Klaukien, A., Shepherd, D. A. & Patzelt, H. (2013). Passion for work, nonwork-related excitement, and innovation managers' decision to exploit new product opportunities. Journal of Product Innovation Management, 30(3), 574–88.
Klein, P. G. (2008). Opportunity discovery, entrepreneurial action, and economic organization. Strategic Entrepreneurship Journal, 2(3), 175–90.
Knight, F. H. (1921). Risk, uncertainty and profit. New York: Houghton Mifflin.
Krueger, N. & Dickson, P. R. (1994). How believing in ourselves increases risk taking: Perceived self-efficacy and opportunity recognition. Decision Sciences, 25(3), 385–400.
Leibenstein, H. (1978). General X-efficiency theory and economic development. Oxford: Oxford University Press.
Magnusson, D. & Torestad, B. (1993). A holistic view of personality: A model revisited. Annual Review of Psychology, 44(1), 427–52.
McAdams, D. P. & Pals, J. L. (2006). A new Big Five: Fundamental principles for an integrative science of personality. American Psychologist, 61(3), 204.
McGee, J. E., Peterson, M., Mueller, S. L. & Sequeira, J. M. (2009). Entrepreneurial self-efficacy: Refining the measure. Entrepreneurship Theory and Practice, 33(4), 965–88.
McMullen, J. S., Plummer, L. A. & Acs, Z. J. (2007). What is an entrepreneurial opportunity? Small Business Economics, 28(4), 273–83.
Morgenstern, O. & von Neumann, J. (1953). Theory of games and economic behavior. Princeton., NJ: Princeton University Press.
Obschonka, M., Silbereisen, R. K. & Schmitt-Rodermund, E. (2010). Entrepreneurial intention as developmental outcome. Journal of Vocational Behavior, 77(1), 63–72.
Obschonka, M., Silbereisen, R. K. & Schmitt-Rodermund, E. (2011). Successful entrepreneurship as developmental outcome: A path model from a lifespan perspective of human development. European Psychologist, 16(3), 174.

Obschonka, M., Schmitt-Rodermund, E., Silbereisen, R. K., Gosling, S. D. & Potter, J. (2013). The regional distribution and correlates of an entrepreneurship-prone personality profile in the United States, Germany, and the United Kingdom: A socioecological perspective. Journal of Personality and Social Psychology, 105(1), 104.

O'Connor, G. C. & Rice, M. P. (2001). Opportunity recognition and breakthrough innovation in large established firms. California Management Review, 43(2), 95–116.

Read, S., Song, M. & Smit, W. (2009). A meta-analytic review of effectuation and venture performance. Journal of Business Venturing, 24(6), 573–87.

Rentfrow, P. J., Gosling, S. D. & Potter, J. (2008). A theory of the emergence, persistence, and expression of geographic variation in psychological characteristics. Perspectives on Psychological Science, 3(5), 339–69.

Sarasvathy, S. D. (2001). Causation and effectuation: Toward a theoretical shift from economic inevitability to entrepreneurial contingency. Academy of Management Review, 26(2), 243–63.

Sarasvathy, S. D., Dew, N., Velamuri, S. R. & Venkataraman, S. (2010). Three views of entrepreneurial opportunity. In Handbook of Entrepreneurship Research. New York: Springer, 77–96.

Schmitt-Rodermund, E. (2004). Pathways to successful entrepreneurship: Parenting, personality, early entrepreneural competence, and interests. Journal of Vocational Behavior, 65, 498–518.

Schumpeter, J. A. (1911). Theorie der wirtschaftlichen Entwicklung. Berlin: Duncker und Humblot.

Schumpeter, J. A. (1934). The theory of economic development. Cambridge, MA: Harvard University Press.

Schumpeter, J. A. (1939). Business cycles. New York: McGraw-Hill.

Schwartz, H. (2002). Herbert Simon and behavioral economics. The Journal of Socio-Economics, 31(3), 181–9.

Senyard, J., Baker, T., Steffens, P. & Davidsson, P. (2014). Bricolage as a path to innovativeness for resource-constrained new firms. Journal of Product Innovation Management, 31(2), 211–30.

Shane, S. (2000). Prior knowledge and the discovery of entrepreneurial opportunities. Organization Science, 11(4), 448–69.

Simon, H. A. (1955). A behavioral model of rational choice. The Quarterly Journal of Economics, 69(1), 99–118.

Simon, H. A. (1963). Problems of methodology: Discussion. American Economic Review, 53, 229–31.

Singh, R. P. (2001). A comment on developing the field of entrepreneurship through the study of opportunity recognition and exploitation. Academy of Management Review, 26(1), 10–12.

Sombart, W. (1909). Der kapitalistische unternehmer. Archiv für Sozialwissenschaft und Sozialpolitik, 29, 689–758.

Stuetzer, M., Obschonka, M. & Schmitt-Rodermund, E. (2013). Balanced skills among nascent entrepreneurs. Small Business Economics, 41(1), 93–114.

Talhelm, T., Zhang, X., Oishi, S., Shimin, C., Duan, D., Lan, X. & Kitayama, S. (2014). Large-scale psychological differences within China explained by rice versus wheat agriculture. Science, 344(6184), 603–8.

Zhao, H. & Seibert, S. E. (2006). The Big Five personality dimensions and entrepreneurial status: A meta-analytic review. Journal of Applied Psychology, 91(2), 259–71.

14

A BOUNDED RATIONALITY ASSESSMENT OF THE NEW BEHAVIORAL ECONOMICS

Morris Altman

Introduction

I explore the evolution of behavioral economics, from a multidisciplinary rational agent or bounded rationality approach that was pioneered and championed by Herbert Simon (1959, 1978, 1987) from the 1950s, to the heuristics and biases approach that currently dominates the field. I argue that although the heuristics and biases approach pioneered by Kahneman and Tversky (1979; Kahneman, 2003, 2011; Tversky and Kahneman, 1981) has made significant contributions to the field, the bounded rationality approach holds most promise because of its focus on methodology and related causal analyses and modeling, smart decision-makers, capabilities, and institutional design.[1]

The heuristics and biases approach, where heuristics refers to decision-making shortcuts, is more focused on documenting deviations from the neoclassical or conventional behavioral norms, where the latter is considered to be the normative ideal. This normative ideal is typically rejected in the bounded rationality approach when inconsistent with the evidence. The heuristics and biases approach also pays considerable attention to how heuristic-based biased behavior better describes and explains a good deal of economic behavior and outcomes than the conventional wisdom.

This descriptive narrative raises questions about the analytical relevance of conventional economics, in many domains, and remains vitally important not only to the behavioral economics narrative, but also to economics in general. For all perspectives in economics the dynamic interaction, the passionate tango, between facts and theory, is supposed to be a linchpin of scientific analysis.

A common thread running through behavioral economics is that many economic outcomes are inconsistent with the predictions of conventional economic theory. Documenting this inconsistency represents key contributions of Herbert Simon, but especially that of Daniel Kahneman and Amos Tversky, all of whom are considered to be among the core founding fathers of contemporary behavioral economics. Significant efforts to document these inconsistencies with conventional theory have also been made by Vernon Smith (2003), one of the founding fathers of experimental economics, and by Gerd Gigerenzer (2007), a pioneer in developing the notion of rational decision-making heuristics (shortcuts). This documented inconsistency opens the door wide open to various alternative models of human decision-making and their determinants. This is particularly true if one concludes that these inconsistencies are persistent and represent an important subset of choice outcomes, not just some interesting outlier anomalies.

Behavioral economics sometimes affords us with quite different and opposing perspectives on what the deviations from the conventional or neoclassical economic norms mean for our understanding of human behavior, the causes of such deviations, and for the development of robust economic theory and policy. These points of difference are a central theme of this chapter.

Assumptions-matter and behavioral economics

In the contemporary literature on behavioral economics (the heuristics and biases approach), attention is drawn to behavioral economics as better describing economic reality than conventional theory in terms of both choice behavior and the outcomes of these choices, which tend to deviate from what is predicted by conventional economics. These outcomes are interpreted as being all too often a product of error prone and biased decision-making processes, where decisions are often driven by "irrational" emotional considerations as opposed to careful and considered calculating behavior. Apart from this interpretation of choice outcomes, an objective of documenting deviations from predicted conventional outcomes (a point of commonality with the bounded rationality approach) is to demonstrate that conventional theory too often fails to predict choice behaviors and choice outcomes.[2]

But this worldview is completely contrary to the methodological perspective of conventional economics, one that permeates other approaches to economic analysis as well. This outlook stems from the classic 1953 methodological paper by Friedman (1953), where he argued that the realism of simplifying modeling assumptions is not of any significance in building robust economic models or theories. Getting the description right as regards choice behavior is not of importance—all that counts is predicting the outcomes of choice behavior correctly. Of course, behavioral economists have additionally found that all too many of the predictions of the conventional model are incorrect. Related to this, Simon (1987) and the bounded rationality approach make a critical point—the realism of the simplifying assumptions of models is vitally important to achieve rigorous analytical predictions and causal analyses (Altman, 2005a, 2005b, 2012, 2015).

Friedman (1953) argues that trying to be more accurate in the realism of one's assumptions "only confuses the issue, promotes misunderstanding about the significance of empirical evidence for economic theory ... [and] ... wildly inaccurate descriptive representations of reality, and, in general the more significant the theory, the more unrealistic the assumption (in this sense)." A realistic modeling of assumptions is, therefore, of no consequence. The ultimate test of whether modeling assumptions are "good enough" or appropriate is the model's predictive power, even if the assumptions are markedly inaccurate. In other words, inaccurate assumptions and, even more extremely, assumptions that have no bearing on how decision-makers actually behave are quite acceptable when they generate reasonably robust predictions. From this methodological perspective, causality, cause and effect, as opposed to correlation, is difficult to determine. And, correlation can be misinterpreted as causation (Altman, 2006).

A critical facet of the bounded rationality approach is that causality can only be determined with reference to simplifying assumptions that are empirically derived. Only in this manner can one test whether a model's analytical predictions are robust and impute causation to the independent variables of the model and, more specifically, to the particular behaviors of decision-makers and their decision-making environment. This also reduces the probability of generating omitted variable problems. It also changes the analytical rules of the game away from necessarily assuming that individuals make decisions in optimally yielding optimal results (an analytical default option in the conventional wisdom) towards determining how decision-makers actually behave and their decision-making constraints. Because Friedman assumes that individuals behave in a manner consistent with "optimal" economic behavior, it is also often assumed that outcomes are optimal even if, on the surface, they appear not to be so. This too runs contrary to the behavioral economics narrative where what appear to be suboptimal outcomes are interrogated and tested for suboptimality, and then related to the choice behavior of decision-makers.

In addition, this bounded rationality approach is not consistent with the modeling by some behavioral economists who introduce various psychological or sociological assumptions, as replacements for the conventional neoclassical ones, that yield robust predictions but which are not derived empirically. Although this approach to model building might appear reasonable, derived from the decision-making literature, the model's underlying assumptions are not derived from the actual decision-making process. For example, this approach would *not* assume that individuals behave as if they compute simultaneously hundreds of equations to optimize their results—which is the Milton Friedman approach modeling—but it would allow for assumptions that don't appear "absurd" but are equally unreasonable as are Friedman's deliberately wildly unrealistic assumptions. The common core here is that assumptions are not being empirically derived and what matters is that the predictions are robust (Altman, 2015; Berg and Gigerenzer, 2010). In the bounded rationality approach, behavioral and context-related assumptions need to be sensible and realistic given the context of decision-making, the hypothesis being tested, and the outcomes being explained. This assumptions-matter perspective also allows us to test the reasonableness and the implications of different sets of plausible behavioral assumptions for causality, prediction, and for improved decision-making outcomes.

The conventional wisdom and the different faces of behavioral economics

According to Simon (1987), bounded rationality refers to rational choice behavior. But bounded rationality refers to the type of rational choice behavior that one finds in the real world. Such choice is bounded by a variety of factors, such as the cognitive limitations of decision-makers, including limitations to their knowledge of pertinent information (and their ability to acquire such knowledge), and to their computational capabilities and capacities (see Akerlof, 1970, on information asymmetries). The institutional factors that can hinder or improve the decision-making process and outcomes are also important. More recently, behavioral economists and others have increasingly introduced psychological (Kahneman and Tversky, 1979; Kahneman, 2003, 2011; Tversky and Kahneman, 1981; Lewis, Webley, and Furnham, 1995) and sociological factors in models of decision-making (Akerlof and Kranton, 2010).[3]

But what are the conventional economic or neoclassical norms for optimal behavior? Not everyone would completely agree. However, there are certain core assumptions that are often referenced by both neoclassical economic and behavioral economists:

1 Individuals can and do make consistent choices across all possible bundles of goods and services and through time.
2 It is assumed that all individuals have thorough knowledge of all of the relevant available options at any given point in time and they all have the means to process and understand this information in a timely manner—the brain is assumed not to be scarce resource and individuals' computational ability is unlimited.
3 Individuals can forecast the implications of their decisions through time and, hence, calculate at least in a measurable probabilistic sense the consequences of their choices.

4 Individuals are assumed to make choices across alternatives that maximize utility or well-being. It is typically assumed either explicitly or implicitly that, controlling for risk, utility maximization is consistent with wealth or income maximization.
5 It is assumed that individuals are effective and efficient calculating machines or at least they behave as if they are, irrespective of age, experience, or education.
6 It is assumed that all individuals independent of context should behave in the same calculating manner (following conventional behavioral norms) to maximize utility or efficiency.

The "new" behavioral economics, emanating from the initial research outcomes and initiatives of Kahneman and Tversky, sets out to develop theories that are better able to describe human behavior, where often such behavior is related to economic issues. In this vein, for example, they developed prospect theory as an alternative to subjective expected utility theory. Certainly, Kahneman and Tversky view their scientific project as bearing down on better describing choice behavior than conventional economic theory. In the Kahneman and Tversky approach, such descriptive theories are typically related to the behavior of the average individual. The focus on the average has also been a mainstay of conventional economics. This implicitly assumes that the average is the most appropriate point of reference for descriptive and analytical purposes.

This "new" behavioral economics also interprets the "average" individual's deviations from the conventional economic norms for optimal decision-making to be error prone and biased, and typically persistently so. On the one hand, this perspective on behavioral economics maintains and adheres to a fundamental premise of conventional economics, that there is particular way of behaving in the economic realm resulting in a particular set of choices and, therefore, outcomes that are optimal (most effective, efficient, unbiased). But it represents a big break with conventional economics in that individuals tend not to behave optimally in a large array of choice scenarios. It is argued that individuals tend to engage in biased and error prone behaviors. And they do so because they do not conform to conventional or neoclassical behavioral norms.

The bounded rationality approach in context

The bounded rationality approach breaks with conventional economics by recognizing that individuals and organizations all too often behave in a manner that deviates from the conventional economic norms for optimal and even rational behavior. But unlike with the "new" behavioral economics, in the bounded rationality approach such deviations often signal decision-making processes and outcomes that are optimal and rational given the preferences of the decision-makers and the constraints that they face. These constraints can be of a physiological, neurological, psychological, or institutional nature. Hence, the bounded rationality approach rejects, on an empirical basis, that individuals and organizations generate decisions that are typically consistent with conventional economic theory predicted outcomes, while also rejecting the null hypothesis that one should typically use conventional economic theory benchmarks to determine which outcomes are optimal from either an individual or social perspective. This approach does not deny the possibilities of errors and even biases in decision-making. Moreover, there is a focus here on causal analysis. Modeling is important. Identifying which particular behaviors yield particular outcomes is critical. This shifts attention from correlation-based prediction to cause-and-effect modeling. The former remains the basis of much of conventional economics.

Herbert Simon developed the key analytical concepts of bounded rationality and satisficing as an alternative to the conventional economic concepts of rationality and maximizing or minimizing behavior. He argued that these alternative analytical tools were better able to describe and explain (causally) the behavior of human decision-makers in the real world, as well as providing more reasonable normative benchmarks for rational behavior. He accepted a basic premise of conventional economics that most individuals (the typical individual) are goal-oriented and have reasons for what they do, for the decisions they make. Being goal-oriented and having reasons behind one's actions is what Simon considered to be fundamental to any reasonable definition of rationality. But determining rationality required placing human action in the context of an individual's and an organization's decision-making environment (Simon, 1987; Todd and Gigerenzer, 2003).

One of Simon's main differences with and concerns about conventional economics throughout his career was that conventional economics decontextualized the meaning of rationality. It thereby defines rationality in terms of norms that are often dissociated from the overall decision-making environment. Conventional economics also tends to assume that individuals and organizations behave in a manner consistent with these decontextualized norms, where such behavior is considered to be the only behavior that is rational. In this case, if individuals are rational, which is a bread-and-butter assumption of conventional economics, one must assume that behavior is consistent with conventional norms of rational behavior.

But if, as Simon argues, rationality needs to be more broadly defined and defined in a contextualized manner, conventional norms should not necessarily be used as a benchmark of rational behavior. What is rational from the perspective of conventional economics might be irrational from a bounded rationality perspective. And, what conventional economics considers to be an irrational behavior, might very well be rational behavior. Market forces should, according to the conventional wisdom, wipe out the former in a short enough period of time such that irrational behavior from a conventional economic perspective should not be of analytical significance (Reder, 1982). But the bounded rationality approach would consider deviations from the conventional norm to be not uncommon and to persist over time, especially if such deviations are the product of some rational decision-making process.

One example of the bounded rationality approach is provided by James March (1978), a close associate of Simon during the golden years of the foundational period of behavioral economics in Carnegie-Mellon University. March argued that one should approach the determination of the rationality of decision-making in the context of the decision-making environment. March, therefore, concludes that in the first instance one should assume that choice behavior is sensible and, therefore, rational, even if this behavior deviates from conventional economic norms, even by a significant extent:

> Engineers of artificial intelligence have modified their perceptions of efficient problem solving procedures by studying the actual behavior of human problem solvers. Engineers of organizational decision-making have modified their models of rationality on the basis of studies of actual organizational behavior . . . Modern students of human choice behavior frequently assume, at least implicitly, that actual human choice behavior in some way or other is likely to make sense. It can be understood as being the behavior of an intelligent being or group of intelligent beings . . .
>
> *(p. 589)*

This does not imply that all choices are rational or sensible. But one should not determine rationality, sensibility, or optimality, by the extent to which choice behaviors and outcomes deviate from conventional norms of rationality. Moreover, one should not attempt to achieve superior outcomes by inducing individuals or organizations to conform to or adhere to conventional economic behavioral norms.

More recently, Vernon Smith, a pioneer of contemporary experimental economics concluded in a similar vein, but based his conclusion on evidence derived from classroom experiments. One of his key findings is that behaviors that generate economic success are all too often not consistent with what contemporary economic theory considers to be rational or smart decision-making. But then this implies that there is something fundamentally wrong with the theory, in this case the assumption that profit maximizing behavior generates economic success and optimal economic outcomes. One should not challenge the rationality of decision-making that is consistent with economic success, when economic success is the normative end-game of the theory. Moreover, in this scenario the conventional economic model's prediction is also wrong. Profit maximization would not result in firm success whereas forms of non-maximization would.

Smith finds that:

> It is shown that the investor who chooses to maximize expected profit (discounted total withdrawals) fails in finite time. Moreover, there exist a variety of nonprofit-maximizing behaviors that have a positive probability of never failing. In fact it is shown that firms that maximize profits are the least likely to be the market survivors. My point is simple: when experimental results are contrary to standard concepts of rationality, assume not just that people are irrational, but that you may not have the right model of rational behavior. Listen to what your subjects may be trying to tell you. Think of it this way. If you could choose your ancestors, would you want them to be survivalists or to be expected wealth maximizers?
>
> *(2005: 149–50; see also Smith, 2003)*

Simon developed the concepts of bounded and procedural rationality, as well as satisficing, as alternatives to conventional economic rationality and maximizing/minimizing/optimizing behavior. These alternative concepts have embodied in them alternative sets of rational behavior which differ from those embodied in conventional economic modeling. Simon provided these alternative sets of concepts to capture rational or sensible behavior that was inconsistent with conventional economic norms. It was not enough to simply critique conventional economics as being descriptively incorrect. It was imperative to also provide conceptional vehicles to facilitate modeling human decision-making.

Bounded rationality (BR) refers to goal-oriented and even deliberative and, therefore, rational behavior. Unlike the conventional economics definition of rationality, BR is more broadly defined and is empirically derived, based on how smart people behave in the real world situations given the various parameters or constraints faced by the decision-maker and the decision-making environment.

BR is a contextualized and operational definition of rationality. Rational decision-making is bounded by a number of factors. And these bounds generate decision-making and outcomes and processes different from what one would predict or assume from the perspective of conventional economics. Of particular importance are the cognitive limitations of decision-makers, including limitations to their knowledge of pertinent information (and their ability to acquire such knowledge) and the limitations to their computational capabilities and capacities. The latter acknowledges the brain as a scarce resource—we are not endowed with unlimited cognitive capability or capacity. Our processing capacity can be potentially increased through the development of new products, such as calculators and computers—a crucial point made by Simon. An additional point that needs to be made is that this potential can only be realized if individuals can afford these computational aids and know how to use them. Hence, one integrates into one's modeling framework the importance of income and education affecting the type of decisions made by rational but constrained individuals.

In this context, what appears to be a suboptimal choice or an error or bias in decision-making from a strictly conventional economics perspective or even from the heuristics and biases approach (Kahneman and Tversky, 1979; Kahneman, 2003, 2011) is rather a product of cognitive, educational or income constraints faced by the decision-maker. So, when a decision appears to be odd or irrational, this modeling framework demands that one should determine if there are BR constraints that can explain these "odd" decisions as rational. Here, improvements to decisions relate to improving individuals' decision-making capabilities. And, one of Simon's passions was to develop mechanical decision-making aids to improve individuals' decisions and, therefore, economic efficiency and also better meet the preferences of decision-makers. Overall, what might appear to be an irrational choice is quite rational within the bounds of reason—individuals are doing the best that they can given their constraints, capabilities, and opportunities.

Also important are institutional factors that can hinder or improve the decision-making process and outcomes. Institutional parameters, either formal or informal rules of the game, impact on the decision-making process and rules of the game. This is a point emphasized by Simon and of importance to the BR approach to behavioral economics. Choices that appear to be irrational or suboptimal might simply be a product of perverse institutional parameters that induce suboptimal choices. On the other hand, a different set of institutional parameters might be necessary for optimal decisions to be made from either an individual or social perspective (Simon, 1987; North, 1971). Simon places considerable weight on the importance of the old institutional economics, exemplified by Commons (1931) in explaining rational but non-neoclassical choice behavior.

Also, as mentioned above, sociological factors can impact on choice behavior, generating choices that might also appear to be irrational or suboptimal. This is a point made by Gary Becker, one of founding fathers of contemporary or mainstream economic theory. But he breaks with his peers by arguing for integrating social variables into his modeling of human decision-making. Price theory alone cannot explain choice behavior, at least in many critical instances. Relations with others in the past and present and one's place and standing in ones community are of vital importance to explain behavior that in the first instance might appear to be irrational. Sociological factors are typically not given due consideration in behavioral economics, but can be vitally important in better explaining and predicting choice behavior. A clear exception to this "rule" is Akerlof and Kranton (2010) who develop identity economics, where a person's utility maximizing behavior is driven by desire of individuals to fit into their group or community. One can go back in time to the contributions of Thorsten Veblen (1899) and there is also James Duesenberry (1949) who developed the concept of relative positioning in income as key to a person's utility as opposed to a person's absolute state of wealth. The latter concept is key to the work of Kahneman and Tversky's prospect theory, with an emphasis on how this yields suboptimal behavior by focusing on relative as opposed to absolute states of wealth or income.

Overall, institutional and sociological factors can also be important to explain and predict both suboptimal and optimal choices, where the latter are conditional upon an appropriate institutional and sociological environment. This is apart from the state of cognitive and related variables. Introducing such non-economic variables is most consistent with the BR approach given that they help explain rational choices that appear irrational from the perspective of the conventional wisdom. It is important to note that rational choices need not generate optimal outcomes, given the constraints faced the individual. This point is not emphasized enough in either perspective of behavioral economics (Altman, 2005b, 2015). Rational or smart decision-makers can yield inefficient outcomes (Altman, 2005b, 2015). One can end up with rational inefficiencies as opposed to errors and biases in decision-making, which is a focal point of the heuristics and biases approach to behavioral economics. Where constraints and capabilities can be changed, rational individuals can be expected to adjust their decisions yielding improved choices.[4] Better education, improved access to computers (and computer literacy programs), improved institutional and sociological parameters, for example, can yield choices that can be more economically efficient and yield a higher level of utility or wellbeing to the individual.

Within the BR analytical framework one also has heuristics as possible efficient shortcuts in the decision-making process. In this case, individuals do not engage the careful and detailed calculating behavioral assumed by and considered to be normatively ideal in conventional economics. Heuristics are considered to be an effective means to make decisions in a cost effective manner given the various constraints and limitations faced by individuals in the decision-making process. Hence, Simon and those adhering to and developing the BR approach to decision-making, begin their analysis with the assumption that heuristics are used because they are the smart or rational means of engaging in the decision-making process.

This analytical approach has been further refined by Gerd Gigerenzer (2007) and colleagues who have advanced what is referred to as the fast and frugal heuristics toolbox. Evidence suggests that heuristics typically outperform conventional economic behavioral norms. It is important to note, however, that it is not assumed here that heuristics necessarily refer to gut reactions to challenges and opportunities. Gut reactions, however, are often based on prior learning and experience and generate efficient boundedly rational outcomes. But heuristics can be a product of careful deliberation where and when time permits. And, they need not always be correct. There can be errors in decision-making. Inappropriate heuristics can be chosen given the decision-maker's constraints and capabilities. However, in the bounded rationality approach, the norms for optimal behavior are empirically derived from the circumstances surrounding real world decision-making as opposed to being imposed exogenously without any connection to the empirics underlying decision-making. But the assumption that non-conventional behavioral norms (aka heuristics) typically outperform conventional behavioral norms in terms of outcomes, is another key distinction between the conventional wisdom and the BR approach to behavioral economics, and between the BR and the heuristics and biases analytical frameworks.

To reiterate what we have discussed above, in the conventional model a core assumption is that rational individuals must behave in a rigorously calculating manner and this will yield optimal outcomes. And, because we all behave in this manner, outcomes should be optimal. The BR perspective stands in stark contrast to this conventional scenario, and to the heuristics and biases approach to behavioral economics. The latter typically starts with the hypothesis that heuristics are biased and error prone because they deviate from the conventional economic norms for optimal decision-making behavior.

More recently, Kahneman (2011; Altman, 2015) has himself presented a more nuanced argument whereby heuristics can represent a relatively effective decision-making tool, under certain circumstances. Kahneman argues that individuals use or should use different types of mental processes to engage in decision-making, broadly categorized as System 1 and System 2. In System 1, decision-making tends to be fast, emotionally driven, and intuitive and, therefore, often based on deep-grained habits (or hardwired), and is consequently very difficult to modify and control. In System 2, decision-making tends to be thoughtful and deliberative involving much more effort and time than System 1 related decision-making. Kahneman argues that System 1 behavior can be more efficient in certain circumstances but is more subject to systematic errors and biases. System 2 behavior is more efficient in other circumstances and is less subject to systematic errors and biases. So, an important aspect of this type of more nuanced categorization of decision-making behavior is to determine which system works best and when, where, and for whom.

But still, even in this approach, heuristics remain error prone and predisposed to biases, and are especially inefficient when decisions can and should take place (providing that the time to think and analyze is available) over a longer period of time. Consistent with the BR approach there are a wide array of heuristics that are possible, not all of which will be error-free, unbiased, or best practice. However, in the real world, heuristics as opposed to conventional economic norms are almost always used to make decisions. In the BR approach, the default assumption is that heuristics are superior to conventional decision-making norms, having evolved over time and through experience. The critical question then becomes, again, under which circumstances are particular heuristics optimal and under which circumstances are they not?

Satisficing and procedural rationality in context

With regard to satisficing, there is no denying here that individuals are assumed to be purposeful and even contemplative about their decisions at least in the longer term. Nor does satisficing deny, based on the evidence, that most individuals at least most of the time attempt to do the best they can. But it does deny that rational or smart individuals typically engage in the type of calculating marginal analysis that the conventional wisdom assumes. Moreover, most successful decision-makers do not behave in accordance with conventional behavioral norms, according to the evidence (Simon, 1959, 1978, 1987; Altman, 2012, 2015).

Satisficing is posited as an alternative to optimizing, foreshadowing the literature on heuristics. It is argued that individuals and organizations develop and adopt decision-making shortcuts or heuristics based on experience. When satisficing, an individual makes choices based on what meets predetermined criteria for what is good enough. There is often a form of stopping rule that is applied. The argument here is that given the constraints, capabilities, and opportunities faced by decision-makers in the real world, using heuristics and, therefore, satisficing, generates superior choices in a more efficient and effective manner than engaging in what conventional economics would define as optimizing behavior. This is especially the case when individuals update their heuristics as errors are uncovered and when better heuristics are discovered or developed. Satisficing heuristics need to evolve over time. When they do not, we can end up with errors in decision-making and suboptimal results.

Procedural rationality relates to BR, satisficing, and the use of heuristics in decision-making. Simon sets procedural rationality in stark contrast to the rationality of conventional or neoclassical economics, where the latter is referred to as substantive rationality. With substantive rationality the objective world is easily identified by the decision-maker who has unlimited computational capacity. And, one can deduce how an individual should behave to maximize efficiency or utility from the utility function of the individual. So, Simon argues that if the world is as the conventional wisdom assumes, there would be no problem with its modeling of choice behavior. One could take this particular argument to task. But, be this as it may, a critical point made by Simon (1986: S211) states that:

> . . . if we accept the proposition that knowledge and the computational power of the decision maker are severely limited, then we must distinguish between the real world and the actor's perception of it and reasoning about it . . . we must construct a theory (and test it empirically) of the processes of decision. Our theory must include not only the reasoning processes but also the processes that generate the actor's subjective representation of the decision problem, his or her frame . . . The rational person of neoclassical economics always reaches the decision that is objectively, or substantively, best in terms of the given utility function. The rational person of cognitive psychology

> goes about making his or her decisions in a way that is procedurally reasonable in the light of the available knowledge and means of computation [it is context dependent].

Procedural rationality is a form of BR. It relates to what are the best procedures to achieve the objectives (the utility or preference function) of an individual or an organization, given the decision-making environments faced by the individual or organization and the decision-making capacities and capabilities of the individual and organization. The benchmark for what are the best practice behavior cannot be given exogenously. There might also be alternative paths to achieve a given objective. Hence, what is procedural rationality can only be empirically derived, based on the capabilities and capacities of decision-makers and their preferences at any given point of real or historical time (Simon, 1986: S212):

> To move from substantive to procedural rationality requires a major extension of the empirical foundations of economics. It is not enough to add theoretical postulates about the shape of the utility function, or about the way in which actors form expectations about the future, or about their attention or inattention to particular environmental variables. These are assumptions about matters of fact, and the whole ethos of science requires such assumptions to be supported by publicly repeatable observations that are obtained and analyzed objectively . . . The application of this procedural theory of rationality to economics requires extensive empirical research, much of it at micro-micro levels, to determine specifically how process is molded to context in actual economic environments and the consequences of this interaction for the economic outcomes of these processes.

Satisficing, to reiterate, is a general term that relates heuristics in decision-making in contrast to maximizing or minimizing behavior. It is part and parcel of the concept of procedural rationality. It is a conceptual term that encapsulates how goal-oriented individuals tend to behave in the real world of decision-making. But what is procedurally rational—which satisficing heuristics are developed, adapted or adopted—is contingent upon goal and circumstance. Exogenously determined and imposed standards for optimality are rejected in this approach, in contrast to the worldview of both the conventional economic wisdom and the heuristics and biases approach.

X-efficiency theory and external benchmarks for optimal behavior

There is another approach to procedural rationality and BR that uses rough conventional or neoclassical benchmarks for optimal performance but which rejects logically derived neoclassical procedures to achieve optimal performance. Note that the heuristics and biases approach also uses neoclassical benchmarks to determine optimality but in a less nuanced and in a much more generalized manner. Leibenstein (1966, 1979; Frantz, 1997) argues that for firms to be economically efficient the workers, managers, and employers, must be working as hard and as smart as they can, irrespective of their preference function. For efficiency to be achieved, certain behaviors must be realized. In the conventional model, the quantity and quality of effort input per unit of time, ceteris paribus, is assumed to be constant, but it is also typically and implicitly assumed to be fixed at some maximum.

But because, in reality, individuals and organizations deviate from conventional economic norms of effort maximization, firms tend to be economically inefficient; they are not as productive as they might otherwise be. Leibenstein refers to this scenario as x-inefficiency in production. Individuals and organizations that are x-inefficient are considered to be irrational or quasi-rational at best, according to Leibenstein. Such quasi-rational behavior is assumed to be a function of individuals maximizing their utility, where utility maximization is consistent with x-inefficiency in production. In this case, a Darwinian-survival of the fittest process that forces individuals to maximize effort inputs is not in place. The latter process is assumed in the conventional model.

In the BR approach x-inefficient behavior would be considered rational because the decision-makers are achieving their goals and objectives. But outcomes are suboptimal in the sense that the firm's output is less than it might otherwise be. We have rational inefficiencies (Altman, 2005b, 2006, 2015). The fact that Leibenstein refers to x-inefficient decision-makers as quasi-rational or irrational is beside the point since, he argues, their choices are purposeful and deliberate as well as utility maximizing. Their choices derived from the decision-makers' utility maximizing preferences simply do not generate economically efficient outcomes.

For Leibenstein, the conventional economic norm of effort maximization is a reasonable one if productivity is to be maximized, but one that is typically not realized in the real world economy. A critical difference between Leibenstein and conventional economics is that he does not assume that organizations necessarily perform x-efficiently in production. Whether they do or do not cannot simply be assumed. It becomes an empirical question—a key methodological point among behavioral economists. In addition, a key point of focus for Leibenstein is the process by which an organization might achieve x-efficiency or the conditions under which suboptimal levels of production (x-inefficiency) are realized. This is well situated in the BR approach with its focus on procedural rationality—the actual behaviors required to meet a set of objectives are investigated and articulated (Cyert and March, 1963). According to Leibenstein, one can identify market structures, decision-makers' preferences, and industrial relations structures that are most conducive to x-efficiency in production. This cannot be done by framing one's analysis in terms of maximizing or minimizing behavior—this is too simplistic and not empirically based. X-efficiency is more related to cooperative forms of governance than to mechanistic maximizing-minimizing behavior (Altman, 2005b, 2006). Leibenstein also argues that there is no natural imperative for x-efficiency in production to take place, hence the importance of garnering an understanding of how firms behave inside of the black box of the firm. And, assuming that x-efficiency always exists generates serious missing variable problems, thereby misspecifying some of the key causes of a firm's suboptimal performance. Overall, from this perspective, although the conventional overarching behavioral norms might be correct (effort maximization is required to maximize productivity), this does not imply that these norms will be achieved or that the path to achieve these norms can be reduced into a simplistic optimization space.[5]

Nudging versus constraints change and redesign

In popular lore, behavioral economics is very much about getting the individual to do what the expert perceives to be in the best interest of the individual. This is somewhat exaggerated, but is consistent with important aspects of the heuristics and biases approach to behavioral economics. This stems from the fact that an individual's choices tend to systematically deviate from conventional economic behavioral norms, assumed to be the benchmark for rational-optimal behavior, and that individuals are hardwired to behave in this deviant fashion. This has given rise to the nudge literature spearheaded by Thaler and Sunstein (2009). Although some of the nudge literature is oriented towards improving information stocks and flows and processing capabilities (arguably consistent with enhancing the freedom of choice afforded to decision-makers), the substance of the nudge argument is that individuals need to be either softly (soft paternalism) and or to much more forcefully induce individuals to make choices which do not necessarily correspond with their preferences. This is achieved through what is referred to as choice architecture.

Thaler and Sunstein (2009: 6) maintain that:

> Individuals make pretty bad decisions in many cases because they do not pay full attention in their decision-making (they make intuitive choices based on heuristics), they don't have self-control, they are lacking in full information, and they suffer from limited cognitive abilities.

They also argue that those who oppose choice architecture make the false assumption that individuals typically make choices that are in their own best interest or that their choices are better than those that would be made on their behalf by the expert or choice architect (Thaler and Sunstein, 2009: 6). The essence of this approach is imposing external norms for what is deemed to be in the best interest of the individual on the individual's preferences and choices.

In the BR approach, the null hypothesis is that individuals do the best that they can (satisficing) given the constraints, capabilities, and opportunities that bound their choice sets. Hence, errors in decision-making or individuals' inability to realize their preferred preferences are often viewed as being a function of the constraints, capabilities, and opportunities faced by decision-makers—their decision-making environment. The core problem is typically viewed as not being a function of the hardwiring of the individual. Hence, the focus is on improving the decision-making environment, which would include improving the capabilities of the individual to process, understand, and access relevant information sets. Also, mechanisms could be put in place to resolve social dilemmas, or to provide a more equitable environment where such dilemmas can be resolved.[6] Hence, in the BR approach, the focus is on institutional design and improving decision-making technology as opposed to nudging individuals to make decisions that best fit into the experts' worldview of what is in the best interest of some average individual.

Conclusion

A summary of the differences between conventional economics and the BR as well as heuristics and biases approaches to behavioral economics is presented in Figure 14.1. A critical difference between the BR approach and the heuristics and biases approach is that the former does not necessarily use conventional behavioral norms as the ideal for rational and optimal behavior. Deviations from conventional norms demonstrate a critical weakness of the conventional economic wisdom but, according to the BR approach, do not necessarily imply errors, biases, or irrationality in decision-making. On the other hand, one cannot assume that simply because individuals adopt heuristics as opposed to conventional decision-making rules that these heuristics and related decisions are in some sense necessarily optimal. Errors and biases can exist. Needless to say, in the BR approach the typical prior assumption is that individuals do the best that they can give their decision-making capabilities and their decision-making environment. But this does not mean that such rational decisions, from the perspective of the individual, are best for the organization or society at large. As a footnote, one should point out that the individual might not achieve her objective because of flaws in the overall decision-making environment.

From the BR perspective, which behavioral and related norms should be used as optimal decision-making benchmarks must be empirically derived and contextualized by the individual's

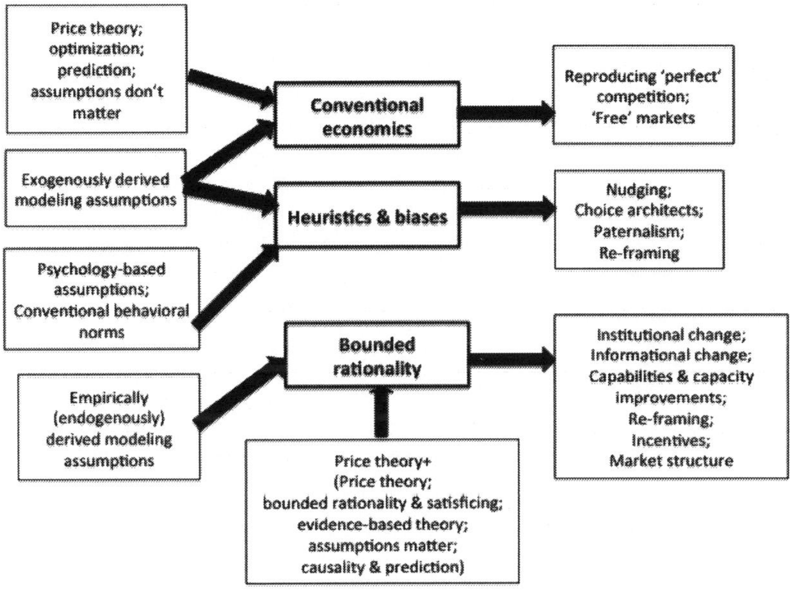

Figure 14.1 The different faces of behavioral economics and the conventional wisdom

decision-making capabilities and their decision-making environment. These benchmarks should not be externally imposed, as it is the conventional economic wisdom and in the heuristics and biases approach.

For this reason, in the BR approach much attention is paid to changing the capabilities and constraints that bound an individual's decision-making environment. This would include education, improvements to information availability, asymmetries, and understandings, changes to incentives, and changes to the broader decision-making and related institutional environment. In contrast, from the heuristics and biases perspective, the tendency has been to correct or fix decision-making problems from the perspective that individuals need to be nudged towards choices that they might not otherwise make due to hardwired behavioral flaws. The ideal or optimal choices are prescribed exogenously. To reiterate, in the BR approach the ideal choices are derived from individual preferences and what these would be in an ideal decision-making environment (Altman, 2010, 2011).

When particular individual preferences generate negative externalities, then one has a social dilemma that needs to be resolved, going well beyond articulating a framework to facilitate the realization of the ideal choices of the individual decision-maker. Examples of these social dilemmas are:

- A firm's decision-makers might prefer a low wage, even conflictual, x-inefficient firm to one that is relatively high wage, cooperative, and x-efficient even if both are equally cost competitive, in contrast to the preferences of most employees.
- Smokers might not care about the secondhand smoke that they impose on others, which violates the preferences of non-smokers.
- For some individuals, utility is enhanced by freeriding on others, which can cause common pool problems.

These conflicting preference and free rider issues and problems cannot be resolved simply by addressing individualized choice problems, which have been a major point focus of behavioral economics. But behavioral economics can inform the resolution of such social dilemmas by informing the conversation about the actual preferences of individuals and their formation and how this might contribute towards resolving social dilemmas.

Notes

1 See Tomer (2007) for detailed and nuanced discussion of behavioral economics. See Keynes (1936) for many early insights and applications of what has become known as behavioral economics.
2 It is important to note the research on emotions which suggests that emotions and intuition (based on experience) often play an important and positive role in decision-making (Damasio, 1996).
3 One can also refer to Becker (1996), who is very much immersed in price theory but who argues that sociological variables are vital to understand decision-making and choice behavior.
4 The importance of capabilities was later refined and articulated by Sen (1985) and Nussbaum (2011).
5 See Akerlof (2002) for an application of efficiency wage theory, a variant of x-efficiency theory, to macroeconomic theory and policy. See Akerlof and Shiller (2009) for a broader application of behavioral economics principles to an understanding of macroeconomic phenomenon.
6 There is still the possibility of individuals not having the capability of making optimal self-interested decisions because of psychological and physiological issues (such as addiction and mental illness). But this is another matter.

Bibliography

Akerlof, G. A. (1970). The Market for "Lemons": Quality Uncertainty and the Market Mechanism. Quarterly Journal of Economics, 84, 488–500.

Akerlof, G. A. (2002). Behavioral Macroeconomics and Macroeconomic Behavior. American Economic Review, 92, 411–33.

Akerlof, G. A. & Kranton, R. E. (2010). Identity Economics: How our Identities Shape our Work, Wages, and Well-Being. Princeton, NJ: Princeton University Press.

Akerlof, G. A. & Shiller, R. J. (2009) Animal Spirits: How Human Psychology Drives the Economy, and Why it Matters for Global Capitalism. Princeton, NJ: Princeton University Press.

Altman, M. (2005a). Reconciling Altruistic, Moralistic, and Ethical Behavior with the Rational Economic Agent and Competitive Markets. Journal of Economic Psychology, 26: 732–57.

Altman, M. (2005b). Behavioral Economics, Power, Rational Inefficiencies, Fuzzy Sets, and Public Policy. Journal of Economic Issues, 39, 683–706

Altman, M. (2006). What a Difference an Assumption Makes: Effort Discretion, Economic Theory, and Public Policy. In M. Altman, ed., Handbook of Contemporary Behavioral Economics: Foundations and Developments. Armonk, NY: M.E. Sharpe, 125–64.

Altman, M. (2010). A Behavioral and Institutional Foundation of Preference and Choice Behavior: Freedom to Choose and Choice X-inefficiencies. Review of Social Economy, 69, 395–411.

Altman, M. (2011). Behavioural Economics, Ethics, and Public Policy: Paving the Road to Freedom or Serfdom? In J. Boston ed., Ethics and Public Policy: Contemporary Issues. Wellington: Victoria University Press, 23–48.

Altman, M. (2012). Behavioral Economics for Dummies. Mississauga, ON: Wiley.

Altman, M. (2015). Introduction. In M. Altman, ed., Real-World Decision Making: An Encyclopedia of Behavioral Economics. Santa Barbara, US: Greenwood, ABC-CLIO.

Becker, G. S. (1996). Accounting for Tastes. Cambridge, MA: Harvard University Press.

Berg, N. & Gigerenzer, G. (2010). As-If Behavioral Economics: Neoclassical Economics in Disguise? History of Economic Ideas, 18, 133–66.

Commons, J. R. (1931). Institutional Economics. American Economic Review, 21, 648–57.

Cyert, R. M. & March, J. C. (1963). A Behavioral Theory of the Firm. Englewood Cliffs, NJ: Prentice-Hall.

Damasio, A. R. (1996). Descartes' Error. London: Penguin.

Duesenberry, J. S. (1949). Income, Saving, and the Theory of Consumption Behavior. Cambridge, MA: Harvard University Press.

Frantz, R. S. (1997). X-Efficiency Theory, Evidence and Applications. Topics in Regulatory Economics and Policy 23. Boston, Dordrecht, and London: Kluwer Academic.
Friedman, M. (1953). The Methodology of Positive Economics. In Essays in Positive Economics. Chicago: University of Chicago Press, 3–43.
Gigerenzer, G. (2007). Gut Feelings: The Intelligence of the Unconscious. New York: Viking.
Kahneman, D. (2003). Maps of Bounded Rationality: Psychology for Behavioral Economics. American Economic Review, 93, 1449–75.
Kahneman, D. (2011). Thinking, Fast and Slow. New York: Farrar, Straus and Giroux.
Kahneman, D. & Tversky, A. (1979). Prospect Theory: An Analysis of Decision under Risk. Econometrica, 47, 263–91.
Leibenstein, H. (1966). Allocative Efficiency vs. "X-Efficiency". American Economic Review, 56, 392–415.
Leibenstein, H. (1979). A Branch of Economics is Missing: Micro-Micro Theory. Journal of Economic Literature, 17, 477–502.
Lewis, A., Webley, P. & Furnham, A. (1995). The New Economic Mind. New York: Harvester Wheatsheaf.
March, J. G. (1978). Bounded Rationality, Ambiguity, and the Engineering of Choice. Bell Journal of Economics, 9, 587–608.
North, D. C. 1971. Institutional Change and Economic Growth. Journal of Economic History, 31, 118–25.
Nussbaum, M. (2011). Creating Capabilities: The Human Development Approach. Cambridge, MA: Harvard University Press.
Reder, M. W. (1982). Chicago Economics: Permanence and Change. Journal of Economic Literature, 20, 1–38.
Sen, A. (1985). Commodities and Capabilities. Amsterdam: North-Holland.
Simon, H. A. (1959). Theories of Decision Making in Economics and Behavioral Science. American Economic Review, 49, 252–83.
Simon, H. A. (1978). Rationality as a Process and as a Product of Thought. American Economic Review, 70, 1–16.
Simon, H. A. (1986). Rationality in Psychology and Economics. Journal of Business, 59, S209–24.
Simon, H. A. (1987). Behavioral Economics. In The New Palgrave: A Dictionary of Economics, edited by J. Eatwell, M. Millgate, and P. Newman. London: Macmillan, 221–5.
Smith, V. L. (2003). Constructivist and Ecological Rationality in Economics. American Economic Review, 93, 465–508.
Smith, V. L. (2005). Behavioral Economics Research and the Foundations of Economics. Journal of Socio-Economics, 34, 135–50.
Thaler, R. H. & Sunstein, C. (2009). Nudge: Improving Decisions about Health, Wealth, and Happiness. New Haven and London: Yale University Press.
Todd, P. M. & Gigerenzer, G. (2003). Bounding Rationality to the World. Journal of Economic Psychology, 24, 143–65.
Tomer, J. F. (2007). What Is Behavioral Economics? Journal of Socio-Economics, 36, 463–79.
Tversky, A. & Kahneman, D. (1981). The Framing of Decisions and the Psychology of Choice. Science, 211, 453–8.
Veblen, T. (1899). Theory of the Leisure Class: An Economic Study of Institutions. New York and London: Macmillan.

PART II

Specific domains of behavioral economics

Introduction

Modern economics has extensive influence across many disciplines. Its clear and straightforward methods of valuation allow for quantification of costs and benefits associated with both individual and collective choices. Thus legislators, regulators, and policy makers can benefit from economics principles in making their decisions, as can the firms, households, and individuals that are affected by those decisions. The first part of this handbook introduced scientists whose work has bearing on the field of behavioral economics. In the second part of this handbook, each chapter magnifies a specific domain of behavioral economics. Whether emotions, regulations, computation, or morality, all aspects of human cognition and environment play a role in the resulting observed behavior. By collecting these in one place, we aim to portray a holistic picture of these varied aspects.

The first two chapters provide an overview of cognitive studies pertinent to the design of effective regulatory structures. Sunstein argues that the assumed consequences and impact of regulations have been transformed through lawmakers' recent awareness of cognitive science. Following the architecture of cognition proposed by Kahneman (in his Nobel Prize lecture), Sunstein proposes a choice architecture view of social behavior in the regulatory environment. He provides an overview of findings and practices whereby public policy making has been informed by this view, warns of potential traps along the way, and shares his vision of what lies ahead in this trend.

Humans ignore information pertinent to the consequences of their choices either freely or because they cannot reliably specify the outcomes. Roy and Zeckhauser define this state in which some outcomes cannot be identified, as in Knightian uncertainty, as *ignorance*. They provide a review of their joint research focused on the human desire to forecast the future, demonstrated in the likes of hunches and prophecies. In their view, expected utility theory is unable to capture such phenomena, whereas their conceptualization of ignorance constitutes a promising direction for behavioral decision-making studies in economics and beyond.

In their chapter, Chen, Chie, and Tai question whether smart (or digital) societies make better decisions. Their elaborate literature review concludes that concerns about information and choice overload still persist. However, their review also reveals that smart societies promote prosocial behavior, as evident in phenomena such as crowdsourcing. The reason is that digital societies are better equipped to match teams. Moreover, members of smart societies strive for even higher aspirations because higher goals appear more achievable once tackled by a team rather than an individual.

The animal spirit of Keynes has left lasting traces in our ways of understanding, teaching, and formulating macroeconomic phenomena. In an artfully composed piece, Baddeley interweaves the old idea of animal spirit with current attention in the field to optimism and then uses the role of time as a central constraint in the making of decisions to deliver ways in which behavioral macroeconomics can complement its neoclassical foundation in a coherent manner while incorporating psychological insight.

Has behavioral economics ignored relevant psychology findings? This is what Mousavi, Gigerenzer, and Kheirandish consider when introducing the fast-and-frugal heuristics study program. They provide an overview of the way heuristics can be analyzed and modeled according to their ecological—as opposed to neoclassical—rationality and walk the reader through the steps of building a testable heuristic model that accounts for long-lasting anomalies such as the Allais paradox.

Chen, Kao, and Venkatachalam investigate the role of machines and computation in the analysis of human behavior while noting the more qualitative notions of psychology that enhance understanding of human cognition. Machine learning and human behavior share the use of heuristics in problem solving. Starting from this overlap, they take the reader on a journey to explore how developments in machine learning can be employed to make sense of intelligent human behavior. Their discussion of the challenges of analyzing human behavior by coding and computation points out our technical limits and raises exciting questions and areas of exploration for the computationally inclined.

Ever since Hume wrote his treatise the role of emotions in human action has been acknowledged by empiricists, and nowadays by game theorists such as Ken Binmore. Bandelj, Kim, and Tufail take a leap into the heart of the human psyche by directly linking emotions to economics. They provide an account of the growing number of studies over the past two decades on both the role of emotions in individual and organizational decision making and the economics of happiness.

In the eighteenth century, Adam Smith moved beyond the wealth of nations to ponder on moral sentiments. His introspections and inferences have been highly influential in the formation of modern economics. In his chapter, Friedman takes a formal approach to morality, strictly attempting to formulate it as a constraint in the study of economic behavior. Using the conception of morality as a variable constraint to self-interest, Friedman elaborates on the coevolution of moral systems and market-oriented institutions.

Although economics declared independence from political economy as a discipline a good while ago, the ties were never completely severed. Foster and Frijters courageously introduce the long neglected yet most powerful human emotion of love into the equations of economics and political science. In their framework, love is the counterpart to greed, where greed constitutes individual wealth maximization. They work out a way to think about behavioral political economy, where politics emerge from group interactions, by using love as the catalyst.

How do we learn and teach? This question lies at the heart of all academic inquiries, and is also a most debated topic in both household and government decision making. Leaver develops a behaviorally informed framework that moves beyond mere cost-benefit analysis to include essential psychological factors such as identity and self-control in the economy of education and also in the evaluation of students and educational systems.

Advances in all areas are almost always owed, at least in part, to innovation. Governments and private institutions alike promote it, and entrepreneurs move the markets in unseen directions with their innovations. Potts takes a systematic approach to reconcile the psychological and economic aspects of innovation within a theoretical framework that he calls behavioral innovation economics.

Agent-based modeling is an increasingly growing field that connects computation with the study of behavior in complex systems. It offers accuracy and techniques for the analysis of economic markets without having to deal with traditional methods of optimization and equilibrium solutions. Mueller and Pyka demonstrate how agent-based modeling accommodates the actual complexity of human behavior and thus has the potential to generate insights that were not deliverable in the traditional framework that is limited by too many simplifying assumptions about humans as a consequence of making models tractable.

Labor economists do not consider their field as a segment of macroeconomics but as a field on its own merit. The mechanisms of the labor market sufficiently differ from other markets to justify such independence. Wang provides a comprehensive overview of deviations from neoclassical labor models inspired and fueled by behavioral phenomena and presents the resulting policy implications.

The chapters stand alone and can be read in any order. Clearly, the future of economics involves considerable interactions and exchanges between scholars across many fields of study. Our collection offers but a glimpse at such potentials. We hope that this handbook inspires many more interactions and look forward to hearing your feedback and thoughts. Enjoy!

15

BEHAVIORALLY INFORMED REGULATION, PART 1

Cass R. Sunstein

Introduction

In recent decades, cognitive psychologists and behavioral economists have been incorporating empirical findings about human behavior into economic models. These findings have transformed our understanding of regulation and its likely consequences. They are also providing instructive lessons about the appropriate design of "nudges"— low-cost, choice-preserving, behaviorally informed approaches to regulatory problems, including disclosure requirements, default rules, and simplification (Thaler & Sunstein, 2008).

The most general lesson is that *choice architecture*, understood as the background against which decisions are made, has major consequences for both decisions and outcomes. Small, inexpensive policy initiatives, making modest design changes, can have large and highly beneficial effects in areas that include health, energy, the environment, savings, education, and much more. The purpose of this chapter is to explore relevant evidence, to catalogue behaviorally informed practices and reforms, and to discuss some implications for regulatory policy.

I write in part on the basis of my experience as Administrator of the White House Office of Information and Regulatory Affairs, where I was privileged to serve between 2009 and 2102. In that period, a number of people in the Obama Administration took the findings of behavioral economics quite seriously. We adopted a large number of initiatives that count as nudges. One of my main goals here is to catalogue those initiatives and to explore their implications for the future.

In the United States, regulatory efforts have been directly informed by behavioral findings, and behavioral economics has played an unmistakable role in numerous domains. The relevant initiatives enlist tools such as disclosure, warnings, norms, and default rules, and they can be found in multiple areas, including fuel economy, energy efficiency, environmental protection, health care, and obesity. As a result, behavioral findings have become an important reference point for regulatory and other policymaking in the United States. In 2015, President Barack Obama issued a historic Executive Order, directing the agencies of his government to incorporate behavioral insights in their work (see Appendix).

In the United Kingdom, Prime Minister Cameron created a Behavioural Insights Team, starting in 2010, with the specific goal of incorporating an understanding of human behavior into policy initiatives. The official website states that its "work draws on insights from the growing body of academic research in the fields of behavioral economics and psychology which show how often subtle changes to the way in which decisions are framed can have big impacts on how people respond to them" (Cabinet Office, n.d.). The team has used these insights to promote initiatives in numerous areas, including smoking cessation, energy efficiency, organ donation, consumer protection, and compliance strategies in general (Halpern, 2015). A great deal of money is being saved. In 2013, the United States created a Behavioral Insights Team of its own, which President Obama formally institutionalized, and made permanent, in 2015. Other nations have expressed keen interest in such work, and are adopting, or considering adopting, similar initiatives. In 2014, Germany created its own team to explore behavioral insights.

Behavioral economics has drawn attention in Europe more broadly. The Organization for Economic Development and Cooperation (OECD) has published a Consumer Policy Toolkit that recommends a number of initiatives rooted in behavioral findings (OECD, 2010). In the European Union, the Directorate-General for Health and Consumers has also shown the influence of behavioral economics (DG SANCO, 2010). A report from the European Commission, called *Green Behavior*, enlists behavioral economics to outline policy initiatives to protect the environment (European Commission, 2012; inudgeyou.com, n.d.). Private organizations are making creative use of behavioral insights to promote a variety of environmental, health-related, and other goals (see inudgeyou.com, n.d.; see also greeNudge.no).

It is clear that behavioral findings are having a large impact on regulation, law, and public policy all over the world and with increasing global interest in low-cost regulatory tools, that impact will inevitably grow over the next decades. In these circumstances, it is particularly important to have a sense of what we know, what we do not know, and how emerging understandings can inform sensible policies and reforms.

I. What we know

A. Findings

For purposes of regulation, the central findings of behavioral research fall in four categories. What follows is not meant to be a comprehensive account; the focus is on those findings that have particular importance to regulatory policy.

1. Inertia and procrastination

A) DEFAULT RULES OFTEN HAVE A LARGE EFFECT ON SOCIAL OUTCOMES

Both private and public institutions often establish "default rules"—rules that determine the result if people make no affirmative choice at all. In part because of the power of inertia, default rules can be extremely important. In the domain of retirement savings, for example, the default rule has significant consequences. When people are asked whether they want to opt in to a retirement plan, the level of participation is far lower than if they are asked whether they want to opt out. Automatic enrollment significantly increases participation.

More generally, people may decline to change from the status quo, even if the costs of change are low and the benefits substantial. In the context of energy and the environment, for example, we might predict that people might neglect to switch to fuel-efficient alternatives even when it is in their interest to do so. It follows that complexity can have serious adverse effects, by increasing the power of inertia, and that ease and simplification (including reduction of paperwork burdens) can produce significant benefits. These benefits include increased compliance with law and greater participation in public programs. Often people do not act in advisable ways, not because they do not want to do so, but because the best path is obscure or difficult to navigate.

B) PROCRASTINATION CAN HAVE SIGNIFICANT ADVERSE EFFECTS

According to standard economic theory, people will consider both the short term and the long term. They will take account of relevant uncertainties; the future may be unpredictable, and significant changes may occur over time. They will appropriately discount the future; it may be better to have money, or a good event, a week from now than a decade from now. In practice, however, some people procrastinate or neglect to take steps that impose small short-term costs but that would produce large long-term gains. They may, for example, delay enrolling in a retirement plan, starting to exercise, ceasing to smoke, or using some valuable, cost-saving technology.

When procrastination is creating significant problems, automatic enrollment in relevant programs might be helpful. Moreover, complex requirements, inconvenience, and lengthy forms are likely to make the situation worse and perhaps unexpectedly so.

C) WHEN PEOPLE ARE INFORMED OF THE BENEFITS OR RISKS OF ENGAGING IN CERTAIN ACTIONS, THEY ARE FAR MORE LIKELY TO ACT IN ACCORDANCE WITH THAT INFORMATION IF THEY ARE SIMULTANEOUSLY PROVIDED WITH CLEAR, EXPLICIT INFORMATION ABOUT HOW TO DO SO (LEVENTHAL, SINGER, & JONES, 1965; NICKERSON & ROGERS, 2010)

For example, those who are informed of the benefits of a vaccine are more likely to become vaccinated if they are also given specific plans and maps describing where to go (Leventhal, Singer, & Jones, 1965). Similarly, behavior has been shown to be significantly affected if people are informed, not abstractly of the value of "healthy eating," but specifically of the advantages of buying 1 percent milk (as opposed to whole milk) (Heath & Heath, 2010). In many domains, the identification of a specific, clear, unambiguous path or plan has an important effect on social outcomes; complexity or vagueness can ensure inaction, even when people are informed about risks and potential improvements. What appears to be skepticism or recalcitrance may actually be a product of ambiguity.

2. Framing and presentation

A) PEOPLE ARE INFLUENCED BY HOW INFORMATION IS PRESENTED OR "FRAMED" (LEVIN, SCHNEIDER, & GAETH, 1998)

If, for example, people are informed that they will *gain* a certain amount of money by using energy efficient products, they may be less likely to change their behavior than if they are told that they will *lose* the same amount of money by not using such products. When patients are told that 90 percent of those who have a certain operation are alive after five years, they are more likely to elect to have the operation than when they are told that after five years, 10 percent of patients are dead (Redelmeier, Rozin, & Kahneman, 1993). It follows that a product that is labeled "90 percent fat-free" may well be more appealing than one that is labeled "10 percent fat." It also follows that choices are often not made based solely on their consequences; assessments may be affected by the relevant frame.

B) INFORMATION THAT IS VIVID AND SALIENT USUALLY HAS A LARGER IMPACT ON BEHAVIOR THAN INFORMATION THAT IS STATISTICAL AND ABSTRACT

With respect to public health, vivid displays can be more effective than abstract presentations of statistical risks. This point bears on the design of effective warnings. Attention is a scarce resource, and vivid, salient, and novel presentations may trigger attention in ways that abstract or familiar ones cannot.

In particular, salience greatly matters. Why, for example, do people pay bank overdraft fees? One of the many possible answers is that such fees are not sufficiently salient to people, and the fees are incurred as a result of inattention or inadvertent mistakes. One study suggests that limited attention is indeed a source of the problem, and that once overdraft fees become salient, they are significantly reduced (Stango & Zinman, 2011). When people take surveys about such fees, they are less likely to incur a fee in the following month, and when they take a number of surveys, the issue becomes sufficiently salient that overdraft fees are reduced for as much as two years. In many areas, the mere act of being surveyed can affect behavior by, for example, increasing use of water treatment products (thus promoting health) and the take-up of health insurance. One reason for this is that being surveyed increases the salience of the action in question (Zwane et al., 2011).

A more general point is that many costs (or benefits) are less salient than purchase prices; they are "shrouded attributes" to which some consumers do not pay much attention. Such "add-on" costs may matter a great deal but receive little consideration, because they are not salient.

C) PEOPLE DISPLAY LOSS AVERSION; THEY MAY WELL DISLIKE LOSSES MORE THAN THEY LIKE CORRESPONDING GAINS (THALER, KAHNEMAN, & KNETSCH, 1991; MCGRAW, LARSEN, KAHNEMAN, & SCHKADE, 2010; CARD & DAHL, 2011)

Whether a change counts as a loss or a gain depends on the *reference point*, which can be affected by mere description or by policy decisions, and which is often the status quo. A small tax—for example, on grocery bags—can have a large effect on behavior, even if a promised bonus has no effect at all; one reason is loss aversion. It follows that very small charges or fees can be a surprisingly effective policy tool. In part as a result of loss aversion, the initial allocation of a legal entitlement can affect people's valuations. Those who have the initial allocation may value a good more than they would if the allocation were originally elsewhere, thus showing an *endowment effect*.

3. *Social influences*

A) IN MULTIPLE DOMAINS, INDIVIDUAL BEHAVIOR IS GREATLY INFLUENCED BY THE PERCEIVED BEHAVIOR OF OTHER PEOPLE (HIRSHLEIFER, 1995; DUFLO & SAEZ, 2003)

With respect to obesity, proper exercise, alcohol consumption, smoking, becoming vaccinated, and much more, the perceived decisions of others have a significant influence on individual behavior and choice. The behavior of peers has been found to have a significant effect on risky behavior among adolescents, including tobacco smoking, marijuana use, and truancy (Card & Giuliano, 2011; Bisin, Moro, & Topa, 2011).

In particular, food consumption is greatly affected by the food consumption of others, and indeed the body type of others in the relevant group can affect people's responses to their food choices, with a greater effect from those who are thin than those who are heavy (McFerran et al., 2011). Perception of the norm in the pertinent community can affect risk taking, safety, and health.

The norm conveys significant information about what ought to be done; for that reason, those who lack private information may follow the apparent beliefs and behavior of relevant others, sometimes creating *informational cascades*.

In addition, people care about their reputations, and for that reason, they may be influenced by others so as not to incur their disapproval. In some contexts, social norms can help create a phenomenon of *compliance without enforcement*—as, for example, when people comply with laws forbidding indoor smoking or requiring buckling of seat belts, in part because of social norms or the expressive function of those laws. These points bear on the value and importance, in many domains, of private–public partnerships.

B) IN PART BECAUSE OF SOCIAL INFLUENCES, PEOPLE ARE MORE LIKELY TO COOPERATE WITH ONE ANOTHER, AND TO CONTRIBUTE TO THE SOLUTION OF COLLECTIVE ACTION PROBLEMS, THAN STANDARD ECONOMIC THEORY PREDICTS (CAMERER, 2003)

People's willingness to cooperate is partly a product of an independent commitment to fairness; but it is partly a product of a belief that others will see and punish a failure to cooperate or to act fairly. Norms of reciprocity can be exceedingly important. In many contexts, the result is a situation in which people cooperate on the assumption that others are cooperating as well—and might punish those who fail to do so.

4. Difficulties in assessing probability

A) IN MANY DOMAINS, PEOPLE SHOW UNREALISTIC OPTIMISM (JOLLS, 1998; SHAROT, 2011)

The "above average" effect is common (Weinstein, 1987); many people believe that they are less likely than others to suffer from various misfortunes, including automobile accidents and adverse health outcomes. One study found that while smokers do not underestimate statistical risks faced by the population of smokers, they nonetheless believe that their personal risk is less than that of the average smoker (Slovic, 1998). Unrealistic optimism has neurological foundations, with people incorporating good news far more readily than bad news (see Sunstein, 2013, for an overview). A predictable result of unrealistic optimism is a failure to take appropriate precautions.

B) PEOPLE OFTEN USE HEURISTICS, OR MENTAL SHORTCUTS, WHEN ASSESSING RISKS (KAHNEMAN & FREDERICK, 2002)

For example, judgments about probability are often affected by whether a recent event comes readily to mind (Tversky & Kahneman, 1973). If an event is cognitively "available," people may well overestimate the risk. If an event is not cognitively available, people might well underestimate the risk. In short, "availability bias" can lead to inaccurate judgments about the probability of undesirable outcomes.

C) PEOPLE SOMETIMES DO NOT MAKE JUDGMENTS ON THE BASIS OF EXPECTED VALUE, AND THEY MAY NEGLECT OR DISREGARD THE ISSUE OF PROBABILITY, ESPECIALLY WHEN STRONG EMOTIONS ARE TRIGGERED (LOEWENSTEIN ET AL., 2001)

When emotions are strongly felt, people may focus on the outcome and not on the probability that it will occur (Rottenstreich & Hsee, 2001). (This point obviously bears on reactions to extreme events of various sorts.) Prospect theory, which does not depend on emotions at all, suggests that for low and moderate changes, people may be risk averse with respect to gains but risk seeking with respect to losses; for very large changes, people may be risk seeking with respect to gains but risk averse for losses (Kahneman & Tversky, 1979).

B. Incentives and choice architecture

These various findings are hardly inconsistent with the conventional economic emphasis on the importance of material incentives; actual and perceived costs and benefits certainly matter. When the price of a product rises, or when it becomes clear that use of a product imposes serious health risks, the demand for the product is likely to fall (at least, and this is a significant qualification, if these effects are salient). But apart from strictly material incentives of this kind, evidence suggests the independent importance of (1) the social environment and (2) prevailing social norms. If, for example, healthy foods are prominent and easily accessible, then people are more likely to choose them; one study finds an 8 to 16 percent decrease in intake simply by making food more difficult to reach (as, for example, by varying its proximity by ten inches or altering the serving utensil) (Rozin et al., 2011). The problem of childhood obesity is, at least in part, a result of the easy availability of unhealthy foods. The same point bears on smoking and alcohol abuse.

In fact small nudges can have surprisingly large effects. For example, automatic enrollment in savings programs can have far larger effects than significant economic incentives—a clear testimonial to the potential power of choice architecture and its occasionally larger effect than standard economic tools (Chetty et al., 2012). Some evidence suggests that if people are asked to sign forms first rather than last—an especially minor change—the incidence of honesty increases significantly (Shu et al., 2012). Reminders and warnings can make a large difference.

Here is another way to put the point. The existing social environment and current social norms provide the backdrop for many outcomes. Consumer products are accompanied by default rules of various sorts; consider, for example, rental car and cell phone agreements, where it is possible to opt in or to opt out of a range of features, and where the default rule may much matter. With respect to water quality, air quality, sewage treatment, immunization, and health care, the social environment provides relevant background, which is often taken for granted, and which need not, for many people much of the time, become a serious source of deliberation and choice. In particular for people who are well-off, the relevant background, which need not be an object of reflection, is highly desirable and may be taken for granted without causing harm. For others, the background is not so benign, and it should in any case be an object of reflection and choice.

II. Concerns

A. Are predictions possible?

It is tempting to respond that these diverse findings might point in different directions, even for the same subpopulation faced with the same problem, and hence that clear predictions cannot be made in particular cases. For example, will people save too little or too much? Will they take optimal, excessive, or insufficient precautions against the risks associated with poor diet?

By itself and in the abstract, an understanding of loss aversion, the availability heuristic, and social influences does not produce clear answers. Such an understanding could, on plausible assumptions, suggest that people may save too much or take excessive precautions, or on other plausible assumptions, suggest the opposite conclusions. And it may well be the case that loss aversion, unrealistic optimism, the availability heuristic, and social influences are simultaneously at work and will point in different directions, making predictions difficult or impossible. For example, unrealistic optimism may lead people to underestimate certain risks, while the availability heuristic may lead people to overestimate the same risks. And although procrastination will cause delay, loss aversion may lead people to act promptly.

It is true that if these findings are taken as a whole and in the abstract, they will not lead to a clear or unique prediction about behavior. Particular situations must be investigated in detail in order to understand likely outcomes. Predictions often cannot and should not be made in the abstract. For the purposes of this chapter, it is not necessary to engage these questions in detail. We know that automatic enrollment usually has a large effect, and we know when it does not (Sunstein, 2013; see also Chetty et al., 2012). Low-cost regulatory policies, such as disclosure, reminders, and simplification, may be justified even if we do not have a clear understanding, in the abstract, of whether relevant behavior is affected by loss aversion or social influences. Of course it is also true that the design of a disclosure policy should be based on an understanding of how people process information, and that a sensible approach to simplification will require an understanding of whether and why complexity can create problems and of what kinds of simplification can eliminate those problems.

B. Markets, government, and the vexing problem of paternalism

It is natural to wonder whether an understanding of the findings outlined above justify paternalism, or operate as a defense of "more" regulation. With respect to paternalism in particular, it is true that some of the relevant findings supplement the standard accounts of market failures, suggesting that in some settings, markets may fail, in the sense that they may not promote social welfare even in the presence of perfect competition and full information. We are now in a position to identify a series of *behavioral market failures*, and these do appear to justify regulatory controls. Responses to behavioral market failures might be counted as paternalistic.

If, for example, people focus on short-term costs and neglect long-term benefits, then it is possible that disclosure policies that specifically emphasize the long-term, or even regulatory requirements (involving, for example, energy efficiency), may be justified. It is also possible to identify "internalities"—problems of self-control and errors in judgments that produce within-person harms, as, for example, when smoking behavior leads to serious risks because of the victory of short-term considerations over the longer view. These too count as behavioral market failures, and responses may be paternalistic in character.

Richard Thaler and I have argued in defense of "libertarian paternalism" (Thaler and Sunstein, 2008; see also Sunstein, 2013), understood as approaches that preserve freedom of choice while also steering people in directions that will make their lives go better (by their own lights). And it would be possible to think that at least some behavioral market failures justify more coercive forms of paternalism.

But even if the standard accounts of potential market failures are supplemented, it does not necessarily follow that paternalism, or more regulation, is justified. Perhaps markets will eventually address the problem better than regulators would, and for multiple reasons, the cure might be worse than the disease. And indeed, many behaviorally informed approaches should be seen as an effort to increase *navigability*. Those efforts need not be characterized as paternalistic at all.

Indeed, some of the findings might argue in favor of less rather than more regulation and less rather than more paternalism. When, for example, people are able to solve collective action problems on their own, government is not needed. In certain circumstances, automatic enrollment is preferable to mandates and bans. Moreover, market forces can provide a great deal of help in the face of human error. For example, the private sector has relied increasingly on automatic enrollment in savings plans, and countless companies attempt to promote better diet and more exercise (perhaps expecting to obtain more customers as a result).

It should not be necessary to emphasize that public officials are subject to error as well. Indeed, errors may result from one or more of the findings traced above; officials are human and capable of error too. The dynamics of the political process may or may not lead in the right direction. It would be absurd to say that behaviorally informed regulation is more aggressive than regulation that is not so informed, or that an understanding of recent empirical findings calls for more regulation rather than less. The argument is instead that such an understanding can help to inform the design of regulatory programs.

With respect to the particular concerns, it would be valuable to have a better understanding of how the relevant findings apply within heterogeneous groups; the findings are far from uniform within the population, and for purposes of policy, heterogeneity may matter. It would also be valuable to have a better understanding of actual conduct within diverse settings—for example, the decision whether or not to purchase fuel-efficient cars and appliances in the face of short-term costs and long-term benefits. We have good reason to believe that many people do not buy energy efficient products even when it would be in their economic interest to do so, but the conceptual and empirical issues are complex and have not been fully sorted out.

But even at this stage, existing research offers helpful lessons for regulatory policy, which helps account for both the popularity and the impact of recent initiatives. Relevant research suggests that four such approaches have particular promise: (1) using disclosure as a regulatory tool, especially if disclosure policies are designed with an appreciation of how people process information; (2) simplifying and easing choices through appropriate default rules, reminders, reduction of complexity and paperwork requirements, and related strategies; (3) increasing the salience of certain factors or variables; and (4) enlisting or promoting social norms through private–public partnerships and other approaches that operate in the service of agreed-upon public goals. Behaviorally informed approaches of this kind are already in place, including a large set of reforms in both the United Kingdom and the United States (Halpern, 2015; White House Social and Behavioral Sciences Team, 2015).

Acknowledgments

This chapter and the following draw heavily, and are largely based, on Cass R. Sunstein, Empirically Informed Regulation, 78 U. Chi. L. Rev. 1349 (2011), and readers interested in relevant details might consult that discussion. There are, however, some significant additions, revisions, and changes in emphasis. I am grateful to Cassie Chambers for excellent research assistance.

Bibliography

Bisin, A., Moro, A., & Topa, G. (2011). The Empirical Content of Models with Multiple Equilibria in Economies with Social Interactions (Working Paper No. 17196, June 2011). Retrieved from the National Bureau of Economic Research website: www.newyorkfed.org/research/economists/topa/multimay11b.pdf.

Camerer, C. F. (2003). Behavioral game theory: Experiments in strategic interaction. Princeton: Princeton University Press.

Card, D. and Dahl, G. B. (2011). Family violence and football: The effect of unexpected emotional cues on violent behavior. Quarterly Journal of Economics, 126(4), 1879–907.

Card, D. and Giuliano, L. (2011). Peer effects and multiple equilibria in the risky behavior of friends (NBER Working Paper No. 17088) Retrieved from the National Bureau of Economic Research website: www.nber.orgers/w17088.pdf.

Chetty, R., Friedman, J., Leth-Petersen, S., Nielsen, T, and Olsen, T. (2012). Active vs. Passive Decisions and Crowdout in Retirement Savings Accounts: Evidence from Denmark (NBER Working Paper No. 18565) Retrieved from the National Bureau of Economic Research website: www.nber.org/papers/w18565

DG SANCO (2010). Consumer affairs. Retrieved from http://ec.europa.eu/consumers/docs/1dg-sanco-brochure-consumer-behavior-final.pdf.

Duflo, E., & Saez, E. (2003). The role of information and social interactions in retirement plan decisions: Evidence from a randomized experiment. Quarterly Journal of Economics, 118(3), 815–42.

European Commission (2012). Science for environment policy, Future brief: Green behavior. Retrieved from http://ec.europa.eu/environment/integration/research/newsalert/pdf/FB4.pdf.

Halpern, D. (2015). Inside the Nudge Unit. London: W.H. Allen.

Heath, C., & Heath, D. (2010). Switch: How to change things when change is hard. New York: Broadway.

Hirshleifer, D. (1995). The blind leading the blind: Social influence, fads, and informational cascades. In M. Tommasi and K. Ierulli (Eds.) The new economics of human behavior Cambridge, UK: Cambridge University Press, 188–215.

Jolls, C. (1998). Behavioral economics analysis of redistributive legal rules, Vanderbilt Law Review, 51(6), 1653188–21577.

Kahneman, D., & Frederick, S. (2002). Representativeness revisited: Attribute substitution in intuitive judgment. In T. Gilovich, D. Griffin, and D. Kahneman (Eds.) Heuristics and biases. Cambridge, UK: Cambridge University Press, 49–81.

Kahneman, D., & Tversky, A. (1979). Prospect theory: An analysis of decision under risk. Econometrica, 47(2), 263–92.

Leventhal, H., Singer, R. & Jones, S. (1965). Effects of fear and specificity of recommendation upon attitudes and behavior. Journal of Personality and Social Psychology, 2(1), 20–9.

Levin, I. P., Schneider, S. L., & Gaeth, G. J. (1998). All frames are not created equal: A typology and critical analysis of framing effects. Organizational Behavior and Human Decision Processes, 76(2), 149–88.

Loewenstein, G. F., Weber, E. U., Hsee, C. K., & Welch, N. (2001). Risk as feelings, Psychological Bulletin, 127(2), 267–86.

McFerran, B. et al. (2011). How the body type of others impacts our food consumption. In R. Batra, P. Keller, and V. Strecher (Eds.) Leveraging consumer psychology for effective health communications. Armonk, NY: M.E. Sharpe, 151–70.

McGraw, P., Larsen, J., Kahneman, D., & Schkade, D. (2010). Comparing gains and losses. Psychological Science, 21(10), 1438–45.

Nickerson, D. W., & Rogers, T. (2010). Do you have a voting plan? Implementation intentions, voter turnout, and organic plan making. Psychological Science, 21(2), 194–9.

Organization for Economic Cooperation and Development (2010). Consumer policy toolkit. Retrieved from www.oecd.org/sti/consumerpolicy/consumerpolicytoolkit.htm.

Redelmeier, D. A., Rozin, P. & Kahneman, D. (1993). Understanding patients' decisions: Cognitive and emotional perspectives. Journal of the American Medical Association, 270(1), 72–6.

Rottenstreich, Y. & Hsee, C. K. (2001). Money, kisses, and electric shocks: On the affective psychology of risk. Psychological Science, 12, 185–90.

Rozin, P. et al., (2011). Nudge to nobesity I: Minor changes in accessibility decrease food intake, Judgment and Decision Making, 6(4), 323–32.

Sharot, T. (2011). The optimism bias: A tour of the irrationally positive brain. New York, NY: Knopf Publishing.

Shu, L., Mazar, N., Gino, F., Ariely, D., & Bazerman, M. (2012). Signing at the beginning makes ethics salient and decreases dishonest self-reports in comparison to signing at the end. PNAS 109: 15197–200.

Slovic, P. (1998). Do adolescent smokers know the risks? Duke Law Journal, 47(6), 1133–41.

Stango V. & Zinman, J. (2011). Limited and varying consumer attention: Evidence from shocks to the salience of bank overdraft fees (Working Paper No. 11–17) Retrieved from Federal Reserve Bank of Philadelphia website: http://papers.ssrn.com/sol3/papers.cfm?abstract_id=1817916.

Sunstein, C. R. (2013). Simpler. New York, NY: Simon & Schuster.

Thaler, R. H., & Sunstein, C. R. (2008). Nudge. New Haven: Yale University Press.

Thaler, R. H., Kahneman, D. & Knetsch, J. L. (1991). Experimental tests of the endowment effect and the Coase theorem, in R. H. Thaler (Ed.) Quasi rational economics. New York: Russell Sage, 167–88.

Tversky, A. & Kahneman, D. (1973). Availability: A heuristic for judging frequency and probability. Cognitive Psychology, 5(2), 207–32.

Weinstein, N. (1987). Unrealistic optimism about susceptibility to health problems: Conclusions from a community-wide sample, Journal of Behavioral Medicine, 10(5), 481–500.
White House Social and Behavioral Sciences Team. (2015). Annual Report. Available at www.whitehouse.gov/sites/default/files/microsites/ostp/sbst_2015_annual_report_final_9_14_15.pdf
Zwane, A. P. et al. (2011). Being surveyed can change later behavior and related parameter estimates. Proceedings of the National Academy of Sciences, 108(5), 1821–6.

Appendix: Executive Order: using behavioral science insights to better serve the American people

A growing body of evidence demonstrates that behavioral science insights—research findings from fields such as behavioral economics and psychology about how people make decisions and act on them—can be used to design government policies to better serve the American people.

Where Federal policies have been designed to reflect behavioral science insights, they have substantially improved outcomes for the individuals, families, communities, and businesses those policies serve. For example, automatic enrollment and automatic escalation in retirement savings plans have made it easier to save for the future, and have helped Americans accumulate billions of dollars in additional retirement savings. Similarly, streamlining the application process for Federal financial aid has made college more financially accessible for millions of students.

To more fully realize the benefits of behavioral insights and deliver better results at a lower cost for the American people, the Federal Government should design its policies and programs to reflect our best understanding of how people engage with, participate in, use, and respond to those policies and programs. By improving the effectiveness and efficiency of Government, behavioral science insights can support a range of national priorities, including helping workers to find better jobs; enabling Americans to lead longer, healthier lives; improving access to educational opportunities and support for success in school; and accelerating the transition to a low-carbon economy.

Now, therefore, by the authority vested in me as President by the Constitution and the laws of the United States, I hereby direct the following:

Section 1. Behavioral Science Insights Policy Directive.

a Executive departments and agencies (agencies) are encouraged to:

  i identify policies, programs, and operations where applying behavioral science insights may yield substantial improvements in public welfare, program outcomes, and program cost effectiveness;
  ii develop strategies for applying behavioral science insights to programs and, where possible, rigorously test and evaluate the impact of these insights;
  iii recruit behavioral science experts to join the Federal Government as necessary to achieve the goals of this directive; and
  iv strengthen agency relationships with the research community to better use empirical findings from the behavioral sciences.

b In implementing the policy directives in section (a), agencies shall:

  i identify opportunities to help qualifying individuals, families, communities, and businesses access public programs and benefits by, as appropriate, streamlining processes that may otherwise limit or delay participation—for example, removing administrative hurdles, shortening wait times, and simplifying forms;

- ii improve how information is presented to consumers, borrowers, program beneficiaries, and other individuals, whether as directly conveyed by the agency, or in setting standards for the presentation of information, by considering how the content, format, timing, and medium by which information is conveyed affects comprehension and action by individuals, as appropriate;
- iii identify programs that offer choices and carefully consider how the presentation and structure of those choices, including the order, number, and arrangement of options, can most effectively promote public welfare, as appropriate, giving particular consideration to the selection and setting of default options; and
- iv review elements of their policies and programs that are designed to encourage or make it easier for Americans to take specific actions, such as saving for retirement or completing education programs. In doing so, agencies shall consider how the timing, frequency, presentation, and labeling of benefits, taxes, subsidies, and other incentives can more effectively and efficiently promote those actions, as appropriate. Particular attention should be paid to opportunities to use nonfinancial incentives.

c For policies with a regulatory component, agencies are encouraged to combine this behavioral science insights policy directive with their ongoing review of existing significant regulations to identify and reduce regulatory burdens, as appropriate and consistent with Executive Order 13563 of January 18, 2011 (Improving Regulation and Regulatory Review), and Executive Order 13610 of May 10, 2012 (Identifying and Reducing Regulatory Burdens).

Sec. 2. Implementation of the Behavioral Science Insights Policy Directive.

a The Social and Behavioral Sciences Team (SBST), under the National Science and Technology Council (NSTC) and chaired by the Assistant to the President for Science and Technology, shall provide agencies with advice and policy guidance to help them execute the policy objectives outlined in section 1 of this order, as appropriate.

b The NSTC shall release a yearly report summarizing agency implementation of section 1 of this order each year until 2019. Member agencies of the SBST are expected to contribute to this report.

c To help execute the policy directive set forth in section 1 of this order, the Chair of the SBST shall, within 45 days of the date of this order and thereafter as necessary, issue guidance to assist agencies in implementing this order.

16

BEHAVIORALLY INFORMED REGULATION, PART 2

Cass R. Sunstein

If policymakers are using behavioral science, what exactly will they do? Building on actual practice in the United States, the United Kingdom, and elsewhere, I offer a set of answers here. As we shall see, the policy initiatives raise an assortment of questions, many of them empirical. The most important of these is simple: Will they work? As we shall also see, an examination of actual practices helps to show the problems with what we might call the *trap of abstraction*, which evaluates behaviorally informed approaches, or nudges, without engaging with concrete practices (Halpern, 2015; White House Social and Behavioral Sciences Team, 2015).

I. Disclosure as a nudge

In this section, I explore the uses of disclosure as a behaviorally informed regulatory tool. It is important to distinguish between *summary disclosure*, often provided at the point of purchase, and *full disclosure*, typically provided on the Internet. A central point is that disclosure policies should be based on an understanding of how people actually process information. On this count, behavioral findings are essential.

A. Actually informing choice

1. Examples

Many statutory programs recognize that information disclosure can be a useful regulatory tool, replacing or complementing other approaches. Central examples include legislative efforts to require disclosure of the risks associated with smoking, of potential savings from energy efficiency, and of information that bears on health. Recent initiatives have drawn directly from behavioral economics, emphasizing the importance of plain language, clarity, and simplicity (White House Social and Behavioral Sciences Team, 2015; Sunstein, 2013).

A) CREDIT CARDS

The Credit Card Accountability, Responsibility, and Disclosure Act of 2009 (Credit CARD Act, 2009) is designed in large part to ensure that credit card users are adequately informed. Specifically, the Act prohibits an increase in annual percentage rates (APR) without forty-five days' notice, prohibits the retroactive application of rate increases to existing balances, and also requires clear notice of the consumer's right to cancel the credit card when the APR is raised.

The Act also requires a number of electronic disclosures of credit card agreements. Specifically, it requires that (1) "[e]ach creditor shall establish and maintain an Internet site on which the creditor shall post the written agreement between the creditor and the consumer for each credit card account under an open-end consumer credit plan"; (2) "[e]ach creditor shall provide to the Board, in electronic format, the consumer credit card agreements that it publishes on its Internet site"; and (3) the "Board shall establish and maintain on its publicly available Internet site a central repository of the consumer credit card agreements received from creditors pursuant to this subsection, and such agreements shall be easily accessible and retrievable by the public" (Credit CARD Act, 2009).

B) NUTRITION

In the domain of nutrition, a number of disclosure requirements are in place. To take just one example, a final rule has been issued by the US Department of Agriculture (USDA), requiring provision of nutritional information to consumers with respect to meat and poultry products. Nutrition facts panels must be provided on the labels of such products. Under the rule, the panels must contain information with respect to calories and both total and saturated fats (9 CFR § 317.309).

The rule clearly recognizes the potential importance of framing. If a product lists a percentage statement such as "80 percent lean," it must also list its fat percentage. This requirement should avoid the confusion that can result from selective framing; a statement that a product is 80 percent lean, standing by itself, makes leanness salient, and may therefore be misleading.

C) HEALTH CARE

The Patient Protection and Affordable Care Act of 2010 (Affordable Care Act) contains a large number of disclosure requirements designed to promote accountability and informed choice with respect to health care. Indeed, the Affordable Care Act is, in significant part, a series of disclosure requirements, many of which are meant to inform consumers, and to do so in a way that is alert to behavioral findings. Under the Act, a restaurant that is part of a chain with twenty or more locations doing business under the same name is required to disclose calories on the menu board. Such restaurants are also required to provide in a written form (available to customers upon request) additional nutrition information pertaining to total calories and calories from fat, as well as amounts of fat, saturated fat, cholesterol, sodium, total carbohydrates, complex carbohydrates, sugars, dietary fiber, and protein (Affordable Care Act, 2010).

In a similar vein, § 1103 of the Act calls for "[i]mmediate information that allows consumers to identify affordable coverage options." It requires the establishment of an Internet portal for beneficiaries to easily access affordable and comprehensive coverage options, including information about eligibility, availability, premium rates, cost sharing, and the percentage of total premium revenues spent on health care, rather than administrative expenses.

It should be clear from this brief survey that the range of recent disclosure requirements is very wide. Such approaches have considerable promise.

2. How, not only whether

As social scientists have emphasized, disclosure as such may not be enough; regulators should devote care and attention to *how, not only whether, disclosure occurs*. Clarity and simplicity are often critical. In some cases, accurate disclosure of information may be ineffective if the information is too abstract, vague, detailed, complex, poorly framed, or overwhelming to be useful (White House Social and Behavioral Sciences Team, 2015). Disclosure requirements should be designed for *Homo sapiens*, not *Homo economicus* (the agent in economics textbooks). In addition, emphasis on certain variables may attract undue attention and prove to be misleading. If disclosure requirements are to be helpful, then they must be designed to be sensitive to how people actually process information.

A good rule of thumb is that disclosure should be concrete, straightforward, simple, meaningful, timely, and salient. If the goal is to inform people about how to avoid risks or to obtain benefits, disclosure should avoid abstract statements (such as, for example, of "healthy eating" or "good diet") and instead clearly identify the steps that might be taken to obtain the relevant goal (by specifying, for example, what specific actions parents might take to reduce the risk of childhood obesity).

In 2010, the Department of Health and Human Services (HHS) emphasized the importance of clarity and salience in connection with its interim final rule entitled "Health Care Reform Insurance Web Portal Requirements," which "adopts the categories of information that will be collected and displayed as Web portal content, and the data we will require from issuers and request from States, associations, and high risk pools in order to create this content" (Department of Health and Human Services, 2010b). The preamble to the interim final rule is behaviorally informed in the sense that it is directly responsive to how people process information:

> In implementing these requirements, we seek to develop a Web site (hereinafter called the Web portal) that would empower consumers by increasing informed choice and promoting market competition. To achieve these ends, we intend to provide a Web portal that provides information to consumers in a clear, salient, and easily navigated manner. We plan to minimize the use of technical language, jargon, or excessive complexity in order to promote the ability of consumers to understand the information and act in accordance with what they have learned. . . . [W]e plan to provide information, consistent with applicable laws, in a format that is accessible for use by members of the public, allowing them to download and repackage the information, promoting innovation and the goal of consumer choice.

That web portal can be found at www.healthcare.gov/.

3. Testing disclosure

To the extent possible, agencies should study in advance the actual effects of alternative disclosure designs to ensure that information is properly presented and will actually inform consumers. The "Nutrition Facts" labels on many food products followed such a process of advance study, with careful investigation of consumer responses to different presentations of the relevant material. Actual experience can, of course, provide valuable information.

Because they are more likely to yield information about actual behavior, experimental or quasi-experimental studies are preferred to focus groups; randomized experiments have particular advantages. At the same time, focus groups can also be useful, especially if they are carefully designed to assess likely behavior (rather than simply asking people which presentations or formats they most like).

4. Behavioral economics, cognitive illusions, and avoiding confusion

If not carefully designed, disclosure requirements can produce ineffective, confusing, and potentially misleading messages. Behaviorally informed approaches are alert to this risk and suggest possible improvements.

For instance, automobile manufacturers are currently required to disclose the fuel economy of new vehicles as measured by miles per gallon (MPG). This disclosure is useful for consumers and helps to promote informed choice. As the Environmental Protection Agency (EPA) has emphasized, however, MPG is a nonlinear measure of fuel consumption (Environmental Protection Agency, 2009a). For a fixed travel distance, a change from 20 to 25 MPG produces a larger reduction in fuel costs than does a change from 30 to 35 MPG, or even from 30 to 38 MPG. To see the point more dramatically, consider the fact that an increase from 10 to 20 MPG produces more savings than an increase from 20 to 40 MPG, and an increase from 10 to 11 MPG produces savings almost as high as an increase from 34 to 50 MPG.

Evidence suggests that many consumers do not understand this point and tend to interpret MPG as linear with fuel costs. When it occurs, this error is likely to produce inadequately informed purchasing decisions when people are making comparative judgments about fuel costs. For example, people may well underestimate the benefits of trading a low MPG car for one that is even slightly more fuel-efficient. By contrast, an alternative fuel economy metric, such as gallons per mile, could be far less confusing. Such a measure is linear with fuel costs and hence suggests a possible way to help consumers make better choices.

A closely related finding is that because of the MPG illusion, consumers tend to *underestimate* the cost differences between low-MPG vehicles and tend to *overestimate* the cost differences between high-MPG vehicles (Allcott, 2011). Recognizing the imperfections and potentially misleading nature of the MPG measure, the Department of Transportation and EPA proposed in 2010 two alternative labels that are meant to provide consumers with clearer and more accurate information about the effects of fuel economy on fuel expenses and on the environment (Environmental Protection Agency, 2009a).

After a period of public comment, the Department of Transportation and EPA ultimately chose a label that borrows from both proposals (Environmental Protection Agency, 2009a). This approach calls for disclosure of the factual material included in the first option but adds a clear statement about anticipated fuel savings (or costs) over a five-year period. The statement of fuel savings (or costs) should simultaneously help counteract the MPG illusion and inform consumers of the economic effects of fuel economy over a relevant time period (Environmental Protection Agency, 2009a). At the same time, the chosen approach does not include the letter grades, on the ground (among others) that it might be taken to suggest a governmental evaluation of the overall merits of the car (Sunstein, 2013).

In a related vein, the USDA abandoned the "Food Pyramid," which was used for decades as the central icon to promote healthy eating. The Pyramid has long been criticized as insufficiently informative; it does not offer people with any kind of clear "path" with respect to healthy diet. According to one critical account, "its meaning is almost completely opaque.... To learn what the Food Pyramid has to say about food, you must be willing to decipher the Pyramid's markings.... The language and concepts here are so hopelessly abstracted from people's actual experience with food... that the message confuses and demoralizes" (Heath & Heath, 2010). In response to these objections, and after an extended period of deliberation, the USDA replaced the Pyramid with a new, simpler icon, consisting of a plate with clear markings for fruit, vegetable, grains, and protein.

The plate is accompanied by straightforward guidance, including "make half your plate fruits and vegetables," "drink water instead of sugary drinks," and "switch to fat-free or low-fat (1 percent) milk." This approach has the key advantage of informing people what to do, if they seek to have a healthier diet.

In a related vein, the HHS, implementing a provision of the Affordable Care Act, issued a rule to require insurance companies to provide clear, plain language summaries of relevant information to prospective customers. The rule includes basic information, including the annual premium, the annual deductible, a statement of services that are not covered, and a statement of costs for going to an out-of-network provider (Healthcare.gov, 2011).

In some circumstances, the tendency toward unrealistic optimism may lead some consumers to downplay or neglect information about statistical risks associated with a product or an activity. Possible examples include smoking and distracted driving. In such circumstances, disclosure might be designed to make the risks associated with the product less abstract, more vivid, and salient. For example, the Family Smoking Prevention and Tobacco Control Act of 2009 (Smoking Prevention Act) requires graphic warnings with respect to the risks of smoking tobacco, and the Food and Drug Administration (FDA) has finalized such warnings for public comment, with vivid and even disturbing pictures of some of the adverse outcomes associated with smoking.

5. Behavioral economics and promoting competition

If disclosure requirements are straightforward and simple, then they should facilitate comparison shopping and hence market competition. Drawing on social science research, the Treasury Department's account of financial regulation emphasizes the value of requiring that "communications with the consumer are reasonable, not merely technically compliant and non-deceptive. Reasonableness includes balance in the presentation of risks and benefits, as well as clarity and conspicuousness in the description of significant product costs and risks" (Department of the Treasury, 2009b). The department's analysis goes on to say that one goal should be to

> harness technology to make disclosures more dynamic and adaptable to the needs of the individual consumer. . . . Disclosures should show consumers the consequences of their financial decisions. . . . [The regulator] should mandate or encourage calculator disclosures for mortgages to assist with comparison shopping. For example, a calculator that shows the costs of a mortgage based on the consumer's expectations for how long she will stay in the home may reveal a more significant difference between two products than appears on standard paper disclosures.
>
> *(Department of the Treasury, 2009b)*

In keeping with this theme, the Consumer Financial Protection Bureau is authorized to ensure that "consumers are provided with timely and understandable information to make responsible decisions about financial transactions" (Dodd–Frank Act, 2010). The Bureau is also authorized to issue rules that ensure that information is "fully, accurately, and effectively disclosed to consumers in a manner that permits consumers to understand the costs, benefits, and risks associated with the product or service, in light of the facts and circumstances" (Dodd–Frank Act, 2010).

To accomplish this task, the Bureau is authorized to issue model forms with

> A clear and conspicuous disclosure that, at a minimum—(A) uses plain language comprehensible to consumers; (B) contains a clear format and design, such as an easily

readable type font; and (C) succinctly explains the information that must be communicated to the consumer.

(Dodd–Frank Act, 2010; Riis & Ratner, 2011)

In addition, the director of the Bureau is required to "establish a unit whose functions shall include researching, analyzing, and reporting on . . . consumer awareness, understanding, and use of disclosures and communications regarding consumer financial products or services" and "consumer behavior with respect to consumer financial products or services, including performance on mortgage loans." Note that new technologies make it possible to inform consumers of their own choices and usages, an approach that may be especially important when firms have better information than consumers do about such choices and usages.

In the same general vein, the Department of Labor issued a final rule requiring disclosure to workers of relevant information in pension plans. The rule is designed to require clear, simple disclosure of information about fees and expenses and to allow meaningful comparisons, in part through the use of standard methodologies in the calculation and disclosure of expense and return information (29 CFR § 2550.404a-5).

Yet another example is provided by a final rule of the Department of Education that promotes transparency and consumer choice with respect to for-profit education by requiring institutions to provide clear disclosure of costs, debt levels, graduation rates, and placement rates (Department of Education, 2010a). The rule states that relevant institutions must disclose, among other things, the occupations that the program prepares students to enter, the on-time graduation rate for students completing the program, the tuition and fees charged to students for completing the program within a normal time, the placement rate for students completing the program, and the median loan debt incurred by students who completed the program. These disclosures must be included "in promotional materials [the institution] makes available to prospective students" and be "[p]rominently provide[d] . . . in a simple and meaningful manner on the home page of its program Web site" (34 CFR § 668.6); Department of Education, 2010b).

B. Behaviorally informed tools: summary disclosure and full disclosure

Disclosure requirements of this kind are designed to inform consumers at the point of purchase, often with brief summaries of relevant information. Such "summary disclosures" are often complemented with more robust information, typically found on public or private websites. For example, the EPA offers a great deal of material on fuel economy online, going well beyond the information that is available on stickers, and the nutrition facts label is supplemented by a great deal of nutritional information on government websites. Approaches of this kind provide information that private individuals and institutions can adapt, reassemble, and present in new, helpful, imaginative, and often unanticipated ways. Some of the most valuable and creative uses of full disclosure are made by the private sector.

Other disclosure requirements are not specifically directed to consumers or end users at all. They promote public understanding of existing problems and help produce possible solutions by informing people about current practices. One example is the Emergency Planning and Community Right-to-Know Act of 1986 (Emergency Planning Act, 1986). At first, this law seemed to be largely a bookkeeping measure, requiring a "Toxic Release Inventory" in which firms reported what pollutants they were using. But available evidence indicates that it has had beneficial effects, helping to spur reductions in toxic releases throughout the United States (Hamilton, 2005). One reason for this involves public accountability: public attention can help promote behavior that fits with statutory purposes.

In 2009 and 2010, the Occupational Safety and Health Administration (OSHA) placed a significant subset of its fatality, illness, and injury data online, in a step that should promote both accountability and safer workplaces (Department of Labor, 2011). In 2009, the EPA issued a greenhouse gas reporting rule, requiring disclosure by many of the most significant emitters (Environmental Protection Agency, 2009b). The data may well allow businesses to find innovative ways to track their own emissions, to compare them to similar facilities, and eventually to identify low-cost reductions.

The Department of Justice (DOJ) has similarly published dozens of data sets involving crime, enforcement, and prison (Department of Justice, 2012; Data.gov, n.d.), and is preparing many more for future release. Similarly, the Department of Labor's "Searchable Enforcement Database" provides the public with one-stop access to enforcement data across the department (for example, Mines and Chemical Hazards) (Department of Labor, n.d.). The EPA has taken a similar approach (Environmental Protection Agency, n.d.). Generalizing from these practices, President Obama has issued a memorandum requiring agencies "with broad regulatory compliance and administrative enforcement responsibilities" to "develop plans to make public information concerning their regulatory compliance and enforcement activities accessible, downloadable, and searchable online" (Presidential Memorandum, 2011).

These steps fit well with the goals of the Office of Management and Budget's (OMB) "Open Government Directive," which is intended in part to ensure that high-value data sets are placed online (Orszag, 2009). Posting these data sets online can promote regulatory goals by virtue of the power of publicity. Indeed, many high-value data sets count as such because their publication helps agencies further their statutory missions. The directive explicitly emphasizes this point (Orszag, 2009), and numerous agencies have disclosed high-value data sets (Department of Health and Human Services, 2010a; Department of the Treasury, 2009a; Department of Housing and Urban Development, n.d.; Department of Energy, n.d.) and developed open government plans (Environmental Protection Agency, 2010; Department of Transportation, 2010; Department of Health and Human Services, 2010b; Department of Labor, 2010; Asamoah & Sharfstein, 2010). Disclosure of many of the data sets (for example, in the domain of safety and health) should promote agency missions; the open government plans enlist openness for the same reason.

Disclosure is also used as a check on certain increases in health insurance premiums. For plan years beginning in 2010, Affordable Care Act § 1004 requires that the secretary and states establish a process for the annual review of "unreasonable increases" in premiums for health insurance coverage (Affordable Care Act, 2010). That process shall "require health insurance issuers to submit to the Secretary and the relevant State a justification for an unreasonable premium increase prior to the implementation of the increase" (Affordable Care Act, 2010). Moreover, "such issuers shall prominently post such information on their Internet websites," and the "Secretary shall ensure the public disclosure of information on such increases and justifications for all health insurance issuers" (Affordable Care Act, 2010).

In addition to making data more accessible, some agencies are attempting to make the data more readily usable. An example of this kind of clean, clear, and flexible transparency technology is eXtensible Business Reporting Language (XBRL)(XBRL, n.d.). XBRL is an open standard for creating electronic reports and exchanging data via the web. Using a standardized series of "tags" for labeling information, XBRL essentially allows anyone to download and analyze huge amounts of data using a simple spreadsheet. By June of this year, companies with a market capitalization over $5 billion that use US accounting rules will need to submit all filings via the XBRL format, according to a recently announced Securities and Exchange Commission (SEC) rule, entitled "Interactive Data to Improve Financial Reporting," which requires

> companies to provide financial statement information in a form that is intended to improve its usefulness to investors. In this format, financial statement information could be downloaded directly into spreadsheets, analyzed in a variety of ways using commercial off-the-shelf software, and used within investment models in other software formats. . . . The new rules are intended not only to make financial information easier for investors to analyze, but also to assist in automating regulatory filings and business information processing. Interactive data has the potential to increase the speed, accuracy, and usability of financial disclosure, and eventually reduce costs.
>
> *(Securities and Exchange Commission, 2009)*

The requirement will be phased in over three years for smaller public companies and mutual funds.

To be sure, mandatory disclosure can impose costs and burdens on both private and public institutions, and to the extent permitted by law, those costs and burdens should be considered when deciding whether and how to proceed. Empirical evidence on the actual effects of disclosure policies is indispensable (Greenstone, 2009; Schwartz et al., 2011; Sunstein, 2010a).

II. Default rules and simplification as nudges

Social science research provides strong evidence that starting points, or "default rules," greatly affect social outcomes (Sunstein, 2015; Johnson et al., 1993). In some contexts, it may be possible to promote statutory goals with sensible default rules that preserve freedom of choice and that might help to avoid the rigidity, cost, and unintended adverse consequences of mandates and bans. Default rules are one way of easing people's choices, and they are used in countless domains by both public and private institutions. There are other ways of easing choices. One example is simplification, as with communications and forms that are shorter, easier, more intuitive, electronic, and in some cases prepopulated with information, thus reducing burdens on those who are asked to fill them out (White House Social and Behavioral Sciences Team, 2015).

A. Automatic enrollment and default rules: examples

1. Savings

In the United States, employers have long asked workers whether they want to enroll in 401(k) plans; under a common approach, the default rule is nonenrollment. Even when enrollment is easy, the number of employees who enroll, or opt in, has sometimes been relatively low (Madrian & Shea, 2001; Gale et al., 2009). Recently, a number of employers have responded by changing the default to automatic enrollment, by which employees are enrolled unless they opt out. The results are clear: significantly more employees end up enrolled with an opt-out design than with opt-in (Gale et al., 2009). This is so even when opting out is easy. Importantly, automatic enrollment has significant benefits for all groups, with increased anticipated savings for Hispanics, African Americans, and women in particular (Orszag & Rodriguez, 2009; Papke, Walker, & Dworsky, 2009; Chiteji & Walker, 2009).

The Pension Protection Act of 2006 (PPA) (Pension Protection Act, 2006) draws directly on these findings by encouraging employers to adopt automatic enrollment plans. The PPA does this by providing nondiscrimination safe harbors for elective deferrals and for matching contributions under plans that include an automatic enrollment feature, as well as by providing protections from state payroll-withholding laws to allow for automatic enrollment. Building on these efforts,

President Obama has asked the IRS and the Treasury Department to undertake initiatives to make it easier for employers to adopt such plans (Obama, 2009; Internal Revenue Service, 2009).

2. Health care

A provision of the Affordable Care Act requires employers with over two hundred employees automatically to enroll employees in health care plans, while also allowing employees to opt-out (Affordable Care Act, 2010). This provision requires implementing regulations, which, once issued, should significantly ease the process of ensuring compliance with the Act's "individual mandate" (which requires health insurance coverage).

On February 4, 2010, the Center of Medicare and Medicaid Services (CMS) provided guidance to states via a State Health Official (SHO) letter (Centers for Medicare and Medicaid Services, 2010). In cases where states are able to obtain all the information necessary to determine eligibility, the new option permits States to automatically enroll and renew eligible children in Medicaid or Children's Health Insurance Program (CHIP). This approach allows states to initiate and determine eligibility for Medicaid or CHIP without a signed Medicaid or CHIP program application, as long as the family or child consents to be enrolled in Medicaid or CHIP.

3. School meals

The National School Lunch Act (Healthy Hunger-Free Kids Act, 2012) takes steps to allow "direct certification" of eligibility, thus reducing complexity and introducing what is a form of automatic enrollment. Under the program, children who are eligible for benefits under certain programs will be "directly eligible" for free lunches and free breakfasts, and hence will not have to fill out additional applications (Healthy, Hunger-Free Kids Act, 2012).

To promote direct certification, the USDA issued an interim final rule that is expected to provide up to 270,000 children with school meals (Department of Agriculture, 2011). Total participants in the direct certification program now exceed 12 million (Department of Agriculture, 2015).

4. Payroll statements

The Department of Homeland Security changed the default setting for payroll statements to electronic from paper, thus reducing costs (Orszag, 2010). In general, changes of this kind may save significant sums of money for both private and public sectors. It would be useful to identify other contexts in which sensible default rules—or automatic or simplified enrollment—might operate in the service of legal requirements and agreed-upon social goals. Of course it is possible to imagine default rules, or approaches to automatic enrollment, that are harmful or counter-productive; this risk is discussed below.

5. Childhood obesity

A great deal of empirical work identifies a noteworthy contributor to the problem of obesity, including childhood obesity. If healthy foods are easily accessible, then people are far more likely to choose them, and the same is true for unhealthy foods. Indeed, convenience and accessibility can significantly increase caloric intake (Rozin et al., 2011; Wansink, Just, & McKendry, 2010) some studies have found that when fast food restaurants are located near schools or residences, significant weight gain occurs in both children and pregnant women (Currie et al., 2010).

Even small differences have large effects on food choices and consumption. For example, the sizes of plates and portions have been increasing over time, and they affect how much people eat; when unhealthy foods are made slightly less accessible, their consumption is reduced (Rozin et al., 2011; Wansink, 2010; Wisdom et al., 2010; Dayan & Bar-Hillel, 2011). These and related issues are discussed in the report of the White House Task Force on Childhood Obesity, which places a great emphasis on the importance of accessibility (White House Task Force on Childhood Obesity, 2010).

In a sense, social settings produce something akin to "default rules" for food choices. These findings—about the importance of seemingly small features of context—have implications for continuing efforts to reduce childhood obesity and many other problems. One study, for example, finds that if people are prompted to consider whether to "downsize" their meals through a simple question, they will eat significantly less at fast food restaurants (Schwartz et al., 2011). Indeed, the effect of this prompt was found to be greater than that of calorie labeling.

B. Automatic enrollment and default rules: mechanisms and complexities

A great deal of research has attempted to explore exactly why default rules have such a large effect on outcomes (Sunstein, 2015; Gale, Iwry, & Walters, 2009; Dinner et al., 2009; Carroll et al., 2009). There appear to be three contributing factors. The first involves *inertia and procrastination*. To alter the effect of the default rule, people must make an active choice to reject the default. In view of the power of inertia and the tendency to procrastinate, people may simply continue with the status quo. It follows that self-consciously and well-chosen default rules by individuals, or by private or public institutions, can operate as commitment devices; consider, for example, a default rule in favor of monthly transfer of money into a savings account, or in favor of savings for retirement.

The second factor involves what might be taken to be an *implicit endorsement* of the default rule. Many people appear to conclude that the default was chosen for a reason; they believe that they should not depart from it unless they have particular information to justify a change.

Third, the default rule might establish the *reference point* for people's decisions; the established reference point has significant effects because people dislike losses from that reference point. If, for example, the default rule favors energy-efficient light bulbs, then the loss (in terms of reduced efficiency) may loom large and there will be a tendency to continue with energy-efficient light bulbs. But if the default rule favors less efficient (and initially less expensive) light bulbs, then the loss in terms of upfront costs may loom large, and there will be a tendency to favor less efficient light bulbs.

In a significant number of domains, it might be possible to achieve regulatory goals, and to do so while maintaining freedom of choice and at low cost, by selecting good default rules and by avoiding harmful ones. The initial task, of course, is to identify the requirements of the law. Within the context of such requirements, one approach is to select the default rule that reflects what most people would choose if they were adequately informed. Suppose, for example, that a particular default rule would place a strong majority of the relevant population in the situation that they would favor if they made an informed choice. If so, there is a legitimate reason to adopt that default rule (with the understanding that for those who differ from the majority, it remains possible to opt out).

Of course, it may be necessary to do a great deal of work in order to identify the approach that informed people would choose, and on this count, actual evidence about informed choice is extremely important. The issue is simplified if the law requires a particular set of outcomes. A default rule might well make sense if it promotes automatic compliance with the law.

Hence, it is important to see that use of default rules may serve either as an independent approach, used instead of a mandate or a ban, or as a complementary approach, operating to facilitate compliance with statutory or regulatory requirements.

It is also important to see that default rules can be badly chosen or misused by private and public institutions alike, and that some such rules can be harmful. The FTC has expressed serious concerns about "negative option marketing," which occurs when those who accept a "free" product are automatically enrolled in a plan or program that carries a monthly fee (unless they explicitly opt out) (16 CFR § 425; Federal Trade Commission, 2009). In some cases, negative option marketing has the unfortunate effect of using a default rule to exploit the tendency toward inertia in a way that is harmful to people's welfare; it is easy to imagine both private and public analogues (consider, for example, an automatic enrollment policy that puts an unreasonably large amount of salary into savings).

To evaluate the use of automatic enrollment, the particular circumstances certainly matter. If automatic enrollment is not made transparent to those who are enrolled, then it can be considered a form of manipulation, and the problem is worse if it is not in their long-term interest.

Some default rules apply to all of the relevant population, subject to the ability to opt out. Other default rules are *personalized*, in the sense that they draw on available information about which approach best suits individuals in the relevant population. A personalized default might be based on geographical or demographic variables; for example, income and age might be used in determining appropriate default rules for retirement plans. Alternatively, a personalized default might be based on people's own past choices to the extent that they are available.

An advantage of personalized default rules is that they may well be more accurate than "mass" default rules. As technology evolves, it should be increasingly possible to produce personalized defaults, based on people's own choices and situations, and likely to be far more accurate than more general ones. There will be excellent opportunities to use default rules to promote people's welfare (Sunstein, 2015). To be sure, any such rules must respect the applicable laws, policies, and regulations involving personal privacy and should avoid unduly crude proxies.

It is important to note that default rules may not "stick" when the relevant population has strong contrary preferences. For example, a study in the United Kingdom found that most people rejected a savings plan with an unusually high default contribution rate (12 percent of before-tax income) (Beshears et al., 2010). Only about 25 percent of employees remained at that rate after a year, whereas about 60 of employees remained at a lower default contribution rate. One implication is that "extreme" defaults are less likely to stick; another implication, based on the lower incomes of those who stayed with the default, is that default rules may be more influential for low-income workers than for their higher-earning counterparts (Beshears et al., 2010).

A related finding is that workers were not much affected by a default allocation of a fraction of their tax refund to US savings bonds, apparently because such workers had definite plans to spend their refunds (Bronchetti et al., 2011). A general lesson is that default rules will have a weaker effect, and potentially no effect, when the relevant population has a strong preference for a certain outcome.

C. Active choices

An alternative approach, sometimes worth serious consideration, is to avoid any default rule and *to require active choices* (Carroll et al., 2009). Under this approach, people are required to make an actual choice among the various options; they are not defaulted into any particular alternative. With respect to savings, for example, an employer might reject both opt-out and opt-in and simply require employees to indicate their preferences. Evidence suggests that active choices result in far higher levels of savings than a default rules that requires people explicitly to opt in (Carroll et al., 2009).

If inertia and procrastination are playing a significant role, then active choosing may be better than opt-in, in which people end up with outcomes that they would not prefer if they were to make a choice. In such circumstances, active choosing increases the likelihood that people will end up with their preferred outcomes (Sunstein, 2015).

Active choosing might also be preferred when public officials lack relevant information, so that the chosen default rule might be harmful. This is an especially important point. If officials are inadequately informed, and if the default rule is no better than a guess, then that rule might lead people in the wrong direction. The same point argues against a default rule when self-interested private groups have managed to call for it, even though it is not in the interest of those on whom it is imposed. Active choosing is much less risky on these counts.

As compared with either opt-in or opt-out, active choosing can have significant advantages when the relevant group has a great deal of diversity, so that a single approach is unlikely to fit variable circumstances. In such contexts, a default rule may also be harmful, because the power of inertia, or the force of suggestion, may mean that many people will end up in a situation that is not in their interest. For this reason, active choosing may be better.

On the other hand, active choosing can have significant disadvantages. One disadvantage is that in situations of unfamiliarity or great complexity, in which people lack information or experience, active choosing may impose unjustified or excessive burdens. These burdens include the resources required to enforce the requirement to choose and the time required for people to obtain relevant information and to make the choice. As compared with a default rule, active choosing increases the costs of decisions, possibly significantly; it also might increase errors, possibly significantly, if the area is unfamiliar and confusing. In such situations, opt-in or opt-out might produce better outcomes for people (Sunstein, 2015).

In the private sector, default rules are often in people's interests, and active choosing would impose unnecessary burdens. When public officials have good reason for confidence that a particular default rule will fit with the informed preferences of the relevant group, and thus promote its interests, it may be preferable to select that default rule rather than to require active choosing (Sunstein, 2010a). Personalized default rules, by virtue of their accuracy, may have particular virtues on this count.

D. Simplification as nudge

Where it is not possible or best to change the default, a similar effect might be obtained merely by simplifying and easing people's choices. Complexity can have serious unintended effects (including indifference, delay, and confusion), potentially undermining regulatory goals by reducing compliance or by decreasing the likelihood that people will benefit from various policies and programs (White House Social and Behavioral Sciences Team, 2015).

For example, a series of steps have been taken toward simplifying the Free Application for Federal Student Aid (FAFSA), reducing the number of questions through skip logic (a survey method that uses previous responses to determine subsequent questions) and allowing electronic retrieval of information (Office of Management and Budget, 2010). Use of a simpler and shorter form is accompanied by a pilot initiative to permit online users to transfer data previously supplied electronically in their tax forms directly into their FAFSA applications.

These steps are intended to simplify the application process for financial aid and thus to increase access to college; there is good reason to believe that such steps will enable many students to receive aid for attending college when they previously could not do so. Similar steps might be taken in many other domains. Considerable thought should be given to the question whether complexity is having unintended adverse effects and undermining regulatory programs.

The Department of Treasury has also launched an important initiative in the domain of Social Security and Supplemental Security Income: the "Direct Express" card program. Many people are now automatically receiving their money via a prepaid debit card. This measure increases, at the same time, both convenience and accuracy, thus reducing paperwork and costs. It provides particular help for those who lack bank accounts. Other programs might build on this approach by considering the choice between an opt-in and opt-out design and simplifying people's choices. Some such programs might be designed to help those without bank accounts, by giving them such accounts or the functional equivalent.

In 2010, the Treasury Department also took several steps to increase simplicity by moving to electronic systems. Perhaps most importantly, the department finalized a rule to provide electronic payments to people receiving Social Security, Supplemental Security Income, Veterans, Railroad Retirement, and Office of Personnel Management benefits (29 CFR § 1926).

It is estimated that these steps will save over $400 million in the first five years. The initiatives from the Treasury Department are in line with a 2010 request from the OMB asking agencies for initiatives that would promote electronic filing through "fillable fileable" forms, substitute electronic for paper signatures, increase administrative simplification, and reduce burdens on small business (Sunstein, 2010b). That request in turn produced seventy-two initiatives from various agencies, all designed to reduce burdens and to increase simplification (Office of Information and Regulatory Affairs, 2009). In total, those initiatives are expected to eliminate over 60 million hours of paperwork and reporting burdens each year.

In 2011, OMB followed the 2010 request with another one, also emphasizing simplification and focusing in particular on small business and benefit programs (Sunstein, 2011). The request drew particular attention to the potential harms of complexity, noting that

> the process of renewing or applying for benefits can be time-consuming, confusing, and unnecessarily complex, thus discouraging participation and undermining program goals. Sometimes agencies collect data that are unchanged from prior applications; in such circumstances, they might be able to use, or to give people the option to use, pre-populated electronic forms.
>
> *(Sunstein, 2011)*

And indeed, there is reason to believe that imperfect take-up of existing benefit programs, including those that provide income support, is partly a product of behavioral factors such as procrastination and inertia. It follows that efforts to increase simplicity, including automatic enrollment, may have substantial benefits.

E. Structuring choices

Complexity can also create problems through a phenomenon known as *choice overload*. In the traditional view, having more choices helps, and never harms, consumers or program participants. This view is based on the reasonable judgment that, if an additional option is not better than existing options, people will simply not choose it. In general, more choices are indeed desirable, but an increasing body of research offers certain potential qualifications, especially in unusually complex situations (Sethi-Iyengar, Huberman, & Jiang, 2004). For example, there is some evidence that enrollment may decline (Sethi-Iyengar, Huberman, & Jiang, 2004) and asset allocations may worsen (Iyengar & Kamenica, 2010) as the menu of investment options in a 401(k) plan expands.

Responding to this general problem in the context of prescription drug plans, CMS has taken steps to maintain freedom of choice while also reducing unhelpful and unnecessary complexity (Gruber & Abaluck, 2011). The CMS Medicare Part D program rules require sponsors to ensure that when they provide multiple plan offerings, those offerings have meaningful differences. The rules also eliminate plans with persistently low enrollments, on the ground that those plans increase the complexity of choices without adding value.

III. Salience as nudge

It is often possible to promote regulatory goals by making certain features of a product or a situation more *salient* to consumers. As a simple example of salience effects, consider alcohol taxes. There is evidence that when such taxes are specifically identified in the posted price, increases in such taxes have a larger negative effect on alcohol consumption than when they are applied at the register (Chetty, Looney, & Kroft, 2009; Finkelstein, 2009). Incentives matter, but in order to matter, they must be salient. Sensible regulatory policies, especially those that involve disclosure, are attentive to the importance of salience.

People's attention is limited, and regulatory goals are not always served merely by altering policy or disclosing information. The relevant policy or information must also be salient. In the context of fiscal policy, consider the question whether to provide payments in the form of a one-time check or instead in the form of reduced withholding. Would one or another approach lead to increased spending?

In the abstract, it may be predicted that there would be no difference as a result of delivery method. But evidence suggests that a one-time stimulus payment may have greater effects in increasing spending than does an economically equivalent reduction in withholding (Sahm, Shapiro, & Slemrod, 2011). A potential explanation, with support in the evidence, involves the importance of salience or visibility. Indeed, a majority of households did not notice the withholding changes in the relevant study, and households who found "a small but repeated boost to their paychecks" appear to be less likely to use the money for significant purchases.

There are many potential applications. With respect to smoking prevention, for example, increased salience is a central purpose of disclosure requirements. The Smoking Prevention Act reflects recognition of this point in calling for new and more graphic warnings; the chosen images are vivid and will be highly salient. Similarly, OSHA has proposed a regulation that would require chemical manufacturers and importers to prepare labels for hazardous chemicals that include pictograms and signal words that can be easily understood by workers (29 CFR §§ 1910, 1915, 1926). Well-designed labels make relevant factors salient to those who will see them. The significant consequences of easy accessibility and convenience (return to the issue of obesity) can be seen as a close cousin of salience effects.

A similar point applies in the domain of energy efficiency. For many consumers, the potential savings of energy-efficient products may not be salient at the time of purchase, even if those savings are significant. The "energy paradox" refers to the fact that some consumers do not purchase energy-efficient products even when it is clearly in their economic interest to do so. Empirical work suggests that nonprice interventions, by making the effects of energy use more salient, can alter decisions and significantly reduce electricity use. There is evidence that such interventions can lead to private as well as public savings (Howarth, Haddad, & Paton, 2000). Consider, for example, the fact that energy costs are generally salient only once a month, when people are presented with the bill. Efforts to increase the salience of such costs, by displaying them in real time, can produce significant savings, Recall as well the finding that if people are asked to sign at the beginning rather than the end, the incidence of dishonesty decreases; early signing makes honesty salient (Shu et al., 2012).

A related approach attempts to identify and consider the frame through which people interpret information. There is some evidence that some consumers may not seriously consider annuities in retirement to insure against longevity risk—the risk that they will outlive their assets—because they do not fully appreciate the potential advantages of annuities (Brown, 2007). One hypothesis is that some people evaluate annuities in an *investment frame* that focuses narrowly on risk and return (Brown et al., 2008). Looking through such a frame, consumers focus on the risk that they could die soon after annuity purchase and lose all of their money. Some evidence suggests that efforts to shift consumers into a *consumption frame*, which focuses on the end result of what they can consume over time, help consumers appreciate the potential benefits of annuities. The goal here is not to suggest a view on any particular approach to retirement; it is merely to emphasize that the relevant frame can increase salience.

IV. Social norms as nudges

Social scientists have emphasized the importance of social practices and norms, which have a significant influence on individual decisions. If people learn that they are using more energy than similarly situated others, then their energy use may decline—saving money while also reducing pollution. The same point applies to health-related behavior. It has long been understood that people are more likely to engage in healthy behavior if they live or work with others who so engage. And if people are in a social network with other people who are obese, they are significantly more likely to become obese themselves. The behavior of relevant others can provide valuable information about sensible or appropriate courses of action. As noted above, informational cascades are a possible consequence, as people rely on, and thus amplify, the informational signals produced by the actions of their predecessors. Similarly, those actions can provide information about what others will approve and disapprove.

Research suggests that efforts to use social comparisons can alter decisions and significantly reduce economic and environmental costs. For example, people can be informed of how much energy they use, how their use compares with that of their neighbors, and how much they spend compared with what their neighbors spend. In the private sector, these points are being put to creative use. Opower, an American company that makes impressive use of behavioral economics, specializes in providing people with social comparisons, above all through its innovative Home Energy Report. Opower's nudges have had a major effect. Over four million households now receive Home Energy Reports, and they are saving people hundreds of millions of dollars as a result. (See opower.com for details.) These and related interventions can save consumers a great deal of money and also reduce pollution.

These points have implications for regulatory policy. For example, smoking and seat belt regulations appear to have worked hand in hand with emerging social norms, helping to reduce deaths and injuries. In the context of seat belt usage, there has been a dramatic change in behavior, with an increase in a few decades from usage rates under 15 percent to usage rates over 70 percent, in significant part as a result of social norms that operated in concert with regulatory changes. In some domains, social norms have helped to promote compliance with law even without active enforcement. Public–private partnerships can be especially important in this domain, as those in the private sector emphasize norms that increase compliance with law and promote safer choices.

Consider as well the problem of distracted driving. On October 1, 2009, President Obama issued an executive order that bans federal employees from texting while driving. Such steps can help promote a social norm against texting while driving, thus reducing risks. This same approach—emphasizing social norms—might be applied in many domains. In the domain of childhood obesity, for example, a social norm in favor of healthy eating and proper exercise could produce significant health benefits. Here, as elsewhere, public–private partnerships can play a key role, with those in the private sector helping to spur emerging norms that promote better choices by and for children.

In particular, the "Let's Move" initiative has emphasized such partnerships. First Lady Michelle Obama has collaborated with Walmart to promote healthier choices (Mulligan, 2011). As part of that initiative, Walmart has committed to reformulating thousands, of everyday packaged food items by 2015 by reducing sodium by 25 percent and added sugars by 10 percent, and by removing all remaining industrial produced trans fats. It has also committed to reduce the costs of healthier options, thus making those costs comparable to the costs of less healthy choices, and at the same time to reduce the costs of fruits and vegetables. Finally, Walmart has agreed to develop a "healthy seal" to help consumers to identify healthy choices.

In a similar vein, a number of companies, including Kraft Foods, General Mills, Coca-Cola, Pepsi, and Kellogg, have pledged to remove 1.5 trillion calories from their products by 2015, in an effort to combat childhood obesity (*USA Today*, 2010). The relevant steps include reduction of product sizes and introduction of lower calorie foods. Finally, the Food Marketing Institute and the Grocery Manufacturers Association have agreed to promote informed choice through a "Nutrition Keys" label, designed in part to combat childhood obesity (Food Market Institute, 2011).

Well beyond incentives

In general, we can conclude that while material incentives (including price and anticipated health effects) greatly matter, outcomes are independently influenced by choice architecture, including (1) the social environment and (2) prevailing social norms. When some people, cities, and nations do well and others less so, it is often because the former, and not the latter, are able to benefit from aspects of the environment, and from prevailing norms, that enable them to take for granted, and perhaps not even to think much about, a set of practices that serve them well. And as we have seen, some behaviorally informed tools, such as automatic enrollment, can have very large effects—larger, in fact, than significant economic incentives (Chetty et al., 2012).

While disclosure of information is an important regulatory tool, steps must be taken to ensure that disclosure will be not merely technically accurate but also meaningful and helpful. Such steps require careful attention to how people process and use information. It is useful to distinguish between summary disclosure, typically provided at the point of purchase, and full disclosure, typically provided on the Internet. Summary disclosure should be clear, simple, and salient, and it should emphasize factors that matter to people (such as annual dollar value of fuel economy or energy-efficient choices).

Full disclosure should provide information that can be used in multiple ways, thus improving the operation of markets; often the most important uses come from the private sector. In all cases, disclosure is most useful if it informs people of what, precisely, they might do in order to avoid significant risks or obtain significant benefits.

Default rules can greatly affect social outcomes, and in some circumstances, sensible defaults can serve as a complement or alternative to mandates and bans. One of the advantages of well-chosen default rules is that they can simplify and ease choices—for example, by producing automatic enrollment in programs that are generally beneficial while also allowing people to opt out. A potential problem is that regulators may not know which default rule is best and one size may not fit all. When the relevant group is diverse and the domain is familiar, active choosing is likely to be preferable to default rules.

Because complexity can often have undesirable or unintended side effects—including high costs, noncompliance with law, and reduced participation in useful programs—simplification helps to promote regulatory goals. Indeed, simplification can often have surprisingly large effects. Reduced paperwork and form-filling burdens (as, for example, through fewer questions, use of skip patterns, electronic filing, and prepopulation) can produce significant benefits. It is also desirable to take steps to ease participation in both private and public programs by increasing convenience and by giving people clearer signals about what, exactly, they are required to do.

As behavioral research has shown, people are far more likely to respond when certain facts, risks, or possibilities are salient; effective warnings take account of this fact. Finally, regulation can work in concert with social norms, helping to promote agreed-upon public goals and to increase compliance with legal requirements. The result can be to save both money and lives. Public–private partnerships, enlisting the creativity of the private sector, are especially helpful in this regard, above all because they build on, and sometimes help promote, emerging social norms.

Bibliography

Affordable Care Act (2010). The Patient Protection and Affordable Care Act of 2010. Pub L No 111–148, 124 Stat 119, codified in various sections of Title 42.

Allcott, H. (2011). Consumers' perceptions and misperceptions of energy costs. American Economic Review, 101(3), 98–104.

Asamoah, A. K., and Sharfstein, J. M. (2010). Transparency at the Food and Drug Administration. New England Journal of Medicine, 362, 2341–3.

Beshears, J., Choi, J. Laibson, D., and Madrian, B. (2010). The limitations of defaults. Unpublished manuscript. Retrieved from: www.nber.org/programs/ag/rrc/NB10-02,%20Beshears,%20Choi,%20Laibson,%20Madrian.pdf.

Bronchetti, E. T., Dee, T. S., Huffman, D. B., and Magenheim, E. (2011). When a nudge isn't enough: Defaults and saving among low-income tax filers (Working Paper Series 16887). Retrieved from National Bureau of Economic Research website: www.nber.org/papers/w16887.

Brown, J. R. (2007). Rational and behavioral perspectives on the role of annuities in retirement planning (NBER Working Paper No. 13537). Retrieved from the National Bureau of Economic Research website: www.nber.org/papers/w13537.

Cabinet Office (n.d.). The behavioural insights team. Retrieved from www.cabinetoffice.gov.uk/behavioural-insights-team.

Carroll, G. et al. (2009). Optimal defaults and active decisions. Quarterly Journal of Economics, 124(4), 1639–74.

Centers for Medicare and Medicaid Services (2010, February 4). Re: Express lane eligibility option. Retrieved from http://peerta.acf.hhs.gov/uploadedFiles/Express%20Lane%20Eligibility%20SHO%20final%202-4-10%20508%20ready.pdf.

Chetty, R., Looney, A., and Kroft, K. (2009). Salience and taxation: Theory and evidence. American Economic Review, 99(4), 1145–77.

Chetty, R., Friedman, J., Leth-Petersen, S., Nielsen, T., and Olsen, T. (2012). Active vs. Passive Decisions and Crowdout in Retirement Savings Accounts: Evidence from Denmark (NBER Working Paper No. 18565). Retrieved from the National Bureau of Economic Research website: www.nber.org/papers/w18565.

Chiteji, N., and Walker, L. (2009). Strategies to increase the retirement savings of African American households. In W. G. Gale et al. (Eds.), Automatic: Changing the Way America Saves. Washington, DC: Brookings Institution, 231–60.

CLASS Act (2010). Pub L No 111–148, title 8, 124 Stat 828, codified at 42 USC § 300.

Credit CARD Act (2009). Pub L No 111–24, 123 Stat 1734, codified in various sections of Titles 15 and 16.

Currie, J. et al. (2010). The effect of fast food restaurants on obesity and weight gain. American Economic Journal: Economic Policy, 2(3), 32–63.

Data.gov (n.d.). Home: data.gov. Retrieved from www/data.gov.
Dayan, E., and Bar-Hillel, M. (2011). Nudge to nobesity II: Menu positions influence food orders. Judgment and Decision Making, 6(4), 333–42.
Department of Agriculture (2011). Direct certification and certification of homeless, migrant and runaway children for free school meals. 76 Federal Register 22785-02, 22793.
Department of Agriculture (2015). Direct Certification in the National School Lunch Program Report to Congress: State Implementation Progress, School Year 2013–2014. Available at www.fns.usda.gov/direct-certification-national-school-lunch-program-report-congress-state-implementation-progress.
Department of Education (2010a). Program Integrity Issues, 75 Federal Register 66832, codified in various sections of Title 34 of the CFR.
Department of Education (2010b). Department of Education establishes new student aid rules to protect borrowers and taxpayers. Retrieved from www.ed.gov/news/press-releases/department-education-establishes-new-student-aid-rules-protect-borrowers-and-tax.
Department of Energy (n.d.). Residential energy consumption survey (RECS) files. Retrieved from www.data.gov/raw/10.
Department of Health and Human Services (2010a, May 1). Centers for Disease Control and Prevention, Community health status indicators (CHSI) to combat obesity, heart disease and cancer. Retrieved from www.data.gov/raw/2159.
Department of Health and Human Services (2010b, June 25). HHS open government plan version 1.1 12. Retrieved from www.hhs.gov/open/plan/opengovernmentplan/openplanversion1_1.pdf.
Department of Housing and Urban Development (n.d.). Public housing physical inspection scores. Retrieved from www.data.gov/raw/1258.
Department of Justice (2012). Open government at DOJ. Retrieved from www.justice.gov/open/data.html.
Department of Labor (n.d.). Enforcement data. Retrieved from http://ogesdw.dol.gov/search.php.
Department of Labor (2010, April 7). Open government plan version 1.0 3. Retrieved from www.dol.gov/open/OGDplan.pdf.
Department of Labor (2011). Workplace Injury, Illness and Fatality Statistics, Retrieved from www.osha.gov/oshstats/work.html.
Department of Transportation (2010, June 25). Open government plan version 1.2 10. Retrieved from www.dot.gov/open/pdf/DOT_Open_Gov_Plan_V1.2_06252010.pdf.
Department of the Treasury (2009a). Financial regulatory reform: A new foundation. Retrieved from www.treasury.gov/initiatives/wsr/Documents/FinalReport_web.pdf.
Department of the Treasury (2009b, December 4). FinancialStability.gov TARP transactions data: Asset guarantee program (Dec 4, 2009). Retrieved from www.data.gov/raw/1260.
Dinner, I. et al. (2009). Partitioning default effects: Why people choose not to choose (unpublished manuscript). Retrieved from http://ssrn.com/abstract=1352488.
Dodd–Frank Act (2010). § 1021, 12 USC § 5511 (2010).
Emergency Planning and Community Right to Know Act (1986). Pub L No 99–499, 100 Stat 1728, codified at 42 USC § 11001 et seq.
Environmental Protection Agency (2009a). Fuel Economy Labeling of Motor Vehicles: Revisions to Improve Calculation of Fuel Economy Estimates. 74 Federal Register 61537-01, 61542, 61550–53 (amending 40 CFR Parts 86, 600).
Environmental Protection Agency (2009b). Mandatory Reporting of Greenhouse Gases. 74 Federal Register 56269-01, codified in various sections of Title 40 of the CFR.
Environmental Protection Agency (2010, June 25). Open government plan 1.1 1 Retrieved from www.epa.gov/open/EPAOpenGovernmentPlan_11.pdf.
Environmental Protection Agency (n.d.). Enforcement & compliance history online (ECHO). Retrieved from www.epa-echo.gov.
European Commission (2012). Science for environment policy, Future brief: Green behavior. Retrieved from http://ec.europa.eu/environment/integration/research/newsalert/pdf/FB4.pdf.
Federal Trade Commission (2009, January). Negative options: A report by the staff of the FTC's division of enforcement. Retrieved from www.ftc.gov/os/2009/02/P064202negativeoptionreport.pdf.
Finkelstein, A. (2009). E-ZTAX: Tax salience and tax rates. Quarterly Journal of Economics, 124(3), 969–1010.
Food Market Institute (2011). Press release: Food & beverage industry launches nutrition keys front-of-pack nutrition labeling initiative to inform consumers and combat obesity: Nutrition icon to be supported by $50 million industry-funded consumer education campaign. Retrieved from www.fmi.org/news_releases/index.cfm?fuseaction=mediatext&id=1207.

Gale, W., Iwry, J., and Walters, S. (2009). Retirement savings for middle- and lower-income households: The Pension Protection Act of 2006 and the unfinished agenda. In W. G. Gale, et al. (Eds.), Automatic (11–27), Harrisburg, VA: R. R. Donnelley.

Greenstone, M. (2009). Toward a culture of persistent regulatory experimentation and evaluation. In D. Moss and J. Cisternino (Eds.) New perspectives on regulation. Cambridge, MA: The Tobin Project, 111–25.

Gruber, J., and Abaluck, J. T. (2011). Choice inconsistencies among the elderly: Evidence from plan choice in the Medicare Part D Program. American Ecnonomic Review, 101(4), 1180–210.

Halpern, D. (2015). Inside the Nudge Unit. London: W.H. Allen.

Hamilton, J. T. (2005). Regulation through revelation: The origin, politics, and impacts of the toxics release inventory program. Cambridge, UK: Cambridge University Press.

Healthcare.gov (2011). Providing Clear and Consistent Information to Consumers about Their Health Insurance Coverage. Retrieved from www.healthcare.gov/news/factsheets/labels08172011a.html and www.healthcare.gov/news/factsheets/labels08172011b.pdf.

Healthy, Hunger-Free Kids Act (2012). Pub L No 111–296, 124 Stat 3183.

Heath, C., and Heath, D. (2010). Switch: How to change things when change is hard. New York: Broadway.

Howarth, R. B., Haddad, B. M., and Paton, B. (2000) The economics of energy efficiency: Insights from voluntary participation programs. Energy Policy, 28(6–7), 477–86.

Internal Revenue Service (2009, September). Retirement & savings initiatives: Helping Americans save for the future. Retrieved from www.irs.gov/pub/irs-tege/rne_se0909.pdf.

iNudgeYou.com (n.d.) Resources. Retrieved from www.inudgeyou.com/resources.

Iyengar, S., and Kamenica, E. (2010). Choice proliferation, simplicity seeking, and asset allocation. Journal of Public Economics, 94(7–8), 530–9.

Johnson, E. J., Hershey, J., Meszaros, J., and Kunreuther, H. (1993). Framing, probability distortions, and insurance decisions. Journal of Risk and Uncertainty, 7, 35–51.

Madrian, B. C., and Shea, D. F. (2001). The power of suggestion: Inertia in 401(k) participation and savings behavior. Quarterly Journal of Economics, 116(4) 1149–87.

Mulligan, J. (2011, January 26). First Lady Michelle Obama announces collaboration with Walmart in support of Let's Move Campaign. Retrieved from www.letsmove.gov/blog/2011/01/25/first-lady-michelle-obama-announces-collaboration-walmart-support-lets-move-campaign.

Obama, B. (2009, September 5). Weekly Address.

Office of Information and Regulatory Affairs (2009). Information collection budget of the United States government. Retrieved from www.whitehouse.gov/sites/default/files/omb/assets/inforeg/icb_2009.pdf.

Office of Management and Budget, Office of Information and Regulatory Affairs (2010). Information collection budget of the United States government. Retrieved from: www.whitehouse.gov/sites/default/files/omb/inforeg/icb/icb_2010.pdf.

Organisation for Economic Cooperation and Development (2010). Consumer policy toolkit. Retrieved from www.oecd.org/sti/consumerpolicy/consumerpolicytoolkit.htm.

Orszag, P. R. (2009, December 8). OMB Memorandum for the Heads of Executive Departments and Agencies, Open Government Directive 2, 7 (OMB Memorandum M-10-06, Dec 8, 2009). Retrieved from www.whitehouse.gov/omb/assets/memoranda_2010/m10-06.pdf.

Orszag, P. (2010, March 29). OMB, Director, SAVEings. Retrieved from www.whitehouse.gov/omb/blog/10/03/29/SAVEings/.

Orszag, P. R., and Rodriguez, E. (2009). Retirement security for Latinos: Bolstering coverage, savings, and adequacy. In W. G. Gale, et al. (Eds.), Automatic: Changing the Way America Saves. Washington, DC: Brookings Institution, 173–98.

Papke, L. E., Walker, L., and Dworsky, M. (2009). Retirement savings for women: Progress to date and policies for tomorrow. In W. G. Gale, et al. (Eds.) Automatic: Changing the Way America Saves. Washington, DC: Brookings Institution, 199–30.

Pension Protection Act (2006). Pub L No 109–280, 120 Stat 780, codified in various sections of Titles 26 and 29.

Presidential Memorandum (2011, January 18). Regulatory compliance. Retrieved from www.whitehouse.gov/the-press-office/2011/01/18/presidential-memoranda-regulatory-compliance.

Riis, J., and Ratner, R. (2011). Simplified nutrition guidelines to fight obesity. In Leveraging consumer psychology for effective health communications: The obesity challenge. R. Batra, P. A. Keller, and V. J. Strecher (Eds.). Armonk, NY: M.E. Sharpe.

Rozin, P. et al., (2011). Nudge to nobesity I: Minor changes in accessibility decrease food intake. Judgment and Decision Making, 6(4), 323–32.

Sahm, C. R., Shapiro, M. D., and Slemrod, J. (2011). Check in the mail or more in the paycheck: Does the effectiveness of fiscal stimulus depend on how it is delivered? (Finance and Economics Discussion Series 2010–40). Retrieved from Federal Reserve Website: www.federalreserve.gov/pubs/feds/2010/201040/201040pap.pdf.

Schwartz, J. et al. (2011). Would you like to downsize that meal? Activating self-control is more effective than calorie labeling in reducing calorie consumption in fast food meals (unpublished manuscript).

Securities and Exchange Commission (2009). Interactive Data to Improve Financial Reporting, 74 Federal Register 6776.

Sethi-Iyengar, S. Huberman, G., and Jiang, W. (2004). How much choice is too much? Contributions to 401(k) retirement plans. In O. S. Mitchell and S. P. Utkus (Eds.) Pension design and structure: New lessons from behavioral finance. Oxford, UK: Oxford University Press.

Sharot, T. (2011). The optimism bias: A tour of the irrationally positive brain. New York, NY: Knopf Publishing.

Shu, L., Mazar, N., Gino, F., Ariely, D., and Bazerman, M. (2012). Signing at the beginning makes ethics salient and decreases dishonest self-reports in comparison to signing at the end. PNAS 109: 15197–200.

Sunstein, C. R. (2010a). Administrator, OIRA, Memorandum for the Heads of Executive Departments and Agencies, Disclosure and Simplification as Regulatory Tools. Retrieved from: www.whitehouse.gov/sites/default/files/omb/assets/inforeg/disclosure_principles.pdf.

Sunstein, C. R. (2010b, April). Data call for the 2010 information collection budget. Retrieved from www.whitehouse.gov/omb/assets/inforeg/2010_icb_datacall.pdf.

Sunstein, C. R. (2011, February). Memorandum for chief information officers: Minimizing paperwork and reporting burdens. Retrieved from www.whitehouse.gov/sites/default/files/omb/inforeg/icb/2011_ICB_Data_Call.pdf.

Sunstein, C. R. (2013). Simpler. New York, NY: Simon & Schuster.

Sunstein, C. R. 2015. Choosing not to choose. Oxford: Oxford University Press.

USA Today (2010, May 21). Food giants pledge to cut 1.5 trillion calories out of products. Retrieved from www.usatoday.com/money/industries/food/2010-05-17-cutting-calories_N.htm.

Wansink, B. (2010). Mindless eating, New York: Bantam Dell.

Wansink, B., Just, D., and McKendry, J. (2010). Lunch line redesign, NY Times at A35.

White House Social and Behavioral Sciences Team. 2015. Annual Report. Available at www.whitehouse.gov/sites/default/files/microsites/ostp/sbst_2015_annual_report_final_9_14_15.pdf.

White House Task Force on Childhood Obesity (2010, May). Report to the President: Solving the problem of childhood obesity within a generation 49–55. Retrieved from www.letsmove.gov/pdf/TaskForce_on_Childhood_Obesity_May2010_FullReport.pdf.

Wisdom, J., Downs, J., and Loewenstein, G. (2010). Promoting healthy choices: Information versus convenience. American Economic Journal: Applied Economics, 2, 164–78.

XBRL (n.d.). About XBRL International. Retrieved from www.xbrl.org/AboutXBRL.

9 CFR § 317.309.

16 CFR § 425.

29 CFR §§ 1910, 1915, 1926.

29 CFR § 1926.

29 CFR § 2550.404a-5 (2011).

34 CFR § 668.6 (2010).

17
IGNORANCE
Literary light on decision's dark corner

Devjani Roy and Richard Zeckhauser

Introduction

Rational decision theory requires that the decision maker attach von Neumann–Morgenstern utilities to possible outcomes. Each outcome represents the combination of the state of the world and a decision taken. In a broad range of decision problems, however, the decision maker is unable to identify important outcomes, hence potential significant outcomes remain unknown. Ignorance represents a situation in which some potential outcomes cannot be identified. Ignorance has received surprisingly scant attention in the behavioral economics literature.[1] This chapter examines the concept of ignorance and identifies the behavioral propensities that arise when it is present—some well known and others specific to decision situations that involve ignorance. It also introduces a new methodological approach to behavioral decision, drawing on the choices of characters in great literature as qualitative evidence of human behavior. Portions of this chapter draw on our recent studies (Roy and Zeckhauser, 2015).

The impulse to forecast the future is etched indelibly in our DNA. Hunches, prophecies, divining the future through patterns found in nature or in our palms or our food, and speculations about divine intention inferred through oracular utterances—intelligent and rational human beings have attempted it all to make sense of a universe that continually challenges our predictive capabilities. Early-nineteenth-century French mathematician Pierre-Simon Laplace posited what is known today as "Laplacian determinism": if blessed with omniscience, or a complete knowledge of the universe and the laws of nature, the human intellect would be able to predict accurately every detail of the future.[2] But, as Laplace concluded, since omniscient intelligence is nowhere to be found, our best hope is probabilistic prediction. But Laplace was an optimist; probabilistic prediction trips us up as well.

Frank Knight (1921) first drew the critical distinction between risk—wherein potential outcomes and their probabilities are both known—and uncertainty, or conditions in which potential outcomes are known, but not their probabilities.[3] Knight also categorized probability situations by degree of predictability, into "*a priori* probability," "statistical probability," and "estimates," adding that forecasting "estimates" is the most challenging of all since "there is *no valid basis of any kind* for classifying instances" for this unique form of probability. In the past century since Knight, decision scientists have focused broadly on engaging uncertainty so that it can be treated like risk. A principal tool has been refining unknown probabilities. Thus, we have become skilled at predicting the likelihood of precipitation tomorrow, and assessing the probability of whether or not someone with particular characteristics will complete college. Fancy models and large data sets support such efforts. For many problems, however, there are no data sets to distill. Decision scientists then turn to methods that calibrate subjective probabilities,[4] which are then treated no differently from objective probabilities. With these methods, they need not shrink from assessing the likelihood that China and Japan will be involved in a shooting war in the next decade, or that an interview will lead to a job offer.

However, with ignorance, the embrace of subjective probability methods is not sufficient for rational decision, because the decision maker cannot know all of the possibilities to which probabilities should be attached. Ignorance commonly arises with unique events, such as the rise of ISIS or the long-term consequences of climate change. These events encounter deep uncertainties, and deep uncertainties both defy traditional predictive methods and challenge the usual procedures for assessing subjective probabilities.

On the continuum that proceeds from risk to uncertainty, ignorance lies beyond both. Ignorance, as we show below, is the starting point of a fertile, untapped area for decision research. Given that ignorance adds the additional complexity of unidentified outcomes, it encounters all the behavioral biases of uncertainty (some magnified), plus additional biases of its own. The rational decision paradigm (see Savage, 1954 and Raiffa, 1968) employs the expected utility (EU) framework. This normative framework attaches a probability, often subjective, and a utility to each potential outcome. Finally, it prescribes that the decision maker assess the decision tree and choose the preferred branch. Alas, ignorance defeats the straightforward application of such methods: metaphorically, some branches of the tree remain shrouded in darkness. Compounding these difficulties, the presence of ignorance often goes unrecognized: what is unseen is not considered.

The EU model, if embraced, must be extended to allow for ignorance in every life area, from international diplomacy to intimate relationships. Decision making under ignorance suffers crucial errors, affecting governments, financial institutions, and individuals alike. Here we identify a path forward, highlighting broad prescriptions that incorporate the approach of rational decision theory while recognizing the challenges that ignorance introduces.

Ignorance falls into two broad categories: *primary* and *recognized*. *Primary ignorance* characterizes situations where the decision maker does not see its presence. *Recognized ignorance* applies when the decision maker knows that important potential outcomes exist that remain hidden in darkness.

The concept of the *consequential amazing development* (CAD) is at the heart of ignorance. Where ignorance is present, a CAD may follow. While a CAD may be good or bad, it will always be memorable. To be consequential, a CAD must be better or worse than the extreme events in a typical month. To be amazing, it must lie beyond the decision maker's horizon of contemplation. Not every event of significance is a CAD. It is not an objective concept but a subjective one, defined from the standpoint of the individual affected. A mere outlier would not qualify, nor would a Black Swan event, such as a plummeting financial market or windfall spectacular job promotion, because such outcomes can be easily foreseen as a possibility.

We classify CADs according to the difficulty involved in conjecturing them: CADs are *deep*, *conventional*, or *blindered*.[5] *Deep* CADs describe events that could not possibly have been contemplated and often emerge "out of the blue." *Conventional* CADs are those that are difficult to envision, but through some cognitive effort we might have envisioned them.[6] *Blindered* CADs are outcomes that might easily be visualized but are not, often due to the role of visceral factors such as drive states, feeling states, and negative emotions (Loewenstein, 2000). Such forces act in the manner of blinders on a horse, thus restricting the field of view, in this case blocking the recognition of possible outcomes. In short, cognitive efforts can potentially transform conventional and blindered CADs into contemplated outcomes, but such efforts would be futile where deep CADs are concerned.

We also classify CADs according to impact. This chapter is predominantly addressed to CADs that strike one or a few individuals; we label them *narrow* CADs. Think of being cheated by one's long-term trusted business partner. *Broad* CADs impact large swaths of society. The implosion of the Soviet Union, the 2007–8 financial meltdown, and the rise of ISIS are prime examples of broad CADs. Professionals were paid to predict these broad CADs. That they failed suggests that cognitive effort alone would not have led to their anticipation. Broad CADs inevitably trickle down into multitudes of narrow CADs, beginning life as society-wide developments that end up changing the life circumstances of thousands, sometimes millions. Deng Xiaoping's 1979 opening of China to market reforms provides a salient example, ultimately affecting the lives of multitudes not merely in China but also throughout the world.

What makes ignorance a challenge for decision scientists? First, they present the problem of chronicling and classification: namely, situations of ignorance rarely get recorded in the same manner as, say, sports performances or corporate profits. Since CADs are unique occurrences, they defy easy classification, and classification is often the *sine qua non* of serious investigation and study. Second, though potential CADs are many, those that actually occur are few. Third, most potential CADs reside below the stage of contemplation. Absent data sets, statistical methods—the forecaster's prime weapon—are rendered impotent. Fourth, behavioral biases complement these statistical challenges. For example, when contemplating the future, people tend to be limited by the parameters of what they have already seen or experienced. CADs do not repeat; at their second appearance they become predictable phenomena. The third section delves into heuristics and biases that afflict ignorance.

Ignorance will always be with us, and it will particularly afflict highly consequential choices. Thus, just as decision theory developed the concept of subjective probability to cope with decisions under uncertainty, it should provide methods to grapple with ignorance. Thus this chapter does not merely describe; it sets forth four prescriptive recommendations as a first step.

1 *Build intellectual capital.* Understand that ignorance is both widespread and important. Beware of the behavioral biases that humans suffer when they fail to recognize ignorance, and when they respond to it. Build intellectual capital on ways to recognize and respond to ignorance, as best as possible.
2 *Scan for potential CADs.* Scan choice situations inexpensively for the potential for CADs. Cognitive computation and information gathering cost time and effort (Payne, Bettman, and Johnson, 1993), but the scanning we recommend is neither a detailed investigation nor a foolproof method; rather, it is intended to sound a warning when one should seriously attend to ignorance. The scan should be particularly on the lookout for conventional or blindered CADs, since they are possible to anticipate. Given a negative scan, employ traditional decision procedures.
3 *Devote attention to a decision after a positive scan.* A CAD threatens when the product of estimated likelihood for CADs times their expected magnitude is substantial. Particularly for deep CADs, one may not know its nature but be aware of its potential.
4 *Adjust choices given ignorance.* If ignorance is substantial, undertake actions that may prevent adverse CADs or improve the outcome if a CAD does strike.

Ignorance, behavioral decision, and literature

Uncertainty is the favored child of behavioral decision. It gets disproportionate attention relative to certainty and risk. Ignorance, in contrast, suffers neglect. One explanation for this is that ignorance is difficult to study. While studying future conditions and future preferences under uncertainty is difficult enough, predicting preferences under conditions never before encountered, indeed not even foreseen as a possibility, is a daunting challenge. The tried-and-tested ways of examining human behavior empirically do not work in the study of ignorance:

1 The behavioral scientist's familiar tools—namely, the randomized controlled studies in the field or online, the laboratory experiments with small economic payouts, the large data sets subjected to statistical analyses—are poorly suited to or simply unavailable for the study of ignorance. Poetically expressed, ignorance has been behavioral decision's will-o'-the-wisp—a shapeless ephemeron.
2 For both theoretical and practical reasons, primary ignorance defies study in laboratory settings. Merely raising the possibility of ignorance would give away the game.
3 CADs tend to be unique, *sui generis*, one-time-only incidents. As such, they are difficult to categorize, much less predict. And events not even conjectured, a prime characteristic of CADs, are still more unfathomable.
4 CADs are low in frequency, and most potential CADs never occur. Even if we take protective actions to avoid potential CADs, we have no way to learn or study whether or not these actions have had any effect. In contrast, empiricists overwhelmingly investigate phenomena that occur regularly. Even if single individuals encounter events rarely, if the events are roughly the same across individuals—think heart attacks—they can be readily tallied and studied.

Given these difficulties, perhaps the most promising way to study ignorance is to draw lessons from multiple realms, such as personal medical thunderbolts, stock market crashes, and spontaneous events of human contagion, such as the Arab Spring. Here we concentrate on insights from literature, with strong justification: authors chronicle the way individuals confront ignorance and CADs that occur in their lives. Literature offers adaptive value in two ways: it models social life and it also molds our cognitive models of social life (Oatley and Mar, 2005). Literary fiction offers what evolutionary psychologists call "universals": behavioral and cognitive traits that remain true across cultures (Brown, 1991; Dunbar, 1996, 2004). We draw on insights from the choices of literary characters in some of the world's best-known stories.[7] This qualitative "database" provides us with a descriptive model of behavior when facing ignorance. Such a model is the first step toward our ultimate goal—to produce prescriptive recommendations for making decisions facing possible ignorance.

Literature brings six great virtues to the study of human behavior in general and of ignorance in particular:

1 *Scope.* Literature sketches decision making under ignorance on a large canvas. CADs frequently provide the fuel and the fodder for fictional narratives. Authors, unlike social scientists, have little interest in predictive models but are greatly interested in how literary characters face unprecedented situations.
2 *Induction.* Authors depict how literary characters make choices within everyday decision-making contexts such as love, marriage, education, and saving for the future, to name only a few. Through a process of induction, the nimble-minded decision scientist can extrapolate from these stories to build general descriptive models of behavior. Literature also depicts broad CADs such as revolutions and natural disasters, and the unanticipated consequences in wars and financial upheavals, including the behavior of humans confronting broad CADs. Here the induction task is more challenging, since the circumstances tend to be disparate, but literature still provides a great deal of qualitative data.

3 *Cultural learning*. Discussing how to prepare for uncertainty, Weber and Johnson (2008) observe: "Individuals who live in cooperative groups with the ability to communicate information in symbolic form can use the experience of others not just by direct observation, but also receive it in condensed form."[8] We add that stories *are* the "condensed form" of the "experience[s] of others," honed finely against the whetstone of time. Authors from Aeschylus to Angelou have transmitted didactic content about both human ability and fallibility (the latter is what the decision scientist would call a "bias") within the descriptive boundaries of the fictional narrative.

4 *Anticipation*. "What happens next?" This single question prompts us to read, and keep reading, a work of literature. This impulse—to predict the future while knowing that a great margin of error underlies our speculations—is one of the joys of fiction. It can also provide subject matter for study by behavioral economists, many of whom investigate the psychological motivations behind anticipation and expectation through such concepts as intertemporal choice and risk-taking behavior. The mere title of perhaps the most famous paper in behavioral decision, "Prospect Theory," is revealing of the central role of anticipation in that field.

5 *Contemplation*. Recent decision research emphasizes the importance of noticing, and the dangers of not noticing, information that is easily available but often ignored (Bazerman, 2014). Literary fiction teaches us the importance of contemplation and of exercising the imagination through timely noticing, both qualities critical to envisioning the nature of CADs or merely their potential.

6 *Insights into behavioral decision making*. Decision theory came late to behavioral decision making, given the implicit assumption, which leaked from economics, that descriptive behavior would be driven to the standards of its prescriptive model. Literature never suffered from this handicap, starting instead by being built on observations of human behavior.

Fiction depicts human beings across a range of social, cognitive, and behavioral environments. Thus, reading fiction brings an awareness of how humans actually make decisions in a range of situations, usually banal, frequently consequential, and occasionally astonishing. Fiction also documents severe violations of EU maximization in choices made under risk, uncertainty, and ignorance. Although behavioral decision has now come into its own, it has shown its ignorance of ignorance.

The rich history of literature as a mimetic, or imitative, model, both ideal and cautionary, for human behavior begins with Plato's recommendation to banish poets from the republic, because their stories represent attractive and often undesirable behavior for the future philosopher-ruler. Aristotle builds on this concept to promulgate his more positive theory of mimesis in *The Poetics*, according to which a poet (or writer) should imitate (i.e., portray) things not simply as they are but also as they should be. That concept has had a long-reaching influence on Western literature and theater. Roman poet Horace posits literature as learning for life by providing exemplars of behavioral strategies to writers. Storey (1996) and Scalise Sugiyama (2001) hypothesize that literature transmits accurate psychological information and functions as a storage device for a range of behaviors.

Ignorance serves as the foundation for deception, as Shakespeare shows in many of his plays. From mistaken identities (*A Comedy of Errors*) to psychological ignorance, or obliviousness to the true motives of others (*Much Ado about Nothing*), from gender-based disguise (a woman impersonating a man in *As You Like It*) to masquerading as someone else (King Henry disguising himself as a common soldier and circulating among his troops in *Henry V*)—in each of these instances, the deceived suffer from primary ignorance and fail to imagine the possibility of what is real.

Stories are universal in their descriptive illustration of behavior in a world of ignorance. For instance, over two millennia, the Bible has shown human beings the importance of ignorance, something decision theorists have overlooked. Usually its message takes the form of parables and stories with deeper, metaphorical meaning. Abraham is commanded by God to sacrifice his son Isaac. Abraham proceeds, but at the last moment, Isaac is saved—it was all a test of faith. Ignorance was critical. Abraham's faith would hardly have been tested had he suspected the outcomes that occurred. When the Israelites sought to flee Egypt but the Pharaoh refused, God sent plagues to afflict Egyptians. The Pharaoh, convinced of the power of his own gods, could not imagine any of these catastrophes as sent by a rival deity. The tenth plague, death of the first-born son in each Egyptian family, finally changed the Pharaoh's mind.

Literature, particularly wisdom literature, has long been sought out as a source of insight in a world of unexplained events.[9] It is fitting that economist Thomas Schelling (1984), a lifelong practitioner of the literary form of the essay, despite practicing the dismal science, describes fiction thus: "Novels, plays ... and stories give the reader ... a stake in the outcome. ... The characteristic that interests me is the engrossment[,] the participation, the sense of being in the story or part of it, caring, and wanting to know."[10]

Writers represent the human experience through a range of emotional and cognitive processes. They provide an unconventional, and entirely unexplored, education in behavioral decision making. The central problem with ignorance—the complete lack of information that could serve as the basis for establishing a prior probability distribution on potential outcomes—may be illuminated through greater exposure to literary fiction.

Heuristics and biases associated with ignorance

Human beings have always relied on simple cognitive mechanisms, termed "heuristics," to make decisions within the natural restraints of information-gathering and processing power (Simon, 1957). The word "heuristic," in the decision-making sense of "relating to, or enabling discovery or problem-solving [...] through relatively unstructured methods such as experimentation, evaluation, trial and error" first appeared in eighteenth-century German philosopher Immanuel Kant's *Essays and Treatises on Moral, Political, and Various Philosophical Subjects* (1798).[11] Heuristics conserve cognitive effort. However, while some are valuable, others can lead us astray.[12] Heuristics that put us off-track are labeled "biases." The word "bias" first appears in the English language in 1530 and it originally meant "an oblique or slanting line," a sense that we retain today when using "bias" as automatic thinking in favor of something or someone, independent of the evidence.[13]

In the mid-twentieth century, Herbert Simon (1955) introduced the concept of *satisficing*, or adaptive thinking to find a satisfactory decision instead of the optimal one. Psychologists Amos Tversky and Daniel Kahneman's initial research on heuristics and biases (1973, 1974) addressing *availability*, *anchoring and adjustment*, and *representativeness* was supplemented over the next thirty years by a generation of behavioral scientists identifying dozens of additional proclivities in this realm. These range from Fischhoff and Beyth's *hindsight bias* (1975), Samuelson and Zeckhauser's *status quo bias* (1988), Johnson and Goldstein's *default heuristic* (2003), to the sports-related *gaze heuristic* (Gigerenzer, 2004).

A general pattern observed with behavioral decision is that as we move from certainty to risk to uncertainty, heuristics and biases play an ever-greater role. Indeed, many biases—such as the non-linear weighting of probabilities or the law of small numbers—could not even exist under either certainty or risk. Ignorance adds a dimension of the unknown beyond uncertainty. Thus, decision makers confronting it also suffer more from biases and heuristics than when faced merely with uncertainty. We address three that arise under primary ignorance:

1 *Overconfidence*. Individuals are frequently overconfident in their assessment of the future. In the simple case of predicting a numerical magnitude, their assessed distributions are too

tight (Alpert and Raiffa, 1982). CADs, which hardly fall on a defined quantitative spectrum, are much harder to assess. They are often ignored; when not, they are likely underestimated.

2 *Availability*. In predicting the future, individuals tend to focus on prior events already experienced and cognitively available (Tversky and Kahneman, 1973; Epley and Gilovich, 2006). When CADs occur, the availability heuristic tends to impede successful decision making. For example, since 9/11, it is not surprising that the United States has invested vast amounts in airplane safety and relatively very little on protecting our ports.

3 *Selective attention*. Individuals recall and retell some events more prominently than others, notably surprising events with non-trivial consequences. Idiosyncratic circumstances thus find their way more easily into cultural narratives such as stories, films, and historical anecdotes, or, for that matter, accounts from personal experiences. CADs presumably get over-represented in these sources, a possible counterbalance to our natural tendency to miss situations of ignorance. When CADs occur, selective attention complements the availability heuristic: it makes us overestimate the likelihood of these events reoccurring merely because they are available to us.

When ignorance does get recognized, additional biases impede measured decision making. We identify four:

1. Action bias

Action bias (AB) is the excess inducement to take action when gains seem likely and individuals seek recognition or acclaim for their choices (Patt and Zeckhauser, 2000). There is thus a close connection between ignorance, the anticipation of favorable CADs, and AB.[14] Given ignorance, we often will not know what would have happened on the road not taken. If so, it will never be known whether sticking with what was would have proved superior to taking action. Blame comes from bad outcomes, or even from good outcomes if another choice would have been demonstrably superior. Given ignorance, when outcomes including surprises are likely to be good, action bias can claim credit yet avoid blame.

Throughout recorded history, the value of action has been upheld and endorsed. No doubt selective recall contributes, since history is written mostly by the victors—a process that publicizes conquerors and suppresses the tales of agents who took actions and lost. Such endorsements make AB both hard to critique and hard to overcome. In philosophical literature, for instance, the widespread recommendation is that taking action is good; it is the path towards self-improvement and justification of human existence.[15]

2. Status quo bias

Status quo bias (SQB) refers to the tendency to stick to a pre-existing choice, particularly when moving away from this choice, whose outcome serves as a reference point, might incur losses (Samuelson and Zeckhauser, 1988). Loss aversion is a prime promoter of SQB, but other forces also contribute. These include the desire to avoid the cost (in time and money) of studying of new options, and the fear of going against the consensus if a popular status quo already exists.

We hypothesize that ignorance reinforces SQB. Behavioral decisions research supports this conjecture. Weber et al. (2005) demonstrate that familiarity with asset name ("recognition bias") and or location ("home bias") makes assets more appealing, since they are judged to be less risky than unfamiliar assets. Cognitively speaking, the individual adheres to the familiar ("better the devil you know than the one you don't") when ignorant of what the future holds.[16]

We should observe, as the reader has no doubt noted, that AB and SQB pull in opposite directions. There is no tension, however, because AB tugs when the weather conjecture is sun, that is, favorable CADs seem likely, and SQB when it is rain. Most surprises are unpleasant, as Warren Buffett once observed, and CADs surely are surprises. Thus, SQB will prevail in most situations where ignorance abounds.

With its high degree of reliance on unknown-unknowns, detective fiction provides some of the best examples of ignorance as a promoter of SQB. Edgar Allan Poe's "Murders in the Rue Morgue" is hailed as the world's first detective story. An old woman Madame L'Espanaye and her daughter Camille are violently murdered in a Parisian apartment, respectively by decapitation and strangling, inside a room locked from the inside. Who is the murderer and how has s(he) managed to escape? The tale reveals how SQB afflicts thought processes, and not merely choices. Various printed reports in the Parisian newspapers follow established and seemingly logical lines of thinking; they thus demonstrate status quo framing.

The brilliant detective C. Auguste Dupin exposes the flaws in this ratiocination and reveals the real murderer: an orangutan on the loose. The escaped primate, owned by a sailor who acquired the animal overseas, mimicked his owner's daily ritual of shaving (learned by observing his master) by similarly "shaving" Madame L'Espanaye. Strangling the daughter Camille, he stuffs her body up a chimney in an attempt to hide his crime and escapes through the window. The combination of an understanding of simian psychology and the willingness to bounce to new alternatives when ignorance abounds despite the cognitive costs involved—both require moving one's mindset beyond the familiar—is required to solve the crime. In most detective fiction, the local police force makes an initial decision and hysteresis sets in. The initial decision constrains their choices at each subsequent juncture. Often this status quo force is reinforced by concerns about sunk costs, anxiety about errors of commission (not wanting to lose face with their superiors), regret avoidance, and a drive for consistency and safety in the face of uncertainty. Mere mortals have a hard time thinking in new directions, though detective stories shine a spotlight on ignorance and regularly demonstrate that fresh thinking is needed. Only brilliant detectives—Auguste Dupin, Sherlock Holmes, Hercules Poirot—are able to step psychologically to "out-of-the-box" hypotheses.

3. *Indecision bias*

Indecision bias (IB) arises when individuals who recognize that they are ignorant get frozen with indecision; inaction sets in. IB is far from SQB. It is not a choice to stick with what they have. Rather, they consciously steer clear of making a decision, perhaps standing by waiting for an ill defined something to happen. Even shreds of knowledge may give them hope that a critical indicator will appear. When confronted with ignorance, the already indecisive become doubly so. They frequently require far too much positive evidence before switching from a choice where probabilities are known to one where they are unknown. They fail to recognize that choosing the unknown probability often offers valuable learning opportunities, opportunities that would otherwise be missed. In short, they neglect option value (Trautmann and Zeckhauser, 2013). The magnification of indecision bias by ignorance is particularly disturbing given that consequential decisions often need to be made under conditions of little or no information.

Indecisiveness has been studied as fostering "worst-case scenario" reasoning, and has been explained as a fear of the threat of ambiguity. Indecisiveness has been said to influence not only the decision-making process (e.g., time taken) but also decision-making content or quality (Rassin and Muris, 2005). In effect, indecision bias makes individuals seek out more-than-optimal information before making a decision. CADs, by their very nature, do not announce their coming arrival, rendering information gathering fruitless. Recognized ignorance could magnify indecision bias, since it highlights the fear of possibly committing to an inappropriate course of action, a variant of the fear of an error of commission.

Characters in literature commonly display indecision bias. They "play safe" or delay inordinately because uncertainty or ignorance tends to paralyze the choice process. Some characters are much more indecisive than others. Writers frequently identify great intelligence and capacity for affect as promoting indecision. Shakespeare, a master student of human psychology, portrays Hamlet's indecisiveness in his "To be or not to be" speech. *Macbeth* presents a noble, sensitive, and courageous military general who becomes the king of Scotland by murdering the *in situ* king Duncan. However, courage hardly assures swift or effective decision making. Macbeth worries pathologically and obsessively before he commits the murder, only acting after his wife derides his indecisiveness and his masculinity. In Edith Wharton's *The Age of Innocence*, the morally upright lawyer Newland Archer is strongly attracted to the separated-but-not-divorced Countess Ellen Olenska, the cousin of his fiancée, May Welland. Fearful of flouting social conventions, Archer waffles endlessly, but ultimately chooses the easy path and marries May, even though he is aware they are ill suited. His indecision persists to the end of his life when, many years after May's death, he has the chance to reunite with Ellen but decides not to do so.[17]

4. Herd behavior

Herd behavior is the tendency of humans who would pick A in isolation to choose B so as to conform with the choices of others. As with herding in animals, moving with the herd can be individually rational, even though the collective outcome can be far from optimal (Schelling, 1978a). Sometimes an inferior equilibrium is reached. Other times no equilibrium is optimal, because the individuals' actions impose externalities on one another.

Herd behavior by humans has been attributed to three causes (Zeckhauser et al., 1991):

1. Free-riding in information acquisition, whereby individuals hope that others know better what decision should be made.
2. Protection from adhering to the group. For example, if individuals are to be judged by their performance relative to others, choosing like others reduces the risk that could come from being an outlier. Similarly, one cannot be blamed for one's beliefs if one adjusts those beliefs, or at least one's expression of beliefs, to accord with the beliefs of others.
3. Adherence to group norms as a means to curb self-reproach.

The famed Asch conformity experiments (1956) demonstrate the strong attraction of sticking with the herd. All three of the causes above have been presented as explanations.

Ignorance has the potential to reinforce these tendencies. We provide two examples:

1. *Regret avoidance*. Once ignorance is recognized, aversive events may occur at any time. Thus, regret as a concern looms large. But regret from our own bad choices may be reduced when other members of the herd have fared equally badly. (One might call this an insidious, yet common form of schadenfreude.)
2. *Safety*. When judged by others, or even oneself, there is always safety in numbers. Ignorance magnifies concerns for safety. Wandering alone in the vast unknown is threatening, both cognitively and to one's reputation. If you know nothing, others may know something, hence imitation may bring protection from danger. Equally important, when all are acting alike, none can be blamed for choosing differently and receiving a poor outcome. Following this logic, the major investment banks all bought commercial mortgage-backed securities, an instrument they did not understand, before the 2008 financial meltdown.

Literary fiction frequently recounts herd behavior in many of the same domains as real life: politics and finance. In *A Tale of Two Cities* by Charles Dickens, the mob mentality under Robespierre's reign during the French Revolution creates untold violence and deaths, making for a situation expressed by the idiom, "the blind leading the blind." The purported goal of the revolutionaries is to bring about social change but the herd behavior produces chaos, not coherence.

In Anthony Trollope's *The Way We Live Now*, based partly on the financial panics of the 1870s, the unprincipled but rich financier Augustus Melmotte draws members of the British upper class to invest in his dubious railway schemes. While individually contemptuous of Melmotte as a social *arriviste*, the aristocrats function collectively as a herd attracted to the future prospect of economic gains and "safety in numbers"—since other established members of their clique also invest with Melmotte. At a historical period when investment schemes were in a nascent stage, and railway investments particularly dubious, Melmotte's investors are collectively ignorant of the future. Their herd behavior proves calamitous when Melmotte is revealed as a forger. Bernard Madoff capitalized on similar herd effects to promote his Ponzi scheme.

Literature frequently portrays gossip, or the creation and social dissemination of reputation, as a facilitator of herd behavior. Gossip, in real life as in fiction, is rarely used to spread honest information or praise. More likely, we see malicious or erroneous gossip that is used to lead the herd in the wrong direction. Mr. Darcy in Jane Austen's *Pride and Prejudice* has the disadvantage of being proclaimed a disagreeable, arrogant man for much of the novel, because his reputation precedes him, nearly all of it circulated by his enemy George Wickham. In Richard Brinsley Sheridan's play *The School for Scandal*, one brother spreads gossip about the other brother's spending habits, seeking to damage his reputation. Lily Bart, the tragic heroine of Edith Wharton's *The House of Mirth*, is banished from the herd in affluent New York society when her reputation is called into question through a series of inaccurate accounts of her behavior spread by prominent members of her former in-group.

After a CAD strikes, two additional biases come into play:

1. Retrospective recollection of contemplation

Retrospective recollection of contemplation (RRC) represents a self-deluding effort to gain comfort with our past failure to recognize ignorance. RRC essentially whitewashes our cognitive failings. We failed to contemplate the CAD that transpired (although with a conventional CAD we *might* have and with a blindered CAD we *should* have). RRC handily leads us to recollect erroneously that the CAD was on our menu of possible outcomes. Falling prey to RRC is akin to creating a "highlight reel" of images of a reconstituted, "cherry-picked" past. It enables us to avoid self-blame in the present because, as we tell ourselves, we saw this coming in the past.

RRC may arise from the human imperative to believe that life makes sense, intuitively speaking; and that as intelligent beings on this planet, we can envision the events will transpire according to some mostly discernible patterns. RRC may be described as the impulse to make sense of apparently anomalous events, much as religious faith does for some individuals.

In William Shakespeare's *Othello,* a CAD strikes the newly married Othello when his meaningful gift of a handkerchief to his wife Desdemona is discovered with Othello's lieutenant, the young and handsome Cassio. Othello's scheming ensign, the "trusty" Iago, has been gradually convincing Othello that Desdemona and Cassio are having an affair. The discovery of the handkerchief (it once belonged to Othello's mother) ignites Othello's already suspicious mind, and sets off a cascade of events: Othello's sexual jealousy produces ever successive lows. First, he smothers his innocent wife to death. Then a new CAD follows: he realizes his error. That CAD in turn leads him to commit suicide.

The "handkerchief episode," upon closer examination, provides crucial understanding of how RRC works on the mind. When a CAD occurs, the past is reconstituted to repress or submerge evidence of our past ignorance. "Of course we saw this coming," we tell ourselves. Desdemona, always of irreproachable, pristine conduct, is now, in Othello's deluded mind, recast as a woman who was always capable of adultery. Falling prey to RRC, he concludes he was too infatuated, and he rebukes himself for failing to recognize Desdemona's true character. Action bias springs forward and Othello murders Desdemona, since he knows he will credit himself for appropriate revenge. The Othello story is a cautionary tale against indulging in impetuous action bias when a CAD strikes. Othello would have been better served by considering alternative strategies, such as openly discussing his concerns with his wife. Ultimately, he might come to question the motives of his source, Iago, who is the only informant to Desdemona's adultery. Othello, however, ricochets from deep love to deep suspicion of Desdemona. Where was Ann Landers when he needed her?

Othello goes to his death lamenting he is a man "that loved not wisely, but too well." And while the world of sixteenth-century Cyprus may seem eons away from ours, we too erroneously recollect that we had contemplated a specific CAD once this CAD has become a reality. To do otherwise would be a betrayal of our past self (Schelling, 1978b). As in fiction so in life, the individual fails to draw inferences from the presence of clues that, were they more carefully noticed, would be warning bells for ignorance, sometimes before a CAD strikes, and sometimes after.

2. Barn door closing

This describes post-CAD behavior when one encounters a chance at a similar decision, albeit in a new environment. Patel et al. (1991) apply the concept to investors who make the investment choices today that they should have made yesterday, figuratively securing the barn door after the horse has bolted. When victims of a negative CAD, decision-makers attempt to rectify history by making today's decision the right retrospective decision. Flawed reasoning leads to poor decisions. Barn door closing provides temporary comfort at the risk of compounding errors. If today's context differs from yesterday's, for example if we are buying equities now when we should have bought them a year ago, the past becomes an oracle of false guidance. Economists have written extensively about the problematic conception of the self when dealing with future behavior (Thaler and Shefrin, 1981; Schelling, 1984; Ainslie and Haslam, 1992), but the phenomenon of barn door closing after a CAD has not hitherto been investigated.[18]

Barn door closing represents a cognitive attempt to look at what lies ahead not through the windshield, but through the rear-view mirror. We tell ourselves, "I can do better this time around." The investor who, with grim tenacity, attempts to avoid mistakes from the past by employing a by now outmoded, investment strategy in effect creates a new barn door to be closed tomorrow.[19]

In literary fiction, we encounter barn door closing most commonly in the domain of intimate relationships—a domain in which individuals are compelled, through some vicious, inexorable force, to draw inappropriate lessons from history. And who can forget Jay Gatsby's cloying desperation as he attempts to rectify his past error in letting the now-married Daisy Buchanan slip out of his life, in *The Great Gatsby*:

> "Can't repeat the past?" [. . .] "Why of course you can!" He looked around him wildly, as if the past were lurking here in the shadow of his house, just out of reach of his hand. "I'm going to fix everything just the way it was before," he said, nodding determinedly. "She'll see."

Prescriptions for ignorance

Our strategy for dealing with ignorance incorporates the four recommendations presented in the first section: first, build a repository of intellectual capital; second, scan the decision environment for potential CADs; third, dedicate attention once a scan has revealed that CADs are imminent; and finally, adjust choices through cognitive diversity and flexibility.

We advocate building intellectual capital by developing decision-theoretic methods, but on an expedient basis from empirical study of instances of ignorance. For that empirical study, we recommend adding to the literature on behavioral and rational decision studies from the world of fiction—specifically, the decision-making adventures of literary characters who are frequently grappling with the complexities of ignorance. Writers, poets, and dramatists know that decisions are not made in environments such as those in decision theory texts, where potential future outcomes are readily identified. A large body of research, from evolutionary psychology to cognitive studies, has noted the evolutionary benefits of storytelling in helping human beings deal with physical and social environments that are hard to predict. Most notably, this body of research speaks loudly and concertedly that stories, disseminated first orally and then through the medium of writing, have instructed human beings in understanding the thoughts and actions of other human beings.[20]

Ignorance poses big challenges. In coping with it, we should first dampen aspirations. For example, we will never foresee deep CADs, and conventional and blindered CADs may just be missed. A systematic approach, however, can improve performance.

Often, the recognition of ignorance changes our choices. Recognizing that emotions are strong, implying that a blindered CAD may lurk, we may opt to delay a life decision, such as getting married. In other contexts we might pursue a more flexible strategy—for example, renting not buying in the new city in case the job does not pan out. For many consequential decisions, advice from the outside is worth gathering. With adverse CADs, prevention is better than mitigation, and actions may be available that reduce a CAD's likelihood. To be sure, such actions entail costs, which are wasted if the CAD would not have occurred. But on an expected value basis, these costs may be worth paying, particularly once we recognize that a CAD is a reasonable possibility.

Analytic tools are often most helpful when they are hardest to employ. Knowledge of decision theory provides modest benefit when shopping at the supermarket, but can be of great value when dealing with a complex medical decision or an elaborate R&D undertaking, both CAD-related events, even if we employ only the theory's basic approach. Thus, we propose a decision-theoretic approach to ignorance. We call our approach *measured decision*, hoping to suggest doing something reasonable and "good enough," if not optimal.

Let us start with CAD magnitude. Many CADs involve consequences that are not readily assessed on a monetary basis: a marriage destroyed, a betrayal by a dear friend. Prescriptive decision theory has just the measuring tool, von Neumann–Morgenstern (VN-M) utilities. An excellent reference outcome would be pegged at 100.0, which would be the status quo. Then a poor outcome would get a value –X.[21] Each CAD outcome would then be placed on this scale using traditional lottery procedures.

If the concern is about the consequences of CADs and the assessment of ignorance, negative or positive values of the same magnitude would get the same weight. Thus, we would compute the expected absolute value of a CAD. These are VN-M utilities; thus weighting them by probabilities is appropriate. No doubt, this calibration process would be challenging: assessing the magnitude of consequences that you often cannot even identify. However, making a crude estimate is better than simply not considering the problem.

Figure 17.1 shows the expected consequences of consequential amazing developments. Any individual CAD would be represented by a point on the graph, where greater probability or greater consequences imply greater importance. The figure darkens and the expected consequences of ignorance grow as we move in a north-easterly direction. The figure shows two points, A and B, each representing a CAD. Their aggregate contribution to ignorance is point S, computed by adding together the two points' probabilities and computing the expected value of their consequences. The expected consequences are the same at any point along a rectangular hyperbola.

How should we respond when we recognize our consequential ignorance? What, in such a context, would characterize a "measured" decision? One strategy would be to conceptualize decisions most favorable to a potential CAD, with an emphasis on diversity and flexibility. But "diversity" and "flexibility" are easier to recommend than to implement. Diversity would imply having at our disposal a miscellany of cognitive prototypes of decision making, some from real life and some from literature—let us call it a mental warehouse—filled with decision-making "anecdotes" that we draw from in times of need.[22] Flexibility could imply gathering more information before we bite the bullet, and testing the waters with a range of strategies when early indications of dark CAD clouds threaten on the horizon.

Diversity and flexibility are also adaptive strategies for macro institutions—namely, governments, financial institutions, policy-making bodies—since the decisions they make when CADs threaten or happen affect us all. (Think of the Western world in 2015 as it confronts ISIS.)

These macro institutions frequently get trapped in a warren of bureaucratic and political processes when attempting to protect against unfavorable CADs, or indeed after CADs happen. We recommend that the body of intelligentsia that works for these institutions—that is, the policy researchers and the analysts—create a depository of decisions to draw upon and learn from in parlous and unprecedented situations.

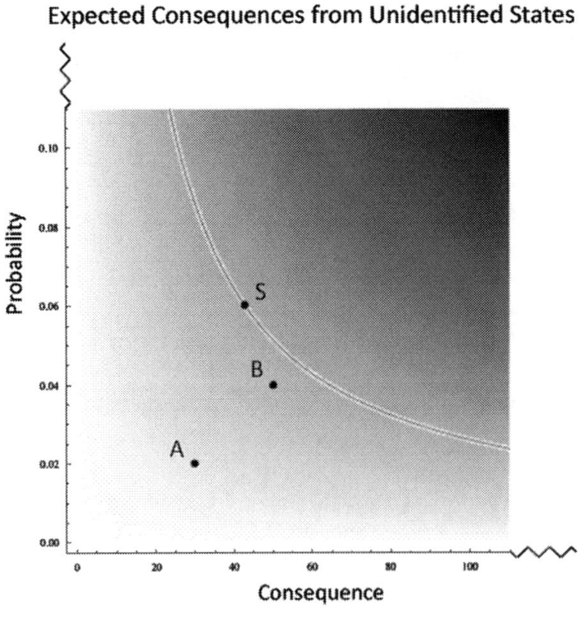

Figure 17.1 Expected consequences from unidentified states

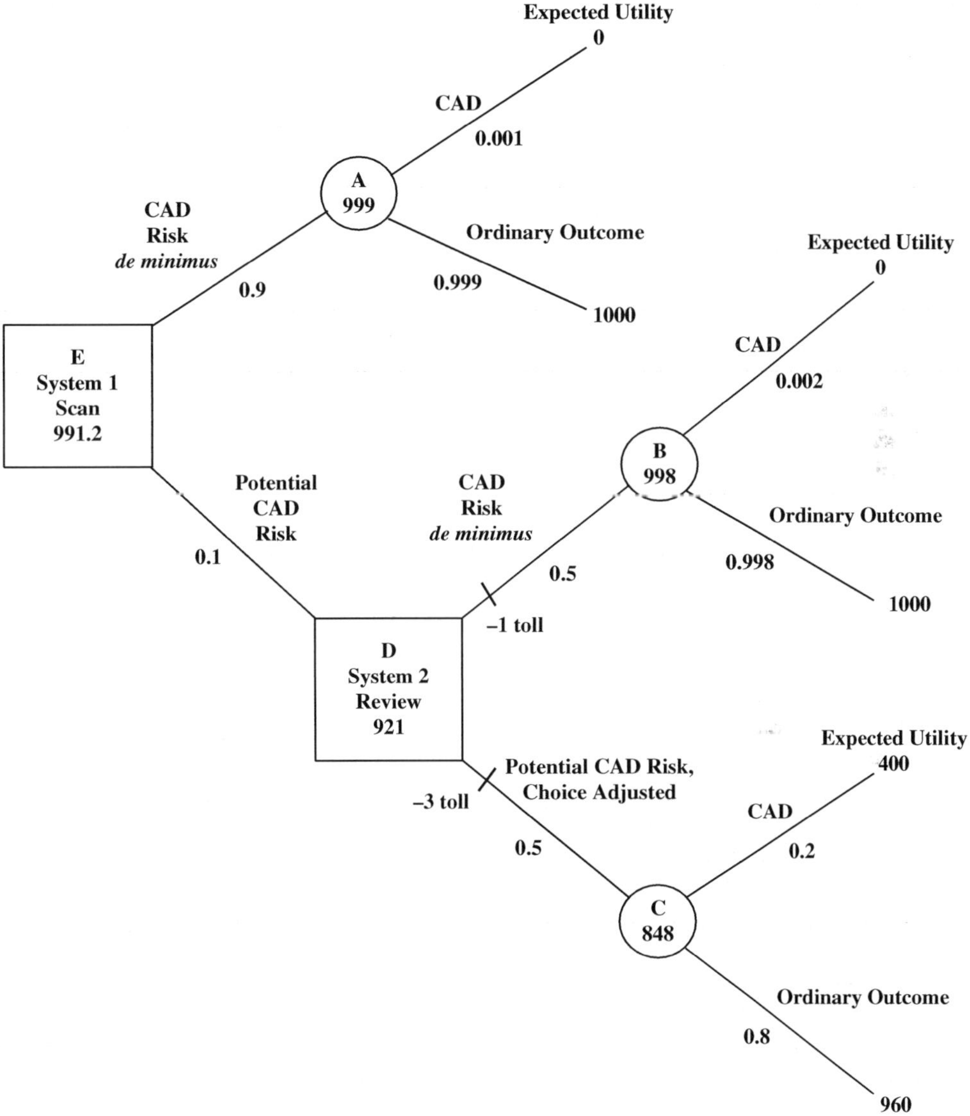

Figure 17.2 Prescriptive illustration attending to ignorance

Say we have built capital to understand ignorance and CADs. What next? Figure 17.2 illustrates our prescriptive recommendations given hypothetical numerical values. We assume that an individual first employs fast and intuitive System 1 (Stanovich and West, 2000; Kahneman, 2003, 2011) to scan each potentially important decision to vaguely assess the base rate for CADs in that decision. That scan might show 10 percent of decisions to have CAD potential.[23] Those 10 percent are then addressed by cautious and deliberate System 2 (Evans and Stanovich, 2013). Posit that half the time (5 percent), System 2 determines that CADs do threaten. System 2 then adjusts choices for those one in 20 decisions.

To put this all together, we need utility values and some further probabilities. The expected utility payoffs are as follows: normal outcome, 1000; CAD outcome, 0; CAD outcome with an adjusted choice, 400;[24] and normal outcome with an adjusted choice, 960.[25] The CAD occurs 0.1 percent of the time when System 1 finds it insignificant, 0.2 percent when System 1 alerts but System 2 finds it insignificant,[26] and 20 percent when System 2 assesses a threat and choices get adjusted. System 1 effectively costs nothing to employ. The initial System 2 review has a utility cost of 1. System 2 costs an additional 2 if CAD risk is identified and the choice is adjusted.

On the decision tree, expected utilities—computed by folding back—are shown at each choice or chance node. Let us proceed. If ignorance is simply neglected, there is a 0.021 chance of a CAD. Expected utility will be 0.021*0 + 0.979*1000 = 979. If ignorance is recognized and a choice is adjusted, as shown in box E, expected utility is 991.2. Attending to ignorance cuts the expected cost of CADs by 58%, from 1000-979 = 21 to 1000 – 991.2 = 8.8.

Discussion and conclusions

What might have been is an abstraction

Remaining a perpetual possibility

Only in a world of speculation.

(T. S. Eliot, Burnt Norton)

These lines from T. S. Eliot provide the perfect coda to our study of ignorance. They elegantly delineate the challenge of anticipating CADs. They also indicate that the type of mental processes represented by the lower branch of Figure 17.2 represent our hope to both anticipate and grapple reasonably effectively with ignorance. Our natural proclivity is to proceed along Figure 17.2's upper branch—namely, to pay ignorance no heed. While we cannot predict deep CADs, human beings have the potential to employ System 2 methods and foresee the two other categories: conventional CADs and blindered CADs. In terms of strategies for ignorance, our strongest endorsement goes to developing vigilance by engaging cognitive assists from multiple sources.[27]

One of the world's most trusted sources of decision making wisdom, the Bible notes the virtues of looking ahead and planning, observing, "A prudent man foreseeth the evil, and hideth himself: but the simple pass on, and are punished" (Proverbs 22.3). The Proverbs, the Book of Job, Ecclesiastes, among other biblical texts, lead us to conclude that ignorance abounds in the universe, unpleasant CADs intervene constantly in our lives, and sometimes people deserve these CADs and sometimes they do not. But, as our opening verse exhorts, it is in preparation that lies our victory over ignorance. The Bible, like much of wisdom literature, is replete with situations where human beings failed to envision the extreme events that happened. Job loses his family, riches, and health, with no divine explanation offered (until God's final appearance at the end). The author(s) of Ecclesiastes cautions that risk underscores human existence ("chance happeneth to [us] all") and that "[w]isdom is better than strength" and "better than weapons of war" (Ecclesiastes 9.16-18).

Literature provides powerful insights on the subject of ignorance. Great works of literature often represent the theater of life with its scenes of drama, conflict, and resolution. And the characters it portrays frequently tread paths not knowing to what outcomes they lead. We can recreate from these narratives cause-and-effect prototypes of decision making that translate to real-life situations.[28]

A central lesson from life is to learn from the past and stay alert to the future. With literature, we can learn from the lives of myriad others, and the ignorance and CADs they experience, not merely from our own experience. Putting these lessons to work alongside those emerging from our analytic framework, we can better anticipate CADs. When CADs seem to threaten, focused attention and System II thinking can replace naïve complacency and reflexive responses. Ignorance will always be a threat, but if we draw effectively on both literature and decision theory, ignorance will be a less-frequent and less-harmful surprise visitor.

Notes

1 Although, see Gomory (1995) and Zeckhauser (2006) and their discussions of the unknown and unknowable. See also Congar and Maniquet (2010).

2 As Laplace eloquently puts it:

> We may regard the present state of the universe as the effect of its past and the cause of its future. An intellect which at a certain moment would know all forces that set nature in motion, and all positions of all items of which nature is composed, if this intellect were also vast enough to submit these data to analysis, it would embrace in a single formula the movements of the greatest bodies of the universe and those of the tiniest atom; for such an intellect nothing would be uncertain and the future just like the past would be present before its eyes.
>
> *(Laplace, 1951: 4)*

3 Frank Knight (1921: 224–5). For a fresh, innovative reading of intuition and Knight's work on risk and uncertainty, see Frantz (2005).

4 Howard Raiffa (1968: 273).

5 We recognize that the word "blindered" does not exist in the dictionary. We use it in the sense of having blinders on, in the manner of a horse.

6 The dual characteristics of contemplation and cognitive effort intersect also with Herbert Simon's (1957) concept of "bounded rationality." Because we have limited cognitive processing power that is typically applied towards "good enough" choices as opposed to the "best possible" ones, a CAD will fly in and turn our lives inside out, leaving us at sixes-and-sevens because we were "bounded" in our ability to envision it.

7 In this chapter, we use "literature," "literary fiction," "stories," and "fiction" interchangeably, a usage apt to shock the purist. Our reader should take these terms to imply any story created by the imagination, including novels, plays, epics, and short stories.

8 Elke Weber and Eric Johnson (2008: 132).

9 The term "wisdom literature" is applied primarily to selected biblical texts that impart didactic wisdom on certain common themes: family, ethics, faith, and making sense of suffering, among others. From the Old Testament, they include the Book of Job, Proverbs, Ecclesiastes, and the Song of Solomon. From the Aprocrypha (or the Deuterocanon), they include Ecclesiasticus and Wisdom of Solomon. James L. Crenshaw (1993).

10 Thomas Schelling (1984: 331).

11 "heuristic, n. and adj.". OED Online. September 2014. Oxford: Oxford University Press. Available at: www.oed.com/view/Entry/86554 (accessed November 27, 2014).

12 Some scholars hold a contrary view. For example, Gigerenzer and Brighton (2009) assert that despite the widely held view (also advanced here) that faster processing—hence less cognitive effort—impairs accuracy, it actually fosters decision making, noting: "Contrary to the belief in a general accuracy–effort tradeoff, less information and computation can actually lead to higher accuracy, and in these situations the mind does not need to make tradeoffs. Here, a *less-is-more* effect holds." Gigerenzer and Brighton (2009: 109).

13 "bias, adj., n., and adv.". OED Online. June 2014. Oxford University Press. Available at: www.oed.com/view/Entry/18564 (accessed July 23, 2014).

14 We digress for a moment to observe it is not coincidental that the distinguishing feature of epics—from Virgil's *Aeneid* to the Mesopotamian *Epic of Gilgamesh*—is their depiction of action as a means towards

the resolution of uncertainty. Beowulf, the English epic hero, takes on both the monster Grendel and Grendel's mother because the hope for the halo of heroism outweighs the presence of the possibility of death. The Old English poems *The Seafarer* and *The Wanderer* describe the hardships of life on the vast, uncaring seas, based on the knowledge that, despite the inevitability of suffering, sailors would venture forth impelled by AB.

15 For instance, the Hindu spiritual text the *Bhagavad Gita* posits action as virtue, stating, in its most famous passage, that only action performed selflessly and continually will free human beings from the never-ending cycle of attachment and loss, and success and failure: "You have the right to work [action], but never to the fruit of work. You should never engage in action for the sake of reward, nor should you long for inaction" (2.47). (The absence of reward seeking, of course, would prevent the action bias that arises in the Western canon.)

16 The recommendation to stick with the known when ignorant, thus promoting SQB, is a frequent theme in fairytales, folklore, and myths, which, as Carl Jung, Joseph Campbell, Claude Lévi-Strauss, and Roland Barthes have argued, depict behavioral and cognitive archetypes. Characters—consider Hansel and Gretel in the nineteenth-century Brothers Grimm fairytale—are punished when they tread into unknown paths in deep woods.

17 Wharton ends her novel in Paris where Archer and his now-adult son are visiting Ellen and Archer has the chance to reunite with her at a time when he is widowed. He chooses not to go up to her apartment: "'[Ellen's image is] more real to me here than if I went up,' he suddenly heard himself say; and the fear lest that last shadow of reality should lose its edge kept him rooted to his seat as the minutes succeeded each other." Archer's inner monologue, which portrays his struggle with the anxiety produced when contemplating an act of commission, shows his indecision bias at work in an environment of ignorance.

18 In "Egonomics, or the Art of Self-Management" (1978b), Schelling observes wryly that whether quitting smoking or adhering to diets "everybody behaves like two people, one who wants clean lungs and long life and another who adores tobacco, or one who wants a lean body and another who wants dessert. The two [selves] are in a continual contest for control; the 'straight' one often in command most of the time, but the wayward one needing only to get occasional control to spoil the other's best laid plan." To this we would add that barn door closing is a way for the "wise" present self to wipe clean the errors of the "foolish" past self.

19 Many investors act as if securities markets are like physics experiments, where what happened yesterday will happen again today. They fail to recognize that investors learning from and responding to yesterday's market will change the behavior of the market today.

20 For seminal research in this area, see Storey (1996), Scalise Sugiyama (1996), and Carroll (2004).

21 Note: We do not require that the bad outcome get a utility value of exactly -100, because no plausible outcome may have that value, and any bottom value can serve as a reference point.

22 Evolutionary scholars describe stories as cognitive models of cause-and-effect representations of goals and strategies for pursuing these goals within certain environments (Scalise Sugiyama, 2001). Our recommendation is that decision researchers should create a depository of stories as cause-and-effect models generally, and that they draw on them in particular when confronted with consequential ignorance.

23 We simplify by assuming that the capital-building step imposes negligible cost on a decision when amortized over the individual's lifetime, and that System 1 scanning is effectively costless, not unlike looking both ways before crossing the street. We scale the top outcome to 1,000, not the more conventional 100, to reduce decimals. All calculations are carried through without rounding. However, the values at nodes in the decision tree are rounded to the nearest tenth.

24 Some CAD outcomes may be favorable, which presents no problem since this is an expected utility.

25 If it were known that a CAD would not occur, it would be better not to adjust one's choice.

26 Even though System 2 is much more thorough than System 1, it is screening decisions pre-selected for high CAD risk. Hence, there is the 0.2% probability here versus 0.1% when System 1 finds an insignificant risk.

27 Consider the blindered CAD of the subprime market crisis. Both its occurrence and that it triggered the market crash of 2008 demonstrate a complete absence of cognitive vigilance. As early as 2003, economists Karl Case and Robert Shiller cautioned of the impending bubble in the housing market. But despite easily available information, public policy analysts, credit agencies, and lenders chose to ignore "the canary in the coalmine" of runaway house prices unrelated to fundamentals, and continued to extend credit to ever-riskier borrowers.

28 See Tooby and DeVore's (1987) pioneering work on strategic modeling within the context of evolution; one of their observations is that human beings create and transmit models of their environment through culture.

Bibliography

Ainslie, G. & Haslam, N. (1992). Hyperbolic Discounting. In Choice over Time, edited by G. Loewenstein and J. Elster. New York: Russell Sage, 57–92.

Alpert, M. & Raiffa, H. (1982). A Progress Report on the Training of Probability Assessors. In Judgment under Uncertainty: Heuristics and Biases, edited by D. Kahneman, P. Slovic, and A. Tversky. Cambridge, UK: Cambridge University Press, 294–305.

Asch, S. E. (1956). Studies of Independence and Conformity: A Minority of One against a Unanimous Majority. Psychological Monographs, 70(9), 1–70.

Austen, J. (1966). Pride and Prejudice. Edited by D. J. Gray. New York: Norton.

Bazerman, M. H. (2014). The Power of Noticing: What the Best Leaders See. New York: Simon & Schuster.

Bhagavad Gita. (1986). Translated by E. Easwaran. London: Arkana.

Brown, D. E. (1991). Human Universals. Philadelphia: Temple University Press.

Carlson, M. (2003). Mimesis. In The Oxford Encyclopedia of Theatre and Performance. London: Oxford University Press, 2003. Available at: www.oxfordreference.com/view/10.1093/acref/9780198601746.001.0001/acref-9780198601746-e-2643 [accessed June 23, 2014].

Carroll, J. (2004). Literary Darwinism: Evolution, Human Nature, and Literature. New York: Routledge.

Case, K. E. & Shiller, R. T. (2003). Is there a Bubble in the Housing Market? Brookings Papers on Economic Activity, 2, 299–362.

Congar, R. & Maniquet, F. P. (2010). A Trichotomy of Attitudes for Decision-Making under Complete Ignorance. Mathematical Social Sciences, 59(1), 15–25.

Crenshaw, J. L. (1993). Wisdom Literature. In The Oxford Companion to the Bible. London: Oxford University Press. Available at: www.oxfordreference.com/view/10.1093/acref/9780195046458.001.0001/acref-9780195046458-e-0770 [accessed November 26, 2014].

Dickens, C. (1970). A Tale of Two Cities. Edited by G. Woodcock. Harmondsworth, UK: Penguin.

Dunbar, R. (2004). The Human Story: A New History of Mankind's Evolution. London: Faber.

Dunbar, R. & Grooming, I. M. (1996). Gossip and the Evolution of Language. London: Faber.

Eliot, T. S. (1943). The Four Quartets. London: Harcourt.

Epley, N. & Gilovich, T. (2006). The Anchoring-and-Adjustment Heuristic: Why the Adjustments are Insufficient. Psychological Science, 17(4), 311–18.

Evans, J. S. B. T. & Stanovich, K. E. (2013). Dual Process Theories of Higher Cognition: Advancing the Debate. Perspectives on Psychological Science, 8(3), 223–41.

Fischhoff, B. & Beyth, R. (1975). "I Knew it would Happen": Remembered Probabilities of Once-Future Things. Organizational Behaviour and Human Performance, 13(1), 1–16.

Fitzgerald, F. S. (2007). The Great Gatsby. Edited by M. Nowlin. Peterborough, ON: Broadview.

Frantz, R. (2005). Two Minds: Intuition and Analysis in the History of Economic Thought. New York: Springer.

Gigerenzer, G. (2004). Fast and Frugal Heuristics: The Tools of Bounded Rationality. In Blackwell Handbook of Judgment and Decision Making, edited by D. J. Koehler and N. Harvey. Oxford, UK: Blackwell, 62–88.

Gigerenzer, G. & Brighton, H. (2009). Homo Heuristicus: Why Biased Minds Make Better Inferences. Topics in Cognitive Science, 1(1), 107–43.

Gomory, R. E. (1995). The Known, the Unknown and the Unknowable. Scientific American, 272(6), 120.

Johnson, E. J. & Goldstein, D. (2003). Do Defaults Save Lives? Science, 302(5649), 1338–9.

Kahneman, D. (2003). Maps of Bounded Rationality: Psychology for Behavioral Economics. American Economic Review, 93(5), 1449–75.

Kahneman, D. (2011). Thinking, Fast and Slow. New York: Farrar, Straus and Giroux.

Kant, I. (1798). Essays and Treatises on Moral, Political, and Various Philosophical Subjects. London: William Richardson.

Knight, F. H. (1921). Risk, Uncertainty and Profit. Chicago: University of Chicago Press.

Laplace, P.-S. (1951). A Philosophical Essay on Probabilities. Translated by F. Wilson Truscott and F. Lincoln Emory. New York: Dover.

Loewenstein, G. (2000). Emotions in Economic Theory and Economic Behavior. American Economic Review, 90(2), 426–32.
Oatley, K. & Mar, R. A. (2005). Evolutionary Pre-Adaptation and the Idea of Character in Fiction. Journal of Cultural and Evolutionary Psychology, 3(2), 181–96.
Patel, J., Zeckhauser, R. J. & Hendricks, D. (1991). The Rationality Struggle: Illustrations from Financial Markets. American Economic Association Papers and Proceedings, 81(2), 232–6.
Patt, A. & Zeckhauser, R. J. (2000). Action Bias and Environmental Decisions. Journal of Risk and Uncertainty, 21(1), 45–72.
Payne, J. W., Bettman, J. R. & Johnson, E. J. (1993). The Adaptive Decision Maker. Cambridge: Cambridge University Press.
Poe, E. A. (2006). The Murders in the Rue Morgue: The Dupin Tales. Edited by M. Pearl. New York: Modern Library.
Raiffa, H. (1968). Decision Analysis: Introductory Lectures on Choices under Uncertainty. Reading: Addison-Wesley.
Rassin, E. & Muris, P. (2005). Indecision and the Interpretation of Ambiguous Situations. Personality and Individual Differences, 39(1), 1285–91.
Roy, D. & Zeckhauser, R. J. (2015). Grappling with Ignorance: Frameworks from Decision Theory, Lessons from Literature. Journal of Benefit–Cost Analysis, 6(1), 33–65.
Samuelson, W. & Zeckhauser, R. J. (1988). Status Quo Bias in Decision Making. Journal of Risk and Uncertainty, 1(1), 7–59.
Savage, L. J. (1954). The Foundations of Statistics. New York: Wiley.
Scalise Sugiyama, M. (1996). On the Origins of Narrative: Storyteller Bias as a Fitness-Enhancing Strategy. Human Nature, 7(7), 403–25.
Scalise Sugiyama, M. (2001). Food, Foragers, and Folklore: The Role of Narrative in Human Subsistence. Evolution and Human Behavior, 22, 221–40.
Schelling, T. C. (1978a). Micromotives and Macrobehavior. New York: Norton.
Schelling, T. C. (1978b). Egonomics, or the Art of Self-Management. American Economic Review, 68(2), 290–4.
Schelling, T. C. (1984). Choice and Consequence. Cambridge, MA: Harvard University Press.
Shakespeare, W. (1962). Macbeth. Edited by K. Muir. London: Methuen.
Shakespeare, W. (2009). Othello. Edited by J. Bate and Eric Rasmussen. New York: Modern Library.
Sheridan, R. B. (1971). The School for Scandal. Edited by C. J. L. Price. London: Oxford University Press.
Simon, H. A. (1955). A Behavioral Model of Rational Choice. Quarterly Journal of Economics, 69, 99–118.
Simon, H. A. (1957). Models of Man, Social and Rational: Mathematical Essays on Rational Human Behavior in a Social Setting. New York: Wiley.
Stanovich, K. E. & West, R. F. (2000). Individual Differences in Reasoning: Implications for the Rationality Debate? Behavioral and Brain Sciences, 23(5), 645–726.
Storey, R. F. (1996). Mimesis and the Human Animal: On the Biogenetic Foundations of Literary Representation. Evanston: Northwestern University Press.
Thaler, R. H. & Shefrin, H. M. (1981). An Economic Theory of Self-Control. Journal of Political Economy, 89(2), 392–406.
Tooby, J. & DeVore, I. (1987). The Reconstruction of Hominid Behavioral Evolution through Strategic Modeling. In The Evolution of Human Behavior: Primate Models, edited by W. G. Kinzey. Albany, NY: SUNY Press, 183–237.
Trautmann, S. T. & Zeckhauser, R. J. (2013). Shunning Uncertainty: The Neglect of Learning Opportunities. Games and Economic Behavior, 79, 44–55.
Trollope, A. (1951). The Way We Live Now. New York: Oxford University Press.
Tversky, A. & Kahneman, D. (1973). Availability: A Heuristic for Judging Frequency and Probability. Cognitive Psychology, 5(2), 207–32.
Tversky, A. & Kahneman, D. (1974). Judgment under Uncertainty: Heuristics and Biases. Science, 185(4157), 1124–31.
Weber, E. U. & Johnson, E. J. (2008). Decisions under Uncertainty: Psychological, Economic and Neuro-economic Explanations of Risk Preference. In Neuroeconomics: Decision Making and the Brain, edited by P. Glimcher, C. Camerer, E. Fehr, and R. Poldrack. New York: Elsevier.

Weber, E. U., Siebenmorgen, N. & Weber, M. (2005). Communicating Asset Risk: How Name Recognition and the Format of Historic Volatility Information Affect Risk Perception and Investment Decisions. Risk Analysis, 25(3), 597–609.

Wharton, E. (1990). The House of Mirth. Edited by E. Ammons. New York: Norton.

Wharton, E. (1996). The Age of Innocence. Edited by C. Griffin Wolff. New York: Penguin.

Zeckhauser, R. J. (2006). Investing in the Unknown and Unknowable. Capitalism and Society, 1(2), 1–39.

Zeckhauser, R. J., Patel, J. & Hendricks, D. (1991). Nonrational Actors and Financial Market Behavior. Theory and Decision, 31, 257–87.

18
SMART SOCIETIES

Shu-Heng Chen, Bin-Tzong Chie, and Chung-Ching Tai

Introduction

In their 1995 article entitled "Quantitative and Computational Innovation in Investment Management," Leinweber and Arnott (1995) raised two questions: "If you had unlimited computational power, what would you do with it?" and "What would you do differently if you were completely unconstrained by the capacity of your computers?" By slightly rephrasing these two questions, we immediately see a "digital" version of these two questions: "If you could *digitize everything*, what would you do with it?" and "What would you do *differently* if you were completely unconstrained by *the capacity of your digitalization*?"

The motivation to write this chapter from the perspective of behavioral economics is driven by the prevalence of digital societies in various forms, such as digital democracy, digital governance, digital media, and digitalization of the protocols, routines, and archives by which modern society is now defined, shaped, and operated. However, a digital society is not "automatically" equivalent to a smart society; in fact, a number of studies indicate exactly the worrying trend that digitalization can contribute to the dumbness, shallowness and instability of that society (Keen, 2007; Bauerlein, 2008).[1] Despite this shadow, the fundamental question that concerns behavioral economists is: To what extent can digitalization enhance our decision making and choice quality? Hence, we need to ask how the digitalization process changes human behavior or decision rules such that it may be easier to shape a smart society and a good society. Furthermore, from the viewpoint of the behavioral foundations of public policies, we are interested in knowing how the digitalization process can be used in the vein of *nudges* by which a smart society can be generated by smart designs. For example, can the digitalization trend facilitate a design of the *choice architecture* so that better decisions can be nudged (Thaler & Sunstein, 2008)?

The questions outlined above are basically applicable to every new technology, not just the digital ones. The relationship between technology and behavior is bidirectional. Behavioral rules or decision making processes can determine how technology is diffused (i.e., the diffusion dynamics). In turn, the availability of a new technology can, or can be designed to, bring about changes in humans' decision making routines or heuristics in a non-trivial way, for example, the great involvement of decision support systems and data-mining tools in decision making, thanks to the advances in high-performing computer technology (Soares de Mello & Namorado

Clímaco, 2015). Therefore, before we proceed further, it is imperative to know how digital technology is different from other technologies and hence deserves a unique treatment. To answer this question, we shall first present one essential assertion that makes digital technology and the shaped digital society unique. We shall then discuss and reflect upon the validity of this argument.

The rest of the chapter is organized as follows. In the second section, we first review the possibility that the digital society has a characteristic to converge to a frictionless economy. We then review some fundamental limits which may cause the path to deviate from convergence. One related issue is the well-known information overload and choice overload problem. The third section shows why these problems may remain even in the digital era. One reason for that is the powerful information pooling mechanisms supported by Web 2.0. The fourth section reviews the information aggregation mechanism in the digital society, known as big data. We address the behavioral causes and consequences of big data in light of Hayek (1945). The fifth section, in view of the recent spread of peer production, crowdsourcing, and crowdfunding, addresses how the powerful crowd matching mechanism provided by the digital society has helped promote prosocial behavior. The final section gives the concluding remarks.

A frictionless economy?

The role of information had been ignored by economists for a long time. Many standard doctrines such as perfect competition and the no-arbitrage condition are built upon some assumptions for fluid information flow. These assumptions had been taken for granted until the rise of research under the discipline known as *economics of information and uncertainty* in the 1960s (Hirshleifer & Riley, 1979). The formation of this field basically recognizes that it is imperative to distinguish the economic theory built upon the assumption of complete information from the one built without this assumption. The information-imperfection awareness in economic theorizing inevitably has promoted economists to clothe their models with considerations of searching behavior (McCall, 1970), uncertainty (Shackle, 1968), ambiguity (Ellsberg, 1961), learning (Cross, 1973), expectations, and various cognitive biases and heuristics (Tversky & Kahneman, 1974), which in turn partially contribute to the body of behavioral economics. Hence, if behavioral economics is partially built upon the assumption that the information is imperfect, then it is high time to examine whether the nature of imperfect information remains unchanged under the digital society.

The key assertion to be proposed and to be open for debates at the outset is that digitalization is a process toward *perfection* in the sense of *perfect information* and a *frictionless market,* dubbed the *perfect-economy assertion.* The perfect-economy assertion starts with the perception that a digital society creates an information-abundant environment in which each agent can access tremendous information with negligible costs. For example, the information regarding prices and quality has become much more easily available in a digital society than in a conventional economy. In addition to big information, there are various searching robots, known as *pricebots* and *shopbots* (Smith, 2002), and various *price comparison websites* (Ronayne, 2015), designed to help consumers find the lowest prices. On top of that, there are online interviews (Chatterjee, 2001), archived as a part of recommendation systems, and various words of mouth, mediated through social media networks, that make it easier for consumers to ascertain the expected quality of goods or services. In a sense, we have all become avid users of databases and search engines. Ideally, an economy evolving with increasing digitalization brings us closer to an economy with perfect information. Hence, the day might come when, in making a purchasing decision, each consumer may access all available commodities associated with the respective prices and quality on his/her smartphone.

Given that information, some smartphone applications (apps) can even automate the default (the optimal) decision for the consumer.

Is the above smart economy realizable, or is it only limited to Hollywood science fiction movies? On this issue, we propose the *non-convergence assertion*. The reason why a digital society will not converge toward a perfect-economy is mainly because of the *description complexity* of the goods, services, jobs, and capabilities. If all of what can be traded in goods and labor markets is in a finite-dimensional space, that is, the familiar R^n space, with time-invariant attributes, then the digitalization of all tradable goods or labor can be a matter of time, and a perfect search or match with the assistance of some highly performing robots can be possible.

However, not all goods and services can be perfectly captured by a vector of real numbers, and, when they are not, verbal descriptions become indispensable. Nevertheless, unlike automated search over Euclidian space, automated search over spaces of verbal descriptions or texts involves not just syntactic issues but also semantic issues. The current text mining techniques are still quite short in handling the latter. Considering the situation where a job searcher can freely describe his preferred jobs and the compensation package, but his verbal descriptions of job preference may not be entirely captured by the robot, because of the semantic difficulty, and hence the search cannot be fully automated. Under this situation, human involvement cannot be waived. What can be even worse, while rather realistic, is that many events are *undescribable*, also known as *complex events*.[2] On this occasion, human involvement in the search process is not entirely replaceable by machines. It is true that digital societies may not free human involvement in many decision making processes, but would it at least make it easier for humans to make decisions and hence enhance human welfare? In the following, we shall argue that the automated search involving humans can end up with a case of *the second-best theory*.[3]

Information and choice overload

Given the prevalence of complex or undescribable events, objects, or products, it is hard to make search robots harness what the host wants. In this case, the search robot will frequently generate a long list of possible relevant choices, which can trap decision makers in the familiar paradox of choice (Schwartz, 2003). The paradox originates from a series of human-subject experiments which address the behavior related to choice conflicts, choice aversion, or choice deferral. Obviously, in this situation, the subject is not well motivated to make a choice and, instead, prefers indefinite procrastination or simply not to make a choice.

In the literature, the paradox of choice is formally known as the *choice overload hypothesis*. The hypothesis says that "an increase in the number of options to choose from may lead to adverse consequences such as a decrease in the motivation to choose or the satisfaction with the finally chosen option" (Scheibehenne, Greifeneder, & Todd, 2010: 73). The choice overload hypothesis was first proposed by Iyengar and Lepper (2000). In their famous jam promotion experiment, Iyengar and Lepper distinguished the designs with psychologically manageable numbers of choices (limited-choice condition), say, six, from the designs with psychologically excessive numbers of choices (extensive-choice condition), say, twenty-four. They found that while the 24-jam table was able to attract more shoppers than the 6-jam one, it did not successfully beef up their purchasing willingness.

The line of research initiated by Iyengar and Lepper echoes well with a separate but earlier research line initiated by Jacoby, Speller, and Kohn (1974) and Jacoby, Speller, and Berning (1974), known as the *information overload hypothesis*. Psychologists believe that when the amount of information provided to decision makers is beyond a threshold exceeding the limited information processing capabilities of decision makers then the quality of decisions made will be adversely affected (Schroder, Driver, & Streufert, 1967). As shown in Figure 18.1, in the initial stage, information load may help decision makers in terms of their decision quality; however, up to some point, say, x_{max}, there is a U-reversal indicating that the further information load may reduce the decision quality, due to a cognitive deficit to process the excessive amount of information. The stage after the U-turn is then perceived as a stage of information overload.

Figure 18.1 is very basic; two qualifications can be added. First, agents are heterogeneous. The threshold or the turning point can be heterogeneous among agents due to their heterogeneous cognitive capacities (Schroder, Driver, & Streufert, 1967).[4] Second, agents are adaptive. From a proactive aspect, they may develop various information filtering strategies to push the threshold forward. This progress may further depend on some innovations in information compression technology. However, information compression, measured based on *Kolmogorov complexity* and *maximal compressibility*, cannot be done indefinitely (Li & Vitányi, 2009). Hence, from a more reactive aspect, agents may rely on various *fast and frugal heuristics* to cope with the overload issues (Gigerenzer & Gaissmaier, 2011).

While the research on information overload was initially conducted outside the context of digital societies, its relevance to digital societies may be even stronger (Lee & Lee, 2004; Chen, Shang, & Kao, 2009).[5] Furthermore, the "primitive" digital societies are operated by the Internet; information suppliers are mainly from the supply side of the economy. However, the modern digital societies are operated by Web 2.0 and various social networks and social media; information suppliers can be all users and cover the entire demand side of the economy.[6] Therefore, we have reasons to believe that the information overload issue can be severer in the modern digital societies. For example, more and more consumers use Web 2.0 tools, such as online discussion forums, consumer review sites, weblogs, and social network sites, to communicate their opinions and exchange product information. This new form of word-of-mouth has now been another source of information overload (Park & Lee, 2009). In this regard, one can expect an increasing relevance of behavioral economics in the digital society.

In fact, recent research on information seeking and searching behavior is greatly influenced by Herbert Simon's notion of bounded rationality (Simon, 1955, 1956). Under the influence of Simon, behavioral economists characterize each decision process with three main stays,

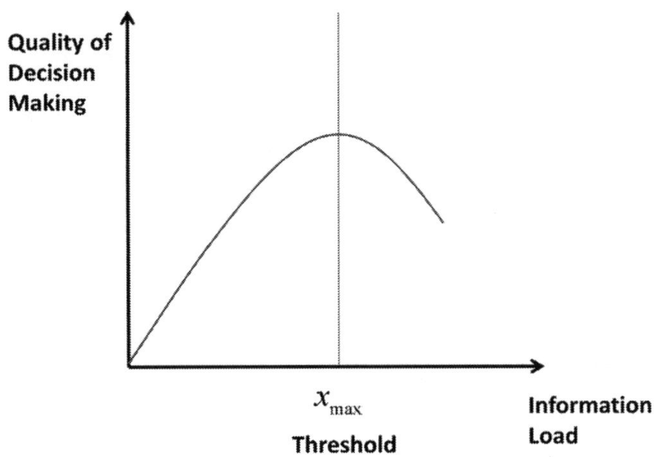

Figure 18.1 Information overload

namely, a *search rule*, a *stopping rule*, and a *decision rule* (Gigerenzer, 2007). It is clear that information seekers in general and Web users in particular are mainly "satisficers" rather than "maximizers". When the object to search is not entirely describable and the search robot fails to pinpoint the desirable target, decision makers are frequently bombarded with an immense list of candidates. In this case, if a stopping rule is not imposed, there may be no limit for human involvement.

To sum up, due to the nature of undescribable objects, digital societies may not be smart enough to bring us closer to the frictionless economy. The information is rich, but it is unclear whether it will be translated into better quality of decisions. Additionally, information overload remains a problem, probably even more severe than before. If so, then like designing choice architecture, the information displayed also needs to be smartly structured before it can beef up decision quality. Not only does this show the significance of "nudging" (Thaler & Sunstein, 2008), but it also indicates that behavioral economics, as a discipline to understand the importance of heuristics and emotion in decision making, may become even more relevant in digital societies.

When Herbert Simon (Simon, 1971) stood on the issue which we currently address, he did not immediately exclude the possibility that a computer may compound the information overload problem instead of solving or mitigating it. He acutely proposed the following general principle:

> *An information processing subsystem … will reduce the net demand on the rest of the organization's attention only if it absorbs more information previously received by others than it produces.*
>
> *(Ibid.: 42; italics, original)*

As we shall see in the next section, it is entirely possible that the digital society may *produce* more than it can absorb.

Big data

One issue related to digital societies and information overload is *big data*. Data become big when our communication, leisure, and commerce have moved to the Internet and the Internet has moved into our phones, our cars and even our glasses, and life can be recorded and quantified in a way that was unimaginable just a decade ago. With the advancement of digital societies, more and more people are placed in this big data or information-rich environment in the following two prototypes.

First, each agent is equipped with some portable digital devices, such as notebooks or smart phones. Each of these devices, through the Internet, is connected to a platform. The platform pools the information received from this and other agents (Figure 18.2, the left panel), and may further aggregate and process this information and then send back signals to these or other agents online or offline to facilitate or *influence* their decisions and communications.[7] Examples abound, such as the United Nations' project on Global Pulse, Google Flu Trends, Google Glass, and Street Bump (Table 18.1). Second, each agent is situated in an environment surrounded by digital devices which may interact with the agent or the portable device carried by the agent (Figure 18.2, the right panel). Based on the on-time information received, the device can provide timely information for the agent or other stakeholders. Examples are BinCam, Environmental Teapot, smart mirror, smart carpet, or smart belt (Table 18.1).[8]

Long before the availability of big data, economists had already noticed the value and the use of big data, although in those days the term was not in the dictionary of economic science. Friedrich

Table 18.1 New data collection device

	Descriptions and Related Research
Global Pulse	Kirkpatrick (2014)
Google Flu Trends	Ginsberg et al. (2009)
Google Glass	Ackerman (2013)
Street Bump	Schwartz (2012)
Traffic D4V	Picone, Amoretti, and Zanichelli (2012)
BinCam	Comber and Thieme (2013)
Environmental Teapot	Marres (2012)
Smart Mirror	Pantano and Nacarato (2010)
Smart Carpet	Aud et al. (2010)
Smart Belt	Shieh, Guu, and Liu (2013)

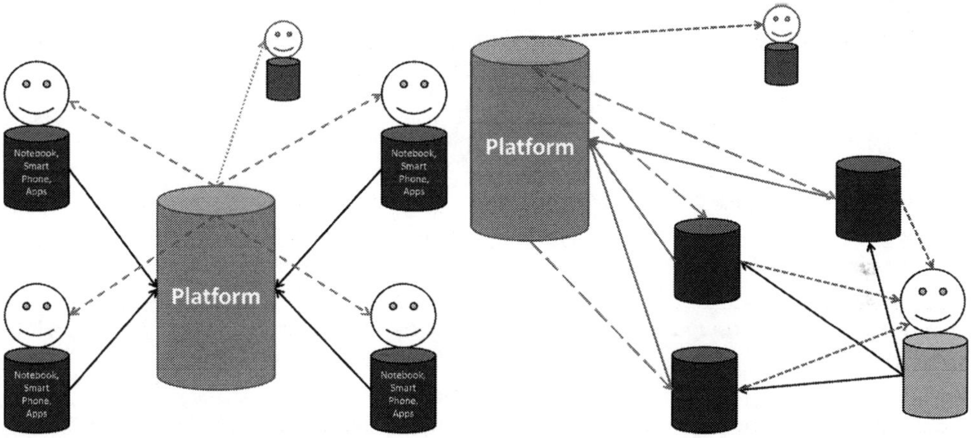

Figure 18.2 Ubiquitous computing (left panel) and Internet of Things (right panel)

Hayek, in his classic work (Hayek, 1937, 1945), rightly addressed this issue. In response to the possible information overload, he was wondering how much we really need to know.

> How much knowledge does he need to do so successfully? Which of the events which happen beyond the horizon of his immediate knowledge are of relevance to his immediate decision, and *how much of them need he know*?
>
> *(Ibid.: 525; italics added)*

The solution that Hayek proposed for the information overload problem is an *information aggregation mechanism*. With the market as an information aggregation mechanism, decision makers may be able to be free from information anxiety (Wurman, 2001) by "*watching the hands of a few dials*, in order to adjust their activities to changes of which they may never know more than is reflected in the price movement" (Hayek, 1945: 527; italics added). In his active participation in the Socialist Calculation Debate, Hayek did not consider that a central planner by incorporating all relevant data into a supercomputer and carrying out the Walrasian tâtonnement process, as suggested by Oskar Lange and Abba Lerner, can be an effective alternative to the market mechanism (Boettke, 2000). It is not even theoretically possible.

From a glance of the smart devices listed in Table 18.1, one can see that a take-off to characterize digital societies is, indeed, *information aggregation*. For example, Google Flu Trends uses search engines to collect unstructured posts, messages, searches, updates, and tweets from the users of social media sites and uses these data to predict influenza patterns ahead of the Centers for Disease Control and Prevention (CDC) and to strengthen public health preparedness. Similarly, the Street Bump app relies on ubiquitous motion detectors which are available in many citizens' smartphones to map out potholes on Boston's roads with almost no time delay without the need for city workers to patrol the streets. It seems that these digital devices are catching every "man on the spot" (Hayek, 1945: 524) and placing them on the screen.

In this way, digital societies may then introduce a *non-market information aggregation mechanism* as the alternative to the conventional market mechanism and it may be even more direct and immediate. With a degree of optimism, one can ask whether the information will be aggregated in such a way that we can envision a future without auto accidents and traffic jams, when human fallibility is kept in check (Picone, Amoretti, & Zanichelli, 2012). In the same vein, would the cobweb model instability due to misalignments of production with lags be avoided in the future? From the current majors of PhD students, can the education system be quickly informed that a decade from now college teachers in humanities will be in short supply (Ehrenberg et al., 2009)? Would various environment, energy and health issues related to poor decisions, due to near-sightedness constraints or the ignorance of possible social and individual consequences, be managed better in a growing digital society?

Needless to say, the list of the above issues above can indefinitely extend, and they have been broached in the recent literature on big data (Morozov, 2014; Harford, 2014; Hargittai, 2015). From the viewpoint of behavioral economics, what concerns us is the possibility or the limitation of non-market information aggregation mechanisms with big data. The essence of Hayek (1945) on information aggregation involves two major functions: *information pooling* and *processing*. Both introduce some difficulties which have concerned Hayek and his contemporaries, but are now equally troubling the big data theorists and pragmatists.

On information pooling, Hayek has emphatically pointed out the tacitness of knowledge (Hayek, 1937, 1952). It is fundamentally difficult to make tacit knowledge explicit. However, even though tacit knowledge is not a problem, information pooling requires individuals' cooperation. On this, Hayek (1945) states

> the knowledge of the particular circumstances of time and place. It is with respect to this that practically every individual has some advantage over all others in that he possesses unique information of which beneficial use might be made, but of which can be made only if the decisions depending on it are left to him or are made with his *active cooperation*.
>
> *(Ibid.: 521–2; italics added)*

The required active cooperation has challenged the incubation of many big data ideas. For example, it has been documented that one problem for BinCam, as a solution to waste control and recycling enhancement, is that engagement with social media remains low (Comber et al., 2013). In economics, this issue is known as a *thin market*. The performance of the prediction market, an idea directly inherited from Hayek (1945), is known to be adversely affected by market thinness (Berg et al., 2008). From a statistical viewpoint, we do not demand that the whole population or a very large sample serve as the foundation of decisions, but small samples may introduce biasedness, which can ruin the performance of prediction markets as well as big data intelligence.

Assume that all people are cooperative: they join social media and carry smartphones. Then ubiquitous computing,[9] as demonstrated in Figure 18.2 (left panel), will paint a picture of the world with immense detail. In this sense, big data is the modern equivalent of a microscope. When the amount of information is measured by zettabytes or even yottabytes, we may actually be totally blind unless some automated procedure can mine the hidden gold for us. However, in Web 2.0, the main data type is texts, images or videos, and not just numbers. Intelligent algorithms are required to recognize, interpret, and process opinions, attitudes, sentiments, emotions, and implications inherent in natural language, images, and videos. The current state of the art with its reliance on searching for key terms, phases, or geometric patterns is, at best, rather limited for us to access the knowledge inside the box.

Crowd matching

While human nature remains a long-standing debatable issue in philosophy, from Aristotle, Plato, Mencius, and Xunzi to Thomas Hobbes and Jean-Jacques Rousseau, the recent interdisciplinary scientific studies on prosocial behavior tend to suggest that it would be oversimplified or even misleading to assume that humans are selfish (Schroeder & Graziano, 2015). Even those who hold opposite views may agree that prosocial behavior can be enhanced or corrupted through different social institutions or social structures. It is, therefore, interesting to inquire about the possible impacts of digital societies on prosocial behavior.

Earlier we mentioned that digital societies may enhance the quality of decisions by providing more "smart" information aggregation (pooling and processing). This implies that this "smart" information aggregation mechanism may enhance *pairing* or *grouping* decisions; after all, the other side of the information aggregation mechanism is the *matching mechanism*. Digital societies have already helped match demand and supply through a large pool of products with the aid of online customer reviews (see the second section). In economics, matching theory starts from dating (Gale & Shapley, 1962) and, over the last two decades, we have seen that online dating has revolutionized these "economic" activities by providing participants with more opportunities to access potential partners. As we have mentioned in the second and third sections, whether this will facilitate decision making depends on how efficiently information is aggregated. If the information to be pooled is not overwhelming and hence can be effectively processed, it may be possible that online dating can help participants make better decisions (Hitsch, Hortaçsu, & Ariely, 2010; Rosenfeld & Thomas, 2012; Konrad, 2015).

In this section, we consider a more general form of matching—matching a team or a crowd since this is a place where we probably can closely observe how people cooperate, sometimes altruistically or voluntarily, to achieve some common goals that could not be realized alone. The three most shining demonstrations are *peer production*, *crowdsourcing* and *crowdfunding* (Figure 18.3).

Peer production refers to the activity whereby individuals voluntarily collaborate to produce knowledge, goods, and services. This form of production, distinguished from production activity through markets and hierarchies, is the third alternative of the production paradigm (Benkler, 2002, 2006). The work, from the time of its inception by some initiators, can be constantly modified and extended by a dynamically evolving self-organizing team comprised of volunteer workers who have no binding commitments to the team. This emerging production paradigm in digital societies, also known as *digitally enabled peer production*, has been an important source of value or wealth creation and public goods provision in many domains, such as open source

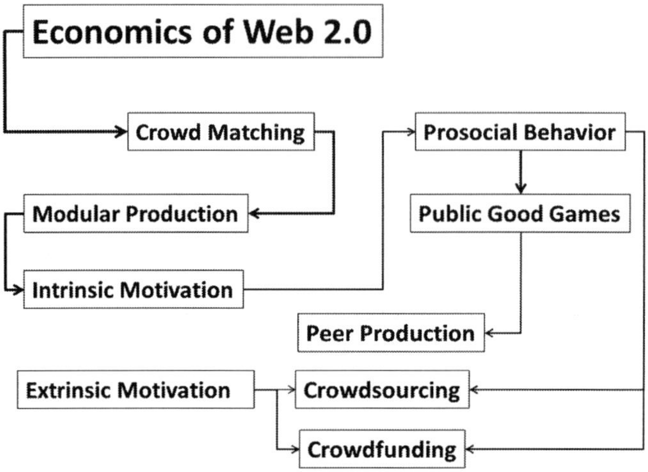

Figure 18.3 Prosocial behavior in the form of the digital society

software projects, citizen science (Bonney et al., 2014; Franzoni & Sauermann, 2014), library science, politics, education, journalism, and culture. It is still not clear as to the limit of the applicability of digitally enabled peer production in other domains (Kreiss, Finn, & Turner, 2011), but a required key element is *modular production* or, simply, *modularity*.

Modular production is an idea largely ignored in mainstream economics, although it can be long traced back to Herbert Simon (Simon, 1962), specifically, in his story on the competition between two watchmakers, Tempus and Hora. A technical formulation of the modular economy and modular production is given in Chen and Chie (2007), Chie and Chen (2013), and Chie and Chen (2014). Technically speaking, a production process is referred to as modular production if it can be modeled by a *context-free grammar*. By a context-free grammar, each work (product), depending on the grammar (technology), and the current alphabets (materials, knowledge, or expertise), can be reshaped and extended; Wikipedia provides such an example. Even though the work is completed, it can still be reused as a module of another more synergetic work or product; open source software projects are cases in point.

Modular production has already existed long before the advent of digital societies. What digital societies have done is to facilitate modular production by efficiently matching various modules distributively owned by different volunteers. In terms of the context-free grammar, the minimal module is an alphabet, which indicates that the threshold for volunteer work can be low. In other words, digital societies allow peers with skills for specific modular tasks to be easily matched in various public good projects, and the match can be so fine that even the minimum threshold required for the corresponding public good, perceived as a threshold public good game, is low.

The access to a great diversity of public good games helps the formation of intrinsic motivation for a heterogeneous population of agents, whereas the low threshold, acting in a form of "even a penny will help", promotes volunteerism. The latter is the familiar *legitimization of paltry donations*, which satisfy the donor's need for self-presentation of being helpful and socially responsible (Shearman & Yoo, 2007; Guéguen, 2013). In sum, digital societies enable efficient matches of intrinsically motivated volunteers; hence, it helps promote prosocial behavior. Our theoretical explanation above is basically consistent with the experimental findings of Algan et al. (2013), who showed that reciprocity and social image are both strong motives for sustaining cooperation in peer production environments, while altruism is not.

The second form is crowdsourcing (Figure 18.3). Crowdsourcing is a term coined in 2006 by Jeff Howe (Howe, 2006, 2008), who defined it as the outsourcing of a function or task traditionally done by a designated agent to an undefined network of laborers carried out by a company or a similar institution through an open call for solutions over the Internet or social media. Crowdsourcing is, therefore, another collaborative model of production which involves prosocial behavior. However, it is different from peer production in its property regime. As mentioned earlier, peer production is mainly used to produce public goods or commons, such as Wikipedia or open source software; however, in crowdsourcing, both inputs and outputs are governed by proprietary or contractual models. Some frequently cited examples of crowdsourcing are Amazon Mechanical Turk, an online labor market (Paolacci, Chandler & Ipeirotis, 2010), and reCAPTCHA, which uses optically scanned book fragments as gateways to secure services (von Ahn et al., 2008).

Crowdsourcing is not new to economists. This development is in the vein of the market mechanism as the efficient use of knowledge (Hayek, 1945). Before the advent of Web 2.0, we had already seen two stages of its early development in economics, namely, experimental markets and prediction markets (Arrow et al., 2008). The idea of creating a *market* such that knowledge distributed over the crowd can be used (pooled and processed) has become the idea of creating a *platform* to do that. In fact, the prediction market can be considered as the earliest form of crowdsourcing. Since the middle 2000s, we have experienced the quick development and evolution of various forms of crowdsourcing. Partially because of this trend, even the prediction market has evolved into its second generation, namely, the idea market (Slamka, Jank, & Skiera, 2012).

Working a crowd begins with constructing a crowd; the motivation for participating in a crowd becomes an important issue. On this issue, while extrinsic motivation is found to be crucial in many crowdsourced domains, intrinsic motivation or the internalized extrinsic motivation is also found to be key driver of the formation of crowds (Brabham, 2010; Füller, 2010; Roth, Brabham, & Lemoine, 2015). From these studies, people participating in crowdsourcing are *not just for the money* (Frey, 1997). Some are participating for the love of the underlying community, for the enjoyment of being jointly creative, or, more generally, for the pleasure of being part of the process of a participatory culture. Through the Schelling–Axelrod model (Axelrod, 1997), we know that homophily, in the form of sharing some common interests, may play an important role in giving a cohesive structure to the formed culture and community. Therefore, crowdsourcing shows again how the proliferation of the Internet, the explosion of social media, and matching technologies have promoted prosocial behavior, accompanied by a cultural formation process.

The last form is crowdfunding (Figure 18.3). Crowdfunding platforms allow the kind of search and assembly of information that can bring up crowds of otherwise diverse investors with similar focuses to jointly turn entrepreneurs' ideas into a reality. Examples of crowdfunding platforms include Kickstarter, Indiegogo, RocketHub, Fundable, Crowdfunder, etc. The starters of small and medium-sized businesses may find it easier to succeed through the kind of communication and search that those platforms provide. As Robert Shiller pointed out, crowdfunding draws on modern behavioral economics (Shiller, 2013). It is "based on concepts of motivating drives in people, on their ability to respond to incentives, and the diversity of types of people that may be brought together creatively in enterprises" (Ibid.: 80).

The two essential characteristics which enhance prosocial behavior in peer production also appear here, namely, fine modularity and low threshold. Some fundraisers modularize their project at a fine level and rank the modules by the required investment, from moderate size to pocket money. This division helps distinguish investors not only by their shared vision but also by their financial affordability. Hence, just like the paltry contribution seen in peer production, the threshold required for a crowdfunded project can be low. For example, in Kiva, a non-profit micro-loans organization with a mission to connect people through lending to alleviate poverty, one can loan merely $25 to a seamstress in Guatemala or to a pig farmer in Senegal.

Crowdfunding differs from the conventional capital markets in the sense that through Web 2.0 it is embedded with a kind of participatory culture. A number of studies have already noticed the significance of intrinsic motivation to invest in crowdfunded projects. For example, Gerber, Hui, and Kuo (2012) found that in addition to anticipated extrinsic motivators, such as securing funding (for creators) and consuming products and experiences (for backers), participants were also motivated by social interactions realized through crowdfunding platforms, such as the strengthening commitment to an idea through feedback and feelings of connectedness to a community with similar interests and ideals. Beaulieu and Sarker (2013) conducted a discourse analysis of the contents over the course of a crowdfunding campaign. They argued that understanding the creation of meaning is important because this meaning inspires backers not only to contribute financially to a given project but also to share the project within their own social networks. The intrinsic motivation may become even more important when we consider a special type of crowdfunding, namely, micro-crowdfunding or civic crowdfunding, in which a crowdfunding concept is used to encourage a community to act to solve critical social problems (Davies, 2015).

Concluding remarks

In this chapter, we provide probably the first comprehensive reflection on digital societies, or so-called smart societies, from the viewpoint of behavioral economics. What particularly concerns us is whether smartness, if there is any, can be translated into goodness at both the individual level and the social level. We basically address two issues along these lines. First, we ask whether a "smart" society can actually enhance the quality of individual decisions, either through more information or better nudges. We point out that, although a "smart" society is strong in terms of information pooling as manifested by big data, it is not immediately clear whether this vastly pooled information, particularly in the form of transcripts, audio, or video data, can be efficiently processed.

Therefore, based on Simon's economics of attention (Simon, 1971), the net gain of a "smart" society is not guaranteed to be positive, and hence the concern with the information overload or choice overload hypothesis remains or is amplified. When that happens, we should be alerted to the situation where a "smart" society may not make decision making easier, but harder. This is mainly because people are more easily exposed to an information-rich environment, while at the same time the intelligence tools which can help them grasp the essence of the big pile of various types of data may not keep pace with the speed of pooling. Facing this conundrum, agents may have heuristics to which they can resort to circumvent this situation. Some of these heuristics can be fast and frugal, but some can be herding and biased. While it is now a trend for people to keep on watching the dynamics of everything from their smartphones as if they were checking for the presence of any arbitrage condition, we have yet to see up to when they will find that the leisure which they have given up for this "work" may not be worth the effort made. However, under limited attention, smartphones and the "smart" society can cause the entire society to become addicted to this "diligent" social norm and may have adverse effects on the quality of life and degree of happiness (Lohmann, 2015).

From the social viewpoint, we notice that a "smart" society is strong in its matching mechanism. In fact, this enhancement is not simply due to technological feasibility, but more to the participation of humans (the crowd). Web 2.0 enables agents to self-organize through search and discovery. This function is also provided by the conventional market (Hayek, 1945), but Web 2.0 makes this function even more powerful, thanks to various platforms and social media. As a result, it makes Adam Smith's invisible hand bigger; in fact, it is the search and discovery process initiated and driven by humans that modularizes production to achieve a finer division of labor and then pack the platforms in a well-structured manner.

Hence, on the one hand, this enhanced matching mechanism helps people to discover what they are initially endowed with in terms of labor, skills, and talents; some of these "advantages" naturally become part of their intrinsic motivation to participate in market activities, a part to which mainstream economics has paid less attention. On the other hand, since the matches are flexible and adaptive with size, this facilitates the formation of a crowd. This promotes prosocial behavior because the contribution from each participant can be small, and the aspired intrinsic motivation is sufficient to incentivize such size of contribution. Peer production, crowdsourcing, and crowdfunding can all or partially be seen as a consequence of prosocial behavior.

In sum, digital societies will neither create a frictionless economy nor an omniscient agent, and that in fact enhances the relevance of behavioral economics. It provides us with better technological support to design various nudges or choice architectures, and a more flexible space to design field or policy experiments to realize various prosocial behaviors by coordinating good incentives. In his forward to the second edition of Axelrod's book, *The Evolution of Cooperation*, Richard Dawkins began with "THIS IS A BOOK OF OPTIMISM. But it is a believable optimism, more satisfying than naïve, unrealistic hopes of pie in the sky (or rapture in the revolution)" (Axelrod, 2006: xi; capitals, original). Since Axelrod (1984), game theory has constantly shown that social networks or social structures that facilitate prosocial behavior do exist and can emerge from network evolutions.[10] Digital societies have demonstrated their great potential to form such social networks.

Acknowledgments

The first author is grateful for the research support in the form of the Ministry of Science and Technology (MOST) Grant, MOST 103-2410-H-004-009-MY3.

Notes

1 Since the term "smart society" is often used with the term "digital society", in this chapter they shall be used interchangeably. To be exact, the reader should keep in mind that smart society used in this chapter can be given quotation marks, that is, "smart" society, due to the existence of both optimism and skepticism toward the future of digital societies. Therefore, with this understanding, we do not intend to make a further distinction between those digital societies which are considered to be smart and those which are not.

2 The undescribable or complex event has been an idea well established in the incomplete contract literature (Chen, 1992; Al-Najjar, Anderlini, & Felli, 2006; Kunimoto, 2008, 2010).

3 The second-best theory was first formulated by Lipsey and Lancaster (1956). It says that if we are away from the optimal conditions on more than one dimension, then satisfying some optimization conditions, but not all of them, is not guaranteed to be superior to a situation in which fewer conditions are fulfilled. For a survey, the interested reader is referred to Lipsey (2007).

4 See Chen (2015), part VI, for a comprehensive treatment of this subject.

5 The reader, however, should be reminded of some mixtures of the results in the literature on these two overload hypotheses, namely, information overload and choice overload. The interested reader is referred to the existing survey articles (Eppler & Mengis, 2004; Scheibehenne, Greifeneder & Todd, 2010).
6 O'Reilly & Battelle (2009) give a systematic guide to the origin and the development of Web 2.0.
7 It is important to emphasize that in some cases, such as the Environmental Teapot, BimCam, smart mirror (Table 18.1), the processed information or output signals are not just passively used to help decision makers make a decision; it may even actively persuade or "coerce" them to behave in a certain way. This design involves the elements of both social norms and social preferences to place decision-makers in a more social-awareness decision frame. This kind of design is also known as *persuasive technology* (Fogg, 2002; Hamari, Koivisto, & Pakkanen, 2014).
8 More generally, any object can be attached to a digital sensor to constantly collect surrounding information, from temperature, humidity and chemical particles to pedestrian intensity, mass psychology and public conversations. All local information can be pooled in a platform, also known as the *Internet of Things* (Westerlund, Leminen, & Rajahonka, 2014), to get a grasp of the global environment.
9 The term *ubiquitous computing* was first introduced by Mark Weiser in 1989, to distinguish it from conventional desktop computing (Weiser, 1991). For recent developments more related to the scope of this chapter, the interested reader is referred to Kinder-Kurlanda & Nihan (2015).
10 For a literature review of the pile of studies, the interested reader is referred to Namatame & Chen (2015).

Bibliography

Ackerman, E. (2013). Google gets in your face. IEEE Spectrum, 50(1), 26–9.

Algan, Y., Benkler, Y., Morell, M., & Hergueux, J. (2013). Cooperation in a peer production: Economy experimental evidence from Wikipedia. In Workshop on Information Systems and Economics, Milan, Italy. Avialable at: www.parisschoolofeconomics.eu/IMG/pdf/hergueuxpaper-2.pdf.

Al-Najjar, N., Anderlini, L., & Felli, L. (2006). Undescribable events. Review of Economic Studies, 73(4), 849–68.

Arrow, K. J., Forsythe, R., Gorham, M., Hahn, R., Hanson, R., Ledyard, J. O., Levmore, S., Litan, R., Milgrom, P., Nelson, F. D., Neumann, G. R., Ottaviani, M., Schelling, T. C., Shiller, R. J., Smith, V. L., Snowberg, E., Sunstein, C. R., Tetlock, P. C., Tetlock, P. E., Varian, H. R., Wolfers, J., & Zitzewitz, E. (2008). The promise of prediction markets. Science, 320(5878), 877–8.

Aud, M., Abbott, C., Tyrer, H., Neelgund, R., & Shriniwar, U. (2010). Developing a sensor system to detect falls and summon assistance. Journal of Gerontological Nursing, 36(7), 8–12.

Axelrod, R. (1984). The Evolution of Cooperation. Basic Books, New York.

Axelrod, R. (1997). The dissemination of culture: A model with local convergence and global polarization. Journal of Conflict Resolution, 41(2), 203–26.

Axelrod, R. (2006). The Evolution of Cooperation. Basic Books, New York. Second Edition.

Bauerlein, M. (2008). The Dumbest Generation: How the Digital Age Stupefies Young Americans and Jeopardizes Our Future (Or, Don't Trust Anyone under 30). Penguin.

Beaulieu, T., & Sarker, S. (2013). Discursive meaning creation in crowdfunding: A socio-material perspective. Proceedings on the 34th International Conference on Information Systems. Available at: http://aisel.aisnet.org/icis2013/proceedings/ResearchInProgress/80/.

Benkler, Y. (2002). Coase's penguin, or Linux and the "Nature of the Firm". Yale Law Journal, 112, 369–446.

Benkler, Y. (2006). The Wealth of Networks: How Social Production Transforms Markets and Freedom. Yale University Press.

Berg, J., Forsythe, R., Nelson, F., & Rietz, T. (2008). Results from a dozen years of election futures markets research. In: C. Plott, & V. Smith (Eds.), Handbook of Experimental Economics Results 1, Elsevier, 742–51.

Boettke, P. (2000) (Ed.). Socialism and the Market: The Socialist Calculation Debate Revisited. Routledge.

Bonney, R., Shirk, J., Phillips, T., Wiggins, A., Ballard, H., Miller-Rushing, A., & Parrish, J. (2014). Next steps for citizen science. Science, 343(6178), 1436–7.

Brabham, D. (2010). Moving the crowd at Threadless: Motivations for participation in a crowdsourcing application. Information, Communication & Society, 13(8), 1122–45.

Chatterjee, P. (2001). Online reviews: Do consumers use them? In: M. Gilly, & J. Meyers-Levy (Eds), Advances in Consumer Research Volume 28, Association for Consumer Research, 129–34.
Chen, S.-H. (1992). On the complexity in adaptive economic systems: The relation between RBS and PDP in adaptive economic systems. Doctoral dissertation, University of California, Los Angeles.
Chen, S.-H. (2015). Agent-Based Computational Economics: How the Idea Originated and Where it is Going. Routledge.
Chen, S.-H., & Chie, B.-T. (2007). Modularity, product innovation, and consumer satisfaction: An agent-based approach. In: H. Yin, P. Tino, E. Corchado, W. Byrne, & X. Yao (Eds.), Intelligent Data Engineering and Automated Learning, Lecture Notes in Computer Science (LNCS 4881), Springer, 1053–62.
Chen, Y.-C., Shang, R.-A., & Kao, C.-Y. (2009). The effects of information overload on consumers' subjective state towards buying decisions in the internet shopping environment. Electronic Commerce Research and Applications, 8(1), 48–58.
Chie, B.-T., & Chen, S.-H. (2013). Non-price competition in a modular economy: An agent-based computational model. Economica Politica: Journal of Analytical and Institutional Economics, 30(3), 273–300.
Chie, B.-T., & Chen, S.-H. (2014). Competition in a new industrial economy: Toward an agent-based economic model of modularity. Administrative Sciences, 4(3), 192–218.
Comber, R., & Thieme, A. (2013). Designing beyond habit: Opening space for improved recycling and food waste behaviors through processes of persuasion, social influence and aversive affect. Personal and Ubiquitous Computing, 17(6), 1197–210.
Comber, R., Thieme, A., Rafiev, A., Taylor, N., Krämer, N., & Olivier, P. (2013). BinCam: Designing for engagement with Facebook for behavior change. In Human-Computer Interaction-INTERACT 2013. Springer, 99–115.
Cross, J. (1973). A stochastic learning model of economic behavior. Quarterly Journal of Economics, 87(2), 239–66.
Davies, R. (2015). Three provocations for civic crowdfunding. Information, Communication & Society, 18(3), 342–55.
Ehrenberg, R., Zuckerman, H., Groen, J., & Brucker, S. (2009). Educating Scholars: Doctoral Education in the Humanities. Princeton University Press.
Ellsberg, D. (1961). Risk, ambiguity, and the Savage axioms. Quarterly Journal of Economics, 75, 643–69.
Eppler, M., & Mengis, J. (2004). The concept of information overload: A review of literature from organization science, accounting, marketing, MIS, and related disciplines. The Information Society, 20(5), 325–44.
Fogg, B. (2002). Persuasive Technology: Using Computers to Change what we Think and Do. Morgan Kaufmann.
Franzoni, C., & Sauermann, H. (2014). Crowd science: The organization of scientific research in open collaborative projects. Research Policy, 43(1), 1–20.
Frey, B. S. (1997). Not Just for the Money: An Economic Theory of Personal Motivation. Edward Elgar.
Füller, J. (2010). Refining virtual co-creation from a consumer perspective. California Management Review, 52, 98–122.
Gale, D., & Shapley, L. (1962). College admissions and the stability of marriage. American Mathematical Monthly, 69(1), 9–15.
Gerber, E., Hui, J., & Kuo, P. (2012). Crowdfunding: Why people are motivated to post and fund projects on crowdfunding platforms. In Proceedings of the International Workshop on Design, Influence, and Social Technologies: Techniques, Impacts and Ethics.
Gigerenzer, G. (2007). Gut Feelings: The Intelligence of the Unconscious. Penguin Books.
Gigerenzer, G., & Gaissmaier, W. (2011). Heuristic decision making. Annual Review of Psychology, 62, 451–82.
Ginsberg, J., Mohebbi, M., Patel, R., Brammer, L., Smolinski, M., & Brilliant, L. (2009). Detecting influenza epidemics using search engine query data. Nature, 457(7232), 1012–14.
Guéguen, N. (2013). "Even a donation one time in your life will help ...": The effect of the legitimizing paltry contribution technique on blood donation. Transfusion and Apheresis Science, 49(3), 489–93.
Hamari, J., Koivisto, J., & Pakkanen, T. (2014). Do persuasive technologies persuade? A review of empirical studies. In: A. Spagnolli, L. Chittaro, & L. Gamberini (Eds.), Persuasive Technology, Springer, 118–36.

Harford, T. (2014). Big data: Are we making a big mistake? Financial Times, 28, 2014.
Hargittai, E. (2015). Is bigger always better? Potential biases of big data derived from social network sites. ANNALS of the American Academy of Political and Social Science, 659(1), 63–76.
Hayek, F. A. (1937). Economics and knowledge. Economica, 4, 33–54.
Hayek, F. A. (1945). The uses of knowledge in society. American Economic Review, 35(4), 519–30.
Hayek, F. A. (1952). The Sensory Order: An Inquiry into the Foundations of Theoretical Psychology. University of Chicago Press.
Hirshleifer, J., & Riley, J. (1979). The analytics of uncertainty and information: An expository survey. Journal of Economic Literature, 17, 1375–421.
Hitsch, G. J., Hortaçsu, A., & Ariely, D. (2010). Matching and sorting in online dating. American Economic Review, 100(1), 130–63.
Howe, J. (2006). The rise of crowdsourcing. Wired Magazine, 14(6), 1–4.
Howe, J. (2008). Crowdsourcing: How the Power of the Crowd is Driving the Future of Business. Random House.
Iyengar, S., & Lepper, M. (2000). When choice is demotivating: Can one desire too much of a good thing? Journal of Personality and Social Psychology, 79(6), 995–1006.
Jacoby, J., Speller, D., & Berning, C. (1974). Brand choice behavior as a function of information load: Replication and extension. Journal of Consumer Research, 1, 33–42.
Jacoby, J., Speller, D., & Kohn, C. (1974). Brand choice behavior as a function of information load. Journal of Marketing Research, 11(1), 63–9.
Keen, A. (2007). The Cult of the Amateur: How Today's Internet is Killing our Culture. Doubleday.
Kinder-Kurlanda, K., & Nihan, C. (2015) (Eds.). Ubiquitous Computing in the Workplace: What Ethical Issues? An Interdisciplinary Perspective. Springer.
Kirkpatrick, R. (2014). A conversation with Robert Kirkpatrick, Director of United Nations Global Pulse. SAIS Review of International Affairs, 34(1), 3–8.
Konrad, K. (2015). Affection, speed dating and heartbreaking. Journal of Population Economics, 28(1), 159–72.
Kreiss, D., Finn, M., & Turner, F. (2011). The limits of peer production: Some reminders from Max Weber for the network society. New Media & Society, 13(2), 243–59.
Kunimoto, T. (2008). Indescribability and asymmetric information at the contracting stage. Economics Letters, 99(2), 367–70.
Kunimoto, T. (2010). Indescribability and its irrelevance for contractual incompleteness. Review of Economic Design, 14(3–4), 271–89.
Lee, B.- K., & Lee, W.-N. (2004). The effect of information overload on consumer choice quality in an on-line environment. Psychology & Marketing, 21(3), 159–83.
Leinweber, D. (2009). Nerds on Wall Street: Math, Machines and Wired Markets. John Wiley and Sons.
Leinweber, D., & Arnott, R. (1995). Quantitative and computational innovation in investment management. Journal of Portfolio Management, 21(2), 8–15.
Li, M., & Vitányi, P. (2009). An Introduction to Kolmogorov Complexity and Its Applications. Springer.
Lipsey, R. (2007). Reflections on the general theory of second best at its golden jubilee. International Tax and Public Finance, 14(4), 349–64.
Lipsey, R., & Lancaster, K. (1956). The general theory of second best. Review of Economic Studies, 24(1), 11–32.
Lohmann, S. (2015). Information technologies and subjective well-being: Does the Internet raise material aspirations? Oxford Economic Papers, 67(3), 740–59.
Marres, N. (2012). The Environmental Teapot and other loaded household objects: Reconnecting the politics of technology, issues and things. In: P. Harvey, E. Casella, G. Evans, H. Knox, C. McLean, E. Silva, N. Thoburn, & K. Woodward (Eds.), Objects and Materials: A Routledge Companion. Routledge.
McCall, J. (1970). Economics of information and job search. Quarterly Journal of Economics, 84 (1), 113–26.
Morozov, E. (2014). To Save Everything, Click Here: The Folly of Technological Solutionism. Public Affairs.
Namatame, A., & Chen, S.-H. (2015). Agent Based Modelling and Network Dynamics. Oxford University Press.
O'Reilly, T., & Battelle, J. (2009). Web Squared: Web 2.0 Five Years On. O'Reilly Media.

Pantano, E., & Nacarato, G. (2010). Entertainment in retailing: The influences of advanced technologies. Journal of Retailing and Consumer Services, 17(3), 200–4.
Paolacci, G., Chandler, J., & Ipeirotis, P. (2010). Running experiments on Amazon Mechanical Turk. Judgment and Decision Making, 5(5), 411–19.
Park, D., & Lee, J. (2009). eWOM overload and its effect on consumer behavioral intention depending on consumer involvement. Electronic Commerce Research and Applications, 7(4), 386–98.
Picone, M., Amoretti, M., & Zanichelli, F. (2012). A decentralized smartphone-based traffic information system. In IEEE Intelligent Vehicles Symposium (IV), IEEE, 523–8.
Ronayne, D. (2015). Price comparison websites. Working Paper. Coventry: University of Warwick. Department of Economics. Warwick economics research papers series (TWERPS), 2015(1056).
Rosenfeld, M., & Thomas, R. (2012). Searching for a mate: The rise of the Internet as a social intermediary. American Sociological Review, 77(4), 523–47.
Roth, Y., Brabham, D., & Lemoine, J. (2015). Recruiting individuals to a crowdsourcing community: Applying motivational categories to an ad copy test. In: F. Garrigos-Simon, I. Gil-Pechuán, & S. Estelles-Miguel (Eds.), Advances in Crowdsourcing, Springer, 15–31.
Scheibehenne, B., Greifeneder, R., & Todd, P. (2010). Can there ever be too many options? A meta-analytic review of choice overload. Journal of Consumer Research, 37(3), 409–25.
Schroder, H., Driver, M., & Streufert, S. (1967). Human Information Processing. Holt, Rinehart and Winston.
Schroeder, D., & Graziano, W. (2015). The field of prosocial behavior: An introduction and overview. In: D. Schroeder, & W. Graziano (Eds.), The Oxford Handbook of Prosocial Behavior, Oxford University Press, 3–34.
Schwartz, A. (2012). Street Bump: An app that automatically tells the city when you drive over potholes. Fast Company.
Schwartz, B. (2003). The Paradox of Choice: Why More is Less. Harper Perennial.
Shackle, G. (1968). Uncertainty in Economics and other Reflections. Cambridge University Press.
Shearman, S., & Yoo, J. (2007). "Even a penny will help!": Legitimization of paltry donation and social proof in soliciting donation to a charitable organization. Communication Research Reports, 24(4), 271–82.
Shieh, W.-Y., Guu, T.-T., & Liu, A.-P. (2013). A portable smart belt design for home-based gait parameter collection. In: Proceedings of IEEE Conference on Computational Problem-Solving (ICCP), IEEE Press, 16–19.
Shiller, R. (2013). Finance contributing to the good society. Business Economics, 48(1), 77–80.
Simon, H. (1955). A behavioral model of rational choice. Quarterly Journal of Economics, 69(1), 99–118.
Simon, H. (1956). Rational choice and the structure of the environment. Psychological Review, 63(2), 129–38.
Simon, H. (1962). The architecture of complexity. Proceedings of the American Philosophical Society, 106(6), 467–82.
Simon, H. (1971). Designing organizations for an information-rich world. In: M. Greenberger (Ed.), Computers, Communications and the Public Interest, Johns Hopkins University Press, 37–72.
Slamka, C., Jank, W., & Skiera, B. (2012). Second-generation prediction markets for information aggregation: A comparison of payoff mechanisms. Journal of Forecasting, 31, 469–89.
Smith, M. (2002). The impact of shopbots on electronic markets. Journal of the Academy of Marketing Science, 30(4), 446–54.
Soares de Mello, J. C., & Namorado Clímaco, J. C. (2015). Preface to the special issue on decision support systems. International Transactions in Operational Research, 22(2), 203.
Thaler, R., & Sunstein, C. (2008). Nudge: Improving Decisions about Health, Wealth, and Happiness. Penguin.
Tversky, A., & Kahneman, D. (1974). Judgment under uncertainty: Heuristics and biases. Science, 185(4157), 1124–31.
von Ahn, L., Maurer, B., McMillen, C., Abraham, D., & Blum, M. (2008). reCAPTCHA: Human-based character recognition via web security measures. Science, 321(5895), 1465–8.
Weiser, M. (1991). The computer for the twenty-first century. Scientific American, 265(3), 94–104.
Westerlund, M., Leminen, S., & Rajahonka, M. (2014). Designing business models for the internet of things. Technology Innovation Management Review, 4(7), 5–14.
Wurman, R. (2001). Information Anxiety 2. New Riders Publishers.

19

BEHAVIOURAL MACROECONOMICS

Time, optimism and animal spirits

Michelle Baddeley

Introduction

The 2007–8 financial crisis precipitated growing disillusionment with standard macroeconomic tools and models. The most influential macroeconomic models in policy terms are the dynamic stochastic general equilibrium (DSGE) models which assume forward looking agents facing random events within a general equilibrium framework focusing on complete sets of interacting markets, as opposed to a partial equilibrium approach analysing one market at a time. Of the two forms in which DSGE models are generally seen, monetarist/neoclassical versus New Keynesian versions, both are dependent on narrow conceptions of economic behaviour and rationality, and both are founded on rigorous micro-foundations. Neoclassical and monetarist models assume perfect competition in smooth running markets with many buyers and sellers, flexible prices, perfect information and market-clearing—and these assumptions are applied to labour markets as well as goods markets. In this world, unemployment is voluntary, reflecting a worker's choice about working only when the equilibrium real wage is large enough for workers to give up their valuable leisure time. Traditionally, Keynesian models focused on involuntary unemployment and sticky prices and New Keynesian models blend these insights with a softening of some of the strict assumptions associated with neoclassical and monetarist models to allow for imperfect information, sticky prices and transaction costs, including menu costs—and via these routes allow for involuntary unemployment: imperfectly competitive wage bargaining generates labour markets in which the real wage set by negotiations between employers and insiders (and their unions) is too high to clear the labour market. Involuntary unemployment of outsiders excluded from wage bargaining is the consequence of this insider-driven wage bargaining process.

While New Keynesian models and conclusions fit better with what we see in the world around us than neoclassical and monetarist models, they are nonetheless founded on similar conventions about behaviour, made mainly for empirical tractability. Via the representative agents hypothesis, the macroeconomy can be simplified to an analysis of two main groups of rational maximising economic agents: workers/householders, selling labour and buying goods and services; and employers/firms, selling goods and services and buying labour. If the average behaviour of agents is perfectly rational, then the model can be operationalised by assuming that all agents act as if they are identical. The task of understanding a complex macroeconomy can then be simplified to the task of understanding just two types of rational and selfish optimisers, where rationality is defined narrowly in terms of the rational expectations hypothesis. Rational agents (workers and firms) use all currently available information, respond quickly to news, and do not make systematic mistakes—if they make a mistake in one period of time, once that mistake is realised, they are clever enough to know not to repeat it. These models also assume that agents are forward looking optimisers, making decisions taking their whole (often infinite) lifetimes into account. Their preferences—including both discount rates and risk preference—are stable. In these models, people behave as if they are mathematical machines, processing inputs of information to generate outputs in the form of decisions: a firm maximises profits and minimises costs and this drives their investment and production decisions; workers and households maximise utility—and this drives their decisions about work/leisure and consumption/savings—for example, in deciding whether or not to work, they are driven by forward looking judgements about the relative benefits of the real wage they can earn from working versus the utility they can derive from consuming leisure. In this view of the world, work is just about the monetary valuations of the opportunity cost of leisure in the form of lost wages.

These conventional models are obviously highly artificial and unrealistic—and the justification for this is that they are parsimonious abstractions that enable us to simplify the world so that we can better understand and analyse it. Whether or not these models achieve this is not the focus of this chapter—there is already a substantial literature on these methodological issues. Instead, the questions explored here are: Can behavioural economics provide more realistic foundations without losing too much in terms of theoretical and empirical tractability? And can behavioural economics offer anything more in terms of improving macroeconomic theory and policy? This chapter explores some of the ways in which insights from behavioural economics can be incorporated into a new approach to macroeconomic theory, policy, and forecasting. So far, the most promising starting steps in achieving this goal have been in the behavioural economic literature, which focuses on behavioural insights about time, optimism, and animal spirits. This chapter will explore ways in which these phenomena can be embedded into a macroeconomics framework. The chapter also explores some of the constraints facing behavioural macroeconomists, especially in terms of constructing an empirically tractable model of the interactions of different types of agents and the implications of their behaviour for the macroeconomy as a whole.

Behavioural macroeconomic theory: the state of play

A key way in which behavioural economics can offer a different approach to understanding the macroeconomy is by relaxing the standard rational expectations hypothesis, that rational agents make full use of all available information, and do not make systematic mistakes. Behavioural economics allows a broader view of rationality and, following Herbert Simon, allows that rationality can be bounded by information and cognitive constraints, giving a perspective on rationality that can be defined in a broader way than is conventional in standard economic models. Standard economic theory is founded on a substantive form of rationality: there is a substantive, objective basis to decision-making. In mainstream macroeconomics and in microfounded versions of macroeconomics described above—this comes in the form of an optimisation problem defined in terms of an objective function (e.g. utility) and a set of constraints (e.g. the household budget). Substantively rational agents optimise by maximising utility or profits using mathematical tools, for example differential calculus. In this way they can identify the objectively best solution for themselves in a mechanistic and deterministic way. Simon observed however, that economic decision-making is more likely to be characterised by a process of procedural rationality—people often making decisions in a world of fundamental uncertainty, where the information and forms of quantification required to set up decisions as an optimisation problem are neither feasible nor available. In these circumstances, people will use judgement, prior experience, intuition and gut feel to guide their decision-making (Simon, 1976; Baddeley, 2006).

Behavioural macroeconomics can use insights from behavioural economics to devise behavioural assumptions that are more consistent with softer conceptions of rationality and our intuitions about what drives human action. If behaviour in the macroeconomy is driven by wider variety of decision-making tools than those needed for rational optimisation, then the approach to macroeconomic modelling and forecasting, as well as macroeconomic policy tools, will be profoundly different, but not necessarily easier. This section outlines the key ways in which insights from behavioural economics are being used in the development of macroeconomic models and approaches, either via refinements that relax assumptions embedded into macroeconomic models, or by introducing a profoundly different approach to macroeconomic analysis which embeds socio-psychological influences alongside economic fundamentals. Key insights from behavioural economics can be embedded into macroeconomic models in a number of ways—but the literature so far has concentrated mainly on efficiency wage theory; heuristics and biases; time and risk preferences; and animal spirits.

Efficiency wage theory

Efficiency wage theory, while focused on the labour market rather than the macroeconomy as a whole, does have important macroeconomic implications in terms of labour supply–demand relationships that drive macroeconomic performance, specifically in terms of labour productivity, employment and involuntary unemployment. Efficiency wage theory allows that the role played by the real wage is more nuanced than that described in standard labour market theory in which employers pay a real wage reflecting marginal productivity of labour, with labour productivity determined by labour supplied (assuming diminishing marginal productivity of labour), capital–labour ratios and human capital investment. It is dominated by standard, non-behavioural approaches but the literature is growing to incorporate insights from behavioural economics and social psychology. For example, New Keynesian models allow for the possibility that the market-clearing wage is not necessarily the optimal wage, even for an employer: paying a higher wage can lead to proportionately greater increases in productivity and/or proportionately greater decreases in unit labour costs, and in this way paying a wage above the market-clearing wage can raise a firm's profits rather than lower them (see Katz (1986) for a comprehensive survey of efficiency wage theories and explanations). For example, Shapiro and Stiglitz (1984) show, in a world of asymmetric information, that firms will pay a wage higher than the market-clearing wage in the hope that it will discourage shirking by encouraging workers to value their jobs more highly. But Shapiro and Stiglitz also demonstrate that this can lead to a perverse consequence—if all firms in a perfectly competitive market raise their wages to discourage working shirking, then the real wage moves beyond the equilibrium level that would clear the market, generating involuntary employment in the macroeconomy, which in turn disciplines the insiders who do have a job: it is not the higher wage that dis-incentivises shirking; it is the threat of involuntary unemployment.

Behavioural economics can also expand understanding of labour markets and their impacts on macroeconomic employment, unemployment and productivity by allowing that workers face a broader range of motivations than purely extrinsic monetary rewards—there may be other extrinsic rewards, for example reciprocity and social approval. The role of exchange in a social context captures the impact of effort and loyalty, for example via gift exchange between employer and employee (e.g. see Akerlof, 1982). Behavioural economists have also explored the idea that working relationships involve trust and social norms—and these are also associated with wages above a market-clearing level—an insight that can feed into macroeconomic models. Existing behavioural research also captures the impact of worker incentives and motivations more broadly defined, linking with insights about intrinsic motivation and extrinsic incentives and their impacts on worker effort (e.g. see Kreps, 1997; Frey & Oberholzer-Gee, 1997; Bénabou & Tirole, 2006). Worker effort reflects not just the wage paid but also intrinsic rewards associated with motivation and the inherent satisfaction that can come from working in a job that is rewarding either in terms of its intrinsic rewards or in terms of its social rewards. For behavioural macroeconomics, the problem is that these insights have yet to be embedded within a full macroeconomic model.

Heuristics and biases

Instead of decision-making as the outcome of an objective, mathematical process, people use heuristics and are prone to make systematic mistakes, especially when their decisions are distorted by social influences and herding. A range of heuristics could have macroeconomic impacts. The availability heuristic, which is about people making decisions on the basis of information easy to recall rather than all relevant information, could generate disproportionate responses to short-term events, contributing to instability. The representativeness heuristic, capturing decision-making via (sometimes spurious) reference to apparently similar events, could connect to inertia, feeding into macroeconomic problems such as unemployment hysteresis for example. Anchoring and adjustment would also feed into inertia and play a role in driving herding behaviours if, for example, financial markets are driven by people anchoring their financial investment decisions around conventional valuations; for example in housing markets, buyers may anchor their willingness to pay around socially driven valuations.

Not all heuristics and biases will necessarily have negative consequences. Some cognitive biases may have positive impacts—for example: optimism bias may boost entrepreneurship ensuring higher levels of investment and production than there might have been otherwise—and this could link to animal spirits, as discussed below. Social influences including herding and social learning drive behaviour and, if other people's actions are genuinely informative, this may have positive impacts on fixed asset investment (for example, see Acemoglu, 1993). Other biases may have detrimental effects, for example if present bias, where decisions are biased towards current rewards ahead of future rewards, leads to disproportionately short-termist decisions about saving and investment.

Time and risk preferences

Standard macroeconomic models generally assume that people are substantively rational—they make their decisions via a mathematical optimising process. In this, people are assumed to be forward looking, judging the present value of future rewards using an exponential discounting process. This leads to decisions over time which are time consistent with no present bias or preference reversals, that is, people do not change their mind over time; for example if they decide in November to give up smoking on New Year's Day then they do not change their mind on New Year's Eve. The behavioural literature brings in a range of alternative assumptions about time preference, to replace the standard economic assumption of exponential discounting.[1] With quasi-hyperbolic discounting, standard discount factors are nested within a specification that allows for present bias capturing the fact that people are disproportionately impatient in the short term and disproportionately patient in the long run. This is potentially a strong link to develop in macroeconomic theory, as the discount function is an essential component of most mainstream macroeconomic models because these tend to assume that people are making decisions over long time horizons. One example of a way in which this behavioural insight can link with macroeconomic behaviour is in explaining trends in consumption, savings and investment—Laibson's "golden egg" hypothesis that people hold onto illiquid wealth and short-term borrowing simultaneously in the hope that their golden eggs will deliver positive returns in the distant future is an important insight for macroeconomics (Laibson, 1997; Harris & Laibson, 2001). Behavioural discounting functions can be embedded into otherwise conventional structural models of the macroeconomy to generate simulations of liquid/illiquid wealth, borrowings and investment, for example see Angeletos et al. (2001). This type of behavioural innovation is a relatively simple tweaking of conventional models via the addition of a present bias parameter, but whilst it is not a radical re-think, nonetheless offers some potential for development in behavioural macroeconomic theory. In the context of short-term versus long-term behavioural adaptation, one example of short-run momentum versus preference reversals in the long run is explored by De Bondt and Thaler (1985) in their analysis of market over-reaction, associated with long-term reversals and winner–loser effects. It also connects with Bernatzi and Thaler's (1995) analysis of the equity premium puzzle as a reflection of short-term myopia alongside loss aversion.

Given uncertainty, actions are driven by interplays of risk preferences and time preference, as captured in discount functions. Risk plays a less direct role in standard DSGE macroeconomic models, perhaps reflecting implicit assumptions that risk preferences are stable and therefore not a driver of macroeconomic fluctuations and/or that, in aggregate, heterogeneity of risk preferences balances out. An issue to address in behavioural macroeconomic models is the separation versus conflation of risk preference and time preference. Uncertainty is in essence about the interaction of attitudes towards risk and time. If risk attitude is about decisions taken now with unpredictable future consequences, how to separate time and risk preferences in macroeconomic models is an important question. There is a growing literature exploring these themes, for example Andreoni and Sprenger (2012, 2015) and Andersen et al. (2008) argue that time preference and risk preference are different types of preference whereas empirical/experimental evidence can appear to suggest that risk and time preference are the same thing. This interchangeability is possibly an artefact resulting from imposition of theoretical assumptions. Experimental tests are being developed that are aimed to enable researchers to separate the two, but more theoretical work is needed to unravel the difference between the two, because there will be key implications for macroeconomic theory and policy.

Risk preference has received far more attention in the financial literature—for example portfolio theory and the capital asset pricing model are constructed around expected utility theory in which risk preferences and parameters are stable and constant, with a concave utility function usually assumed, which is consistent with risk aversion. One of the problems with modern macroeconomics is that money is a veil, and specific features of financial decision-making are given no independent role follows the Modigliani–Miller theorem of financing neutrality—the corporate finance structure of a firm makes no difference to fixed asset investment decisions because the costs of different financing instruments will equilibrate given perfect capital markets. While the assumptions underlying this theorem are problematic and unrealistic, nonetheless the relevant point here is that risk could be captured within macroeconomic models in some form, by embedding a financial sector properly within macroeconomic models. In terms of behavioural insights, prospect theory perhaps has some potential to fill the gap with a more realistic model of risk, moving beyond the expected utility theory approach in which risk preferences are assumed to be stable. The pioneers are Markowitz (1952), and Kahneman and Tversky (1979) who analysed the importance of reference points when people are making decisions about risky prospects, which explains some anomalies identified in experimental evidence. It is also associated with conceptions of the fourfold pattern or risk, as more recently elucidated by Scholten and Read (2014). The fourfold pattern captures shifting risk preferences in domains of losses versus gains, and large outcomes versus small outcomes. Large outcomes are associated with risk aversion in gains and risk seeking in losses; on the other hand, small outcomes are associated with risk aversion in losses and risk seeking in gains. These shifting risk preferences cannot be explained by expected utility theory. These insights are useful in understanding real-world features of macroeconomic and financial instability; for example, as explored by Genesove and Mayer (2001) who analyse housing market instability in the context of loss aversion, consistent with prospect theory, and also explored by Bernatzi and Thaler (1995) on myopic loss aversion in the context of the equity premium puzzle, as noted above.

Prospect theory is well explored in behavioural finance, but there is currently little research done in behavioural macroeconomic modelling to capture shifting, unstable risk preferences—except via a connection with animal spirits and confidence, as discussed below.

Animal spirits, optimism and pessimism

The most developed literature in behavioural macroeconomics is the literature on animal spirits in the macroeconomy. Animal spirits are most commonly associated with John Maynard Keynes (1936), who built on a concept first introduced by the classical Greek medic and physiologist Galen. Galen understood animal spirits as drivers of action and his conception was linked to the Hippocratic division of temperaments into the four humours: choleric, melancholic, sanguine and phlegmatic—with animal spirits associated with the sanguineous humour. Galen also developed conception of animal spirits as a type of nutrient that flows through the digestive system, eventually propelling action (Costandi, 2006). Keynes's animal spirits link most easily to the sanguine temperament, which is characterised by optimism, leadership and positive action. Keynes took Galen's concept of animal spirits and used it to argue that, in a market economy, private investment is subdued by uncertainty about the future and this leads the macroeconomy into persistent periods of under-investment and involuntary unemployment. Given uncertainty, most entrepreneurs would not be persuaded by a purely mathematical business case based around net present value calculations. Animal spirits play an important role in overcoming this barrier but what Keynes meant by animal spirits is not exactly clear. There is a link with optimism and spontaneity, and in Keynes's analysis, entrepreneurs' animal spirits drive them to act, reflecting a "spontaneous urge to action", and also reflecting a "delicate balance of spontaneous optimism" (Keynes, 1936: 161–2). This spontaneity contrasts with the forward looking assumption associated with neoclassical and monetary models and therefore, animal spirits are a concept that could be linked with analyses of present bias and short-termism, as seen in behavioural discounting models.

In modern behavioural macroeconomic models, Keynes's concept of animal spirits has been simplified and mostly they are equated with business/consumer confidence and/or general psychological influences. In some behavioural macroeconomic models, they are essentially an additional source of variance. For example, Woodford (1988), and Howitt and McAfee (1992) model animal spirit cycles, in which animal spirits are exogenous random noise in a two-state Markov switching model, with switching between high/low demand states.[2] Similar insights are developed by Topol (1991) in the context of financial markets to show how animal spirits, herding, and mimetic contagion operate and affect financial decision-making, again within an approach in which behaviour is driven by statistical judgements in a world of quantifiable "Knightian risk" versus unmeasurable "Knightian uncertainty." This distinction is explored by Knight (1921) and Keynes (1921), one of the few insights on which Knight and Keynes agreed.

The problem with these approaches is the assumption that risk and uncertainty are quantifiable, yet many of the most important socio-psychological influences driving macroeconomic outcomes are not inherently quantifiable in a straightforward way. In this sense, these models are suited to a world of substantively rational agents rather than procedurally rational agents.

Are there other ways in which these influences can be captured without requiring strong assumptions about the objective and quantifiable high levels of quantification? Akerlof and Shiller (2009) describe animal spirits as a set of five generalised psychological influences with macroeconomic implications, including confidence, fairness, corruption, money illusion, and storytelling. Akerlof and Shiller's broad approach is not necessarily a faithful account of Keynes's original insights and, more importantly in terms of constructing a tractable behavioural macroeconomic model, animal spirits are defined essentially as a synonym for psychological influences (Baddeley, 2009).

Other animal spirits models grounded in an alternative heterodox approach include Dow (2011), and Dow and Dow (2011) who focus on animal spirits as drivers of action and, in a world of uncertainty, the issue of whether or not these animal spirits are rational or irrational is moot because animal spirits are context dependent and their nature and role will vary across different sectors and firms. Nonetheless, their analysis does not explore how animal spirits might be incorporated into an analytical framework that could be useful in policy-making terms.

Overall, animal spirits models have much potential to offer in the development of behavioural macroeconomic models, but need to be set within a clearer analytical structure. This can be done by using animal spirits as a link that connects emotional influences, separates time preferences from risk preferences and captures different forms of motivation. The following section develops some ideas about how animal spirits models can be incorporated in more coherent and tractable versions of behavioural macroeconomic theory.

The role of rhetoric

A complete macroeconomic theory should include not only socio-psychological influences alongside economic fundamentals but also political and institutional contexts. The political environment will play a role via politicians' rhetoric, and this rhetoric does not necessarily have a clear connection with economic fundamentals, especially if it is obfuscating rhetoric designed for political purposes rather than a genuine desire to communicate objective information to the public. For example, rhetoric about reducing deficits and debt is not necessarily accompanied by significant movement in these policy variables. Nonetheless this political rhetoric affects the macroeconomic psychological state via its impact on consumer and business confidence, animal spirits and expectations—though evidence is needed to establish if fierce austerity rhetoric from government agencies either reassures businesses and makes them more confident in building up productive capacity in expectation of smoother macroeconomic conditions ahead, or depresses private consumption and investment activity. Either way, behavioural factors and socio-economic influences will play a crucial role in transmitting political events through to the real economy via verbal and online communication and conversation. These relationships and processes are not captured within conventional macroeconomic approaches and behavioural macroeconomic models perhaps offer a solution, if some of the empirical constraints can be resolved (some of the empirical constraints are discussed below).

A behavioural macroeconomic model

The approaches outlined in the section above provide some valuable insights about the potential impact of socio-psychological influences in the macroeconomy, but building these insights convincingly into a coherent behavioural macroeconomic model is not straightforward. The key influences on individual decision-making that feed through into macroeconomic outcomes include heuristics and biases, time and risk, broader forms of motivation and incentives beyond the standard monetary incentives, and animal spirits as a proxy for personality and emotion. In addition, influences beyond the individual will have an impact—for example embedding insights about social mood can link with some of social and political influences that drive confidence among businesses and consumers, linking with insights from Keynes (1936, 1937) as well as with socionomic models in which social mood is the ultimate independent variable (Prechter & Parker, 2007; Casti, 2010). All these factors together can be incorporated into a model that uses socio-psychological influences as the grounding for macroeconomic fluctuations driven by macroeconomic psychological phenomena, linking into consumer and business confidence, as well as by influences from individual firms and workers in the form of entrepreneurial activity and workers' effort.

Key behavioural assumptions

As a first step in developing a new approach to macroeconomic modelling, some key assumptions can be introduced as alternatives to the standard economic assumptions of rational expectations: agents make full use of all available information and do not make systematic mistakes and the efficient financial markets (with rational agents, asset markets efficiently process information, ensuring that perfect arbitrage generates current asset prices are an unbiased indicator of future asset prices). The overarching approach is one in which macroeconomic actors are procedurally rational, not substantively rational.

Assumption 1: Macroeconomic phenomena are driven by procedurally rational behaviours, including heuristics, biases and socio-psychological influences.
Assumption 2: Propensities to exhibit systematic biases correlate with individual differences including demographic factors, socio-economic characteristics and personality traits.
Assumption 3: Decision-making is affected by a range of intrinsic as well as extrinsic motivations and incentives. For example, labour market outcomes are driven by efficiency wages and so worker productivity reflects social rewards and intrinsic motivations as well as real wages. Also, entrepreneurs' animal spirits drive positive actions in the form of investment and production, and these constitute a form of intrinsic motivation, in addition to the extrinsic monetary incentive of expected profits.
Assumption 4: Discount functions and discount rates are endogenously determined, varying across individuals and over time, reflecting social influences and psychological factors.
Assumption 5: Decisions today with future consequences, e.g. entrepreneurs' investment decisions, are driven by animal spirits and predispositions towards optimism and pessimism.
Assumption 6: Animal spirits are determined by a mix of individual traits and social influences including personality traits and social mood. Positive animal spirits are associated with an optimistic, sanguine temperament and therefore a propensity to act now to ensure future rewards, rather than procrastinating.

An approach combining these elements could form the basis for a behavioural business cycle theory in which fluctuating animal spirits drive up discount factors and encourage more forward looking behaviour via pro-cyclical future bias and optimism during upswings, in contrast to anaemic animal spirits driving counter-cyclical pessimism and present bias during downswings. Instead of assuming that the discount rate is an exogenously determined stable preference and/or that the discount factor evolves in a stable and deterministic way (as assumed even in analyses of hyperbolic and quasi-hyperbolic discounting), an alternative approach would be to specify discount functions determined endogenously, as well as being neither constant nor deterministic. The truly independent explanatory variables within the macroeconomic system would be the socio-psychological factors, depending on whether animal spirits are positive and buoyant, during upswings, or dimmed and in abeyance, during recessionary/depressive episodes. For example when the economy is in the doldrums, a mood of pessimism will take hold and this will lower everyone's discount factors.

This approach to specifying the discount function goes beyond the hyperbolic discounting models that allow behavioural time inconsistency as a facet of an individual's boundedly rational decision-making at a microeconomic level. It is distinct from the dynamic inconsistency problem identified by rational expectations theorists, which is associated market/institutional failures reflecting sub-optimal interactions between strictly rational agents (e.g. as outlined by Kydland & Prescott, 1977), though the interactions between time inconsistency at a microeconomic level versus dynamic inconsistency as a market failure is an interesting theme to explore. The behavioural approach outlined here allows not only for present bias and time inconsistent preferences but also for the discount function to be driven by socio-psychological factors and intrinsic incentives, as well as economic fundamentals.

The factors driving the discount function are also determined by individual differences and this allows for heterogeneity amongst the populations that constitute the macroeconomy. For example, there may be a mixture of impatient consumers and patient savers and investors, and the difference between them can be modelled by allowing that these different groups have different discount functions. The problem in macroeconomics is that this complicates aggregation. Conventional models assume homogeneity of agents; that is, everyone is behaving in the same substantively rational maximising way. With this simplifying assumption, it is easy to aggregate individual behaviours just by multiplying the relationship that describes the behaviour of the two representative agents. When we allow not only that people are different, in terms of personality, preferences and demographics but also allow that their preferences are shifting, the empirical problem of modelling this behaviour becomes much more complex.

Combining these influences allows that the present bias parameter from the quasi-hyperbolic discount function (*DF*) to be re-specified as:

$$DF = f(t, X, Z)$$

where t is a time trend, X is a vector of socio-psychological factors including animal spirits, risk attitudes, mood and business confidence; and Z is a vector of contextual influences including economic fundamentals (output growth, employment, unemployment, inflation), financial market conditions and contextual factors including the socio-political environment. The latter also has the potential to capture the impact of political events that affect macroeconomic policies and outcomes. A current example is the impact of political events on the fate of the euro and financial system including substantial real-world impacts of austerity and migration flows (from policy or enforced by recent events in Greece and the euro zone and also more recently in response to conflict in the Middle East and Africa).

Behavioural macroeconomic modelling: empirical constraints

What are the empirical constraints? A key problem is that socio-psychological influences are much less easily measurable than the conventional macroeconomic data regularly collected by national and international statistical agencies. One reason why mainstream DSGE models have power is that they are relatively easy to use, estimate and forecast using standard monetary-based statistics easily available from published statistical sources, with widely agreed (though not infallible) conventions about the best ways to collect the data. The mathematics of DSGE models is also relatively easy to analyse because the models are based on a limited number of key variables. In a behavioural macroeconomic model, data is harder to collect and socio-psychological influences are harder to capture—not least because of the aggregation problem. As noted above, in DSGE models, the representative agents hypothesis enables easy aggregation—the whole is the sum of the identical parts so describing one set of representative agents is enough. But once we allow that social interactions are an essential feature of economic relationships then the whole is not equal to the sum of the parts and simple aggregation is misplaced. Another question is the extent to which GDP and GNP, as money-based measures of economic performance, are good measures of macroeconomic performance more widely. The limitations of conventional measures of macroeconomic performance are being more widely recognised in recent years. In parallel, measures of happiness and subjective wellbeing are increasingly being accepted by the mainstream as legitimate indicators of macroeconomic performance. The award of the 2015 Economics Nobel Prize to Angus Deaton is a testament to this because some of his most important empirical work has been in the analysis of happiness and wellbeing. In response, governments are re-orienting their data collection to focus on collection of wellbeing and happiness statistics: the OECD and a number of national statistical agencies are collecting measures of wellbeing and devising robust econometric solutions to the problems of sampling and self-reporting biases that limit the accuracy of many measures of collecting wellbeing statistics (e.g., see O'Donnell et al. (2014) for a survey of the possibilities for wellbeing statistics and analysis). Given data constraints, another promising empirical route is to use computational methods such as agent based modelling to model the macroeconomic impact of decisions driven by socio-psychological factors.

Another approach would be to use public mental health indicators as proxies for macroeconomic performance, such as suicide rates and mental health statistics. These could be statistical proxies for social mood and/or novel methods for measuring collective mood. Additional methods include incorporating other novel data such as weather data, as applied for example by Hirshleifer and Shumway (2003), and Kamstra, Kramer and Levi (2003).

Policy implications and conclusions

Behavioural macroeconomic theory introduces a new set of insights for policy-makers, but insights that could supplement rather than replace standard policy approaches. The policy insights from models building within a DSGE framework tend to focus on ameliorating market failures—especially in terms of reducing uncertainty and improving information via greater transparency about government and central bank policy-making. How will a behavioural macroeconomic model change textbook accounts of standard goals and instruments? In the pre-crisis years the focus in macroeconomic policy was on inflation targeting and anchoring inflationary expectations by promoting the transparency and credibility of central bank decision-making. The real-side goals of boosting employment and promoting growth and productivity were assumed to follow from the decreased uncertainty associated with a low inflation environment. Other standard instruments included manipulation of interest rates and, in recent years, boosting the money supply and bank lending via quantitative easing. Expansionary fiscal policies have fallen out of favour for most governments, while the contractionary fiscal policies associated with austerity and deficit-debt reduction are now fashionable.

How might a behavioural approach affect these policy prescriptions? Once the psychology of the macroeconomy as a whole, as well as the potential biases and socio-psychological influences on the economic decision-makers that make up the macroeconomy are considered, the impacts of socio-psychological factors on increased instability in periods of profound uncertainty suggest that macroeconomic and financial policies should be designed to stabilise the macroeconomic psychology. This could include ameliorating or compensating for the negative consequences of moods, emotions and present bias. Political rhetoric could play a role in this. Austerity rhetoric might reassure financial markets, increasing the supply for lending and thereby putting downward pressure on commercial lending rates, enabling entrepreneurs to embark on more new fixed asset investment projects. On the other hand, it may have a dampening effect on business confidence, optimism and entrepreneurs' animal spirits, putting downward pressure on discount factors (upward pressure on discount rates) generating an atmosphere driven by caution and delay, with increasing short-termism, present bias and risk aversion contributing to under-investment in private fixed capital, with knock-on effects in the short term on aggregate demand and an erosion of future productive capacity for the long term. The mood of pessimism would lead to under-investment, with knock-on effects in terms of falling employment, rising unemployment and deflation.

Conventional policies have additional backing once socio-psychological factors are taken into account—for example if pessimism and social mood mean that the private sector is floundering, the justification for expansionary fiscal policy can be expanded to include the positive impact that public investment for example in infrastructure, can achieve, not only in promoting future productivity and growth, but also concrete returns in the long term via a boost to entrepreneurs' animal spirits and consumer and business confidence. Financial policies are primarily designed by central bankers to increase the availability of finance and supply of bank lending. In addition, there will be knock-on socio-psychological effects associated with positive sentiment in the financial sector—what Keynes (1936) refers to as the "state of credit". Relaxing private sector financing constraints may reduce pessimism and present bias, as well as generating cheaper finance. Both will work in concert to lower the hurdle rate of return on projects, making more fixed asset investment projects viable. There will be feedback effects as the increased volume of investment boosts the hopefulness of entrepreneurs and consumers, partially overcoming self-fulfilling prophecies of sluggishness and stagnation. For example, Akerlof and Shiller (2009) identify housing market instability as an example of this: before the sub-prime mortgage crisis, a narrative emerged that house prices could never fall, fuelling housing demand and contributing to self-fulfilling prophecies of rising house prices. Many other examples of speculative episodes from throughout history reflect similar factors.

To conclude, there is pressing need to re-think macroeconomic theory and analysis, especially in the wake of financial crisis, global recession and fiscal pressures. If insights from behavioural economics can be embedded into macroeconomic models, then this might lead to significant advances in the design of effective macroeconomic policies to achieve a wide range of macroeconomic goals, from lowering unemployment, boosting growth and productivity, and also increasing levels of wellbeing and happiness. The problem, however, is that the logistics of blending behavioural economics with macroeconomic theory are complicated. If ways can be found to bring the two subjects together convincingly, then the potential benefits for economies and societies as a whole will be significant.

Notes

1 See Frederick et al. (2002) for a review of the literature.
2 See also Farmer & Guo (1994), and de Grauwe (2011, 2012a).

Bibliography

Acemoglu, D. (1993). Learning about others' actions and the investment accelerator, The Economic Journal, 103(417), 318–28.

Akerlof, G. (1982). Labor contracts as partial gift exchange, Quarterly Journal of Economics, 97(4), 543–69.

Akerlof, G. & Shiller, R. (2009). Animal Spirits: How Human Psychology Drives the Economy and Why it Matters for Global Capitalism, Princeton: Princeton University Press.

Andersen, S., Harrison, G. W., Lau, M. I. & Rutström, E. E. (2008). Eliciting time and risk preferences, Econometrica, 76(3), 583–618.

Andreoni, J. & Sprenger, C. (2012). Risk preferences are not time preferences, American Economic Review, 102(7), 3333–56.

Andreoni, J. & Sprenger, C. (2015). Risk preferences are not time preferences: Reply, American Economic Review, 105(7), 2287–93.

Angeletos, G. M., Laibson, D., Repetto, A., Tobacman, J. & Weinberg, S. (2001). The hyperbolic consumption model: Calibration, simulation, and empirical evaluation. Journal of Economic Perspectives, 15(3), 47–68.

Avery, C. & Zemsky, P. (1998). Multi-dimensional uncertainty and herd behavior in financial markets. American Economic Review, 88, 724–48.

Baddeley, M. (2006). Behind the black box: A survey of real-world investment appraisal approaches, Empirica, 33(5), 329–50.

Baddeley, M. (2009). Far from a rational crowd: Review of Akerlof and Shiller's Animal Spirits. Science, 324, 883–4.

Baddeley, M. (2010), Herding, social influence and economic decision-making: Socio-psychological and neuroscientific analyses. Philosophical Transactions of the Royal Society B, 27, 365(1538), 281–90.

Baddeley, M. C. (2013). Behavioural Economics and Finance, Basingstoke: Routledge.

Baddeley, M. (2014), Rethinking the microfoundations of macroeconomics: Insights from behavioural economics. European Journal of Economics and Economic Policies: Intervention, 11(1), 99–112.

Baddeley, M. & McCombie, J. (2004). An historical perspective on speculative bubbles and financial crises: Tulipmania and the South Sea Bubble. In What Global Economic Crisis? (eds P. Arestis, M. Baddeley & J. McCombie), London: Palgrave Macmillan.

Baddeley, M., Curtis, A. & Wood, R. (2005) An introduction to prior information derived from probabilistic judgments: Elicitation of knowledge, cognitive bias and herding. In Geological Prior Information: Informing Science and Engineering, edited by A. Curtis and R. Wood, Geological Society, London, Special Publications No. 239, 15–27.

Banerjee, A. (1992). A simple model of herd behavior. Quarterly Journal of Economics, 107(3), 797–817

Bechara, A. & Damasio, A. R. (2005). The somatic marker hypothesis: A neural theory of economic decision. Games and Economic Behavior, 52(2), 336–72.

Bénabou and Tirole (2006). Incentives and prosocial behaviour. American Economic Review, 96(5), 1652–77.

Bernatzi, S. & Thaler, R. (1995). Myopic loss aversion and the Equity Premium Puzzle. Quarterly Journal of Economics, 110(1), 73–92.

Bernheim, B. D. & Rangel, A. (2004). Addiction and cue-triggered decision processes. American Economic Review, 94(5), 1558–90.

Bikhchandani, S., Hirshleifer, D. & Welch, I (1992). A theory of fads, fashions, custom and cultural change as informational cascades. Journal of Political Economy, 100(5), 992–1026.

Bikhchandani, S., Hirshleifer, D. & Welch, I. (1998). Learning from the behavior of others: Conformity, Fads, and Informational Cascades. Journal of Economic Perspectives, 12(3), 151–70.

Burke, C., Baddeley, M., Tobler, P. & Schultz, W. (2010b). Striatal BOLD response reflects the impact of herd information on financial decisions. Frontiers – Human Neuroscience, 4, article 48. Available at: http://frontiersin.org/human%20neuroscience/10.3389/fnhum.2010.00048.

Burke, C., Tobler, P., Baddeley, M. & Schultz W. (2010a). Neural mechanisms of observational learning. Proceedings of the National Academy of Sciences, 107(32), 14431–6.

Casti, J. L. (2010). Mood Matters: From Rising Skirt Lengths to the Collapse of World Powers. Berlin: Springer-Verlag.

Costandi, M. (2006). Exorcising animal spirits: the discovery of nerve function. Neurophilosophy. Posted on: http://neurophilosophy.wordpress.com/2006/11/16/exorcising-animal-spirits-the-discovery-of-nerve-function/.

Damasio, A. R. (1994). Descartes' Error: Emotion, Reason, and the Human Brain. London: Vintage.
Davidson, P. (1997). Are grains of sand in the wheels of international finance sufficient to do the job when boulders are often required? The Economic Journal, 107(442), 671–86.
Davidson, P. (2008). Securitization, Liquidity, and Market Failure. Challenge.
De Bondt & Thaler (1985). Does the stock market over-react? Journal of Finance, 40(3), 793–805.
De Grauwe, P. (2011). Animal spirits and monetary policy. Economic Theory, 47, 423–57.
De Grauwe, P. (2012a). Lectures on Behavioural Macroeconomics. Princeton: Princeton University Press.
De Grauwe, P. (2012b). Booms and busts in economic activity: A behavioural explanation. Journal of Economic Behavior and Organisation, 83(3), 484–501.
Dow, A. & Dow, S. (1985). Animal spirits and rationality. In Lawson, T. & Pesaran, H. (eds) Keynes' Economics: Methodological Issues. Beckenham: Croom Helm.
Dow, A. & Dow, S. (2011). Animal spirits revisited. Capitalism & Society, manuscript no. 1087.
Dow, S. C. (2011). Cognition, sentiment and financial instability: Psychology in a Minsky framework. Cambridge Journal of Economics, 35(2), 233–50.
Elster, J. (1996). Rationality and the emotions. Economic Journal, 106(438), 136–97.
Elster, J. (1998). Emotions and economic theory. Journal of Economic Literature, 36(1), 47–74.
Farmer, R. E. A., & Guo, J.-T. (1994). Real business cycles and the animal spirits hypothesis. Journal of Economic Theory, 63, 42–73.
Frederick, S., Loewenstein, G. & O'Donoghue, T. (2002). Time discounting: A critical review. Journal of Economic Literature, 40(2), 351–401.
Frey, B. S. & Oberholzer-Gee, F. (1997). The cost of price incentives: An empirical analysis of motivation crowding-out. American Economic Review, 87(4), 746–55.
Genesove, D. & Mayer, C. (2001). Loss aversion and seller behavior: Evidence from the housing market. Quarterly Journal of Economics, 116, 1233–60.
Gigerenzer, G. (2007). Gut Feelings: The Intelligence of the Unconscious. London: Penguin.
Gigerenzer, G. & Goldstein, D. G. (1996). Reasoning the fast and frugal way: Models of bounded rationality. Psychological Reviews, 103, 650–69.
Harlow, J. M. (1868). Recovery from the passage of an iron bar through the head. Publications of the Massachusetts Medical Society, 2, 327–47.
Harris, C. & Laibson, D. (2001). Dynamic choices of hyperbolic consumers. Econometrica, 69(4), 935–57.
Hirshleifer, D. & Shumway, T. (2003). Good day sunshine: Stock returns and the weather. Journal of Finance, 58(3), 1009–32.
Howitt, P. (1997). Expectations and uncertainty in contemporary Keynesian models. In Harcourt, G. C. & Riach, P. A. (eds) A 'Second Edition' of *The General Theory*. London: Routledge.
Howitt, P. & McAfee, R. P. (1992), Animal spirits, American Economic Review, 82(3), 493–507.
Kahneman, D. & Tversky, A. (1979). Prospect theory: An analysis of decision under risk. Econometrica, 47(2), 263–92.
Kamstra, M. J., Kramer, L. A. & Levi, M. D. (2003). Winter blues: A SAD stock market cycle. American Economic Review, 93(1), 324–43.
Katz, L. F. (1986). Efficiency wage theories: A partial evalution. In Fischer, S. (ed.) NBER Macroeconomics Annual 1986, Volume 1. Cambridge, MA: MIT Press.
Keynes, J. M. (1921). A Treatise on Probability. London: Macmillan.
Keynes, J. M. (1930). A Treatise on Money. London: Macmillan.
Keynes, J. M. (1936). The General Theory of Interest, Employment and Money. London: Macmillan.
Keynes, J. M. (1937). The general theory of employment. Quarterly Journal of Economics, 51, 209–23.
Knight, F. (1921). Risk, Uncertainty and Profit. Boston MA: Houghton-Mifflin.
Koppl, R. (1991). Retrospectives: Animal spirits. Journal of Economic Perspectives, 5(3), 203–10.
Koppl, R. (2002). Big Players and the Economic Theory of Expectations. Palgrave: Basingstoke.
Kreps, D. M. (1997). Intrinsic motivation and extrinsic incentives. American Economic Review, 87(2), 359–64.
Kydland, F. E. & Prescott, E. C. (1977). Rules rather than discretion: The inconsistency of optimal plans. Journal of Political Economy, 95(3): 473–91.
Laibson, D. (1997). Golden eggs and hyperbolic discounting. Quarterly Journal of Economics, 112, 443–78.
Loewenstein, G (1996). Out of control: Visceral influences on decision making. Organizational Behavior and Human Decision Processes, 65(3), 272–92. Reprinted in Camerer et al. (2004), Advances in Behavioral Economics.

Loewenstein, G. F. & O'Donoghue, T. (2004). Animal spirits: Affective and deliberative processes in economic behaviour. Center for Analytic Economics, CAE Working Paper 04–14. New York: Cornell University.

Loewenstein G. F., Weber, E. U., Hsee, C. K. & Welch, N. (2007). Risk as feelings. In Exotic Preferences: Behavioral Economics and Human Motivation (ed. G. F. Loewenstein), Oxford: Oxford University Press, 567–611.

Markowitz, H. (1952). The utility of wealth. Journal of Political Economy, 60, 151–8.

Martins, N. (2011). Can neuroscience inform economics? Rationality, emotions and preference formation. Cambridge Journal of Economics, 35(2), 251–67.

Mini, P. (1990). Keynes, Bloomsbury and The General Theory. London, Macmillan.

Minsky, H. P. (1978). The Financial Instability Hypothesis: A Restatement. Thames Papers in Political Economy, London: North East London Polytechnic.

Minsky, H. P. (1986). Stabilizing an Unstable Economy, New Haven: Yale University Press.

Minsky, H. P. (1992). The Financial Instability Hypothesis. Levy Institute Working Paper No. 74.

O'Donnell, G., Deaton, A., Durand, M., Halpern, D. & Layard, R. (2014). Wellbeing and Policy. London: Legatum Institute.

O'Donoghue, T. & Rabin, M. (1999). Doing it now or later. American Economic Review, 89(1), 103–24.

Prechter, R. R. & Parker, W. D. (2007). The financial/economic dichotomy in social behavioral dynamics: The socionomic perspective. Journal of Behavioral Finance, 8(2), 84–108.

Scharfstein, D. S. & Stein, J. C. (1990). Herd behaviour and investment. American Economic Review, 80(3), 465–79.

Scholten, M. & Read, D. (2014). Prospect theory and the "forgotten" fourfold pattern of risk preferences. Journal of Risk and Uncertainty, 48(1), 67–83.

Shapiro, C. & Stiglitz, J. (1984). Involuntary unemployment as a worker discipline device. American Economic Review, 74(3), 433–44.

Simon, H. (1976). From substantive to procedural rationality. In T. J. Kastelein, S. K. Kuipers, W. A. Nijenhuis & G. R. Wagenaar (eds) 25 Years of Economic Theory. New York: Springer, 65–86.

Thaler, R. & Sunstein, C. (2008). Nudge: Improving Decisions about Health, Wealth and Happiness. New Haven: Yale University Press.

Topol, R. (1991). Bubbles and volatility of stock prices: Effect of mimetic contagion. The Economic Journal, 101, 786–800.

Tversky, A. & Kahneman, D. (1974). Judgement under uncertainty: Heuristics and biases. Science, 185, 1124–31.

Woodford, M. (1988). Expectations, finance constraints, and aggregate instability. In M. Kohn and S. C. Tsiang (eds), Finance Constraints, Expectations, and Macroeconomics, New York: Oxford University Press, 230–61.

Woodford, M. (1990). Learning to believe in sunspots. Econometrica, 58, 277–307.

20

RETHINKING BEHAVIORAL ECONOMICS THROUGH FAST-AND-FRUGAL HEURISTICS

Shabnam Mousavi, Gerd Gigerenzer, and Reza Kheirandish

> How do humans reason when the conditions for rationality postulated by the model of neoclassical economics are not met?
>
> *Herbert A. Simon, 1989*

Introduction

The goal of behavioral economics is to develop models that extend the explanatory and predictive power of economic theory, to address violations of expected utility theory, and to account more realistically for individual choice behavior that does not adhere to calculative rationality. In mainstream behavioral economics, two defining practices have been to list so-called cognitive fallacies and to extend existing expected utility models by adding parameters to account for behavioral factors. Both practices have met their limits. Many cognitive fallacies have been shown to be most likely error on the part of researchers, and adding parameters has been shown to improve fitting but not necessarily the predictive power of the revised utility model. In view of this situation, we review fast-and-frugal heuristics as an alternative vision of behavioral economics that leads to testable process models with superior predictive power. Such a theory satisfies Herbert Simon's criteria of developing process models rather than as-if Bernoulli functions, deals with genuine uncertainty rather than reducing uncertainty to calculable risk, and postulates ecological rather than logical rationality.

In their opening chapter of *Advances on Behavioral Economics* (2004), Camerer and Loewenstein present their "final thoughts":

> Critics have pointed out that behavioral economics is not a unified theory, but is instead a collection of tools or ideas. This is true. It is also true of neoclassical economics. A worker might rely on a "single" tool—say, a power drill—but also use a wide range of drill bits to do various jobs. Is this one tool or many? ... The goal of behavioral economics is to develop better tools that, in some cases, can do both jobs at once ... *all too often economists fail to conduct intellectual trade with those who have a comparative advantage in understanding individual human behavior.* ... Our hope is that behavioral models will gradually replace simplified models based on stricter rationality, as the behavioral models

prove to be tractable and useful in explaining anomalies and making surprising predictions. Then strict rationality assumptions now considered indispensable in economics will be seen as useful special cases . . . , they help illustrate a point which is truly established only by more general, behaviorally grounded theory.

(pp. 41–2, emphasis added)

What is called behavioral economics consists of two different programs. The first catalogues a list of cognitive fallacies, and the second accounts for psychological phenomena through minimal alterations of expected utility theory. This twin research program has run into two severe problems. First, many so-called cognitive fallacies have since been shown to be mainly statistical or measurement artifacts and thus do not represent genuine psychological phenomena that provide insight into human behavior. For example, the hot hand fallacy introduced by Gilovich, Vallone, and Tversky (1985), which attributed systematic errors to coaches and players, has been argued to result from researchers' systematic error in measurement (Miller & Sanjurjo, 2015). Likewise, overconfidence defined as miscalibration (Lichtenstein, Fischhoff, & Phillips, 1982) has been shown to be mainly due to researchers' misinterpretation of regression to the mean (see Erev, Wallsten, & Budescu, 1994); the same holds for Slovic, Fischhoff, and Lichtenstein's (1982) reported overestimation of low risk and underestimation of high risk (see Hertwig, Pachur & Kurzenhäuser, 2005). In both cases, researchers mistook the participants' unsystematic errors for systematic ones. Other alleged systematic errors have been similarly set in a different light (see Gigerenzer, 2015; Gigerenzer, Fiedler & Olsson, 2012). Equally important, systematic literature searches show lack of evidence that these cognitive illusions, even if they existed, would cause actual harm in terms of less wealth, health, or happiness (Arkes, Gigerenzer & Hertwig, 2016; Berg & Gigerenzer, 2010).

The second problem has to do with an issue inherent to the functional form underlying behavioral economics models. Behavioral economists have attempted to build behavioral models by adding free parameters to expected utility models that generally have Bernoulli functional forms. Adding parameters to Bernoulli functions can increase their data fitting power but is no remedy for their poor out-of-sample prediction power (Friedman, Isaac, James & Sunder, 2014). On the contrary, adding more adjustable parameters ultimately decreases the predictive power because of increasing estimation error (Geman, Bienenstock & Doursat, 1992). Thus, achieving better prediction power for behavioral models developed through such practices is problematic. An alternative can be found in a program of study inspired by Herbert Simon's version of behavioral economics, which differs from the described two practices in three respects: by developing process models rather than as-if Bernoulli functions to achieve higher predictive power, openly dealing with genuine uncertainty rather than reducing uncertainty to risk, and utilizing an ecological notion of rationality that rectifies mistaken claims of cognitive fallacies. These properties characterize the fast-and-frugal heuristics study program.

This chapter provides a selective survey of fast-and-frugal heuristics (Gigerenzer, Hertwig & Pachur 2011; Gigerenzer, Todd and the ABC Research Group, 1999) that addresses the characteristics and goals of behavioral economics as described in the above passage by Camerer and Loewenstein, which are still valid today (Pope & Sydnor, 2016). Our respective position can be summarized as follows. We partially share the tool-with-bits view, wholeheartedly agree that understanding individual behavior is central to developing a behavioral theory, and seriously doubt that such a theory will develop around the "strict rationality" maxim. To clarify our position, we introduce the concept of the mind as an adaptive toolbox replete with tools, including heuristics (Gigerenzer & Selten, 2001). However, we regard heuristics not as a defective tool or merely a drill bit but as an altogether new set of tools (or drills) for the study of human behavior at par with logic and statistics. This characterization of heuristics emerges from studying them with respect to their match to the environment in which they are used, which constitutes their *ecological rationality*, as opposed to exclusively evaluating them against logic or statistical benchmarks (Gigerenzer, 2008). Moreover, we advocate comparative evaluation of models based on predictive accuracy, demonstrate the high explanatory power of fast-and-frugal heuristics and tractability of heuristic models, and highlight normative implications of their ecological rationality.

In the development and examination of testable models of heuristic decision making, conditions have been brought to light under which less information, calculation, and in general expenditure of cognitive, technical, and material resources can lead to higher predictive accuracy, more efficiency, and easier attainment of goals. This seeming paradox is referred to as the less-is-more phenomenon. The important realization that heuristics do not necessarily trade accuracy for effort opens the way to a better understanding of the phenomenon through exploring environmental structures that favor heuristic strategies, that is, through revealing conditions under which heuristics are ecologically rational. Note that an accuracy–effort trade-off is commonly assumed in traditional heuristics/adaptive behavior literature (see Payne, Bettman & Johnson, 1993, for a rational account of such trade-offs based on the cost of effort; see Shah & Oppenheimer, 2008, for an argument to the same effect based on cognitive limitations).

Alternatively, the study of fast-and-frugal heuristics focuses on exploring the criteria for functionally matching a strategy with the environment in which it succeeds in completing a task, making a good choice, or resolving a problem. These conditions signify the ecological rationality of a strategy in a given environment. In this framework, the mind is seen as an adaptive toolbox that includes heuristics, their building blocks, and the capacities that they exploit. By exploiting evolutionary or learned capacities, heuristic strategies can be frugal, fast, and robust while simple. Additionally, heuristics are not universal rules but rather elements in the adaptive toolbox that contains both domain-specific heuristics and non-heuristic strategies. In this view, bias is not simply predisposition to make error. A complete statistical configuration of predictive error—composed of both "bias" and "variance" (see below)—clarifies why retaining some bias can play a beneficial role in reducing the total error of prediction models by reducing error due to variance. Notably, the study of less-is-more effects calls for new norms that adequately reflect environmental structures. We elaborate on the superior predictive power of heuristic models in relation to particular environmental structures such as dominance and noncompensatoriness. The evaluation of heuristic models in comparison with traditional models in terms of their predictive power is a promising but underexplored path, which we aim to bring to researchers' attention.

In the very same manner that simple heuristics can help people make better decisions under uncertainty, some simple models and modeling techniques offer a wealth of explanatory power to scientists. By way of example, we introduce the priority heuristic. For the assessment of choice behavior through gambling tasks, the priority heuristic as a model of preferential choice considers payoffs and probabilities one at a time in a lexicographic order rather than by adding flexible parameters that add analytical sophistication to value maximization. Brandstätter, Gigerenzer, and Hertwig (2006) explain how they derived the order of this sequence from psychological insights into human inclinations such as regret aversion as opposed to value maximization based on transitive preference. This simple lexicographic model with no free parameters responds directly to Camerer and Loewenstein's (2004) vision of behaviorally grounded models in more than one way. The priority heuristic model both yields a surprisingly high explanatory power and logically implies the Allais paradox, the certainty effect, the fourfold pattern of risk attitudes, and other so-called anomalies. Hence, moving beyond calculative rationality does not necessitate adding to the complexity of models. Several testable and empirically verified models of heuristics listed in this chapter are evidence of this claim.

The rest of this chapter is organized in three sections, which are followed by closing remarks. The first section focuses on definitions and characteristics of heuristics in the adaptive toolbox, which constitutes the descriptive study of heuristics. In it, we provide clarifying explanations as to why the widely presumed economics-based principles of accuracy–effort trade-off and more-is-better constitute common misunderstandings within the study and analysis of heuristic decision making. Picking up from there, the second section formally discusses less-is-more effects and the bias–variance dilemma. This section describes the normative study of the ecological rationality of heuristics and presents a novel direction not yet explored in mainstream behavioral economics. Here, we elaborate on situations in which less information and computation can lead to more predictive accuracy and present three environmental structures that lend themselves to heuristic exploitation. The third section then leads the reader through the steps of constructing a heuristic process model—the priority heuristic—for preferential choice, the very type of problem that preoccupies many economists. The priority heuristic is a simple lexicographical model that logically implies a number of behavioral puzzles. Finally, a few remarks and highlights close the chapter.

Adaptive toolbox: models of heuristics

The Oxford dictionary defines *heuristic* (adj.) as "enabling a person to discover or learn something for themselves." Used as a noun, *heuristic* refers to "a heuristic process or method." A survey by Groner, Groner, and Bischof (1983) shows the extensive and long ongoing use of the term across disciplines in relation to theories of rationality, knowledge, and action. The behavioral economics literature largely follows the tradition of the heuristics-and-biases program (Tversky & Kahneman, 1974), which considers heuristics as mental shortcuts that are the source of cognitive illusions. Dividing the "architecture of cognition" into two systems, Kahneman (2003) classifies heuristics into the low- or no-effort category of System 1, in contrast to the deliberate reasoning of System 2 that consumes cognitive resources:

> The difference in effort provides the most useful indications of whether a given mental process should be assigned to System 1 or System 2. Because the overall capacity for mental effort is limited, effortful processes tend to disrupt each other, whereas effortless processes neither cause nor suffer much interference when combined with other tasks.
>
> *(p. 1451)*

Attributing the use of heuristics to saving on effort is not our position. In fact, we hold the idea of a general accuracy–effort trade-off (as proposed by Payne et al., 1993; and Shah & Oppenheimer, 2008) to be an enduring misconception associated with heuristic mental processes (this point will be further elaborated on in our discussion of the bias–variance dilemma). Instead, we promote analyzing heuristics with respect to their degree of adaptation to the environment (ecological rationality) and developing testable models of heuristic judgment. Moreover, unlike proponents of Systems 1 and 2, we view heuristics as strategies that can be used both consciously and subconsciously.

Here, we focus on heuristics as simple rules of thumb that effectively ignore less relevant information and exploit environmental uncertainty. This shifts the focus from avoiding uncertainty to yielding efficient results (Neth, Meder, Kothiyal & Gigerenzer, 2014). Consequently, uncertainty does not necessarily have to be reduced to a calculable representation of risk in the study of choice behavior (Neth & Gigerenzer, 2015: 6).

Definition: Heuristics are adaptive tools that ignore information to make fast-and-frugal decisions that are accurate and robust under conditions of uncertainty. A heuristic is considered ecologically rational when it functionally matches the structure of environment.

Many strategies, including heuristic ones, can be understood when they are decomposed into: (i) *a search rule* that provides direction to the search in the information space, (ii) *a stopping rule* that defines when to stop search, and (iii) *a decision rule* that defines the final choice. Each of these three rules itself can be a heuristic rule (Gigerenzer et al., 1999). For example, search can be nonexhaustive, it can stop before all pieces of information are looked up (as in satisficing behavior), and a decision can be made based on a rule of thumb. Search rules, stopping rules, and decision rules are referred to as *building blocks* in the adaptive toolbox. Below is an example of decomposing the take-the-best heuristic—which represents a process of sequential binary comparisons—into its building blocks (Gigerenzer, 2006: 125):

1. *Search rule*: Search through cues in order of their validity. Look up the cue value with the highest validity first.

2. *Stopping rule*: If one object has a positive cue value and the other does not (or is unknown), then stop search and proceed to Step 3. If no more cues are found, guess.

3. *Decision rule*: Predict that the object with the positive cue value has the higher value on the criterion.

The take-the-best heuristic was the first in a series of formal models generated in the fast-and-frugal heuristics study program (Gigerenzer & Goldstein, 1996). Gigerenzer and Gaissmaier (2011) surveyed the literature on testable models of heuristics with a focus on inferential judgment. Drawing on this survey in addition to other work (references herein), Table 20.1 provides a classification of heuristics alongside examples in each class and related studies in the fields of economics and business decision making. Here, heuristics are assigned to four classes: recognition-based decision making, sequential consideration, satisficing, and equal weighting. This classification is neither complete nor unique. It provides a frame of reference for our discussion and serves as an example of the type of work that brings us closer to theorizing heuristics.

Recognition-based heuristics process the information on alternative options based on recognition and assign a higher value to the recognized option. Table 20.1 lists two heuristics in this class that have been studied in economic and other domains. The recognition heuristic was formally introduced by Goldstein and Gigerenzer (2002).

Recognition heuristic: If one of two alternatives is recognized and the other is not, then infer that the recognized alternative has the higher value with respect to the criterion.

Ortmann, Gigerenzer, Borges, and Goldstein (2008) show the merits of simple and low-cost strategies such as the recognition heuristic that outperform sophisticated analysis of financial markets, drawing on a study in which portfolios of stocks recognized by laypeople in the US and Germany outperformed the market index, whereas experts-recognized based portfolios did not (Borges, Goldstein, Ortmann & Gigerenzer, 1999). One reason for their failure is that experts

Table 20.1 A classification of models of heuristics and examples of economic applications

Classes of heuristics in the adaptive toolbox	*Example heuristics*	*Applications in economics/business*
Recognition-based decision making: Evaluate options based on their being recognized	Recognition heuristic	Investment portfolio performance (Borges et al., 1999; Ortmann et al., 2008)
	Fluency heuristic	Performance of IPOs, and value estimates in the market (Alter & Oppenheimer, 2006, 2008)
Sequential consideration: Consider cues in a simple order such as lexicographical; stop consideration as soon as a decision can be made (Special case: Base decision on a single cue)	One-clever-cue heuristics	Identifying active customers: the hiatus heuristic (Wübben & von Wangenheim, 2008) Pricing by intuition (Rusetski, 2014) Crisis management: the credibility heuristic (MacGillivray, 2014)
	Priority heuristic	Logically implies the Allais paradox, certainty effect, and fourfold pattern of risk attitudes (Brandstätter et al., 2006)
	Take-the-best	Forming consideration sets for purchase (Hauser, 2014)
Satisficing: Choose the first option that meets an aspiration level. (Information consideration does not follow a sequence ordering.)	Setting and adjusting aspiration levels	Aspiration adaptation theory (Selten, 1998) Investing in malls/high-rises (Berg, 2014) Pricing used cars (Artinger & Gigerenzer, 2016)
*Equal weighting**: Assign simple—0/1 or equal—weights. Forgo estimating weights to reduce estimation error.	Tallying	Emergency room decisions (Kattah et al., 2009)
	1/N heuristic	Equal allocation of resources to investment options (DeMiguel et al., 2009)

*Equal weighting can be perceived as a special case of a larger class of heuristics with rules that assign simple weights to cues. This is a potential area for future studies.

cannot benefit from the recognition heuristic in the same way that laypeople do; experts know too much. The other heuristic in this class, the fluency heuristic, assigns a higher value to the option that is recognized more rapidly (Schooler & Hertwig, 2005).

> *Fluency heuristic*: If both alternatives are recognized but one is recognized faster, then infer that this alternative has the higher value with respect to the criterion.

Alter and Oppenheimer (2006) report that the fluency of pronouncing the name of a stock has a clear positive correlation with its immediate performance in initial public offerings. In 2008, the same authors report experimental studies wherein the valuation process is based on familiarity and fluency, and extend the implications of their findings to marketing experts and policymakers.

Sequential heuristics consider cues/reasons (or pieces of information) in a simple sequence, such as a lexicographic order, and stop as soon as a decision can be made. A subclass of these, one-clever-cue heuristics, ignores all but one of the observable cues. Wübben and von Wangenheim (2008) report the use of one threshold value, which they call the hiatus heuristic, to identify active customers in an airline industry, an online CD retailer, and in an apparels business.

> *Hiatus heuristic*: If a customer has not purchased within a certain number of months (the hiatus), the customer is classified as inactive; otherwise, the customer is classified as active.

They showed that this heuristic, which uses only one threshold and ignores all else, is as good as or better than complex algorithms such as Pareto/NBD at identifying active customers.[1] Similarly, Rusetski (2014) finds no evidence for the use of complex compensatory algorithms by brand managers when making price decisions. His survey of more than 100 managers reveals a simple pricing strategy that considers only the competitors' price levels, followed by a consistent positioning above, equal to, or below that price. In the area of crisis management, MacGillivray (2014) introduces the credibility heuristic used by managers in detecting contaminated water sources and presents evidence from the field on how these decisions are made based simply on "the perceived trustworthiness of the message conveyor." The credibility heuristic can be effective because situations in crisis management are subject to a high level of uncertainty and decisions need to be made without delay.

In the class of sequential heuristics, two further heuristic models are listed in Table 20.1: the priority and take-the-best heuristics. The priority heuristic models information processing for the preferential choice between gambles, as discussed in detail later in this chapter. The take-the-best heuristic, whose building blocks were described above, orders cues unconditionally without taking their interdependencies into account. In a similar manner, consumers who are faced with many products and/or several attributes for each product follow a sequential consider-then-choose process in a heuristic-based form (for a survey of evidence and literature on this topic see Hauser, 2014). Hauser (2014) emphasizes that understanding this process of choice, which he names *consideration set heuristic*, is essential to successful managerial decisions on product development and marketing communication, where "consideration sets are key to business strategy" (p. 1688). The heuristic process used in the formation of consideration sets is particularly prevalent and successful in noncompensatory environments (see the next section for a definition).

Famously proposed by Simon (1955), satisficing is a heuristic-based behavior and the initial inspiration for many studies in heuristic decision making. Here, the search among options follows no specific order and stops simply once the option under consideration *satisfices*, that is, is "good enough" to meet an aspiration level. This does not rule out the possibility of adjusting an initial aspiration level during the process of search/examination.

> *Satisficing*: Set an aspiration level α and start the search in any order. Choose the first object with value $\geq\alpha$. If no object is found after time β, lower aspiration level by δ. Continue search with the updated aspiration level $\alpha-\delta$. Repeat the process until a choice can be made.

Theorized by Selten (1998), this nonoptimizing process is described under the title of *aspiration adaptation*. Its noteworthy distinction lies in satisficing an aspiration level as opposed to satisfying a mathematical criterion, the latter requiring strict adherence to the criterion but the former accepting "good enough" adherence. Configuration of behavior as a satisficing process especially fits the way in which humans resolve ill-defined problems such as choice of a lifetime partner or a job/career. Two empirical studies listed in Table 20.1 provide evidence from markets for satisficing behavior. In one of these, Berg (2014) interviewed entrepreneurs to discover the process of information that leads to the choice of location for large construction investments such as building commercial high-rises. His data could not be described by a model of search cost but instead support simple satisficing search and limited consideration of information. Interestingly, "locations are frequently discovered by chance." Developers reportedly make high-impact decisions based on satisficing a simple aspiration criterion such as a fixed return over a fixed period of time. Moreover, they do not update their initial aspirations in the process of search, thereby resorting to the simplest form of satisficing behavior. Another example for satisficing behavior is found in the market for second-hand cars, where BMW dealers set the price by determining an initial aspiration level, followed by gradual (in fixed percentage) adjustments over fixed (monthly) intervals (Artinger & Gigerenzer, 2016).

The last class of heuristics in Table 20.1 is the class of *equal weighting*, where equal weights are allocated to all cues or options in order to reduce the error incurred when estimating weights. The efficiency of simple unit weighting schemes when dealing with small samples has been long investigated in mathematical psychology and organizational behavior (Einhorn & Hogarth, 1975), but relatively rarely incorporated in econometrics. Tallying heuristics belong to this class. A simple tallying heuristic counts only the favored cues, that is, assigns them a weight of one and ignores the rest by assigning them a zero weight. Tallying is routinely used, for instance, in emergency rooms for making vital calls (Kattah, Talkad, Wang, Hsieh & Newman-Toker, 2009), and by hikers for avoiding avalanche accidents (McCammon & Hägeli, 2007). Another member of this class is the *1/N* heuristic, which allocates resources to *N* options equally. Although equal allocation of resources to options has been observed as a frequent behavior, behavioral economists have considered it an inferior allocation strategy. For example, Benartzi and Thaler (2001) refer to equal allocation of assets in retirement portfolios as *naive diversification*. Yet when empirically tested, 1/*N* outperformed Markowitz's mean-variance portfolio in six out of seven tests and could not be consistently outperformed by any of another dozen sophisticated portfolio diversification algorithms (DeMiguel, Garlappi & Uppal, 2009).

Situations where simple strategies can outperform complex ones are instances of the less-is-more effect. The study of the ecological rationality of heuristics explains when and why less can be more.

Ecological rationality: bias–variance dilemma and less-is-more effects

The goal of the study of ecological rationality is to specify the environmental conditions under which a given strategy or heuristic can be expected to succeed compared to competitors. It is based on two methodological principles: to test a model in its predictive accuracy (as opposed to data fitting) and to test a model competitively against the best existing models. In our view, these two methodological principles should become standard in behavioral economics.

Error in predictive accuracy stems from two sources: (i) bias, that is, the difference between the true value and the average predicted value; and (ii) variance, that is, the variance of the predictions around the average predicted value. Bias corresponds to the mis-specification of a model, and variance to overfitting. Variance is influenced by sample size. Predictive accuracy increases when the sum of both errors is reduced, and it is subject to a trade-off between the two. Total systematic error in prediction can be expressed as

$$Error = Bias^2 + Variance. \qquad (1)$$

This bias–variance dilemma (Geman et al., 1992; Grenander, 1952) can be best understood in the context of over- and underfitting for prediction models (Hastie, Tibshirani & Friedman, 2009). An optimum level of model complexity corresponds to the optimal trade-off between bias reduction and variance reduction. When the complexity of the model exceeds this optimum level, overfitting occurs, whereas underfitting occurs when complexity is inadequate. These relations are depicted in Figure 20.1.

Simple heuristic models for binary comparisons can reduce total prediction error by beneficially trading less variance for more bias (or, if certain environmental conditions hold—see below—, without increasing bias). In their analysis of the relative predictive accuracies of take-the-best and other simple strategies with respect to the way in which cues are weighted, choice sets characterization, and error, Hogarth and Karelaia (2006: 237) called for future studies to address a crucial question:

> An important question … is to understand the types of environments that people encounter in their decision making activities. For example, to what extent do the data sets compiled by Czerlinski et al. (1999) characterize the kinds of situations people face in their natural ecologies? *We simply do not know.* (emphasis added)

Şimşek (2013) responded to this call. First, we now know of three environmental structures for which the "bias" component of error is the same for a lexicographic heuristic as for a linear model (assuming same order of cue weights). These are defined in Table 20.2. Dominance is the most obvious: if the cue (attribute) values of option *A* are never smaller than those of option *B*, and at least one value is larger, then *A* dominates *B*. Here, every strategy will arrive at the same choice. Cumulative dominance extends dominance to the cumulative values of the cues, and noncompensatoriness holds if the cue weights (assuming, without loss of generalization, that the

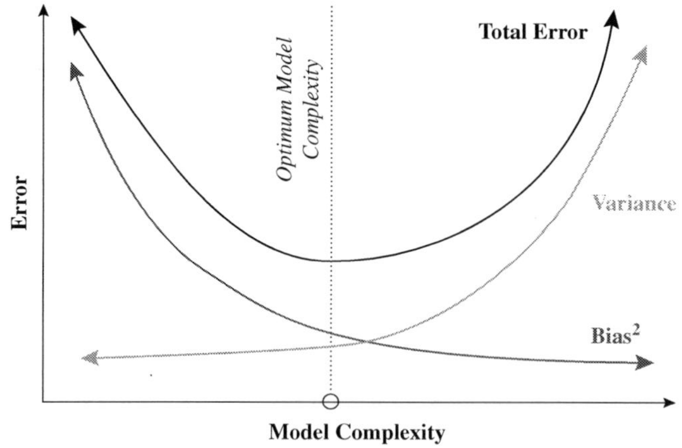

Figure 20.1 Bias–variance trade-off versus model complexity

Source: Adapted from Fortman-Roe (2012).

cues are binary and weights are nonnegative) are ordered in decreasing value, each weight is greater than the sum of all weights that come after it. An example is the set of weights 1, 1/2, 1/4, and 1/8. In this case, a lexicographic strategy that relies only on the first cue that allows for a decision will always end up with the same choice as a linear model (that has the same cue order). The question is how prevalent are these conditions in natural environments?

For paired comparison tasks, Şimşek (2013) examined the structure of 51 data sets from online repositories, textbooks, research publications, field data, and packages for R statistical software. These diverse areas span business, economics, engineering, and medicine. How often was one or more of these three structures—dominance, cumulative dominance, and noncompensatoriness—satisfied? The median for the 51 data sets was 90 percent. That is, in half of the data sets, a lexicographic heuristic yielded the same choice as a linear model for more than 90 percent of the decisions encountered, but more quickly and with less effort. When the cues (predictors) were dichotomized at the median, this number increased to 97 percent (Şimşek, 2014). In other words, in the majority of decisions, a lexicographic heuristic has the same bias as a linear model. Together with lexicographic heuristics' potential for reducing variance, this result explains why and when simple heuristics outperform linear models in prediction.

This section provided a case study in ecological rationality[2] by specifying the conditions under which simple heuristics can outperform more information-greedy strategies. It explains why the accuracy–effort trade-off does not generally hold and why the bias–variance trade-off allows for a better understanding of the rationale of heuristics. In addition, these results clarify that there is nothing irrational per se about relying on heuristics. If one of the conditions in Table 20.2 is in place and people rely on lexicographic heuristics instead of linear rules, this does not imply a lack of rationality because of cognitive limitations, as has been commonly assumed in the heuristics-and-biases program. On the contrary, due to higher estimation error, choosing a simple rule can lead to better predictions.

In the next section, we address in detail the question of how to build a model of heuristics based on empirical data and the objective to reduce error due to variance.

Table 20.2 Environmental structures that lexicographic heuristics exploit (in paired comparison tasks). If one of these structures holds, a lexicographic heuristic has the same "bias" as a linear model

Environmental structure	*Definition*
Dominance	For two options A and B with k attributes x_{iA} and x_{iB}, where $\Delta x_i = (x_{iA} - x_{iB})$, A dominates B if $w_i \Delta x_i \geq 0, \ \forall i, \text{ and } w_i \Delta x_i > 0, \ \exists i.$ *Example*: In the decimal system, $A = 642$ does not dominate $B = 351$ because 6>3 and 2>1, but 4<5.
Cumulative dominance	For two options A and B with attributes x_{iA} and x_{iB}, where $\Delta x_i = (x_{iA} - x_{iB})$, $\Delta x_i' = \sum_{j=1}^{i} \Delta x_j, \ \forall i$, and $w_i' = w_i - w_{i+1}, 1 \geq i < k$. A cumulatively dominates B if $w_i' \Delta x_i' \geq 0, \ \forall i, \text{ and } w_i' \Delta x_i' > 0, \ \exists i.$ *Example*: In the decimal system, A=642 cumulatively dominates B=351 because 6>3, 6+4>3+5, and 6+4+2>3+5+1.
Noncompensatoriness	For an option with binary attributes x_i that take values 0 or 1, a set of (nonnegative) weights is called noncompensatory if $w_i > \sum_{j=i+1}^{k} w_j, i = 1, 2, ..., k-1.$ *Example*: 1, 0.5, 0.25, 0.125.

Source: Extracted from Şimşek (2013).

Building a heuristic model for preferential choice: the priority heuristic

The classes of heuristics listed in Table 20.1 can be used for both inference and preference. Studying inferential choice requires an external metric and thus avoids the difficulty of uniquely specifying a metric as in the study of preferential choice. However, preferential choice is the centerpiece of economic modeling of human behavior. Paul Samuelson, who redefined and mainstreamed modern economics, developed the theory of revealed preferences (Samuelson, 1938a, 1938b, 1948), which remains to date the cornerstone for theoretical analysis and empirical testing of choice behavior in accordance with utility maximization. Its underlying idea is that people consider all options and have a clear and stable order of preferences for the options. The act of rational choice simply reflects such an order.

The behavioral revolution in economics ensued from accumulation of evidence on systematic violations of rationality axioms such as stable ordering of options, transitivity of choices, and other requirements of internal logical consistency. Formal attempts to capture the observed violations, such as intransitivity and inconsistency of preferences, have been chiefly shaped by adding free or adjustable parameters to the expected utility model (Berg & Gigerenzer, 2010). Cumulative prospect theory (Tversky & Kahneman, 1992) is a case in point, where three parameters fit the shape of the value function, and another two the shape of the probability weighting function.[3] In this approach, flexible parameters are modeling elements that extend the explanatory power of the expected utility theory to account for the observed violations. Yet cumulative prospect theory is not meant to model the process of decision making but is used instead as an as-if model that demands estimations and computations that are even less realistic than expected utility theory (Berg & Gigerenzer, 2010). Moreover, although such models may fit the data better as a result of using more parameters, the very practice can cause overfitting and even reduce the predictive power. The bias–variance dilemma accounts for why adding free parameters can increase error due to "variance" and diminish predictive power.

Rather than adding parameters, the idea that led to the development of the priority heuristic model took another approach: Why not study what people actually do when they make decisions? What if people actually use simple rules when the problem at hand becomes more complex? If that is the case, then a model without adjustable parameters can potentially capture such processes and should logically imply systematic deviations from expected utility theory. In pursuit of this conjecture, Brandstätter, Gigerenzer, and Hertwig (2006, BGH herein) constructed the priority heuristic by taking the following steps.

> *Step 1*: Which heuristic form? From the set of all possible heuristics for two-alternative choice problems, the candidates were narrowed down to lexicographic rules and tallying (see Table 20.1 for definitions). Then, tallying was ruled out because empirical evidence does not support equal treatment of reasons in choice between monetary gambles. Once the lexicographic form was chosen, reasons for consideration needed to be specified.
>
> *Step 2*: Which reasons? Start with simple gambles that contain only nonnegative payoffs, or "gains." These contain three separate reasons: (i) a maximum gain, M; (ii) a minimum gain, m; and (iii) the probability of minimum gain p_m, where $p_M + p_m = 1$. Three reasons have six possible orderings, from which one order must be chosen by investigating the evidence on choice behavior.
>
> *Step 3*: Which order? Choice experiments by Brandstätter and Kühberger (2005) suggest that people consider value of gains before their probabilities. This eliminates

two possible orders in which probabilities are the first reason, leaving four. Because people are risk averse in the gain domain (Edwards, 1954), they consider m first in order to avoid the worst outcome. Which of the remaining two possible orders is actually followed needs to be further elicited. To examine the remaining two orders of consideration, m-p-M versus m-M-p, BGH conducted an experiment in which m was kept constant to elicit the order for p and M. Their results agree with Slovic, Griffin, and Tversky (1990, Study 5) in that p preceded M in consideration order. Thus, the order of reasons was specified as m-p-M which is called the priority (or search) rule.

Step 4: When to stop search? This can be determined by finding empirically supported satisficing rules. For two simple gambles A and B, one starts by comparing their minimum gain values, $\Delta m = |m_A - m_B|$. Evidence suggests that whether Δm is considered large enough to stop the consideration of reasons depends on the maximum gain. Taking a simple aspiration that corresponds to the decimal system, BGH postulated that people stop search if Δm is larger than or equal to $0.1M$, where $M = max\{M_A, M_B\}$. Notice that 0.1 is an empirically informed fixed (not flexible) parameter. (i) if $\Delta m < 0.1M$ then consider the second reason (probabilities of minimum gains). If $\Delta p_m = |p_{mA} - p_{mB}| \geq 0.1$ then stop; otherwise consider the last reason (maximum gains).

Step 5: Which gamble to choose? For the choice between gambles BGH defined a decision rule based on "attractiveness." Once the search is stopped, the priority heuristic predicts that the gamble with the more attractive decisive feature, either gain or probability, will be chosen.

Steps 1 to 5 describe the procedure of constructing the priority heuristic model, which is a lexicographic model for preferential choice. The resulting model has the following three building blocks (BGH, 2006: 413):

Priority Rule: Go through reasons in the order of minimum gain, probability of minimum gain, maximum gain.

Stopping Rule: Stop examination if the minimum gains differ by 1/10 (or more) of the maximum gain; otherwise stop examination if probabilities differ by 1/10 (or more) of the probability scale.

Decision Rule: Choose the gamble with the more attractive gain (probability).

This model is generalized to both gambles with nonpositive gains (losses) and nonnegative gambles with more than two outcomes. How does this simple model with no flexible parameters fare in predicting choice behavior, where systematic violations of expected utility are prevalent? Because one can always construct a set of choices between gambles in which one's model fares well, BGH (2006) tested the priority heuristic using four "hostile" data sets designed by Kahneman, Tversky, and others. The competitors were three modifications of expected utility theory, including cumulative prospect theory, and ten previously studied heuristics, including tallying. Across all 260 problems, the priority heuristic topped them all with a predictive accuracy of 87 percent; cumulative prospect theory predicted only 77 percent of people's choices correctly. Note that cumulative prospect theory excelled in data fitting, that is, explaining data already known, but not in prediction. The reason for that discrepancy follows from the bias–variance dilemma: Cumulative prospect theory suffers from prediction error due to the variance in parameter estimation, whereas the priority heuristic, having no free parameters, incurs no error from variance but only from bias.

The priority heuristic is not the only heuristic people use. A detailed analysis showed that different strategies are adapted to either easy or difficult choices (BGH, 2006). Choices are considered easy when the expected values differ by a factor of 2 or more and difficult when the factor is smaller (<2). Whereas the priority heuristic predicted people's behavior best for difficult choices, cumulative prospect theory was better at predicting easy choices. For easy choices, however, the best strategy was simple expected value theory. Thus, two strategies—each with zero adjustable parameters—might be sufficient to predict the data for difficult and simple problems, respectively. This shows how risky choice can be modeled without Bernoulli functions, which are notoriously unreliable in out-of-sample prediction (Friedman et al., 2014; Stewart, Reimers & Harris, 2014).

In summary, BGH (2006) showed how to construct a process model from empirical observations. The resulting priority heuristic was better at predicting people's choices for two- and multiple-outcome gambles and for certainty equivalent problems than are cumulative prospect theory and similar modifications of expected utility theory, and logically implies the major violations of utility theory (Katsikopoulos & Gigerenzer, 2008). This model is emphatically not meant to be the last word but rather exemplifies a new behavioral economics that builds realistic process models rather than more complicated as-if models and that can be more successful in predicting actual choice behavior.

Final remarks

In the past, heuristics were commonly associated with cognitive biases and generally considered to be second-best strategies. This view focused on reducing the bias—and developing debiasing techniques—while ignoring the variance component of errors. As we illustrated, however, reducing either component of error can reduce the total prediction error. Fast-and-frugal heuristics are simple yet robust tools in the adaptive toolbox of individuals and institutions that produce a beneficial trade-off between bias and variance so that people can make effective choices under uncertainty. This trade-off highlights the importance of two methodological principles: to test models in out-of-sample prediction, not by fitting their parameters to known data; and to test models competitively against the best existing candidates.

In this chapter, we introduced several testable models of heuristics. Particularly, by going through the steps of formulating the priority heuristic model, we illustrated the way in which a simple model is constructed that logically implies violations of the expected utility theory without adding more free parameters. Thus we established that heuristic models can satisfy the eventualities required by economists for proper formalization. However, the methodology we introduced here takes an alternative, algorithmic approach in that optimization is not the main method. Nor are flexible parameters added to account for the psychological aspects of behavior. Viewed in perspective, examination of constructing the priority heuristic demonstrates that the methodology of investigation is never neutral. It directs and limits the type and shape of the outcomes of scientific inquiry, as can be observed in the emerging trends in behavioral economics in comparison with the study of fast-and-frugal heuristics.

Whereas behavioral economics operates mainly in the explanatory domain, the fast-and-frugal heuristics program works in parallel on explanatory and normative aspects of a science of heuristics. Indeed, what humans ought to do cannot be understood without acknowledging what they can do. And what humans can do is the most reliable basis for developing norms for what they should do. As such, our position concurs with that of James March:

> If behavior that apparently deviates from standard procedures of calculated rationality can be shown to be intelligent, then it can plausibly be argued that models of calculated rationality are deficient not only as descriptors of human behavior but also as guides to intelligent choice.
>
> *(1978: 593)*

In particular, we maintain that extending behavioral insights to policy design and to recommendations for improving individual and collective choice necessarily entails an ecological approach to human behavior, including the development of a systematic theory of behavior that regards heuristics at par with logical and statistical rules. Steps in this direction have been taken in finance (Forbes, Hudson, Skerratt & Soufian, 2015) and business (a series of papers in *Journal of Business Research*, 67, 2014).

In this chapter, we provided a classification of heuristics and an introduction to the normative study of heuristics, that is, their ecological rationality. These heuristics are empirically found to produce robust and effective outcomes by ignoring information, using less calculation, and relying on exploitation of human capacities and environmental uncertainty. Given that informational efficiency is at the heart of the formal study and modeling of markets in economics, the analysis of heuristics that efficiently ignore information can provide a new framework for behavioral economics.

Acknowledgments

We are thankful to Özgür Şimşek and Konstantinos Katsikopoulos for their careful feedback and suggestions, and to Rona Urnau for providing many helpful improvements to our article.

Notes

1 NBD stands for negative binomial distribution.

2 Two forms of rationality in economics à la Smith (2008) are constructivist and ecological forms. Whereas Smith adopts the definition of ecological rationality formulated in the study of fast-and-frugal heuristics, his account remains descriptive. The shared definition and juxtaposition of these two views is reported in Mousavi and Kheirandish (2014).

3 *Prospects* are gambles. Gambles have been used to represent risky decision making in a tradition that can be traced back to the origins of probability theory in the seventeenth century (Hacking, 1975).

Bibliography

Alter, A. L., & Oppenheimer, D. M. (2006). Predicting short-term stock fluctuations by using processing fluency. Proceedings of the National Academy of Sciences of the United States of America, 103(24), 9369–72.

Alter, A. L., & Oppenheimer, D. M. (2008). Easy on the mind, easy on the wallet: The roles of familiarity and processing fluency in valuation judgments. Psychonomic Bulletin & Review, 15(5), 985–90. doi: 10.3758/PBR.15.5.985.

Arkes, H. R., Gigerenzer, G., & Hertwig, R. (2016). How bad is incoherence? Decision, 3, 20–39. doi: 10.1037/dec0000043.

Artinger, F., & Gigerenzer, G. (2016). Aspiration-adaptation, price setting, and the used-car market. Unpublished manuscript.

Benartzi, S., & Thaler, R. H. (2001). Naive diversification strategies in defined contribution saving plans. American Economic Review, 91(1), 7998.

Berg, N. (2014). Success from satisficing and imitation: Entrepreneurs' location choice and implications of heuristics for local economic development. Journal of Business Research, 67(8), 1700–9. doi: 10.1016/j.jbusres.2014.02.016.

Berg, N., & Gigerenzer, G. (2010). As-if behavioral economics: Neoclassical economics in disguise? History of Economic Ideas, 18(1), 133–66.

Borges, B., Goldstein, D. G., Ortmann, A., & Gigerenzer, G. (1999). Can ignorance beat the stock market? In G. Gigerenzer, P. M. Todd, & the ABC Research Group. Simple heuristics that make us smart. New York: Oxford University Press, 59–72.

Brandstätter, E., & Kühberger, A. (2005). Outcome priority in risky choice. Unpublished manuscript, Department of Psychology, Johannes Kepler University Linz, Linz, Austria.

Brandstätter, E., Gigerenzer, G., & Hertwig, R. (2006). The priority heuristic: Making choices without trade-offs. Psychological Review, 113(2), 409–32.

Camerer, C. & Loewenstein, G. (2004). Behavioral economics: Past, present, future. In C. F. Camerer, G. Loewenstein, & M. Rabin (Eds.), Advances in behavioral economics. New York, NY: Princeton University Press, 3–51.

Czerlinski, J., Gigerenzer, G., & Goldstein, D. G. (1999). How good are simple heuristics? In G. Gigerenzer, P. M. Todd, & the ABC Research Group. Simple heuristics that make us smart. New York: Oxford University Press, 97–118.

DeMiguel, V., Garlappi, L., & Uppal, R. (2009). Optimal versus naive diversification: How inefficient is the 1/N portfolio strategy? Review of Financial Studies, 22(5), 1915–53.

Edwards, W. (1954). The theory of decision making. Psychological Bulletin, 51(4), 380–417.

Einhorn, H. J., & Hogarth, R. M. (1975). Unit weighting schemes for decision making. Organizational Behavior and Human Performance, 13(2), 171–92.

Erev, I., Wallsten, T. S., & Budescu, D. V. (1994). Simultaneous over- and underconfidence: The role of error in judgment processes. Psychological Review, 101(3), 519–27. doi: 10.1037/0033-295X.101.3.519.

Forbes, W., Hudson, R., Skerratt, L., & Soufian, M. (2015). Which heuristics can aid financial decision making? International Review of Financial Analysis, 42, 199–210.

Fortmann-Roe, S. (2012). Understanding the bias–variance tradeoff. Retrieved from http://scott.fortmann-roe.com/docs/BiasVariance.html.

Friedman, D., Isaac, R. M., James, D., & Sunder, S. (2014). Risky curves: On the empirical failure of expected utility. New York, NY: Routledge.

Geman, S., Bienenstock, E., & Doursat, R. (1992). Neural networks and the bias/variance dilemma. Neural Computation, 4(1), 1–58.

Gigerenzer, G. (2006). Bounded and rational. In R. J. Stainton (Ed.), Contemporary debates in cognitive science (Contemporary Debates in Philosophy No. 7). Oxford, UK: Blackwell, 115–33.

Gigerenzer, G. (2008). Why heuristics work. Perspectives on Psychological Science, 3(1), 20–9.

Gigerenzer, G. (2015). On the supposed evidence for libertarian paternalism. Review of Philosophy and Psychology, 6(3), 361–83.

Gigerenzer, G., & Gaissmaier, W. (2011). Heuristic decision making. Annual Review of Psychology, 62, 451–82.

Gigerenzer, G., & Goldstein, D. G. (1996). Reasoning the fast and frugal way: Models of bounded rationality. Psychological Review, 103(4), 650–69.

Gigerenzer, G., & Selten, R. (Eds.). (2001). Bounded rationality: The adaptive toolbox. Cambridge, MA: MIT Press.

Gigerenzer, G., Fiedler, K., & Olsson, H. (2012). Rethinking cognitive biases as environmental consequences. In P. M. Todd, G. Gigerenzer, and the ABC Research Group, Ecological rationality: Intelligence in the world. New York, NY: Oxford University Press, 80–110.

Gigerenzer, G., Hertwig, R., & Pachur, T. (2011). Heuristics. New York, NY: Oxford University Press.

Gigerenzer, G., Todd, P. M., & the ABC Research Group. (1999). Simple heuristics that make us smart. New York, NY: Oxford University Press.

Gilovich, T., Vallone, R., & Tversky, A. (1985). The hot hand in basketball: On the misperception of random sequences. Cognitive Psychology, 17(3), 295–314.

Goldstein, D. G., & Gigerenzer, G. (2002). Models of ecological rationality: The recognition heuristic. Psychological Review, 109(1), 75–90.

Grenander, U. (1952). On empirical spectral analysis of stochastic processes. Arkiv för Matematik, 1(6), 503–31.

Groner, M., Groner, R., & Bischof, W. F. (1983). Approaches to heuristics: A historical review. In M. Groner, R. Groner, & W. F. Bischof. Methods of heuristics. New York, NY: Routledge, 1–18.

Hacking, I. (1975). The emergence of probability: A philosophical study of early ideas about probability, induction and statistical inference. London, UK; New York, NY: Cambridge University Press.

Hastie, T., Tibshirani, R., & Friedman, J. (2009). The elements of statistical learning: Data mining, inference, and prediction. New York, NY: Springer.

Hauser, J. R. (2014). Consideration-set heuristics. Journal of Business Research, 67(8), 1688–99. doi: 10.1016/j.jbusres.2014.02.015.

Hertwig, R., Pachur, T., & Kurzenhäuser, S. (2005). Judgments of risk frequencies: Tests of possible cognitive mechanisms. Journal of Experimental Psychology: Learning, Memory, and Cognition, 31(4), 621–42. doi: 10.1037/0278-7393.31.4.621.

Hogarth, R. M., & Karelaia, N. (2006). "Take-the-best" and other simple strategies: Why and when they work "well" with binary cues. Theory and Decision, 61(3), 205–49.

Kahneman, D. (2003). Maps of bounded rationality: Psychology for behavioral economics. American Economic Review, 93(5), 1449–75.

Katsikopoulos, K. V., & Gigerenzer, G. (2008). One-reason decision-making: Modeling violations of expected utility theory. Journal of Risk and Uncertainty, 37(1), 35–56.

Kattah, J. C., Talkad, A. V., Wang, D. Z., Hsieh, Y. H., & Newman-Toker, D. E. (2009). HINTS to diagnose stroke in the acute vestibular syndrome: Three-step bedside oculomotor examination more sensitive than early MRI diffusion-weighted imaging. Stroke. A Journal of Cerebral Circulation, 40(11), 3504–10. doi: 10.1161/STROKEAHA.109.551234.

Lichtenstein, S., Fischhoff, B., & Phillips, L. D. (1982). Calibration of probabilities: The state of the art to 1980. In D. Kahneman, P. Slovic, & A. Tversky (Eds.), Judgment under uncertainty: Heuristics and biases. New York, NY: Cambridge University Press, 306–34.

MacGillivray, B. H. (2014). Fast and frugal crisis management: An analysis of rule-based judgment and choice during water contamination events. Journal of Business Research, 67(8), 1717–24.

March, J. G. (1978). Bounded rationality, ambiguity, and the engineering of choice. Bell Journal of Economics, 9(2), 587–608.

McCammon, I., & Hägeli, P. (2007). An evaluation of rule-based decision tools for travel in avalanche terrain. Cold Regions Science and Technology, 47(1), 193–206.

Miller, J. B., & Sanjurjo, A. (2015). Surprised by the gambler's and hot hand fallacies? A truth in the law of small numbers. IGIER Working Paper #552. Available at SSRN: http://ssrn.com/abstract=2627354 or doi: 10.2139/ssrn.2627354.

Mousavi, S., & Kheirandish, R. (2014). Behind and beyond a shared definition of ecological rationality: A functional view of heuristics. Journal of Business Research, 67(8), 1780–5.

Neth, H., & Gigerenzer, G. (2015). Heuristics: Tools for an uncertain world. In R. Scott & S. Kosslyn (Eds.), Emerging trends in the social and behavioral sciences: An interdisciplinary, searchable, and linkable resource. New York, NY: Wiley, 1–18. doi: 10.1002/9781118900772.etrds0394.

Neth, H., Meder, B., Kothiyal, A., & Gigerenzer, G. (2014). Homo heuristicus in the financial world: From risk management to managing uncertainty. Journal of Risk Management in Financial Institutions, 7(2), 134–44.

Ortmann, A., Gigerenzer, G., Borges, B., & Goldstein, D. G. (2008). The recognition heuristic: A fast and frugal way to investment choice? In C. Plott and V. Smith (Eds.), Handbook of experimental economics results, Volume 1. Amsterdam, The Netherlands: North-Holland, 993–1003.

Payne, J. W., Bettman, J. R., & Johnson, E. J. (1993). The adaptive decision maker. Cambridge, UK: Cambridge University Press.

Pope, D. G., & Sydnor, J. R. (2016). Behavioral economics: Economics as a psychological discipline. In G. Keren, & G. Wu (Eds.), The Wiley-Blackwell handbook of judgment and decision making. Wiley-Blackwell, 800–27. doi: 10.1111/b.9781118468395.2015.00029.x.

Rusetski, A. (2014). Pricing by intuition: Managerial choices with limited information. Journal of Business Research, 67(8), 1733–43. doi: 10.1016/j.jbusres.2014.02.020.

Samuelson, P. A. (1938a). A note on the pure theory of consumer's behaviour. Economica, 5(17), 61–71.

Samuelson, P. A. (1938b). The empirical implications of utility analysis. Econometrica, 6(4), 344–56.

Samuelson, P. A. (1948). Consumption theory in terms of revealed preference. Economica, 15(60), 243–53. doi: 10.2307/2549561.

Schooler, L. J., & Hertwig, R. (2005). How forgetting aids heuristic inference. Psychological Review, 112(3), 610–28.

Selten, R. (1998). Aspiration adaptation theory. Journal of Mathematical Psychology, 42(2), 191–214.
Shah, A. K., & Oppenheimer, D. M. (2008). Heuristics made easy: An effort-reduction framework. Psychological Bulletin, 134(2), 207–22. doi: 10.1037/0033-2909.134.2.207.
Simon, H. A. (1955). A behavioral model of rational choice. Quarterly Journal of Economics, 69(1), 99–118.
Simon H. A. (1989). The scientist as problem solver. In D. Klahr & K. Kotovsky (Eds.), Complex information processing: The impact of Herbert A. Simon [21st Carnegie-Mellon symposium on cognition]. Hillsdale, NJ: Erlbaum, 373–98.
Şimşek, Ö. (2013). Linear decision rule as aspiration for simple decision heuristics. In C. J. C. Burges, L. Bottou, M. Welling, Z. Ghahramani, & K. Q. Weinberger (Eds.), 27th Annual Conference on Neural Information Processing Systems 2013 (Online-Version, pp. 2904–12). Red Hook, NY: Curran Associates. Retrieved from http://papers.nips.cc/paper/4888-linear-decision-rule-as-aspiration-for-simple-decision-heuristics.pdf.
Şimşek, Ö. (2014). How natural environments support simple decision heuristics. Talk held at the Center for Adaptive Behavior and Cognition Workshop, Max Planck Institute for Human Development, Berlin, Germany. October 2014.
Slovic, P., B. Fischhoff, and S. Lichtenstein. (1982). Facts versus fears: Understanding perceived risk. In D. Kahneman, P. Slovic, & A. Tversky (Eds.), Judgment under uncertainty: Heuristics and biases. Cambridge, UK: Cambridge University Press.
Slovic, P., Griffin, D., & Tversky, A. (1990). Compatibility effects in judgment and choice. In R. M. Hogarth (Ed.), Insights in decision making: A tribute to Hillel J. Einhorn (pp. 5–27). Chicago, IL: University of Chicago Press.
Smith, V. L. (2008). Rationality in economics: Constructivist and ecological forms. New York, NY: Cambridge University Press.
Stewart, N., Reimers, S., & Harris, A. J. L. (2014). On the origin of utility, weighting, and discounting functions: How they get their shapes and how to change their shapes. Management Science, 61(3), 687–705.
Tversky, A., & Kahneman, D. (1974). Judgment under uncertainty: Heuristics and biases. Science, 185(4157), 1124–31.
Tversky, A., & Kahneman, D. (1992). Advances in prospect theory: Cumulative representation of uncertainty. Journal of Risk and Uncertainty, 5(4), 297–323.
Wübben, M., & von Wangenheim, F. (2008). Instant customer base analysis: Managerial heuristics often "get it right". Journal of Marketing, 72(3), 82–93.

21
COMPUTATIONAL BEHAVIORAL ECONOMICS

Shu-Heng Chen, Ying-Fang Kao, and Ragupathy Venkatachalam

Introduction

Computational intelligence has been frequently applied to modeling artificial agents in agent-based computational economics. Commonly used applications include reinforcement learning (Chen, 2013), classifier systems (Vriend, 2002), genetic algorithms, genetic programming (Chen, 2002a,b), swarm intelligence (Boyer, Brorsen & Zhang, 2014), and instance-based learning (Pape & Kurtz, 2013). They are considered as alternative toolkits for the classical or Bayesian statistical models in modeling bounded-rationality and adaptive behavior (Sargent, 1993). However, these toolkits, except for reinforcement learning, are not explicitly grounded in psychology. It, therefore, remains to be seen whether these "machines" (artificial agents) are related to the bounded-rational agents as conceived by behavioral economists. Or, alternatively, to what extent can we relate the general principles or practices that are frequently applied in behavioral economics to the designs of these machines?

This issue has generally been ignored in the literature on behavioral economics, since machine learning and artificial intelligence remain a focus only for few branches of behavioral economics, specifically those following the legacy of Herbert Simon. On the other hand, this issue has not been well noticed in the literature on the machine learning community either. Although the machine learning community is well aware of the prevalence of ill-defined or poorly structured problems, this understanding is rarely extended to the context of economic decision making. Specifically, these two communities do not systematically share a background of the methodological controversy related to the divide between Homo Economicus and Homo Sapiens (Thaler, 2000). Therefore, given this dual ignorance, the fundamental connection between computational intelligence and behavioral economics is either missing or it only exists in an implicit manner.

The purpose of this chapter is to uncover this fundamental connection and to give it a systematic treatment. We attempt to do so by reviewing the behavioral economic principles behind computational intelligence tools. On the basis of this fundamental connection that we establish, we can see how agents, equipped with some "intelligence designs", substantiate the behavioral constraints and heuristics through implementable (computational) procedures. We refer to this substantiation or implementation and to the implied general approach as *computational behavioral economics*.

The rest of the chapter is organized as follows. The second section reviews some general features of decision making. This review motivates the framework used in this chapter.

The framework begins with routines, defaults or automated decisions. The third section addresses the role of computational intelligence in shaping this kind of decision process. This connection between computational intelligence and behavioral economics is illustrated by the instance-based decisions, such as K nearest neighbors, and other related algorithms, such as K-means, self-organizing maps and reinforcement learning. To cope with information or choice overload, heuristics based on instances need to be structured in a hierarchical form. The fourth section addresses how computational intelligence can be applied to examine this more advanced decision making behavior. The fifth section discusses the formation of novel heuristics, including the discovery of new attributes, new instances, and new hierarchies. The formation processes involve the idea of autonomous agents, whose behaviors are driven by the modularity heuristic. Computational modeling of these behaviors can be assisted by evolutionary computation, which provides an effective representation of behavioral heterogeneities among decision makers. Decision making can be affected by peers, colleagues, neighbors, and social norms. These behaviors have also been found in entomological experiments and some of them have been well formulated in computational intelligence. The sixth section provides a brief account of this development. The seventh section discusses some problems of treating randomization as a heuristic in decision making. Concluding remarks are presented in the final section.

Decision making and choices

Before we proceed, it may be useful to notice a common feature shared by both behavioral economists and machine learning scholars. For both, the "real world" is a world filled with ill-structured and vaguely defined problems. Many intelligent toolkits were proposed mainly to deal with these challenges. These challenges involve a kind of uncertainty, ambiguity or vagueness, which cannot be well formulated in a probabilistic environment and hence cannot be solved using standard rational (optimization) procedures that are built upon statistical decision theory or the von Neumann–Morgenstern expected utility maximization paradigm (von Neumann & Morgenstern, 1944). One of the most telling examples was given by Gerd Gigerenzer (Gigerenzer, 2007):

> A professor from Columbia University was struggling over whether to accept an offer from a rival university or to stay. His colleague took him aside and said, "Just maximize your expected utility—you always write about doing this." Exasperated, the professor responded, "Come on, this is serious."
>
> *(Ibid.: 3)*

A little reflection on this somewhat embarrassing situation highlights some important facets of decision making. First, many decisions are inconsequential, but some are not. Second, some choice or decision problems are encountered frequently; some less often. Accepting a new job offer or keeping the current job is not an inconsequential decision and is not the kind of decision which we make frequently; nevertheless, this kind of decision problem is prevalent in a normal economic life. Third, while it may be difficult to figure out the exact number of decisions that we make in a typical day, this number can be large and definitely larger than we might think (Wansink & Sobal, 2007). Fourth, we spend very little time making many choices or decisions and due to time constraints, many of us do not allow ourselves to spend too much time making those decisions (Mormann, Koch & Rangel, 2011). Fifth, many decisions are often made by processes that may be unclear for us, say, by emotion or gut feeling, or even automated (Damasio,

1994; Kahneman, 2011; Newell & Shanks, 2014). It is fortunate that many decisions do not take up much of our time or even need our conscious effort; therefore, we are still able to handle a sizable number of decisions in a typical day, including those with sizable consequences and for which we have very little past experience.

These facets of decision making problems suggest that there are two types of decision modes. The first are the *automated decision modes* that can handle frequently encountered decisions, specifically, those inconsequential ones. The second are the *manual decision modes* that can address less frequent, less experienced, but consequential decisions. The first type of decision mode typically refers to those *defaults* and *routines*, whereas the second type of decision mode is a meta-level decision model, which can identify novel elements, and constantly review and revise all routines and defaults, thereby facilitating the discovery of new routines or defaults.

Routine decision modes can be viewed as being organized in a hierarchical form (i.e., *the routine over routines*) as shown in Figure 21.1. The familiar decision problem will trigger our memory of the past similar situations, and the associated routines being followed in the past, but only the most relevant routine will be followed. The chosen routine will then be reviewed and revised based on its performance each time after its application, and will be added to the memory of routines. In this way, the set of routines can be updated, even occasionally. This hierarchy has often been mentioned in behavioral economics, but probably the most prominent quotation is the following one from Friedrich Hayek (Hayek, 1945).[1]

> We make constant use of formulas, symbols and rules whose meaning we do not understand and through the use of which we avail ourselves of the assistance of knowledge which individually we do not possess. We have developed these practices and institutions by building upon habits and institutions which have proved successful in their own sphere and which have in turn become the foundation of the civilization we have built up.
>
> *(Ibid.: 528)*

In the following sections, we elaborate more on this notion of hierarchical decision making processes, involving routines or rules, that are based on the experiences of the agents.

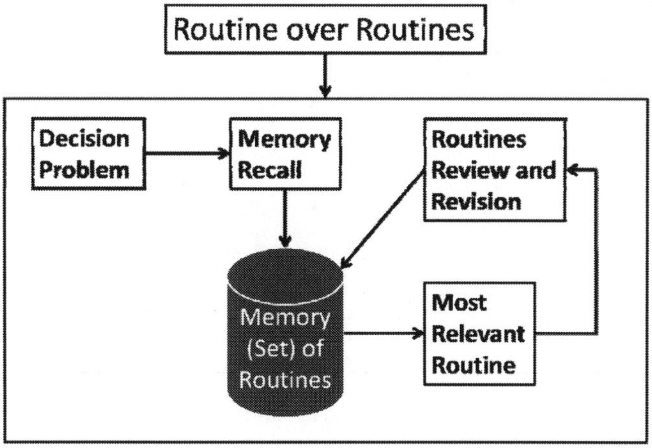

Figure 21.1 Routine formulation

Routines and instance-based decisions

The two-level hierarchical decision framework begins with the idea of defaults or routines, a subject well studied in behavioral economics (Thaler & Sunstein, 2008; Betsch & Haberstroh, 2014; Madrian, 2014). Routines help specify the rules concerning the default behavior for various problem instances. They allow us to economize on the time required for decision making and enhance the automated procedures for decision making. In this section, we shall address the behavioral features of using routines, and hence defaults, from the perspective of computational intelligence.

Routine formulation plays an important role in computational intelligence. The essence of the idea is that, until otherwise stated, similar simulations tend to evoke similar responses (decisions, actions, and choices). The key then is to consider an appropriate notion of similarity. David Hume, in his book *An Enquiry concerning Human Understanding*, has the following remark on experience and similarity.

> In reality all arguments from *experience* are founded on the *similarity* which we discover among natural objects, and by which we are induced to expect effects similar to those which we have found to follow from such objects. . . . *From causes which appear similar we expect similar effects.* This is the sum of all our experimental conclusions.
>
> *(Ibid.: section IV; italics added)*

Among many computational intelligence toolkits, an illustration concerning the first of the two modes (i.e., default or routine mode) that is most familiar to economists is the *case-based decision* (Gilboa & Schmeidler, 1995, 2001). In computational intelligence, the case-based decision is also popularly known as *instance-based learning* (Aha, Kibler, & Marc, 1991) or *lazy learning* (Aha, 1997).[2]

In instance-based decisions, the decision environment (instance) is characterized by its related features (attributes); for example, a vector $\boldsymbol{a}$ in an M-dimensional Euclidean space $\boldsymbol{R}^M$, $\boldsymbol{a} \in \boldsymbol{R}^M$. When the decision maker at time t faces a situation (instance) characterized by $\boldsymbol{a}_t$, we assume that she will recall her actions from her experience in similar situations in the past. Let $\boldsymbol{A}_t$ be the memory space of the past instances,

$$A_t = \{\boldsymbol{a}_s : S < t\}, \tag{1}$$

and $\boldsymbol{R}_t$ be the subset of similar instances, that is,

$$\boldsymbol{R}_t = \{\boldsymbol{a}_k : k < t, \|\boldsymbol{a}_k, \boldsymbol{a}_t\| = \epsilon_{k,t} < \epsilon\}, \tag{2}$$

where $\|\cdot\|$ is a metric which may be subjectively determined by the decision maker, and the distance ϵ, also subjectively determined, dictates what are perceived as similar instances by the decision maker. Furthermore, let d_t be the decision corresponding to an instance $\boldsymbol{a}_t$. The instance-based decision rule $d_t(\boldsymbol{a}_t)$ is then the function:

$$d_t = f(\boldsymbol{D}_t), \tag{3}$$

where the set $\boldsymbol{D}_t = \{d_k{:}\boldsymbol{a}_k \in \boldsymbol{R}_t\}$, that is., the set of all past decisions that were taken in "similar" instances.

Depending on the application domain, there are a number of possible functional forms that have been suggested in the literature. For example, if d_t is a numerical decision, that is, just a number, then a simple average of the past decisions under similar instances can form a new decision.

$$d_t = \frac{\sum_{d_k \in \boldsymbol{D}_t} d_k}{Card(\boldsymbol{D}_t)}, \tag{4}$$

where *Card* indicates cardinality. In addition to the simple average, weights or weighting functions can be further used to differentiate the similarity among different $\mathbf{a}_k$ to $\mathbf{a}_t$.

$$d_t = \sum_{d_k \in \boldsymbol{D}_t} w_k d_k, \tag{5}$$

where

$$w_k = \frac{g(\epsilon_{k,t})}{\sum_{\{s: \boldsymbol{a}_s \in \boldsymbol{R}_t\}} g(\epsilon_{s,t})}, \tag{6}$$

The function g is a transformation of the similarity index $\epsilon_{s,t}$. If we let $\pi_k(t)$ be the most updated *strength* of the rule d_k, that is, the past experience (evaluation) of the performance of the rule d_k, then in addition to similarity $\epsilon_{k,t}$, the weight can also be adjusted based on $\pi_k(t)$. Hence,

$$w_k = \frac{g(\epsilon_{k,t}, \pi_k(t))}{\sum_{\{s: \boldsymbol{a}_s \in \boldsymbol{R}_t\}} g(\epsilon_{s,t}, \pi_k(t))}. \tag{7}$$

If the decision is in the form of discrete choices, then the function can be given with a stochastic choice formulation.

$$\text{Prob}(d_t = d_k) = \frac{g(\epsilon_{k,t}, \pi_k(t))}{\sum_{\{s: \boldsymbol{a}_s \in \boldsymbol{R}_t\}} g(\epsilon_{s,t}, \pi_k(t))}. \tag{8}$$

The above general discussion of the instance-based decision, with slight modifications, applies to a number of computational intelligence algorithms. Equations (4) to (6) constitute the basic form of K nearest neighbors (Chan et al., 1999). Equation (8) is a more general version of reinforcement learning.

K nearest neighbors

The method of K nearest neighbors (KNNs) is a typical experience-based computational behavioral model. In KNNs the idea of neighborhood, that is, Equation (2), is altered and instead of imposing an upper limit ϵ to define the set $\boldsymbol{R}_t$, KNNs select the K most similar instances or the K most nearest neighbors. We can rank $\epsilon_{s,t}$ in an ascending order and let the rank of $\epsilon_{s,t}$ be denoted as $R(\epsilon_{s,t})$. The set of similar instances, Equation (2), is then modified as follows.

$$\boldsymbol{R}_t = \{\boldsymbol{a}_k : k < t, \boldsymbol{R}(\epsilon_{k,t}) \leq K\}. \tag{9}$$

KNNs has been initiated thrice by different academic communities, first, by engineers (Cover & Hart, 1967), then by statisticians (Stone, 1977; Cleveland, 1979), and finally by physicists (Farmer & Sidorowich, 1987). From these three origins, we can see how the *similarity heuristic* is introduced as a heuristic in information processing and statistics, and then later on to serve a computational model of behavioral economics (Chan et al., 1999).

When our knowledge of the environment is incomplete or vague, our decisions naturally rely on or are biased towards familiar or similar experiences. The nearest neighbor was first used by Cover and Hart (1967) to give a notion of *similarity*:

> In the classification problem there are two extremes of knowledge which the statistician may possess. Either he may have complete statistical knowledge of the underlying joint distribution of the observation x and the true category θ, or he may have no knowledge of the underlying distribution except that which can be inferred from sample . . .
>
> *(Ibid.: 21)*

In the second extreme case, "a decision to classify x into category θ is allowed to depend only on a collection of n correctly classified samples $(x_1, \theta_{1,}), (x_2, \theta_{2,}), \ldots, (x_n, \theta_{n,})$, and *the decision procedure is by no means clear*" (Ibid.: 21; italics added). With the absence of a clear decision procedure, Cover and Hart (1967) proposed the following heuristic:

> Thus to classify the unknown sample x we may wish to weight the evidence of the nearby x_i's most heavily. Perhaps the simplest nonparametric decision of this form is the *nearest-neighbor* (**NN**) rule, which classifies x in the category of its nearest-neighbor.
>
> *(Ibid.: 21; bold and italics original)*

KNNs was later introduced in the literature on robust local regression by Cleveland (1979). However, instead of having closeness or similarity as the main pursuit, the key focus here is on *smoothness*, specifically, the smoothness of the conditional density function. As commonly seen in functional approximation; its main goal is to regulate the polynomial degree of curve fitting. However, in addition to functional approximation, it is also fundamentally connected to the pursuit of simplicity in the science of discovery (Li & Vitanyi, 2008).

The *smoothness heuristic* is related to the *closeness heuristic* under the instance-based reasoning principle, where similar inputs are expected to have similar outputs. This principle implies a response surface which is simple in terms of its *descriptive complexity* or *algorithmic complexity*.[3] In other words, the instance-based decision model helps the decision maker to give a more concise description of her decision making process, specifically explaining why such a decision is made. Without the closeness and smoothness constraints, the simplicity of the decision-response surface may be lost, and, given the increased complexity, an automated decision becomes hardly available, and the decision will have to be left to "the man on the spot" (Hayek, 1945: 524–5). Such kinds of non-smooth decisions may be time-consuming, but their frequency must be limited, given the time constraint to which each decision maker is subjected.

In agent-based computational economics, *NN agents* were first used in an agent-based artificial stock market (Chan et al., 1999). The NN agent forecasts the price based on a moving window with a length l, which is also known as the *embedding dimension*. Let $p_t = ln^{(P_t/P_{t-1})}$, where P_t is the asset price at time t and ln denotes the natural log. Furthermore, let

$$\boldsymbol{p}_t^l = (p_t, p_{t-1}, \ldots, p_{t-(l-1)}). \tag{10}$$

To forecast p_{t+1}, the NN agent will find the past K historical windows (instances) which are most similar to $\boldsymbol{p}_t^l$, that is,

$$\boldsymbol{R}_t = \{\boldsymbol{p}_k^l : R(\epsilon_{k,t}) \leq K\}, \tag{11}$$

where $\epsilon_{k,t} = corr(\boldsymbol{p}^l_k, \boldsymbol{p}^l_t)$. An average of the price p_{k+1} will then be used as the forecast of p_{t+1}.

$$p^{\epsilon}_{t+1} = \frac{\sum_{\{k:\boldsymbol{p}^l_k \in \boldsymbol{R}_t\}} p_{k+1}}{K} \tag{12}$$

A difficult part of the instance-based decision is to address how instances are formed in the first place. In many real-life situations, it can be hard to tell whether two instances are closely related or similar. A proposed distance or similarity measure can be sensitive to different attribute spaces. Some critical but hidden attributes could be ignored and may never be found. Nevertheless, what matters is not whether the decision maker has built her decision upon the "true" attribute space, but instead whether they actually follow instance-based reasoning to streamline their decisions. It can be argued that without such a framework, the decisions can be harder and may be less satisfactory. Accordingly, as shown in Figure 21.1, the instance-based decision making addresses the needs of a less loaded decision making process. Amartya Sen termed the situation *decisional inescapability*, in that a decision or a choice has to be made even before the completion of a judgement process (Sen, 1997). To cope in such instances, decision makers may have to learn and evolve to develop various heuristics, such as the instance-based decisions, to handle these otherwise inescapable situations. The often observed decision making based on *stereotypes* can be interpreted as an instance-based decision (Bodenhausen, 1990; Chaxel, 2015; Fabre et al., 2015). Again, here, the stereotype attached to a specific instance, say, a person, a city, a country, a gender, a culture, or a brand, etc., can be imprecise, but what matters is that this frame facilitates decision making, particularly when a reason is needed or when the time available for making the decision is severely limited. In fact, as we shall see below, evolutionary computation can allow agents to discover useful instances, which constitutes a part of the learning for agents (Figure 21.1).

K-means and self-organizing maps

The number of nearest neighbors, that is, *K*, obviously, is a key parameter in the KNN algorithm. The question of the optimum number of *K* has been addressed in the third of the above-mentioned intellectual origins of KNNs, that is, the chaotic-dynamics origin (physicist approach) (Takens, 1981).[4] In this stream of the literature, it has been shown that, based on the Takens theorem, KNNs can help forecast the chaotic time series, specifically, the deterministic chaotic time series. To do so, the parameter K is determined by the embedding dimension l (Equation 10). It has been suggested that $k = 2(l + 1)$ (Casdagli, 1991), but, under the case of stochastic non-linear systems, it also depends on the noise level: the higher the added noise level, the higher the K. Nonetheless, the above analysis is entirely from a mathematical viewpoint. From a cognitive viewpoint, a number of other considerations need to be incorporated.

First of all, how can humans actually retrieve similar instances from their memory? And how many such instances can be retrieved? Considering the brain with its limited capacity for memory, a pertinent question concerns how the brain deals with increasing information by not memorizing all of it or by forgetting some of it. How does it do the much necessary *pruning*? This is still a non-trivial issue pursued by neuroscientists today.[5] This suggests a role for redundancy-reduction behavior. Hence, similar instances, given a certain tolerance level of noise, may be combined into one instance. A large number of instances are then substantially reduced to a few representative instances. Hence, when making a new decision, the number of referred neighbors may be very low, say, close to those magic numbers which psychologists normally refer to (Miller, 1956; Mathy & Feldman, 2012).[6] The computational model of the aforementioned compression behavior is known as a clustering algorithm in computational intelligence, and the two popularly used clustering algorithms are *K-means* and *Kohonen's self-organizing maps* or SOMs (Kohonen, 1995). *K*-means clustering, developed by MacQueen (1967), is one of the widely used clustering algorithms that groups data with similar characteristics or features together. SOMs resemble *K*-means. They both involve minimizing some measure of dissimilarity, called the cost functions, in the instances within each cluster. The difference between the *K*-means and the SOM lies in their associated cost functions. Consider a series of n instances, each of which has M numeric attributes:

$$\boldsymbol{a}_1^M, \boldsymbol{a}_2^M, \ldots, \boldsymbol{a}_n^M, \boldsymbol{a}_i^M \in \boldsymbol{R}^M, \forall i = 1, 2, \ldots, n \tag{13}$$

where

$$\boldsymbol{a}_i^M \equiv \{a_{i,1}, a_{i,2}, \ldots, a_{i,m,}\}.a_{i,l} \in \boldsymbol{R}, \forall l = 1, 2, \ldots, M \tag{14}$$

The *K*-means clustering is to find a series of k clusters, the centroids of which are denoted, respectively, by

$$C_1, C_2, \ldots, C_k, C_j \in \boldsymbol{R}^M, \forall j = 1, 2, \ldots, k \tag{15}$$

such that each of the observations is assigned to one and only one of the clusters with a minimal cost, and the cost function is defined as follows:

$$C_{K-means} = \sum_{i=1}^{n} \sum_{j=1}^{k} \|\boldsymbol{a}_i^M, C_j\| \delta_{i,j}, \tag{16}$$

where $\|\boldsymbol{a}_i^M, C_j\|$ is the standard Euclidean distance between $\boldsymbol{a}_i^M$ and $\boldsymbol{C}_j$, and $\delta_{i,j}$ is the delta function:

$$\delta_{i,j} = \begin{cases} 1, & if\ \boldsymbol{a}_i^M \in C_j \\ 0, & if\ \boldsymbol{a}_i^M \notin C_j \end{cases} \tag{17}$$

To minimize the cost function (16), one can begin by initializing a set of k cluster centroids. The positions of these centroids are then adjusted iteratively by first assigning the data samples to the nearest clusters and then recomputing the centroids. Corresponding to (16), the cost function associated with SOM can be roughly treated as follows:

$$C_{SOM} = \sum_{i=1}^{n} \sum_{j=1}^{k} \|\boldsymbol{a}_i^M, C_j\| \cdot h_{\omega(\boldsymbol{a}_i^M),j} \tag{18}$$

where $h_{\omega(\boldsymbol{a}_i^M),j}$ is the neighborhood function or the neighborhood kernel, and $\omega(\boldsymbol{a}_i^M)$, the winner function, outputs the cluster whose centroid is nearest to the input $\boldsymbol{a}_i^M$. In practice, the neighborhood kernel is chosen to be wide at the beginning of the learning process to guarantee the global ordering of the map, and both its width and height decrease slowly during learning. For example, the Gaussian kernel whose variance monotonically decreases with iteration times is frequently used. By comparing Equation (16) with (18), one can see that in SOM the distance of each input from all of the centroids is weighted by the neighborhood kernel h, instead of just the closest one being taken into account. Through either KNNs or SOM, our experiences of the past can then be constantly processed by clustering, which provides us with *points of reference* or *anchors* upon which the subsequent decisions can be based and facilitated.

Reinforcement learning

In the context of *discrete choice*, Equation (8) is a more general version of reinforcement learning. To see this, simply impose the requirement that ε to zero, that is, only consider those perfectly identical instances, and require g to be a Gibbs–Boltzmann distribution with the temperature parameter λ,

$$\text{Prob}(d_t = d_t) = \frac{exp^{\lambda \pi_k(t)}}{\sum_{\{s:\boldsymbol{a}_s \epsilon R_t\}} exp^{\lambda \pi_s(t)}}, \tag{19}$$

in which case we have a Roth–Erev version of reinforcement learning (Roth & Erev, 1995).

Reinforcement learning has already been applied to explain or predict human behavior in the context of game experiments. It is considered to be consistent with the robust properties of learning observed in the large experimental psychology literature on both human and animal learning, specifically, the *Law of Effect* (Roth & Erev, 1995).[7] The recent progress in neuroscience indicates that humans, and more generally, mammals are naturally endowed with a reinforcement learning mechanism in their brains. In fact, one of the most impressive recent results in neuroscience is the discovery of the relationship between the dopamine neural system and reinforcement learning.[8] Technically, reinforcement learning has been extended to take into account a number of psychological factors in learning, such as memory (Roth & Erev, 1995), counterfactual thinking (Camerer & Ho, 1999), aspiration (Erev & Roth, 1998) and attention (Chen & Hsieh, 2011).

The standard version of reinforcement learning only considers a fixed and finite set of alternatives, since the decision environment is homogeneous. The typical example used to illustrate this decision environment is the *multi-armed bandit problem* (Bush & Mosteller, 1955). The decision maker at each time is always offered a fixed number of bandits, and, since instances are always the same, the decision can be automated by using the stochastic choice formulation given in Equation (19). In a special case where $\lambda = 0$, the default turns out to be the one with the highest updated strength (most successful experience), or simply, the best one so far. In this special case, it is similar to the *take-the-best heuristic* (Gigerenzer, 2007), a member of *one-good-reason heuristics*.[9] The generalized version, Equation (7), simply adds a hierarchical structure to the set of rules by classifying them according to their applicability to a certain instance.[10] Hence, each instance corresponds to a specific set of rules with different strengths. The set of rules may be globally the same over different instances, but their respective weights (strengths) and hence priorities can differ from one instance to another. In behavioral economics, reinforcement learning has been proposed as a model of *low rationality* (Erev & Roth, 1998; Duffy, 2006; Chen, 2013). This original intention may lead people to misperceive it as a mere model fitting for very simple behavior in a rather recurrent decision environment.[11] However, as we shall see, this is not the case. Not only can reinforcement learning serve as a model to handle novel situations, but it can also serve as a meta-level learning model, that is, *to learn how to learn*. Vriend (2002) is the best illustration to exemplify these two features.

Vriend (2002) considers the kind of decisions which are unique and, hence, not repeated (not similar). Examples can be buying a car, buying a house, choosing a restaurant in Pinamar, and booking a hotel in Reykjavik. Hence, strictly speaking, reinforcement learning cannot be directly applied in these situations, since available alternatives (available experiences) are not transferrable (commutable) from one place to the other. Nevertheless, with such a series of novel situations, one can learn from the experiences of others, the so-called *social learning*, and there are different ways to learn from others (Nowak, 2006; Scott, 2012). Vriend considered three types of rules, namely, randomly behaving rules (throwing a coin), following what the majority did (herding), or replicating the good experiences of others.

These three types of rules can always be applicable to any novel situation, as long as the decisions made by others and their resultant experiences are available. In fact, Vriend (2002) can be read as a contribution to the economy of Web 2.0 and the agent-based study of Big Data in the following sense. First, as mentioned in Chen, Chie and Tai (Chapter 18), the essential characteristic of the Web 2.0 economy concerns the user-initiated and user-supplied content, and the online customer review is one major form of digital content. Second, while online customer review reports can help consumers acquire more information on the quality of the product, their fast accumulation can result in an overload of information for consumers. To understand how consumers make use of this digital content, the aforementioned three types of rules seem to be a reasonable beginning. The randomized rule does not require any cognitive effort from the decision maker. The second one needs only a counting of heads. The last one needs to read the reviews and to know users' experiences; hence, it may be more time-consuming. Reinforcement learning can then be applied to these three levels of learning: no learning, shallow learning, and deep learning. Reinforcement learning can then serve as a model of meta learning.

Hierarchical structure of decisions

Quite contrary to what is usually taught in economics, many of our decisions or choices are not always based on insufficient information, but on overloaded information. In behavioral economics, this conundrum is known as the *information overload hypothesis.*[12] A typical heuristic to make a decision in such a situation is not to look at all information at once; instead, information will be given a sequential or hierarchical structure so that one needs to get access to more information only when the decision cannot be made based on the "abridged" version. Because of this practical need, a tree or a hierarchical structure can play quite a crucial role in decision making or choice making.

Decision trees

The decision tree, a canonical model in computational intelligence, can be interpreted as a computational behavioral model corresponding to the hierarchical structure of decision making. Suppose that we are interested in knowing how a tennis player decides whether to play tennis. We have a sequence of observations of her past decisions,

$$(\boldsymbol{D}_T, \boldsymbol{A}_T) = \{(d_t, \boldsymbol{a}_t)\}_{t=1}^{T}$$

where d_t is a binary decision variable, either to play $d_t = 1$ or not to play $d_t = 0$. $\boldsymbol{a}_t$ can be a vector of attributes which may help define an instance; for example, outlook, humidity and wind, if she is only concerned with the weather condition.

A decision tree is constructed based on a *top-down greedy algorithm*, known as the ID3 in machine learning (Quinlan, 1986). The key idea is fairly straightforward. First, one finds the attribute a^*, say, outlook, that *best* classifies $\boldsymbol{D}_t$, and then uses this attribute as the *root* of the decision tree. The process is then repeated for each subtree. The main issue in this greedy algorithm concerns the criterion regarding the choice of the best classifying attribute. A common solution to this problem is to select the attribute with the *highest information gain*, which is defined as the expected reduction in the *entropy* of the dataset $\boldsymbol{D}_t$ caused by knowing the value of the attribute $\boldsymbol{A}_T^* = \{a_t^*\}_{t=1}^T$.

An illustration of a decision tree which is built is given in Figure 21.2. In this illustration, among a sequence of information, the tennis player will first look at the outlook, and there are three values for the outlook: sunny, overcast, and rainy. If the outlook is overcast, then the tennis player will simply disregard the unread information and will decide to play tennis. On the other hand, if it is not overcast, then the information (the second attribute) to be further examined depends on whether the outlook is sunny or rainy. The second attribute is humidity if the outlook is sunny, and wind, if the outlook is rainy. In each of these two branches, the decision can always be made without further looking into the remaining information. In other words, although each instance is defined by three attributes, at any given time at most two attributes are required in order to make a decision.

Decision tree has been considered to be a fast and frugal heuristic in behavioral economics (Gigerenzer, 2007). It might, therefore, be worth discussing the connection between machine learning and behavioral economics in their respective use of decision trees. First of all, the top-down greedy algorithm as introduced by the artificial intelligence (AI) community is applicable to the study of the real decision process; for example, in using it for analyzing the observations of human-subject experiments. In fact, the idea of decision trees has already been used as a model to analyze and understand the decision making observed in human-subject experiments, such as the prisoner's dilemma games (Axelrod, 1984), ultimatum games (Duffy & Engle-Warnick, 2002), and trust games (Rieskamp & Gigerenzer, 2002; Engle-Warnick & Slonim, 2004, 2006). The heuristics studied in these papers, such as the TIT-FOR-TAT, can be presented in the form of a decision tree heuristic. However, none of these studies has formally applied the top-down greedy

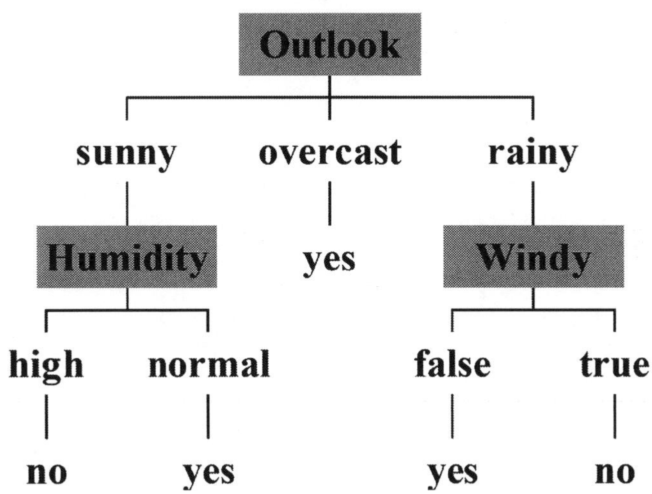

Figure 21.2 The decision tree of the *play tennis* decision

algorithms to build and formulate a decision tree heuristic; therefore, there is room for applying the decision tree model to discover the decision tree heuristics followed by human subjects in experimental or real data (Tagiew, 2012; Rosenfeld et al., 2015).

Second, while the top-down greedy algorithm can be useful for data mining and rule extraction, the algorithm per se may not provide a good description of the process of formation of these heuristics from a behavioral viewpoint. For example, humans may find the root attribute, "outlook" in Figure 21.2, based on their intuition, experience or preferences. In the case of the tennis player, putting outlook as the root attribute may be entirely due to the player's enjoyment in playing, but it may also be due to her past performance under different weather conditions. Hence, what is needed in behavioral economics is a learning (formation) process for the decision tree heuristics that are employed.

Incremental reinforcement decision tree construction[13]

The learning (formation) process includes two parts: first, the list of all relevant attributes, and, second, their ranks (positions) in the decision tree. The first issue is more complex and involves the discovery process, which we will show later on. Once a_t is determined, the second issue can be answered by reinforcement learning. Assume that decision makers begin with the *one-reason heuristic* and try to find out the best attribute, and then make a decision based on that attribute. In our tennis player example, the three attributes will compete for the attention of the tennis player at the first stage. After a while, overcast is selected through reinforcement learning as the first attribute, and the decision is:

IF ((Outlook=overcast)

THEN YES (Play Tennis))

As time goes on, the player may then discover that when the outlook is not overcast, he could still have fun playing tennis, and a competition for the second attribute is triggered again through another reinforcement learning cycle, which leads to the identification of humidity and wind as the second attribute under different branches of Figure 21.2, and the newly developed decision tree is: IF ([(Outlook=overcast)] OR [(Outlook=sunny) AND (Humidity=normal)] OR [(Outlook=rain) AND (Wind=weak)]) THEN YES (Play Tennis)).

In sum, the above proposal is to replace the original top-down greedy algorithm with incremental reinforcement learning. In this way, a learning (formation) process of the decision tree heuristic is articulated. The essence of the proposed behavioral algorithm is that it is *incremental*; basically, it decomposes the entire tree formation process into many "multi-armed bandit problems" and applies reinforcement learning to each of these bandit problems. Hence, as we have learned from Vriend's model, reinforcement learning can be applied generally to a meta-level of learning, and hence is much more powerful than it might seem.

In terms of understanding the human decision making process, decision trees can also be compared to the frequently used multivariate regression models, including the probit and logit models. First, human decisions may be fitted well by both these approaches, but multivariate regression only gives a summary of decision making, rather than a *process* of decision making. Hence, when trying to give an account of how a specific decision is made, it is easier to communicate using decision trees rather than by using multivariate regression. Second, when making a decision, multivariate regression essentially needs decision makers to pay attention *simultaneously* to multiple attributes, whereas decision trees only require them to focus on one attribute at a time.

From the viewpoint of cognitive loading, decision trees are less demanding than multivariate regression.[14]

Evolutionary computation

Autonomous agents

Evolutionary computation plays a critical role in the development of behavioral economics, in particular, the contribution to crystallizing the idea of *autonomous agents*, that is, agents who are able to discover chances or novelties without external guidance, in particular, without those "interventions" from modelers themselves. Behavioral economics has long criticized the notion of *Homo economicus* used in mainstream economics, but their proposed alternative, *Homo sapiens*, also suffers from operational emptiness. John Tomer's recent proposal on the notion of *smart persons* may not be an entirely new idea, but it clearly reveals the fact that the boundedly rational agents in behavioral economics have a blurred face (Tomer, 2015).[15] The *missing ingredient*, as Tomer calls it, in our view is exactly a notion of autonomous agents. One reason that the autonomous agents have not been well incorporated into behavioral economics is the lack of toolkits. It would probably be fair to say that the tools available for economists to build chance-discovering or novelty-discovering agents[16] with a moderate degree of autonomy were rather limited before the early 1990s.

In the early 1990s, genetic algorithms were formally introduced to economics as a tool to construct autonomous agents (Holland & Miller, 1991). The notion of autonomous agents is crucial for behavioral economics since a set of heuristics, be they biased or frugal, should not be taken as given, except those which are proved to be genetically driven and are innate. In general, the employed heuristics are constantly evolving and, as time goes on, new heuristics may be discovered. In a nutshell, heuristics should not be treated as scientific laws; instead, they can be best understood as an evolutionary process.

A good illustration of the evolution of heuristics as well as personal traits is the integration of gambling psychology in an agent-based lottery market (Chen & Chie, 2008). In their model, Chen and Chie (2008) incorporated three characteristics into their gambling decision making model; these three are the halo effects (lottomania)—related to participation ratio, conscious selection, and aversion to regret. What differentiates their model from the typical behavioral models is that these three characteristics are not imposed *exogenously*, but are probabilistic emergent properties.

A bit string, also known as a *chromosome* in genetic algorithms, is used to code the three characteristics of agents, and after decoding one can know the state of each characteristic, as shown in (20).

$$\overbrace{\underbrace{1001\ldots\ \ldots\ \ldots.0001}_{20\,bits}}^{participation\ ratio} \mid \overbrace{\underbrace{100\ldots\ \ldots\ \ldots..111}_{16\,bits}}^{conscious\ selection} \mid \overbrace{\underbrace{0\ldots\ \ldots\ \ldots\ \ldots\ \ldots 1}_{4\,bits}}^{degree\ of\ regret\ aversion} \tag{20}$$

The standard single-population genetic algorithm is then applied to evolve a population of these randomly-generated bit strings, characterizing the initial heterogeneities of gamblers on these characteristics. One can then observe how each of these characteristics changes over time, both at the individual level and aggregate level. From a market design perspective, Chen and Chie (2008) studied the effect of the lottery tax rate on the population size of non-gamblers (agents with a zero lottery participation rate). While the expected return of "investing" in a lottery is negative, the gamblers will not be driven out by the market selection mechanism defined by genetic algorithms. In addition, from probability theory, while conscious selection of winning numbers does not make any sense, Chen and Chie, however, showed that a rather moderate degree of conscious selection behavior will remain in the market; hence, the market also fails to drive out this "irrational" behavior. Perhaps the most intriguing part concerns their analysis of the regret aversion behavior. It was found that the attention to other gamblers' rewards (jackpots), a kind of social preference, may co-evolve with their devotion to gambling; both are co-determined by the lottery design (the lottery tax rate). Specifically, when the lottery tax rate is high, the size and the winning probability of jackpots become low and the gamblers' devotion also decreases, accompanied by their greater pleasure in being released from the possible regrets of not gambling. This exemplifies how evolutionary computation can work with behavioral economics by making the implicit selection process explicit and by providing a test for the stability of these behavioral patterns.

Hierarchical modularity

If behaviors (routines and heuristics) are not static but are constantly evolving, then one has to ask what the universal representation of the behavior of the evolution of behaviors is. In this section, inspired by Simon (1962), we propose hierarchical modularity as the fundamental representation.[17] Generally speaking, modularity refers to the idea of self-encapsulated, independently operationable, and reusable (evolvable) routines, procedures or programs. It provides us with a constructive way to think about what a decision making system is, and, in particular, how a decision maker can cope with complexity and survive in the constantly evolving environment. Take decision trees as an example. Each decision tree can be perceived as a module, and, therefore, can be used to construct a bigger decision tree if the root of the child tree is an emanating node of some mother trees. In other words, decision trees can be considered as a special case of hierarchical modularity.

In computational intelligence, the idea of modularity can be realized by genetic programming (Koza, 1992). Instead of working on finite-length strings (bits), genetic programming directly operates on the space of computation programs which are represented using the formal language theory, specifically, the context-free grammar (Linz, 2006). Starting with a finite set of alphabets (primitives) and following the given grammar (production rules), one can develop phrases, sentences, paragraphs, chapters, books, all the way up without a limit. In each stage of this development, simpler or lower-level modules are used to construct sophisticated or higher-level modules, and this process can continue without an end. To understand the meaning of a decision rule, one only needs to harness its immediate constituents (modules). Since each module is already encapsulated, there is no need to go further down to their modules, and their modules' modules, and so on. The modular structure, therefore, reduces the huge amount of information required in applying a rule or making a decision.

Genetic heterogeneity

In addition to being a tool for the computational behavioral model of searching and discovery, evolutionary computation also contributes to behavioral economics by generating agents with heterogeneous traits. Recently, there has been a growing attempt to explore the genetic influence that concerns human decision making. Some recent areas of focus in behavioral economics, such as self-control, impulsivity, addiction, patience, risk preference, and cognitive capacity, are being examined for possible heritable factors. The literature on this area continues to grow.

In 2007, Daniel Benjamin and his colleagues gave this nascent field a neologism: *genoeconomics* (Benjamin et al., 2007).

The relation between cognitive capacity and decision making has become an issue of focus in this stream of the literature. Earlier genoeconomic studies have indicated a possible pathway from genetic causes to cognitive capacity, to education and to income. Recently, the decision making capability under an uncertain environment has also been included as a part of this pathway (Beauchamp et al., 2011; Callaway, 2012; MacKillop, 2013; Ashraf & Galor, 2013). In parallel, experimental economists have also begun to design human-subject experiments to examine the possible effects of cognitive capacity on economic decisions.[18]

If cognitive capacity does affect decision making, including both processes and outcomes, then what will be the ideal computational model to take account of this factor? Recently, it has been suggested that the *population size*, a key parameter used in evolutionary computation, can be regarded as a proxy variable for cognitive capacity (Casari, 2004; Chen, Tai, & Wang, 2010). In physical terms, population size is related to space complexity in computation theory. The logistics of a complex product requires many intermediate steps and, hence, needs a large space to store and to integrate intermediate products. If the space is not large enough, then a complex product may be beyond the affordability of all available logistics. Hence, population size directly determines the capability of parallel processing of many intermediate tasks.

On the other hand, the working memory capacity of a human being is frequently tested based on the number of cognitive tasks that humans can simultaneously process (Cappelletti, Guth & Ploner, 2008). Dual tasks have been used in hundreds of psychological experiments to measure the attentional demands of different mental activities (Pashler, 1998). Hence, the population size seems to be an appropriate choice with regard to mimicking the working memory capacity of human agents; in this sense, evolutionary computation can directly control the 'cognitive capacity' of a computational behavioral model through varying population size. The heterogeneity of cognitive capacity of different human subjects can be represented by a society of artificial agents driven by genetic algorithms or genetic programming with different population sizes.

The proposed computational behavioral model of cognitive capacity, working memory capacity (WMC), has been applied to agent-based double auction markets to examine the effect of WMC on earning performance (Chen, Tai, & Wang, 2010).[19] It is found that the artificial traders with larger WMC can earn more than the artificial traders with smaller WMC. However, this dominance becomes less (statistically) significant when WMC increases further. Moreover, if we allow artificial traders with lower WMC more time to learn so that their deficiency in terms of WMC can be compensated by the longer time of learning (evolution), then the above income gap can disappear if the difference in WMC among traders is limited; otherwise, the gap can only be narrowed, but it will not disappear. Therefore, the above simulation shows that even though the double auction market is an easy environment, it can still generate persistent income inequality if the heterogeneity in the cognitive capacity of traders is significant enough.

Ant as a model of human behavior

Our next section focuses on the ant colony optimization algorithm, another computational intelligence tool that is frequently used in the context of optimization, such as the travelling salesman problem (Dorigo & Stützle, 2010). Compared to some other CI tools, such as reinforcement learning and evolutionary computation, the ant algorithm or, more generally, swarm intelligence is relatively less familiar to behavioral economists. Due to the important contributions by Alan Kirman (1991, 1993), economists have a chance to access interesting findings and puzzles related to ants' foraging behavior.

Earlier entomological experiments, cited in Kirman (1993), have shown that ants' foraging behavior over two identical equidistant food sources can demonstrate constant asymmetric distribution over the two sources; say, one source attracts the majority of ants and the other source attracts the minority of ants. Furthermore, as time goes on, the majority side and the minority side will switch without any external environmental changes. In other words, ants can collectively generate an endogenous fluctuation of their foraging distribution over the two sources of food. While this is an entomological finding, it has some significant implications for economics and other social sciences. Its possible implications have been well surveyed in Kirman (1993), including providing support for a fundamental instability in financial markets.

The underlying mechanism for this endogenous switching is known as a communication mechanism called *stigmergy*. The communication among ants is not necessarily direct, but more indirect, partially due to their poor visibility. The ants' reliance on indirect communication has been noticed by the French biologist Pierre-Paul Grasse (1895–1985), and he termed this style of communication or interaction *stigmergy* (Grosan and Abraham, 2006). He defined stigmergy as: "Stimulation of workers by the performance they have achieved." Stigmergy is a method of communication in which the individuals communicate with each other via modifying their local environment. For ants, this is achieved by the release of pheromone along their foraging trails.

However, the essence of these algorithms is to have an explicit modeling of social interactions on individual behavior. These algorithms are again built on empirical grounds, in this case, entomological experiments. Due to the nature of entomology, one would hardly argue whether these ants or locusts or other low-level swarms are consciously choosing to do anything "rational"; studies of their behavior tend to be more in the biological or neurological direction (Garnier, Gautrais & Theraulaz, 2007; Beekman, Sword & Simpson, 2010). Hence, the experimental results obtained here seem to put more focus on the effect of social interactions on emission or release of chemical materials, such as pheromone in the case of ants, or neurotransmitters, such as serotonin in the case of locusts (Paula et al., 2015).

We have known that social interactions have many channels to affect agents' decision and behavioral rules, such as social norms, social conformity, homophily, etc. In Kirman's ant model, the proposed social interaction mechanism is binary so that only a simple stochastic process, an urn process, is introduced to determine how one agent's decision can be affected by a randomly encountered agent. In computational intelligence, the behavioral algorithm is more explicitly related to the accumulated pheromone or accumulated serotonin, hence even though the decision can still be random, it is stochastic in a way related to various characteristics of social interactions, such as the degree of social polarization and the size of social network (for the concern of social conformity) (Valentini & Hamann, 2015). This type of algorithm essentially allows us to address the connection between social interactions and individual decisions through the biological and neural mechanisms. In this regard, the development of swarm intelligence stands in a unique position in computational behavioral economics in the sense that it can effectively incorporate the findings of neuroscientific experiments with these insects into the behavioral algorithms proposed for these swarms. Since entomological experiments are easier to implement, we hope that the behavioral economists can gain some useful insights, which are more difficult to glean from human fMRI experiments.

Can randomization be a heuristic?

All the heuristics reviewed up to this point correspond to some degree of learning from either one's own or others' experiences and reasoning with them. There is, however, a heuristic which requires no memory, no learning, and no reasoning. This is known as the *zero-intelligence heuristic*, to which we now turn.

The zero-intelligence (ZI) agent has been one of the widely employed characterizations of an agent in agent-based models and it has had a remarkable impact in both economics and finance (Ladley, 2012). The supposed simplicity of this kind of agent stems from their lack of strategy and their random behavior. Gode and Sunder (1993), and many since then, have employed this device to illustrate the irrelevance of a high level of sophistication in strategies and learning at the individual level in achieving market level efficiency.[20]

ZI agents or randomly behaving agents have been employed in wider contexts that range beyond a mere device to separate the effect of strategies from that of the market mechanism. The rationale for this agent design is that the individual level details become worn out in the aggregate with a large number of heterogeneous agents. Another reason advanced is the lack of precise knowledge about strategies used by different agents, at any given point in time. Hence, modeling them as if they behave in a random fashion (from a bounded set of strategies) allows one to not commit to one strategy *a priori*. Consequently, "zero intelligence agent" may be a misnomer and *entropy maximizing agents* can serve as a better term. This is because the relationship between zero intelligence, cognitive ability and the ease or the simplicity of random behavior may not be as obvious or straightforward.[21]

While there may be a case to start with entropy maximizing agents in the face of ignorance, their behavioral underpinnings ought to be scrutinized. The *entropy maximizing* role needs to be distinguished from *random behavior* as being a proxy for simplicity or naivety in terms of strategies (or a lack of them). By relating "zero intelligence" to random behavior, the implicit assumption is that random behavior is simple to execute and that it requires very little sophistication. To design artificial economic agents more like human agents, we need to examine whether the programmed actions have a psychological or behavioral foundation. Hence, the plausibility of human beings to be able to "behave" in an analogous fashion and the associated cognitive demands need to be studied. In this context, it is therefore natural to question the ability and the extent to which human agents can choose strategies randomly. More generally, we need to examine whether it is behaviorally plausible for an agent to act randomly and for the others to perceive such an action to be random.

Studies from psychology indicate that the human ability to perceive randomness and act randomly may be limited (Wagenaar, 1972). This problem can be subdivided into the ability to perceive, discriminate and generate random behavior, each of which is far from easy. In the light of limited memory, cognitive limitation (Hahn & Warren, 2009) and finiteness of data, detection and execution of random or patternless behavior seems notoriously hard (Kahneman & Tversky, 1972). This is further complicated by difficulties in the characterization of randomness when the data are finite. Even a supposedly elementary task of generating random sequences has been found to be a non-trivial, difficult exercise for human subjects in experimental environments.[22] In addition, the distinction between the perception and identifiability of randomness raises further questions about the indiscriminate use of randomly behaving agents in strategic and interactive environments that one often encounters in economics and agent-based models (Zhao, Hahn, & Osherson, 2014). If randomness is interpreted as a lack of a pattern or rule in the sequence of responses generated, then such random behavior requires the avoidance of any discernible pattern. Interpreted this way, random behavior may require far more intelligence, cognitive ability, and sophistication than otherwise assumed.

In sum, although randomization in the form of entropy maximization may be often considered as a cognitively effortless heuristic, our review indicates that this "stereotype" may not be entirely correct; hence, without relying on an external device, such as a coin, dice, or an oracle, making a truly random decision may not be that easy for the human brain.

Concluding remarks

Computational intelligence or machine learning has been developed independently of behavioral economics over a period of about three decades. Before this, and even through this period, the dominating approach regarding decision making in economics has been probability and statistics, upon which the rational expectations revolution has been built. The formulation of decision making in the mainstream economics literature is basically the application of statistical decision theory, which, in turn, is the application of von Neumann and Morgenstern's expected utility maximization framework (Ferguson, 2014). Computational intelligence is a credible alternative to this paradigm. Instead of a model driven approach, it is mainly a data-driven or an experience-based approach. Instead of being restricted to a "small world" (Savage, 1972), it mainly deals with uncertainty in a "large world" in which a proper probabilistic formulation of the world is often infeasible.

Computational intelligence relies on various heuristics to build another set of guidelines to learn from the past, to cope with complexity, and to make decisions. Some of these heuristics that are reviewed in this chapter include similarity, closeness, smoothness, reinforcement, default, automation, hierarchy, and modularity. These heuristics together help shape what is known as *behavioral AI*, to be distinguished from classical AI or symbolic AI (Wooldridge, 2009).[23] We believe that computational intelligence can consolidate and enrich the study of behavioral economics by providing the computational underpinnings of decision making processes. This direction, referred to as computational behavioral economics, will also enhance the interdisciplinary conversations between behavioral economics and other related disciplines.

Acknowledgments

The authors have benefitted from two excellent referee reports, and we are grateful to Manuel Scholz-Wäckerle and Andreas Duus Pape for their painstaking review of the paper with many valuable and constructive comments and suggestions. The first author and the third author are grateful for the research support in the form of Ministry of Science and Technology (MOST) grants, MOST 103-2410-H-004-009-MY3, and MOST 104-2811-H-004-003, respectively.

Notes

1 For a comprehensive treatment of Hayek's contribution to behavioral economics, the interested reader is referred to Frantz and Lesson (2013).

2 In the literature, it is also known as instance-based decision or instance-based reasoning; in this chapter, we shall use these terms interchangeably.

3 Descriptive complexity looks into the amount of information required to "describe" a given, finite, binary sequence, but more generally to mathematical objects. The notion stems from the work of Andrey Kolmogorov (1903–87), Ray Solomonoff (1926–2009) and Gregory Chaitin in the 1960s, and the description needs to be understood in terms of output of ideal Turing machines. This is different from computational complexity. See Li and Vitanyi (2008).

4 Takens' paper was in the context of fluid dynamics, identifying procedures to decide whether or not to attribute experimental data to the presence of strange attractors. By *the physicist approach* what we mean is those from the dynamical systems origin.

5 The same issue can interest economists as well, because it concerns the efficient use of limited space. An early study on reward-motivated memory formation by neural scientists may provide an economic foundation for the memory formation (Adcock et al., 2006). Adcock et al. (2006) reports brain-scanning studies in humans that reveal how specific reward-related brain regions trigger the brain's learning and memory regions to promote memory formation.

6 The magic number *seven*, originally proposed by Miller (1956), is a measure related to short memory capacity or working memory capacity, characterized by the number of items that an individual can

discriminate or remember over very short periods of time, say, seconds. Based on a few experiments that he reviewed, Miller concluded that most people can correctly recall about 7 ± 2 items. Different numbers have been proposed in this stream of literature.

7 Reinforcement learning has also been used to explain institutional change, more precisely, the interdependence between economic behavior of agents and institutional change. See, for example, Heinrich and Schwardt (2013).

8 See Montague (2006), chapter 4, for a vivid historical review of the research on the dopamine system and reinforcement learning.

9 By one-good-reason heuristics, agents focus on *only one good reason* or *cue* to make a decision, rather than considering all cues and weighting them. Contrary to expectations, they are not just fast, but also more accurate in a variety of environments (Snook et al., 2005; Gigerenzer and Gaissmaier, 2011).

10 While we use the term hierarchy, Equation (7) is not the *hierarchical reinforcement learning* normally formulated in the context of a Markov decision process (Barto and Mahadevan, 2003) and recently applied to computational neuroscience (Botvinick, 2012). The kind of decision considered by us in this chapter is not Markovian, but a type of reinforcement learning model frequently used by experimental economists. The usual hierarchical reinforcement learning models use the idea of subroutines, macro procedures, modularity, or the so-called abstraction states to deal with the curse of dimensionality. We shall come back to this idea in the fifth section.

11 This ideal environment is very similar to the situation depicted by the movie *Groundhog Day* as briefly mentioned in Thaler (2000).

12 Given that there are other chapters devoted to this subject, for example, Chen, Chie and Tai (chapter 18), to avoid redundancy, we shall not elaborate on this hypothesis further.

13 We are grateful to Andreas Pape for suggesting this term to replace our originally proposed term, incremental reinforcement learning.

14 This is specific when we consider some cognitive constraint, such as Miller's magic number, *seven* (Miller, 1956). The point we wish to make in this paragraph is not on which decision model is real, i.e., the actual mechanisms/processes that exist in people's heads, since both multivariate regressions and decision trees may not be real decision processes. Instead, we address the transparency of a decision model in its dynamics.

15 In a spectrum between Homo Economicus and Homo Sapiens, Tomer (2015) tries to position an agent called the *smart person*, who differs from those at both ends. To do so, Tomer identifies the missing ingredients in both ends.

16 While chance-discovering is tied to the notion of random behavior, the idea and the process of novelty-discovery does not necessarily have to be random. Also, see Witt (2009).

17 By Simon (1962), the reason that one can harness complex systems is because they tend to be near decomposable and evolving hierarchical.

18 For a survey of these experiments, the interested reader is referred to Chen (2015), chapter 17.

19 See Wäckerle, Rengs and Radax (2014) for the role of different memory sizes on social trust and institutional change analyzed within an agent-based framework.

20 For a critical discussion on the cognitive ability of the ZI agents, see Tubaro (2009).

21 See Chen (2012) for a discussion on the relationships.

22 There are studies which argue that random behavior can be learned in the presence of feedback (Neuringer, 1986). However, in the standard version of ZI, agents do not learn.

23 About behavioral AI, Wooldridge (2009) made the following remarks:

> The workers in this area were not united by any common approaches, but certain themes did occur in this work. Recurring themes were the rejection of architectures based on symbolic representations, an emphasis on a closer coupling between the agent's environment and the action it performs, and the idea that *intelligent behavior can be seen to emerge from the interaction of a number of much simpler behaviors.*
>
> *(Ibid.: 395; italics added.)*

Bibliography

Adcock, A., Thangavel, A., Whitfield-Gabrieli, S., Knutson, B. & Gabrieli, J. (2006). Reward motivated learning: Mesolimbic activation precedes memory formation. Neuron, 50(3), 507–17.

Aha, D. (1997). Lazy Learning. Kluwer.

Aha, D., Kibler, D. Marc, K. (1991). Instance-based learning algorithms. Machine Learning, 6(1), 37–66.
Ashraf, Q. & Galor, O. (2013). The "Out of Africa" hypothesis, human genetic diversity, and comparative economic development. American Economic Review, 103(1), 1–46
Axelrod, R. (1984) The Evolution of Cooperation. New York: Basic Books.
Barto, A. & Mahadevan, S. (2003). Recent advances in hierarchical reinforcement learning. Discrete Event Systems Journal, 13, 41–77.
Beauchamp, J., Cesarini, D., Johannesson, M., van der Loos, M., Koellinger, P., Groenen, P., Fowler, H., Rosenquist, J., Thurik, A., & Christakis, N. (2011). Molecular genetics and economics. Journal of Economic Perspectives, 25(4), 57–82.
Beekman, M., Sword, G. & Simpson, S. (2010). Biological foundations of swarm intelligence. In Blum, C. & Merkle, D. (eds.), Swarm Intelligence: Introduction and Application. Springer, 3–41.
Benjamin, D., Chabris, C., Glaeser, E., Gudnason, V., Harris, T., Laibson, D., Launer, L., & Purcell, S. (2007). Genoeconomics. In: Weinstein, M., Vaupel, J. & Wachter, K. (eds.), Biosocial Surveys. National Academic Press, 303–35.
Betsch, T. & Haberstroh, S. (eds.) (2014). The Routines of Decision Making. Psychology Press.
Bodenhausen, G. (1990). Stereotypes as judgmental heuristics: Evidence of circadian variations in discrimination. Psychological Science, 1(5), 319–22.
Botvinick, M. (2012). Hierarchical reinforcement learning and decision making. Current Opinion in Neurobiology, 22(6), 956–62.
Boyer, C., Brorsen, W. & Zhang, T. (2014). Common-value auction versus posted-price selling: An agent-based model approach. Journal of Economic Interaction and Coordination, 9(1), 129–49.
Bush, R. R. & Mosteller, F. (1955). Stochastic Models for Learning. New York: JohnWiley & Sons.
Callaway, E. (2012). Economics and genetics meet in uneasy union. Nature, 490(7419), 154–5.
Camerer, C. & Ho, T.-H. (1999). Experienced-weighted attraction learning in normal form games. Econometrica, 67(4), 827–74.
Cappelletti, D., Guth, W. & Ploner, M. (2008). Being of two minds: An ultimatum experiment investigating affective processes. Jena Economic Research Papers, 2008-048.
Casari, M. (2004). Can genetic algorithms explain experimental anomalies? An application to common property resources. Computational Economics, 24, 257–75.
Casdagli, M. (1991). Chaos and deterministic versus stochastic nonlinear modeling. Journal of the Royal Statistical Society B, 54, 303–28.
Chan, N., LeBaron, B., Lo, A. & Poggio, T. (1999). Information dissemination and aggregation in asset markets with simple intelligent traders, Working paper, MIT.
Chaxel, A. (2015). How do stereotypes influence choice? Psychological Science, 26(5), 641–5.
Chen, S.-H. (ed.) (2002a). Evolutionary Computation in Economics and Finance. Physica-Verlag.
Chen, S.-H. (ed.) (2002b). Genetic Algorithms and Genetic Programming in Computational Finance. Kluwer.
Chen, S.-H. (2012). Varieties of agents in agent-based computational economics: A historical and an interdisciplinary perspective. Journal of Economic Dynamics and Control, 36(1), 1–25.
Chen, S.-H. (2013). Reasoning-based artificial agents in agent-based computational economics. In: Nakamatsu, K & Jain, L. (eds.), Handbook on Reasoning-based Intelligent Systems, World Scientific, 575–602.
Chen, S.-H. (2015). Agent-Based Computational Economics: How the Idea Originated and Where it is Going. Routledge.
Chen, S.-H. & Chie, B.-T. (2008). Lottery markets design, micro-structure, and macrobehavior: An ACE approach. Journal of Economic Behavior and Organization, 67(2), 463–80.
Chen, S.-H. & Hsieh, Y.-L. (2011). Reinforcement learning in experimental asset markets. Eastern Economic Journal, 37(1), 109–33.
Chen, S.-H., Tai, C.-C. & Wang, S.-G. (2010) Does cognitive capacity matter when learning using genetic programming in double auction markets? In: Di Tosto, G. & Parunak, V. (eds), Multi-Agent-Based Simulation X. Springer, 37–48.
Cleveland, W. (1979). Robust locally weighted regression and smoothing scatterplots. Journal of the American Statistical Association, 74(368), 829–36.
Cover, T. & Hart, P. (1967). Nearest neighbor pattern classification. IEEE Transactions on Information Theory, 13(1), 21–7.
Damasio, A. (1994). Descartes' Error: Emotion, Reason and the Human Brain. Grosset: Putnam.
Dorigo, M. & Stützle, T. (2010) Ant colony optimization: Overview and recent advances. In: Gendreau, M. & Potvin, J. (eds.), Handbook of Metaheuristics. Springer, 227–63.

Duffy, J. (2006). Agent-based models and human subject experiments. In: Tesfatsion, L. & Judd, K. (eds), Handbook of Computational Economics: Agent-based Computational Economics, Vol. 2., Oxford: Elsevier, 949–1011.
Duffy, J. & Engle-Warnick, J. (2002). Using symbolic regression to infer strategies from experimental data. In Chen, S. (ed.), Evolutionary Computation in Economics and Finance, Springer, 61–82.
Engle-Warnick, J. & Slonim, R. (2004). The evolution of strategies in a repeated trust game. Journal of Economic Behavior and Organization, 55(4), 553–73.
Engle-Warnick, J. & Slonim, R. (2006). Inferring repeated-game strategies from actions: Evidence from trust game experiments. Economic Theory, 28, 603–32.
Erev, I. & Roth, A. (1998). Predicting how people play games: Reinforcement learning in experimental games with unique, mixed strategy equilibria. American Economic Review, 88, 848–81.
Fabre, E., Causse, M., Pesciarelli, F. & Cacciari, C. (2015). Sex and the money: How gender stereotypes modulate economic decision-making: An ERP study. Neuropsychologia, 75, 221–32.
Farmer, J. & Sidorowich, J. (1987). Predicting chaotic time series. Physical Review Letters, 59(8), 845–7.
Ferguson, T. (2014). Mathematical Statistics: A Decision Theoretic Approach (Vol. 1). Academic Press.
Frantz, R. & Leeson, R. (eds.) (2013). Hayek and Behavioral Economics. Palgrave Macmillan.
Garnier, S., Gautrais, J. & Theraulaz, G. (2007). The biological principles of swarm intelligence. Swarm Intelligence, 1(1), 3–31.
Gilboa, I. & Schmeidler, D. (1995). Case-based decision theory. Quarterly Journal of Economics, 110(3), 605–39.
Gilboa, I. & Schmeidler, D. (2001). A Theory of Case-Based Decisions. Cambridge University Press.
Gigerenzer, G. (2007). Gut Feelings: The Intelligence of the Unconscious. Penguin Books.
Gigerenzer, G. & Gaissmaier, W. (2011). Heuristic decision making. Annual Review of Psychology, 62, 451–82.
Gode, D. & Sunder, S. (1993). Allocative efficiency of markets with zero intelligence traders: Market as a partial substitute for individual rationality. Journal of Political Economy, 101, 119–37.
Grosan, C. & Abraham, A. (2006). Stigmergic optimization: Inspiration, technologies and perspectives. In Abraham, A., Gorsan, C. & Ramos, V. (eds.), Stigmergic Optimization. Springer, 1–24.
Hahn, U. & Warren, P. (2009). Perceptions of randomness: Why three heads are better than four. Psychological Review, 116(2), 454–61.
Hayek, F. (1945). The use of knowledge in society. American Economic Review, 35(4), 519–30.
Heinrich, T. & Schwardt, H. (2013) Institutional inertia and institutional change in an expanding normal-form game. Games, 4, 398–425.
Holland, J. & Miller, J. (1991). Artificial adaptive agents in economic theory. American Economic Review, 81(2), 365–70.
Kahneman, D. (2011). Thinking, Fast and Slow. Farrar, Straus and Giroux.
Kahneman, D. & Tversky, A. (1972). Subjective probability: A judgment of representativeness. Cognitive Psychology, 3, 430–54.
Kirman, A. (1991). Epidemics of opinion and speculative bubbles in financial markets. In: Taylor, M. (ed.), Money and Financial Markets. Blackwell, Cambridge, 354–68.
Kirman, A. (1993). Ants, rationality, and recruitment. Quarterly Journal of Economics, 108, 137–156.
Kohonen, T. (1995). Self-organizing Maps. Springer.
Koza, J. (1992). Genetic Programming: On the Programming of Computers by Means of Natural Selection. MIT Press.
Ladley, D. (2012). Zero intelligence in economics and finance. Knowledge Engineering Review, 27(2), 273–86.
Li, M. & Vitanyi, P. (2008). An Introduction to Kolmogorov Complexity and its Applications. Springer.
Linz, P. (2006). An Introduction to Formal Languages and Automata. 4th edition. Jones & Bartlett.
MacKillop, J. (2013). Integrating behavioral economics and behavioral genetics: Delayed reward discounting as an endophenotype for addictive disorders. Journal of the Experimental Analysis of Behavior, 99(1), 14–31.
MacQueen, J. (1967). Some methods for classification and analysis of multivariate observations. Proceedings of 5th Berkeley Symposium on Mathematical Statistics and Probability. University of California Press, 1, 281–97.
Madrian, B. (2014). Applying insights from behavioral economics to policy design. Annual Review of Economics, 6, 663–88.

Mathy, F. & Feldman, J. (2012). What's magic about magic numbers? Chunking and data compression in short-term memory. Cognition, 122, 346–62.
Miller, G. (1956). The magical number seven plus or minus two: Some limits on our capacity for processing information. Psychological Review, 63, 81–97.
Montague, R. (2006). Why Choose This Book? New York: Dutton.
Mormann, M., Koch, C. & Rangel, A. (2011). Consumers can make decisions in as little as a third of a second. Judgment and Decision Making, 6(6), 520–30.
Neuringer, A. (1986). Can people behave "randomly"?: The role of feedback. Journal of Experimental Psychology: General, 115(1), 62–75.
Newell, B. & Shanks, D. (2014). Unconscious influences on decision making: A critical review. Behavioral and Brain Sciences, 37(1), 1–19.
Nowak, M. (2006). Evolutionary Dynamics: Exploring the Equations of Life. Harvard University Press.
Pape, A. & Kurtz, K. (2013). Evaluating case-based decision theory: Predicting empirical patterns of human classification learning. Games and Economic Behavior, 82(1), 5265.
Pashler, H. (1998). The Psychology of Attention. Cambridge, MA: MIT Press.
Paula, J., Messias, J., Grutter, A., Bshary, R. & Soares, M. (2015). The role of serotonin in the modulation of cooperative behavior. Behavioral Ecology, arv039.
Quinlan, R. (1986). Induction of decision trees. Machine Learning, 1(1), 81–106.
Rieskamp, J. & Gigerenzer, G. (2002). Heuristics for social interactions: How to generate trust and fairness. Paper presented at a colloquium at the Workshop in Political Theory and Policy Analysis, Indiana University, Bloomington, on April 8, 2002.
Rosenfeld, A., Bareket, Z., Goldman, C., LeBlanc, D. & Tsimhoni, O. (2015). Learning drivers, behavior to improve adaptive cruise control. Journal of Intelligent Transportation Systems, 19(1), 18–31.
Roth, A. & Erev, I. (1995). Learning in extensive-form games: Experimental data and simple dynamic models in the intermediate term. Games and Economic Behavior, Special Issue: Nobel Symposium, 8, 164–212.
Sargent, T. (1993). Bounded Rationality in Macroeconomics. Oxford.
Savage, L. (1972). The Foundations of Statistics. Courier Corporation.
Scott, J. (2012). Social Network Analysis. 3rd edition, Sage Publications, London.
Sen, A. (1997). Maximization and the act of choice. Econometrica, 65(4), 745–79.
Simon, H. (1962). The architecture of complexity. Proceedings of the American Philosophical Society, 106(6), 467–82.
Snook, B., Zito, M., Bennell, C. & Taylor, P. J. (2005). On the complexity and accuracy of geographic profiling strategies. Journal of Quantitative Criminology, 21, 1–26.
Stone, C. (1977). Consistent nonparametric regression. Annals of Statistics, 5(4), 595–620.
Tagiew, R. (2012). Mining determinism in human strategic behavior. In: Tagiew, R., Ignatov, D., Neznanov, A. & Poelmans, J. (eds.), Experimental Economics in Machine Learning. Workshop co-located with the 10th International Conference on Formal Concept Analysis, May 2012, Leuven, Belgium. 84–91.
Takens, F. (1981). Detecting strange attractors in turbulence. In: Rand, D. & Young, L.-S. (eds.), Dynamical Systems and Turbulence. Springer-Verlag, 366–81.
Thaler, R. (2000). From Homo economicus to Homo sapiens. Journal of Economic Perspectives, 14(1), 133–141.
Thaler, R. & Sunstein, C. (2008). Nudge: Improving Decisions about Health, Wealth, and Happiness. Penguin Books.
Tomer, J. (2015). Smart persons and human development: The missing ingredient in behavioral economics. In: Altman M. (ed.), Behavioral Economics with Smart People, Edward Elgar.
Tubaro, P. (2009). Is individual rationality essential to market price formation? The contribution of zero-intelligence agent trading models. Journal of Economic Methodology, 16(1), 1–19.
Valentini, G. & Hamann, H. (2015). Time-variant feedback processes in collective decision making systems: Influence and effect of dynamic neighborhood sizes. Swarm Intelligence, 9(2–3), 153–76.
von Neumann, J. & Morgenstern, O. (1944). Theory of Games and Economic Behavior. Princeton University Press, Princeton.
Vriend, N. (2002). Was Hayek an ACE? Southern Economic Journal, 68(4), 811–40.
Wäckerle, M., Rengs, B. & Radax, W. (2014). An agent-based model of institutional life-cycles. Games, 5, 160–87.

Wagenaar, W. (1972). Generation of random sequences by human subjects: A critical survey of literature. Psychological Bulletin, 77(1), 65–72.

Wansink, B. & Sobal, J. (2007). Mindless eating: The 200 daily food decisions we overlook. Environment & Behavior, 39(1), 106–23.

Witt, U. (2009). Propositions about novelty. Journal of Economic Behavior & Organisation, 70, 311–20.

Wooldridge, M. (2009). An Introduction to Multi-Agent Systems, 2nd Edition. Wiley.

Zhao, J., Hahn, U. & Osherson, D. (2014). Perception and identification of random events. Journal of Experimental Psychology: Human Perception and Performance, 40(4), 1358–71.

22
EMOTIONS IN ECONOMY

Nina Bandelj, Julie Kim, and Zaibu Tufail

Introduction

About twenty years ago, George Loewenstein (1996: 289) concluded that "[with] all its cleverness . . . decision theory is somewhat crippled emotionally, and thus detached from the emotional and visceral richness of life." Since then, research on emotions and economy has grown substantially. A search in EconLit database in 2015 produced about 200 articles with the word emotions in their titles, with the bulk of these articles appearing after 2000.

In this body of work, which is growing across disciplines, researchers use notions such as emotions, affect, physical drive states, or mood, and link them to various economic processes. While there are conceptual distinctions between these terms, we will subsume them under the general term "emotion" for the purposes of this review. In social psychological and sociological analyses emotional states include visceral physiological reactions as well as interpretation of these reactions. We also include in this review research on economics of happiness, recognizing that this research deals with not just emotions but more general understandings of subjective wellbeing.

Many writers on the role of emotions in economic processes note that early economic theory considered emotions as peripheral to decisions. As Figure 22.1 illustrates, this framework treats emotions as a byproduct of decision-making and not related to the outcome. With the rise of behavioral economics and increasing experimental evidence, economic analysts started to take emotions seriously, and have found it useful to distinguish between "expected" and "immediate" emotions (Loewenstein et al., 2001; Loewenstein & Lerner, 2003). Expected emotions refer to those emotional states that are anticipated ahead of time to occur as the outcome of a certain decision occurs (Figure 22.2). For instance, a person buying a car may anticipate feeling happiness after the purchase is complete, which can become a part of her subjective expected utility. Such a role for anticipated emotions is entirely consistent with the assumption that people assess the desirability and likelihood of consequences of particular courses of action and choose the action that promises maximum expected utility. Here, anticipated emotions are just one additional factor to take into account when assessing expected utility.

In contrast, immediate emotions are, just as the term implies, immediately experienced as the decision process is ongoing, often as visceral reactions that shape the ongoing decision-making process. Immediate emotions are not merely a byproduct of decision-making, but have an

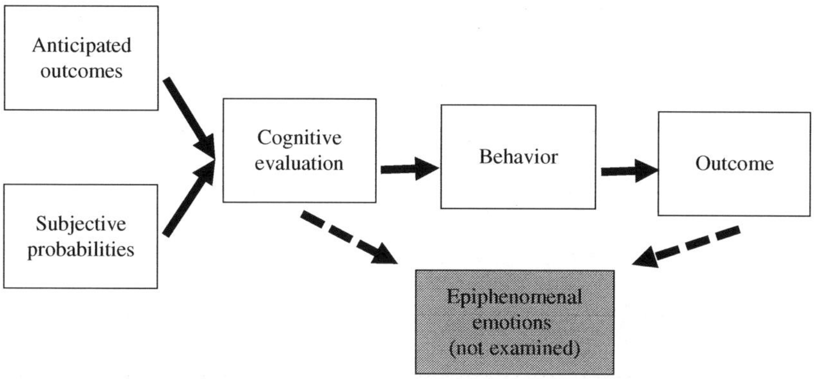

Figure 22.1 Emotion and classical economic theory

Source: Adapted from Loewenstein et al. (2001).

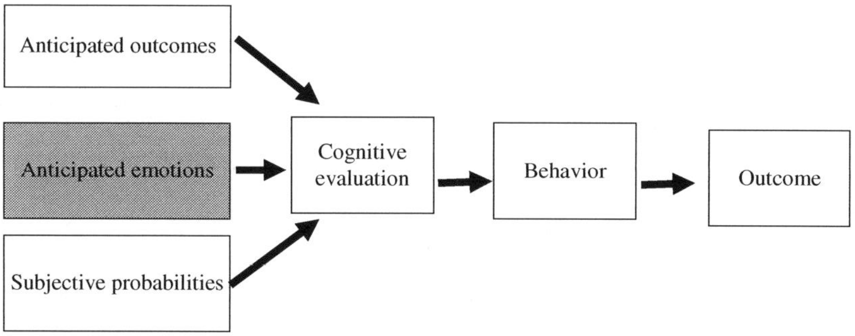

Figure 22.2 Anticipated emotions integrated into classical theory

Source: Adapted by authors from Loewenstein et al. (2001).

influence on what kind of a decision takes place, what Loewenstein and colleagues (2001) summarized in a "risk-as-feelings" perspective (Figure 22.3). We can distinguish between two kinds of immediate emotions, integral and incidental (Rick & Loewenstein, 2008). On the one hand, integral emotions arise while individuals consider the consequences of their decisions and are experienced at the moment of choice. For example, in the process of deciding whether to buy a car, a person might experience immediate elation and pride at envisioning her driving this car, or immediate fear at the thought of investing a large amount of money in a durable that will lose its value as soon as she drives off the parking lot. On the other hand, incidental emotions, while also experienced during the process of decision-making, "arise from dispositional or situational sources objectively unrelated to the task at hand" (Rick & Loewenstein, 2008: 138), such as the crying of a child that may happen to be in that car dealership shop, or spilling coffee on the way to buy a car, which makes the buyer upset for reasons unrelated to the purchase. Integral immediate emotions may be incorporated into a classical decision-making framework, if we relax the assumption that people have known preferences. In this case, the integral immediate emotions would help articulate tastes and clarify what expected emotions of a decision maker truly are, as the incremental decision process is ongoing. Taking incidental emotions seriously presents a challenge to the classical perspective because, by definition, incidental emotions are an

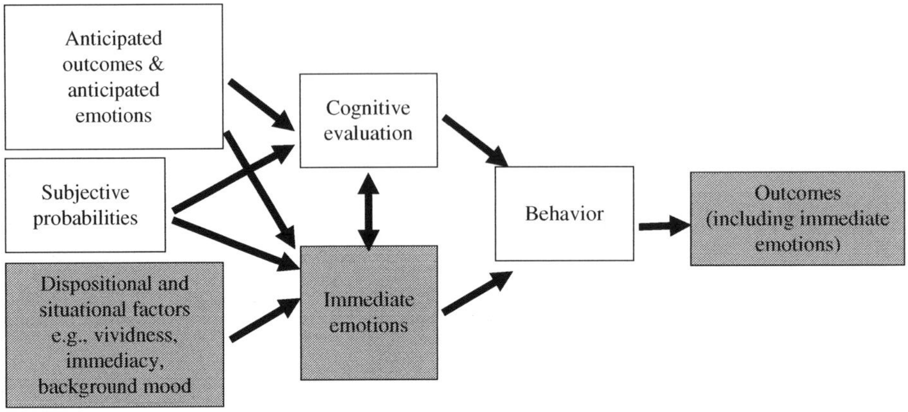

Figure 22.3 Risk-as-feelings perspective

Source: Adapted by authors from Loewenstein et al. (2001).

unexpected byproduct of the decision situation (such as vividness, immediacy, background mood, etc.) and thus irrelevant to the decision at hand. This means that a factor unrelated to the expected utility may influence decisions.

Social psychologists and sociologists provide what we call an emotional embeddedness perspective because they go beyond the individual decision-making framework to point to the influence of social interaction between individuals during one's economic decision-making process, and how such interaction induces immediate emotions that shape economic outcomes in often unanticipated ways (Bandelj 2009, Rivera 2015). Moreover, this emotional embeddedness perspective also stipulates the impact of organizational context and occupational roles on emotional experience (Figure 22.4).

Integrating findings across disciplines, this chapter provides a brief overview of the classical statements on the role of emotions in decision-making, and then proceeds to review recent experimental evidence on anticipated and immediate emotions in economic decision-making, economics of happiness, and emotions in organizations and corporations.

Central theoretical contributions on emotions in economic decision-making

Considerations in the literature on emotions and economy dovetail with the perennial debate about the link between emotion and cognition, to which psychologists, economists and neuroscientists have contributed. We review these statements here before we provide the outline of theoretical contributions by behavioral economists.

Theories of the emotion–cognition link

Providing a classical statement, Zajonc (1980, 1984) argued that emotion does not require cognition. "Affect and cognition are separate and partially independent processes and although they ordinarily function cojointly, affect could be generated without a prior cognitive process" (Zajonc, 1984: 117). Imagine that you suddenly face a barking dog. According to Zajonc, your physiological emotional reaction of fear will occur before you have processed the sensory image of the dog cognitively. Zajonc bases his conclusions on the "mere exposure" effect experiments,

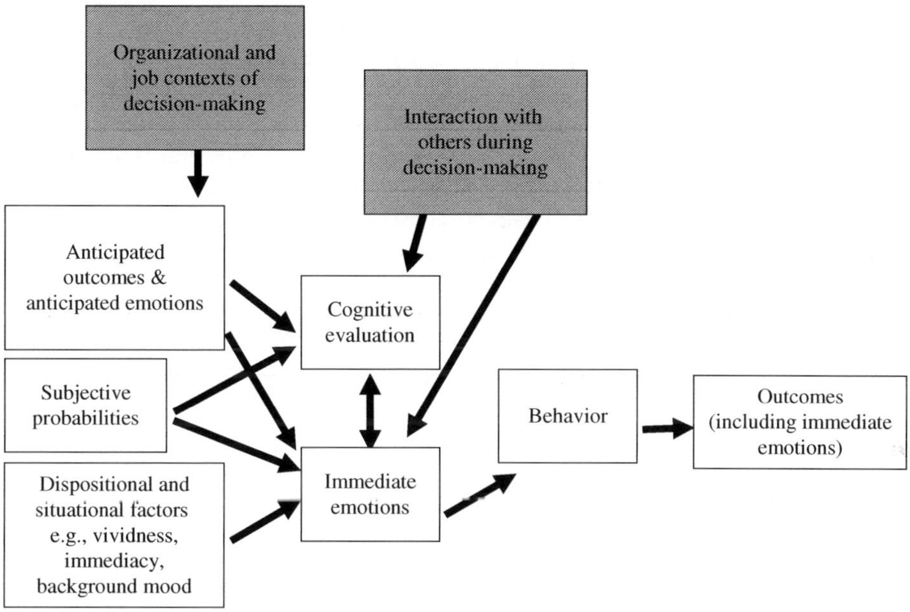

Figure 22.4 Emotional embeddedness perspective

which show that people will tend to like something simply because they have been exposed to it (or seen it) before. Lazarus (1982) has criticized conclusions about emotion and cognition based on mere exposure experiments. He warns us about equating awareness and cognition. For Lazarus, if subjects like more things they have seen subliminally then they may still have processed these things cognitively. It follows then, for Lazarus, that the cognitive process of detecting or determining affect has primacy over any elicitation of emotion.

Along these lines, Damasio (1994) made a crucial intervention using neuroscientific and psychological experimental evidence to argue that affect is essential to rational action. Damasio posited that human thought is made largely from images (i.e. symbolic and perceptual representations), and that through a lifetime of learning, people link these images to positive or negative feelings, or what he calls somatic markers. This means that when a future outcome is considered and an acquired link between the image of this outcome and affect is positive, this is perceived as a prompt for action. On the other hand, if contemplating a future outcome triggers negative somatic markers, this sounds an alarm. Damasio concludes that "the effective deployment [of reasoning strategies] probably depends, to a considerable extent, on a continued ability to experience feelings" (1994: xii). Subjects in his studies who due to injuries sustained to the prefrontal and somatosensory cortices of the brain had a diminished capacity to experience emotion were severely hindered in their ability to make intelligent practical decisions. More recently, Damasio and colleagues developed a somatic marker hypothesis (Bechara & Damasio, 2005), which states that decision-making is influenced by marker signals in bioregulatory processes that express themselves in emotions and feelings. In this neural model of economic decision, emotions are treated as a major component in the interaction between environmental conditions and decision-making processes. Emotional systems are seen as providing implicit or explicit knowledge for making efficient and sound decisions.

In a different vein, economist Robert Frank (1988) emphasized the strategic role of emotions. Frank focuses on the intersection between emotion and economy in the so called "commitment problem." The gist of this problem is that commitment appears irrational because it is based on emotions such as love or anger. However, Frank reasons that it is in one's interest to engage in commitment often because otherwise one's position in a reference group would suffer if one did not make these commitments, which would worsen one's wellbeing in the long term. Hence, there is a calculus of rationality even in apparently irrational behavior, which Frank (1988) calls "shrewdly irrational." In this case, emotions seem to facilitate rational action because they permit us to act in ways compatible with our long-term interests.

Theoretical foundations on emotions from behavioral economists

Integral to the development of the field of behavioral economics, a fundamental intervention to understand emotions in decision-making came from the work of Daniel Kahneman and Amos Tversky, which substantiates how the use of heuristics leads to significant departures from synoptic rationality. Kahneman and Tversky's (1979) prospect theory emphasizes that people are rather narrow in their focus of assessing alternative courses of action, and use heuristics to do so. Moreover, what matters more to people are changes in wealth or welfare relative to a reference point rather than absolute values. The part of the prospect theory most relevant to emotions is preference for loss aversion, or the tendency of people to prefer avoiding losses than acquiring gains, perhaps even twice as much (Tversky & Kahneman, 1992). This may be because people feel losses more deeply than the elation of gains, and have a stronger visceral reaction against losses, not wanting to be hurt by them.

Kahneman and colleagues have also studied what Thaler (1980) termed the "endowment effect," or a tendency of people to value an object more highly if they possess it than they would value the same object if they did not possess it. Kahneman et al. (1990) conducted an experiment where individuals possess an object and are given the option of trading it for various amounts of cash while other participants do not possess the object but are given a series of choices between receiving the object and receiving various amounts of cash. Although the objective wealth position and possible choices of the two groups are identical, those participants who possess the object are willing to sell it at high prices, which are significantly higher than the price that those sellers who do not possess the object identify, presumably because it is painful to part from objects that we already possess and are emotionally attached to. In fact, further elaboration by Loewenstein and Adler (1995) suggested that participants who are not endowed with an object fail to predict how painful it is to part with it once they possess it.

While most research tends to focus on anticipated emotions, which are expected to be experienced in the future as opposed to at the time of decision-making, Loewenstein (2000) has been influential in calling attention to immediate emotions, experienced at the time of decision-making. He urges economic analysts to consider visceral factors, which include a range of negative emotions such as anger and fear, drive states such as thirst and hunger, and feeling states such as pain to motivate their behavior, because they underpin daily experiences and propel behavior contrary to long-term costs and benefits analyses. Loewenstein argues that visceral factors play a critical role in decision-making in three domains of economic behavior. The first is bargaining behavior clouded by anger, fear, and embarrassment. For instance, pre-existing anger toward the people an individual is in negotiation with could drive that individual to behave in ways that work against her own economic interests. Second is intertemporal choice (e.g., visceral factors may help to explain inconsistencies, such as among those in the entertainment industry who do not stick to their diets despite the possibility of long-term gains by maintaining attractiveness). Lastly, visceral factors play a crucial role when making decisions under conditions of market risk and uncertainty. For instance, fear may increase over time as risk becomes temporally relevant while cognitive risk evaluations may remain unchanged. Such divergence between emotional reactions to risks and cognitive evaluations of risks could result in "chickening out."

Taking on the bias in economic theory toward cognitivism and consequentialism, Loewenstein and colleagues (2001) develop a risk-as-feeling proposition, which emphasizes the role of affect experienced in the moment of decision-making. They propose that emotional reactions to risky situations are often quite different from cognitive assessments of those risks. It is not so much that "people make decisions on the basis of an assessment of the consequences of possible choice alternatives" (p. 267) but that the emotional reactions often drive behavior. The authors distinguish between anticipatory emotions and anticipated emotions, where the former refer to immediate visceral reactions, such as anxiety or fear experienced in the immediate present, and the latter to emotions anticipated in the future. While we need more research on the role of anticipatory emotions, a few studies point to their influence. For instance, Harle and Sanfey (2010) test and confirm that incidental emotions bias decision-making. When psychology undergraduates were asked to play the ultimatum game in which they were asked to accept or reject monetary offers among themselves, incidental moods elicited through simple emotional priming altered decision-making. Similarly, in Rick's (2007) experiment, tightwads and spendthrifts had to decide whether or not to purchase a variety of goods while listening to neutral or sad music. Due to incidental immediate emotions the tightwads spent more when sad than when in a neutral state, and spendthrifts spent less when sad than when in a neutral state.

Loewenstein's work is part of what has become known as affective forecasting research (Wilson & Gilbert, 2005). This involves examining how people estimate their future emotional states, finding that we are relatively poor judges of our future emotions, their intensity, or duration. For instance, researchers find that people succumb to impact bias (Gilbert et al., 1998), which is one where we tend to overestimate the impact that a particular future event may have on us emotionally, such as the extent to which a future winning of lottery is thought to increase our feelings of happiness. Likewise, the durability bias captures the fact that people overestimate the length or the intensity of future feeling states. In a study of consumer choices, Wood and Bettman (2007) found that people make their choices based on estimated pleasure they will derive from a good, but they often overestimate this pleasure, as affective forecasting would predict. However, if people overestimate the duration of pleasure derived from a good, then they are more likely to purchase it, something that advertisers can manipulate. Research on attachment to objects that individuals are asked to sell, or predictions of future attachments, points to "projection bias" (Galanter, 1992; Kermer et al., 2006; Conlin et al., 2007), whereby people tend to overestimate the degree to which their future tastes will resemble their current tastes.

Experimental evidence on anticipated and immediate emotions in economic decision-making

Empirical evidence from research in behavioral economics, experimental economics and economic psychology focuses on various types of emotions that people experience when different outcomes are realized, people's predictions of what emotions they will experience, and the degree to which decisions are in fact guided by anticipated and immediate emotions. In general, researchers find that emotions have multifaceted functions, such as provide information on pleasure and pain, enable rapid decision-making under time constraints, focus attention on decision relevance, and generate commitment, meaning sentiments or commitment to stick to morally/socially significant decisions (Pfister & Bohm, 2008).

Much research concerns the role of regret that potentially arises by comparing the outcome one experiences once the decision is made with the outcome one could have experienced should one have made a different choice (Loomes & Sugden, 1982; Mellers et al., 1997), finding that regret is an important influence when the possibility of regret is salient (Zeelenberg & Beattie, 1997), which is often more in prospect rather than in retrospect (Gilbert et al., 2004).

Emotions have also been considered influential when making risky decisions. Bechara et al. (1997) drew on neuropsychological evidence with patients who suffered damage to the ventromedial prefrontal cortex and found that these patients were more willing to make risky decisions in a game where they were asked to try to win as much money as possible, because of their failure to experience fear when contemplating different risk decisions. Also examining risk, Johnson et al. (1993) found that participants were not treating all possibilities of risk the same and were willing to pay slightly more for insurance protecting against terrorism as a cause of plane crash than other crash risks. In considering choices among consumer products, Kahn and Isen (1993) found that a positive mood may make decision makers more risk-averse so as to not disturb the experience of positive feelings.

When manipulating emotions in determining buying and selling prices, Lerner, Small and Loewenstein (2004) found that disgust leads to reducing buying and selling prices, whereas sadness increased buying prices but reduced selling prices. When manipulating feelings related to fairness, researchers found that the experience of pain, as shown on brain scans, was greater in ultimatum games when receiving unfair offers from human proposers than for fair offers from non-human proposers (Knutson et al., 2007). Inducing anger or happiness during the ultimatum game, Andrade and Ariely (2009) found that happy responders were less likely than angry responders to reject unfair offers.

Studies also considered the role of time in receiving pleasure from consumption choices. Ainslie (1975) identified a general pattern called "hyperbolic time discounting," which says that people are distressed more about the delay that is proximate rather than distant, and they do not discount the future exponentially (Kirby & Herrnstein, 1995; Rachlin & Raineri, 1992). For instance, people will be more unhappy with delaying consumption of a pleasurable good from today to tomorrow rather than from 50 to 51 days.

Research on immediate emotions undermines the idea that individual decisions are guided by strict considerations of opportunity costs. For instance, Frederick et al. (2009) asked participants whether they would (hypothetically) be willing to purchase a desirable video for $14.99. They framed this decision in two ways. One was to say that you are deciding not to buy this entertaining video, and the other was to say that you can keep the $14.99 for other purchases. These two options were objectively equivalent, however, the former framing highlighted the pleasure from other purchases that would be forgone by purchasing the video, and more participants decided not to purchase when the opportunity costs were directly highlighted to them. This suggests that many people do not spontaneously consider opportunity costs, unless these are explicitly brought to their attention by evoking immediate emotions. Moreover, in charity giving and helping behavior, researchers pointed to an "identifiable-victim effect" (Small & Loewenstein, 2003), which refers to the tendency to give more to, or help more readily, identifiable victims than to statistical victims, suggesting that immediate emotions play a role in generosity toward others (Kogut & Ritov, 2005).

Although traditional finance theories assume that securities in financial markets should be priced according to their technical quality, market participants gauged the price of securities using factors other than technical information. MacGregor et al. (2000) asked 57 advanced business students in a securities analysis course to evaluate a number of industry groups on the New York Stock Exchange using a set of judgment variables. Participants were first provided with imagery and affective evaluations for each industry group and then asked to judge their likelihood of investing in companies associated with each industry. Their results suggest that while imagery and affect make up a psychological framework for evaluating securities, that framework may have low validity for predicting actual market performance.

There is also some research on the role of optimism, or positive emotional inclinations, finding that optimists work harder (Carver, Scheier & Segerstrom, 2010), and make more money (Mohanty, 2012). The mechanism suggested for these outcomes is that optimists are less likely to give up when things get difficult than pessimists, and are quicker than pessimists to switch to alternative tasks with higher chances of success when given the opportunity. However, extreme optimists may carry things too far, as Puri and Robinson (2007) found that overly optimistic people made bad financial decisions.

Economics of happiness

A growing body of research on emotion in economy is what many have termed happiness economics (Bruni & Porta, 2008; Frey & Stutzer, 2001). This research asks about the relationship between "happiness" and macroeconomic variables, such as income, economic growth, unemployment, inflation and governance. To understand "happiness" researchers used various notions of positive emotional states, wellbeing, quality of life, or life-satisfaction, which they try to quantify (van Praag & Ferrer-i-Carbonell, 2004). Emotions are most often conceptualized here as subjective wellbeing. Researchers use aggregated self-reports of individuals, from established data sets with questions on wellbeing, such as those from the World Values Survey or European Social Survey (MacKerron, 2012).

What does this research find?

Income

One of the interesting findings is the effect of income on subjective wellbeing. There is a positive relationship (Gardner & Oswald, 2007), but the magnitude of the effect is relatively small (Clark et al., 2008). In fact, Layard and colleagues (2008) find that the marginal utility of income declines somewhat faster than in proportion with the rise in income. Moreover, past income is negatively associated with individuals' current subjective wellbeing (Clark et al., 2008) as is the reference group income, which seems to matter even more than individual's own income (Knight et al., 2009). However, despite the relationship between happiness and income at the individual level, there appears to be little corresponding relationship between the rising GDP on average national happiness levels over time (but see DiTella et al., 2003), which researchers have termed an Easterlin paradox (Easterlin, 2004).

Unemployment, inflation, welfare

Economists have also studied the effect of unemployment on subjective wellbeing, and find a negative impact, and that high local unemployment rates ameliorate the impact of an individual's own unemployment (Dolan et al., 2008). Inflation may also have a negative influence on subjective wellbeing, but evidence on income inequality is mixed and varies by real and perceived mobility (MacKerron, 2012). There is little evidence concerning the effects of the welfare state on subjective wellbeing (Dolan et al., 2008).

Emotions in organizations and corporations

Social psychologists, sociologists, and organizations scholars have developed three broad lines of research on emotions in an economic sphere. One concerns the influence of organizational structure and culture on emotional states, the other on emotional intelligence as linked to corporate performance, and the third focuses on so called "positive organizations."

Organizational impacts as a cause of our emotional states

Researchers have identified a multitude of organizational events with emotional impact for workers including those related to interactions among coworkers, with customers, and superiors (Mastenbroek, 2000; Weiss & Brief, 2001; Bono et al., 2007; Elfenbein, 2007). A key contribution from sociologists is about the effect of occupational roles on emotion management in organizations. Hochschild (1983) developed this concept based on a study of flight attendants, underscoring that service workers are trained to express particular emotional reactions as part of their job, so that managing emotions becomes work (cf. Pierce, 1996; Bolton & Boyd, 2003). The consequences of emotional labor for the self have also been a subject of research. The most consistent finding is that surface acting (changing one's outward appearance) is associated with emotional exhaustion (Wharton, 2009), but deep acting (changing one's inner feelings) does not necessarily lead to emotional exhaustion (Grandey, 2003). Rather, emotional labor effects are conditioned by the workers' level of job autonomy and involvement and the workers' self-monitoring/regulating abilities (Wharton, 1993). Morrill's (1995) work on conflict management in corporations shows that how conflict and emotions are managed depends on organizational cultures and informal social networks shaped by the organizational structure of companies. In another study of how organizational contexts moderate emotional experiences, Grant et al. (2009) found that under different conditions, the same corporate-sanctioned values can lead to different emotional experiences.

With the rise of financialization, researchers have also paid attention to emotions in finance organizations. Pixley (2002) argues that finance organizations routinely use emotions in formulating expectations. She states that "emotions are prevalent all the time" and "necessarily play some part in actually fostering 'rational' decision-making in finance organizations" (2000: 42) because they enable economic actors to formulate expectations. Based on interviews and ethnographic observations of financial fund managers, Chong and Tuckett (2015) develop the notion of conviction narratives, which is a way of dealing with uncertainty and ambivalence of everyday financial decision-making that produces emotional conflicts for decision makers. In the authors' view, conviction narratives both enable participants to become excited about opportunities they identify as well as repel any doubts associated with those opportunities and therefore mitigate anxiety. Chong and Tuckett's work is in line with research that finds emotions have an analogous role to trust in permitting financial action (Bachmann, 2006; Nooteboom, 2006; Pixley, 2009). Barbalet (2009) argues that this is because financial decisions are always uncertain and dealing with this uncertainty involves emotional work.

Environmental factors within organizations, such as temperature or noise, are also found to impact emotions within organizations (Isen & Baron, 1991), as are physical artifacts, such as colors and symbols (Rafaeli & Vilnai-Yavetz, 2004). Scholars have also examined how external factors that carry over to work, such as family concerns, matter for emotional experience in work organizations (Brief & Weiss, 2002).

Emotional intelligence as a cause of organizational performance

Business literature has increasingly focused on emotions by expounding the notion of emotional intelligence (EI) and its impact on organizational performance. Defined as the ability to perceive and understand emotions of the self and others to inform and guide self-behavior (Salovey & Mayer, 1990), a social psychological and organizational approach shapes much of the theoretical and empirical development of EI. For Goleman (1995) EI is comprised of five features—understanding your emotions, managing them, emotional self-control such as delaying gratification, empathy, and relationship management—that are particularly pertinent in leadership performance, leadership processes, and group achievement (Goleman, 1998; George & Jones, 2000; Prati et al., 2003). Empirical studies find a positive association between EI and leadership skills and assert that EI enhances managerial effectiveness by influencing workplace attitudes and behavior and, ultimately, organizational performance outcomes (Carmeli, 2003). The link between EI and leadership offers an explanation for why managers with both knowledge and industry experience sometimes do not succeed at the workplace, suggesting that cognitive intelligence, personality traits, and competence do not fully account for work success (Rosete et al., 2005). Though most studies examine the role of EI in enhancing leadership skills, some focus on how employee EI is related to their job satisfaction, job stress, job control, commitment, turnover intentions, and emotional labor (Petrides & Furnham, 2006; Wong & Law, 2002). Other studies specifically explore the impact of EI on occupations requiring extensive emotion work, such as nursing in care work (Carson & Carson, 1998; McQueen, 2004) and hospitality in service work (Jung & Yoon, 2012). EI also affects organizational capability and influence organizational change (Huy, 1999). However, not all studies point to positive associations between EI and team performance outcomes. When multifaceted investigations look at the relationship of the leader, employee, and team, EI is not related to group performance (Feyerherm & Rice, 2002). The relationship between EI and leadership disappears when controlling for ability and personality (Cavazotte et al., 2012). EI can also facilitate self-serving interests for high-EI individuals at the cost of others (Kilduff et al., 2010). Because EI is neither tangible nor observable, measurements often entail self-reports (Palmer et al., 2001; Gardner & Stough, 2002) or questionnaires (Barling, 2000). Frequently used questionnaires include Goleman's 10-item measure, Seligman Attributional Style Questionnaire, EI Inventory, and the Mayer–Salovey–Caruso EI Test, among others. The self-report approach is limited, however, and some measures are not suitable in the organizational context (Wong & Law, 2002).

Positive emotions as a cause of organizational performance

Another strand of organizational research explicitly concerned with emotions is positive organizations scholarship (Cameron, Dutton, & Quinn, 2003), which examines how a *positive* lens or an orientation that focuses on strengths rather than weaknesses, on optimism rather than pessimism, and on the supportive rather than critical actions (Cameron, 2008), influences the organization in its decision-making, behavior, and judgment (Forgas, 2001). Organizations may have positive organizational social capital, meaning that members of an organization maintain high-quality relationships and reciprocity among each other (Baker & Dutton, 2007) through organizational practices that motivate employees to pursue such relationships and attitudes. This literature finds that interpersonal trust among employees affects both the behavior and performance of the firm (McAllister, 1995). Other studies focus on positive psychological capital (Luthans et al., 2004; Youssef & Luthans, 2007; Toor & Ofori, 2010), which includes individual capacities of hope, optimism, resilience, and efficacy as well as character strengths such as feelings of vigor, physical strength, emotional energy, and cognitive liveliness (Shirom, 2003). These are found to affect job performance and employee attitudes such as perceived organizational support, emotional commitment to the firm, job satisfaction, and work happiness. Positive organizations are also negatively associated with undesirable employee attitudes such as anxiety, job stress, turnover intentions, and cynicism (Avey et al., 2011). Individual-level satisfaction can add up at the aggregate level to engender organizational innovation or generate and implement creative ideas (Shipton, 2006).

Whereas studies examine how individual-level traits and interactions have organizational-level impact, conversely, others examine the implications of a positive organizational structure on organization and individual outcomes. Some firms promote positive affect in the workplace or structure a positive climate such that rather than focusing on individual error or power control, they focus on building an organization with a hopeful orientation, creating a culture of creativity, or an ethical organizational identity (Avital et al., 2006; Cangemi & Miller, 2007; Verbos et al., 2007). Positive organizations are associated with healthy mental and physical outcomes for employees (Heaphy & Dutton, 2008). Staw, Sutton and Pelled (1994) show an association between positive emotion at work and both work achievement (favorable work evaluations and higher pay) and supportive social context with more support from supervisors and coworkers.

Conclusion

Emotions have received increasing attention by scholars of economic behavior. It is no longer controversial to consider that people anticipate, and take into account, how they are likely to feel about the potential consequences of alternative choices identified in their economic decision-making. Such research on the role of expected emotions in economy has tried to identify the types of emotions that people experience when different outcomes are realized, people's predictions of what emotions they will experience, and the degree to which decisions are in fact guided by predicted emotions. More recent work on emotions has considered the role of immediate emotions. A review of this research concludes that,

> In some cases, these emotions seem to play a beneficial role in decision-making, informing decision makers about their own values. But in other cases, such as the disproportionate fear commonly associated with flying as opposed to driving, integral emotions may cause people to act contrary to their own material interests.
>
> *(Rick & Loewenstein, 2008: 149)*

Other ways in which emotions are considered consequential for the economy have been emphasized in the macro research on the economics of happiness, in the scholarship on emotion management of workers to fit occupational roles, and in studies on the impact of EI and positive organizations on organizational performance.

On the whole, there is much still to be done to understand emotions in economy, including how immediate and anticipated emotions interact. For example, immediate emotions may encourage risk-taking behavior, but contemplation of anticipated emotions associated with such decisions, such as regret, may discourage it. More generally, considerations of immediate emotions pose problems to traditional economic models of rational decision-making. Weighing of costs and benefits requires a deliberative process that immediate emotions likely undermine.

These immediate, unanticipated, emotions result either because of unrelated background moods and states, or because decision makers engage in unpredictable social interaction during the process of decision-making. Moreover, different kinds of emotions, not only regret and pleasure, and different strength of emotions, especially very intense ones, have yet to be examined more rigorously, albeit this is quite challenging to do in laboratory experiments. Finally, economic and psychological models of decision-making do not pay enough attention to social interaction, and how emotional experiences change because of organizational and institutional contexts. This calls for more interdisciplinary research on emotions and economy, and collaboration of behavioral economists with other social scientists.

Bibliography

Ainslie, G. (1975). Specious Reward: A Behavioral Theory of Impulsiveness and Impulse Control. Psychological Bulletin, 82(4), 463–96.

Andrade, E. & Ariely, D. (2009). The Enduring Impact of Transient Emotions on Decision Making. Organizational Behavior and Human Decision Processes, 109, 1–8.

Avey, J. B., Reichard, R. J., Luthans, F. & Mhatre, K. H. (2011). Meta-Analysis of the Impact of Positive Psychological Capital on Employee Attitudes, Behaviors, and Performance. Human Resource Development Quarterly, 22(2), 127–52.

Avital, M., Lyytinen, K. J., Boland Jr., R., Butler, B. S., Dougherty, D., Fineout, M., Jansen, W., Levina, N., Rifkin, W. & Venable, J. (2006). Design with a Positive Lens: An Affirmative Approach to Designing Information and Organizations. Communications of the Association for Information Systems, 18(25), 519–45.

Bachmann, R. (2006). Trust and/or Power: Towards a Sociological Theory of Organizational Relationships. In Bachmann, R. & Zaheer, A. (eds). Handbook of Trust Research, Cheltenham, UK: Edward Elgar.

Baker, W. & Dutton, J. E. (2007). Enabling Positive Social Capital in Organizations. In Exploring Positive Relationships at Work: Building a Theoretical and Research Foundation, edited by J. E. Dutton and B. R. Ragins. Mahwah, NJ: Lawrence Erlbaum, 325–46.

Bandelj, N. (2009). Emotions in Economic Action and Interaction. Theory & Society, 38(4), 347–66.

Barbalet, J. (2009). A Characterization of Trust, and its Consequences. Theory and Society, 38, 367–82.

Barling, J., Slater, F. & Kelloway, E. K. (2000). Transformational Leadership and Emotional Intelligence: An Exploratory Study. Leadership & Organization Development Journal, 21(3), 157–61.

Bechara, A. & Damasio, A. R. (2005). The Somatic Marker Hypothesis: A Neural Theory of Economic Decision. Games and Economic Behavior, 52(2), 336–72.

Bechara, A., Damasio, H., Tranel, D. & Damasio, A. R. 1997. Deciding Advantageously Before Knowing the Advantageous Strategy. Science, 275, 1293–5.

Bolton, S. & Boyd, C. 2003. Trolley Dolly or Skilled Emotion Manager? Moving On from Hochschild's Managed Heart. Work, Employment and Society, 17(2), 289–308.

Bono, J. E., Foldes, H. J., Vinson, G. & Muros, J. P. (2007). Workplace Emotions: The Role of Supervision and Leadership. Journal of Applied Psychology, 92(5), 1357–67.

Bosman, R., Sutter, M. & van Winden, F. (2005). The Impact of Real Effort and Emotions in the Power-to-Take Game. Journal of Economic Psychology, 26(3), 407–29.

Brief, A. P. & Weiss, H. M. (2002). Organizational Behavior: Affect in the Workplace. Annual Review of Psychology, 53, 279–307.

Bruni, L. & Porta, P. L. (eds.) (2008). Handbook on the Economics of Happiness. Edward Elgar Publishing.

Cameron, K. S. (2008). Paradox in Positive Organizational Change. Journal of Applied Behavioral Science, 44, 7–24.

Cameron, K. S., Dutton, J. E. & Quinn, R. E. (2003). Positive Organizational Scholarship: Foundations of a New Discipline. San Francisco, CA: Berrett-Koehler.

Cangemi, J. & Miller, R. (2007). Breaking-Out-of-the-Box in Organizations: Structuring a Positive Climate for the Development of Creativity in the Workplace. Journal of Management Development, 26(5), 401–10.

Carmeli, A. (2003). The Relationship between Emotional Intelligence and Work Attitudes, Behavior and Outcomes. Journal of Managerial Psychology, 18(8), 788–813.

Carson, K. D. & Carson, P. P. (1998). Career Commitment, Competencies, and Citizenship. Journal of Vocational Behavior, 6(2), 195–208.

Carver, C. S., Scheier, M. F. & Segerstrom, S C. (2010). Optimism. Clinical Psychology Review, 30, 879–89.

Cavazotte, F., Moreno, W. & Hickmann, M. (2012). Effects of Leader Intelligence, Personality and Emotional Intelligence on Transformational Leadership and Managerial Performance. Leadership Quarterly, 23(3), 443–55.

Chong, K. & Tuckett, D. (2015). Constructing Conviction through Action and Narrative: How Money Managers Manage Uncertainty and the Consequence for Financial Market Functioning. Socio-Economic Review, 13(2), 309–30.

Clark, A. E., Frijters, P. & Shields, M. A. (2008). Relative Income, Happiness, and Utility: An Explanation for the Easterlin Paradox and Other Puzzles. Journal of Economic Literature, 46(1), 95–144.

Conlin, M., O'Donoghue, T. & Vogelsang, T. J. (2007). Projection Bias in Catalog Orders. The American Economic Review, 97(4), 1217–49.

Cubitt, R. P., Drouvelis, M. & Gächter, S. (2011). Framing and Free Riding: Emotional Responses and Punishment in Social Dilemma Games. Experimental Economics, 14(2), 254–72.

Damasio, A. R. (1994). Descartes' Error: Emotion, Reason and the Human Brain. New York: Grosset/Putnam.

DeSteno, D. (2009). Social Emotions and Intertemporal Choice: "Hot" Mechanisms for Building Social and Economic Capital. Current Directions in Psychological Science, 18(5), 280–4.

Di Tella, R., MacCulloch, R. J. & Oswald, A. J. (2003). The Macroeconomics of Happiness. Review of Economics and Statistics, 85(4), 809–27.

Dolan, P., Peasgood, T. & White, M. (2008). Do we Really Know What Makes us Happy? A Review of the Economic Literature on the Factors associated with Subjective Well-Being. Journal of Economic Psychology, 29, 94–122.

Easterlin, R. A. (2004). The Economics of Happiness. Dædalus, 133(2), 26–33.

Elfenbein, H. A. (2007). Emotion in Organizations: A Review and Theoretical Integration. Academy of Management Annals, 1(1), 315–86.

Feyerherm, A. E. & Rice, C. L. (2002). Emotional Intelligence and Team Performance: The Good, the Bad and the Ugly. International Journal of Organizational Analysis, 10(4), 343–62.

Forgas, J. P. & George, J. M. (2001). Affective Influences on Judgments and Behavior in Organizations: An Information Processing Perspective. Organizational Behavior and Human Decision Processes, 86(1), 3–34.

Frank, R. H. (1988). Passions within Reason: The Strategic Role of the Emotions. New York, NY: WW Norton & Co.

Frederick, S., Novemsky, N., Wang, J., Dhar, R. & Nowlis, S. (2009). Opportunity Cost Neglect. Journal of Consumer Research, 36, 553–61.

Frey, B. S. & Stutzer, A. (2001). Happiness and Economics: How the Economy and Institutions Affect Human Well-Being. Princeton, NJ: Princeton University Press.

Fritz, C. & Sonnentag, S. (2009). Antecedents of Day-Level Proactive Behavior: A Look at Job Stressors and Positive Affect during the Workday. Journal of Management, 35(1), 94–111.

Galanter, E. (1992). Utility Functions for Nonmonetary Events. American Journal of Psychology, 65, 45–55.

Gardner, J. & Oswald, A.J. (2007). Money and Mental Wellbeing: A Longitudinal Study of Medium-Sized Lottery Wins. Journal of Health Economics, 26(1), 49–60.

Gardner, L. & Stough, C. (2002). Examining the Relationship between Leadership and Emotional Intelligence in Senior Level Managers. Leadership & Organization Development Journal, 23(2), 68–78.

Gaudine, A. & Thorne, L. (2001). Emotion and Ethical Decision-Making in Organizations. Journal of Business Ethics, 31(2), 175–87.

George, J. M. & Jones, J. H. (2000). Emotions and Leadership: The Role of Emotional Intelligence. Human Relations, 53(8), 1027–55.

Gilbert, D. T., Morewedge, C. K., Risen, J. L. & Wilson, T. D. 2004. Looking Forward to Looking Backward: The Misprediction of Regret. Psychological Science, 15(5), 346–50.

Gilbert, D. T., Pinel, E. C., Wilson, T. D., Blumberg, S. K. & Wheately, T. (1998). Immune Neglect: A Source of Durability Bias in Affective Forecasting. Journal of Personality and Social Psychology, 75, 617–38.

Goleman, D. (1995). Emotional Intelligence. New York, NY: Bantam Dell.

Goleman, D. (1998). Working with Emotional Intelligence. New York, NY: Bantam Dell.

Grandey, A. A. (2003). When "The Show Must Go On": Surface Acting and Deep Acting as Determinants of Emotional Exhaustion and Peer-Rated Service Delivery. Academy of Management Journal, 46(1), 86–96.

Grant, D., Morales, A. & Sallaz, J. J. (2009). Pathways to Meaning: A New Approach to Studying Emotions at Work. American Journal of Sociology, 115(2), 327–64.
Hanselmann, M. & Tanner, C. (2008). Taboos and Conflicts in Decision Making: Sacred Values, Decision Difficulty, and Emotions. Judgment and Decision Making, 3(1), 51–63.
Hareli, S. & Rafaeli, A. (2008). Emotion Cycles: On the Social Influence of Emotion in Organizations. Research in Organizational Behavior, 28, 35–59.
Harlé, K. M. & Sanfey, A. G. (2010). Effects of Approach and Withdrawal Motivation on Interactive Economic Decisions. Cognition and Emotion, 24(8), 1456–65.
Heaphy, E. D. & Dutton, J. E. (2008). Positive Social Interactions and the Human Body at Work: Linking Organizations and Physiology. Academy of Management Review, 33(1), 137–62.
Hochschild, A. R. (1979). Emotion Work, Feeling Rules, and Social Structure. American Journal of Sociology, 85(3), 551–75.
Hochschild, A. R. (1983). The Managed Heart: Commercialization of Human Feeling. Berkeley: University of California Press.
Huy, Q. N. (1999). Emotional Capability, Emotional Intelligence, and Radical Change. Academy of Management Review, 24(2), 325–45.
Isen, A. M. & Baron, R. A. (1991). Positive Affect as a Factor in Organizational Behavior. Research in Organizational Behavior, 13, 1–53.
Johnson, E. J., Hershey, J., Meszaros, J. & Kunreuther, H. (1993). Framing, Probability Distortions, and Insurance Decisions. Journal of Risk and Uncertainty, 7(1), 35–51.
Jung, H. S. & Yoon, H. H. (2012). The Effects of Emotional Intelligence on Counterproductive Work Behaviors and Organizational Citizen Behaviors among Food and Beverage Employees in a Deluxe Hotel. International Journal of Hospitality Management, 31(2), 369–78.
Kahn, B. E. & Isen, A. M. (1993). The Influence of Positive Effect on Variety Seeking among Safe, Enjoyable Products. Journal of Consumer Research, 20(2), 257–70.
Kahneman, D. & Tversky, A. (1979). Prospect Theory: An Analysis of Decision under Risk. Econometrica, 47(2), 263–91.
Kahneman, D., Knetsch, J. L. & Thaler, R. H. (1990). Experimental Tests of the Endowment Effect and the Coase Theorem. Journal of Political Economy, 98(6), 1325–48.
Kermer, D. A., Driver-Linn, E., Wilson, T. D. & Gilbert, D. T. (2006). Loss Aversion is an Affective Forecasting Error. Psychological Science, 17(8), 649–53.
Kilduff, M., Chiaburu, D. S. & Menges, J. I. (2010). Strategic Use of Emotional Intelligence in Organizational Settings: Exploring the Dark Side. Research in Organizational Behavior, 30, 129–52.
Kirby, K. N. & Herrnstein, R. J. (1995). Preference Reversals due to Myopic Discounting of Delayed Reward. Psychological Science, 6(2), 83–9.
Knight, J., Song, L. & Gunatilaka, R. (2009). Subjective well-being and its determinants in rural China. China Economic Review, 20(4), 635–49.
Knutson, B., Rick, S., Wimmer, G. E., Prelec, D. & Loewenstein, G. (2007). Neural Predictors of Purchases. Neuron, 53, 147–56.
Kogut, T. & Ritov, I. (2005). The "Identified Victim" Effect: An Identified Group, or just a Single Individual? Journal of Behavioral Decision Making, 18(3), 157–67.
Layard, R., Mayraz, G. & Nickell, S. (2008). The Marginal Utility of Income. Journal of Public Economics, 92, 1846–57.
Lazarus, R. S. (1982). Thoughts on the Relation between Cognition and Emotion. American Psychologist, 37, 1019–24.
Lerner, J. S., Small, D. A. & Loewenstein, G. (2004). Heart Strings and Purse Strings: Carryover Effects of Emotions on Economic Decisions. Psychological Science, 15(5), 337–41.
Loewenstein, G. (1996). Out of Control: Visceral Influences on Behavior. Organizational Behavior and Human Decision Processes, 65(3), 272–92.
Loewenstein, G. (2000). Emotions in Economic Theory and Economic Behavior. American Economic Review, 90(2), 426–32.
Loewenstein, G. & Adler, D. (1995). A Bias in the Prediction of Tastes. The Economic Journal, 105(431), 929–37.
Loewenstein, G. & Lerner, J. (2003). The Role of Affect in Decision Making. In Handbook of Affective Science, edited by R. J. Dawson, K. R. Scherer & H. H. Goldsmith. Oxford: Oxford University Press, 619–42.

Loewenstein, G. & Small, D. A. (2007). The Scarecrow and the Tin Man: The Vicissitudes of Human Sympathy and Caring. Review of General Psychology, 11, 112–26.
Loewenstein, G., Weber, E., Hsee, C. & Welch, N. (2001). Risk as Feelings. Psychological Bulletin, 127(2), 267–86.
Loomes, G. & Sugden, R. (1982). Regret Theory: An Alternative Theory of Rational Choice under Uncertainty. The Economic Journal, 92, 805–24.
Luthans, F., Luthans, K. W. & Luthans, B. C. (2004). Positive Psychological Capital: Beyond Human and Social Capital. Business Horizons, 47(1), 45.
MacGregor, D. G., Slovic, P., Dreman, D. & Berry, M. (2000). Imagery, Affect, and Financial Judgment. Journal of Psychology and Financial Markets, 1(2), 104–10.
MacKerron, G. (2012). Happiness Economics from 35,000 Feet. Journal of Economic Surveys, 26(4), 705–35.
Mastenbroek, W. (2000). Organizational Behavior as Emotion Management. In Emotions in the Workplace: Research, Theory, and Practice, edited by N. M. Ashkanasy, C. E. J. Härtel, and W. J. Zerbe. Westport, CT: Quorum, 19–35.
McAllister, Daniel J. (1995). Affect and Cognition-Based Trust as Foundations for Interpersonal Cooperation in Organizations. Academy of Management Journal, 38(1), 24–59.
McQueen, A. C. H. (2004). Emotional Intelligence in Nursing Work. Journal of Advanced Nursing, 47(1), 101–8.
Mellers, B. A., Schwartz, A., Ho, K. & Ritov, I. (1997). Decision Affect Theory: Emotional Reactions to the Outcomes of Risky Options. Psychological Science, 8(6), 423–9.
Mirchandani, K. (2003). Challenging Racial Silences in Studies of Emotion Work: Contributions from Anti-Racist Feminist Theory. Organization Studies, 24(5), 721–42.
Mohanty, M. S. (2012). Effects of Positive Attitude and Optimism on Wage and Employment: A Double Selection Approach. Journal of Socio-Economics, 41, 304–16.
Morrill, C. (1995). The Executive Way. Chicago University Press.
Nooteboom, B. (2006). Forms, Sources and Processes of Trust. In Handbook of Trust Research, edited by Bachmann, R. and Zaheer, A. Northampton, Edward Elgar, 247–63.
Palmer, B., Walls, M., Burgess, Z. & Stough, C. (2001). Emotional Intelligence and Effective Leadership. Leadership & Organization Development Journal, 22(1), 5–10.
Petrides, K. V. & Furnham, A. (2006). The Role of Trait Emotional Intelligence in a Gender-Specific Model of Organizational Variables. Journal of Applied Social Psychology, 36(2), 552–69.
Pfister, H. R. & Böhm, G. (2008). The Multiplicity of Emotions: A Framework of Emotional Functions in Decision Making. Judgment and Decision Making, 3(1), 5–17.
Pierce, J. L. (1996). Gender Trials: Emotional Lives in Contemporary Law Firms. Berkeley: University of California Press.
Pixley, J. (2002). Finance Organizations, Decisions and Emotions. British Journal of Sociology, 53(1), 41–65.
Pixley, J. (2009). Time Orientation and Emotion-Rules in Finance. Theory and Society, 38, 353–400.
Prati, M. L., Douglas, C., Ferris, G. R., Ammeter, A. P. & Buckley, M. R. (2003). Emotional Intelligence, Leadership Effectiveness, and Team Outcomes. International Journal of Organizational Analysis, 11(1), 21–40.
Puri, M. & Robinson, D. T. (2007). Optimism and Economic Choice. Journal of Financial Economics, 86, 71–99.
Rachlin, H. & Raineri, A. (1992). Irrationality, Impulsiveness, and Selfishness as Discount Reversal Effects. In Choice over Time, edited by G. Loewenstein and J. Elster. New York: The Russell Sage Foundation, 93–118.
Rafaeli, A. & Vilnai-Yavetz, I. (2004). Emotion as a Connection of Physical Artifacts and Organizations. Organization Science, 15, 671–86.
Rick, S. (2007). The Influence of Anticipatory Affect on Consumer Choice. Doctoral dissertation, Department of Social and Decision Sciences, Carnegie Mellon University.
Rick, S. & Loewenstein, G. (2008). The Role of Emotion in Economic Behavior. In Handbook of Emotions, edited by M. Lewis, J. M. Haviland-Jones, and L. Feldman Barrett. New York, NY: Guilford Press, 138–156s.
Rivera, L. (2015). Go with your Gut: Emotion and Evaluation in Job Interviews. American Journal of Sociology, 120(5), 1339–89.
Rosete, D. & Ciarrochi, J. (2005). Emotional Intelligence and its Relationship to Workplace Performance Outcomes of Leadership Effectiveness. Leadership & Organization Development Journal, 26(5), 388–99.
Salovey, P. & Mayer, J. D. (1990). Emotional Intelligence. Imagination, Cognition and Personality, 9(3), 185–211.

Schieman, S., McBrier, D. B. & Gundy, K. V. (2003). Home-to-Work Conflict, Work Qualities, and Emotional Distress. Sociological Forum, 18(1), 137–64.

Shipton, H. J., West, M. A., Parkes, C. L., Dawson J. F. & Patterson, M. G. (2006). When Promoting Positive Feelings Pays: Aggregate Job Satisfaction, Work Design Features, and Innovation in Manufacturing Organizations. European Journal of Work and Organizational Psychology, 15(4), 404–30.

Shirom, A. (2003). Feeling Vigorous at Work? The Construct of Vigor and the Study of Positive Affect in Organizations. In Research in Organizational Stress and Well-Being. Vol. 3, Emotional and Physiological Processes and Positive Intervention Strategies, edited by P. L. Perrewe, and D. C. Ganster. Emerald Group, 135–64.

Slovic, P., Finucane, M., Peters, E. & MacGregor, D. (2004). Risk as Analysis and Risk as Feelings: Some Thoughts about Affect, Reason, Risk and Rationality. Risk Analysis, 24(2), 311–22.

Small, D. A. & Loewenstein, G. (2003). Helping a Victim or Helping the Victim: Altruism and Identifiability. Journal of Risk and Uncertainty, 26(1), 5–16.

Spreitzer, G. M. & Cameron, K. S. (2012). A Path Forward: Assessing Progress and Exploring Core Questions for the Future of Positive Organizational Scholarship. In The Oxford Handbook of Positive Organizational Scholarship. New York, NY: Oxford University Press, 1034–48.

Staw, B. M., Sutton, R. I. & Pelled, L. H. (1994). Employee Positive Emotion and Favorable Outcomes at the Workplace. Organization Science, 5(1), 51–71.

Thaler, R. (1980). Toward a Positive Theory of Consumer Choice. Journal of Economic Behavior and Organization, 1(1), 39–60.

Toor, S. R. & Ofori, G. (2010). Positive Psychological Capital as a Source of Sustainable Competitive Advantage for Organizations. Journal of Construction Engineering and Management, 136(3), 341–52.

Tversky, A. & Kahneman, D. (1992). Advances in Prospect Theory: Cumulative Representation of Uncertainty. Journal of Risk and Uncertainty, 5(4), 297–323.

van Praag, B. & Ferrer-i-Carbonell, A. 2004. Happiness Quantified: A Satisfaction Calculus Approach. Oxford University Press.

Verbos, A. K., Gerard, J. A., Forshey, P. R., Harding, C. S. & Miller, J. S. (2007). The Positive Ethical Organization: Enacting a Living Code of Ethics and Ethical Organizational Identity. Journal of Business Ethics, 76(1), 17–33.

Walter, F. & Bruch, H. (2008). The Positive Group Affect Spiral: A Dynamic Model of the Emergence of Positive Affective Similarity in Work Groups. Journal of Organizational Behavior, 29(2), 239–61.

Weiss, H. & Brief, A. (2001). Affect at Work: A Historical Perspective. In Emotions at Work: Theory, Research, and Applications for Management, edited by R. L. Payne and C. L. Cooper. Chichester, UK: Wiley, 133–72.

Wharton, A. S. (1993). The Affective Consequences of Service Work: Managing Emotions on the Job. Work and Occupations, 20(2), 205–32.

Wharton, A. S. (2009). The Sociology of Emotional Labor. Annual Review of Sociology, 35, 147–165.

Wharton, A. S. & Erickson, R. J. (1995). The Consequences of Caring: Exploring the Links between Women's Job and Family Emotion Work. Sociological Quarterly, 36(2), 273–96.

Wilson, T. D. & Gilbert, D. T. (2005). Affective Forecasting: Knowing What to Want. Current Directions in Psychological Science, 14(3), 131–4.

Wong, C.-S. & Law, K. S. (2002). The Effects of Leader and Follower Emotional Intelligence on Performance and Attitude: An Exploratory Study. Leadership Quarterly, 13(3), 243–74.

Wood, S. L. & Bettman, J. R. (2007). Predicting Happiness: How Normative Feeling Rules Influence (and Even Reverse) Durability Bias. Journal of Consumer Psychology, 17(3), 188–201.

Youssef, C. M. & Luthans, F. (2007). Positive Organizational Behavior in the Workplace: The Impact of Hope, Optimism, and Resilience. Journal of Management, 33(5), 774–800.

Zajonc, R. B. (1980). Feeling and Thinking: Preferences Need No Inferences. American Psychologist, 35, 151–75.

Zajonc, R. B. (1984). On the Primacy of Affect. American Psychologist, 39, 117–23.

Zapf, D. & Holz, M. (2006). On the Positive and Negative Effects of Emotion Work In Organizations. European Journal of Work and Organizational Psychology, 15(1), 1–28.

Zeelenberg, M. & Beattie, J. (1997). Consequences of Regret Aversion: Additional Evidence for Effects of Feedback on Decision Making. Organizational Behavior and Human Decision Processes, 72(1), 63–78.

Zeelenberg, M., Nelissen, R. M., Breugelmans, S. M. & Pieters, R. (2008). On Emotion Specificity in Decision Making: Why Feeling is for Doing. Judgment and Decision Making, 3(1), 18–27.

23

MORALITY AS A VARIABLE CONSTRAINT ON ECONOMIC BEHAVIOR

Daniel Friedman

Introduction: the third branch of behavioral economics

Standard neoclassical analysis assumes *equilibrium* among economic agents who *maximize* preferences based on material *self-interest*. Behavioral economics is concerned with systematic deviations from standard neoclassical analysis, so one can say that it has three main branches. The first branch, exemplified in learning or adaptive processes, relaxes the assumption that the economy is always in equilibrium. The second branch, exemplified in the biases and anomalies literature, relaxes the assumption of maximization. Although there is much to say about these matters (some of it contained elsewhere in this volume), it can be argued that behavior in these branches often is transient. People usually improve their choices once they become aware of substantially better alternatives, and many economic processes tend towards equilibrium, at least under favorable circumstances.

The third branch of behavioral economics is different. It studies deviations from self-interested behavior, and in many circumstances, such deviations are not transient. People who deviate from material self-interest are typically well aware of that fact, and often are proud of it. Serving the greater good at moderate personal expense is considered the right thing to do, and in some circumstances following personal self-interest is considered reprehensible.

This chapter will examine the enduring deviations from self-interest that are guided by moral principles. We argue informally that such deviations can be understood using tools familiar to economists, and that they can be economically important. Examples abound in all stages of life, from child raising to bequests.

Two side issues perhaps deserve mention before proceeding. First, the title of this chapter will strike some readers as oxymoronic: in mathematics, constraints are not variable. True enough, but a major theme of this chapter is that the contents of moral codes are very context- and culture-dependent. Hence the constraints they impose also vary over time and by location, context and status.

Second, emphasizing such variability may cause some readers to wonder whether the chapter assumes (or even espouses) moral relativism. Of course, *descriptive* moral relativism is a simple and not very controversial fact. Clearly the content of moral codes varies considerably from culture to culture, and even within a culture from context to context. To cite one example, the age of consent is 15 to 18 in most Western societies, but arranged marriages of very young children are an accepted practice in some parts of the world. On the other hand, this chapter will take no stand on more controversial versions of moral relativism such as *meta-ethical* relativism, the claim that nobody can judge one set of ethical beliefs morally superior to another. We will only go so far as to claim that in some situations, one moral code may be more efficient than another.

The next four sections rely largely on material presented more fully in Friedman (2008, chapter 1), Friedman and Sinervo (2016, chapter 13), and Rabanal and Friedman (2015).

An evolutionary puzzle

Everyday experience tells us that cooperation is common, and yet it is a puzzle to biologists as well as to economists. For the moment, take as given that fitness is the biological counterpart of material self-interest; later we will consider the point more carefully. The fundamental tenet of evolution is that fitter behavior becomes more prevalent over time. It seems to follow that evolution favors the selfish, so that behavioral deviations from self-interest should also be transient.

Figure 23.1 elucidates the puzzle from the perspective of an economic agent called Self, who interacts with other economic agents, collectively called Other. Relative to the status quo, each alternative action available to Self potentially increases or decreases her own fitness, and at the same time has an impact on other individuals. That net fitness impact (summing across all agents other than Self) may also be positive or negative, and is shown on the vertical axis labeled Other.

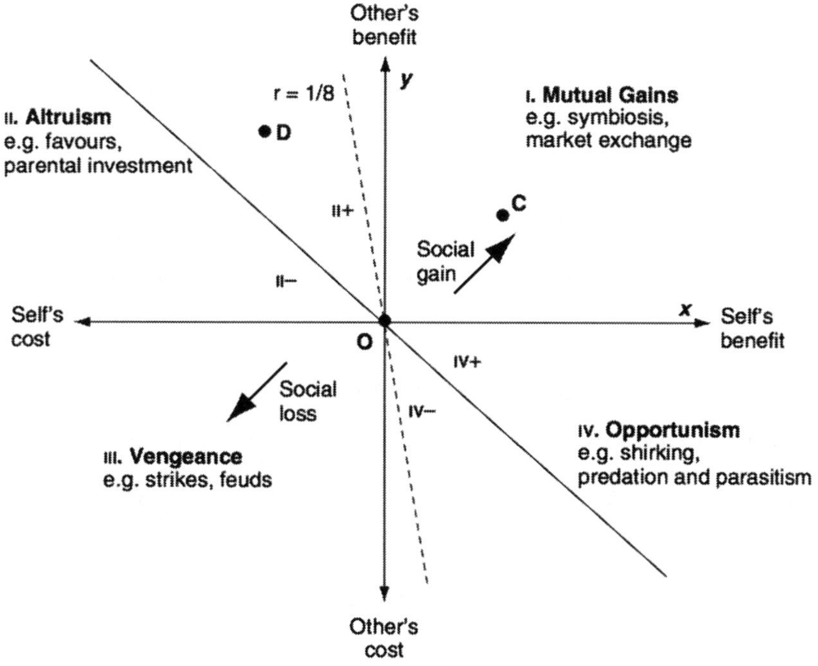

Figure 23.1 The origin O = (0, 0) marks the status quo fitness. In quadrant I, both the actor ("Self") and all others affected by her action ("Other") benefit from a departure from the status quo. In quadrant II, the action helps Other at a cost to v; the fitness sum is positive in subquadrant II+ (shaded) and negative in II-. In quadrant III, both Self and Other incur fitness costs. In IV, Self gains at the expense of Other, and the fitness sum is positive in IV+ but negative in the shaded subquadrant IV

Evolution directly favors actions whose fitness impact on Self is positive, regardless of the impact on Other. Self's iso-fitness lines in Figure 23.1 are parallel to the vertical axis, and lines further East (i.e., to the right) represent higher fitness. Hence, shares should increase most rapidly for actions whose fitness is furthest East. We conclude that unaided evolution pushes agents into quadrants I and IV.

By contrast, the group as a whole gains fitness when the sum (or average) of the members' payoffs is as high as possible. Social efficiency is best promoted by actions that equally weight fitness of Other and Self, so social iso-efficiency lines are parallel to the line of slope-1 through the origin. The group does best when actions are chosen that are farthest to the Northeast.

Actions in quadrant I serve self-interest and group interest simultaneously, that is, bring mutual gains. However, efficient altruism (subquadrant II+) is not favored by unaided evolution, while inefficient opportunism (IV−) is favored. In these subquadrants we have a direct conflict between what is good for the individual and what is good for the group.

A standard example is the two-player Prisoner's Dilemma, with payoff matrix (1)

1, 1	−1,2
2,−1	0,0

The status quo is for both players to choose the second action ("Defect"), yielding the payoff sum $0 + 0 = 0$. A unilateral move by Self to instead play the first action ("Cooperate") yields the payoff vector (−1,2) in subquadrant II+, an increase in social efficiency since the payoff sum is $-1+2 = 1 > 0$. Social efficiency is maximized if Other reciprocates, yielding payoff vector (1,1) in quadrant I and payoff sum 2. But unaided evolution increases the share of Defect because it is the dominant action.

In general, social efficiency requires seizing opportunities in shaded region II+ and preventing activities in shaded region IV−, contrary to the push from unaided evolution. How might this happen? There are several different ways, as we will now see. From the perspective of Figure 23.1, however, they all do the same thing—they all rotate the vertical axis (or Self's iso-fitness lines) counterclockwise. In other words, they all internalize the externalities and thereby convert social dilemmas into coordination games.

Two standard solutions

The first way to resolve social dilemmas is to funnel the benefits to kin (Hamilton, 1963). Here is the basic algebra, which interested readers can extend to more general scenarios. Suppose that, relative to status quo, Self bears fitness cost C for some genetically controlled cooperative behavior, and other individuals $i=1, \ldots, n$ each enjoy benefit b. Let $r_i \in [0, 1]$ denote i's degree of relatedness to Self, that is, the probability that i and Self share a rare gene. Let $r = (1/n)\Sigma\, r_i$ be the average degree of relatedness of the beneficiaries, and let $B=nb$ be the total benefit to Other. Then, relative to status quo, the prosocial gene has fitness $-C + rB$. Therefore, it will increase share if and only if

$$rB > C. \qquad (1)$$

Equation (1) is known as Hamilton's rule, and says that a prosocial trait will spread if its personal cost is less than the total benefit B times the beneficiaries' average relatedness r.

Figure 23.1 illustrates the geometry. When r=1.0, as between clones, the locus B=C where equation (1) holds with equality coincides with the $-45°$ line that separates the efficient from the inefficient portions of quadrants II and IV. A gene benefits exactly to the extent that the group benefits. That is, when genes are identical within the group, the vertical line (representing zero fitness increment for Self) is rotated counterclockwise 45°. Then, the externality is completely internalized and the conflict between group and self-interest evaporates. For lesser values of r, the conflict is ameliorated but not eliminated. The dashed line in Figure 23.1 is the locus rB=C when $r = 1/8$, as with first cousins. The line has slope $-1/r = -8$, and it represents counterclockwise rotation by about a sixth of that required to eliminate the conflict between Self and group.

Kin selection is an important solution to social dilemmas, but it has its limits. To work properly, non-kin must be largely excluded from the benefits of altruistic behavior. Otherwise, as the fraction of non-kin beneficiaries increases, the average relatedness r drops until equation (1) fails, which implies by Hamilton's rule that cooperation fails. To exclude non-kin, there must be reliable kin recognition and/or limited dispersal.

Game theorists developed a second solution to social dilemmas, this one purely rational. By the early 1960s many leading game theorists came to realize that the key was repeated interaction and patience. Their insight is contained in what is now called the Folk Theorem. As explained in almost every game theory textbook, a simple version runs as follows. Suppose that Self interacts repeatedly with Other, and each can bestow benefit B on the other at personal cost C. If the discount factor (due to delay and uncertainty) in receiving return benefit is δ, then the repeated game has an equilibrium in which everyone always cooperates (i.e., always bestows the benefit) if and only if $\delta B > C$.

Readers will quickly realize that the condition is exactly the same as Hamilton's rule except that the discount factor $\delta \in [0, 1]$ replaces the relatedness coefficient $r \in [0, 1]$. The geometry and the economic interpretation is also the same: a larger δ implies more counterclockwise rotation of the vertical axis in Figure 23.1, and more internalization of the externality. The dilemma is ameliorated for $\delta > 0$, and eliminated only for $\delta = 1$.

Note that, in order to work well, this sort of cooperation requires reliable repeat business (and the ability to recognize who is owed a favor); otherwise δ will be too low to support significant departures from direct self-interest.

Taken together, these two different solutions can explain a lot of cooperation observed in nature. The standard explanation for the remarkable degree of cooperation among sister ants and bees is that they are very closely related, with r as high as 0.75. The standard example of cooperation explained by the Folk Theorem (or of reciprocal altruism, as biologists have called it since Trivers, 1971) is mutual grooming by chimpanzees and many other primate species—unrelated adults literally scratch each other's backs to mutual benefit.

Social preferences: half of a third solution

We humans are especially good at exploiting once-off opportunities with a variety of different partners, so bilateral reciprocity cannot be the whole story. Nor can kin selection, since even in tribal groups average relatedness r is typically less than 1/8 (e.g., Smith, 1985).

What other explanations might there be? Could it be that we just like to help our friends? Introspection tells us that most people really do care about others, at least their friends, and are willing to make some sacrifices to benefit them. That is, we have *social preferences*. Let us pick a simple specification and examine it in light of the discussion so far.

Suppose that your utility function is $u(x, y) = x + \theta y$, that is, you are willing to sacrifice up to θ units of personal payoff x in order to increase others' payoff by a unit. In other words, you would take an action with personal cost C as long as the benefit B to others satisfies $\theta B>C$. Once again, you follow a variant of Hamilton's rule, now with the preference parameter θ replacing the relatedness coefficient r. And once again, we have the same geometry and economic intuition. Friendly preferences of the sort just described partially internalize the externality, and parameter values $\theta \in [0,1]$ potentially can explain exactly the same range of social behavior as genetic relatedness and repeated interaction.

But this explanation is too glib. The relatedness coefficient r and the discount factor δ are given features of the environment, while θ is an evolved preference parameter. The puzzle has not been solved, just pushed down a level. Now the question is: how can friendly preferences evolve? How can $\theta>0$ arise, and how can it resist invasion?

Before trying to answer that question we should probe the nature of preferences. Economists usually take preferences as a starting point that is not subject to further analysis but, if pushed, some will say that preferences really just summarize (and are revealed by) contingent choices.

Evolutionary economists have recently begun to develop a different perspective, and see evolved preferences as Nature's way of delegating choices that must respond to local contingencies. For example, tribeswomen may gather only certain kinds of root vegetables and only in certain seasons, and prepare them only in certain ways. They and their families would lose fitness if they ate poisonous roots, or did not cook some good roots properly. It is implausible that evolving hardwired contingent behavior could deal with so much complexity—one needs about 2^{100} alternatives to fully specify contingent behavior with only five root species in four seasons with five preparation methods. Even worse, changes in the environment can make the hardwiring obsolete before it can become established. As Robson and Samuelson (2011, section 2.3) put it,

> A more effective approach may then be to endow the agent with a goal, such as maximizing caloric intake or simply feeling full, along with the ability to learn which behavior is most likely to achieve this goal in a given environment. Under this approach, evolution would equip us with a utility function that would provide the goal for our behavior, along with a learning process, perhaps ranging from trial-and-error to information collection and Bayesian updating, that would help us pursue that goal.

To return to the question of how a social preference parameter like θ evolves, we must distinguish between fitness payoff and utility payoff. Evolution is driven purely by fitness, that is, by own material payoff x arising from one's own acts and those of others. Choice, on the other hand, is driven by preferences, that is, by utility payoff that may include other components such as θy, the joy of helping others.

Creatures (including people) who make choices more closely aligned with fitness should, it would seem, displace creatures whose choices respond to other components. But social interactions complicate the analysis because fitness payoffs depend on others' choices as well as one's own, and one's own behavior can affect others' choices. For a given sort of preferences to evolve, creatures with such preferences must receive at least as much material payoff (or fitness) as creatures with feasible alternative preferences. Evolution here is indirect (Guth and Yaari, 1992) in that it operates on the preference parameters (such as θ) that determine behavior, rather than directly on behavior.

Thus, the crucial evolutionary question is whether people with larger θ gain more material payoff than those with smaller θ in [0,1]. The extreme $\theta = 1$ applies to individuals who follow the Golden Rule and value Other's material payoff equally with own material payoff, and the other extreme $\theta = 0$ represents a selfish Self who is indifferent to the impact his actions have on others.

Hirshleifer (1978) refers to such behavior as the Brass Rule. Compared to those with larger θ, individuals with smaller θ would seem to have lower costs, since they bear the cost of donation in fewer circumstances. If so, evolutionary forces will undercut friendly preferences and they will eventually disappear, or never appear in the first place.

Vengeful preferences rescue friendly preferences. The idea here is that social preferences are state dependent: my attitude θ towards your material well-being depends on my emotional state (such as friendly or hostile) and your behavior systematically alters my emotional state. If you help me or my friends, then my friendliness increases, as captured in the model applying a larger positive θ to your material payoff. But if you betray my trust, or hurt my friends, then I may become quite angry with you, as captured by a negative θ. In this emotional state, I am willing at some personal material cost to reduce your material payoff, that is, I seek revenge. I would thus follow Hirshleifer's (1978) Silver Rule: be kind to others who are kind to you, but also seek to harm those who harm you or your friends.

The algebra of vengeance involves double negatives but is otherwise very simple. An action in Quadrant III of Figure 23.1 is represented by $x, y<0$, that is, both Self and Other incur losses relative to the status quo. In an angry state with $\theta < 0$, punishing (imposing the loss $y<0$ on) a culprit Other will bring Self satisfaction $\theta y>0$, which may more than offset her personal fitness loss $x<0$.

Everyone loses fitness from such punishment and in that sense it directly impairs efficiency, but the indirect positive effects can more than compensate. If Others punish Self for being insufficiently friendly, then the material advantage of having a lower θ shrinks or disappears. Cheaters no longer prosper. That is, although less friendly people still incur fewer costs of altruistic acts, they now incur increased costs due to punishment by vengeful group members. If vengeance is sufficiently intense, it supports a high average value of θ, and thus promotes efficient social behavior.

But we are still not done. Punishment is also costly to the avenger, so less vengeful preferences seem fitter. What then supports vengeful preferences: who guards the guardians? This is called the *second order free rider problem*, and it has provoked a considerable literature in its own right. Samuelson (2001) summarizes the early work as follows. There is no second order free rider problem when Others can see Self's degree of vengefulness. In this case, sometimes called "transparent disposition," a high degree of vengefulness brings high material payoff because it deters free riding and no costly punishment is necessary. However, in the opposite case of "opaque disposition," in which Others can not directly tell whether Self is quite vengeful or not at all vengeful, then the second order free rider problem is fatal: less vengeful types indeed drive out more vengeful types and cooperation fails.

Morals: the missing half

As we see it, morals are the human solution to the second order free rider problem and hence (in conjunction with Silver Rule preferences) are the other half of our solution to underlying social dilemmas. The second order free rider problem is greatly ameliorated when the costs of vengeful behavior are shared widely within a group—the group as a whole can impose large costs on a single culprit at small cost to each individual member. The cost is even lower when such group sanctions deter most selfish behavior, so that vengeful episodes are rare. Gossip (or, in economic jargon, information sharing within the group) may be imperfect but it still enables these advantages.

The Rabanal and Friedman (2015) model captures some of the crucial ideas. Consider the Prisoner's Dilemma in extensive form, also known as the Trust Game, as a population game with two roles: first mover (or Trustor) and second mover (or Trustee). Starting with the payoff matrix in equation (1) above, the payoff is 0 to both players if the Trustor defects, is (−1,2) if he cooperates but the Trustee defects, and is (1,1) if both cooperate. When a Trustee defects, Trustors with vengeful preferences and constant marginal punishment cost c want to (personally or as a group) incur total cost v to inflict a utility-maximizing degree of harm v/c on the culprit. In the basic model where aggrieved Trustors personally punish culprit Trustees, it turns out that second order free riding brings higher fitness to Trustors with lower v, who therefore displace the more vengeful types. Cooperation is not evolutionarily viable.

But now suppose that vengeance is backed by a moral code that calls on each Trustor (a) to share equally the cost of punishing all Trustees who defect, and (b) to share information via gossip on which Trustees defect so that they can be avoided in the future. We have in mind a coherent group of Trustors who interact frequently and know each other well, and so can discipline anyone who tries to gain the benefits of gossip without sharing the punishment cost. Thus (a) and (b) are a package. Some Trustors, the code compliers (K), adopt the package. Possibly there are other Trustors, called non-compliers (N), who avoid the costs of punishing third parties but have no access to gossip. Of course, gossip is imperfect, so there is some error rate e at which defecting Trustees are encountered.

Cost sharing boosts Ks' expected payoff when D is relatively rare and K is relatively common. It turns out that the model supports an equilibrium of that sort, that is, with a high degree of cooperation but less than 100%. Even better, that equilibrium has a large basin of attraction under perturbed best response (logit) dynamics for plausible parameter values, that is, the populations of Trustors and Trustees converge to this equilibrium, via damped oscillations, from a broad set of initial conditions. The basin of attraction is larger when, for example, gossip is more reliable.

The point of the model is that a functioning moral code can promote a high degree of flexible cooperation within a coherent small group of people who know each other and can share information about code compliance. Examples include tribesmen, and members of a small unit within a modern organization. The model says nothing about cooperation in a wider world where people often interact with strangers.

Before moving on, it may be worth underlining the distinction between compliance to a moral code and responding to social preferences. Social preferences trade off self-interest against the greater good, while compliance to a moral code is a constraint that admits no tradeoff. The constraint depends on the content of the particular moral code, and that varies by context even in simple societies. In the modern world the moral constraints are even more variable, yet still crucial in many realms. They deserve closer scrutiny by economists.

Morals, civilization, markets, and modernity

All of the evidence suggests that the moral system co-evolved with our hunter-gatherer ancestors, and that their moral codes were very egalitarian (see, for example, chapters 1 and 2 of Friedman, 2008). The contents of the moral code changed drastically with the appearance of large scale river valley agriculture. First seen along the Tigris and Euphrates, soon after along the Nile and then on the great rivers of India and China, this sort of agriculture demands cooperation of large numbers of individuals to construct and maintain irrigation facilities, and to store and defend a large annual harvest.

Meeting those logistical requirements marked a new chapter in human sociality, and ushered in civilization. No longer did humans interact mainly with people they knew personally. In a city of thousands of inhabitants (Uruk, the world's leading city 6,000 years ago, had a population of 50,000), cooperation becomes qualitatively different. Gossip cannot keep up, and people often have to deal with perfect strangers. Egalitarianism then fails to ensure cooperation.

Moral codes adapted. In contrast to hunter-gatherers' egalitarian codes, the codes of river valley civilizations all emphasize hierarchy, obedience to authority, and third party enforcement.

Markets originate in gift exchange, first practiced by our prehistoric ancestors. Gift exchange continues in new guises in river valley civilizations, but spot markets began to emerge. So did written contracts and other promises verifiable by third parties with no personal connection—indeed, writing seemed to develop largely to support contracting (e.g., Van De Mieroop, 2005). But all market activity was subordinate to the moral system as enforced by political and religious authorities, backed by laws and soldiers. The authorities tended to favor monopolies run by their friends, limiting innovation and disruption.

A very different social order began to take hold in England and the Netherlands about 200 years ago. The long absence of unified political control in Europe, together with active long-distance trade, allowed markets to slip their feudal bonds. For the first time, market imperatives became a force comparable to moral imperatives, sometimes able to trump traditional political and religious authority. It was the dawn of the modern world.

The rise of markets caused (and was caused by) another great transition in moral codes. Bourgeois virtues—prudence, punctuality, respect of private property and wealth accumulation, autonomy, skepticism of authority—worked better with the emerging modern economy, and tended to displace more traditional moral codes. Our interest in this chapter, however, is the reverse influence: How do modern moral codes constrain modern markets?

Existential constraints

The most fundamental constraint is whether a market exists at all. Markets for slaves existed for millennia, but they did not survive the sea change in moral codes. Notions of human rights and democracy gained traction in the late 1700s, and by the late 1800s laws backed by military force had killed off international slave markets. Moral forces similarly helped terminate the market for child labor in Western world in the early twentieth century.

A number of other potential markets fail to exist due to moral strictures backed by well-enforced laws. In the twenty-first century United States, these include direct purchase of votes for elective office, direct purchase for transplant of organs such as kidneys, and selling horsemeat for human consumption. Despite often vigorous suppression, black markets continue to exist for many illegal drugs, for sexual services, and for venues for soccer's World Cup. In the nineteenth century, it was legal (if less than honorable) to hire a substitute to avoid military service, but that became illegal in the twentieth century. Readers can surely add to the list of markets that were or are non-existent because of morally grounded legal prohibitions, and to the list of black or gray markets that exist despite prohibition.

Conversely, some markets exist only by virtue of moral impulses. Philanthropy can be explained in part by our tax laws and some donors' desire for public recognition, but only in part. Likewise, the war on drugs has been funded willingly (at least until quite recently) by taxpayers who by all objective measures get a meager or perhaps negative return for their generous support.

Such lists beg the question: How do particular sorts of markets come to be considered moral or immoral? Indeed, are some sorts of transactions inherently corrupt, and others inherently legitimate? Since we are not prepared to reject (or accept) meta-ethical moral relativism, the follow up question remains beyond the scope of this chapter. Readers may, however, want to scan chapters 4–6 of Friedman (2008), which recount the moral revulsion to early capitalism and urban squalor expressed by Romantic poets such as William Blake, the subsequent hostility to many sorts of markets that informed nineteenth and twentieth century socialism, and the moral constraints that paralyzed Japan's economy after 1990. Roth (2007) is the seminal article on this topic.

Neoclassical economists may have part of the answer to the begged question. The Law and Economics literature posits that the key is (and should be) economic efficiency. Does opening some market increase aggregate wealth? If so, then morals and laws should support it. Does graft or nepotism slow the growth of the economic pie? If so, such activities should be efficiently suppressed. One could perhaps extend the test to economic equality, if it is associated with growth or desired for its own sake. To the extent that economic efficiency helps one jurisdiction outcompete another, evolutionists would use the same criterion. Economic efficiency evidently provides an advantage in meme competition, so in the long run it should help determine which sorts of markets are encouraged or discouraged by our moral codes.

Pricing constraints

To see how a firm's everyday pricing decisions are constrained by morals, consider the following hypothetical scenario from Kahneman, Knetsch and Thaler (1986):

> A hardware store has been selling snow shovels for $15. The morning after a large snowstorm, the store raises the price to $20. Please rate this action as Completely Fair, Acceptable, Unfair [or] Very Unfair.

The authors report that 82 percent of respondents rate the price increase as unfair or very unfair. Other parts of the study suggest that customers are okay with raising prices due to cost increases, but not due to demand increases. An actual hardware store that surmised that its customers had similar reactions would probably not raise prices after a snowstorm, and the likely result would be a stockout, reducing both consumer surplus and firm profits.

In 2000, Amazon's customers became aware that some got lower prices than others for the same DVD movies. Intense outrage led Amazon to offer refunds to those who bought at the higher prices in their "dynamic pricing experiment" (Streitfeld, 2000). Since then, firms have been very circumspect in conducting such experiments, despite their obvious value to the firm and perhaps even to most customers.

On the other hand, airline passengers have become accustomed to paying wildly different prices. On any given flight, a typical customer might have paid hundreds of dollars more (or less) than the person sitting next to her. Why does such extreme price discrimination provoke only grumbles and not outrage? Why is there no pressure to allow secondary markets in airline tickets? These would quickly eliminate most of the price discrepancies, but they are forbidden by law. (Why? Supposedly for security reasons, but that claim falls apart when examined.)

The moral constraint thus seems especially variable when it comes to pricing. It seems manipulable by choice of framing and force of habit. One conjecture perhaps worth exploring is that the moral instincts are efficiency-enhancing in proper context, but sometimes are improperly generalized. In the snow shovel example, our outrage at the price increase may spill over from hold-up problems. A first mover who expects exploitation by the second mover will not invest, to the detriment of both. However, as in the Trust Game described earlier, a second mover who expects moral outrage and sanctions in response to an attempted hold-up will be deterred from such antisocial behavior, enabling efficient cooperation. Perhaps our moral instincts are not yet finely tuned enough to distinguish the snow shovel allocation problem from the classic hold-up problem.

Wage constraints

Moral constraints play a central role in the workplace. Neoclassical principal/agent models assume that workers will shirk whenever that is in their direct interest, but everyday observation suggests otherwise. Organizations with a positive "corporate culture" get a major boost from workers trying to act in the organization's best interest even when they are not monitored. It is a form of gift exchange, where the workers reciprocate with organizations that offer good working conditions and wages. Friedman (2008, chapter 7) argues that these organizations harness our small group moral system and profit from it.

But things can also go badly in organizations. When employees resent their peers or their bosses, they can cripple productivity and worse. Krueger and Mas (2004) document an egregious example at Firestone's Decatur Illinois tire plant. In 1995, management won a bitter battle with the labor union, but defective tires from that plant subsequently caused hundreds of traffic fatalities. Firestone and its main customer, Ford, barely survived.

The macroeconomic implications may be even more serious. Textbooks attribute jumps in unemployment largely to downward nominal wage rigidity: when demand slackens, firms have traditionally been more inclined to lay off workers than to cut wages to clear the market. Akerlof (1982) was among the first to argue that the reason is gift exchange. The positive reciprocity described two paragraphs ago might, following wage cuts, become more like the negative reciprocity described in the previous paragraph. Cyclical bouts of unemployment, recessions and occasional depresssions may well be the unintended consequence of moral constraints in the workplace.

Brosnan and de Waal (2003) point to another aspect of fair pay. They famously show how one capuchin monkey that had been happy to perform routine tasks for a cucumber slice reward becomes enraged, and stops performing the task, when he sees another monkey getting a better reward, a grape, for the same task. It is easy to overinterpret this study, but it has traction at my school. Viewing de Waal's video enlivened discussions of salary compression—some recently hired junior faculty receive salaries similar to those of more accomplished senior faculty. This "compression" is due to the disconnect between the external job market and internal pay scales based on seniority and merit. Of course, there is also a long-running controversy on the extent of, and the reasons for, lower pay for women whose qualifications seem similar to men. Pay equity is an issue in most large organizations, and there is no easy answer when internal notions of fair pay collide with external market trends.

Financial market constraints

Finance has always faced severe moral constraints. Laws against usury crippled finance in the medieval world, and still distort financial arrangements in the Islamic world. In the United States today, there are still laws that cap the interest rate lenders can charge, but the more interesting and consequential constraints concern home mortgages.

Twentieth century home mortgages were rather straightforward. After saving for years a family would shop for an affordable home. The down payment would cover at least 20 percent of the price, and the rest would be financed by a 30 year loan whose monthly payments required at most 1/3 of verified monthly income. The lender was a local savings and loan or commercial bank, and the lending officer would often build a personal relationship with the borrower. If the family got into trouble, they would often be able to negotiate an accommodation that worked for both borrower and lender.

Things changed around the turn of the century. Financial innovations, especially securitization, broke the personal connection between borrow and lender. Since the loan would not stay long on the lender's books, the loan officer became concerned mainly with whether the loan would be accepted into a pool that could be securitized and sold to investors.

Demand boomed for high-yielding mortgage-backed securities in the early years of the twenty-first century. Moral and legal responsibility diffused between the institutions that originated loans, the mortgage brokers who first bundled them, the investment banks that sliced and diced the bundles, the rating agencies who blessed the resulting products with AAA ratings, and the investors who purchased them. Booming demand and diffuse responsibility naturally led to lower standards—loans soon required only a 10 percent or 5 percent, or eventually 0 percent down payment; some borrowers were encouraged to lie about their income, and some never understood the teaser loans they received with artificially low initial monthly payments. Savvy financial professionals up and down the securitization food chain knew that lots of these mortgages would go bad, but thought that they were insulated from the problem and that someone else would be left holding the bag.

This moral morass was, it is widely acknowledged, the primary cause of financial market turmoil in 2008–9 and the subsequent great recession, from which the world has not yet fully recovered; see, for example, Gorton and Metrick (2012) and Lo (2012).

Moral constraints can bind when financial markets are behaving well. The insurance industry is emblematic, and not just for trying minimize submission of fraudulent claims. The term "moral hazard" was invented by Victorian-era insurance analysts to describe the propensity to engage in riskier behavior after purchasing insurance. The term is now part of standard lexicon, but like shirking on the job, it is less prevalent in advanced economies than standard selfish optimization models would predict.

Recent financial innovations work with moral constraints in new ways. In many emerging economies, roscas (see, e.g., Anderson and Baland, 2002) and other sorts of microfinance (e.g., Armendáriz and Morduch, 2010) leverage small group personal connections to improve repayment rates. In the United States and other advanced economies, crowdfunding platforms like Prosper.com, Kickstarter.com and GiveForward.com (see, e.g., Belleflamme et al., 2014) and innovative companies like SoFi help small investors find and directly fund individuals and businesses with whom they share some sort of affiliation.

Discussion

This chapter has aimed to highlight many of the significant roles that moral considerations play in economic life. It began with perspectives on the social purpose of a moral code, and hinted at the reasons why codes vary so much in terms of which behaviors they encourage or discourage. The economic consequences include creating markets where they might not otherwise exist, including black or gray markets for some goods, while killing off markets for other goods and services. Moral constraints reshape financial markets and labor markets, and constrain pricing behavior, even in markets for everyday consumer items.

These points are worth making to an academic audience because moral constraints are not yet an established part of economists' research agenda. New questions begin to come into focus. Some seem trivial—for example, why do people who would be distressed if the home team lost the big game not use the cheap insurance policy of betting on the rival team? More often, they compound their risks by betting on the home team. Other open questions are deep, and perhaps interdisciplinary—for example, how can we model the evolution of norms, the contents of moral codes? If some readers are inspired to tackle such questions, this chapter has served its purpose.

Bibliography

Akerlof, G. A. (1982). Labor contracts as partial gift exchange. Quarterly Journal of Economics, 97(4), 543–69.

Anderson, S. & Baland, J.-M. (2002). The economics of roscas and intrahousehold resource allocation. Quarterly Journal of Economics, 117(3), 963–95.

Armendáriz, B. & Morduch, J. (2010). The Economics of Microfinance. MIT Press.

Belleflamme, P., Lambert, T. & Schwienbacher, A. (2014). Crowdfunding: Tapping the right crowd. Journal of Business Venturing, 29(5), 585–609.

Brosnan, S. F. & de Waal, F. B. M. (2003). Monkeys reject unequal pay. Nature, 425(6955), 297–9.

Friedman, D. (2008). Morals and Markets: An Evolutionary Account, Palgrave Macmillan.

Friedman, D. & Sinervo, B. (2016). Evolutionary Games in Natural, Social, and Virtual Worlds, Oxford University Press.

Gorton, G. & Metrick, A. (2012). Securitized banking and the run on repo. Journal of Financial Economics, 104(3), 425–51.

Güth, W. & Yaari, M. (1992). An evolutionary approach to explain reciprocal behavior in a simple strategic game. In U. Witt (ed.), Explaining Process and Change: Approaches to Evolutionary Economics. Ann Arbor, 23–34.

Hamilton, W. D. (1963), The evolution of altruistic behavior. American Naturalist. 97(896), 354–6.

Hirshleifer, J. (1978). Natural economy versus political economy. Journal of Social and Biological Structures, 1(4), 319–37.

Kahneman, D., Knetsch, J. L. & Thaler, R. (1986). Fairness as a constraint on profit seeking: Entitlements in the market. American Economic Review, 76(4), 728–41.

Krueger, A. B. & Mas, A. (2004). Strikes, scabs, and tread separations: Labor strife and the production of defective Bridgestone/Firestone tires. Journal of Political Economy, 112(2), 253–89.

Lo, A. W. (2012). Reading about the financial crisis: A twenty-one-book review. Journal of Economic Literature, 50(1), 151–78.

Rabanal, J. P. & Friedman, D. (2015). How moral codes evolve in a trust game. Games, 6(2), 150–60.

Robson, A. & Samuelson, L. (2011). The evolution of decision and experienced utilities. Theoretical Economics, 6(3), 311–39.

Roth, A. E. (2007). Repugnance as a constraint on markets. Journal of Economic Perspectives, 21(3), 37–58.

Samuelson, L. (2001). Introduction to the evolution of preferences. Journal of Economic Theory, 97(2), 225–30.

Smith, E. A. (1985). Inuit foraging groups: Some simple models incorporating conflicts of interest, relatedness, and central-place sharing. Ethology and Sociobiology, 6(1), 27–47.

Streitfeld, D. (2000) Amazon pays a price for marketing test. Los Angeles Times, October 2, C1.

Trivers, R. L. (1971) The evolution of reciprocal altruism. Quarterly Review of Biology, 46(1), 35–57.

Van De Mieroop, M. (2005). The invention of interest: Sumerian loans. In W. N. Goetzmann & K. G. Rouwenhorst (eds.), The Origins of Value. Oxford University Press, 17–30.

24
BEHAVIORAL POLITICAL ECONOMY

Gigi Foster and Paul Frijters

Introduction

A major element in the success of economics is its production of simple ideas to describe many complex phenomena. Crudely speaking, mainstream economists view the world as made up of optimizing actors looking to become as wealthy as possible within the rules of the game set down by a political process. Consequently, approximating perfect markets as closely as possible is the means by which a society can achieve the greatest overall welfare from the natural competition between individuals. Economists, therefore, analyze situations in terms of their divergence from perfect markets; for example, because of asymmetric information, missing markets, returns to scale, limited property rights, and/or market power. Economists then rely on implicit rules of thumb about what can be done to overcome market imperfections, such as 'seek to reduce entry barriers', 'promote public access to trade-relevant information', and 'avoid concentrations of market power'. Feasible interventions based on such rules of thumb might include public oversight over natural monopolies, contract enforcement, managing interest rates and the money supply, setting up new property rights, creating markets, and so forth.

Policy is frequently informed by these core ideas and rules of thumb: modern societies feature state production of public goods (such as education and a national currency) and a plethora of regulatory institutions largely concerned with spotting and alleviating market imperfections. It is no exaggeration to say that the utopian vision of mainstream economics has become the 'main vision in town' as to how welfare can be improved by politicians and other social actors. As a result, economists enjoy a standing in the policy community unparalleled by that of any other social science, as well as an enviable academic position relative to other social sciences (Fourcade, Ollion & Algan, 2014).

Behavioral economics has in recent decades extended the mainstream *Homo Economicus* model of microeconomic behavior to 'explain' aspects of the wider economy that were previously mysterious. This approach has given us useful working paradigms, such as Robert Shiller's 'bubbles' arising from Keynesian 'animal spirits' (Shiller & Akerlof, 2009) and the idea that 'warm glow' effects underpin more giving behavior than greed would imply (Kolm, 2013). Yet the connection of such additions as animal spirits and warm glow to general economics is still shallow, in the sense that the picture of the individual lying at their base is not well-developed or integrated with the institutions and patterns observed in our broader society.

More broadly, the discipline has blind spots in its image of society as a whole, and opponents of economics have repeatedly pointed them out. For example, the scope of the state's ability to improve matters is not well understood. How do the rules of the democratic game actually come about? And how robust are they? Which behaviors of market players can realistically be monitored or enforced by the state? For that matter, why would one trust any state official to enforce anything that goes against his own personal interests? Despite a large body of work in institutional economics, and whole literatures in sociology and political science describing the state as the winner of an evolutionary struggle for supremacy (and thus as an institution with strengths and weaknesses), mainstream economic textbooks do not seriously consider the nature of the state and individuals' relation to it.

Ironically, an entire integrated set of blind spots in economics concerns trade—arguably the activity that the discipline is best known for championing. How prices are actually formed, what is involved when an agent searches for trading partners, and the role of trust in key aspects of the system underpinning trade (specifically, money, the division of labor, and the rule of law) remain strikingly absent from the mainstream economics curriculum. This makes it hard for economists to view recessions as anything other than mass holidays in which potential workers are simply not willing to accept wage reductions. Many reflective and experienced economists (e.g., Larry Summers and John Maynard Keynes) have understood that in recessions, workers are willing to work and firms have things they want to sell, but these two sides cannot find each other and get organized quickly enough to trade, and that this leads to unemployment and bankruptcy. Yet this description of what goes on during recessions can be viewed with incredulity by freshly minted PhD economists, as they will often never have encountered such a notion during their training.

There is also no guidance provided by the 'microeconomic foundations' approach, behavioral or otherwise, about which core ideas should be used in modelling any concrete problem. Is a particular policy scenario best modelled as a public-goods problem, or as a problem of barriers to entry? Externalities, or fixed costs? Structural inefficiencies, or returns to scale?

We submit that to fill in these blind spots, it is preferable 'to consider whole clusters of ideas rather than to target just one at a time' (Frijters, 2013: 342). Taking Daniel Kahneman's cue to move beyond rational economic man, we propose in this chapter a more integrated picture of not only the individual, but also his groups and his institutions. While we cannot solve all of the problems that modern mainstream economics leaves unsolved, we aim to show how expanding economists' view of individual and group processes, by accommodating more behavioral realism and directly modelling processes traditionally considered the purview of social psychology, can yield an improved understanding not only of microeconomic behavior but of the broader political economy in which we operate.

The individual and the greed–love dichotomy

Modern mainstream economics depicts a person as an 'individually rational agent', seeking to attain maximum personal gain from scarce material resources. This stylized individual simply takes resources and dominates others whenever he can in the pursuit of more wealth. Yet moral philosophers, including many modern economists, know that this is not a realistic depiction of human behavior: people's behavior reflects not only their search for money and status but also their love for their children, their love for their gods, and their commitment to notions of right and wrong. Yet how can we make our view of the individual more realistic without sacrificing the simplicity and tractability of the *Homo Economicus* model? A workable alternative should retain the elegance and the myriad contributions of the old model lest we fall into the trap of throwing away a very successful model just because it does not explain everything. Yet, the call to jettison what has been learned because of what is not yet explained is made by many (see, for example, Hodgson, 2013). Sensing the threat of admitting that the standard model fails to address important economic phenomena, economists have offered ever more fanciful rationalizations for retaining the old model, including such behaviors as voting (Downs, 1957), paying taxes (Allingham & Sandmo, 1972), and giving away money (Tiehen, 2001).

Significant mental gymnastics are required, however, to rationalize why a wealth maximizer would agree to serve his country as a front-line soldier; why a voter would expend effort to vote even though his chances of changing the outcome of the election are minimal; or why any one of us should be a tax-paying, law-abiding citizen when the probability of getting caught engaging in tax avoidance or petty crime is minimal. Either an individual must be stupid, uninformed, deluded, or unseen strings must be attached in order for mainstream economics to make sense of behavior that appears to be misaligned with the material interests of the individual. Perhaps our care for our children is the clearest case of the limits of the explanatory power of wealth-maximization: you would have to believe very unlikely arguments, such as that the only reason parents buy things for their children is so that the parents themselves look good in front of their friends and thus get more status, or that parents secure the highest possible income in adulthood for their children, the better to then beg, borrow or steal some of it for themselves.

Cognitive limitations, habits, and poor information (Pingle, 2010; Fehr & Zych, 2008; Altman, 2012) have frequently been offered as justifications for 'suboptimal' behavior, with some *ad hoc* acknowledgment of the possible contributions of true generosity or love. Variants of 'altruism' have been observed in many settings, in the lab and elsewhere (e.g., Andreoni, 1995), but this phenomenon has not been theoretically integrated into the economic model of decision-making. Even the motivating ideals of economics as a science and a profession are mysterious from the point of view of the very *Homo Economicus* lying at the discipline's heart, who cares nothing for helping society as a whole, searching for 'the truth' or helping 'his colleagues'.

While we freely acknowledge the greed of people and their willingness—seen in examples throughout history and around the world—to lie, cheat, steal, and kill in order to amass more for themselves, we think it is impossible to fully explain human behavior solely by greed. To dismiss the many situations in which people give freely of their resources with no personal material reward as merely unusual-looking attempts to dominate requires too many acrobatic flips of logic and suspensions of disbelief. Taking a serious alternative stance, however, requires an objective examination of what 'non-greed' really is.[1]

What the economist requires is a simple statement of the truly non-greedy side of human motivation that makes sense from the evolutionary and economic perspectives, fits most observed behaviors stemming from something other than greed, and is also flexible and general enough to inform and be woven into a larger story of how individuals interact.

Our main argument is that the non-greedy side of human motivation, which we call interchangeably love or loyalty, can be seen as a resource-acquisition strategy based on submission: an individual gives up part of his current identity and resources to a person or entity in the hope of a return favor.[2]

When do we use this strategy? Crucially, as it is impossible to consciously choose to love or stop loving something or someone, something uncontrolled by our conscious will must be at work in determining whether or not we will use this 'non-greedy' submission strategy in a given situation. For lack of a better word, we refer to this part of the mind as the 'unconscious.'

We propose that love is initialized in the unconscious mind because of a combination of desire (the lover must desire something from the loved object) and power (the lover must perceive the loved object as so powerful that it cannot be directly dominated). We thus contend that objects, ideals or people are loved when have been assessed by those beholding them as possessing something of value, but as being unable to be forced into surrendering it. Love is then essentially an implicit offer of care made by the unconscious mind towards the loved object, made in the hope that the loved object will reciprocate by providing the lover with what he wants. Once ensnared by this offer, the lover's conscious mind becomes bound to its promise, and treats the loved object as an extension of himself, irrespective of whether the hoped-for reciprocation happens.

We contend that economic agents act under the influence of greed when they consciously try to get the most for themselves by taking it or trading for it, and that they act under the influence of love or loyalty when they give towards others (people, objects, gods, or ideals) when there is no material reward for their generosity. There may be a hoped-for material reward, and there is also a true reward for seeing the loved entity thrive, but these are only perceived inside the mind of the lover. Figure 24.1, reproduced from Frijters (2013), provides a simple schematic of the two different strategies: greed, based on the domination response; and love or loyalty, based on the submission response.

It is hard to overstate the policy relevance of this mechanism. If loyalty is the outcome of beholding a power that is deemed to control something desired, then those with actual power can use this mechanism to create loyalty towards themselves and their ideals. Hence, nation states can create loyalty to themselves by means of national curricula, national armies, national festivities, and the national media. Through its power over the next generation in schools, army institutions, universities, and ministries, the nation state molds its citizens into loyal subjects who then man the state institutions and organize the loyalty formation of the next generation. In a similar way do academic disciplines and large corporations influence new recruits towards adopting new ideals and goals. Simply put, the love mechanism provides a natural means for the creation of group loyalty and hence for the creation and maintenance of groups themselves.

Naturally, some people pretend to be acting out of loyalty when in actual fact they are merely being calculating (i.e., greedy). This situation normally requires a social component, since pretense is normally a social activity. Hence, to further explore this and other consequences of our enhanced view of the individual, we must proceed to examine a higher level of aggregation than the individual himself: groups of people.

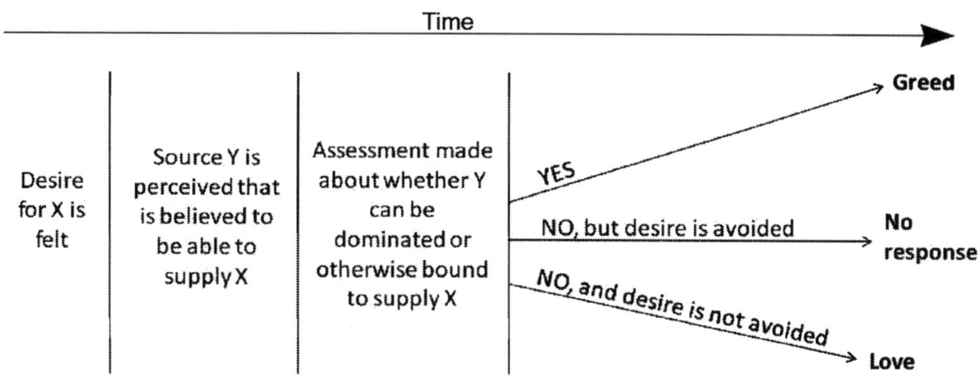

Figure 24.1 The stylized dichotomy between the strategies of dominance and submission

Groups

We now put forth a view of human groups that is consistent with the above view of the individual, and that can underpin an understanding of the wide array of economic and social institutions that we see today and have seen throughout history.

We draw inspiration in this section from studies in sociology and social psychology of how people interact in different types of groups. The Milgram studies (Milgram, 1974), for example, demonstrate our high degree of willingness to follow orders from a figure of authority when we are in the role of an underling. Other studies in psychology also show how a particular interpretation of reality can be upheld through social pressure within a group of relative equals (Asch, 1956) and how groups can form quickly where there are clear and immediate returns to being part of a group rather than on one's own (Peters, 1971). Like love, groups clearly matter for how we behave, meaning again that economists require a simple, tractable understanding of them that can be integrated with the discipline's existing models of behavior.

Our proposal is that every human group and organization is made up of elements of two core archetypes: hierarchies, and what we will call circles of reciprocity. Hierarchies feature clear lines of authority, with one person or group of people 'in charge' and others playing the role of followers. The number of hierarchical layers may vary, but the distinguishing feature is that orders of the leaders must be obeyed by the followers, whether or not these orders make sense to the followers. People operating in archetypical hierarchies are not motivated by any abstract common purpose shared by everyone in the hierarchy, other than the simple desire to amass wealth or status. The hierarchy is the social group type most associated with greed, as it operates on the basis of cold calculation by everyone in the hierarchy that their best chance to get ahead—possibly by rising in the ranks of the hierarchy itself—is to continue to be part of the hierarchy, whether as a follower or as a leader.

The other group archetype that we propose is characterized by the absence of lines of authority. A pure circle of reciprocity consists of people who see themselves as equals. The group runs not on the basis of its members' conscious pursuit of more for themselves and obedience to authority, but rather through the existence of abstractions in everyone's minds to which all members contribute. Due to the exceptional power of the human mind to conjure up and be motivated by unseen things, the abstractions defining a circle of reciprocity need not be specified exactly in order to perform the function of coordinating the group's actions. Such vague notions as 'fairness', 'our nation', 'my family', 'the school', or 'our ethnicity' are perfectly serviceable, even if what is meant by each of these things is subject to personal interpretation. Some fraction of the members of any circle of reciprocity will sacrifice towards the ideals of the group out of true loyalty to those ideals (one might call these members 'true believers'), where that loyalty has developed over time following the process sketched previously. Others in the circle may not be truly loyal to the ideals but nevertheless wish to benefit from membership in the group, and hence will play along.

A hierarchy offers high returns for those at the top, and each individual member must only monitor the activities of underlings one layer down. Hence, hierarchies naturally attract ambitious people, and are efficient ways to organize large-scale, generic activities whose successful performance requires only minimal (i.e., one-layer-down) checking to ensure that orders are being followed. The main economic cost of a hierarchy is that its members are not loyal to a group ideal and are continuously looking to benefit personally at the expense of other members. In modern societies featuring nation states with monopolies on violence, individuals can usually just walk away from hierarchies, which means that a successful modern hierarchy must obtain a rent to share among its members. This rent might be an effective monopoly, generated via a patent or returns to scale, or a political rent, in the case of a hierarchical ministry established by the political system.

The economic advantage of a circle of reciprocity is that its members are motivated to advance the interests of the group even when unmonitored. This makes circles of reciprocity the preferred group type with which to organize activities that require the coordinated activity of many individuals whose choices are based on locally available information and are complementary with other individuals' choices. This is partially why schools, army units, and teams operate as circles of reciprocity. Activities of the productive members of these groups amplify each other in production: successful performance of the group goal requires coordinated effort at myriad local levels contributed by willing cooperators.

Circles of reciprocity can be usefully subdivided into small ones—where all members are personally known to all others—and large ones. Both types feature individuals sustaining mental relations with the group abstraction: one's relation with 'Russia', 'Hinduism', or 'sociology' is equivalent for our purposes as one's relation with one's mother or one's neighbors. Yet small circles of reciprocity involve a cost, borne by members, of keeping mental score sheets as to who has contributed what. Even when there is a core of 'true believers', this score-keeping is required in order for circles of reciprocity to prevent and punish the free-riding of those who are not true believers, and thereby to maintain behavioral commitment to the joint group ideal. The cost of mutual monitoring goes up quadratically in the number of group members, which limits the size of small circles of reciprocity. In large circles of reciprocity, such as a religion or a nation state, the required monitoring happens instead via dedicated institutions. Members of a large reciprocal group do not personally know all of the group's other members, but everyone shares a similar understanding as to how the 'group-as-a-whole' rewards and punishes each member. Cohesion is maintained via formal institutions that indoctrinate new members, reward faithful service to the group, and punish conspicuous deviants—in line with that shared understanding and essentially following the recipe for generating loyalty in our love/greed theory above. Of course, the monitoring of large circles is not perfect, and individuals may compete for control of the common understanding or 'story' of what it means to be a 'good' member of the group.

These core archetypes are rarely seen in their pure form: most real human groups are patchworks of hierarchies and circles of reciprocity. Nonetheless, the nation state is the best modern example of a large reciprocal group. It wields the greatest power over us in many ways, including in terms of taxation and military potential, and even in terms of our self-image.

We propose that an economist can better understand the incentives faced by people, who are invariably members of multiple groups, when he first determines what lines of authority exist and what abstractions are at play in those groups. Any individual behavior that the economist would like to understand better can be viewed in the context of those group pressures most relevant to the individual at the time. For example, a father teaching his small child arithmetic will respond very differently to his child's questions than he would have responded earlier that day in response to questions from his marketing colleagues around the boardroom about his most recent proposed initiative to increase sales. This is because he is facing different powers in the two situations. With his child, he is motivated mainly by love, together with a mild sense of being in a position of authority over the child; in the boardroom, he is motivated by a desire to be seen to be trying to advance the financial interests of the company, and also to be seen as a valued member of his group of marketing colleagues who view each other roughly as equals sharing a particular outlook on the world. His answers to his colleagues' questions would, therefore, be framed in terms of financial benefit to the company and adherence to principles of marketing; his answers to his child would be framed in terms of information provision and training (possibly both about math and about obedience) that will best assist his child to learn and feel good.

Power

Power is a very slippery term. Our working definition of power is that it is about the believed potential to call upon resources in service of an objective. The power faced by underlings in a hierarchy is wielded mainly by their overseers, who can call upon their own physical force, and ultimately the physical force of others of higher rank, in order to ensure compliance with orders. The power faced by a member of a circle of reciprocity is not only that wielded over him by his unconscious mind if he is a true believer, essentially telling him that he himself will ensure his compliance, but also ultimately—for true believers and others alike—the power of the entire group. Every member of a circle of reciprocity is bound to adhere to the ideals of that circle in part because he believes those ideals to be backed up by the potential of everyone in the group. This is why, when decisions about the strategic objectives of a circle of reciprocity (such as a nation) are taken by one person or a small group of people (such as a president, or a cabinet of ministers) who temporarily hold the potential of all the members of the circle in their hands, it is common to talk of that person or small group as having a lot of power. In reality, the elite that is temporarily in charge of guiding a circle of reciprocity is almost as tightly constrained as any ordinary member by adherence to the group's ideals. Straying too far from those ideals will result in the ousting of a temporary leader from headship of a circle of reciprocity, and the consequent loss of virtually all of his 'power'.

We propose that power almost always derives from group roles; that it is about believed potential to draw upon resources; and that it is created in greatest measure by large circles of reciprocity. Much of the power wielded in smaller groups and hierarchies is derivative of the rules agreed upon centrally in our large circles of reciprocity, such as family law, contract law, labor law, and general expectations of proper behavior.

Networks

The final element that we propose here operates, like hierarchies and circles of reciprocity, at an intermediate level of aggregation—yet it differs from the two above-mentioned group archetypes in that there are no group-derived behavioral expectations. No lines of authority exist that are expected to be respected by members, and no ideals exist to which members are expected to show allegiance. People are instead allowed and even expected to behave in an entirely self-promoting fashion, with no one in a position to tell anyone else what to do. This interactive realm is what we refer to as a trade network.

The basic building block of a network is a trade relation, also called a link or a business relation, which is in essence an expected trade between two entities over some period of time. The expectation can be formal, such as when a worker holds an employment contract with a firm, or implicit, such as when a shopkeeper rationally expects to be able to sell his goods to one in twenty of the tourists in his part of town. The trade can be one-off or sustained, specialized or generic, and may involve prior investments. At the macro level, the aggregate concept of 'networks in the economy' is very similar to the concept of aggregate demand and aggregate supply, but we speak in terms of individual trade links at the micro level in order to support a conception of networks at the individual, firm, industry, and country level.

Like power, a trade link exists as a believed potential rather than necessarily a tangible, easily quantifiable object, even though many links will be expressed in quantifiable and tangible formats (such as delivery contracts). When someone says that his 'network' is large, it means that he believes he could call upon (and expect to receive an answer from) a large number of people in regard to a new opportunity. For example, a baker might notice that his new millet rolls are selling well, and might call his 'network' of suppliers to find out who can quickly increase their supply of millet flour. A chemist might hear about a new drug at a conference, and later contact his 'network' of suppliers to find out who can sell him the drug; he might also promote the drug among his 'network' of clients and even among other chemists in his professional 'network'. The expected response from a member of someone's network to information about a new opportunity is to be interested in the potential to achieve some type of personal gain from that opportunity. Still, the value of a network is often recognized by its members, which somewhat constrains their behavior: people do not routinely defraud other people in their networks, even if they are presently competing with them, since those same people may be of use in a future period. More important for our view of the aggregate economy, a network's members are constrained by the rules and behavioral expectations that accompany the hierarchies and circles of reciprocity to which those members belong.

Within this view, an unemployed person is someone without a particular type of link, that is, someone with no partners with whom to trade his labor. Job search consists of looking for partners with whom to enjoy the benefits of trading on the basis of comparative advantage. Private firms are primary bundles of networks, both among workers inside a firm (who are sorted into functional units and teams) and between any given firm and its external clients and suppliers. Bankruptcy is often caused by the collapse of these trading ties: that is, the reneging on explicit or implicit expectations of intentions to buy or sell particular goods at particular prices. The strong interdependence of network-related decisions taken every moment by actors in the modern economy has immediate implications for how to conceptualize economic downturns. As we discuss in more detail below, the links of trade and expectations defining an economy can suffer rapid and catastrophic destruction due to the externalities that accompany every decision in a given network. Once existing trade links break, it takes time for all directly affected parties to find new partners—something already recognized in existing search models—but our model predicts the cost of this search to be even higher because of the negative externality of others' links having also been broken. In this way, the interconnectedness of trade networks that characterizes a modern, advanced economy leads to protracted periods of economic doldrums after catastrophic crashes.

Networks have been identified by some economists as important catalysts for trade (Coase, 1937; Calvo-Armengol, 2004), but in our view they are more than that. They are a necessary input for trade and ultimately for economic growth. It is via networks that opportunities are broadcast, new combinations of inputs trialed in production processes, and innovations spread. It was not only through war, migration, and theft but also via trade networks that spices were brought to Europe, horses to America, and cotton to Africa. Traders have a keen interest and economic stake in preserving their autonomy—only a free hand can capture opportunities when they arise—and we contend that this dynamic in the longer run shapes the political systems under which we live, since many of the large circles of reciprocity that now dominate the political landscape started out as ideas bandied around in trade networks (Frijters, 2013).

Implications

We now combine the above ingredients to offer a behavioral interpretation of the structures of modern society, maintained not only by greed, but also the conditioned loyalty of individuals towards the abstractions supporting the circles of reciprocity in the economy. We first examine important components of the wider economy, and then offer observations about economic crises such as the GFC.

The legal system

The structure of laws and courts underpinning our economies is an outgrowth of the ideals that define the large circle of reciprocity that is the modern democratic nation state. The idea of 'the rule of law' precedes the nation state, but its current form is as an instrument, serving the goals of the country as a whole. The legal system is seen as an efficient means of guaranteeing desirable outcomes, such as the separation of powers and the ability to plan for the future on the basis that the rules of society in the future will be upheld much as they are today.

Ideas like human rights, egalitarian treatment, fairness, and justice are by implication only as powerful as they are today due to the power of the nation states with which these ideas are aligned. Those who operate within our legal system, including lawyers, judges, and bureaucrats, are beholden more or less to those nation-state ideals, but also hold other loyalties and face other material incentives. For example, the standing of lawyers is heavily influenced by what other lawyers think of them, which in turn is influenced by factors such as whether they are perceived to know their case law or to be effective arguers. Their ideals are partially shaped in law school as young, aspiring lawyers wanting something from the legal profession (i.e., a job and social standing) and judging unconsciously that submission to the ideals of that profession was the optimal strategy for satisfying those desires.

At the same time, lawyers face opportunities for personal material advancement that exploit their reputation but do not actually further the ideals of either the nation or their profession. Hence, lawyers and judges—like many other professionals in society—constantly balance a tension between their impulse to dominate and acquire more wealth while secretly disregarding the ideals that support their role and reputation in the economy, and 'toeing the line' in regard to those ideals. This tension is of a different caliber for those legal professionals who have developed true loyalty to the ideals of fairness and justice, but even those who have not are constrained by what they believe to be the ideals of others. Those legal professionals who are seen to use their position to further their own ends (e.g., by taking bribes, or devoting insufficient effort to determining 'fair' sentences) without regard to the ideals of their profession may find themselves out of a job.

Central banks

Central bankers are also part of the machinery of the nation state and are hence somewhat beholden to the ideals that it promulgates. In this case, however, the ideal most relevant to their professional decisions is not fairness or human rights, but the growth desired by the state.

Growth requires stability and predictability. This is because people will not plan or make long-term investments in the areas of their comparative advantages (i.e., they will not specialize) unless they are relatively sure that later possibilities for trade with other specializing people will materialize. Ultimately, the ability to create the circumstances in which economic growth occurs is a large part of what lends the nation state its perpetual pull on people's loyalty: this is a power that pushes citizens into adopting a submission strategy rather than a domination strategy when interacting with 'the nation'. Central bankers operate as a group with growth as the guiding ideal, following particular notions of what the group is supposed to do, such as maintaining purchasing power stability through setting appropriate interest rates.

As with judges, temptations arise for bankers to stop subjugating themselves to this ideal and instead to exploit their positions for personal benefit, and such temptations are easier to resist the stronger the true loyalty of bankers to the economic success of the nation state. Again, this loyalty is developed over time, in proportion to bankers' perception of the nation as a powerful force that offers benefits. With a measure of independence from the government bureaucracy, central bankers can distance themselves from the fiscal realities of everyday government, giving them more freedom to act in accordance with their ideals but also some independence from bureaucratic oversight, opening opportunities for corruption.

The independence of both the legal system and the central bank from the main political actors in the nation state (e.g., parliament and the political executive, such as a cabinet or president) is not inevitable, but is rather the outcome of a learning process regarding how to efficiently organize institutions that support the nation state. Distance between the politicians and these groups is, in the dominant nation-state vision of today, believed to be in the interests of the members of the nation state. Whether that is actually true, and whether better mechanisms are possible, are both subject to debate.

Government ministries

The nation state's daily operations are overseen by a vast patchwork of small circles of reciprocity (the elite groups in charge of government ministries) that dominate and direct the large hierarchy of the national bureaucracy, which in turn dominates and directs both smaller hierarchies (e.g., at the state level) and the small circles of reciprocity that direct them. The small circles of reciprocity at the top of ministries—like those at the top of any hierarchy, even an autocratic one—are essential, for without them the leaders of the hierarchy would not achieve the level of cooperation required to ensure the effective functioning of the entire (ministerial) hierarchy. Each of the small circles at the top is in part dependent for its existence upon its reputation for advancing the nation as a whole, but also acts to promote its own interests, such as when it tries to grab resources and administrative oversight from other ministries. The arguments made in any such attempts at domination and subgroup advancement will be made in terms of the interests of the whole nation or its ideals, rather than in terms of advancing merely the interests of the subgroup. Here again, the ideals upheld by the larger circle of reciprocity act to restrain the personal greed of those operating within it.

Watchdog groups

Competition watchdog groups, such as the Fair Trade Commission, are also outgrowths of nation-state ideals. They are staffed by professionals bound not only to the ideals of the nation state but also to their professional ideals, lest they lose their posts. An economist who takes a five-year job with a watchdog group and is seen by his peers during that time not to have upheld the ideals of the profession of economists—namely, to seek higher social welfare and efficiency, and to push markets towards the perfect-competition, laissez-faire ideal—will likely find himself out of a job once his term ends. The prospect of this reputation damage constrains the behavior even of similarly drafted economists who believe in neither the ideals of the nation state nor the ideals of economics. The same can be said of economic advisors to governments or non-governmental organizations.

Corporations and their lobby groups

Corporations are primarily wealth-maximizing hierarchies that can, in our modern societies, gain financial advantages by latching onto the ideals of various circles of reciprocity, and even by pretending to be circles of reciprocity. They can only exist because the nation state reinforces their hierarchical elements with contract laws and enforcement mechanisms (e.g., police, courts, and habits of obedience taught at school). Within a corporation, as within the government bureaucracy itself, lie many small circles of reciprocity, often organized around productive units—Accounts Payable, or the Board of Directors—that seek gain for themselves but are constrained by the need to be seen to adhere to the objectives of the whole corporation. The more that the corporation's employees have developed true corporate loyalty, the less direct monitoring from the top is required. Corporate lobby groups, which represent the interests of corporations to the government, are institutionalized rent-seekers. Playing the system by appealing to nation-state ideals while really having only partisan interests at heart, lobby groups are a good example in the modern world of a wolf in sheep's clothing: an entity that is powered by greed but that relies for its own productivity on appeals to loyalty. This view accords with what is known as 'capture theory' in political economy (Stigler, 1971; Peltzman, 1976), although unlike ours, that theory does not provide an explanation for the countervailing force of nation-state ideals in the decision-making of the government officials who are lobbied.

Economic crises

Through the lens of our theory, most economic crises are due to stagnation in the creation of new trade links together with the destruction of existing trade links, often through bankruptcies and lay-offs. The resultant crumbling of networks leads to idle labor (unemployment) and idle capital (unused buildings and machinery). Trade links, which take time to rebuild, are broken in rapid cascades because the destruction of any individual link creates externalities on the trading partners of those previously linked. This is why economic busts in our theory are predicted to be rapid but followed by long periods of slow recovery, in which capacity continues to be under-utilized. By contrast, most traditional economic theories, such as theories of unemployment that rest on sluggish price movements, understate the difficulties of finding trading partners and overstate the ease with which information and opportunities are available and recognized.

Business cycles result in our theory from interconnected trade networks combined with the agency problem afflicting large hierarchical organizations, like banks. Like other professionals, bankers face a constant temptation to gamble with the resources of their organization in order to achieve private gain. When there is substantial discretion on the part of a bank's top brass and technical decision makers (e.g., key investment managers), one should expect unproductive networks to be formed during the boom phase of the economic cycle. This is because those professionals who are neither true believers nor closely monitored will hire their friends as suppliers, waste money on trades that only benefit themselves and their cronies, package bad loans in complex and non-transparent ways so investors can be fooled into buying them and thereby taking on excessive risk, and so on. Similar things will happen in other large hierarchical organizations. Once these bad investments become visible, a period of stagnation in new link formation ensues in which large organizations switch to 'no risk' mode as managers try to learn more about what they actually invested in, and organizations pay off their accumulated debts and collect on outstanding debts.

A type of endogenous regime-switching ensues, where a regime is described by the degree to which the more entrepreneurial actors in large organizations find themselves able to set up new networks. In 'normal times', the limited liability of these decision makers gives them an incentive to invest in new projects and gamble with the resources of their organizations and investors. The investments and projects that are undertaken by such actors are interconnected and complementary to one another. This results in phases in which many projects are successful, and lead to more investments, until there is a conspicuous failure that leads to an initial destruction of business links, at which point the general expectation switches. This switch then causes many investments existing at that moment to fail, and throws up blockades against new investments. Because of the interconnectedness of investments via trade links, what starts out as a small shock can grow into a large cyclical slow-down involving the destruction of many networks without the creation of new networks to replace them.

Even large organizations that do not themselves enter a 'no risk' mode once the switching point arrives face the problem that when many others do enter that mode, new ventures will be more likely to fail: chains of trade links are required to make new ventures productive, and many parts of each chain will experience knock-on effects from the decisions made in other parts.

This interpretation of recessions, fairly close in spirit to the views of Keynes, explains why large volumes of government and private debt can prevent new economic activities from being started and funded. The difficulties of servicing large debts when other organizations are also reducing their activities lead many organizations into 'no risk' mode, which implies that they are unavailable—at least temporarily—for the creation of new links. Other organizations in the economy then face higher costs of finding new connections. In a recession, the chances that something new will fail are much greater than in normal times because new connections must be formed by many different players in order to make new ventures productive—and in a recession, many players are unavailable.

Observations on the Global Financial Crisis

The Global Financial Crisis of 2008–13, also known as the Great Recession, involved many elements relevant to our theory. For the sake of brevity we enumerate and explain below a few aspects particular to the GFC that are not recognized in standard economic discussions and that underscore the importance of groups, links, and loyalty in society.

Debt and the move from informal to formal links

The rise of household indebtedness that accompanied the property bubble, whose bust is a core characteristic of the GFC, is a measure of the entanglement of claims among individuals due to the fact that one person's loan is another's investment. One might argue that having more debts makes an individual more vulnerable to shocks, since people who cannot pay back their debts thereby sever many trade ties with investors who in turn might well sever some of theirs. This may be true, but why did debts rise so much in the first place? Put differently, what did the larger and larger debts observed in recent times replace?

Pre-GFC, the level of household debt had grown over a long period in both the US and, even more noticeably, in the richest countries of the EU. Figure 24.2 (reproduced from Weisenthal (2012)) shows a time series of debt-to-disposable income percentages for the US that climbed steadily from the mid-1980s through the start of the GFC. Figure 24.3 shows a rise in the same measure starting from the mid-to-late 1990s, using similar data for many EU member states.

Part of the explanation for the slow rise in normalized debts pre-GFC is that economic relations gradually changed in the twentieth century from being strongly mediated by families and small communities (small circles of reciprocity) to being reflected in anonymous, trackable trades (anonymous networks). Instead of living in their parents' house that they would inherit when the parents died, partially in exchange for looking after the parents in their dotage, younger people started owning their own homes and insuring themselves against health shocks, unemployment, and old age via anonymous financial markets. The Netherlands and Denmark, which saw the greatest rise in debts as shown in Figure 24.3, not coincidentally also had the largest assets in the form of huge public pension funds. Households had both debts and large pension assets, both operating via formal, visible financial institutions. Thus, what were previously invisible debts and implicit rights inside households and communities—informal links—became openly visible links,

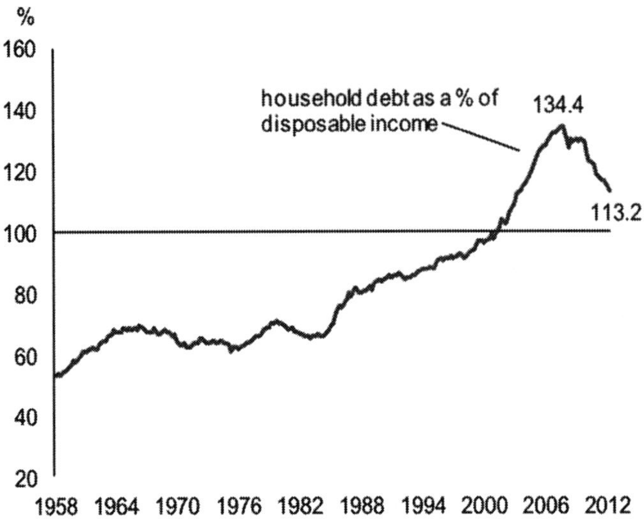

Figure 24.2 US debt to disposable income

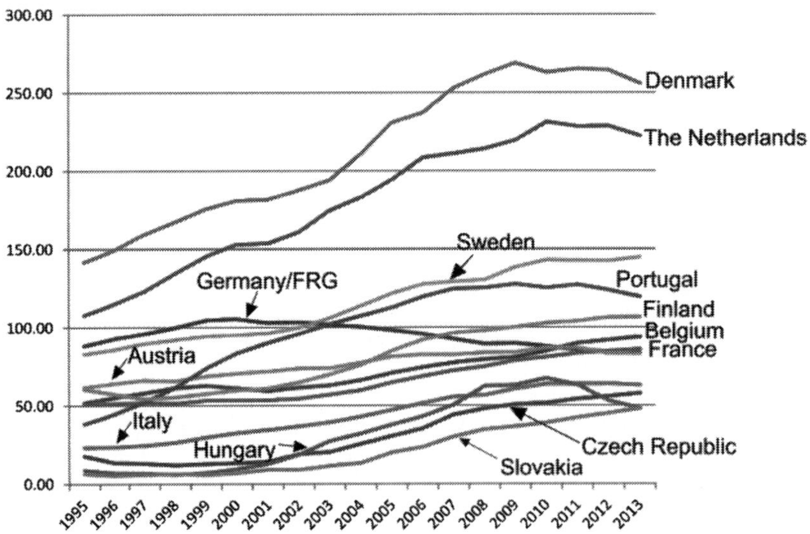

Figure 24.3 European debt to disposable income, in percentages

Source: Eurostat.

whereby the relatively young and poor borrowed money from the relatively old and rich via banks, insurance companies, and pension companies.

Because the unraveling of implicit debts and rights inside less visible small circles (families and communities) has gone unmeasured, it is not obvious whether the increased formal debt levels replaced equal, lesser, or greater amounts of previously invisible debts. Measures of changes in the hidden insurance and wealth claims within families and communities would be needed in order to gauge whether there are more claims on the average young person today than in the past.

Nation-state identities and accountability I: the Fed versus the ECB

The US Federal Reserve reacted to the GFC more quickly and in a different fashion than the EU financial institutions, notably the European Central Bank. The Fed was able to buy up large amounts of US treasury bonds and bad loans made by US financial institutions, and to make cheap loans available to banks so as to increase the money supply (a policy known as 'quantitative easing'). In contrast, the ECB could buy up only a very limited number of member states' government bonds, and could not directly buy up bad loans.

The difference arises because the United States is a nation state, with the nation-state ideals and members' loyalties that come with that, and the EU is not. Decision makers within the Fed have the explicit mandate from the whole of the United States to ensure price stability and to try to prevent and ameliorate recessions. The ECB by contrast only has a mandate to ensure price stability, and must also navigate the conflicting interests of member states, which made it unable to buy bonds and engage in quantitative easing on the same scale as the Fed. During the crisis, member countries with divergent financial interests have effectively vetoed expansions in the ECB's minimalist mandate. A recent report financed by the Bruegel Foundation (Mody, 2013) summarizes the financial events in the European Union thus:

> Five years of crisis have pushed Europe to take emergency financial measures to cushion the free fall of distressed countries. However, efforts to turn the crisis into a spur for 'an ever closer union' have met with political resistance to the surrender of fiscal sovereignty. If such a union remains elusive, a perpetual muddling ahead risks generating economic and political dysfunction.

By comparison, the Fed's behavior shows the advantages of being a fully integrated nation state.

Nation-state identities and accountability II: people, power, and politics

During the crisis, all players focused on the decisions taken by the institutions of nation states. This is a clear demonstration of the true underlying distribution of power. Populations, banks, and investors all knew on which side their bread was buttered, and lobbied governments for favorable treatment—governments, not banks, investment agencies, or mortgage holders. Virtually no one saw the point of appealing to the generosity of bankers or homeowners. Why? Because it is well understood by most economic agents that, as our theory proposes, the private sector and financial institutions aim to make money and are hence not likely to be responsive to moral requests, whereas nation states, and their politicians and representative institutions, are in part accountable to their citizens. The citizenry voiced its concerns within the frameworks that organize political power in nation states: by appealing to the politicians, the ministries, and the representative institutions (like the Fed) for solutions. Whether the entities receiving these appeals were to blame for the problems, or even whether they had any idea how to solve them, was immaterial: as the current wielders of the power of the group as a whole, politicians and institutions were expected to deliver a solution.

Many accusations were made (and often proven) about how small vested interest groups had taken advantage of society's trust by means of securing subsidies or favorable legislation before the GFC (such as the repeal of the Glass–Steagall act in the United States that made high-risk investments easier for banks to take). This type of ex-post accusation is further proof of the power of the story of the nation state, that is, the story of what is in the interests of the population and what, in hindsight, should have been done to serve those interests. Institutions and ministries eventually suggested new mechanisms to prevent another GFC, for example by increasing the capital requirements of banks and by having a bank watchdog inside the ECB. In sum, the GFC provided the population with a focal point as to what it did not want, after which the politicians were forced into promising to learn lessons and improve regulation. This very interaction demonstrates the faith by citizens in the long-run oversight provided by the institutions of their nation states.

Trade links and personal incentives in hierarchies with limited monitoring and liability

The high degree of risk-taking inside financial and commercial institutions (which also borrowed heavily) is a key feature of the pre-GFC 'Keynesian boom.' We see such booms as inevitable because of a central trade-off in the economic and legal institutions that surround risk-taking behavior: limited liability versus limited appropriability.

The legal institution of limited liability supports stock-traded companies in which others can invest, but whose managers are not personally responsible for company losses. The worst that can happen to such managers is that they are fired by the stockholders: there is no grand moral ideal they must be seen to uphold for the sake of their reputations. This legal institution has many advantages, including that managers need not be rich and that investors need not be particularly knowledgeable (only enough to smell a rat), but there is a natural disadvantage: the managers will take excessive risks with other people's money, since they stand to share more in gains than in losses. This description applies to a whole layer of decision makers in society, leading them to be optimistic and risk-taking. Because of the interconnectedness of business links, the system as a whole will be swept along with this optimism in good times.

At the societal level, the benefit of this risk-taking comes from the widespread existence of limited appropriability: the benefits that flow from investments and inventions that work out cannot be entirely appropriated by the organization doing the investing or innovating. Inevitably—again because of interconnected business links—the clients and suppliers in the instigating firm's network benefit too, and often whole countries can benefit from new inventions and technologies that were originally the product of some single company or ministry. Those individuals who made the initial investment decisions can only cash in to a limited degree, since intellectual property cannot be perfectly monitored or guarded. As usual in economics, these externalities should lead to under-provision, or in this case under-investment in projects by individuals whose personal gain upon the project's success is less than the social gain.

So, on balance, over-optimistic limited-liability managers finance innovation that they would not finance with their own money, with the social benefit that if things work out, others gain from the new project and technology. The balance between the forces of limited liability and limited appropriability, coupled with imperfect monitoring, makes cycles virtually inevitable in our theory: during booms, societies enjoy the spillovers of successful investments and feel optimistic without knowing the full details of all investments made, and in busts, societies discover the extent of the over-optimism which they could not know beforehand because of the imperfect monitoring of each individual actor in the network, and then become pessimistic.

While we can only guess at whether the balance between these forces is optimal at the moment, it would not surprise us if it were socially optimal to have even more risk-taking on average than we see presently. It may be also turn out to be optimal for our societies to introduce more liability and less risk-taking in some areas (e.g., mortgage markets) and more in other areas, depending on just how important the positive spillovers from limited appropriability are in that area compared to the negative consequences of a cascade of broken links due to over-investment.

Conclusions

The political institutions that support our economies are outgrowths of hundreds of years of social evolution in which the nation state, nurturing a large private sector, has emerged as the currently best vehicle for producing mass loyalty and economic growth. It is clear that national institutions have a great deal of influence on the functioning of our economies, but capturing that influence in a simple way that can be integrated with standard mainstream economic thought has so far eluded the discipline. To fully understand modern political economy, we argue that one must first understand its structures in a way consistent with an expanded view of individuals that includes not only their greedy nature but also their submissive side: how people behave with respect to their groups, and how they respond—and particularly, how they develop loyalty—to power.

We began this chapter by proposing to offer both a way of expanding the core ideas included in the umbrella of economics, and an explicit heuristic for deciding which ideas apply to which particular scenarios. The heuristic that we propose—reflecting facets of both behavioral economics and social psychology—is grounded in an understanding of not only the material aspects of a particular situation, but of the groups, loyalties, and networks relevant to the people operating in that situation. While a full exposition of this heuristic is beyond the scope of this chapter, interested readers can find such a description together with several detailed applications showing its value in our recent book, Frijters (2013). In simplified form, we suggest that instead of asking merely—cui bono? —the behavioral political economist should also ask himself or herself: 'Where have I seen this problem before?', 'Which big groups are involved?', and finally, 'Who faces which powers?'.

Notes

1 Research in behavioral finance has sometimes pointed to fear as an additional non-greedy motivation for behavior (Lo, Repin & Steenbarger, 2005), but we contend that fear of wealth loss (often termed loss aversion) can still be understood as greed, since it derives from the same goal—that is, maximizing wealth.

2 We are less interested in describing the feelings involved in love, as already done in social psychology (Rubin, 1970), but more in offering an explanation about why and how love afflicts an advanced social animal with highly developed survival strategies. We talk at great length in Frijters (2013) about how the 'love program' described here could arise and be evolutionarily stable.

Bibliography

Allingham, M. & Sandmo, A. (1972). Income tax evasion: A theoretical analysis. Journal of Public Economics, 1, 323–38.

Altman, M. (2012). Implications of behavioural economics for financial literacy and public policy. Journal of Socio-Economics, 41, 677–90.

Andreoni, J. (1995). Warm-glow versus cold-prickle: The effects of positive and negative framing on cooperation in experiments. Quarterly Journal of Economics, 110, 1–22.

Asch, S. (1956). Studies of independence and conformity: I. a minority of one against a unanimous majority. Psychological Monographs: General and Applied, 70(9), 1–70.

Calvo-Armengol, A. (2004). Job contact networks. Journal of Economic Theory, 115, 191–206.

Coase, R. (1937). The nature of the firm. Economica, 4(16), 386–405.

Downs, A. (1957). An Economic Theory of Democracy. New York: Harper & Row.

Fehr, E. & Zych, P. K. (2008). Intertemporal choice under habit formation, in C. R. Plott & V. L. Smith, eds, Handbook of Experimental Economics Results, Volume 1, North Holland Publishers.

Fourcade, M., Ollion, E. & Algan, Y. (2014). The superiority of economists. Maxpo Discussion Paper, Number 14/3.

Frijters, P. (2013). An Economic Theory of Greed, Love, Groups, and Networks, Cambridge, UK: Cambridge University Press. [With Gigi Foster.]

Hodgson, G. M. (2013). From Pleasure Machines to Moral Communities: An Evolutionary Economics without Homo Economicus Chicago, IL: University of Chicago Press.
Kolm, S.-C. (2013). Gifts and gratuitousness. In S. Zamagni & L. Bruni, eds, Handbook on the Economics of Philanthropy, Reciprocity and Social Enterprise, Cheltenham: Edward Elgar Publishing.
Lo, A. W., Repin, D. V. & Steenbarger, B. N. (2005). Fear and greed in financial markets: A clinical study of day-traders, American Economic Review, 95(2), 352–9.
Milgram, S. (1974). Obedience to Authority: An Experimental View. Harper & Row.
Mody, A. (2013). A Schuman compact for the euro area. Available at: www.bruegel.org/publications/publication-detail/publication/802-a-schuman-compact-for-the-euro-area/.
Peltzman, S. (1976). Toward a more general theory of regulation. Journal of Law and Economics, 19, 211–40.
Peters, W. (1971). A Class Divided. New York: Doubleday.
Pingle, M. (2010). Looking under the hood: Exploring assumptions and finding behavioral economics. Journal of Economic Behavior and Organization, 73, 73–6.
Rubin, Z. (1970). Measurement of romantic love. Journal of Personality and Social Psychology, 16(2), 265–73.
Shiller, R. & Akerlof, G. (2009). Animal Spirits: How Human Psychology Drives the Economy, and Why it Matters for Global Capitalism. Princeton, NJ: Princeton University Press.
Stigler, G. (1971). The theory of economic regulation. Bell Journal of Economics, 2, 3–21.
Tiehen, L. (2001). Tax policy and charitable contributions of money. National Tax Journal, 54(4), 707–23.
Weisenthal, J. (2012). Chart of the day: Where we are in the deleveraging. Business Insider Australia. Available at: www.businessinsider.com/chart-of-the-day-debt-to-disposable-income-ratio-2012-9?IR=T/.

25

BEHAVIORAL LABOR ECONOMICS

Xianghong Wang

Introduction

The emergence of behavioral economics has advanced the field of labor economics just as it has done many fields of economics. Labor economics is probably where the assumptions and methods of behavioral economics were most welcome (Winter-Ebmer, 2014). This might be true for the following reasons. First, labor economists are mostly concerned with decisions of workers and firms based on their repeated human interactions. Second, the relationship between worker and employer is characterized by incomplete contracts because many dimensions of their interactions, especially worker's effort, cannot be fully specified (Fehr et al., 2009; Leibenstein, 1966). Therefore, the approach of behavioral economics that deviates from standard neoclassical economics regarding the assumptions about the nature of human interactions and motivation helps explain observed behavior of workers and employers. Third, labor economists are much engaged in empirical studies that try to understand causal relationships between individual decisions and labor market conditions. This has benefited from the methods of laboratory and field experiments that have become more influential due to the advancement of behavioral economics. Finally, the combination of behavioral theories and experimental methods has provided promising tools for design and evaluation of labor economic policies.

A few authors have written survey articles about the development of behavioral labor economics. The earliest may be Kaufman's essay on the behavioral foundations of labor economics (Kaufman, 1999), in which he reports that over a six-year period between 1992 and 1997, only two papers are found in the *Journal of Labor Economics* that substantively modified the rational choice model. Less than a decade later, Berg's (2006) survey article suggests that the gap between traditional and behavioral labor economics seems less dramatic than in other subfields of economics since traditional labor economics also has to deal with the feature of repeated human interactions in labor markets. This is probably why scholars are not all in consensus about what is or is not behavioral in labor economics (Dohmen, 2014; Winter-Ebmer, 2014).

In the most recent review, Dohmen (2014) argues that behavioral economics has impacted labor economics mainly in three aspects: theoretical insights; micro studies of decision-making and human interactions; and experimental methods. He discusses the theoretical impact by focusing on the themes outlined by DellaVigna (2009): nonstandard preferences, nonstandard beliefs, and nonstandard decision-making. Social preference is one of the main nonstandard preferences of employees and employers. Fehr et al. (2009) provide a focused discussion on the impact of social preferences and fairness concerns on labor market issues. Nonstandard decision-making is shown in a strand of studies that analyze how biases affect workers' job search and training decisions. Nonstandard beliefs in labor markets may refer to workers' overconfidence in principal–agent relations, and their over-pessimism or over-optimism in job markets.

The methods of experimentation including laboratory experiments and field experiments have been widely used for testing behavioral theories and studying decisions in labor markets. Charness and Kuhn (2011) review laboratory experiments that study various topics of labor economics and provide design strategies to avoid pitfalls. List and Rasul (2011) provide a thorough review of the method of field experiments and its applications in labor economics. In addition to the advantages of all experimental methods, field experiment allows for engaging in primary data collection and working closely with practitioners, which makes it important for study of mechanism design and policy evaluation. The authors argue that insights are most enhanced when field experiments are combined with other approaches in economics.

As shown by the existing literature, behavioral labor economics has become a very important part of labor economics. This chapter will focus on reviewing behavioral insights that appear to be most influential in studies of labor market issues. Compared with previous reviews, this chapter will pay more attention to the exploration of labor policy designs based on behavioral insights. The second section briefly describes relevant behavioral insights, focusing on social preferences, reference-dependence, and self-serving biases. The third section reviews the role of social preferences in understanding workers' motivation issues. The fourth section reviews studies about reference-dependence and relative position, and their impacts on wage and wage distribution. The fifth section reviews the role of self-serving biases in wage settings and wage negotiations. The final section discusses labor economic policies that can benefit from behavioral nudge methods.

Behavioral insights for labor economics

Labor economics covers a wide range of topics mostly related to supply, demand, and the organization of labor markets. We focus our attention on topics that have benefited most from the insights and methods of behavioral economics: workers' motivation or effort provision, firms' incentive schemes, wage determinants and bargaining, and policy interventions for labor participation, training and employment. The main behavioral theories covered include social preferences, fairness concern, reciprocity; reference-dependence of utility; and biased beliefs. These concepts are in contrast to the following main assumptions of standard neoclassical economic theories: economic agents care about their self-interest only, and only in absolute terms of payoff; they have consistent preferences and make labor supply decisions based on rational tradeoff between leisure and consumption in a life-cycle; and they have the cognitive capacity and strong-will to follow through their plans.

Social preferences

Social preference refers to people's tendency of paying attention to others' gains or welfare when interacting with each other in economic activities, which deviates from the neoclassical assumption of people's pure selfishness. The concept was first put forward by Camerer (1997) and it has been researched by many other scholars. Social preferences may include altruism, reciprocity, fairness and other types of interdependent preferences.

Fehr et al. (2009) review how different aspects of social preferences are modeled and tested using various games in laboratories and in the field. Evidence confirms that fairness concerns exert some weak effects in one-shot interactions, and plays more important roles in repeated interactions. Evidence of altruism, reciprocity, or fairness concern comes from ultimatum games (Güth et al., 1982; Roth, 1995; Camerer et al., 2003), dictator games (Kahneman et al., 1986), public goods games (Ledyard, 1995; Fehr and Gächter, 2000b), and trust games (Berg et al., 1995). Studies also show considerable individual heterogeneity in the strength of social preferences, that is, a significant share of individuals also exhibit fairly selfish behaviors, which has implications for studying effects of personal traits and institutions (Fehr et al., 2009).

Individuals with social preferences are willing to pay to punish unfair behaviors (Bolton and Ockenfels, 2000; Charness and Rabin, 2002; Dufwenberg and Kirchsteiger, 2004; Falk and Fischbacher, 2006; Fehr and Schmidt, 1999; Rabin, 1993). Positive reciprocity is an in-kind favorable response to friendly actions while negative reciprocity entails punishment of hostile acts (Fehr and Gächter, 2000a). Various experiments have studied positive and negative reciprocity (Charness, 2004; Cox, 2004; Cox and Deck, 2005; Cox et al., 2008). The general result of experimental evidence is that negative reciprocity is stronger than positive reciprocity.

Reference-dependence and loss aversion

Whereas the standard economic model assumes that only the absolute level of payoffs matters for people's utility, evidence suggests that these levels are valued relative to a reference level. The reference level can come from comparing one's own payoff with other people's payoff (see Veblen, 1899; Duesenberry, 1949; Pollak, 1976; Frank, 1985a, b, 2005; Festinger, 1954; Olson et al., 1986). Various empirical studies have argued that income comparisons affect life satisfaction and decision-making (e.g., Luttmer, 2005; see also Clark et al., 2008, and Clark et al., 2010, for surveys). The chosen comparison targets are likely to be people sharing some common characteristics. Such comparisons have implications for fairness judgments and other preferences in the labor market.

Reference level can also come from comparing with one's own past history, which is consistent with the concept of reference-dependence and loss aversion proposed by Kahneman and Tversky (1979) in Prospect Theory. This will affect preferences of wage profiles for individual workers.

Self-serving biases

Self-serving bias refers to the fact that when people make judgments, they unconsciously tend to favor themselves or the party that is more associated with them. Biases can lead to non-standard beliefs as noted in DellaVigna (2009). Self-serving bias can make people overestimate their own achievements and abilities; obtain and interpret information in their own interests; define fairness based on a standard of self-interest instead of impartial standards.

While people care about fairness in their economic interactions, people do switch between different fairness rules as their decision-making context changes (Frohlich et al., 2004). Experimental study has provided evidence that inconsistency of fairness rules is mainly driven by a self-serving bias (Ubeda, 2010).

Self-serving bias is affected by availability of information. Therefore, improvement in information completeness might lead to a deadlock of the negotiation (Babcock et al., 1995). In a cross-culture negotiation experiment involving subjects from the United States and China, Kriss et al. (2011) show that when people do not know the identity of the object they are judging about, the two sides' judgments of fairness are not different from each other. However, their opinions diverge when revealed identity of object leads to self-serving judgment of fairness.

To save space, we are not going to review all behavioral insights that are used in labor market studies. The next section focuses on how the above behavioral insights have helped advance the studies of labor markets often with combined forces.

Motivation and effort: the role of social preferences

Gift-exchange game, fairness, and reciprocity

To model the behavior of employer and worker under incomplete contracts, most of the research has focused on gift-exchange and the role of fairness norms and reciprocity (see Fehr et al., 2009, for a review). Akerlof (1982), Akerlof and Yellen (1990) first proposed a fair-wage hypothesis about this relation: the employer pays the employee higher wages than the equilibrium wages, and the staff reward the employer through exerting more effort. The resulting positive wage–effort relation helps solve principal–agent problems in settings of contractual incompleteness.

This gift-exchange theory is consistent with the X-efficiency theory proposed by Leibenstein (1966; 1978), in which productive-inefficiency can persist from imperfect competition or psychological factors. Because of incomplete contracts in labor markets, effort discretion plays an important role in determining employees' performance. There exists an inert area of effort within which the individual is mobile. The inert area is determined by factors both internal and external of the individual. Leaving the inert area is caused by a change in internal or external pressure sufficient enough to make the cost of remaining in the inert area exceed the benefit, and thus changes in effort are determined by an interaction of psychological factors and economic considerations. Therefore, the employer can pay employees higher wages than the equilibrium wages so that the cost of remaining in the inert area exceeds the benefit, and employees make more effort.

The gift-exchange theory and various versions of the game have been extensively used to study the effect of labor market institutions in experimental labor market outcomes (see Fehr and Falk, 2002), including hiring decisions (Fehr and Falk, 1999), wage setting behavior of firms (e.g., Abeler et al., 2010), wage rigidity and involuntary unemployment (Altmann et al., 2014), and effects of minimum wage laws (Falk et al., 2006). The main findings of these studies are as follows: first, effort is increased with wage increase; second, effort is more responsive to wage cuts than to wage increase; and third, firms may pay wages higher than the equilibrium.

Fairness concern can result in negative reciprocity in labor relationships, which has been shown by evidence in the field. Krueger and Mas (2004) find that a labor strike at a US tire production site coincided with the production of substantially lower-quality tires, likely due to workers' negative reciprocity in response to what they perceive as unfair treatment. Harmful reciprocations in labor relationships are also documented by Mas (2006, 2008), Kube et al. (2013) and Montizaan et al. (2012).

Altruism, selfishness, heterogeneity, and market conditions

People's willingness to give in to dictator games and public good games can be referred to as altruism or other-regarding behavior. Such preferences can be observed between employer and employee, or among workers. Employers pay wages above the equilibrium due to both altruism and concern for reciprocity.

Altruistic concern among workers can lead them to reduced effort in collusion when high effort creates externality to others. Bandiera et al. (2005) conducted a field experiment which shows that when workers are paid by relative performance instead of piece rate, productivity is lowered because workers internalized negative externality of relative performance to some extent.

Personnel data from a fruit farm during a picking season show changes in the productivity as a function of changes in the compensation scheme. The average productivity of each worker increased by 51.5 percent when the scheme was switched from relative performance to flat piece rate. Workers internalize the externality of relative incentives more when the share of their personal friends in the group is larger and this effect is stronger in smaller groups. However, productivity under relative incentives was significantly lower only when workers were able to monitor each other. This indicates that workers' social preferences do not make them unconditionally altruistic towards others.

While other-regarding preferences play an important role in the labor market, there is pervasive evidence of pronounced heterogeneity in types of agents (see, e.g., Fischbacher et al., 2001) ranging from completely selfish types to altruistic types. The prevailing labor market outcome is not merely determined by the fractions of the various types, but also by the institutional setting in which heterogeneous types interact. For example, when information about minimum wage policy is complete for both sides of workers and firms, many firms pay wages higher than the minimum level (Falk et al., 2006). However, Wang (2012) finds that, when the minimum wage policy is not known to workers, firms' pay to workers is lower than what's found in Falk et al. (2006) and many more firms now offer wages just at the minimum level. This provides evidence that social preference does not make all firms unconditionally generous. The key to predicting outcomes in labor markets is thus an understanding of the factors, conditions and institutional arrangements under which other-regarding preferences or selfishness govern behavior. As a result, there is a need to assess when and how social preferences govern behavior in long-term labor relationships.

Wage distribution and profiles: reference-dependence and relative income

Reference-dependence means that utility is dependent on relative level in addition to absolute level (Kahneman and Tversky, 1979), which can refer to relative position in social comparisons or relative level compared to oneself. Relative comparison has far-reaching implications for labor markets, as it affects labor supply (Neumark and Postlewaite, 1998), wage profiles (Frank and Hutchens, 1993), effort provision (see e.g., Hamermesh, 1975; Cohn et al., 2014a) and the design of optimal incentive systems (Bartling and von Siemens, 2010).

Relative comparison affects employees' satisfaction about their salary pay. As part of the incentive scheme in the firm, relative position provides a status or positional good, which is viewed as one kind of non-monetary incentive by List and Rasul (2011). The study by Card et al. (2012) among employees of the University of California provides evidence that the disclosure of information on peers' salaries causes a reduction of job satisfaction and an increase in turnover intentions among those earning below median salaries, while employees above the median are unaffected. Liu and Wang (2015) provide evidence in an experimental study, which shows that relative income affects income satisfaction given absolute income.

Relative comparison among workers may have an impact on firms' internal pay structure, employee morale, and wage changes over time. Because of possible externality caused by relative income, firms may need to compress pay scales and reduce inequality within firms (Stark and Hyll, 2011; Frank, 1984) or maintain pay secrecy (Charness and Kuhn, 2011).

How people choose reference groups has a strong impact on labor market outcomes. In general, people tend to compare with others who are similar to themselves. This helps explain the sharp difference between wage dynamics in internal and external labor markets (Fehr et al., 2009). Workers who are looking for a job in a new firm seem to evaluate the fairness of a firm's wage offer relative to the going wage in the labor market. Incumbent workers, in contrast, seem to assess the fairness of proposed wage changes in their ongoing employment relative to the status quo. Accordingly, the firm may adjust the new entrants' wages to labor market conditions, while holding those of the incumbents unchanged. In China, as the country is experiencing reforms and introducing new management practices into organizations, for example, there is a saying: "New people new policy, and old people old policy."

Through comparisons with oneself, reference-dependence and loss aversion cause downward nominal wage rigidity. Evidence of such rigidity has been found for managers (Ockenfels et al., 2015) and for workers (Bewley, 1999; Agell and Lundborg, 2003). In contrast, providing an unexpected bonus that is unrelated to past productivity has a significant and positive effect on productivity (Bellemare and Shearer, 2009; Gneezy and List, 2006). Reference-dependence can also affect supply of labor hours when workers set income-targets and do not optimize their payoff as predicted by traditional models. This has been documented by data from taxi drivers (Camerer et al., 1997; Farber, 2005; 2008) and bike messengers (Fehr and Goette, 2007).

Labor relations: role of self-serving biases

Self-serving bias may have implications for many labor market outcomes. First is on the judgment of what constitutes a fair wage. Messick and Sentis (1979) find in an experiment that, when a participant works for a longer time than others, he will tend to ask for a higher fair wage for his work time; however, when he works for a shorter time than others, he will tend to recommend a lower fair wage for others' work time. This tendency suggests that people's judgment on fair wages is mainly based on self-interest.

Biased judgment of fairness may increase conflicts and negotiation impasses between employers and employees. One example is its role in collective wage bargaining (Babcock et al., 1996). Negotiators in wage bargaining consider economic factors as well as fairness and reciprocity. However, there exist systematic differences between "fair wages" in the views of trade unions and management. The negotiator would regard the other party's bargaining as an unfair request. This psychological drive caused negotiators to oppose the conditions below the fairness level that they held, resulting in impasse of the negotiation (Babcock and Loewenstein, 1997). Evidence shows that the degree of difference between negotiators' fairness judgments is correlated to labor strikes (Babcock et al., 1996).

Policy implications

Policymakers in various western economies recognize the potential of a behavioral economic approach in policy analysis because it provides more realistic predictions about behavior than traditional choice models. Some countries have established special groups in the government to apply behavioral insights and methods to policy designs and evaluations. For example, the UK government installed the "Behavioral Insights Team" (BIT) in 2010 and produced some success stories.[1] In the United States, the White House set up the Social and Behavioral Sciences Team (SBST) in 2014, which just released their first annual report. On September 15, 2015, President Obama signed an Executive Order that directs federal agencies to use behavioral science insights in designing and evaluating government programs. In the international domain, behavioral insights are also being applied to world development policies, as documented in World Development Report 2015 issued by the World Bank. Some of these successful policy applications are related to labor market issues. We next review some general policy principles suggested by behavioral economists, and then discuss implications and applications in labor market policies.

Libertarian paternalism and nudging

To make behavioral insights useful for public policy, behavioral economists have proposed some policy guidance and principles. Since individuals' decisions are affected by information and choices, it is desirable to set policies to maximize people's welfare based on predictions about people's behavioral responses. Camerer et al. (2003) call for "asymmetric paternalism" which they define as taking steps to help the least sophisticated people while imposing minimal harm on everyone else. This concept is also called "soft paternalism", "libertarian paternalism", or "nudge" polices. Based on various behavioral biases people may have, libertarian paternalists have suggested some "nudge" methods that help design better policies (Thaler and Sunstein, 2008; Thaler and Sunstein, 2003). For example, the first is called the default rule. Public policies can set default option as the choice that benefits most people. Many organizations in both the public and private sector have discovered the immense power of default options. For example, making a retirement saving plan as a default option significantly increased employees' contributions to their retirement plan (Thaler and Benartzi, 2004; Choi et al., 2004).

Nudge methods advise policy makers to present choices and information to people in ways that help them make better decisions, mitigating their biased expectations, biased judgments, procrastination or other non-optimal behavior. To summarize, the nudging methods may include the following: default option, simplification of complex choices, reminders to prevent expected errors, pre-commitment, feedback or informing of past choices, use of social norms, framing and information disclosure (Camerer et al., 2003; Thaler and Sunstein, 2008; Sunstein, 2014). We next discuss how some of these nudge methods can help improve labor policies.

Applications in the labor market

Labor market policies and programs need to consider behavioral factors in order to help workers get employed, provide education and training opportunities, ensure fairness, safety, and accessibility of workplace, motivate employees, and improve the effectiveness of labor markets. Babcock et al. (2012) review how behavioral insights related to procrastination, difficulties in dealing with complexity, and biased labor market expectations can help design labor market policies including unemployment compensation, employment services, job search assistance, and job training. Following the methods of "libertarian paternalism," we review some behavioral policy approaches for selected labor market issues, including some findings from recent government practices.

Default options and employment assistance

One important type of labor market policies is to facilitate unemployed people to return to work. Some behavioral biases of workers may prolong their unemployed period, including the effects of biased wage expectations, reference dependence or loss aversion, procrastination, and pessimistic views about being hired.

Defaulted training and education can help people become employed. Government policies can be designed to increase workers' tendency to enroll in training programs and their tendency to search for a job. When unemployed people apply for unemployment insurance, for example, they can be defaulted to participate in training programs and job search activities (Director and Englander, 1998; Black et al., 2003; Borghans and Golsteyn, 2014). Johnson and Goldstein (2003) and McKenzie et al. (2006) show that default effects exist even when no effort is required, and many people interpret policy makers' choice of default as the recommended action.

Simplification, reminders, and increased enrollment

Individuals are limited in the attention and the computational capacity they can bring to multifaceted and complex problems (Tversky and Shafir, 1992). To steer people to decisions and behavior that can improve their welfare, government programs often need to present desirable information easily accessible to overcome people's procrastination, or status quo bias. One nudge approach for employment assistance is to simplify and streamline the experience of workers seeking employment services or job search assistance (Babcock et al., 2012). Employment and job search assistance tools should be widely available and easy to use, both online and in public employment service offices. People usually care to compare pay levels with others who are similar to themselves. Job assistance tools could gather information on an individual's background and interests, and provide feedback on the education and employment opportunities pursued by others like them and their projected growth in occupations.

Another direction that appears promising will be to offer small, immediate, and high frequency reminders and incentives to search for jobs. Experimentation can be used to test the possibility of overcoming imperfect self-control by sending various versions of messages and reminders. A recent project in the United States provides such an example. Having a college degree increases earnings and reduces the risk of unemployment. Every year, however, roughly 20 to 30 percent of college-accepted high school graduates in US urban districts fail to matriculate in college in the fall, because they do not complete required pre-matriculation tasks such as filling out course-enrollment forms and financial aid forms, or taking placement tests. Reminders have shown to be effective in increasing low-income students' enrollment in college (SBST report, 2015). SBST collaborated with the Department of Education to unlock access to college for some students. They find that sending personalized text messages to low-income students resulted in increased college enrollment by nearly 9 percent. Improved reminder message is also used to increase veterans' enrollment in Education and Career Counseling Benefits.

Reference effect, framing, and debiasing

Public policies can affect decisions and behavior through economic incentives or through changing perceptions of people about expectations, fairness judgment, and entitlement or status quo. Ariely et al. (2003) show that even arbitrary anchors have strong effects on subjects' reservation prices. Thus, public policies are likely to affect behavior not only through changing incentives but also by shaping perceptions and reservation values.

Labor policies or regulations that provide a standard ceiling or flooring control need to be aware of possible reference effects. For example, evidence shows that the introduction of a minimum wage provides reference points for workers' reservation wages (Falk et al., 2006; Wang, 2012).

Labor programs can make use of the reference effect to debias people's expectation errors. Evidence from other contexts suggests that debiasing of beliefs is possible through carefully designed interventions (Babcock, Loewenstein, and Issacharoff, 1997). This research suggests that having people question their own judgment by explicitly considering counterarguments to their own thinking can be effective. Job search assistance could potentially incorporate such an exercise with respect to wage expectations. Decker et al. (2000) show examples of testing the relative success of differently structured job search assistance programs. Framing consequences as losses instead of gains is known to affect behavior in other contexts (Rothman et al., 2006). This framing can affect the willingness of participants to take risks, such as the risk of interviewing for or starting a new job.

Since information affects how social comparisons are made and how fairness judgment is formed, policy makers can design regulations that make certain information publicly available and some not to reduce biased judgment. For example, Goldin and Rouse (2000) find that "blind" auditions for orchestras increase female musicians' chances of being hired. This is similar to the debiasing tool of "behind the veil of ignorance" used in Kriss et al. (2011).

The World Development Report 2015 provides examples of how productivity can be increased for low-income groups when taking into account behavioral insights. When designing incentive systems, public organizations need to be aware that employees' productivity is affected by how their pay is compared to the outside private system. According to an analysis of nine years of data from the public hospital system, in regions where the nurses earned much less than the wage that prevailed in the external labor market, a 10 percent increase in the outside wage was associated with a 15 percent increase in the fatality rate for patients admitted for heart attacks (Propper and Van Reenen, 2010). Since social comparisons can produce negative externalities, public policies can also use taxation incentives to change labor behavior and reduce such externalities, as suggested by Frank (1985a).

Experiment beyond nudging

Since nudge policies are often aimed at benefiting some targeted group of individuals, a full evaluation of impacts of such policies on other groups should be implemented (Crépon et al., 2013). For example, the default option to help some groups get employed can potentially have displacement (or spillover) effects on the outcomes of other job seekers. While the minimum wage is set to protect the low-income workers, it can potentially affect wages and employment of higher-income groups.

Some nudge type policies seem promising in the abstract, but turn out to fail in practice. Empirical tests, including randomized controlled trials, are indispensable. Experimentation, with careful controls, is a primary goal of the nudge enterprise.

Finally, some scholars argue that stronger paternalism is needed nowadays, especially when information is asymmetric (Bhargava and Loewenstein, 2015). Poor choices cannot easily be remedied through information disclosure (Loewenstein, Golman and Sunstein, 2014). The difficulty in improving choice through information disclosure or education has been demonstrated in the context of savings decisions (Duflo and Saez, 2003). Mandates can be considered for labor related issues, such as safety issues in the workplace, anti-discrimination, and employment development.

Conclusion

Behavioral economics has helped enrich the studies of labor markets in many topics. This chapter first focuses on discussing contributions of the most influential behavioral insights in labor economics: social preferences, relative income, and self-serving biases. A large part is then devoted to applications of behavioral insights in labor market policies. Two main consensuses seem to stand out from surveying the development and current status of behavioral labor economics. First, at this point, research focus may no longer be needed to argue and prove how labor market outcomes deviate from predictions of neoclassical theories. Rather, it is helpful to study how different labor market conditions affect the psychology of heterogeneous types of people and outcomes of the labor market. Second, following the argument of Chetty (2015) for general policy application of behavioral economics, it may be more productive for behavioral labor economists to take a pragmatic approach and distill the list of behavioral anomalies into those that are most relevant in common labor market and policy applications.

Acknowledgments

This paper is supported by the National Natural Science Foundation of China (Project 71173228 and Project 71373273). The author thanks Wanchao Ma for his excellent research assistance.

Note

1 See www.behaviouralinsights.co.uk/publications/

Bibliography

Abeler, J., Altmann, S., Kube, S. & Wibral, M. (2010). Gift exchange and workers' fairness concerns: when equality is unfair. Journal of European Economic Association, 8(6), 1299–324.

Abeler, J., Falk, A., Goette, L. & Huffman, D. (2011). Reference points and effort provision. American Economic Review, 101(2), 470–92.

Agell, J. & Lundborg, P. (2003). Survey evidence on wage rigidity and unemployment. Scandinavian Journal of Economics, 105, 15–30.

Akerlof, G.A. (1980). A theory of social custom, of which unemployment may be one consequence. Quarterly Journal of Economics, 94, 749–75.

Akerlof, G. (1982). Labor contracts as partial gift-exchange. Quarterly Journal of Economics, 97(4), 543–69.

Akerlof, G.A. (1997). Social distance and social decisions. Econometrica, 65, 1005–27.

Akerlof, G.A. & Shiller, R.J. (2009). Animal Spirits: How Human Psychology Drives the Economy, and Why it Matters for Global Capitalism. Princeton, NJ: Princeton University Press.

Akerlof, G.A. & Yellen, J.L. (1990). The fair wage-effort hypothesis and unemployment. Quarterly Journal of Economics, 105(2), 255–83.

Altmann, S., Falk, A., Grunewald, A. & Huffman, D. (2014). Contractual incompleteness, unemployment, and labour market segmentation. Review of Economic Studies, 81, 30–56.

Ariely, D., Loewenstein, G. & Prelec, D. (2003). Coherent arbitrariness: stable demand curves without stable preferences. Quarterly Journal of Economics, 118(1), 73–105.

Babcock, L. & Loewenstein, G. (1997). Explaining bargaining impasse: the role of self-serving biases. Journal of Economic Perspectives, 11(1), 109–26.

Babcock, L., Loewenstein, G. & Issacharoff, S. (1997). Creating convergence: debiasing biased litigants. Law and Social Inquiry, 22, 913–25.

Babcock, L., Loewenstein, G. & Wang, X. (1995). The relationship between uncertainty, the contract zone, and efficiency in a bargaining experiment. Journal of Economic Behavior and Organization, 27, 475–85.

Babcock, L., Wang, & Loewenstein, G. (1996). Choosing the wrong pond: social comparisons in negotiations that reflect a self-serving bias. Quarterly Journal of Economics, 111(1), 1–19.

Babcock, L., Congdon, W.J., Katz, L.F. & Mullainathan, S. (2012). Notes on behavioral economics and labor market policy. Journal of Labor Policy 1(2).

Bandiera, O., Barankay, I. & Rasul, I. (2005). Social preferences and the response to incentives: evidence from personnel data. Quarterly Journal of Economics, 120(3), 917–62.

Bartling, B. & von Siemens, F. (2010). The intensity of incentives in firms and markets: moral hazard with envious agents. Labour Economics, 17, 598–607.

Bellemare, C. & Shearer, B. (2009). Gift giving and worker productivity: evidence from a firm-level experiment. Games and Economic Behavior, 67(1), 233–44.

Berg, J., Dickhaut, J., & McCabe, K. (1995). Trust, reciprocity, and social history. Games and Economic Behavior, 10, 122–42.

Berg, N. (2006). Behavioral labor economics. In M. Altman (Ed.), Handbook of Contemporary Behavioral Economics. M.E. Sharpe, New York, 457–78.

Bernheim, B.D. (1994). A theory of conformity. Journal of Political Economy, 102, 841–77.
Bewley, T.F. (1999). Why Wages Don't Fall during a Recession. Harvard University Press, Cambridge, MA.
Bhargava, S. & Loewenstein, G. (2015). Behavioral economics and public policy 102: beyond nudging. American Economic Review, 105(5), 394–401.
Black, D.A., Smith, J.A., Berger, M.C. & Noel, B.J. (2003). Is the threat of reemployment services more effective than the services themselves? Evidence from random assignment in the UI system. American Economic Review, 93, 1313–27.
Bolton, G. & Ockenfels, A. (2000), ERC: A theory of equity, reciprocity and competition. American Economic Review, 90, 166–93.
Borghans, L. & Golsteyn, B.H.H. (2014). The willingness to learn of the life course. Working Paper. Maastricht University.
Bowles, S., Gintis, H. & Osborne, M. (2001a). Incentive-enhancing preferences: personality, behavior, and earnings. American Economic Review, 91, 155–8.
Bowles, S., Gintis, H. & Osborne, M. (2001b). The determinants of earnings: a behavioral approach. Journal of Economic Literature, 39(4), 1137–76.
Camerer, C. F. (1997). Progress in behavioral game theory. Journal of Economic Perspectives, 11, 167–88.
Camerer, C.F. (2006). Behavioral economics. In: Blundell, R., Newey, W.K., Persson, T. (Eds.), Advances in Economics and Econometrics: Theory and Applications, Ninth World Congress, vol. 2. Cambridge and New York: Cambridge University Press, 181–214.
Camerer, C.F. & Loewenstein, G. (2004). Behavioral economics: past, present, future. In: Camerer, C.F., Loewenstein, G., Rabin, M. (Eds.), Advances in Behavioral Economics. New York and Princeton, NJ: Russell Sage Foundation Press and Princeton University Press, 3–51.
Camerer, C., Babcock, L., Loewenstein, G. & Thaler, R. (1997). Labor supply of New York city cab-drivers: one day at a time. Quarterly Journal of Economics, 112, 407–41.
Camerer, C.F., Samuel I., Loewenstein, G., O'Donoghue, T. & Rabin, M. (2003). Regulation for conservatives: behavioral economics and the case for "asymmetric paternalism". University of Pennsylvania Law Review, 151, 1211–54.
Card, D., Mas, A., Moretti, E. & Saez, E. (2012). Inequality at work: the effect of peer salaries on job satisfaction. American Economic Review, 102(6), 2981–3003.
Charness, G. (2004). Attribution and reciprocity in an experimental labor market. Journal of Labor Economics, 22(3), 665–88.
Charness, G. & Kuhn, P. (2011). Lab labor: what can labor economists learn from the lab? Handbook of Labor Economics, 4, 229–330.
Charness, G. & Rabin, M. (2002). Understanding social preferences with simple tests. Quarterly Journal of Economics, 117(3), 817–69.
Chetty, R. (2015). Behavioral economics and public policy: a pragmatic perspective. American Economic Review, 105(5), 1–33.
Choi, J.J., Laibson, D. & Madrian, B.C. (2004). Plan design and 401(k) savings outcomes. National Tax Journal, 57, 275–98.
Clark, A.E., Frijters, P. & Shields, M.A. (2008). Relative income, happiness, and utility: an explanation for the Easterlin paradox and other puzzles. Journal of Economic Literature, 46, 95–144.
Clark, A.E., Masclet, D. & Villeval, M.C. (2010). Effort and comparison income: experimental and survey evidence. Industrial and Labor Relations Review, 63(3), 407–26.
Cohn, A., Fehr, E., Herrmann, B. & Schneider, F.F. (2014). Social comparison and effort provision: evidence from a field experiment. Journal of the European Economic Association, 12(4), 877–98.
Cox, J.C. (2004). How to identify trust and reciprocity. Games and Economic Behavior, 46, 260–81.
Cox, J.C. & Deck, C. (2005). On the nature of reciprocal motives. Economic Inquiry, 43(3), 623–35.
Cox, J.C., Sadiraj, K. & Sadiraj, V. (2008). Implications of trust, fear, and reciprocity for modeling economic behavior. Experimental Economics, 11, 1–24.
Crépon, B., Duflo, E., Gurgand, M., Rathelot, R. & Zamora, P. (2013). Do labor market policies have displacement effects? Evidence from a clustered randomized experiment. Quarterly Journal of Economics, 128(2), 531–80.
Decker, P.T., Olsen, R.B. & Freeman, L. (2000). Assisting Unemployment Insurance Claimants: The Long-Term Impacts of the Job Search. Office of Workforce Security Occasional Paper.
DellaVigna, S. (2009). Psychology and economics: evidence from the field. Journal of Economic Literature, 47(2), 315–72.

Director, S. & Englander, F. (1998). Requiring unemployment insurance recipients to register with the public employment service. Journal of Risk and Insurance, 55, 245–58. Assistance Demonstration. Mathematica Policy Research, report to the Department of Labor Evidence from a Clustered Randomized Experiment, CREST working paper.

Dohmen, T. (2014). Behavioral labor economics: advances and future directions. Labour Economics, 30, 71–85.

Dohmen, T., Falk, A., Huffman, D., Sunde, U., Schupp, J. & Wagner, G.G. (2011b). Individual risk attitudes: measurement, determinants and behavioral consequences. Journal of European Economic Association, 9(3), 522–50.

Duesenberry, J.S. (1949). Income, Saving, and the Theory of Consumer Behavior. Cambridge and London: Harvard University Press.

Duflo, E. & Saez, E. (2003). The role of information and social interactions in retirement plan decisions: evidence from a randomized experiment. Quarterly Journal of Economics, 118, 815–42.

Dufwenberg, M. & Kirchsteiger, G. (2004). A theory of sequential reciprocity. Games and Economic Behavior, 47, 268–98.

Falk, A. & Fehr, E. (2003). Why labour market experiments? Labour Economics, 10, 399–406.

Falk, A. & Fischbacher, U. (2006). A theory of reciprocity. Games and Economic Behavior, 54, 293–315.

Falk, A. & Heckman, J.J. (2009). Lab experiments are a major source of knowledge in the social sciences. Science, 326, 535–8.

Falk, A. & Ichino, A. (2006). Clean evidence on peer effects. Journal of Labor Economics, 24(1), 39–57.

Falk, A. & Zehnder, C. (2006). Trust and the City: Personal and Environmental Driving Forces of Social Capital, mimeo, University of Bonn.

Falk, A., Fehr, E. & Zehnder, C. (2006). Fairness perceptions and reservation wages: the behavioral effects of minimum wage laws. Quarterly Journal of Economics, 121(4), 1347–81.

Falk, A., Huffman, D. & Sunde, U. (2006). Self-confidence and search (No. 2525). IZA Discussion Papers.

Falk, A., Becker, A., Dohmen, T., Huffman, D. & Sunde, U. (2014). An experimentally-validated survey module of economic preferences. Working Paper. University of Bonn.

Farber, H.S. (2005). Is tomorrow another day? The labor supply of New York City cabdrivers. Journal of Political Economy, 113(1), 46–82.

Farber, H.S. (2008). Reference-dependent preferences and labor supply: the case of New York City taxi drivers. American Economic Review, 98(3), 1069–82.

Fehr, E. & Falk, A. (1999). Wage rigidity in a competitive incomplete contract market. Journal of Political Economy, 107(1), 106–34.

Fehr, E. & Falk, A. (2002). Psychological foundations of incentive. European Economic Review, 46, 687–724.

Fehr, E., Gächter, S., (2000a). Fairness and retaliation: the economics of reciprocity. Journal of Economic Perspectives, 14(3), 159–81.

Fehr, E. & Gächter, S. (2000b). Cooperation and punishment in public goods experiments. American Economic Review, 90(4), 980–94.

Fehr, E. & Goette, L. (2007). Do workers work more if wages are high? Evidence from a randomized field experiment. American Economic Review, 97(1), 298–317.

Fehr, E. & Schmidt, K.L. (1999). A theory of fairness, competition and cooperation. Quarterly Journal of Economics, 114, 817–68.

Fehr, E., Goette, L. & Zehnder, C. (2009). A behavioral account of the labor market: the role of fairness concerns. Annual Review of Economics, 1, 355–84.

Festinger, L. (1954). A theory of social comparison processes. Human Relations, 7(2), 117–40.

Fischbacher, U., Gächter, S. & Fehr, E. (2001). Are people conditionally cooperative? Evidence from a public goods experiment. Economic Letters, 71(3), 397–404.

Frank, R.H. (1984). Are workers paid their marginal products? American Economic Review, 74(4), 549–71.

Frank, R.H. (1985a). The demand for unobservable and other nonpositional goods. American Economic Review, 75(1), 101–16.

Frank, R.H. (1985b). Choosing the Right Pond: Human Behavior and the Quest for Status. Oxford: Oxford University Press.

Frank, R.H. (2005). Positional externalities cause large and preventable welfare losses. American Economic Review, 95, 137–41.

Frank, R.H. & Hutchens, R.M. (1993). Wages, seniority, and the demand for rising consumption profiles. Journal of Economic Behavior and Organization, 21(3), 251–76.

Frohlich, N., Oppenheimer, J. & Kurki, A. (2004). Modeling other-regarding preferences and an experimental test. Public Choice, 119, 91–117.

Gary, B. & Ockenfels, A. (2000). ERC: A theory of equity, reciprocity and competition. American Economic Review, 90, 166–93.

Gneezy, U. & List, J.A. (2006). Putting behavioral economics to work: testing for gift exchange in labor markets using field experiments. Econometrica, 74(5), 1365–84.

Goldin, C. & Rouse, C. (2000). Orchestrating impartiality: the impact of "blind" auditions on female musicians. American Economic Review, 90(4), 715–41.

Güth, W., Schmittberger, R. & Schwarze, B. (1982). An experimental analysis of ultimatum bargaining. Journal of Economic Behavior and Organization, 3(4), 367–88.

Hamermesh, D. (1975). Interdependence in the labor market. Economica, 42, 420–9.

Johnson, E.J., & Goldstein, D.G. (2003). Do defaults save lives? Science, 302, 1338–9.

Kahneman, D. & Tversky, A. (1979). Prospect theory: an analysis of decision under risk. Econometrica, 47, 263–91.

Kahneman, D., Knetsch, J. & Thaler, R. (1986). Fairness and the assumptions of economics. Journal of Business, 59, S285–S300.

Kaufman, B.E. (1999). Expanding the behavioral foundations of labor economics. Industrial and Labor Relations Review, 52, 361–92.

Kriss, P. Loewenstein, G, Wang, X. & Weber, R. (2011). Behind the veil of ignorance: self-serving bias in climate change negotiations. Judgment and Decision Making, 6(7), 602–15.

Krueger, A.B. & Mas, A. (2004). Strikes, scabs, and tread separations: labor strife and the production of defective Bridgestone/Firestone tires. Journal of Political Economy, 112(2), 253–89.

Kube, S., Maréchal, M.A. & Puppe, C. (2013). Do wage cuts damage work morale? Evidence from a natural field experiment. Journal of the European Economic Association, 11(4), 853–70.

Ledyard, J. O. (1995). Public goods: a survey of experimental research. In: J. Kagel and A. Roth (Eds.), Handbook of Experimental Economics. Princeton, NJ: Princeton University Press.

Leibenstein, H. (1966). Allocative efficiency vs. x-efficiency. American Economic Review, 56(3), 392–415.

Leibenstein, H. (1978). General X-Efficiency Theory and Economic Development. Oxford University Press, Oxford.

List, J.A. & Rasul, I. (2011). Field experiments in labor economics. Handbook of Labor Economics, 4a, 104–213.

Liu, K. & Wang, X. (2015). Relative income and income satisfaction: an experimental study. Working paper.

Loewenstein, G., Golman, R. & Sunstein, C.R. (2014). Disclosure: psychology changes everything. Annual Review of Economics, 6(1), 391–419. Russell Golman: Department of Social and Decision Sciences, Carnegie Mellon University, Pittsburgh, Pennsylvania 15213.

Luttmer, E. (2005). Neighbors as negatives: relative earnings and well-being. Quarterly Journal of Economics, 120, 963–1002.

Martin, D. & Kirchsteiger, G. (2004). A theory of sequential reciprocity. Games and Economic Behavior, 47, 268–98.

Mas, A. (2006). Pay, reference points, and police performance. Quarterly Journal of Economics, 121(3), 783–821.

Mas, A. (2008). Labour unrest and the quality of production: evidence from the construction equipment resale market. Review of Economic Studies, 75(1), 229–58.

McKenzie, C.R.M., Liersch, M.J. & Finkelstein, S.R. (2006). Recommendations implicit in policy defaults. Psychological Science, 17, 414–20.

Messick D. & Sentis, K. (1979). Fairness and preference. Journal of Experimental and Social Psychology, 15(1), 418–35.

Montizaan, R., Cörvers, F., de Grip, A. & Dohmen, T. (2012). Negative reciprocity and retrenched pension rights. IZA Discussion Paper: 6955.

Mullainathan, S. & Thaler, R.H. (2001). Behavioral economics. NBER working paper series no. 7948. Cambridge: National Bureau of Economic Research.

Nagel, R. (1995). Unraveling in guessing games: an experimental study. American Economic Review, 85(5), 1313–26.

Neal, D.A. & Johnson, W.R. (1996). The role of premarket factors in black–white wage differences. Journal of Political Economy, 104(5), 869–95.
Neumark, D. & Postlewaite, A. (1998). Relative income concerns and the rise in married women's employment. Journal of Public Economics, 70(1), 157–83.
Ockenfels, A., Sliwka, D. & Werner, P. (2015). Bonus payments and reference point violations. Management Science, 61(7), 1496–513.
Olson, J.M., Herman, C.P. & Zannan, M.P. (Eds.) (1986). Relative Deprivation and Social Comparison. Lawrence Erlbaum, Hillsdale, NJ.
Persico, N., Postlewaite, A. & Silverman, D. (2004). The effect of adolescent experience on labor market outcomes: the case of height. Journal of Political Economy, 112(5), 1019–53.
Piatek, R. & Pinger, P. (2010). Maintaining (locus of) control? Assessing the impact of locus of control on education decisions and wages. IZA Discussion Papers, 5289.
Pollak, R.A. (1976). Interdependent preferences. American Economic Review, 66(3), 309–20.
Propper, C. & Van Reenen, J. (2010). Can pay regulation kill? The impact of labor markets on hospital productivity. Journal of Political Economy, 118(2), 222–73.
Rabin, M. (1993). Incorporating fairness into game theory and economics. American Economic Review, 83(5), 1281–302.
Rabin, M. (2002a). Inference by believers in the law of small numbers. Quarterly Journal of Economics, 117(3), 775–861.
Rabin, M. (2002b). A perspective on psychology and economics. European Economic Review, 46(4–5), 657–85.
Roth, A.E. (1995). Bargaining experiments. In J.H. Kagel and A.E. Roth (Eds.), The Handbook of Experimental Economics Volume 1. Princeton University Press, Princeton, 253–348.
Rothman, A.J., Bartels, R.D., Wlaschin, J. & Salovey, P. (2006). The strategic use of gain- and loss-framed messages to promote healthy behavior: how theory can inform practice. Journal of Communication, 56, S202–20.
Social and Behavioral Science Team Report (2015). Available at: http://sbst.gov/
Stark, O. & Hyll, W. (2011). On the economic architecture of the workplace: repercussions of social comparisons among heterogeneous workers. Journal of Labor Economics, 29(2), 349–75.
Sunstein, C.R. (2014). Nudging: a very short guide. Journal of Consumer Policy, 37, 583–88.
Thaler, R.H. & Benartzi, S. (2004). Save more tomorrow: using behavioral economics to increase employee saving. Journal of Political Economy, 112, 164–87.
Thaler, R.H. & Sunstein, C.R. (2003). Libertarian paternalism. American Economic Review, 93(2), 175–9.
Thaler, R.H. & Sunstein, C.R. (2008). Nudge: Improving Decisions about Health, Wealth, and Happiness. New Haven, CT: Yale University Press.
Tversky, A. & Shafir, E. (1992). Choice under conflict: the dynamics of deferred decision. Psychology Science 3: 358–361.
Ubeda, P. (2010). The consistency of fairness rules: an experimental study. Journal of Economic Psychology, 41, 88–100.
Veblen, T. (1899). The Theory of the Leisure Class. London: Macmillan, George Allen and Unwin.
Wang, X. (2012). When workers do not know: the behavioral effects of minimum wage laws revisited. Journal of Economic Psychology, 33, 951–62.
Weber, R. & Dawes, R. (2010). Behavioral economics. In: Smelser, N.J. & Swedberg, R. (Eds.), The Handbook of Economic Sociology, 2nd edn. Princeton, NJ: Princeton University Press, 90–108.
Wilson, C.M., Garrod, L. & Munro, A. (2013). Default effects, transaction costs, and imperfect information. Economic Letters, 119(2), 213–15.
Winter-Ebmer, R. (2014). What is (not) behavioural in labour economics? Labour Economics, 30, 86–7.
World Bank (2015). World Development Report 2015: 128. Available at: www.behaviouralinsights.co.uk/publications/

26
BEHAVIOURAL EDUCATION ECONOMICS

Sean Leaver

Introduction

The purpose of "behavioural education economics" is to understand the psychological factors influencing educational choice and how individuals optimise these investments within a cognitively hard and complex decision space. Underlying behavioural education economics is the understanding that educational decision making is characterised by choices which are usually not repeated and rely heavily on heuristics to solve complex decisions in the absence of prior learning. By understanding the decision architecture underlying choices in education, causal mechanisms can be identified to guide policy interventions to improve academic outcomes which ultimately influence earnings and other life outcomes such as health. Given that individuals deploy heuristic based decision strategies to arrive at a "good" outcome in the face of incomplete information and limited time (Gigerenzer & Goldstein, 1996), it is important to understand the cognitive processes underlying these strategies and the impact of behavioural biases (Tversky & Kahneman, 1974) which lead to unintended social and economic consequences. Behavioural biases that can affect decisions in education include anchoring, framing, loss aversion, the availability heuristic and prospect theory. Behavioural education economics matters because for the last 30 years rational choice theory based education policy has failed to generate the expected economic outcomes, delivering only marginal overall benefits at best.

Choices in education are complex. Complexity arises from incomplete information, path dependency and the irreversibility of most choices in education. Choices in education are infrequent and rarely repeated. Each stage of investment, such as early childhood or school, comes with its own set of unique opportunities and constraints. Unlike conventional markets, investments in education cannot be readily resold or returned[1] and individuals usually do not benefit from delaying investments.[2] A level of complexity that would challenge seasoned economists not subject to everyday time constraints. Faced with limited time to make decisions and the infrequency of these choices, individuals have little opportunity to optimise utility through repetitive refinement, Arrow's (1962) "learning by doing".

The solution to decision making under complexity, limited time and few opportunities for learning is "bounded rationality". Faced with the uniqueness and complexity of investments in their education, the decision making process individuals undertake operates within the framework of heuristics and biases. Simon (1959) showed that even complex choices under certainty are computationally hard to solve with decreasing marginal returns to computation. This leads to satisficing behaviour where the heuristic "close enough is good enough" is applied for choices which have an acceptability threshold: "Models of satisficing behaviour are richer than models of maximising behaviour, because they treat not only of equilibrium but of the method of reaching it as well" (Simon, 1959). Under uncertainty, conditions of low information availability require decision making to rely on a variety of time efficient heuristics to match the complexity and type of choice context. These may be general purpose intuitive heuristics that involve making inferences under uncertainty (Tversky & Kahneman, 1974), framing heuristics to reduce decision space complexity (Thaler, 1985), or "fast and frugal" decision heuristics (Gigerenzer & Goldstein, 1996) which reduce the complexity of rules applied.

The history of education economics has its foundation in Becker's (1964) seminal work on human capital where individuals, parents and students, are required to make a series of complex inter-generational and intertemporal choices to maximise their utility over time. Education economics has traditionally focused on the impact cognitive ability, wealth constraints, quality of teaching resources and family size have on choices (Becker & Tomes, 1976), the economic returns to investments in education (Mincer, 1958), non-market returns to education (Grossman, 2006), how markets in education should lead to improvements in education quality (Friedman, 1955), how choices in education can be optimised through community sorting (Tiebout, 1956), and how educational preferences associated with school choice are revealed through house prices (Black, 1999). The most important precursor to behavioural education economics are the econometric studies of the impact of educational vouchers (Epple & Romano, 1998) and socio-economic stratification of education (Archbald, 2000) indicating that there are factors rational choice theory is unable in its present form to account for. These studies indicate, for example, that contrary to rational choice predictions low socio-economic families fail to exercise choice and consequentially lag in educational outcomes despite the intervention of economic policies. To understand why policies have failed at the macro-level, focus has turned the mechanics of individual choice associated with investments in education. In a national US study of how students respond to different types of financing in their decisions to study and complete college Avery and Hoxby (2004) found that "a third of the students are probably under investing and our conservative calculations suggest that a typical mistake is worth $76,096 in present value". In particular, Avery and Hoxby found evidence of present bias in student's preferences for front-loaded[3] financial aid and positional framing in their preference for aid presented as scholarships as opposed to aid as grants.

While behavioural education economics is relatively new, its lineage dates back to Rosenthal and Jacobson's 1968 paper on the Pygmalion effect[4] in the classroom, Mischel et al.'s (1972) use of the "marshmallow test" to investigate self-control in children and Kagan et al.'s (1958) research into how exploratory behaviour and curiosity influences changes in cognitive ability over time. Consequently, the focus of education economics has turned to the role non-cognitive behaviours have on choices in education and subsequent labour market outcomes. "Non-cognitive skills strongly influence schooling decisions, and also affect wages given schooling decisions" (Heckman et al., 2006). For a deeper discussion of why non-cognitive skills matter see Heckman and Kautz (2012) and for their long term effects see Fredriksson et al. (2013).

At the heart of behavioural education economics is an understanding that academic outcomes are malleable. That investment decisions associated with education are primarily driven by non-cognitive behaviours and cognitive biases that affect participation in education, and subsequently motivations to commit resources to these investments and maintain these choices over time. This is contrary to the more deterministic view of neoclassical economics where genetic and wealth inherence play the primary roles in an individual's choices leading to academic and earnings outcomes (see Becker, 1976). Instead for behavioural education economics cognitive ability affects the speed of learning but not the ultimate capacity of learning. Consequently, educational outcomes reflect Marcus" (2009) position that while genes pre-wire the brain, the brain is only pre-organised and remains malleable to experience (for instance synaptic pruning during adolescence).

Education is by its very nature a social process where social interactions shape both the willingness of individuals to invest in education and the returns from these investments. Humans are not merely efficient maximisers of self-interest but highly social animals that require new cognitive processes to handle the complexity of social interactions. Importantly, social cognitive processes are key to learning. Regions of the brain associated with social cognition have been shown to have evolved relatively recently in humans compared to our closest evolutionary cousins, the great apes (Tomasello, 2014). Social interactions, however, give rise to the fundamental economic problem of asymmetric information where we do not automatically have complete information as to the motivations and preferences of others. Our most recent cognitive machinery most likely represents an attempt to minimise these information constraints. However, the complexity of our social interactions is now accelerating over a relatively short period of evolutionary time. Automatic cognitive processes such as the general inference heuristics may not only be inappropriate for decision making in educational contexts but also very costly. Small initial errors arising from cognitive biases, such as teacher prejudice (e.g. Pygmalion effect) or peer stereotyping, can compound over time leading to significant student achievement gaps. Consequently, understanding the impact different cognitive processes have on the decision architecture linked to investments in education is crucial for the development of effective policy solutions.

Behavioural economics is generally viewed through the lens of how cognitive biases and heuristics can lead to errors and consequently sub-optimal choice decisions. However, choices in education are unique to the extent to which cognitive biases and heuristics have the capacity to shape preferences. Drawing on McFadden's (2001) choice process model (modified version Figure 26.1), the key insight of behavioural education economics is that social interactions inform "perceptions and beliefs" which via their impact on motivations and attitudes *shape economic preferences*. Critically, social positioning provides a reference point for asymmetric valuations and behaviour linked to loss aversion. This leads to the implication that preferences linked to choices in education appear to be endogenous.[5] Where underlying innate preferences "switch" in a manner similar to Gigerenzer and Todd's (1999) "fast and frugal" heuristics in response to changes in perceptions and beliefs linked to social interaction. Critically, the "if, then" logic of fast and frugal decision heuristics provides an explanation of the contextual responsiveness of identity threat impacting educational choices. Alternatively, broad based "affective states" influenced by emotions such as arousal are able to shape choice preferences in a similar way that a tide raises and lowers all ships (Loewenstein, 2005; Ariely & Loewenstein, 2006).

This is a major departure from the traditional economic approach to decision making where preferences are assumed to be innate and stable, and thereby exogenous. An explicit assumption that preferences are inherited and largely determined by biological processes: "tastes neither change capriciously nor differ importantly between people" (Stigler & Becker, 1977). Indeed, the explanatory power of the standard economic model "lies in its ability to explain most patterns of economic behaviour without having to account for experience or perceptions" (McFadden, 2001). In the standard economic model individuals collect information on alternatives, evaluate the probability of outcomes subject to (usually budget) constraints, and make a choice that reveals their preference.

However, if non-cognitive ability and personality traits shape economic choices in education and are themselves malleable (Kautz et al., 2014) then an economic understanding of preference endogeneity is needed. Specifically non-cognitive behaviour linked to achieving goals, investing effort and willingness to compete. Recently behavioural education economics has been subject

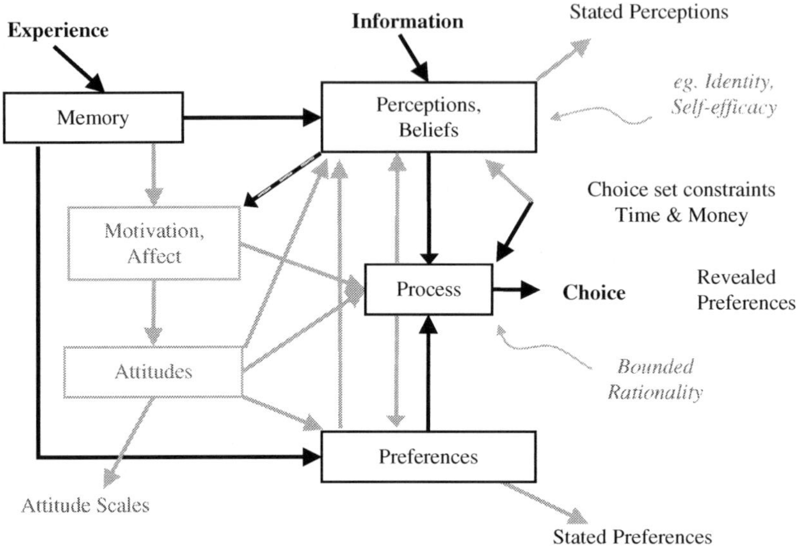

Figure 26.1 The choice process. Dark lines represent rational choice processes. Light lines represent psychological processes. The dashed line indicates how perceptions and belief are able to shape preferences via motivations and attitudes

Source: Modified from McFadden (2001).

to an extensive literature review (Koch et al., 2015) and a review of interventions (Lavecchia et al., 2014). The focus of this chapter will be on the three key non-cognitive behaviours associated with choices in education that play a role in the endogeniety of preferences and lead to malleability of educational outcomes: self-control, self-efficacy and identity.

Self-control: present bias, goals and commitment devices

The relevance of self-control to understanding economic behaviour was first raised by Strotz (1955) as far back as the 1950s, noting that individuals regulate their future economic behaviour in a manner that may seem costly. The implication being that rational behaviour should lead to consistent choices of optimal future outcomes by reason alone and without the need for additional costly commitment devices. From an economic standpoint, self-control allows individuals to avoid dynamic inconsistency in utility maximisation arising from preference reversals. In education, an example of time inconsistent preferences can be seen when a student procrastinates when studying and then subsequently regrets that choice (see Steel, 2007). Preference reversals occur in intertemporal choices when returns are discounted hyperbolically rather than exponentially (Ainslie, 1975; Thaler, 1981; Loewenstein & Prelec, 1992).

Self-control is the "effortful regulation of the self by the self" (Duckworth, 2011) and is key to an individual maintaining educational investments over time. The ability of children to delay gratification has been shown to be a reliable predictor of future academic success. Human self-control begins at school age between three and six years old, and represents a crucial stage of differentiation of humans from our nearest relative the chimpanzee (Herrmann et al., 2014). Suggesting that self-control is a key cognitive development in our evolutionary development, forming a unique component of human decision making processes associated with learning.

In Mischel et al.'s (1972) famous "marshmallow test" four-year-olds were given a choice between eating a marshmallow (or similar treat) now or waiting and receiving an extra marshmallow at the end of the experiment.[6] The marshmallow was placed on a table in front of the children and left unattended to maximise temptation. In this way self-control is seen as a finite resource which can be depleted. In a follow-up study a positive correlation was found between delayed gratification and SAT scores, with the correlations stronger for quantitative test scores than verbal test scores (Shoda et al., 1990). Importantly, studies have shown that self-control is a better predictor of academic outcomes than IQ (Duckworth & Seligman, 2005).

A New Zealand longitudinal study (Moffitt et al., 2011) of 1,000 individuals from birth to 32 years of age showed that self-control was a predictor of health, substance dependence, earnings and criminal behaviour independent of cognitive ability and socio-economic background. A much larger UK longitudinal study (Daly et al., 2015) of two cohorts totalling 16,780 individuals found that low self-control measured in child aged 7 and 11 years predicted unemployment in adulthood as far out as 50 years of age. However, the variation in probability of unemployment was strongest for individuals in their early 20s and declining over successive decades. Significantly, low self-control individuals experienced periods of unemployment 60 percent longer than experienced by high self-control individuals. An earlier study of 351 undergraduates by Tangney et al. (2004) similarly found a strong relationship between measures of self-control and higher academic results, better relationships, and less binge eating and alcohol abuse. The researchers suggest that self-control was important for conforming to social norms or alternatively self-control allows individuals to engage in activities that are socially desirable and require the overriding of self-interest.

It is important to note that self-control is also shaped by social interactions, particularly perceptions of trust. In a modified marshmallow experiment Kidd at al. (2013) added a preceding stage where perceptions of researcher reliability could be shaped. In this pre-stage, children were promised new crayons to draw with while they waited for the marshmallow experiment. One group received the new crayons as promised while the other group received old, clearly used crayons. Children who received the promised new crayons waited significantly longer than those who received the old crayons. Suggesting that self-control is strongly shaped by reasoned beliefs of the reliability of promises made by the researchers. Michaelson et al. (2013) found similar results for experiments with adults that showed social trust having a causal role in the willingness of individuals to delay immediate gratification.

Goal setting is a way to frame the decision space as a smaller set of variables, thereby reducing the cognitive load of complexity (see Thaler, 1985). Within these simpler decision spaces deliberate reasoned choices are more likely to avoid preference reversals. Importantly, when goals are framed as losses individuals are more likely to commit more effort to maintain choices in education. Aspirations framed as losses have been shown to lead to greater persistence by students in achieving their goals (Page et al., 2007). Morisano et al. (2010) showed that when university students asked to plan how to achieve their goals: "students who completed the goal setting . . . raised their grade point averages by 30 percent, and were much less likely to drop courses or quit university altogether." Goals can also take the form of self-imposed deadlines. In a study involving university students, Ariely and Wertenbroch (2002) found that students participating in an incentivised proof-reading task who evenly spaced their deadlines performed significantly better than those that relied on a final deadline for submission of their work.

Another way to overcome preference reversals is the use of self-imposed penalties as pre-commitments. Bryan et al. (2010) "define a commitment device as an arrangement entered into by an agent who restricts his or her future choice set by making certain choices more expensive" and does not provide a strategic advantage with respect to others. For example, students may make binding commitments within groups that provide for penalties if shared individual goals are not achieved. These commitments devices can be very effective in maintaining school attendance and completion independent of any direct intervention by the school or authorities.[7]

Self-efficacy: cognitive biases and the role of incentives

In any decision involving investments in education there needs to be a consideration of the expected return with respect to expected risk over time. Critically, this requires an assessment of an individual's own or in the case of parents their child's ability to achieve an optimal return on their investment in education. The greater the confidence an individual has in achieving a goal, the more resources they will invest. This perception of one's own ability is called self-efficacy and the greater the belief in one's self-efficacy the more productive the individual's efforts (Eden, 1988). However, the complexity of choices in education mean that perceptions are likely to be affected by cognitive biases leading to a problem Bénabou and Tirole (2003) term *imperfect self-knowledge*.

In this regard, the general availability heuristics (Tversky & Kahneman, 1973) play a key role in how individuals resolve information uncertainty and make inferences about their own ability and the perceived ability of others. There are considered to be three general purpose heuristics underlying many intuitive judgements under uncertainty: "availability", "representativeness", and "anchoring with adjustment" (Gilovich & Griffin, 2002). These intuitive heuristics are highly efficient decision rules that achieve a good outcome quickly and with little cognitive effort but at the expense of sizeable type 1 errors.[8] For example in social groups, individuals are usually mindful of behaviours that lead to exclusion from a group. Misperceiving a behaviour as leading to ostracism is psychological costly, requiring effort, but is significantly less costly than missing cues that lead to ostracism (Williams, 2007). However, evolution always lags the environmental fitness space that individuals face and for humans our social interactions have grown in complexity in a relatively short space of evolutionary time. These biases are important for perceptions of group identity but also give rise to prejudice and stereotyping. Cognitive biases that favour false alarms over near misses to avoid social exclusion from tight knit groups in the past have now become a liability as social interactions expand.

Rosenthal and Jacobson (1968) were first to show how an anchoring and adjustment heuristic can affect the motivation of a student to perform and invest effort into their studies. A cognitive bias, the Pygmalion effect, where the greater the expectation placed upon a student the better they perform. In their experiments, teachers were given randomised reports on each student's ability. They found that a teacher's perceptions of a child's ability had a marked impact on the child's subsequent academic performance independent of the child's actual initial ability. This cognitive bias is similar to the "hot hand" effect in basketball (Gilovich et al., 1985) where misperceptions of luck as ability lead to reinforcing improved performance.[9]

In a similar study by Cervone and Peake (1986), undergraduate and high school students were randomly exposed to anchors linked to perceptions of their own ability. Students exposed to a high anchor which indicated high ability persisted longer in tasks than students exposed to a low anchor. Suggesting that task performance is strongly shaped by judgements of self-efficacy independent of innate ability. Perceptions of self-efficacy also influence course choice at university. Hackett and Betz (1989) found that perceptions of self-efficacy were strongly related to choice of mathematics majors at university independent of underlying achievement and performance in mathematics.

A solution to the problem of negative consequences of anchoring and framing is the use of incentives to reinforce positive outcomes. In the workplace the use of incentives is usually linked to a particular job description with defined outcomes rather than individual self-assessment and are thereby less impacted by misperceptions of self-capacity (Bénabou & Tirole, 2005). However, the impact of asymmetric information "of the self by the self" on self-efficacy makes the use of incentives in education more complex and problematic than the traditional focus of incentives reinforcing productive behaviour in workplaces.

Incentives as intrinsic rewards relate to how individuals attribute value to a task with respect to their own personal motivation. The concept of "meaning" plays an important role in attributing value and can be shaped by the context of the task independent of an external reference. The best illustration of the behavioural dynamics behind the attribution of value through "meaning" is the classic novel *Tom Sawyer* by Mark Twain. Tom Sawyer faced with having to whitewash a fence contrived to reposition the activity from being a chore to a rare opportunity which his friends not only find pleasure in doing but also paid to do so (Ariely et al., 2006). This example goes to the heart of economics and the concept of scarcity. Scarcity is not necessarily an objective and fixed constant for all things. Scarcity can be shaped via perceptions of "meaning" and consequently effect the extent to which an individual invests resources into an activity such as a learning task.

Ariely et al. (2008) were able to show experimentally how "meaning" could be manipulated to influence effort and persistence in tasks. They used a simple incentivised experiment where the context of a task, the assembly of Bionicle toys, was changed but the payoffs remained the same. In one context, students were able to line up their completed Bionicle as they went. In the other context a research assistant would disassemble the toy immediately in front of the student after it was assembled.[10] Where Bionicles were disassembled in front of the students, persistence in tasks was significantly lower (7.2 units vs 10.6 units), required a higher marginal value for the last toy completed ($1.40 versus $1.01) and slower speed of construction (0.84/minute versus 0.25/minute).

Incentives as extrinsic rewards on the other hand frame choices with reference to externalised goals in order to overcome negative perceptions of self-efficacy. The impact of extrinsic rewards on academic performance has been shown to decline rapidly when delayed, and non-financial incentives are more cost effective with younger than older children (Levitt et al., 2012). Curiously, Levitt et al. found that framing rewards as losses did not increase the effect of the incentives on student performance. In a study involving 250 schools, Fryer (2011) found that financial incentives tied to academic inputs, such as reading, had a positive impact on academic performance while incentives linked directly to outputs, such as test results, were less effective. Financial incentives also have little impact on increasing participation in education when the objective is to reduce the cost of the choice decision (for school vouchers see Ladd (2002), for school subsidies see Behrman et al. (2005)). Suggesting that financial incentives work best when reducing the complexity of the choice decision rather the costliness of a decision. In an experiment involving 300 students Springer et al. (2015) found that non-financial rewards in the form of certificates of recognition where more than five times more effective at boosting attendance compared to financial incentives relative to a control group (completion of allotted hours: 16.77 percent control, 25.09 percent financial incentives, 59.97 percent certificates). Importantly while meaning and recognition trump financial incentives, meaning and recognition themselves are substitutes (Kosfeld et al., 2014). For a more extensive discussion of how context shapes the effectiveness of different types of incentives see Gneezy et al. (2011) and a review crowding out effects of financial rewards on intrinsic and social motivation see Deci et al. (1999).

Identity: behaviour in groups and social interactions

Choices in education by their very nature are dependent upon social interactions. These social interactions are complex and cognitively demanding due to the number of variables involved, and problems of incomplete and asymmetric information. Consequently, "the ability to sort people (or objects) spontaneously and with minimum effort and awareness into meaningful categories is a universal facet of human perception essential for efficient functioning" (Bodenhausen, Todd & Becker, 2006). A person's identity defines who they are with regards to their social category, the "in-group" (Akerlof & Kranton, 2010). Having a common "identity" in social interactions significantly reduces the amount of information asymmetry present with regard to individuals within the group, thereby decreasing the complexity of decision making.

The same heuristics that are valuable in reducing complexity and cognitive load can also lead to bias-confirming assessments of inter-group relations giving rise to stereotyping. The perception of an individual's identity status via social cues can reinforce confirmation biases associated with maintaining a state of identity threat (Darley & Gross, 1983). Identity threat is one of the mechanisms that lie behind persistent achievement gaps in education outcomes (females: Spencer et al., (1999); African-Americans: Steele and Aronson (1995); students from low socio-economic backgrounds: Croizet and Claire (1998)). However being a socially context dependent behaviour, identity is localised and does not persist beyond its context frame. For example, low achieving boys when changing grades experience large gains when leaving behind old identity norms and expectations (Dweck et al., 1978). For an explanation of the decision processes that underlie poor academic achievement due to identity threat see Cohen and Garcia (2008).

One of the clearest examples of the critical nature of context framing and the malleability of academic performance due to social identity is an experiment by Shih et al. (1999). In their study a group of Asian-American women were randomly split into two groups where either the individual's gender or their ethnicity was made salient using semantic conditioning. Results were compared with a separate, randomly composed control group without any semantic conditioning. For the gender salient group individuals were asked to indicate their gender and answer gender related questions but excluding any reference to ethnicity. Questions for the ethnicity salient group were constructed in a similar manner while the control group answered questions without reference to either gender or ethnicity. Individuals in all groups then completed the same mathematics test. The researchers found that simply switching identity salience produced diametrically opposite levels of performance in the test. When identity was aligned with Asian ethnicity individuals achieved a higher level of accuracy than the control group (54 percent versus 49 percent). However, when identity was aligned with female gender individuals performed worse than the control group for exactly the same test (43 percent versus 49 percent). The important implication of this study is that individuals maintain multiple identities which can be triggered by social context leading to divergent performance in an academic environment.

Social identity has also been shown to affect the willingness of individuals to compete and thereby participate in educational choices. The gender gap in mathematics has been shown by Gneezy et al. (2003), and more recently Niederle and Vesterlund (2010), to be influenced by a screening effect where girls self-select out of mathematics subjects due to the perceived competitiveness of the environment. A similar gender gap has been shown for competitive entrance exams in university choice (Jurajda & Munich, 2011; Pekkarinen, 2014). In studies of girls attending co-educational and single-sex schools, the social context in which students make choices has been shown to change their risk preferences (Booth, Cardona-Sosa & Nolen, 2014). However, negative consequences of identity on academic performance can be remedied by either reducing the salience of a particular identity threat (Cohen & Garcia, 2005) or replacing conflicting identities with a new shared identity[11] (West et al., 2009).

Policy and future directions

Behavioural economics seeks to identify the causal mechanisms linked to non-cognitive behaviour that underlie choices in education so as to inform effective education policy development. Increasingly policy focus is turning to how behaviours can be shaped in early childhood where the gains from policy interventions are greatest. While there is extensive experimental and longitudinal evidence of the substantial positive benefits linked to non-cognitive skills and personality traits, little is known of the causal mechanisms involved and how they impact outcomes over the life of an individual (Heckman et al., 2012). In particular, a nuanced understanding that non-cognitive skills and personality traits that benefit academic outcomes may not necessarily be the same skills and traits that benefit future earnings in the workplace (Lee & Ohtake, 2014).

There is now a substantial and well established literature covering the behavioural economics of public policy (Shafir, 2012). However, most policy interventions in education take the form of either hard or light parentalism (see Lavecchia et al., 2014) which necessarily assumes that policy designers themselves are free of cognitive biases and the constraints of bounded rationality (Viscusi & Gayer, 2015). Light parentalism is most commonly recognised as "nudges" (Sunstein & Thaler, 2012) where preferred choices are framed as defaults.[12] While nudges are useful for policy design in areas such as health and savings, education is more challenging due to the complexity of social interactions that fall outside a formal regulatory framework. For education in particular, social interactions require a deeper understanding of how the macro-behaviour of individuals in groups (see Schelling, 2006) impact on investments in education.

Consideration also needs to be given to behavioural economic policies that increase choices in education rather than constraining choices by framing defaults. That behavioural economics can be used to increase choices in education is not new, although it may not have been recognised as such at the time. It can be considered that the introduction of Chapman's (1988) income-contingent loan scheme for financing higher education in Australia nearly 30 years ago was the first successful application of behavioural economics to education policy. The design of income-contingent loans being effective in overcoming choice inertia, loss aversion, identity threat and willingness to compete which effect participation in higher education by students from low socio-economic backgrounds and women. More consideration needs to be given to these types of "reverse-nudges" that increase both the availability of choice and the social benefits of these choices.

Notes

1 Unlike comparable large investments such as buying a home which are generally fungible and markets liquid.
2 As suggested by real options theory.
3 Front loading is where most of the financial aid is available in the first year of study.
4 A situation whereby the greater the expectation placed upon people, the better they perform.
5 For an example of a discussion on the endogeneity of preferences see Bowles (1998).
6 The marshmallow test is famous for the videos of children desperately trying to distract themselves from the temptation of eating the marshmallow in front of them.
7 From a TV program discussing education and at-risk youth. Student: "Last year we made a bet—there were three of us—and whoever missed a day of school first had to pay the other one $100." "It pushed us to come to school and we did and everything improved." www.sbs.com.au/news/insight/tvepisode/shepparton-3630.
8 Type 1 error is detecting an effect that is not present, while a type 2 error is failing to detect an effect that is present.
9 At least until the "luck" runs out and a "cold hand" leads to reinforcing poor performance.
10 Which Ariely et al. called the Sisyphus condition.

11 Such as replacing racial identities with a common university identity through activities such as sports teams.
12 Light parentalism is sometimes called "libertarian parentalism" while hard parentalism imposes mandatory choice outcomes.

Bibliography

Ainslie, G. (1975). Specious reward: A behavioral theory of impulsiveness and impulse control. Psychological bulletin, 82(4), 463–96.

Akerlof, G. A. & Kranton, R. E.(2010). Identity economics: how our identities shape our work, wages, and well-being, Princeton University Press.

Archbald, D. A. (2000). School choice and school stratification: Shortcomings of the stratification critique and recommendations for theory and research. Educational Policy, 14(2), 214–40.

Ariely, D. & Loewenstein, G. (2006). The heat of the moment: The effect of sexual arousal on sexual decision making. Journal of Behavioral Decision Making, 19(2), 87–98.

Ariely, D. & Wertenbroch, K. (2002). Procrastination, deadlines, and performance: Self-control by precommitment. Psychological Science, 13(3), 219–24.

Ariely, D., Kamenica, E. & Prelec, D. (2008). Man's search for meaning: The case of Legos. Journal of Economic Behavior and Organization, 67(3), 671–7.

Ariely, D., Loewenstein, G. & Prelec, D. (2006). Tom Sawyer and the construction of value. Journal of Economic Behavior and Organization, 60(1), 1–10.

Arrow, K. J. (1962). The economic implications of learning by doing. Review of Economic Studies, 29(3), 155–73.

Avery, C. & Hoxby, C. M. (2004). Do and should financial aid packages affect students" college choices? In C. M. Hoxby (Ed.), College Choices: The Economics of Where to Go, When to Go, and How to Pay for it. University of Chicago Press, 239–302.

Becker, G. S. (1964). Human Capital: A Theoretical and Empirical Analysis, with Special Reference to Education, NBER, Chicago, IL: University of Chicago Press.

Becker, G. S. (1976). Altruism, egoism and genetic fitness: economics and sociobiology. Journal of Economic Literature, 14(3), 817–26.

Becker, G. S., & Tomes, N. (1976). Child endowments and the quantity and quality of children. Journal of Political Economy, 84(4), S143–62.

Behrman, J. R., Sengupta, P. & Todd, P. (2005). Progressing through PROGRESA: An impact assessment of a school subsidy experiment in rural Mexico. Economic Development and Cultural Change, 54(1), 237–75.

Bénabou, R. & Tirole, J. (2003). Self-knowledge and self-regulation: An economic approach. The Psychology of Economic Decisions, 1, 137–67.

Bénabou, R. & Tirole, J. (2005). Incentives and prosocial behaviour. National Bureau of Economic Research (No. w11535).

Black, S. (1999). Do better schools matter? Parental valuation of elementary education. Quarterly Journal of Economics, 114(2), 577–99.

Bodenhausen, G. V., Todd, A. R. & Becker, A. P. (2006). Categorizing the social world: Affect, motivation, and self-regulation. Psychology of Learning and Motivation, 47, 123–55.

Booth, A., Cardona-Sosa, L. & Nolen, P. (2014). Gender differences in risk aversion: Do single-sex environments affect their development? Journal of Economic Behavior and Organization, 99, 126–54.

Bowles, S. (1998). Endogenous preferences: The cultural consequences of markets and other economic institutions. Journal of Economic Literature, 36, 75–111.

Bryan, G., Karlan, D. & Nelson, S. (2010). Commitment devices. Annual Review of Economics, 2(1), 671–98.

Cervone, D. & Peake, P. K. (1986). Anchoring, efficacy, and action: The influence of judgmental heuristics on self-efficacy judgments and behaviour. Journal of Personality and Social Psychology, 50(3), 492.

Chapman, B. J. (1988). An economic analysis of the Higher Education Contribution Scheme of the Wran Report. Economic Analysis and Policy, 18(2), 171–90.

Cohen, G. L. & Garcia, J. (2005). "I am us": Negative stereotypes as collective threats. Journal of Personality and Social Psychology, 89(4), 566.

Cohen, G. L. & Garcia, J. (2008). Identity, belonging, and achievement: A model, interventions, implications. Current Directions in Psychological Science, 17(6), 365–9.

Craik, F. I., & Bialystok, E. (2006). Cognition through the lifespan: Mechanisms of change. Trends in Cognitive Sciences, 10(3), 131–8.

Croizet, J. C. & Claire, T. (1998). Extending the concept of stereotype threat to social class: The intellectual underperformance of students from low socioeconomic backgrounds. Personality and Social Psychology Bulletin, 24(6), 588–94.

Daly, M., Delaney, L., Egan, M. & Baumeister, R. F. (2015). Childhood Self-Control and Unemployment throughout the Life Span: Evidence from Two British Cohort Studies. Psychological Science, 26(6), 709–23.

Darley, J. M. & Gross, P. H. (1983). A hypothesis-confirming bias in labeling effects. Journal of Personality and Social Psychology, 44(1), 20.

Deci, E. L., Koestner, R. & Ryan, R. M. (1999). A meta-analytic review of experiments examining the effects of extrinsic rewards on intrinsic motivation. Psychological Bulletin, 125(6), 627.

Duckworth, A. L. (2011). The significance of self-control. Proceedings of the National Academy of Sciences, 108(7), 2639–40.

Duckworth, A. L., & Seligman, M. E. (2005). Self-discipline outdoes IQ in predicting academic performance of adolescents. Psychological Science, 16(12), 939–44.

Dweck, C. S., Davidson, W., Nelson, S. & Enna, B. (1978). Sex differences in learned helplessness: II. The contingencies of evaluative feedback in the classroom and III. An experimental analysis. Developmental Psychology, 14(3), 268.

Eden, D. (1988). Pygmalion, goal setting, and expectancy: Compatible ways to boost productivity. Academy of Management Review, 13(4), 639–52.

Epple, D. and Romano, R. E. (1998), Competition between private and public schools, vouchers, and peer-group effects. American Economic Review, 88(1), 33–62.

Fredriksson, P., Öckert, B. & Oosterbeek, H. (2013). Long-term effects of class size. Quarterly Journal of Economics, 128(1), 249–85.

Friedman, M. (1955). The Role of Government in Public Education: Economics and Public Interest, New Brunswick: Rutgers University Press.

Fryer, R. (2011). Financial incentives and student achievement: Evidence from randomized trials. Quarterly Journal of Economics, 126, 1755–98.

Gigerenzer, G. & Goldstein, D. G. (1996). 'Reasoning the fast and frugal way: Models of bounded rationality. Psychological Review, 103(4), 650.

Gigerenzer, G. & Todd, P. M. (1999). Fast and frugal heuristics: The adaptive toolbox. In Simple Heuristics that Make us Smart. Oxford: Oxford University Press.

Gilovich, T. and Griffin, D. (2002). Introduction—heuristics and biases: Then and now. In Gilovich, T., Griffin, D. & Kahneman, D. (Eds.), Heuristics and Biases: The Psychology of Intuitive Judgment. Cambridge: Cambridge University Press, 1–18.

Gilovich, T., Vallone, R. & Tversky, A. (1985). The hot hand in basketball: On the misperception of random sequences. Cognitive Psychology, 17(3), 295–314.

Gneezy, U., Meier, S. & Rey-Biel, P. (2011). When and why incentives (don't) work to modify behavior. Journal of Economic Perspectives, 25(4), 191–209.

Gneezy, U., Niederle, M. & Rustichini, A. (2003). Performance in competitive environments: Gender differences. Quarterly Journal of Economics, 118(3), 1049–74.

Grossman, M. (2006). Education and nonmarket outcomes. Handbook of the Economics of Education. Elsevier 1, 577–633.

Hackett, G. & Betz, N. E. (1989). An exploration of the mathematics self-efficacy/mathematics performance correspondence. Journal for Research in Mathematics Education, 20, 261–73.

Heckman, J. J. & Kautz, T. (2012). Hard evidence on soft skills. Labour Economics, 19(4), 451–64.

Heckman, J. J., Pinto, R. & Savelyev, P. A. (2012). Understanding the mechanisms through which an influential early childhood program boosted adult outcomes. National Bureau of Economic Research (No. w18581).

Heckman, J. J., Stixrud, J. & Urzua, S. (2006). The effects of cognitive and noncognitive abilities on labor market outcomes and social behavior. National Bureau of Economic Research (No. w12006).

Herrmann, E., Misch, A., Hernandez-Lloreda, V. & Tomasello, M. (2014). Uniquely human self-control begins at school age. Developmental Science, 18(6), 979–93.

Jurajda, Š. & Münich, D. (2011). Gender gap in performance under competitive pressure: Admissions to Czech universities. American Economic Review, 101(3), 514–18.

Kagan, J., Sontag, L. W., Baker, C. T. & Nelson, V. L. (1958). Personality and IQ change. Journal of Abnormal and Social Psychology, 56(2), 261.

Kautz, T., Heckman, J. J., Diris, R., Ter Weel, B. & Borghans, L. (2014). Fostering and measuring skills: Improving cognitive and non-cognitive skills to promote lifetime success. National Bureau of Economic Research (No. w20749).

Kidd, C., Palmeri, H. & Aslin, R. N. (2013). Rational snacking: Young children's decision-making on the marshmallow task is moderated by beliefs about environmental reliability. Cognition, 126(1), 109–14.

Koch, A., Nafziger, J., & Nielsen, H. S. (2015). Behavioral economics of education. Journal of Economic Behavior & Organization, 115, 3–17.

Kosfeld, M., Neckermann, S. & Yang, X. (2014). Knowing that you matter, matters! The interplay of meaning, monetary incentives, and worker recognition. The Interplay of Meaning, Monetary Incentives, and Worker Recognition. ZEW-Centre for European Economic Research Discussion Paper (14-097).

Ladd, H. F. (2002). School vouchers: A critical view. Journal of Economic Perspectives, 16(4), 3–24.

Lavecchia, A. M., Liu, H., & Oreopoulos, P. (2014). Behavioral economics of education: Progress and possibilities. National Bureau of Economic Research (No. w20609).

Lee, S. and Ohtake, F. (2014). The Effects of Personality Traits and Behavioral Characteristics on Schooling, Earnings, and Career Promotion. RIETI Discussion Paper Series (No. 14023).

Levitt, S. D., List, J. A., Neckermann, S. & Sadoff, S. (2012). The behavioralist goes to school: Leveraging behavioral economics to improve educational performance. National Bureau of Economic Research (No. w18165).

Loewenstein, G. (2005). Hot–cold empathy gaps and medical decision making. Health Psychology, 24(4S), S49.

Loewenstein, G. & Prelec, D. (1992). Anomalies in intertemporal choice: Evidence and an interpretation. Quarterly Journal of Economics, 107(2), 573–97.

Marcus, G. (2009). How does the mind work? Insights from biology. Topics in Cognitive Science, 1, 145–72.

McFadden, D. (2001). Economic choices. American Economic Review, 91(3), 351–78.

Michaelson, L., de la Vega, A., Chatham, C. H. & Munakata, Y. (2013). Delaying gratification depends on social trust. Frontiers in Psychology, 4, 355.

Mincer, J. (1958). Investment in human capital and personal income distribution. Journal of Political Economy, 66(4), 281–302.

Mischel, W., Ebbesen, E. & Raskoff Zeiss, A. (1972). Cognitive and attentional mechanisms in delay of gratification. Journal of Personality and Social Psychology, 21(2), 204.

Moffitt, T. E., Arseneault, L., Belsky, D., Dickson, N., Hancox, R. J., Harrington, H., Houtsa, R., Poultonc, R., Roberts, B., Rossa, S., Searse, M., Thomsong, M. & Caspi, A. (2011). A gradient of childhood self-control predicts health, wealth, and public safety. Proceedings of the National Academy of Sciences, 108(7), 2693–8.

Morisano, D., Hirsh, J. B., Peterson, J. B., Pihl, R. O. & Shore, B. M. (2010). Setting, elaborating, and reflecting on personal goals improves academic performance. Journal of Applied Psychology, 95(2), 255.

Niederle, M. & Vesterlund, L. (2010). Explaining the gender gap in math test scores: The role of competition. Journal of Economic Perspectives, 24(2), 129–44.

Page, L., Garboua, L. L. & Montmarquette, C. (2007). Aspiration levels and educational choices: An experimental study. Economics of Education Review, 26(6), 747–57.

Pekkarinen, T. (2014). Gender differences in behaviour under competitive pressure: Evidence on omission patterns in university entrance examinations. Journal of Economic Behavior and Organization, 115, 94–110.

Rosenthal, R. & Jacobson, L. (1968). Pygmalion in the classroom. Urban Review, 3(1), 16–20.

Schelling, T. C. (2006). Micromotives and Macrobehavior. WW Norton & Company.

Shafir, E. (ed) (2012). The Behavioral Foundations of Public Policy. Princeton, NJ: Princeton University Press.

Shih, M., Pittinsky, T. L. & Ambady, N. (1999). Stereotype susceptibility: Identity salience and shifts in quantitative performance. Psychological Science, 10(1), 80–3.

Shoda, Y., Mischel, W. & Peake, P. K. (1990). Predicting adolescent cognitive and self-regulatory competencies from preschool delay of gratification: Identifying diagnostic conditions. Developmental Psychology, 26(6), 978.

Simon, H. A. (1959). Theories of decision-making in economics and behavioral science. American Economic Review, 49(3), 253–83.

Spencer, S. J., Steele, C. M. & Quinn, D. M. (1999). Stereotype threat and women's math performance. Journal of Experimental Social Psychology, 35(1), 4–28.

Springer, M. G., Rosenquist, B. & Swain-McSurely, W. (2015). Monetary vs. non-monetary incentives: Experimental evidence from after-school tutoring student attendance interventions. Journal of Research on Educational Effectiveness, 8(4), 453–74.

Steel, P. (2007). The nature of procrastination: A meta-analytic and theoretical review of quintessential self-regulatory failure. Psychological Bulletin, 133(1), 65.

Steele, C. M. & Aronson, J. (1995). Stereotype threat and the intellectual test performance of African Americans. Journal of Personality and Social Psychology, 69(5), 797.

Stigler, G. J. & Becker, G. S. (1977). De gustibus non est disputandum. American Economic Review, 67(2), 76–90.

Strotz, R. H. (1955). Myopia and inconsistency in dynamic utility maximization. Review of Economic Studies, 23(3), 165–80.

Sunstein, C. R., & Thaler, R. H. (2012). Nudge: Improving Decisions about Health, Wealth and Happiness. Penguin.

Tangney, J. P., Baumeister, R. F. & Boone, A. L. (2004). High self-control predicts good adjustment, less pathology, better grades, and interpersonal success. Journal of Personality, 72(2), 271–324.

Thaler, R. (1985). Mental accounting and consumer choice. Marketing Science, 4(3), 199 214.

Thaler, R. H. (1981). Some empirical evidence on dynamic inconsistency. Economics Letters, 8(3), 201–7.

Tiebout, C. M. (1956). A pure theory of local expenditures. Journal of Political Economy, 64(5), 416–24.

Tomasello, M. (2014). The ultra-social animal. European Journal of Social Psychology, 44(3), 187–94.

Tversky, A. & Kahneman, D. (1973). Availability: A heuristic for judging frequency and probability. Cognitive Psychology, 5(2), 207–32.

Tversky, A. & Kahneman, D. (1974). Judgment under uncertainty: Heuristics and biases. Science, 185(4157), 1124–31.

Tversky, A. & Kahneman, D. (1981). The framing of decisions and the psychology of choice. Science, 211(4481), 453–8.

Viscusi, W. K., & Gayer, T. (2015). Behavioral Public Choice: The Behavioral Paradox of Government Policy. Vanderbilt Law and Economics Research Paper (15-2).

West, T. V., Pearson, A. R., Dovidio, J. F., Shelton, J. N. & Trail, T. E. (2009). Superordinate identity and intergroup roommate friendship development. Journal of Experimental Social Psychology, 45(6), 1266–72.

Williams, K. D. (2007). Ostracism. Psychology, 58(1), 425.

27

BEHAVIORAL INNOVATION ECONOMICS

Jason Potts

Introduction

Viewed from a distance, the concept of a behavioral innovation economics is relatively easy to frame as the application of behavioral economics (heuristics and biases, bounded rationality in human cognition) (Kahneman, 2003) to innovation economics (investment in R&D, entrepreneurial behavior in new ventures, choice over novel goods). The target discipline is innovation economics and so the problems and subject matter of innovation economics shape the research program of behavioral innovation economics. The behavioral in this is simply to study the cognitive processes involved in choice over novelty, as it were, and under uncertainty. So this would seem to be relatively straightforward application of an approach (behavioral economics) to a field of study (economics of innovation).

In several respects, a behavioral innovation economics is already part of the practical arts of government policy that have sought to adopt behavioral insights into innovative thinking in the public sector (Thaler & Sunstein, 2003; Shafir, 2012; Oliver, 2013). Furthermore, behavioral innovation economics, as a kind of strategic-managerial folk wisdom, is already practiced by many firms (and consultants) that seek to design incentives and choice architecture to 'nudge' innovative decision-making and the sorts of knowledge pooling and collaborative activity that lead to successful innovative activities. And something that we might not unreasonably call 'applied behavioral innovation economics' is also widely practiced by many entrepreneurs and venture capitalists that seek to exploit understandings of cognitive processes embodied in heuristics and biases in order to make better and more effective decisions in choice environments with high uncertainty and the need to rely on entrepreneurial judgment (Foss & Klein, 2012), or to induce others to do so (Hwang & Horowitt, 2012). So in many respects behavioral innovation economics already exists in the wild. What we are talking about here is a domesticated and laboratory version of that, and the assembly of it a coherent body of theory that can be formalized and tested, and then further developed for applications. It is this that barely exists, and this chapter is intended as a way to organize what we know, and to suggest a research program for developing that.

Behavioral innovation economics—as the application of behavioral economic theory and principles to the subject matter of innovation economics (also known as Schumpeterian or evolutionary economics)—is not yet a distinct and recognized field of study, but it is one with much latent potential. Interestingly, this is not because behavioral economics has been neglected from innovation economics, but rather because behavioral assumptions are already deeply embedded in models of the innovating firm. For instance, Nelson and Winter's (1982) 'evolutionary theory of economic change' is constructed atop an explicitly behavioral theory of the firm in which agents are assumed to be boundedly rational (Nelson & Winter, 2002; Nelson, 2008; Cyert & March, 1963; March & Simon, 1958). Furthermore, one can barely shake a stick in the field of entrepreneurial studies without hitting a behavioral explanation for motivations and characteristic features of entrepreneurial actions (Baron, 1998, 2007). Modern Schumpeterian and entrepreneurial economics is built on models with strong and explicit behavioral foundations, yet this is precisely why a distinct field of behavioral innovation economics has not emerged in which behavioral insights are *applied to* innovation economics.

Viewed in this way, an explicitly behavioral innovation economics would have domains of producer and consumer applications. On the supply side, behavioral models would apply to the production of innovation and the coordination necessary to achieve that—that is, to entrepreneurship, the origination and growth of firms, competitive rivalry, and so on. There are applications of behavioral insights to perceptions of opportunities, decisions to invest, and to decisions about cooperative behavior and competitive response. There are also applications to the design of innovation policy and strategy, which is about setting up systems of incentives to induce people to act in ways that are in the group's or society's best interests, even when they are individually risky and uncertain propositions (Greve, 2003; Blinder, 2014).

On the consumer side, a behavioral innovation economics would naturally focus on problems associated with choice over novel goods, the acquisition of new preferences and the adaptation of a consumer lifestyle to innovation (Witt, 2001; Lades, 2013). Innovation means thinking and doing new things, both on the producer and consumer side, and innovation also means pooling and sharing ideas and knowledge, and forming new organizations and institutions. Both aspects of creating and dealing with novelty pose cognitive and behavioral challenges that can be the focus of a behavioral innovation economics.

The challenge here is more than the application of bounded rationality to these problems, as is the standard model in Schumpeterian economics, for instance, and in much modern work on the theory of the firm, starting with Cyert and March (1963). Rather, the focus is to be on the mind and behaviors of the evolutionary adapted human being and the world view that presents and the characteristic decisions that such an agent makes, and why. A behavioral innovation economics will seek to address such basic questions as why innovation is so hard to organize, and why public policy, while often advancing platitudes in its support, often constrains more than it supports. It will focus on why organizations, particularly large organizations, whether public or private, find it so hard to be innovative. It focuses on the question of the reasons why consumers adopt novelty, and the seemingly crucial importance of social context in those decisions. The economic theory of innovation is remarkably straightforward as an application of compound interest: namely, we should invest more, and do so sooner rather than later (*à la* Thaler & Benartzi, 2004). Yet this is nevertheless something that human economic agents find hard to do. Behavioral innovation economics seeks to understand why that is, and to focus on ways to understand how we might improve those situations, both individually and collectively, whether in firms, industries or entire societies.

The starting point in this is to squarely recognize that our minds (and our bodies) were not designed by evolutionary selection forces to live in the current environment that we do. Specifically, we struggle with particular things, and innovation, which I will characterize here as decisions to do new things in uncertain environments, and therefore of choice 'over novelty under uncertainty', is a focus that evolution has not prepared us well for. We are not well adapted to live in a world of rapidly changing knowledge. This problem I suggest is the core subject matter of behavioral innovation economics.

We proceed as follows. In the second section of this chapter we will outline the heuristics and biases approach to behavioral innovation economics. This in effect gathers behavioral innovation economics as it currently exists, and pivots on the work of Dan Kahneman, Richard Thaler, George Loewenstein, Cass Sunstein, and others. In the third section, we set out the case for an 'evolutionary micro-foundations' view of behavioral innovation economics. This is not inconsistent with the 'heuristics and biases' approach, but seeks to go much deeper; it pivots on the work of Herbert Simon, Gerd Gigerenzer, and others. The fourth section concludes.

The heuristics and biases approach to behavioral innovation economics

Innovation economics as choice over novelty under uncertainty

Innovation economics itself has several distinct meanings: these distinguish between the classic Schumpeterian/evolutionary approach and the neoclassical information economics approach. The classic model comes from the work of Joseph Schumpeter who placed the process of innovation in firms at the centre of an economic model of growth and development (Nelson & Winter, 1982). The microeconomic agent responsible for innovation is the entrepreneur, and the macroeconomic consequence is what he called 'creative destruction'. Innovation is in this sense an evolutionary process characterized by a 'meso trajectory' (Dopfer, 2012) that can be arrayed over three phases: (1) entrepreneurial *origination* of the novel idea; (2) *adoption* of the idea through firms and markets; and (3) *retention* of the innovation into economic institutions, including cognitive and behavioral habits and routines.

The neoclassical model of innovation economics is somewhat different, building out of information economics and the problem of the production of new information in a competitive market. The classic statement of this problem is Arrow's (1962) diagnosis of the market failure problem at the heart of the production of new knowledge, due to fixed costs, approriability, and uncertainty. The innovation problem here is focused about the strategic behavior of firms in competitive markets in the production of new information as an investment under uncertainty problem.

The Schumpeterian and neoclassical approaches contain a lot of overlap and at a microeconomic level arrive at a similar diagnosis of the underlying economic problem, namely as the problem of investment under uncertainty in the production of new information—which is the characterization of the problem of a firm in Schumpeterian competition. On the consumer side, the microeconomic problem is choice over novel goods, about which the consumer may not have sufficient information to form well-behaved preferences. Both contexts can be represented as uncertain learning environments in which rational choice is difficult. So there are ample opportunities—as both a producer problem and a consumer problem—to insert behavioral economics into this domain. We characterize the economic choice problem in the context of innovation as the problem of *choice over novelty under uncertainty*.

Using heuristics and biases to decompose the innovation problem

The context of *choice over novelty under uncertainty* can induce systematic behavioral choice implications that can be assembled in the heuristics and biases tradition as set forth by the like of Dan Kahneman, Richard Thaler, et al. We need not elaborate these here, but they run through the full gamut of heuristics and biases such as loss aversion, risk aversion, hyperbolic discounting, status quo bias, sunk cost effects, endowment effects, availability bias, framing bias, optimism bias, confirmation bias, and so on (Gilovich et al., 2002). Behavioral innovation economics then examines the effects of the use of decision heuristics, and the biases they introduce, on the various agents involved in innovation choice, including entrepreneurs, investors, regulators and consumers. There are multiple points at which the innovation process is intersected by problems that are identified by behavioral economics. Potts (2010) identifies ten characteristic such behavioral failures, all associated with the problem of choice over novelty under uncertainty.

Potts' approach was to outline a set of particular choice contexts 'over novelty under uncertainty' (i.e. the producer or consumer context of innovation) that while not necessarily difficult for what Richard Thaler (2000) calls 'Econs' seem to be predictably difficult for humans. These then become likely points of failure in the innovation process that can be analyzed from a heuristics and biases approach to behavioral innovation economics. I will outline these ten forms of failure that affect decision-making in innovation as summarized in Table 27.1 below. Choice over novelty under uncertainty presents many opportunities for systematic behavioral error to manifest in maladaptive heuristics and characteristic biases that cause the innovation process to undershoot some rational benchmark.[1] The implication is that innovation failure may occur for reasons extending beyond standard technology failure, market failure, management failure, or even policy failure arguments that occupy the Schumpeterian and neoclassical approaches to innovation economics, but through a further class of behavioral innovation failure. What this does, then, is to add a further layer reasons why innovation is hard and why we might expect to observe systematic failure (i.e. for cognitive behavioral reasons). The subject matter of behavioral innovation economics in this view would be a way to study the way in which this happens and,

Table 27.1 Ten ways that choice under novelty is hard, leading to innovation failure

Dimension of difficulty	*Mechanism*	*Example*
Awareness of novelty	Human brain routinely filters novelty	Novelty with a smaller 'cognitive distance' is easier to notice
How novelty affects you	Some ideas *sui generis*: no existing routines process them	Novelty that creates new categories is hard to process
Selecting new ideas	Selection over novelty difficult to allocate	Criteria to select people *de facto* mechanism for selecting new ideas
Open innovation	Overvaluing endogenous and undervaluing exogenous novelty	'Not invented here' ideas routinely overlooked
Rational innovation	Identity constructs displace rational choice	Personal, social, political factors enter into choice over novelty
Incentivizing innovation	Status quo bias, conformity bias, loss aversion	Behaviour over novelty must overcome costs to any action at all
Innovation portfolios	Portfolios not a natural cognitive category	Difficulty thinking about multiple novelties simultaneously
Investing in innovation	Myopia, imagination failures	Underinvestment in new ideas & undervaluation of cooperation
Space for innovation	Mental accounts	Tendency to infect novelty with extant context
Innovation failure	Accounting for experimental failure	Failure difficult to rationalize, causing avoidance of experiments

Source: Table copied from Potts (2010: 145).

as with the behavioral policy models (e.g. Oliver, 2013), to suggest possible remedies (call this libertarian innovation paternalism? cf. Loewenstein & Haisley, 2007).

Awareness of novelty is hard

The human mind is not adapted to a world of rapid and continual change; it requires effort to notice such changes and register their actual pace (Paquet, 1998). Human perceptual and cognitive apparatuses are mostly filtering mechanisms. Yet in a world of rapid continual change this mechanism will tend to work too well, causing novelty to be overlooked. Noticing novelty requires cognitive effort. The implication is that behavioral failure can occur due to a bias against seeing novelty. Novelty is easier to notice when it has a small 'cognitive distance' from something familiar. The larger this cognitive distance grows, the more effort is required to see the novelty. This can lead to a systematic underestimation of the amount of change in the environment. This can render radical novelty effectively invisible, which may in part explain how disruptive innovations can actually be so disruptive. Failure to notice novelty can constrain the development of raw ideas into entrepreneurial potential, and can limit adoption when businesses or consumers overlook the value of a novel idea. Furthermore, it can lead to firms systematically underestimating the competitive threat posed by a rival product and inappropriately low innovative response.

Knowing how novelty affects you is hard

Even when noticed, because new ideas are often *sui generis*, and thus in effect 'category creating' or changing the extant categories presently used to partition markets, niches, technologies, etc, this may lead to the use of inappropriate heuristics to evaluate the novelty, leading to an appropriate behavioral response. This causes what I will call 'competition blindness' through failure to see how a novel idea changes the substitution possibilities of producers or consumers, or how the new connections the novel idea makes affect which market a firm is actually in (Earl, 2003).

Selecting among many new ideas is hard

Within a firm, the innovation process can be generically characterized as beginning with the search for opportunities, among those, and development. The selection phase is the most behaviorally difficult because it is never possible to be entirely rational; there always remain significant uncertainties. Selection invariably requires champions: someone must get behind an idea for it to succeed. Because of this, the selection process becomes functionally dependent upon who that is, and why. Mechanisms that select people will thus often function *de facto* to select among new ideas.

Open innovation and learning from outsiders is hard

Novel ideas occurring within a group are often treated differently to novel ideas arising from outside. This asymmetry tends to over-value endogenous novelty and under-value or heavily discount exogenous novelty (Salge, 2011). Cooperation in respect of experimenting with new ideas and sharing knowledge is easy within the boundaries of an organization, but often very difficult across such boundaries with 'outsiders' (Hartley & Potts, 2014). This is why 'open innovation' seems unnatural (Chesbrough, 2003) and large firms, which create a larger population of insiders, can be effective.

Being rational about innovation is hard

Choice under novelty can be as much about the person or organization making the choice as about the substantiative material aspects of the new idea itself. Attitudes with respect to new ideas can serve as important and distinct personality and identity markers, thus overlaying all manner of social identity effects into choice with respect to novelty that can be difficult to decompose. New ideas also present clear opportunities for displays of leadership, adventure and even aggression, or of submission and cooperation, all of which have values and functions that may have little to do with the rational undertaking of innovation. Innovation is by definition a social process, as the value and use of new ideas is 'socially constructed' through continual feedback between users, producers and other parties. It is easy to allow social and behavioral factors to dominate decision-making. Evidence of the difficulties of rational choice can be seen in the extent to which largely 'ceremonial' factors regularly intrude into the innovation process. One example is revenue forecasts made in the context of start-up pitches. These are essentially random numbers (Douglas & Shepherd, 2002). Yet they do nevertheless function as a ritualistic signal of willingness to cooperate. Innovation failure can thus occur for reasons that may have nothing to do with the idea itself but rather with respect to improper observance of the socio-cultural customs associated with the introduction of novelty.

Incentivizing novelty creation and innovation is hard

Incentives to novelty and innovation have to be sufficient to overcome risk and loss aversion that may carry into multiple dimensions. The power of conformity bias makes incentivizing innovative thinking hard, in that the incentive is not that of a marginal substitution, but must fully compensate for potential 'ex-communication' from the tribe. Few people have a high tolerance for this, and most require compensation to be considerable. Even when income and material risks are carried by the organization or by financiers, there still remains the prospect of loss in status or identity if a new idea fails. Expectations will differ and no incentive system will work in all contexts. The costs of discovery of what motivations are at work and in what dimensions losses are salient makes design of incentives for novelty and innovation difficult.

Thinking about innovation portfolios is hard

Portfolio approaches to risk are economically rational because the sum of a bundle of *uncorrelated risks* has lower variance than each individually. Serial entrepreneurship is an effective strategy, as is gathering multiple innovation directions under one organization. Many new ideas pursued at once can be a lower risk strategy than just a single new idea if—and only if—those many ideas are uncorrelated. However, human minds evolved under conditions of social payoffs to being right about risks one at a time. This draws upon instinctive capabilities to lead a journey, to organize a project, to champion an idea, to become a hero, and so on. Single ideas—projects—seem a 'natural unit' for choice under novelty, but they are not: they are a behavioral bias. It is hard to think about innovation from a portfolio perspective—call this bias 'portfolio aversion.'

Investing in innovation is hard; getting cooperation for a new idea is hard

Firms (and people) systematically under-invest in the development of innovation competences and capabilities as well as under-invest in particular innovation projects and portfolios. Two distinct behavioral reasons explain this: first, expectations are hard to form; and second, investment requires persuading others to cooperate. Innovation, by definition, requires cooperation in order to gather and coordinate resources and to induce experimental adoption and learning with respect to the new idea. Yet failure to secure early cooperation is perhaps the most common form of innovation failure. In a network, collaborative or open innovation projects failure commonly arises when cooperative connections fail to form. Yet the opportunity cost of the loss of 'real options' is often difficult to evaluate, especially if others have also not yet signaled their commitment. Risk aversion may thus have a particular manifestation in the form of 'early cooperation aversion' in the often difficult and path-dependent emergence of coalitions about novelty.

Creating space for innovation is hard

Successful innovation requires creating an appropriate 'space' for experimentation to occur. This includes physical space (e.g. a laboratory, an experimental market) and mental space. The creation of mental space for experimentation with novelty can be difficult because it requires letting go or disconnecting from past decisions and knowledge. Endowment effects and sunk cost biases both contribute to this difficulty. A common behavioral bias is the tendency of people to form *mental accounts*, violating the rational principle of fungibility (Thaler, 1985). However, to experiment with novelty often requires a separate mental account (as well as physical and organizational) within which much greater tolerance of failure and heightened attention to feedback occur. The failure to effectively create such an account can result in inappropriate behaviors and heuristics applied to the experimental situation.

Coping with innovation failure is hard

New ideas require experimental learning to ascertain their value and the opportunities they harbor. Yet experimental learning by definition involves failure. This can lead to two often contiguous behavioral failures in the context of experimental learning: (1) the failure to recognize failure when it occurs (either by ignoring it, or reconstructing narratives in which it was not a failure, such as cognitive dissonance); and (2) the failure to learn from failure, in the sense of failing to absorb the feedback information it provided, and thus failing to go on to reconstruct hypotheses and conjectures with that new information. Holding on too long before product release (fear of realizing failure), and staying too long in a failing market (fear of admitting failure, or holding to a belief that a corner will soon be turned) are common behavioral biases that slow the innovation process.

Behavioral innovation economics as evolutionary micro-foundations

Why behavioral innovation economics should be an evolutionary science

The title of this subsection is a reworking of a seminal article of evolutionary economics, by Thorstein Veblen called 'Why is economics not an evolutionary science?' The same point can be argued about behavioral economics in general, not just behavioral innovation economics (Haselton & Nettle, 2006; McDermott et al., 2008). The heuristics and biases approach to behavioral innovation economics in the second section sought to identify characteristic failures in innovation process that could be traced back to characteristic behavioral biases (e.g. loss aversion, sunk cost affects, endowment effects, and so on). That is an effective starting point for a behavioral innovation economics in serving to map out the domain. But simply mapping and labeling is not yet a science (Jones, 2015). What is further required is an endeavor to understand why dealing with choice over novelty under uncertainty is difficult, what aspects of the environment (whether physical or social) makes it so, and how this presents in particular contexts of entrepreneurial action and judgment, carrying risk, forming groups, adopting new ideas and technologies. As indicated in the first section, this is more than simply constructing micro-foundations along the lines of 'we assume agents are boundedly rational, etc' but with an endeavor to understand how evolved cognition is entrained into the task of innovation. Berg and Gigerenzer (2010) call this a program of 'ecological rationality' (a point made in a different context by Vernon Smith (2003), who distinguished between constructivist and ecological rationality) emphasizing that the behavioral departures from perfect rationality identified in the heuristics and biases program may have their own 'ecological' rationality that can be understood from an evolutionary perspective (Witt, 2006).

An evolutionary micro-foundations approach to behavioral innovation economics seeks to get behind the diagnostic approach of the cognitive heuristics and biases approach toward seeking to understand the why and how aspects of human decision-making in the context of innovation. In essence, this seeks to apply evolutionary sciences (evolutionary biology, evolutionary psychology, evolutionary linguistics, evolutionary anthropology) to underpin why and how questions about human choice over novelty under uncertainty. Toward this, I want to outline two particular instances (both involving my own work, not because it is the leading edge, but simply because I know it best) that illustrate what such an approach looks like. The first is a theory of 'universal nomadism' (Potts, 2003), as an evolutionary explanation of the search and discovery mechanism. The second is a model called 'demic concentration' based on the cultural science model of group formation (Hartley & Potts, 2014).

Universal nomadism

Evolutionary economics in both the Veblenian variant and the Schumpeterian variant have both carried some aspiration, and often maintained an ambition to found the model of the economic agent on explicit evolutionary foundations (Nelson & Winter, 2002; Witt, 2006). For example, Kurt Dopfer (2004) develops a theory of the evolutionary economic agent as a 'rule maker and rule user' (see also Dopfer & Potts, 2008). But these approaches tend to be rather abstract at the level of an evolutionary account of bounded rationality, rather than of particular cognitive modules or mechanisms. The model of universal nomadism, however, seeks to account for a particular aspect of choice over novelty under uncertainty.

Universal nomadism (Potts, 2003) is a theory that seeks to explain the origin of novelty (and therefore the well-spring of innovation) in economic systems as a consequence of an adapted instinct in the human mind—the 'nomadic instinct'. In evolutionary psychology (Cosmides & Tooby, 1994; Plotkin, 1997) the human brain is modeled as a suite of cognitive modules, or instincts, evolutionary adapted to the ancestral environment (the Pleistocene). My claim for the existence of a nomadic instinct is that there were particular features of the 'environment of evolutionary adaptedness' (the EEA) that made nomadic behavior, and the cognitive routines that supported it, a successful adaptation. Evidence for this can clearly be seen in the physical adaptations of the human body (upright walking posture, sprung arches, and so on) but the nomadic instinct argues that this is also a neurocognitive adaption too.

Why might this exist? The reason to suspect the existence of such a nomadic instinct is because the EEA was one in which ancestral humans evolved in a complex environment of semi-desert and savannah, where resources were only semi-stable in time and space. There was a complex distribution of the resources that the human population required to survive. We adapted to this complex distribution of resources by ourselves becoming complex in our geographical behavior. We became nomadic. For hundreds of thousands of years, a major force of evolutionary selection (plausibly both natural and sexual selection) over the human and pre-human population, mind and body, was adaptation to climactic variation and shifting and migrating resources.

Universal nomadism is the idea that this nomadic behavior may have levered itself into a new domain of language and ideas, an abstract space (rather than a geographical space) where knowledge itself is the resource that must be constantly tracked and settled. The argument is that the very mechanisms adapted to solve the problem of a complex distribution of physical resources in geographic space (i.e. nomadism) were capitalized as the growth of knowledge process in which knowledge itself is the complex and shifting resource.

In Potts (2003) I make various speculative claims about how the nomadic instinct manifests and the distribution over the human population, and its relation to the long run growth of knowledge processes that have driven modern economic growth. I speculate about its neural correlates associated with language processing rather than visual processing because of the connection to maps of knowledge and the geometry of such maps, and also about the subroutines that such an instinct might comprise: a set of triggers; search heuristics; and a halting function. And I point out the predicted claims that the theory makes. For instance, that the motivation to introduce novelty is only weakly related to price incentives and more strongly related to maps of possible journeys. I suggest that the origin of ideas in the economic system, like the origins of novelty, are explicable in part as a story about the construction of maps of the environment (these are those of technologies and their market opportunities) and nomadic behavior in the presence of these maps.

The point of the thesis of universal nomadism was to furnish an evolutionary consistent story about the nature of human cognitive processing and decision-making (over novelty under uncertainty) by connecting it to an environment of evolutionary selection—which in this case was a complex distribution of resources, which selected for cognitive 'modules' (i.e. the instinct of nomadism) that were adapted to such a complex environment. Universal nomadism is the further claim that this nomadic instinct has been co-opted into the realm of a complex distribution of ideas, and that this behavior now manifests as entrepreneurship and innovation, as opposed to nomadic behavior in the savannah.

The point of this example is not to suggest that this is true—it is a speculative theory, and an untested one at that. The point rather is that it is illustrative of what is meant by an endeavor to go beyond a heuristics and biases approach to behavioral innovation economics in order to assemble an evolutionary consistent account of why and how (Jones, 2015) human decision-making in the context of innovation—that is, over novelty under uncertainty—might have the characteristic features that it does.

Demic concentration

Another key aspect of the behavioral economics of innovation comes from an aspect of entrepreneurship and innovation that is traditionally not well treated in economics, namely the fact that it is generally a highly social process. This occurs at several different levels, from the discovery and assembly of the entrepreneurial opportunity, to the creation of the team that becomes the firm, to the building of the market and community of investors and customers, and so on. In essence, doing new things is not done by an individual—even if there is a somewhat romantic tendency to believe that—but is a highly social, highly cooperative process (Hwang & Horowitt, 2012). It is competitive, intensely so, in that it is groups competing with other groups. The success or failure of innovation often comes down to the effectiveness of these social processes—in effect, we innovate in groups, and for complex group reasons, some of which involves finding solutions to actual problems, but much of which involves complex social signaling. A behavioral innovation economics seeks to understand the evolutionary forces that shape the behaviors that make such groups of knowledge creating agents possible.

A way of approaching this comes from my own more recent work, this time in conjunction with John Hartley, which consists of the development of a general model of what we call 'cultural science'—which is a new approach to the study of culture using evolutionary biology, evolutionary linguistics, evolutionary economics, and semiotics—into a specific model of what we call 'demic concentration' (Hartley & Potts, 2014; Hartley & Potts, 2015), which is based on modern evolutionary theory in which the selective value of culture is that it makes groups, and the selective value of groups is that they make knowledge. Culture acts as the 'survival vehicle' (Pagel, 2012: 12–13) for knowledge and technologies, and thus the group, hence solving the problem of inheritance of knowledge by securing it at group-historical rather than individual-behavioral level. Culture is not something that groups do; rather groups are something that culture does. In this view *Homo sapiens* are a language-using, high-trusting, instinctively cooperative, pro-social groupish animal (Bowles & Gintis, 2011; Nowak, 2011).

A culture-made group is a deme (in biology, a deme refers to an inter-breeding group that shares genes). Ideas and knowledge are 'culturally situated' in the sense that we acquire ideas preferentially from our deme: from within our language, our social references, our (extended) family or trusted non-kin 'honorary relatives' (Pagel, 2012), from within our 'we-group' and against 'they groups'. Innovation occurs as a cultural process when ideas are integrated into the 'we'-group as its boundaries are redrawn to include ideas previously or otherwise part of a 'they-group'. Newness and innovation occur by an evolutionary semiotic process of group-dynamics we call '*demic concentration*'. Demic concentration is the formation of such a bounded group; cf. *demic diffusion* (Cavalli-Sforza, 2000) where the knowledge moves across groups through individual migration. With demic diffusion, knowledge flows out (e.g. farming practices across Neolithic Eurasia, carried by individuals, not by mere copying). With demic concentration, conversely, knowledge flows in: but because of low-trust settings for 'they'-group originated knowledge, it cannot simply be copied but must be *translated* into 'we'-group terms. With demic concentration, the boundaries of a 'knowledge-group' change: this boundary change is innovation.

This 'cultural science' approach derives from a theme arising out of cultural studies—the study of ordinary culture in the Raymond Williams (1958) sense—of culture as productive, and specifically, as productive of novelty. Culture makes groups, groups make knowledge, and new ideas (contributions to knowledge) occur as the tensioned and conflicted boundary of a group changes. Newness and novelty are not the production of an idea, using factor inputs (the production function for ideas), but the reformation of a group boundary such that an idea becomes meaningful. This is the evolutionary model of cultural dynamics through the mechanisms of demic concentration.

Conclusion: toward a research program and policy

Behavioral innovation economics is the application of the approach of behavioral economics to the subject domain of innovation economics, which I have presented here as the problem of choice over novelty under uncertainty. In neoclassical economics, the innovation problem is that of private underinvestment in the research and development that drives innovation from the social welfare perspective. Innovation policy seeks to correct that market failure through a variety of institutions (intellectual property, R&D tax credits, public funding of science, and so forth).

And the research program of innovation economics focuses on understanding these incentive problems, on modeling the process of an innovation trajectory, and on the design of optimal innovation policy.

A behavioral innovation economics looks somewhat different. A mainstream approach that hews to the heuristics and biases behavioral research program will seek to use the various biases and cognitive heuristics identified from the stable of behavioral anomalies and to map these to characteristic points of failure in the innovation process (Potts, 2010). This will explain difficulties and failures in the innovation process by locating the cause of the innovation problem not in the market, as in neoclassical innovation economics, but rather as a decision failure. This different diagnosis would then suggest a different policy approach, based around seeking to correct these decision failures, perhaps through redesign of the choice architecture of the innovation context. At this stage the field is at the phase of beginning to identify possible points of choice failure, and the heuristics and biases that might apply.

A different approach follows more in the manner of Herbert Simon's conception of bounded rationality (and Vernon Smith's conception of ecological rationality) that would seek to furnish explanations of human decision-making in innovation contexts in such a way that these would be consistent with, or even better built upon, foundations in evolutionary theory or neuroscience. This consilience approach was illustrated with two examples (from my own previous work) on an evolutionary theory of novelty generation called 'universal nomadism' (Potts, 2003) and an evolutionary theory of group formation to produce new knowledge called 'demic concentration' (Hartley & Potts, 2014). In this version of behavioral innovation economics the research program seeks to understand human decision-making, both individually and in groups in the context of innovation by drawing on a range of related fields (not just psychology). The policy implications of this approach are also different in that these theories would yield testable predictions about the types of incentive systems and institutional environments that would support endogenous innovation.

Note

1 Potts (2010: 134–5) calls this rational benchmark the 'efficient innovation hypothesis'.

Bibliography

Arrow, K. (1962). Economic welfare and the allocation of resources for invention. In R. Nelson (ed.), The Rate and Direction of Inventive Activity. NBER. 609–26.

Baron, R. (1998). Cognitive mechanisms in entrepreneurship: why and when entrepreneurs think differently than other people. Journal of Business Venturing, 13(3), 275–94.

Baron, R. (2007). Behavioral and cognitive factors in entrepreneurship: entrepreneurs as the active element in new venture creation. Strategic Entrepreneurial Journal, 1(1–2), 167–82.

Berg, N., Gigerenzer, G. (2007). Psychology implies paternalism? Bounded rationality may reduce the rationale to regulate risk-taking. Social Choice Welfare, 28(2), 337–59.

Berg, N., Gigerenzer, G. (2010). As-if behavioral economics: neoclassical economics in disguise? History of Economic Ideas, 18(1), 133–66.

Blinder, M. (2014). Should evolutionary economists embrace libertarian paternalism? Journal of Evolutionary Economics, 24, 515–39.

Bowles, S., Gintis, H. (2011). A Cooperative Species: Human Reciprocity and its Evolution. Princeton, NJ: Princeton University Press.

Cavalli-Sforza, L. (2000). Genes, Peoples, and Languages, New York: North Point Press.

Chesbrough, H., (2003). The era of open innovation. MIT Sloan Management Review, 44(3), 35–41.

Cosmides, L. Tooby, J. (1994). 'Better than rational': evolutionary psychology and the invisible hand. American Economic Review, 84, 327–32.

Cyert, R., March, J. (1963). A Behavioral Theory of the Firm. Englewood Cliffs, NJ: Prentice Hall.

Dopfer, K. (2004). The economic agent as rule maker and rule user: Homo Sapiens Oeconomicus. Journal of Evolutionary Economics, 14, 177–95.

Dopfer, K. (2012). The origins of meso economics. Journal of Evolutionary Economics, 22(1), 133–60.

Dopfer, K., Potts, J. (2008). The General Theory of Economic Evolution. London: Routledge.

Douglas, E., Shepherd, D. (2002). Exploring investor readiness: assessments by entrepreneurs and investors in Australia. Venture Capital, 4(3), 219–36.

Earl, P. (1990). Economics and psychology: A survey. Economic Journal, 100, 718–55.

Earl, P. (2003). The entrepreneur as a constructor of connections. Advances in Austrian Economics, 6, 117–34.

Foss, N., Klein, P. (2012). Organizing Entrepreneurial Judgment. Cambridge: Cambridge University Press.

Frank, R. (2012). The Darwin Economy: Liberty, Competition and the Common Good. Princeton, NJ: Princeton University Press.

Gilovich, T., Griffin, D., Kahneman, D. (eds) (2002). Heuristics and Biases: The Psychology of Intuitive Judgment. Cambridge University Press.

Greve, H. (2003). A behavioral theory of R&D expenditures and innovations: Evidence from shipbuilding. Academy of Management Journal, 46, 685–702.

Hartley, J., Potts, J. (2014). Cultural Science: A Natural History of Stories, Demes, Knowledge and Innovation. London: Bloomsbury.

Hartley, J., Potts, J. (2015). How the social economy produces innovation. SSRN working paper.

Haselton, M., Nettle, D. (2006). The paranoid optimist: an integrative evolutionary view model of cognitive biases. Personality and Social Psychology Review, 10(1), 47–66.

Hwang, V., Horowitt, G. (2012). The Rainforest. Regenwald.

Jones, D. (2015). Why behavioral economics isn't better and how it could be. In J.C. Teitelbaum & K. Zeiler (eds.), Research Handbook on Behavioral Law and Economics. Edward Elgar.

Kahneman, D. (2003). Maps of bounded rationality: psychology for behavioral economics. American Economic Review, 93(5), 1449–75.

Lades, L. (2013). Behavioral and evolutionary economics on impulsive consumption and reflexive thought: nudging ethical consumer behavior. Journal of Economic Psychology, 41, 114–28.

Loewenstein, G., Haisley, E. (2007). The economist as therapist: Methodological ramifications of 'light' paternalism. Available at SSRN 962472.

March, J., Simon, H. (1958). Organizations. Cambridge, MA: John Wiley.

McDermott, R., Fowler, J., Smirnov, O. (2008). On the evolutionary origin of prospect theory preferences. Journal of Politics, 70(2), 335–50.

Nelson, R. (2008). Bounded rationality, cognitive maps and trial and error learning. Journal of Economic Behavior and Organization, 67(1), 78–89.

Nelson, R., Winter, S. (1982). An Evolutionary Theory of Economic Change. Cambridge, MA: Harvard University Press.

Nelson, R., Winter, S. (2002). Evolutionary theorizing in economics. Journal of Economic Perspectives, 16, 23–46.

Nowak, M. (2011). Supercooperators. New York: Free Press.

Oliver, A. (ed.), (2013). Behavioural Public Policy. Cambridge: Cambridge University Press.

Pagel, M. (2012). Wired for Culture: The Natural History of Human Cooperation. London: Allen Lane.

Paquet, G. (1998). Evolutionary cognitive economics. Information Economics and Policy, 10(3), 343–57.

Plotkin, H. (1997). Evolution in Mind. New York: Penguin.

Potts, J. (2003). Toward an evolutionary theory of homo economicus: The concept of universal nomadism. In J. Laurent (ed.), Evolutionary Economics and Human Nature. Edward Elgar. 195–216.

Potts, J. (2010). Toward behavioral innovation economics: Heuristics and biases in choice under novelty. Prometheus, 28(2), 133–48.

Salge, T. (2011). A behavioral model of innovative search: Evidence from public hospital services. Journal of Public Administration Research and Theory, 21(1), 181–210.

Shafir, E. (ed.), (2012). The Behavioral Foundations of Public Policy. Princeton, NJ: Princeton University Press.

Smith, V. (2003). Constructivist versus ecological rationality in economics' American Economic Review, 465–508.

Sugden, R. (2011). The behavioral economist and the social planner: to whom should behavioral welfare economics be addressed? Papers on Economics & Evolution #1121.

Thaler, R. (1985). Mental accounting and consumer choice. Marketing Science, 4(3), 199–214.
Thaler, R. (2000). From Homo Economicus to Homo Sapiens. Journal of Economic Perspectives, 14, 133–41.
Thaler, R., Benartzi, S. (2004). Save More Tomorrow™: using behavioral economics to increase employee saving. Journal of Political Economy, 112(S1), 164–87.
Thaler, R., Sunstein, C. (2003). Libertarian paternalism. American Economic Review, 93(2), 175–9.
Williams, R. (1958). Culture is ordinary. Reprinted in B. Highmore, ed. (2002) The Everyday Life Reader. London: Routledge, 91–100.
Witt, U. (2001). Learning to consume: a theory of wants and the growth of demand. Journal of Evolutionary Economics, 11, 23–36.
Witt, U. (2006). Evolutionary economics and psychology. Max Plank Institute of Economics Papers on Economics and Evolution, no. 0613.

28

ECONOMIC BEHAVIOUR AND AGENT-BASED MODELLING

Matthias Mueller and Andreas Pyka

Introduction

Since the 1980s, continuous improvements in computer technologies have remarkably changed scientists' possibilities to develop and apply computer simulations. Simulations as a scientific tool offer new ways to explore the dynamics of complex models in various disciplines. They enable us to process scientists' thought models into artificial test laboratories in which we can systematically analyse the models' outcomes.

Within the broad field of simulation techniques, the so-called agent-based modelling (ABM) approach has gained increasing momentum, not only for economics but also in many other scientific disciplines. The ABM approach takes the perspective of the system building elements and focuses on the actions and interactions of these entities as the relevant actors within the system. This ABM perspective is accompanied by the attempt to represent actors of economic systems in a more realistic fashion, thereby overcoming the shortcomings of approaches limited to representative agents which by definition ignore heterogeneity and the related implications of interacting heterogeneous agents. In this vein, the research objectives of ABM show a strong similarity with behavioural economics, where deviations from the assumed theoretical behaviour play an outstanding role.

The value of this computational modelling approach becomes clear when we look at the experience gained during the 2010 financial crisis. As Jean-Claude Trichet phrased it:

> When the crisis came, the serious limitations of existing economic and financial models immediately became apparent. [. . .] Macro models failed to predict the crisis and seemed incapable of explaining what was happening to the economy in a convincing manner. [. . .] We need to deal better with heterogeneity across agents and the interaction among those heterogeneous agents. [. . .] Agent-based modelling dispenses with the optimization assumption and allows for more complex interactions between agents. Such approaches are worthy of our attention.
>
> *(Trichet, 2010)*

One reason for the dissatisfaction with the currently dominant paradigm in economics is substantiated in the compulsory assumption of "rational expectations" (Farmer & Foley, 2009). Empirical evidence shows that this assumption is clearly at odds with real human behaviour (see for example the experiments conducted by Güth et al. (1982) and Berg et al. (1995)). To overcome this constrictive paradigm, we clearly need new insight into human behaviour and the development of institutions, which are prominently addressed by the behavioural economics approach. Given the enormous degree of complexity, however, we also need a methodological framework, such as ABM, to incorporate the individual and heterogeneous behaviour of economic actors into models that are capable of portraying the emerging dynamics.

In an early attempt Bob Axelrod characterizes ABM by "the existence of many agents who interact with each other with little or no central direction" (Axelrod, 1997). A final consensus of what ABM is and how scientists can use it to increase our understanding of the complex economic system so far is not existent. The aim of this chapter is to shed some light on the ABM approach as a promising and possibly necessary tool in the scientist's toolbox. We focus, therefore, on the most central methodological issues, reviewing the current state of literature and highlighting the possibilities of this still somewhat disputed approach and emphasizing the complementary relationship of ABM and behavioural economics.

We start in the second section with an introduction to the three pillars of ABM: *modelling, agents and simulation*, which are characteristic for all agent-based models. In the third section we then introduce important methodological aspects that every agent-based modeller must be aware of. Finally, we conclude with a number of remarks and a brief outline of the complementary relationship between ABM and behavioural economics.

The three pillars of ABM

Despite the awareness that ABM has gained for many years, a common protocol for this method is still missing. Driven by the increasing computer resources, different scientific disciplines discovered the versatile possibilities offered by this modelling approach, which lead to different notions and understandings of ABM used in economic science.

Figure 28.1 Flock of birds created by the BOIDS algorithm

To illustrate the diversity of notions and emphasis, ABM also is also labelled as: *ABM* (Epstein & Axtell, 1996), *agent-based simulation modelling* (Polhill et al., 2001), *multi-agent simulation* (Ferber, 1999; Gilbert & Troitzsch, 2005), *multi-agent-based simulation* (Edmonds, 2001), *agent-based social simulation* (Doran, 2001; Downing et al., 2001), *individual-based configuration modelling* (Judson, 1994), *multi-agent systems* (Bousquet & Le Page, 2004), and *agent-based computational economics* (Tesfatsion, 2002).

Despite missing consent concerning the appropriate notion for this scientific method, the understanding of ABM is very similar (see also Hare & Deadman (2004) for a discussion on this issue). In the following section, we will describe three pillars of agent-based modelling: *modelling, agents and simulation*, which will frame our understanding of ABM.

Modelling from an agent-based perspective

The most important element of ABM is its *bottom-up perspective*—describing a system from the perspective of its constituent units, i.e. the agents (Bonabeau, 2002). In short, building the model from the bottom up means, letting complex macroscopic systems emerge from the interactions of microscopic entities (Epstein & Axtell, 1996; Axelrod, 1997). A good example illustrating this underlying principle is the artificial life program BOIDS by Reynolds (1987), which reproduces the complex behaviour of a flock of birds (see Figure 28.1). Instead of treating a flock as a self-contained unit, Reynolds was able to recreate the behaviour of a flock of birds by disaggregating the flock into birds and, therefore, building the model from the bottom up using only three simple behavioural rules for the birds:

1. Separation—avoid crowding neighbours (short range repulsion);
2. Alignment—steer towards average heading of neighbours; and,
3. Cohesion—steer towards average position of neighbours (long range attraction) (Reynolds, 1987).

Although this example could be considered trivial, it shows that the behaviour of complex systems can only be reproduced adequately by taking into account the individual behaviour, that is, the actions and interactions of the system building units. This also illustrates how ABM differs from another numerical method that enjoys a certain popularity in economics, namely system dynamics. On the system level, the rich patterns of possible dynamics remain hidden, whereas it is in the explicit focus of ABM.

In economics, the ABM approach follows the same idea as Reynolds proposed, modelling (macroscopic), such as economic systems through the actions and interactions of (micro-)entities, such as firms, and universities and so on. ABM hereby departs from the top-down perspective of mainstream economic models. Instead of representative individuals constrained by strong consistency requirements associated with equilibrium and an Olympian rationality, ABM describes *heterogeneous* entities living in complex systems that evolve through time (Windrum et al., 2007).

A definition of agents

Although the bottom-up perspective of ABM is without doubt a key characteristic, there are other approaches following the same logic of reasoning. In contrast, for example to the related family of Cellular Automates (Wolfram, 1986) or Microsimulations (Orcutt et al., 1986), the ABM approach centres on a representation of agents in a more realistic way. Focusing on the individual behaviour of economic actors, agent-based models can display important concepts such as for example *heterogeneity* and *bounded rational behaviour* of agents, which leads to all sorts of variation in their modelled behaviour.

An agent represents a dynamic entity, which can be assigned by the modeller with an individual role exhibiting a variety of characteristics. Although a final consensus has not been reached, in the literature it is often claimed that agents may possess the following properties (Wooldridge & Jennings, 1995):

> *Autonomy:* Agents are autonomous entities with little or no central direction and have control of their actions.
> *Social ability:* Agents can interact with other agents (e.g. receiving or sending information about locations or other internal states of others).
> *Reactivity:* Agents have a perception of their environment (e.g. the landscape they are in).
> *Pro-activeness:* Agents exhibit goal-directed behaviour, taking the initiative.

The list of possible characteristics of agents can be extended in several ways. In their original paper, Wooldridge and Jennings (1995) had already named more human characteristics (e.g., knowledge, belief, intention, obligation and emotions) as possible additional features of agents (Wooldridge & Jennings, 1995; Jennings et al., 1998).

In ABM approaches economic actors are what they are, that is, autonomous and heterogeneous entities embedded in an environment that is created by the actions and interactions of these agents (Gilbert & Troitzsch, 2005). In contrast to traditional modelling approaches, the variety of agents and their behaviour are not restricted to fit into an analytical framework. Depending on the problem under investigation and the scope of the corresponding model, agents can flexibly represent any kind of economic actor. On an aggregated level, this can be firms, universities, governmental bodies, and so on; on an individual level, agents can be employees, scientists, consumers, households and so on. However, from an abstract point of view, any independent component of a system can basically be considered to be an agent (Bonabeau, 2002; Macal & North, 2005).

It is important to emphasize that with ABM we can specifically relax unrealistic assumptions about the agents and their behaviour. While in most mainstream models strong assumptions are required in order to guarantee in principle an analytical solvability (Farmer & Foley, 2009), in ABM every agent is endowed with an individual set of initial states, which allows for the representation of characteristic features and a representation of individual behaviour. Consequently, the ABM approach is able to incorporate the manifold insights from behavioural economics about human and institutional behaviour into fruitful models.

In particular, agents within an agent-based model can be assumed to have only limited information about the environment and the behaviour of other agents, limited foresight about the scope of decisions or other resource limitations, such as memory, and so on (Edmonds, 1999). Building on that, agent-based models are capable of displaying true heterogeneity of agents (Macal & North, 2005). Heterogeneity in this sense means that agents are modelled as individual entities with individual states, and with individual behaviours. Heterogeneity in the model can be assigned by the modeller according to the requirements of the problem under investigation, that is, agents may be endowed with different levels of resources, initial knowledge stocks, strategies, reference systems etc. Additionally, heterogeneity is endogenously created within the model through the actions and interactions of agents themselves.

Second, as the behaviour of agent-based models is not restricted to obtain an analytical solution, agents may be assumed to behave as rationally bounded entities (Pyka & Fagiolo, 2007; see also Das (2006) for a detailed discussion). Since the ABM approach focuses directly on the individual, it allows for an intentional non-rational design of economic decisions which, for example, allows for experimental adaption and learning. This enables us to model the effects of psychological principles as for example *reference dependence*, *loss aversion* and *non-linear probability weighting* postulated by the famous prospect theory by Kahneman and Tversky (1979).

The complexity of a model with individual and heterogeneous agents, however, quickly reaches a level where for example the traditional analytical framework fails to offer any solution. A way-out for this problem can be found in computational simulation environments where even complex models can be studied in detail.

Simulation as in-silicio *laboratories*

As a third pillar in our understanding of the ABM approach, we have to consider that agent-based models often are implemented within a simulation environment. Seeing simulation as a form of quasi-experiments, in principle, simple agent-based models can be carried out without the help of simulation tools. A prominent example for this is the famous *Segregation model* by Schelling (1969), which was originally conducted on a chessboard using coins of different colours.

The complexity of any model, however, grows exponentially with the magnitude of the model's assumptions, quickly reaching a level where computational support is necessary, such as in the processing of experimental results. Especially through the steady improvements in computer performance, but also in the progress made on the software side (e.g. object-oriented languages and simulation environments especially dedicated to ABM, such as NetLogo, LSD—Laboratory for Simulation Development, Repast—Recursive Porous Agent Simulation Toolkit etc.), today's simulations act as laboratories where agent-based models can be created and studied *in-silicio* (Pyka & Fagiolo, 2007).

For ABM simulation, tools facilitate a detailed look into the complex interplay between the model's assumptions and the resulting outcome. By building an agent-based model within a computer simulation environment, we have a tool at hand, which helps us to systematically observe and analyse the complex dynamics created by the actions and interactions of agents both on a macro as well as on a micro level. With a computational simulation, we are able to observe all relevant information of the simulation as it progresses. In contrast to real world experiments, simulations offer the possibility of recreating and repeating experiments with the same initial conditions. This gives us the opportunity to systematically alter model parameters and assumptions, and hence leads us to a comprehensive understanding of the model's outcome.

The complexity involved, however, still limits the possible scope of ABM. Although today's computer performance allows for models with an unforeseen range, the complexity of models will always be limited by the capabilities to process the data obtained by the simulation, especially on the researchers' side.

Using ABM as a scientific tool

Despite the new and promising perspective ABM offers, it is also necessary to deal with the question of how ABM can contribute to the scientific endeavour. If used properly, ABM offers researchers a new perspective on complex interplay within economic systems.

Managing the complexity

Although ABM at its core makes a huge step towards a more realistic model of economic systems, one cannot expect a fully detailed picture. As with any model, an agent-based model is designed as a purposeful representation of a system rather than an exact and precise attempt to display real systems (Starfield, 1990). "Purposeful" in the broadest possible sense can be understood as a model that helps the scientist to answer questions that are of interest (Minsky, 1965).

Managing the complexity within a model, that is, finding the right level of complexity, is one of the key challenges for any agent-based modeller. As previously stated, the possibility to implement agent-based models within a simulation environment, the increasing performance of computer systems, and constantly improving methods for data analysis and visualization enable researchers to create models of unforeseen complexity and detail.

To start, almost by definition, we will be hardly able to define something as the optimum level of complexity that should be strived for by ABM in general. Yet there is an extreme that we need to be aware of: if the complexity of the model is reaching a level where we are no longer able to understand the processes involved, then the experiments conducted are of little interest and we cannot understand these artificial complex systems any better than we understand the real ones (Gilbert & Terna, 2000; Axtell & Epstein, 1994).

The level of complexity of an ABM is determined by the actors that the modeller aims to include and the number of assumptions we consider relevant for the model. In particular, for models of economic systems there is a broad range of possible actors and assumptions that can be relevant. The modeller must decide carefully to what extent the elements of the model are necessary or negligible, facing a common trade-off: while models aiming at prediction need descriptive accuracy, models designed for explanatory power should be rather simple (Axelrod, 1997).

Considering the right strategy for building the complexity within ABM, the debate has triggered a rich methodological discussion in which we find three distinct modelling strategies. First, following the *KISS* (*Keep It Simple, Stupid*) strategy one should start with a simple model, which may be extended if necessary. A special case of the KISS strategy is the so called TAPAS approach ("Take A Previous model and Add Something"). Here one starts with an existing model and successively complicates it with incremental additions (Pyka & Fagiolo, 2007).

In contrast, the *KIDS* (*Keep-It-Descriptive, Stupid*) strategy follows the idea of starting with a descriptive model first, which is then, if possible, simplified (Edmonds & Moss, 2005). An illustrative example for the KISS modelling strategy is Schelling's model of segregation in North American cities (Schelling, 1969). In this model, Schelling uses a simple grid for the representation of a city in order to model neighbourhood relationships. He succeeds in identifying the mechanisms that lead to strong clustering patterns of ethnic groups, even if this was only mildly intended in the individual behaviour of agents (Schelling, 1969).

A good example for the KIDS strategy is the model of water demand by Edmonds and Moss (2005), which includes an extremely rich set of varying behaviour rules, preference systems, water consuming devices (power showers, water-saving washing machines etc.), pricing systems, and policy options. With the help of this rich set of elements, backed by empirical observations, the authors intend to model water demand in a region close to the real water demand.

It is important to understand that, in general, the KISS and the KIDS strategies do not differ concerning the degree of complexity. In principle, it is rather a question of how to get there, although in reality it is probably inevitable that the choice for a strategy concerning building the relevant assumptions will end in models with considerably different levels of complexity.

Without going into too much detail, the debate has many facets and a set of additional strategies must be included for a full picture (Pyka & Fagiolo, 2007). It is, however, important to note, that agent-based research should not be oppressed by the fear of complexity. Any claim that ABM is limited to investigate only simple dynamics in small systems is neglecting the possibilities of ABM. Applying ABM for the study of economic systems, however, requires a detailed methodological understanding of this research method and additional inputs from other disciplines; that is, through a profound understanding of realistic behavioural heuristics.

Two ways of using agent-based models

As stated before, the bottom-up perspective of ABM builds on the actions and interactions between heterogeneous agents to analyse the multilevel effects on the overall system, the environment and the agents themselves. Through this, ABM gives a unique understanding of the processes of the interplay between micro and macro levels of a complex system.

The particular role of ABM for the scientific endeavour still is under debate. Facing critiques questioning the scientific value of ABM the modeller needs to be aware of how ABM can be used to deepen our understanding. Based on the literature we can distinguish between two (as will be argued later) complementary perspectives facing different questions.

On the one hand, following the idea introduced by Epstein and Axtell (1996), ABM can be used in a *generative* perspective. ABM in this sense focuses on the possibilities to display the emergence of complex macroscopic system behaviour by the actions and interactions of agents on a micro level. In other words, agent-based models can be designed to find micro-specifications that can explain (from a generative perspective *grow*) a macro level phenomenon of interest (Epstein, 1999). In the literature, this is often put on a level of reproducing stylized facts through ABM to validate models.

To name just a few examples for interesting models reproducing stylized facts, Thomas Schelling (1969) showed, as already mentioned, with his famous Segregation model, that the macroscopic pattern of segregation in cities can be explained by even a minor preferences of inhabitants for neighbourhoods with the same colour. In 1996, Epstein and Axtell reproduced, among other things, right-skewed wealth distributions based on their seminal Sugarscape model. The scope of the model has been extended during the past years continuously, implementing new features carrying forward new aspects to the model (see Epstein (1999) for a list of other interesting models reproducing stylized facts). The logic of reasoning behind the generative perspective of modelling stylized facts constitutes also a severe methodological caveat of the ABM approach which is stressed also by Epstein (1999) or Gilbert and Terna (2000). In principle, it is possible that similar macroscopic system behaviour might be generated by models which refer to different assumptions with respect to the behavioural rules of agents on the micro level. The agent-based modeller simply cannot presume that the microscopic behaviour of agents found to reproduce stylized facts is in fact an accurate and relevant description of the phenomena of interest. For this reason, a final proof for the validity of an agent-based model which reproduces stylized facts is hard to give.

On the other hand, using agent-based models is not limited to reproducing stylized facts and thereby finding *possible* explanations for emerging macroscopic patterns. While the starting point for agent-based models following the generative idea is patterns on the macro level, another strand of models in the literature is based on the possibility to perform a wide range of numerical experiments and, hence, analyse what emerging patterns arise based on micro-specifications of the model. The focus here is on the improvement of our understanding of the dynamic processes within a complex system. ABM from this perspective acts as a laboratory for computational experiments created *in-silicio* (Pyka & Fagiolo, 2007; Leombruni, 2002). As Axelrod puts it:

> Simulation is a third way of doing science. Like deduction, it starts with a set of explicit assumptions. But unlike deduction, it does not prove theorems. Instead, a simulation generates data that can be analysed inductively. Unlike typical induction, however, the

> simulated data comes from a rigorously specified set of rules rather than direct measurement of the real world.
>
> *(Axelrod, 1997)*

Detached from the need to reproduce stylized facts, ABM can also be seen as a scientific method to increase our understanding of complex systems. While the starting point of ABM in a generative sense is macroscopic patterns, the starting point of ABM as an *in-silicio* laboratory is a set of specifications for the micro level; that is, a well-grounded set of behavioural rules on the agent level. Tesfatsion (2006) distinguishes here between two different objectives of ABM. First, ABM can be used to get a *normative understanding*, evaluating whether designs proposed for economic policies, institutions, and processes will result in socially desirable system performance over time. Second, ABM allows for *qualitative insights and theory generation*. The objective here is to understand economic systems through a systematic examination of their potential dynamical behaviours under alternatively specified initial conditions. Using ABM as an *in-silicio* laboratory, however, comes at a cost. To gain wide acceptance, the model need to be validated through a broad set of empirical micro level data.

The need for verification, validation and calibration

The most common critique against agent-based models is perceived lack of robustness. To start, any modeller needs to be aware of the possibility of simple failures in the implementation of the model in a computer simulation. This *verification* of the computer program is a crucial step for the credibility of a model.

Verification simply asks whether the model does what we think it is supposed to do (Ormerod & Rosewell, 2009). Verification, however, is more than just looking for bugs in the computer code. For example, Dawid and Kopel (1998) note: "we have to be aware of the fact that simulation results may crucially depend on implementation details which have hardly any economic meaning". In other words, even though the technical code might be correct, the way the model is translated and implemented in the computer software might lead to biased results which have strong effects on the model's outcome, yet were unintended by the modeller. Especially for complex models, it is therefore necessary to make the implementation of the agent-based model transparent for other researchers. This can be done either by providing the original simulation code or by making main procedures public, including the pseudo code in the publication.

Despite the correct implementation of the simulation model, the modeller is also often confronted with critiques questioning whether the model is an accurate representation of the real world from the perspective of the model's intended applications, that is, the model's validity (Ormerod & Rosewell, 2009). Following the distinction made in the third section, we can differentiate between two ways of *validation*: that is, the *input validation* and *output validation*.

While the latter refers to the matching of model results against acquired real world data, the former regards ensuring that the fundamental structural, behavioural and institutional conditions incorporated in the model reproduce the main aspects of the actual system (Bianchi et al., 2008).

Without going into much detail, this issue is still under great debate and several strategies have been developed to approach the problem of validity of agent-based models, such as the *indirect calibration* approach and the *Werker–Brenner* approach. The underlying concept of these validation strategies is an elaborate multilevel approach where input and output validation are combined. Starting with a model designed to reproduce stylized facts, the modeller can use the micro-specifications found to be valid to replicate the macro patterns as the starting point for a wide set of simulation experiments aiming to give further insights into the dynamical behaviours of the model (see, for example, Windrum et al. (2007), Ormerod & Rosewell (2009), and Werker & Brenner (2004) for interesting discussions on this issue).

Although, without doubt, the validation of an agent-based model is of particular interest, especially if we want to derive valid outcomes such as policy recommendations, we have to be aware that the complexity of ABM always invites criticism. Despite any thorough validation of the model, we may be confronted with questions whether all elements of the model are necessary or if other, so far missing, elements are relevant too and, hence, should be included. Second, the possibility of performing validation is restricted by the set of relevant data available. For validation of agent-based models, we need more than some widely accepted macroeconomic stylized facts. As ABM builds on the actions and interactions of heterogeneous economic actors, this approach requires a fundamentally new understanding of the behaviour of these actors.

Conclusions

Shifting the focus from an oversimplifying perception of economic systems to a more realistic one, ABM is designed to overcome the limiting possibilities of a traditional analytical framework. Central to this new approach is its exceptional perspective of economic actors, treating economic agents as heterogeneous and individual actors that build economic systems from the bottom up.

Using this method, however, comes at a cost. We need to be aware of how ABM can be used to deepen our understanding of complex economic processes. Although ABM at its core makes a huge step towards a more realistic model of economic systems, one cannot expect a fully detailed picture. As with any model, an agent-based model is designed as a purposeful representation of a system. Purposeful in the sense that ABM can be used in a *generative* way, reproducing macro level patterns and hence finding *possible* explanations on the micro level, but also as an *in-silicio* test laboratory where we study the outcome of different micro level specifications.

Especially for the latter case, despite any effort to ensure validity of our models, the complexity created within ABM invites critiques. To counter them, we need a better understanding of the behaviour of economic actors but also well accepted standard models. So far, ABM cannot aim for including all possible aspects of an economy. In contrast, we need at this point to focus on a new joint understanding of basic economic processes, emerging from a profound acknowledgement of human behaviour. Building on that, we can stepwise increase the complexity of our models, gaining descriptive accuracy and hence increasing the predictive power of ABM.

In this light, it is also important to emphasize the complementary relationship of ABM with behavioural economics, offering the possibility for fruitful cross-fertilization. In behavioural economics, instead of a general optimization approach, decision rules are frequently informed by psychological insights of human behaviour, which serve as a heuristic description of decision processes. Empirical observations confirm in many instances a deviation from a theoretically derived optimal solution. As these deviations are systematic and not random, their explanation is of high scientific interest. In many cases, these empirical observations can be explained by behavioural economists with the application of decision heuristics for comparatively simple and artificial cases. ABM now allows for an extension of these comparatively simple and artificial cases towards models with a higher degree of complexity. With this, we can test whether unexpected feedbacks and phase transitions resulting from the interaction of heterogeneous agents might have a strong impact on the expected results. In contrast, ABM finds a rich collection of decision heuristics in the behavioural economics literature that can be used to program agents' decision rules, framing a new and profound understanding of economic systems.

Acknowledgements

This work is part of the research project VISIBLE—Virtual Simulation Lab for the Analysis of Investments in Learning and Education.

Bibliography

Axelrod, R. (1997). Advancing the art of simulation in the social sciences. In R. Conte et al. (eds), Simulating Social Phenomena. Berlin/Heidelberg: Springer, 21–40.

Axtell, R., & Epstein, J. M. (1994), Agent-based modelling: Understanding our creations. Bulletin of the Santa Fe Institute, Winter, 28–32.

Berg, J., Dickhaut, J., & McCabe, K. (1995). Trust, reciprocity, and social history. Games and Economic Behavior, 10(1), 122–42.

Bianchi, C., Cirillo, P., Gallegati, M., & Vagliasindi, P. A. (2008). Validation in agent-based models: An investigation on the CATS model. Journal of Economic Behavior & Organization, 67(3), 947–64.

Bonabeau, E. (2002). Agent-based modeling: Methods and techniques for simulating human systems. Proceedings of the National Academy of Sciences, 99(suppl 3), 7280–7.

Bousquet, F. & Le Page, C. (2004) Multi-agent simulations and ecosystem management: A review. Ecological Modelling, 176(3–4), 313–32.

Box, G. E. (1979). Robustness in the strategy of scientific model building. Robustness in Statistics, 1, 201–36.

Das, S. (2006). On agent-based modeling of complex systems: Learning and bounded rationality. Department of Computer Science and Engineering. La Jolla, CA, 92093-0404.

Dawid, H. & Kopel, M. (1998). On economic applications of the genetic algorithm: A model of the cobweb type. Journal of Evolutionary Economics, 8(3), 297–315.

Doran, J. (2001). Intervening to achieve co-operative ecosystem management: Towards an agent based model. Journal of Artificial Societies and Social Simulation. Available at: www.soc.surrey.ac.uk/JASSS/4/2/4.html.

Downing, T. E., Moss, S., & Pahl-Wostl, C. (2001). Understanding climate policy using participatory agent-based social simulation. In P. Davidsson et al. (eds), Multi-Agent-Based Simulation. Berlin/Heidelberg: Springer, 198–213.

Edmonds, B. (1999). Modelling bounded rationality in agent-based simulations using the evolution of mental models. In Computational Techniques for Modelling Learning in Economics. New York: Springer, 305–32.

Edmonds, B. (2001). The use of models: Making MABS more informative. In P. Davidsson et al. (eds), Multi-Agent-Based Simulation. Berlin/Heidelberg: Springer.

Edmonds, B. & Moss, S. (2005). From KISS to KIDS: An 'anti-simplistic'modelling approach. In P. Davidsson et al. (eds), Multi-Agent-Based Simulation. Berlin/Heidelberg: Springer, 130–44.

Epstein, J. M. (1999). Agent-based computational models and generative social science. Generative Social Science: Studies in Agent-Based Computational Modeling, 4(5), 4–46.

Epstein, J. M., & Axtell, R. (1996). Growing Artificial Societies: Social Science from the Bottom Up. Brookings Institution Press.

Farmer, J. D., & Foley, D. (2009). The economy needs agent-based modelling. Nature, 460(7256), 685–6.

Ferber, J. (1999). Multi-Agent Systems: An Introduction to Distributed Artificial Intelligence. Addison-Wesley, Harlow.

Gilbert, N. (2008). Agent-Based Models. Thousand Oaks, CA: Sage.

Gilbert, N., & Terna, P. (2000). How to build and use agent-based models in social science. Mind and Society, 1(1), 57–72.

Gilbert, N. & Troitzsch, K. G. (2005). Simulation for the Social Scientist. Open University Press, Berkshire.

Güth, W., Schmittberger, R., & Schwarze, B. (1982). An experimental analysis of ultimatum bargaining. Journal of Economic Behavior & Organization, 3(4), 367–88.

Hare, M., & Deadman, P. (2004). Further towards a taxonomy of agent-based simulation models in environmental management. Mathematics and Computers in Simulation, 64(1), 25–40.

Jennings, N. R., Sycara, K., & Wooldridge, M. (1998). A roadmap of agent research and development. Autonomous Agents and Multi-Agent Systems, 1(1), 7–38.

Judson, O. P. (1994). The rise of the individual-based model in ecology. Trends in Ecology & Evolution, 9(1), 9–14.

Kahneman, D., & Tversky, A. (1979). Prospect theory: An analysis of decision under risk. Econometrica: Journal of the Econometric Society, 47(2), 263–91.

Leombruni, R. (2002). The methodological status of agent-based simulations. LABORatorio Riccardo Revelli-Centre for Employment Studies Working Paper (19).

Macal, C. M., & North, M. J. (2005, December). Tutorial on agent-based modeling and simulation. In Proceedings of the 37th Conference on Winter Simulation, 2–15.

Minsky, M. (1965). Matter, Mind and Models. Cambridge, MA: MIT Press.

Müller, M., Buchmann, T., & Kudic, M. (2014). Micro strategies and macro patterns in the evolution of innovation networks: an agent-based simulation approach. In P. Ahrweiler & A. Pyka et al. (eds), Simulating Knowledge Dynamics in Innovation Networks. Berlin/Heidelberg: Springer, 73–95.

Orcutt, G. H., Merz, J., & Quinke, H. (Eds.). (1986). Microanalytic Simulation Models to Support Social and Financial Policy. Amsterdam: North-Holland.

Ormerod, P. & Rosewell, B. (2009) Validation and verification of agent-based models in the social sciences. Epistemological Aspects of Computer Simulation in the Social Sciences. Berlin/Heidelberg: Springer. 130–40.

Polhill, J. G., Gotts N. M. & Law, A. (2001). Imitative versus nonimitative strategies in a land-use simulation. Cybernetics & Systems, 32(1–2), 285–307.

Pyka, A. & Fagiolo, G. (2007). Agent-based modelling: A methodology for neo-Schumpeterian economics. In H. Hanusch & A. Pyka (eds), The Elgar Companion to Neo-Schumpeterian Economics. Cheltenham: Edward Elgar, 467–87.

Reynolds, C. W. (1987). Flocks, herds and schools: A distributed behavioural model. ACM Siggraph Computer Graphics, 21(4), 25–34.

Schelling, T. C. (1969). Models of segregation. American Economic Review, 59(2), 488–93.

Starfield, A. M. (1990). Qualitative, rule-based modelling. BioScience, 40(8), 601–4.

Tesfatsion, L. (2002). Economic agents and markets as emergent phenomena. Proceedings of the National Academy of Sciences, 99(suppl 3), 7191–2.

Tesfatsion, L. (2006). Agent-based computational economics: A constructive approach to economic theory. Handbook of Computational Economics, 2, 831–80.

Trichet, J.-C. (2010). Reflections on the nature of monetary policy, non-standard measures and finance theory, 18 November. Available from www.ecb.int/press/key/date/2010/html/sp101118.en.html.

Werker, C., & Brenner, T. (2004). Empirical calibration of simulation models (No. 0410). Papers on Economics and Evolution.

Windrum, P., Fagiolo, G., & Moneta, A. (2007). Empirical validation of agent-based models: Alternatives and prospects. Journal of Artificial Societies and Social Simulation, 10(2), 8.

Wolfram, S. (1986). Theory and Applications of Cellular Automata (Vol. 1). Singapore: World Scientific.

Wooldridge, M., & Jennings, N. R. (1995). Intelligent agents: Theory and practice. Knowledge Engineering Review, 10(2), 115–52.

INDEX

Page numbers in italics refer to figures and tables.
Page numbers in bold type refer to contributors.

FSC
www.fsc.org
MIX
Papier | Fördert
gute Waldnutzung
FSC® C083411

Kolibri 360 GmbH
Ferdinand-Jühlke-Straße 7
99095 Erfurt, Deutschland
produktsicherheit@kolibri360.de